T0319472

Austrian Reconstruction and the Collapse of Global Finance, 1921–1931

Austrian Reconstruction and the Collapse of Global Finance, 1921–1931

NATHAN MARCUS

Harvard University Press

Cambridge, Massachusetts
London, England
2018

First printing

Library of Congress Cataloging-in-Publication Data

Names: Marcus, Nathan, 1976– author.
Title: Austrian reconstruction and the collapse of global finance, 1921–1931 / Nathan Marcus.
Description: Cambridge, Massachusetts : Harvard University Press, 2018. | Includes
   bibliographical references and index.
Identifiers: LCCN 2017018928 | ISBN 9780674088924 (alk. paper)
Subjects: LCSH: Financial crises—Austria—History. | League of Nations. | Austria—Economic
   conditions—1918–1945. | Austria—History—1918–1938. | Austria—Politics and
   government—1918–1938. | Gold standard—History.
Classification: LCC HB3722 .M33655 2018 | DDC 330.9436 / 0511—dc23
LC record available at https://lccn.loc.gov/2017018928

In memory of my maternal grandparents

LEOPOLDINE NATAN née STORPER

> *Born in Vienna 28 December 1926*
> *Deported to Theresienstadt 9 October 1942*
> *Liberated by the Soviet Army 8 May 1945*
> *Died in Prague 17 April 2003*

ING. FRANTIŠEK NATAN

> *Born in Prague 31 December 1908*
> *Deported to Theresienstadt 4 December 1941*
> *Liberated by the Soviet Army 8 May 1945*
> *Died in Prague 9 May 1965*

Contents

A Note on Austrian Currencies

The Austrian crown (kr.) was stabilized in 1922 at 1/14,400th of its prewar level. One gold crown in 1923 thus equaled 14,400 paper crowns.

One gold crown equaled $0.20 and 71,000 paper crowns were roughly equal to one U.S. dollar.

The Austrian schilling (sch.) replaced the Austrian crown in 1924. One Austrian schilling equaled 10,000 paper crowns or 0.7 gold crowns. From 1924 to 1931, seven Austrian schillings roughly equaled one U.S. dollar.

*Austrian Reconstruction and the Collapse
of Global Finance, 1921–1931*

Introduction

The gates to the Second World War were opened in 1931.

—Eric Hobsbawm, *The Age of Extremes*

THE FINANCIAL HISTORY of interwar Austria is one of precedents. Austria was the first country in Europe to suffer from hyperinflation in the 1920s, followed by hyperinflation in Hungary, the more infamous one in Weimar Germany, and finally in Poland. Austria was also the first country to stop hyperinflation and the first to begin economic reconstruction through the intervention of the League of Nations. The reconstruction program drawn up in Geneva was replicated to help Hungary, and parts of it were incorporated into League schemes for Bulgaria, Danzig, Greece, and, though not sponsored by the League, the German Dawes plan. Last but not least, Austria was also the first European country in the summer of 1931 to battle a banking and then a currency crisis that threatened to take it off the gold standard, followed soon thereafter by Hungary, Germany, and most crucially Britain.

This book tries to give sense to little Austria's chronological preeminence. In fact, many financial historians have been at pains to explain why a small country like Austria should have triggered a Europe-wide financial crisis in 1931 (spoiler alert: it did not), or why it was the first state to receive League assistance after the Great War. To put it succinctly, the reason financial problems surfaced in Austria before posing problems to other countries was that none of these former belligerents suffered from such painful imbalances as the young Austrian Republic. No other country faced such a high war debt in relation to its tax revenues, no other state was forced to spend so much on pensions and wages in per capita terms, and no other economy was so dependent on foreign trade and foreign capital with respect to its gross national product. These imbalances resulted from the discrepancy between the new country's dimensions and the magnitude of its inherited problems. An empire had created the troubles, but the means left by which to tackle them were those of a small nation-state. This meant that in Austria difficulties occurred earlier, inadequate policies broke down sooner, and inconsistencies were observed first. It helps explain why hyperinflation broke out in Austria more than a year before it ravaged Germany, why Austria became the first country to submit to League reconstruction, and why it was the first country to experience a severe financial crisis in 1931.

The Austrian First Republic, therefore, despite and precisely because of its small size, played a pivotal role in the turbulent history of interwar Europe. What makes it furthermore an interesting case study for scholars today is the fact that for much of its short democratic life it was under international financial control. Austria was the first country to appeal to, and receive, financial assistance from a multilateral governmental body: the League of Nations. In return, it had agreed to adhere to a reform program, drafted in cooperation with the League, which was overseen by a foreign General Commissioner residing in Vienna. In the early 1920s, this General Commissioner called Austria "a grand laboratory." For the first time in human history, representatives of different states had gotten together to help a desolate country raise money for economic reconstruction. As much as such schemes have today become commonplace (see, for example, the European Union interventions in Greece since 2010), they remain controversial to many. Modern-day calls of financial colonialism and imperialist banking echo earlier voices of interwar Austrians and their later historiographers.

The Austrian case allows us to address such accusations and to study the genesis of international financial assistance, intervention, and fiscal control. What today still remains shrouded in mystery—enigmatic meetings of central bankers, secret negotiations between creditor and debtor governments, confidential evaluations of ailing economies by international experts and foreign representatives—has become accessible in the case of interwar Austria. The historical archives of the League of Nations, European central banks, and the Austrian First Republic, as well as those of many private banks, are open to today's historians. This book thus desires to study the early cooperation between private financiers, financial experts at the League of Nations, and the staff of European central banks to help reconstruct Austria.

Their common commitment to subjugate narrow national interests in favor of Austrians and a better European future so shortly after the war rested on a new spirit of international cooperation, embodied and put into practice by the League. It was also motivated by the fear of Bolshevik revolution in Central Europe and the belief that a prosperous Austria was essential for stability in the region. Among Austrians, however, the foreign intervention also provoked resentment, xenophobia, and accusations of international capital's conspiracy against their country.

This book aims to settle three larger historiographical debates. First, it provides an answer as to how exactly postwar hyperinflation was stopped in Austria in 1922, and who should be given credit for it. Second, it offers a complete reassessment of the League intervention in Austria from 1922 to 1926 and the reasons for its failures and successes. Finally, it puts to rest the puzzling question as to how failure of the Austrian Credit-Anstalt, the largest Austrian and Central European bank in 1931, might have triggered the European banking crisis during the summer of that year, by showing that it was not so. What links these three questions is Austria's pursuit for economic and financial stability within the larger framework of international diplomacy and global capital markets. Austria is exemplary for a small country that cannot set the larger political and economic conditions that govern its international room to maneuver. By studying the financial history of interwar Austria, we thus gain a better understanding of how smaller countries assert their interests or fall victim to the larger forces of capital and international politics.

What is the agency left to small nations in a world in which the sudden power of capital flows can make or break a state? Under a global order in which international organizations controlled by just a few mighty powers set the global agenda for all? The feeling that larger forces, working for their own specific interests, took away from individuals or smaller nation-states the freedom to decide how to run their lives is widespread not just today. Nor is it only Marxists, sociologists, or neuroscientists who would be quick to start listing the various ways that, say, economic necessities, habits, or biology limit our scope of free will. There exists a view, becoming possibly more prevalent, that the lives of powerless individuals, and also of small, powerless states, are victims of the decisions and policies that more powerful men in more powerful countries make. Such feelings were particularly common-place in post–First World War Austria, which had been created without consulting the wishes of its citizens. Whereas the Wilsonian ideal of national self-determination had embraced the popular desires for nation-states in Czechoslovakia or Poland and supported plebiscites in areas of discord, Austria had been dictated its peace terms and prohibited from pursuing its wish to link its fate with Germany. The foundation of an independent Austrian republic against the will of its people was further unsettling because the notion of Austria had always been intrinsically linked with that of the house of Habsburg, and few could imagine what Austria without its monarchy might stand for. This sense of imposed powerlessness only strengthened the prevalent view among Austrians that their new state was neither economically nor financially viable.

The depreciation of the Austrian crown and the continued price rises, due largely to the need of subsidizing and importing food, culminated in two waves of hyperinflation after the First World War, destroying domestic savings and erasing public debt. Politicians, seeking a way to terminate inflation, largely sought salvation in a foreign loan. But despite the centrality to its future political and economic trajectory, accounts of Austria's First Republic merely discuss hyperinflation as a backdrop to historical developments.[1] The best study of Austrian inflation remains that by Jan van Walré de Bordes from 1924, in which he argued that inflation had been a consequence of accelerated depreciation, due to speculation and capital flight. Austrian inflation, he concluded, had been caused not by excessive money supply but by a deteriorating exchange rate.[2] Later historians trying to identify the causes behind Austrian inflation do little more than describe the course of events, highlighting the trade deficit and a lack of political unity.[3] Some historians confirm van Walré de Bordes's claim that speculation and capital flight were the most important driving forces, while others conclude rather generally that hyperinflation's specific dynamics depended on political, social, and economic factors.[4] Studies by economic historians have focused largely on the economic consequences of inflation. Most argue that inflation increased the participatory share of Austrian banks in industrial enterprises, which had lost much working capital, thereby undermining their own stability, while others discuss inflation's impact on future trade patterns or the cost of stabilization in terms of unemployment.[5]

Economists produced more useful studies of Austrian inflation. Interested in questions of monetary policy, they looked to Austria for answers as to how best to stop hyperinflation successfully. Studying hyperinflation as a homogeneous phenomenon, with commonalities that stretch beyond an individual historical context, they provided solutions to be applied uniformly at any point in time.[6] Phillip Cagan first identified the key importance of people's expectations, which govern the velocity of money. If accommodated by the printing of new notes, these expectations will determine the rates of hyperinflation.[7] Thomas Sargent focuses on the essential role of central banks, which print the new money, noting that once such practice is changed, hyperinflations can be terminated, while Rüdiger Dornbusch stresses the stabilization of exchange rates, because of their immediate effect on prices and the real value of taxes.[8] The economic historian Barry Eichengreen chooses a structural approach, arguing that hyperinflation occurs when people are so reluctant to pay taxes that governments are forced to print money.[9] Eichengreen's call for a complete understanding of the historical context that allows hyperinflations to emerge and to be terminated, before letting economists draw generalized conclusions about what policies guarantee universal success, provided much inspiration for this book's first part.

Largely, Austria's conservatively inspired historiography credits Christian-Social Chancellor and Prelate Ignaz Seipel with bringing about stabilization of Austrian prices and exchange rates after the war. Hailed as the "Savior of Geneva," such hagiographies detect determined activism on his part in August 1922 and see it as instrumental in bringing about the League intervention and the stabilization of Austrian exchange rates that same month.[10] Bereft of access to important historical sources, Socialist histories were largely left with accepting such accounts, criticizing the means of Seipel in bringing about the intervention or the subsequent abuse of the powers it bestowed on him. As I argue in Part I of this book, such a reading stands diametrically opposed to the narrative emerging from primary sources in historical archives. Credit for drafting the League scheme and overcoming international political difficulties in its realization in August 1922 should go to Arthur Balfour and his French colleague Gabriel Hanotaux, who jump-started the League's Austrian reconstruction work. A permanent stabilization of the exchange rate and termination of hyperinflation was not achieved in August, however, but only toward the end of the year, after energetic work by delegates of the League of Nations Financial Committee in Vienna. Meanwhile, Chancellor Seipel and his government, playing a dangerous game of brinkmanship after the League had gotten involved in Austria, stalled on most reforms and legal ratifications, finally requiring the direct intervention of League delegates in Austrian domestic politics to overcome Socialist opposition, create political consensus and bring about stabilization.

After the League's successful intervention restored the credibility of Austrian institutions, confidence about the future had to be consolidated to eventually bring about investments, trade and foreign capital inflows. In Austria this was facilitated by the presence of the League of Nations General Commissioner. The League's intervention scheme gave him some control over Austria's fiscal policies as he had to sign off on monthly budgets, and he had the power to withhold funds raised by the Austrian government on foreign capital markets. His function served as a "credibility technology" that made it appear unlikely in the eyes of citizens and foreigners that the Austrian National Bank (ANB) or government would renege on their pledges. To further consolidate confidence in Austria's economic future and financial stability, the General Commissioner published regular reports that ostensibly provided transparency about the pace and results of reconstruction. The reports could be used to pressure the Austrian government into implementing reforms, and, if providing positive news, to generate public confidence in Austria and abroad. Part II of this book provides the reader with a detailed study of the League presence in Austria and the roles played by the General Commissioner, the League of Nations Financial Committee, and the Bank of England (BoE) on the one side, and the Austrian government and ANB on the other.

The methods of the League intervention scheme in Austria were applied to several other countries in interwar Europe and inspired later interventions, undertaken by bodies such as the International Monetary Fund.[11] Patricia Clavin and Jens-Wilhelm Wessels, as well as Martin David Dubin, argue that work by League officials at its Financial Secretariat and international experts on its Financial Committee facilitated international monetary cooperation. Strongly impacting reconstruction of the global economy and fostering transnational and transgovernmental activities, these functionaries created the basis for the new sort of "international" that emerged in the second half of the twentieth century.[12] According to Andrew Webster, the widespread belief in a novel "League Spirit," meant to overcome national interests, reigned most successfully among these economic and financial experts, who, in the words of Jo-Anne Pemberton, perceived of their work as a novel means to overcome social and economic conflict.[13]

Austrian historiography, however, has largely judged League intervention in Austria negatively. The General Commissioner in Vienna, who undoubtedly possessed an authoritarian character, is accused of having imposed a concoction of monetary and fiscal policies in the interest of foreign financial powers that did more harm than good. The League's intervention is judged as an unwarranted subjugation of Austrian sovereignty, reducing the room for maneuver available to the Austrian government and damaging the Austrian economy. Such accounts tend to exonerate the Austrian government, the ANB, and the country's private sector from responsibility for the country's economic performance.

As noted by the historian F. L. Carsten, Austria under League control was mired by shrinking economic activity and rising unemployment, despite currency stabilization and the rise of state revenues.[14] Hans Kernbauer, Eduard März, and Fritz Weber blame protectionism, lack of competitiveness, and high interest rates for the sluggish economy and rising unemployment.[15] Similarly, Walter Goldinger and Dieter Binder put the blame on the deflationary effects of stabilization, combined with rising taxes and protectionism.[16] But Karl Bachinger and Herbert Matis specifically accuse the League of Nations and the BoE for imposing a regime of budgetary austerity and fiscal retrenchment, which translated into low growth and employment.[17] For Karl Ausch, too, the League of Nations and the BoE were responsible for a harmful deflationary policy, the first by curtailing government expenditures and the second by sanctioning available foreign credit.[18]

Such critical accounts are questioned by the work of others, who find that few alternatives existed to the League's policies. Margaret G. Myers argued as early as 1945 that only the combination of League control, foundation of an independent central bank, and exchange rate stabilization "formed a homogeneous whole" that allowed Austria to borrow foreign capital abroad.[19] Louis Pauly contends that the League intervention was vital because of its demands that the government establish an autonomous central bank, adopt the gold exchange standard, and balance its budget.[20] Peter Garber and Michael Spencer also argue that the presence of the League's General Commissioner

and of a foreign adviser at the central bank were crucial for the long-term
success of Austrian currency stabilization.[21] In the words of economist Julio
Santaella, following hyperinflation the League provided a useful "commitment technology" that ensured stabilization by offering credibility and fresh
capital in return for sound finance.[22]

    The three existing monographs studying the League of Nations interven-
tion based on the extensive archives in Geneva provide more balanced accounts.[23] The impressively detailed three-volume dissertation by Nicole
Piétri identifies the balanced budget as the most important result of League
control, blaming the subsequent high rate of unemployment and lack of financial stability on the failure to reform Vienna's oversized banking sector.[24]
J. L. J. Bosmans's vindication of the General Commissioner's role in Vienna
blames the League's Financial Committee for focusing solely on stable exchange rates and the reduction of expenditure while ignoring the needs of
the domestic economy. Disregarding the causes behind unemployment, Bosmans argues, left Austria in a weak position by the time League control was
terminated in 1926.[25] The most recent and original analysis comes from Michel Fior, whose epistemological account argues that international financial
elites instrumentalized the League to create a global social order in the interest of transnational capital.[26] Accordingly, focusing on budgetary reform
and leaving economic reconstruction to private capital in Austria created a
situation that embodied the seeds for the crisis of 1931, because bankers were
not prepared to lend long term and the Financial Committee did not do
enough to address that problem. Finally, the ambitious study of Jens-Wilhelm
Wessels, though not looking directly at the League's activities, substantiates
claims that there was little alternative to a policy of deflation and credit re-
striction in interwar Austria.[27] Fixed exchange rates and balanced budgets
were the only available options to expert opinion, while high unemployment
and slow economic growth had more to do with a lack of global demand and
the low productivity and competitiveness of Austrian producers than with
the League's reconstruction plan, the BoE's presumed credit embargo, or
policies adopted at the ANB.

    In fact, accusations of financial colonialism or foreign dictatorship in inter-
war Austria are entirely misplaced. The General Commissioner had very
little effective "control," nor did the foreign adviser to the ANB act as a stooge
of foreign financial interests. Instead, both functioned as scapegoats or useful

covers, allowing the Austrian government to blame the League and foreign intervention for unpopular measures that incurred economic hardship or antagonized workers. The Austrian government repeatedly and successfully asserted its independence and retained its agency vis-à-vis the League and other foreign interests. Under Chancellor Seipel, reforms were undertaken with little enthusiasm and the League and its representatives were shunned and even publicly vilified. It was only the initiatives of a successor government that established an effective working relationship with the League of Nations and its representative bodies, bringing control to a belated end. As I find, adversary decisions by Austrian officials often received active support from the foreign adviser at the ANB and even from the General Commissioner in Vienna, contradicting much of the established historical record.

Rectifying the narrative of League intervention in Austria is important because it opens completely new debates regarding the latter's interwar history. Through crediting the League of Nations and its representatives with too much power, historians have ignored the motivations behind Austrian social, economic, and monetary policy. In particular, the most important measures, such as setting domestic interest rates by the central bank, were not dictated by foreign interests, but in fact made against the explicit wishes of the BoE and Geneva. Similarly, while credibility and confidence were restored with the help of the League, the Austrian government reneged on its commitments and ran a vastly larger budget than the League experts in Geneva thought sustainable. Finally, the termination of League control in 1926 was granted despite views among the most influential experts on the League's Financial Committee, who thought it was better that control continue. Austrians quite successfully tried to have their cake and eat it, benefiting from League stabilization and subsequent capital inflows but pursuing largely independent and controversial economic and monetary policies.

The League's hasty departure in 1926 meant that Austria lost its valuable credibility mechanism. While the country remained in need of long-term capital, foreign confidence in Austria's future now rested on the credibility of Austrian institutions alone. Important concessions granted in return for the League's retreat were not enough to bring about the transformation of foreign short-term credits into long-term loans. The departure of the General Commissioner, whose presence had fostered not only foreign confidence but also political peace, opened space for dangerous inter-party violence. Lethal clashes in July 1927 had little impact on investor confidence, but in 1929 fears of civil unrest provoked the withdrawal of foreign capital and savings by concerned citizens, and contributed to the demise of Austria's second largest bank.

In 1931, the Credit-Anstalt had to be bailed out by the Austrian government. Similar action had not produced a panic in 1924, but without the credibility technology of the League, fears of inflation resurfaced. Capital flight ensued and the ANB faced increased demand for foreign exchange. Robert Boyce argues that 1931 was a turning point for world history because the financial crisis that shook the world resulted in Britain abandoning the important global role it had played since the end of the First World War. It put an end to what he calls the first era of globalization, with Britain no longer serving as "the lynchpin of a globalized economic system," turning its back on the gold exchange standard and free trade in favor of its own Imperial economy.[28] For other countries, notably Germany and the United States, 1931 was beset with financial trouble, too. Standard narratives of the European financial crisis of 1931 see a direct link between the collapse of the Credit-Anstalt and the propagation of financial panic across Europe.[29] They claim that Austrian problems triggered a snowball effect that spread beyond its borders across Central Europe and eventually to Great Britain.[30] As argued prominently by Barry Eichengreen, central banks lacked willingness to cooperate and uphold international stability, allowing the crisis to spread.[31] In such narratives, Austria's crisis becomes instrumental in bringing about the Great Depression in Europe.[32]

As I argue in Part III, such an account is neither accurate nor helpful for understanding the origins of the European crisis or the Great Depression. The ANB, with help provided mainly by the BoE, foreign financiers, and the Bank for International Settlements, was able to contain the Credit-Anstalt crisis within just one month, gaining control over the situation by mid-June. To prevent a moratorium or the introduction of capital controls and save the gold exchange standard, Austria's central bank had opted to intervene on exchange markets and spent foreign reserves in defense of its currency's gold value. Encouraged in its policy by central bankers who met at the new Bank for International Settlements in Basel, Austria lost substantial amounts of foreign currency reserves but saw the panic through. It was only when the German crisis struck in mid-July that fright and a run on currency returned, eventually driving Austria practically off the gold exchange standard. Rather than claim that the Credit-Anstalt rescue was a failure and that the bank's collapse was the first in a series of events that led Europe into the Great Depression, I argue that international efforts to save Austria in 1931 were promising if not actually successful, despite significant political obstacles. It was larger developments, particularly the unfolding crisis in Germany, that lay beyond Austria's control, to which it fell victim, and which brought the Great Depression to Europe.

The theses put forward in this book may not all be entirely new, but they are, for the first time, supported by abundant archival evidence to be convincing. They bring together primary sources from public and private archives, originating with governments, diplomats, the League of Nations, central banks, and private financiers, both in Austria and abroad. The notes have been given extensive space, sometimes beyond the usual requirements for referencing, and provide a running illustration of the attention Austrian affairs garnered around the world, attesting to the pivotal role Austria played in European politics and economic reconstruction during the interwar years.

The narrative account is complemented by the analysis of financial data, meant to illustrate and at times substantiate each chapter's claims. Some of the data had been collected by the office of the General Commissioner in Vienna or by the BoE; other figures were obtained from the Austrian daily press. Financial history cannot and must not be written without an understanding and an analysis of the ample financial data that is available. Nor can or should financial history be studied without taking into account political and social contexts. This book in fact attempts to fuse together diverse strands of historical studies, their literatures and methods: financial, cultural, and political. The analyses of financial data are presented as graphic images, with extensive commentaries to make them intelligible to nonspecialist readers. Visual sources in the form of newspaper caricatures are employed to help tease out popular attitudes toward inflation, League reconstruction or political developments. Together with a study of primary source material from historical archives, they provide a well-rounded representation of Austria's interwar past.

Some readers of this book may get the impression that it vindicates capital and provides an apology for the avarice of international finance. This is by no means the case. Now as then, bankers can be guilty of criminal behavior that brings harm to innocent taxpayers or investors. Now as then, government officials can be corrupted, or beholden to private interests. Personally, I think that a tax on certain financial transactions and heavy taxing of the super-rich in First World countries would do a great deal of good. But good historians do not let their political views determine their arguments. If this book goes to great lengths to understand how bankers, financial experts, the General Commissioner, and the Austrian government faced each other over Austrian reconstruction, it is not to defend one or another. It is to show that some of the most popular claims made about Austrian reconstruction and repeated in many a history book are, to paraphrase the German historian Leopold von Ranke, *nicht wie es eigentlich gewesen*—or not as it actually was.

This book proceeds as follows. Part I, "Crisis," covers the period of hyperinflation in Austria from early 1921 to late 1922. Chapter 1, "Making Sense of Hyperinflation," argues that expectations and fears about the future dominated how Austrians made sense of the upheavals brought about by violent depreciation and rising prices. The process of inflation in Austria, as later in Germany, was driven by expectations about the government's ability to cover the budget deficit. Explanations offered by contemporary economists differed, however, and were also determined by their personal visions of Austria's future. Socially, the accelerated monetary dynamics of hyperinflation translated into a heightened sensitivity of individual time, hyperactivity, and a condensed vision of the future. A gender analysis of inflation-themed caricatures shows how men linked fears of society's moral decay with doubts about their future roles as husbands and breadwinners, associated the depreciation of money with the declining value of their own masculine currency, and perceived the future of an economically deprived Austria as open to exploitation by foreign interests.

Chapter 2, "The Road to Geneva," is the account of how Austrian politicians from 1921 to 1922 first failed and eventually managed to obtain a foreign loan to stabilize their economy. Initial attempts miscarried both because foreign powers could not agree on freeing Austrian assets to serve as collateral, and because Austria's government objected to foreign financial control.

Unable to cooperate on a solution to save Austria, the Allied Powers called upon the novel League of Nations to devise a plan. Fearing an unfolding catastrophe in Central Europe, diplomats and politicians cooperated with the League's international financial experts to draw up a scheme that would allow bankrupt Austria to borrow. Covertly, Austria's conservative government now welcomed international financial control over the country's budget policy and use of borrowed funds. Because it ostensibly offered neutrality and technical expertise free from politics, League control could be made palatable to Austrians. The scheme, meant to restore the credibility of Austrian fiscal and monetary policy, was a first in the history of international monetary cooperation and served as a blueprint for similar multilateral interventions that were to follow.

Chapter 3, "How to Kill a Hyperinflation," provides a detailed account of how the League of Nations intervention was initiated in Vienna through the work of a delegation of international financial experts. It demonstrates that these delegates' efforts were vital for getting Austrian politicians to uphold their commitments and implement the pledged measures necessary to restore credibility of Austrian fiscal and monetary policy. International cooperation, as well as a genuine desire among foreign experts and financiers involved in Austrian reconstruction to see it succeed, were the bedrock on which confidence was reestablished, despite Austrian foot dragging and dilatory obstructionism. Notwithstanding the widely held belief that the credit for terminating hyperinflation ought to go to Chancellor Seipel for getting the League to act in August 1922, financial data show that inflationary fears lingered on and that only the incessant efforts of the delegates to ensure Austrian compliance with the League scheme resulted in a change of expectations that eradicated the risk of renewed inflation.

Part II, "Control," is an analysis of the League of Nations' intervention in Austria from 1923 to 1926. It starts out with Chapter 4, "The Inception of Control." The chapter takes the reader from the stabilization of the Austrian crown to the end of the French franc speculation in March 1924. It argues that from the first day of international control, the Austrian government snubbed the General Commissioner, ignoring his requests for accelerated reforms. To secure the initial success of the League intervention, which relied on foreign confidence, the General Commissioner promoted positive news from Austria, but refrained from imposing measures that Geneva considered essential. Increased revenues from taxation allowed the Austrian government to slash the deficit without reducing expenditures. With the help of the League's "credibility technology" and renewed investor confidence in Austria, a loan was issued on foreign capital markets, leading to massive capital inflows, rising revenues from taxation, and steady growth of foreign reserves at the ANB. Because the Austrian government was able to cover expenditures without extra funds, the General Commissioner was largely powerless. But this changed when the perilous bubble that had developed on the Vienna Stock Exchange burst in early 1924.

Chapter 5, "Reconstructions at the Crossroad," covers the period from the French franc crisis in March 1924, which put a successful completion of the reconstruction scheme at risk, to the resignation of Chancellor Seipel in 1925. The League, no longer willing to overlook the high budgetary expenses in Austria, faced off against Chancellor Seipel, who hoped control could be brought to an end by December 1924. Press caricatures depicted the League as a powerful foreign force that subjugated or corrupted Austrian politicians. General Commissioner Alfred Rudolph Zimmerman was shown as a greedy dictator governing Austria in the interest of international capital. But unlike such populist portrayals, the General Commissioner played a conciliatory role, trying to achieve a compromise between Geneva and Vienna. At the same time, the ANB asserted Austria's independence in the face of foreign pressure and interests. Despite explicit wishes from the BoE the Austrians refused to raise their interest level and trigger domestic deflation. This provoked a dangerous deterioration of relations between the two central banks that would become difficult to mend.

Chapter 6, "The Politics of Control," covers the final period of League intervention and Austrian reconstruction, conducted under a new government. Despite the financial crisis of 1924, confidence in Austria's economic and fiscal stability gradually increased and, against the better opinion of the League's own experts, control was terminated in July 1926. Experts on the League's Financial Committee voiced concern about the high level of foreign short-term debt of Austrian banks and about the lack of long-term capital. The Achilles heel of Austria's economy, its current account deficit, made the financial situation particularly unsafe and long-term capital even more important. But political considerations, not least the League's unpopularity in Vienna, timed the end of international intervention in Austria. A foreign advisor at the ANB remained, and though largely unrecognized, helped explain and defend Austrian monetary policy decisions abroad. But the ANB and the BoE did not bridge their disagreement, so a mutual pledge of assistance was impossible, leaving Austria's banks and the currency stability at the mercy of foreign confidence.

Part III, "Collapse," covers two important banking crises that occurred after the League's departure. It begins with Chapter 7, "The Precedence of Politics," in which I argue that following the premature termination of League control, Austria became increasingly politically unstable. The departure of the General Commissioner had left behind a country that looked upon a functioning national economy that was now conceived to be viable. However, even if dependent on foreign developments for economic prosperity, Austrian economic stability was most endangered by its own political troubles. The conflict between labor and capital, fought by the socialist and conservative parties, grew more radical as the reactionary Heimwehr spoke openly of establishing a dictatorship by violent means. Political conflict also prevented the Austrian state from issuing a much-needed foreign loan that would have brought new long-term capital into the country. While riots in 1927 had not (yet) created sufficient concern among foreign lenders or Austrian citizens, political turmoil and the fear of a violent coup d'état in 1929 provoked the withdrawal of foreign deposits and citizens' savings. Though there is little evidence that Heimwehr agitation in the fall brought down Austria's second-largest bank, the sudden and unexplained resignation of Chancellor Seipel in April 1929 certainly contributed to rising financial anxiety that summer.

Chapter 8, "The Credit-Anstalt Crisis and the Collapse of the Gold Exchange Standard," argues that the ultimate collapse of Austrian finance was not due to the Credit-Anstalt's problems, but rather was a consequence of the German and British financial crises. While the Credit-Anstalt's collapse triggered the first national financial crisis of 1931, it was successfully contained within five weeks, by mid-June. Despite the generally accepted belief that central bank cooperation had become an anathema at the time, the Credit-Anstalt affair shows that genuine attempts at international assistance were tried and worked. And while there is evidence that the Credit-Anstalt crisis brought down a Dutch subsidiary, there is no reason to believe that it led directly to the German and British crises. It was only after the unrelated

German crisis provoked capital flight in mid-July that panic returned to Austria. Britain faced its own fiscal crisis and was unable to help, and the ANB had lost too much of its reserves to regain control. The Credit-Anstalt collapse was neither the cause nor the beginning of the European financial crisis of 1931, and Austrian financial stability was ultimately a victim of larger developments that lay to her north, and beyond her control.

Prologue

1908

> In 1900, Austria was an entity unwanted by its subjects.
>
> —Ludwig von Mises, *Memoirs*

THE WEATHER DID ITS PART. Doubtful Viennese who, in the early morning hours of Friday, 12 June 1908, might have still inquired with the municipal switchboards, would have been told that the Imperial Tribute Procession, or Kaiser-Huldigungs-Festzug, was taking place as planned. To honor Emperor Franz Joseph on the occasion of the sixtieth anniversary of his reign, that morning thousands of men and women of all classes and from all over his Austrian lands and kingdoms—though not from the Hungarian half of the realm—had assembled in a long line on the Prater Hauptallee, ready to parade through the inner city. Divided into two processions that together stretched for almost fifteen kilometers, they prepared to perform a succession of historicist and romanticist dramas. Nineteen carefully chosen episodes from 700 years of Habsburg history, composed of mounted knights in full armor, waving ladies in antique carriages, and marching soldiers porting historic arms and uniforms, constituted a choreographed first part. The larger, second sequence was made up of popular delegations representing Franz Joseph's culturally diverse realm. Groups from the outer stretches of the empire and from the closer Austrian heartland, arranged in order of His Majesty's royal title and all clad in their old-fashioned folk costumes, prepared to hail the Emperor in their mother tongues. Members of Vienna's sport societies, professional guilds, and social associations also got into line. Schools, businesses, and even hospitals stayed closed. Hundreds of thousands of festively clad men, women, and children cordoned off by soldiers, cadets, and police, arrived to fill the few open spaces between the spectator stands along the Ringstrasse and inner city boulevards and witness the unusual spectacle.

A temporary festival plaza, the Kaiserfestplatz, guarded by four impressive golden lions carrying pylons and dominated by an opulent tent crowned with a massive double eagle, had been constructed right outside the Hofburg, halfway along the route. By mid-morning, notables in dark morning coats and top hats brandishing their walking sticks, refined ladies in white summer dresses and feathered fedoras, the general staff in parade uniforms, and the diplomatic corps eyed the procession from specially erected terraces. Under the large tent, the Archdukes and Archduchesses had joyfully assembled with their spouses and young children, little boys wearing dark navy costumes and girls wearing white dresses and straw hats. Protected from the strong midsummer sun by a separate baldachin, the seventy-seven-year-old Emperor, in a decorated uniform with sword and plumed hat, uncomfortably received the three-hour tribute crawling before his eyes, impatiently skipping the break with refreshments scheduled for half time, anxious to return to his residence in Schönbrunn on the outskirts of Vienna.

Despite the jubilant and lofty atmosphere that day, some attentive press commentators subtly described the procession as a "colorful fairytale," a "realistic dream," even a "theatric performance."[1] Historians have since carefully dissected how the spectacle, rather than demonstrating the strength of the empire, exposed the principal tribulations challenging the Kaiser, his administration, and the over 50 million subjects living under his rule. Indeed, the forces of nationalism were tearing the dual monarchy apart at its seams, and there appeared to be no easy panacea to save it. Seated among the imperial family was the twenty-year-old grand duke Karl, who had arrived the previous evening from Prague, close to where he was stationed as a first lieutenant, studying law and political science. Little did he know then that he would become the last Emperor of Austria, and would witness, just ten years after that beautiful summer day, the dismemberment of the dual monarchy, followed by his and his family's departure into exile.

The nineteenth century had been one of rapid transformations across all of Europe. Industrialization had given rise to an affluent bourgeoisie, while rapid urbanization had brought about large working-class populations living in the squalor of metropolitan slums and tenements. Since the French Revolution and the widespread but unsuccessful revolts of 1848, monarchical rule and the privileges enjoyed by aristocracy had been on the defensive across much of Europe. In 1908, France, Switzerland, and San Marino might have still been the only republics in Europe, but even the authoritarian Russian Czar Nicholas II had been forced to adopt a constitution and share power with the state Duma following the revolution of 1905. Military rivalry, technological progress, and economic sense had meanwhile underlain the unifications of both Italy and Germany, carried by a surging nationalism that offered an attractive platform for politicians seeking the support of the new urban bourgeoisie.

Franz Joseph was crowned Emperor in the Moravian city of Olomouc on 2 December 1848, where his abdicating uncle, the rather unqualified Emperor Ferdinand, had moved the court fleeing the violent revolution that had taken over Vienna in October that year. The anti-monarchical and revolutionary spirit that had excited people across Europe inspired discontented workers, students, and bourgeois liberals to take to Vienna's streets in March and demand social improvements, the right to vote, and an end to press censorship. There had been rebellions against monarchical rule in Austrian-controlled Milan and Venice, and nationalists in Prague and Budapest had deemed the time right to take up arms and overturn Habsburg rule, but eventually loyal troops reconquered Vienna and put down the revolts in northern Italy and Hungary. As one of his last acts, Emperor Ferdinand professed the indivisibility of the Habsburg Empire, compelling the revolutionary deputies at the first German National Assembly in Frankfurt to accept Prussia as the only power able to generate a true German unification. The Habsburgs, who for centuries had led the Holy Roman Empire of German Nations, chose to continue governing a multinational empire in which Germans were the largest minority, but just one of a dozen or more nationalities. Franz Joseph, eager to strengthen monarchial rule, reintroduced absolutism and suspended the constitution, but only narrowly survived a Hungarian nationalist's attack on his life in 1853.

Beleaguered at home, Franz Joseph was no more fortunate on foreign battlefields, losing Lombardy to the Piedmontese at Solferino in 1859, being defeated by Prussia at Königgrätz in 1866, and losing Veneto to Italy that same year. Unpopular and burdened with war indemnities, the monarchy eventually had to show a conciliatory face and agree to a curtailment of its powers to continue borrowing, shore up precarious state finances, and stabilize the currency. A constitution adopted in 1861 gave a bicameral Reichsrat budgetary powers but was opposed by Hungarian notables on nationalistic grounds, and they continued to refuse to be taxed. The Kaiser disbanded the Reichsrat in 1865 to have a free hand in negotiating a compromise with Hungary, which in 1867 resulted in the historic Ausgleich, an agreement with Hungary that split the empire in two halves. Franz Joseph, Emperor of Austria, was separately crowned King of Hungary so that what was now a double monarchy continued to be ruled by the same monarch, while Vienna and Budapest became home to two separate parliaments. Foreign affairs and matters of war and finance were to underlie joint policies, but in all other matters Hungary was now independent from Austria, or Cisleithania, its politically correct designation.

In Austria the right to vote was gradually extended further until in 1907 the first free, secret, and general elections for all male citizens above the age of twenty-four took place, with no privilege for class, profession, or wealth. Of the three political forces dominating the Austrian Reichsrat, only the largest, the clerical Christian-Socials, were outspokenly sympathetic to the monarchy and old order. The nationalist Pan-Germans saw Austria's future fatefully linked to that of Wilhelmine Germany and disapproved of Habsburg's commitment to a supranational state. The Socialists, inspired by the ideas of Marx and Engels, agitated vocally for the material improvement of the working class and more timidly against existing political hierarchies, but were certainly no supporters of monarchical rule. Ideologies notwithstanding, in parliament, deputies aligned themselves more along national than political lines, with Czech Bohemians and Moravians, Polish Galicians, Slovenians, and Italians from South Tyrol demanding linguistic rights that were opposed by German Austrians who sought to defend and preserve their historic hegemony.

The Czechs, who like the Hungarians had a historical kingdom to harken back to, and who possessed the economic and numerical clout to try to force yet another state-building compromise, most successfully pushed their case by obstructing parliament. In 1897, the initiative of Prime Minister Count Badeni to put Czech on an equal footing with German for all administrative matters in Bohemia and Moravia had been met with disdain by German speakers, provoking violent scenes in the Austrian Reichsrat and bloody unrest in Prague, Vienna, and other cities. Badeni resigned the same year, and there followed eighteen prime ministers in twenty-three years, often ruling by decree, as national animosities paralyzed Austria's parliament. At the same time the populist and anti-Semitic Karl Lueger became mayor of Vienna, much to the dislike of Badeni and the Emperor himself. Austrian liberals, monarchists, aristocrats, and Jews opposed to the rigid and exclusionary categories of national identity were supportive of a multinational Austria and Habsburg Empire and relied on Emperor Franz Joseph and his dynasty for continuity and stability, and for a resolution of the ethnic and linguistic rivalries that threatened the cohesion of the state.

In 1908, Franz Joseph, Europe's oldest and longest ruling monarch, thus looked back on a somewhat unfortunate reign. Privately, he had been forced to endure the suicide of his only son Rudolf and the murder of his beloved wife Elisabeth. He had lost his dynasty's major territories in Italy and its principal position among the German states. Only reluctantly had he introduced constitutions that gave rights and freedoms to citizens, and that delegated power to parliament, curtailing the absolutist rule he had enjoyed as a young Emperor. Naturally, perhaps, none of these events were included among the historical pictures paraded in 1908. Instead, the procession in his honor ended with a mounted Count Josef Radetzky impersonating his legendary grandfather, the Marshall, who in 1848 had successfully put down the Italian revolts, and with the eponymous march accompanying a final contingent of troops. The Socialist *Arbeiterzeitung* rightly commented that, had the flashback continued, it would have had to present not only the crimes of counterrevolution and the madness of absolutism, but also the military catastrophe of Solferino and Austria's loss of leadership in Germany, or "in short, the liquidation of the Habsburg Empire."[2]

The historian Steven Beller argues that the procession of 1908 had been a valuable, rare, but ultimately failed opportunity to instill new meaning and vigor into what it meant to be Austrian and a Habsburg subject. In his view, the organizers of the procession recognized that Austria needed a positive and more inclusive state identity, but the forms chosen for the parade, like other attempts at creating an Austrian self-image, were "a part of the malady for which they claimed to be the cure."[3] According to the historian Daniel Unowsky, the intended message of the procession was in fact that under the Emperor's guardianship all inhabitants, whatever their nationality or language, could enjoy and pursue their own cultures and customs. But, as Unowksy notes, this came with a German centric, civilizational message: Only German Austrian events figured in the historical section, while the nationalities that followed were presented in their folk costumes, as premodern, if not outright backward and primitive.[4] The historic procession thus only served to emphasize German hegemony in a multinational state that was being torn apart by national antagonisms.

More significant, perhaps, Czechs and Hungarians, the two most important non-German groups in the empire, and the Italians of South Tyrol boycotted the festivities. The Hungarians, who had little to celebrate about 1848, insisted on their independence and, arguing that they only recognized Franz Joseph's coronation as Hungarian King in 1867, were conspicuous by their absence. The Czechs were put off by the scornful opposition of Vienna's populist mayor, who orchestrated against the Czech National Theater, which had wished to perform its version of *Hamlet* in honor of the Emperor in Vienna that year.[5] Thus, instead of demonstrating Austrian unity, the tribute revealed the national divisions that ran through the dual monarchy. And finally, the historic section focused entirely on the Habsburg dynasty's record, its German-speaking high aristocracy and German-speaking armies, with soldiers, guns, and cannons dominating much of the procession. Beller argues that to the public the historic scenes seemed meaningless at best, and notes how "the parade said nothing about Austria that was new, changed no minds, and left the state of state consciousness where it had been before."[6] There was no mention of the more recent constitutional, cultural, or social achievements, which might have offered something everyone could have taken some pride in.

Yet, if politically the inhabitants of the Austro-Hungarian Empire were drifting apart, bound together by little else than their allegiance to an aging monarch, economically the Habsburg lands had in many ways grown closer under the reign of Franz Joseph. In Europe, economic development and wealth gradually declined as one traveled from the northwest to the southeast, and this held true for the less developed dual monarchy, too. In the more industrialized areas around Vienna, and in the Czech lands and Silesia, illiteracy had practically been eradicated and skilled laborers earned real wages two or three times higher than illiterate peasants in the poorer regions of Galicia or Bukovina had to make due with. Economic integration was hampered by long distances and bad transportation, but also perhaps by the fact that people felt more comfortable doing business with their own linguistic groups. Nevertheless, technological innovations such as the railways and telegraph had drawn the empire closer and at the turn of the century living standards were slowly converging.

Serfdom had been legally abolished in 1848, freeing farmers to seek new forms of employment. Mechanization of traditional supplementary work in textiles and timber had reduced their additional sources of income and drew peasants to the cities, where they were employed in new industries or as domestic servants. Growing cities stimulated intensified agricultural production in the Hungarian plains, and Hungarian farmers had emerged as the major agricultural producers of the empire, supplying Austrian workers with grain and flour in return for manufactured products. The Austro-Hungarian customs union area was largely autarchic, although it did depend on foreign trade for some specialized or manufactured goods. In Silesia, Bohemia, and Moravia, which were close to the coal mines that fueled the steam engines, but also around Vienna, to which coal could be brought by railways, spinning factories produced cotton and industrialized weaving textiles; iron, steel, and other metal factories were founded; lighting matches were fabricated, beer brewed, sugar refined, coffee roasted in large quantities, paper produced, leather made, ships built, and of course bricks fired. The locomotives for the Ferdinand Nordbahn, the second fully steam-driven railway on the European continent, were still shipped from Britain and painstakingly assembled in Vienna in 1837, but just a couple of years later the first Austrian steam engines were already produced in Viennese railway factories.

Troubled by unhappy military campaigns and constitutional demands, Franz Joseph's neo-absolutist reign was at first pure laissez-faire when it came to business and the economy. The emperor encouraged the foundation of large banks to help finance and run the new industries and the railways they depended on. The Niederösterreichische Escompte-Gesellschaft was founded in 1853, and two years later the Credit-Anstalt für Hand und Gewerbe, which would become the region's largest universal bank, while the Boden-Kredit Anstalt and Anglo-Österreichische Bank followed a decade later. They all grew considerably over time and issued shares for companies, often keeping a sizeable participation to themselves, thereby obtaining large interests in industrial enterprises all over the monarchy, but also promoting protectionism and cartelization. On the Vienna stock exchange, the issue of railway and industrial stocks attracted foreign capital, particularly after the large indemnity paid by France to Prussia following its defeat in 1871. Shares traded at ever higher prices, and when the industrial bubble burst in 1873, the Gründerkrach bankrupted dozens of banks and hundreds of companies, ruining thousands of speculators and investors. To support the market, surviving banks bought shares of healthy companies, further intensifying their existing connections between financial institutions and industrial producers.

Austrian banks and entrepreneurs turned their attention to newly independent Hungary and less developed parts of the empire, such as Carpathia and the Alpine lands, to which capital now flowed in search of returns. And as growth in the Austrian part picked up at a lower pace in the 1890s, there was some convergence across the dual monarchy. Peasants continued to move to urban centers in search of better employment, and the emergence of a class of working poor generated a series of social laws, which were quite progressive for their times. Labor laws prohibited child labor and night work for women and youth, and curtailed work to a maximum of eleven hours a day and six days a week. And as of 1888–1889 there was obligatory health- and workplace insurance, though there were no pension or unemployment benefits. Still, wages of workers hardly covered their most minimal needs and living conditions were dire, working days long, and the pay for children and women particularly low. About 5 million people emigrated between 1876 and 1910, 3.5 million to the United States, even though overall growth rates in Austria-Hungary were now faster than in Western Europe and the Habsburg economy started catching up with wealthier countries. In 1900 the Austro-Hungarian Bank, the monarchy's binational central bank, linked the Austrian currency to gold, loosely pegging the Austrian crown to the British pound.

Of all cities in the monarchy, Vienna underwent the most rapid transformation during the nineteenth century, turning itself into a metropolis akin to London or Paris. Urban expansion and renewal went hand in hand with high population growth and immigration. In the city's noble first district, where every family had at least one domestic, offices and shops replaced apartments on the lower floors and a new, splendidly broad Ringstrasse replaced the old bulwarks. The boulevard surrounded the first district, and while it facilitated traffic, it still served as a physical and visual boundary between the fashionable city center and the adjoining neighborhoods. Surrounding the new boulevard many of the capital's most important and impressive edifices were erected: parliament, the opera, the university, the stock exchange, the Vienna municipality, museums, the Palace of Justice, hotels, banks, and noble residences. As of 1873 a high-line system brought fresh alpine water to the city, and in 1890 the Linienwall, a fortification of brick and moats at the city edge, was torn down and replaced by a circular road (the Gürtel) on which high-line tracks for the Vienna Metropolitan Railway (Stadtbahn) were erected.

Over the nineteenth century, the population of Vienna grew by a staggering 259 percent, from 317,768 inhabitants in 1830 to 1,674,957 in 1900. It was a city of immigrants with more than half of its inhabitants born outside Vienna. One-tenth came from the surrounding countryside and province of Lower Austria; a third came from the Austrian Crown-lands (the Alps, Bohemia, Moravia, Silesia, and the South); one-tenth each came from the rest of the empire or outside it, mainly Hungary and Germany, but also Galicia and Bukovina. In fact, of those born in towns surrounding Prague, more ended up moving to Vienna than to Prague itself. The highest concentration of immigrants could be found in Vienna's second district, known as Leopoldstadt. Around 1900, about one-tenth of these newcomers worked as domestics, forming the bulk of the city's butlers, maids, cooks, nannies, and servants, but most found work in factories, plants, and sweatshops, together with more than half of all other laboring Viennese. Many newcomers were working immigrants, who usually arrived alone and then established a family in Vienna once they were economically secure.

Vienna's garment industry employed more than every tenth immigrant, 30 percent were employed in industries other than garment, and more than 6 percent in restaurants and hotels. Around one-third were self-employed, establishing themselves in trade, commerce, or liberal professions. Men did not outweigh women immigrating to Vienna, partly because of the large demand for female instructors, cooks, and wet nurses, but also because young women from the surrounding areas moved to the city to find a suitable husband. Over 100,000 Czech and Galician Jews arrived in Vienna during the second half of the nineteenth century, many of them settling in the city's second district. The relative success of their integration emerges from the university's student roster of 1903 / 1904. Jews, who at the time represented but 9 percent of the population, made up 22 percent of its student body. Because cheap housing was undersupplied, the city's immigrant poor had to make the best use of existing facilities, and living conditions were crowded. More than half of all two-room apartments had three to five inhabitants, and almost a fifth housed six people or more. Immigrants, apprentices, and day laborers often rented just a bed within a small and usually shared room. Every third apartment in the city housed such Aftermiether (subtenants) or Bettgeher (bed lodgers).

By 1914, Vienna had grown to around 2.1 million inhabitants and was among the largest cities in the world. From all corners of the dual monarchy, migrants flocked to its districts to find work in industry or in the homes of the upper classes, or to establish themselves in trade and commerce. It was home to the Habsburg dynasty, its high nobility, a large and industrious bourgeoisie, and hundreds of thousands of workers. It was the capital of a multilingual and multinational empire, a center for its education, commerce, fashion, industry, and arts. At the same time, it was a city of poverty, squalor, and hard work. In a time before washing machines, running water, widespread elevators, or common electricity, most housework had to be done by manual labor. Thousands of domestics washed, cleaned, cooked, and polished arduously to preserve the elegant lifestyle of their employers. And most Viennese worked long shifts in the sweatshops run by the local garment producers, in the large Wienerberger brick factory, or in the town's many other industries to make a living and feed their families.

On 28 July 1914, the day that Austria declared war on Serbia, exactly one month after the assassination of Archduke Franz Ferdinand by the Yugoslav nationalist Gavrilo Princip in the town of Sarajevo, the editors of the *Neue Freie Presse* still expressed a naïve hope that Russia would stay out of the conflict and thus a World War might be averted.[7] Although enthusiastic crowds in front of Vienna's War Ministry and Rathaus had cheered the upcoming declaration the previous day, the following months and years would show that the dual monarchy was ill prepared for military conflict on such a large scale. Its bifurcated administration made important questions of war, such as food supply, armament production, or resource allocation, a matter of negotiation between Budapest and Vienna, hampering the war effort, and while the army was united under a joint command, prewar military expenditures in Austria-Hungary had been the lowest among all the powers entering the war. Its failed offensives against Russia and Serbia during the early months of fighting came at an enormous human and material cost—over a million dead, missing, or wounded—and its best heavy artillery, locomotives and carriages gone, losses that could not be replaced and that henceforth made hope of a quick victory elusive.

With the outbreak of war the constitutional liberties were suspended. The Austrian parliament was closed indefinitely and freedoms of speech and association were abolished. Censorship was returned and all war-related offenses by civilians, from espionage to undermining morale, were tried without jury under military law. And as men donned uniforms to join the fight, people back home faced material hardships of their own. The Allied blockade made food imports all but impossible, and Hungary, the monarchy's breadbasket, was reluctant to share its poor harvests with Austria. With farms in Galicia and Bukovina destroyed by war against Russia, most able men drafted, and working animals requisitioned, agricultural production in Austria failed to make up for the shortfall. Feeding the army was given priority; consequently food in cities had to be rationed and food shortages appeared early. There were food riots in 1915 and 1916, after which families in Vienna were allotted small plots in the Prater park to grow their own food and the city opened soup kitchens for the poor and hungry.

After Franz Joseph's death in November 1916, his nephew and successor Karl I lifted censorship and reconvened parliament in an attempt to gain legitimacy in face of widespread discontent. In vain he also tried to find ways to exit the war, which was becoming ever more difficult to fight as it dragged on. Unable to import raw materials or replace spare parts, industrial production declined. Scarce metals were confiscated, but even intensified coal and steel production could not meet the large requirements of the armaments industry. By 1917 the railway system was breaking down, leading to coal shortages for industry and civilians, with families allowed to heat only a single room per dwelling. More and more industrial workers joined strikes in demand of better food and pay, with tens of thousands of exhausted workers in key industries laying down tools across Austria in May 1917. In mid-January 1918, infuriated by reduced rations and fears that an intransigent military leadership might fail to make peace with the Soviets at Brest-Litowsk, hundreds of thousands of Austrian workers joined strikers in Germany, demanding an end to the war.

With the army still holding its enemies at bay, Karl I, in order to salvage his dynasty and monarchy, considered granting autonomy to the southern Slaws within a broader federation, including a reconstituted Polish kingdom with him as monarch. Woodrow Wilson's Fourteen Points presented in January 1918 had only demanded the "freest opportunity for autonomous development" of Austria-Hungary's peoples—and only for Poland full independence—while Lloyd George had declared that England did not desire the dismemberment of Austria-Hungary. But Budapest stood opposed to any federalist reforms that would undermine Hungary's position vis-à-vis its own minorities, and over the summer, emboldened by public support from Allied governments, nationalists within the empire or in exile began preparing for national sovereignty. In early October 1918, the central Powers declared themselves in agreement with Wilson's Fourteen Points and Karl officially proposed to parliament a political federation of national, independent states under his reign, without affecting Hungary's rule over Slovaks or Croats. But his tired and underfed army was already disintegrating and national assemblies in Prague and Zagreb were declaring independence from Austro-Hungarian rule. In Vienna, the Reichsrat's German-speaking members announced the constitution of a new German Austria that intended to join with Germany, while in Budapest a new government annulled the 1867 agreement that had bound Hungary to Austria. On 11 November 1918, the day the war officially ended, Karl, without abdicating, announced his retirement from all political affairs. Ten years earlier, on a sunny summer morning, he had sat on a festively decorated dais watching a parade that celebrated the history of a centuries-old empire and its powerful dynasty. Now, under his reign, all of it was quickly coming to an end.

Though Karl I still resided in Vienna, a provisional National Assembly proclaimed the democratic Republic of German-Austria on 12 November 1918. From its initial elections in February 1919, at which women were allowed to participate for the first time, the Social Democrats emerged as the strongest political force, followed by the Christian-Social and Pan-German parties. The first government, formed under Socialist Chancellor Karl Renner, united the two largest parties in a coalition and confirmed his party colleague Otto Bauer as foreign minister. Socialists celebrated as Karl and his family departed Vienna on a train to Switzerland and the Austrian Habsburg laws nationalized their property, forbidding the use of former monarchical titles in the new Republic. Among some of its first legislations, a governmental socialization commission chaired by Socialist Otto Bauer and Christian-Social Ignaz Seipel drafted a wide range of socialist reforms, including the introduction of unemployment insurance, a reduction of working hours, improved conditions at the workspace, vacations, and the installation of workers' councils, which were all quickly put into law.

War-ravaged Austria faced serious economic problems. The currency was depreciating and the government budget suffered heavily from subsidizing basic foodstuffs, paying salaries to the large number of state workers, and covering the deficits at state enterprises, especially the railways. German-speaking civil servants and war veterans flocked to Vienna from all corners of the former empire and the new state had to pay their salaries or pensions, too, without any assistance from other successor states. The new neighbor states of Hungary, Czechoslovakia, Poland, and the Kingdom of Serbs, Croats, and Slovenes (in short SHS and soon renamed Yugoslavia), on which Vienna had long relied for agricultural imports, introduced their own currencies. They viewed the Austrian plight with little sympathy and as refugees continued to arrive in Vienna, food supplies from neighboring countries and Austrian provinces all but ceased. Coal provisions were scarce, too, forcing the partial closure of factories and businesses. Cold and undernourished, the inhabitants of Vienna fell victim to the Spanish flu epidemic and tuberculosis speedily spread among the population. For fear that human misery would bolster sympathies for Bolshevism or strengthen calls for unification with Germany, the Allied blockade was lifted in March 1919 and the Allies extended credits to pay for Austria's food supplies, saving Vienna from starvation. Foreign charitable institutions provided further assistance, particularly for the cities' vulnerable children. In May 1919, the Child Welfare Mission to Austria under the American Relief Administration operated thirty-four soup kitchens in Vienna, delivering 100,000 meals a day, and more than 100,000 deprived children were placed with foreign foster families between 1919 and 1920.

In May 1919, after Germany had been presented with the Treaty of Versailles, which explicitly forbade unification with Austria barring League of Nations consent, the Allies invited the Austrian government to receive its own peace terms at the Peace Conference in Paris. In June, in Saint-Germain-en-Laye, the Austrian delegation led by Chancellor Renner was presented with a draft treaty that foresaw painful losses of territory, but an amended second draft in July showed some economic and territorial improvements. Unlike for Germany, a first installment of reparations was not quantified, as neither Austrians nor Allies expected the impoverished country to pay anything soon. But liens were placed on Austrian state assets until all questions of reparations and the repayment of relief (food) credits were conclusively settled. The Austrian Republic, as it was now officially named, recognized the independence of the other Habsburg successor states and was prohibited from joining with Germany or any other country without League of Nations approval. Its new borders contained about sixty percent of Cisleithanian territory and of its German-speaking inhabitants, leaving out substantial German-speaking minority populations in Poland, Italy and Czechoslovakia. Finally, its army was considerably downsized, its navy and air force dismantled and its armament industry reduced to a minimum.

In September 1919, Austria signed the treaty and was in turn recognized as an independent state. The new country, home to 6.5 million Austrians, of which almost a third lived in Vienna, inherited a disproportionately large part of the monarchy's commercial and industrial apparatus. But output of agricultural producers was far below prewar yields, and industrial production depended almost entirely on the supply of Czechoslovak coal. Furthermore, large industrial firms, such as steel or locomotive producers, relied on sales markets now outside Austria, while important sectors such as textile manufacturers depended on imports for their inputs. Vienna, home to the former monarchy's largest and most important banks, educational institutions, and cultural establishments, now appeared disproportionally large and its multitude of educated state officials far outstripped the number of administrators needed. Before the war, the inhabitants of Vienna had made up around 4 percent of the dual monarchy's total population but had produced and consumed at least three times their demographic share in services and output. Would Austrians manage to fashion their young country into a second Switzerland, smaller but more affluent then Austria, or would the Vienna bourgeoisie have to get used to a permanently much lower standard of living?

Elections in October 1919 left the composition of the Austrian government unchanged. Chancellor Renner set out on drafting a constitution and improving ties with Austria's neighbors, but negotiations with Prague and Rome produced no significant advances on the question of cross-border trade, so Austrians and particularly the Viennese remained dependent on U.S. credits to import food. In February 1920, the Allies and other countries announced the long-term supply of flour and other foodstuffs against the security of unspecified Austrian state assets released by the Reparations Commission. Bread and flour rations could be raised, and although the Austrian government required less foreign exchange to import the food, it had to continue to subsidize the price of all foodstuffs. Austrian policy was to hold the Allies responsible for keeping them alive, and in April the Children's Fund increased the provision of daily meals in Austria from 270,000 to 300,000. During the same month, socialist and communist workers demonstrated in demand of a capital levy, which was passed after long debates in July 1920 but had little effect. The broad government, hampered by mistrust and the ideological disparities of its coalition parties, broke apart and new elections were called for October 1920. The Christian-Socials emerged significantly strengthened from these elections and the Socialists went into opposition. The new government, supported by the Pan-Germans, was headed by the Christian-Social Michael Mayr, a historian born in Upper Austria in 1864, who also acted as his government's Foreign Minister.

A new constitution, voted in October 1920, divided Austria into nine federal provinces, of which one was Vienna, and created a bicameral parliamentary system, with an upper and a lower house. The Bundesrat, made up of deputies sent by the provincial parliaments, and the members of the Nationalrat, voted directly by the electorate, jointly chose the federal President, who had largely ceremonial powers, while the Nationalrat alone elected the government. But finalizing the new state's political structures did little to create a national identity. Many Austrians defined themselves as ethnically German and would have preferred unification of the two countries, commonly known as Anschluss. The fluidity, versatility, and overlap of ethnic and cultural identities that had constituted life in the Habsburg monarchy was replaced with a parochial nationalism, where being Austrian was understood as being exclusively indigenous, German and Roman Catholic. This posed particular problems for Vienna's sizable Jewish community, which saw itself as culturally German, but not nationally so. Lisa Silverman has shown how in the new Austrian republic, Jewishness commonly served as a category to define negatively what it meant to be Austrian. In the new nation-state, being Austrian was frequently understood to also mean not being Jewish.[8]

In January 1920 the League of Nations convened for the first time, after the U.S. Congress had voted in 1919 not to join. The new organization was to safeguard world peace by promoting international cooperation on all matters of security and protecting the rights and safety of smaller nation-states. Its two main bodies were the General Assembly, which met once a year and where all member states were represented, and the League Council, meeting at least four times per year and on which initially only Britain, France, Italy, and Japan had permanent seats. The administration of the League and preparation of its meetings in Geneva were handled by its Secretariat, made up of an idealistic, internationally recruited staff. Historians for a long time viewed the League of Nations as a failure because it did little to prevent the Italian war in Abyssinia or Japan's invasion of Manchuria in the 1930s. But multilateral organizations such as the League are only as strong and effective as their member states allow them to be. On technological, statistical, or health-related questions requiring international cooperation or standardization, the League undoubtedly proved its worth. In the 1920s, with the Marxist threat in Europe already diminishing, the League would play a key role in helping Austria reconstruct its state administration, finances, and economy.

In Hugo Bettauer's 1922 novel *Der Kampf um Wien: Ein Roman vom Tage (The Struggle for Vienna: A Novel of Our Time)*, the American billionaire Ralph O'Flanagan arrives at Vienna's Westbahnhof in December 1922. He moves into the luxurious Hotel Imperial, accompanied by his African American butler, and sets out to find ways to put his enormous fortune to good use. He has read about the destitution and misery governing the city his mother was been born in and wishes to help. But he falls prey to the intrigues of Austria's politicians, bank directors, and Hungarian spies. The good-hearted O'Flanagan is soon disillusioned by the elites, all eager to help their own narrow interests with the American's fortune. O'Flanagan finds no way to help Vienna, but he finds happiness and love, marrying the sweet and innocent Hilde Wehningen three months after his arrival. At their modest wedding meal O'Flanagan berates himself for not having been able to effectively help Vienna's impoverished citizens, but his best man raises a glass and prophesizes that his day might still come: "Der Kampf um Wien beginnt erst!"—The struggle for Vienna is only beginning![9]

I
Crisis

1

Making Sense of Hyperinflation

1921–1922

There are elections in our country—I think in October—
but I see very black for our poor country which has been
entirely smashed.

—Eugen von Rothschild to Anthony de Rothschild
17 September 1921

ON 12 JANUARY 1921, a heated debate in the Austrian parliament's National Assembly turned into a fistfight between Socialist and Christian-Social parliamentarians. The brawl followed upon Vienna's Socialist municipality's deliberate disregard of Christian-Social Interior Minister Egon Glanz's prohibition of staging Arthur Schnitzler's controversial play *Der Reigen*. The liberal *Neue Freie Presse* featured a blanket condemnation of the parliamentarian punch-up, but the conservative Christian-Social *Reichspost* blamed the Socialists for disregarding a government order in support of a "dirty" theater performance.[1] Animosity between the two parties was certainly rife, but the unbecoming exchange of blows in parliament had been more than just an extreme example of their deepening rivalry. Viennese conservatives were outraged because of what they perceived as the play's immoral gist, a series of scenes dealing with adultery, lust, and frivolous sex. Regular demonstrations of concerned citizens took place to protest the play until on 16 February 1921 a mob of six hundred young men stormed its evening performance, swinging canes, hurling tar-filled eggshells, and throwing chairs.[2] Men and women in the audience were beaten, and the violence only stopped after a hydrant was used to flood the stage and dressing rooms, allowing the spectators to escape into night and safety.[3] The *Reichspost* triumphantly reported the next day that young Christians had followed a call of conscience by beating up Jews and foreign speculators while the *Neue Freie Presse* deplored the brutal action and lynching of Viennese theater life.[4]

Seemingly motivated by questions of culture and morals, the violence provoked by *Der Reigen* did not merely reflect the growing schism between Conservatives and Socialists, but was itself fueled by fears and dystopian expectations about Austria's future, stoked by inflation and its dreaded consequences. To Austrians, the initial years following the war were a transition period marked by political uncertainties and economic worries that were amplified by constantly rising prices, an unprecedented depreciation of the crown, and unfulfilled hopes of foreign loans. Anxieties about Austria's prospects, linked to the question of what it meant and should mean to be Austrian and the controversy surrounding *Der Reigen,* reflected deep-seated fears, at least among conservative Viennese, that Socialist ascendancy, inflation, and the deteriorating economic situation were destroying traditional or bourgeois society and making immoral conduct commonplace.[5] Within the multinational Habsburg Empire, being Austrian had meant being a subject of the Emperor. Within the new republic, the meaning of *Austrianess* varied and was hotly debated, but for many it was linked to a history, religion, and culture that could most easily be categorized as simply *non-Jewish.*[6]

Inflation had been a truly global occurrence during the First World War, which no economy, belligerent or neutral, escaped.[7] Great Britain and the United States had experienced only mild inflation during the war; they hoped to restore their price levels by a contraction of money supply below its "natural" level and a return to gold through deflation.[8] In Austria and Germany, central bankers had faced more rapid inflation and could not hope to restore prewar parities in the same way without massive costs to their economy. In Austria, inflation, depreciation and increased money supply continued unabated following the armistice. Despite Allied credits and food supplies, the Austrian government had to borrow fresh notes from the Austrian section of the Austro-Hungarian Bank to finance food subsidies, obtain foreign exchange for additional imports, service national debt, and pay administrative salaries and expenditures. Before the war, one Austrian crown had equaled roughly one Swiss franc. During the war, the crown had lost over two-thirds of its exchange value, so that by 1 January 1919, 3.2575 Austrian crowns had to be paid for a Swiss franc. One year later the exchange rate was 36.75 crowns, and on 1 January 1921 the value had dropped to 109 crowns per Swiss franc. And worse was yet to come. When the Austrian crown finally stabilized after the two hyperinflationary phases of 1921 and 1922, one Swiss franc bought 13,285 Austrian crowns. There was currency speculation as well, but the incessant printing of notes by the Austrian government to cover its expenses was primarily and ultimately to blame.

This chapter offers an analysis of sources from contemporary economic discourse, popular caricatures, and financial and statistical data in order to provide a reflection of how Austrians experienced and made sense of inflation and hyperinflation after the war. It posits that at a time of rapidly increasing prices and depreciating exchange rates, expectations about the future dominated the way in which people made sense of their present. And as the uncanny future drew closer ever more quickly, anxieties about what was to come were amplified. Caricatures played upon and reveal dystopian fears that uncouth materialism and selfishness were replacing the moral values and decency that had ostensibly governed the prewar world. Statistics support the idea that individuals experienced the period of rapid price increases and depreciation as one in which the future became more imminent, amplifying anxieties about their own and society's material prospects. Even economists studying inflation and trying to find ways to stop it were influenced in their choice of economic explanations by their hopes and fears about Austria's economic viability and political future. Crucially, the timing and course of hyperinflation was itself determined by news and people's expectations concerning Austria's fiscal outlook. Thus there existed a reciprocal feedback loop between the social and cultural anxieties suffered by Austrians and the mechanism that drove hyperinflation. Austria was the first country to experience hyperinflation in postwar Europe, with Weimar Germany following one year later; thus hyperinflation was a novelty, associated with Austria's new postwar reality, and one that was little understood.[9]

Economic Debates about Inflation

For most Austrians, rapid inflation was experienced as an uncanny and powerful process of impoverishment and decline. The rapid and erratic deterioration of the crown's exchange rate both resulted from and created fears of a chaotic and unstable future. Economists and politicians tried to understand the reasons for inflation in order to develop measures that would tame the violent price increases and end the unprecedented bouts of depreciation. The way economists made sense of inflation, however, was in itself shaped by their expectations of Austria's possible futures. Experts who thought Austria was economically viable blamed inflation on the budget deficit and the imprudent printing of money. Others who believed Austria could not economically survive sought the causes of inflation in its negative balance of trade and the consequent depreciation of its currency.[10] For the latter group, only unification with Germany (made impossible by the peace treaties of Saint-Germain-en-Laye and of Versailles) or a Danubian Federation (opposed by Czechoslovakia and Hungary) could offer salvation to Austria's structural predicament, while for the former, a large foreign loan might balance the budget and help bring about a permanently stable economy.[11] While economists and financial experts held onto established economic theories, their professional views expressed in debates that played out on the pages of Vienna's daily newspapers seemed informed by this central, albeit theoretical question regarding Austria's political and economic future: whether to demand unification with Germany and therewith antagonize the Allies, or to comply with the Powers and accept their control of loans and pledged revenues in return for financial support.[12]

Stable prices in the nineteenth century had left economists unprepared to deal with inflation and currency depreciation following the First World War. The monetary policies of the nineteenth century had not "produced" stable prices, but rather, by steadily increasing the money supply in line with increased gold production, kept prices stable in a world experiencing high population growth and economic expansion.[13] During the war, Austrian inflation had been somewhat controlled and kept stable through rationing, and through capital and price controls, most of which were discontinued after the armistice. In postwar Austria, however, attempts to curb inflation were made difficult by speculation against the crown and the rising prices for food and primary goods on global markets. Stabilizing the value of the crown through intervention on the exchange market or through obtaining foreign credits to cover expenses repeatedly failed, so that depreciation and inflation rose twice to hyperinflationary levels. Hyperinflations, generally defined by economists as a rate of inflation that exceeds 50 percent per month, are rare and short periods, preceded and often followed by longer stretches of relatively high inflation. The first time monthly inflation rose above 50 percent in postwar Austria was between June and December 1921, the second time from June to August 1922. Both times, over the course of several months, the Austrian crown lost almost 90 percent of its foreign purchasing power.

Throughout these two years, inflation correlated with currency depreciation, which is easier to measure, and which was watched carefully by Austrians as a predictor of prices. Whereas there is only one market exchange rate reported in the press, there are myriad prices in the economy, and while the historian has access to almost continuous data on the exchange rate from multiple sources, it is difficult to come by daily data for even the most important goods. It is thus practical to track the exchange rate to illustrate Austrian inflation (see Graph 1.1). The graph uses the exchange rate to calculate the currency's depreciation per month on a daily basis. For each day it calculates how much the Austrian crown had depreciated over the last thirty days.

There were periods of currency appreciation, notably around the arrival of a first League Delegation in Vienna in the second quarter of 1921, and during March 1922, when Britain provided advances on a future loan, which

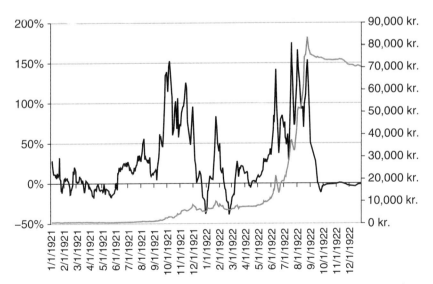

GRAPH 1.1. Daily month-on-month depreciation of Austrian crown vis-à-vis US$ in percent (black line, left axis) and the price of one US$ in Austrian crowns (gray line, right axis), 1 January 1921–31 December 1922. *Source: Neue Freie Presse.*

were employed to stabilize the exchange rate. But these were rather brief and punctuating periods that did not reverse the longer and persistent stretches of currency depreciation. As to be expected, the periods of prolonged severe depreciation coincide with the two phases of hyperinflation. At its most extreme, in late July and early August 1922, month-on-month depreciation reached a staggering 150 percent.

Although Austrian economists were anything but parsimonious when suggesting explanations for continued inflation and depreciation, two main schools of thought can be discerned from their writings.[14] The first view argued that Austria's unfavorable trade balance caused currency depreciation on the exchanges and led to imported inflation, an opinion most vocally advocated by Walther Federn and Gustav Stolper, the two editors of the country's influential *Der Österreichische Volkswirt*. The second view, most prevalent among established economists and government officials, focused on the continuous printing of notes to finance the government's deficitary expenditure, arguing that it increased prices and led to depreciation. Federn, born in Vienna in 1869, had studied economics and trained as a banker before founding his economic weekly, inspired by the London *Economist*, in 1908. Stolper, born in Vienna in 1888, had studied economics and law before joining Federn's magazine in 1911. Both of them also wrote regularly for Austria's daily press, but in 1925 Stolper would move to Berlin to found his own magazine, *Der Deutsche Volkswirt*.

In the view of Federn and Stolper the depreciation of the crown and the increase of prices were due to overconsumption and underproduction, which manifested themselves in a current account deficit (the balance of all trade and capital flows) and excess demand for foreign currency that drove up the exchange rate. Currency depreciation increased the price of imported goods and despite governmental food subsidies, led to demands by state workers for wage increases. As a temporary remedy, *Der Österreichische Volkswirt* recommended reducing state-demand for foreign exchange by abolishing food subsidies, installing higher taxation, and lowering real wages. The two editors were progressive and not anti-socialist, but they considered such radical steps necessary to transition Austria's economy toward a new and lower equilibrium. By pointing to the current account deficit as a structural economic problem, Federn and Stolper argued that Austria faced a poor economic future. If the country did not join Germany or reassert its dominant economic role in Central Europe, either Austrians would have to reduce their standard of living or the Allies, who had after all created Austria, would have to finance its excessive consumption indefinitely.

Stolper's and Federn's writings provide a running commentary to the governmental efforts at curbing inflation. After coming to power following the elections in October 1920 Chancellor Michael Mayr and his coalition of Christian-Socials and Pan-Germans hoped to get a grip on the deteriorating economic situation by terminating the need for new notes through long-term foreign credits.[15] Only a few months after the elections, however, the *Volkswirt* repeatedly called for the incorporation of Austria into Germany as the only realistic means to stop inflation, since no foreign loan would ever be large enough to satisfy Austria's excess demand on foreign exchange.[16] After the Allies referred Austria for help to the League's Financial Committee in March 1921 and a first League delegation arrived in April, the crown rallied on the exchanges in anticipation of foreign credits, but Stolper and Federn warned that the League had failed to take account of Austria's trade deficit and accused its delegates of insufficient knowledge about Austria's need to join Germany.[17] Such explicit calls for Anschluss by Federn or Stolper were rather rare (and disliked by both the Allies and the Austrian government), but the *Volkswirt* editors would often veil their calls for unification with Germany by pointing to Austria's structural overconsumption and underproduction instead. Federn thus repeatedly accused the League of ignoring Austria's fundamental problem: its persistent trade deficit and economically unsustainable existence.[18]

A weakening of the crown ensued in July 1921, after it emerged that the League scheme had failed. Credits from the Allies were unlikely to materialize and the Austrian crown rapidly lost value in July. It stabilized briefly in August upon news that the Allies might consider a new League plan, but after the League's September meeting produced a declaration that no money could be made available until the United States lifted its liens on Austrian assets, the crown went into complete free fall on the exchanges. As prices rose daily, the exchange rate dropped rapidly. At the end of June the U.S. dollar had still cost 950 Austrian crowns; by the end of September its price had risen to 2,500. Toward the end of January 1922, the price of one U.S. dollar was as high as 10,000 Austrian crowns. Within six months, the crown had lost almost 90 percent of its exchange value.

In October 1921, the Social Democrats presented Austria's new conservative government with a financial plan, adopted wholeheartedly by its Finance Minister, calling for increased taxation and reductions in expenditure, foremost in governmental food subsidies.[19] The plan was well received by the *Volkswirt*, but Stolper and Federn seized the occasion to reiterate how increases in money supply and inflation were effectively due to Austrian over-consumption and under-production, which would persist even with a balanced budget.[20] In the popular *Neue Wiener Tagblatt*, Federn wrote in October 1921 that there was no use balancing the budget without balancing the negative current account. Even without governmental food subsidies, Austrian overconsumption would create an excess demand for foreign exchange that would continue to cause depreciation and thus inflation, thereby destroying any increased revenue from taxation.[21] Stolper similarly wrote in the bourgeois, but left-wing *Der Morgen* a few weeks later that an end of food subsidies only meant a new round of inflation, since workers facing market prices for bread would eventually have to be granted higher wages.[22]

Indeed, after food prices were increased, Vienna shuddered from heavy riots led by hungry workers, protesting the end of food subsidies in December.[23] After a small British advance materialized in February 1922, the *Volkswirt* condemned the Finance Minister's intention to use it for a stabilization of the exchange rate, explaining that any appreciation would only increase the perennial current account deficit by widening the trade gap between imports and exports.[24] Government officials tried to reassure the public that negotiations on a foreign loan were proceeding well and that advances would materialize soon, but Stolper doubted that any loan large enough to carry Austria for more than eight months could be obtained. In the *Volkswirt*, Stolper sharply attacked the Austrian government, declaring it incompetent and accusing it of acting irresponsibly: "Never has reconstruction failed so completely, never have politicians acted so irresponsibly with a country entrusted to them."[25] A fresh government plan to found a new central bank to bring about stabilization was characteristically dismissed by Stolper because it would leave Austria's trade deficit unattended.[26] The plan was officially shipwrecked by mid-June 1922, with the crown beginning a renewed descent as the second wave of hyperinflation ensued. The impoverished operators of Vienna's tramway and Austrian state workers went on joint strike, forcing the government to anchor the indexation of state workers' wages into law. Stolper criticized the measure, which undoubtedly helped fuel the second wave of hyperinflation, for further increasing inflation and depreciation, while leaving the substantial current account deficit uncared for.[27]

Although they argued their view on Austria's viability using economic theory, Stolper and Federn lacked enough empirical data to substantiate their claim that Austria was living beyond its means. In a series of articles, Stolper tried to reconstruct the Austrian trade balances for 1919 and 1920, but only had recourse to the total weight of goods, not to their value; this did, however, indicate that the deficit was widening.[28] Yet it was impossible to say whether the trade deficit and the shortfall in the country's balance of payments were structural and irrevocable, nor whether depreciation and inflation resulted primarily from the perceived over-demand for foreign exchange. The fact that both of them were journalists might have informed their choice of the popular position that Austria was not economically viable. But Germany was not only economically stronger, but also socially more progressive, which must have appealed to them, too. Stolper and Federn had no reliable data on which to base their argument, and their conviction of Austria's nonviability was the result of an economic intuition that told them that their own and Austria's future would best be served by unification with Germany.

The other school of thought among Austrian economists argued that inflation was not structural but the result of the increase in money supply from printing new notes for government spending. Higher prices increased the demand for foreign exchange, which resulted in currency depreciation, though much of it was ascribed to speculators and the need of the government to import large amounts of coal and subsidized food. This was the established opinion among Austrian government officials and economists, and their solutions invariably consisted of loans, foreign or domestic, public or private, to cover the budget deficit.[29] Once the budget deficit was eliminated and note issue ceased, they argued, an end of inflation would ensue automatically. According to their judgment, Austria was economically viable, and inflation could be terminated by simply balancing the budget through taxation and reduced expenditure, once a large loan made fiscal reforms possible.

Thus, even though Austrian Chancellor Mayr announced in 1921 that to stop inflation he would balance the budget, much of his efforts concentrated on obtaining foreign loans as the way to make this possible.[30] Mayr and his staff thought that depreciation was temporary and could be stopped with the help of sufficient credits to pay for governmental spending on food imports.[31] Prominent academics shared the view that foreign credit would bring salvation in 1921. Thus Richard Kerschagl, born in Vienna in 1896 and working since 1920 as currency expert for the Austro-Hungarian bank, identified the printing of notes and an increase in consumer demand as the two main causes of inflation. Kerschagl, soon to be a lecturer at the University for World Trade in Vienna, called for a large foreign loan to help eliminate the budget deficit.[32] The banker and lawyer Wilhelm Rosenberg, born in Vienna in 1869 and in 1921 advising Austria's Finance Minister, identified the printing of notes as the driving force behind inflation, too, and wrote an article in favor of a domestic loan to cover the budgetary shortfall.[33] Only Emil Kraft, born in Vienna in 1865 and a board member of the Austro-Hungarian Bank since 1918, sounded a realistic chord and presciently noted in an interview with the *Neue Freie Presse* that without foreign assistance, the Austrian crown could lose all its value. Austrians would be forced to resort to barter if no foreign credits were found to cover the budget shortfall and counter the outflow of capital.[34]

Established economists in Austria thus suggested that inflation was essentially a budgetary problem and Austria no less viable than, say, Switzerland. Stabilization would occur automatically once a foreign or domestic loan allowed the government to cover its deficit, terminate note issue, and stabilize the exchange rate. Their explanations and remedies, though couched in economic theory, were informed by beliefs just as much as those of Federn and Stolper. The two editors of the *Volkswirt* did not think Austria viable and argued that depreciation and inflation were due to structural deficiencies that could only be resolved by integrating Austria into a larger economic sphere, *viz.*, Germany. Officials of Austria's governmental institutions, less worried and quicker to affirm Austria's lasting viability, largely argued that inflation was not structural but contingent on the government's deficit spending and that a remedy was available in the form of a foreign loan to balance the budget. Stolper and Federn were of the opinion that Austria could not continue as an independent state, and this view informed their model just as much as the remedies proposed by government officials presumed its viability. As economic journalists, Federn and Stolper could adopt a dissident position that dovetailed neatly with popular calls for joining

with Germany, whereas politicians and state functionaries accepted and operated within the confines of political realities. Both groups provided a co-
herent model that could explain the steady rise of prices and the currency's
parallel loss of foreign purchasing power, but not why that pace should suddenly pick up dramatically and turn into hyperinflation. The fact that experts appeared divided about the economic causes of inflation and offered
no workable remedies to prevent hyperinflation could only increase popular
feelings of general helplessness and despair in the face of accelerating ruin.

The Role of Expectations

While the mechanisms of inflation were poorly understood and its origins
subject to a divisive debate, the two dominant explanations covered above
were both proven wrong when the crown stabilized in 1922, even though
both note issue and trade deficit continued unabated. The first broad study
of Austrian inflation, published in 1924 by Jan van Walré de Bordes, analyti-
cally refuted both schools of thought. Van Walré de Bordes, born in Utrecht
in 1894, joined the League Secretariat in 1921 before accompanying its General Commissioner to Vienna and preparing the analysis for his doctoral degree from Leiden University. With the benefit of hindsight, he showed that
contrary to established beliefs, increases in money supply could not have
caused the quick rise of prices during hyperinflation (see Graphs 1.2 and 1.3).[35]
Data showed rather that after the war, inflation had preceded the growth in
money supply, and van Walré de Bordes concluded that Austrian postwar
inflation had mainly been imported through exchange depreciation.[36] However, extreme fluctuations of the exchange rate had been due not to current
account deficits either, as argued by Federn and Stolper, but rather to large
and sudden capital flows resulting from speculation and capital flight.[37]
Expectations were an important factor in the formation of the exchange rate
as movements in and out of the crown were determined, according to van
Walré de Bordes, to a large part by *psychological* factors. In his view, the
foreign exchange market was highly susceptible to changes of confidence
and the first market to react to rumors. It was widely acknowledged among
Austrians, van Walré de Bordes wrote, that currency fluctuations were a
guide for future price movements, so that sudden depreciation caused panic

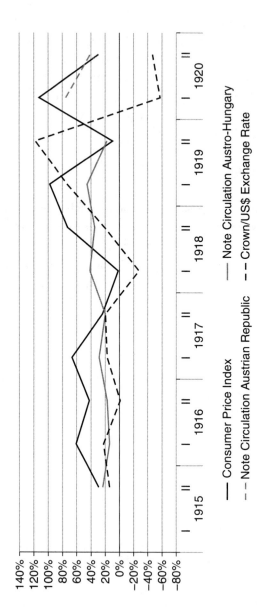

GRAPH 1.2. Biannual change of note circulation, crown / US$ exchange rate and average Consumer Price Index (CPI) in percent, 1915–1920. *Source:* Jan van Walré de Bordes, *The Austrian Crown* (London, 1924).

— Consumer Price Index

-- Note Circulation Austrian Republic

— Note Circulation Austro-Hungary

-- Crown/US$ Exchange Rate

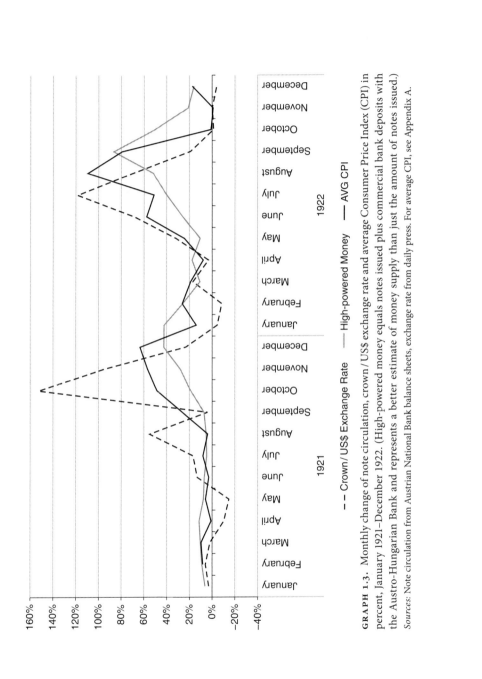

GRAPH 1.3. Monthly change of note circulation, crown/US$ exchange rate and average Consumer Price Index (CPI) in percent, January 1921–December 1922. (High-powered money equals notes issued plus commercial bank deposits with the Austro-Hungarian Bank and represents a better estimate of money supply than just the amount of notes issued.)

Sources: Note circulation from Austrian National Bank balance sheets, exchange rate from daily press. For average CPI, see Appendix A.

about future prices, a flight away from the crown and into the stores in search for goods, which triggered inflation.[38]

Indeed, the importance of psychological factors behind currency depreciation and the rise in prices was noted as early as January 1921.[39] The author and economist Friedrich Hertz, born in Vienna in 1878, had written his doctoral thesis on the discount and foreign exchange policy of the Austro-Hungarian Bank. Now working at the Federal Chancellery, he argued in the *Neue Freie Presse* that sudden falls in the exchange value of the crown were being caused by panic in reaction to rumors, doubts about the future, and lack of trust in Austria and its currency.[40] Around the same time, the German monthly *Die Bank* described how the Austrian crown's exchange rate had reacted to changing news during the last quarter of 1920:

> In September [1920] the crown's exchange rate improves significantly because an international intervention and a large foreign loan are expected. The strong depreciation of the crown in the first half of December is due to rumours that bank notes will soon be stamped in line with certain tendencies within the Government. The crown appreciates in reaction to an official denunciation of these rumours.[41]

Thus the exchange rate of the Austrian crown was driven up and down by expectations about the likelihood of foreign loans or devaluation, and since the exchange rate was understood to impact the price of goods, sudden bouts of depreciation quickly drove up the level of domestic prices as people rushed into stores and cafés to spend their money.

It was the Viennese economist Ludwig von Mises who one year later, at the end of the first hyperinflationary wave, tried to provide a more scientific description of how expectations directly impacted the rate of inflation. Mises argued that when people agreed on the exchange value of a currency, they took into account not only current prices, but also the expected development of prices and other economic variables for the foreseeable future:

> The valuation of money in terms of goods and foreign exchange always includes a speculative aspect, i.e. it always includes the expected development of future conditions. If one expects depreciation to continue because the Government is unwilling to limit its usage of the printing

press, then money will be valued lower than it would have been valued if no more inflation had to be expected. Because one expects deprecia-tion to continue, one tries to get rid of the domestic currency which loses purchasing power on a daily basis by buying goods, stocks or for-eign exchange.[42]

In Mises's view, Austrians were forward-looking and the present-day value of the currency always incorporated the expected risk of future inflation and depreciation. If citizens had reason to believe that money would buy less in the future, then why hold on to it today?

Because prices are slower to react to news or rumors than are exchange rates, depreciation preceded inflation, but today's economists believe that rates of inflation are determined to a large extent by people's expectations about future inflation.[43] In 1956, American economist Phillip Cagan sug-gested that during periods of *hyperinflation* the price level is determined neither by expectations about the increase in money supply nor by the ex-pected rate of currency depreciation, but rather by the expected cost of holding onto cash into the future, that is, the expected rate of inflation itself. Cagan observed that real cash balances (i.e., money supply divided by the price level) fell during high inflation as people wished to hold less and less money and more real assets.[44] In search for real assets, they bid up prices, until, in the aggregate, the new price level created the desired and reduced level of their real cash balances. Thus, although nominal circulation in-creased, prices increased at a faster rate and aggregate real balances declined (see Graph 1.4). Cagan showed that in this way inflation operated as a self-fulfilling prophecy. If expectations of inflation were positive, economic agents would act so as to drive up prices until eventually their expectations were fulfilled.

But what were the price expectations of ordinary Austrians based on? Van Walré de Bordes thought that Austrians looked to currency depreciation as the major indicator of inflation-to-come, but volatility of the exchange rate was itself a consequence of expectations about the future. In 1981, economist Thomas Sargent first speculated that it was the various issues of Treasury Bills to cover government deficits and the likelihood of future budget sur-pluses and deficits that best explained the change in expectations, and thus the course of hyperinflation.[45] Indeed, Austrian changes in money supply

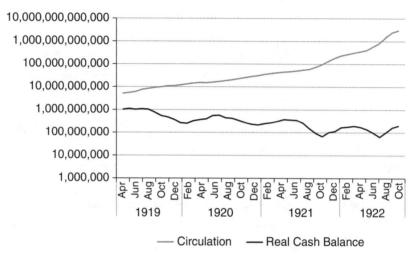

GRAPH 1.4. Austrian crown notes in circulation vs. real cash balance (logarithmic scale, real cash balance in gold crowns), 1919–1922. *Source:* LNA, C 71, La réconstruction financière de l'Autriche 1921–1928 / Balance Sheets (small) Issue Bank: Pierre Quesnay, remarques sur la circulation fiduciaire autrichienne, 3 January 1923.

were largely determined by the size of the government's deficit, as the Austro-Hungarian Bank provided unlimited discounting of Treasury Bills to cover the state's expenditures.[46] When the government issued debt in the form of Treasury Bills, it sold them to the central bank in return for new notes, which, *ceteris paribus,* increased the money supply. Austrians *believed* that a larger money supply led to higher prices, and therefore looked to the amount of Treasury Bills discounted, readily available to any newspaper reader, as an indicator of future inflation. A comparison of the amount of Treasury Bills discounted and the money supply allows us to calculate the percentage of circulation created this way through the issuing of Treasury Bills. In March 1921, Treasury Bills represented less than 20 percent of high-powered money (currency circulating plus money owned by banks), but the unceasing note printing to finance government spending pushed up their share to 80 percent by May 1921 (see Graph 1.5). For most of 1921 and 1922 the continued discounting of Treasury Bills to finance government expenditure was the main cause behind the nominal increase of money supply.

Thus, from June 1921 to August 1922, increases in note circulation and Treasury Bills discounted by the Austro-Hungarian Bank were highly cor-

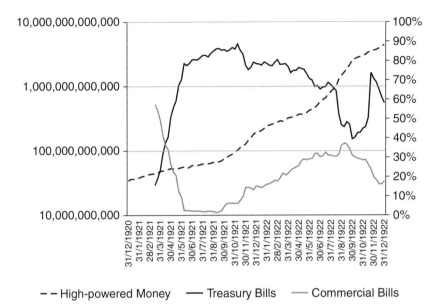

GRAPH 1.5. Percentage share of Treasury Bills and commercial bills backing high-powered money (logarithmic scale in paper crowns). *Source:* Austrian National Bank balance sheets as published in the daily press.

related (see Graph 1.6).[47] Changes in Austrian money supply were determined largely by the government need to finance its budget deficit. If Austrians expected the government to increase borrowing from the central bank and expand money supply, they concluded that inflation would rise and sought to buy foreign exchange, which resulted in depreciation, or real assets, thereby bidding up of domestic prices. When the likelihood of foreign loans rose, and with it the chance that the government might retire some of its debt and reduce money supply, the crown appreciated and prices stabilized. When loan negations failed, the crown fell. At first glance, what might have made stabilization difficult, therefore, was the fact that inflation increased the government's real budget deficit over time. As nominal public expenditures rose, tax revenues incurred weeks or months earlier, or revenues from fixed taxes, failed to keep up. Inflation thus created larger real deficits, which in turn required the discounting of more Treasury Bills, which would increase inflationary expectations. Available monthly budget data from April to August 1922 show how the Austrian government's real

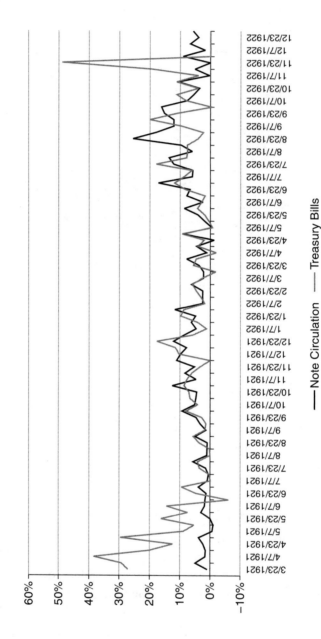

GRAPH 1.6. Weekly changes in percent of note circulation and of Treasury Bills discounted by the Austrian section of the Austro-Hungarian Bank, March 1921–December 1922. *Source:* Austrian National Bank balance sheets as published in the daily press.

Note Circulation —— Treasury Bills

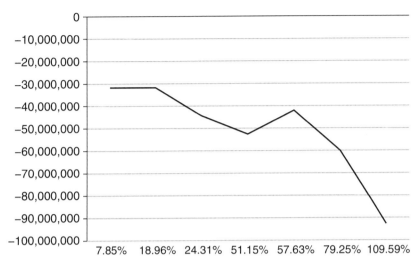

GRAPH 1.7. Relationship between monthly rate of inflation and the real monthly government deficit, March–September 1922. *Source:* Data on expenses, revenue, and deficit are from LNA, C 19, La réconstruction financière de l'Autriche 1922–1925 and deflated with Average Consumer Price Index (CPI). For calculation of the average CPI, see Appendix A.

budget deficit grew as the rate of inflation accelerated toward hyperinflation (see Graph 1.7).

Was there no escaping such a vicious circle? Crucially, when extrapolating the perceived risk of future inflation from the size of real government debt, Austrians would take into account not only future deficits, but also the service and repayment of public debt incurred in the past. High rates of inflation, while producing larger real monthly deficits, could therefore also reduce expected inflation because the *total* real value of past government debt fell. During periods of hyperinflation, the reduction of real value of Treasury Bills discounted throughout the past was larger than the real value of new Treasury Bills added to buy notes and cover the growing deficit. Despite issuing new Treasury Bills, there were periods therefore of high inflation when the Austrian government witnessed a *reduction* in its total debt.[48] From March to June 1921, when the monthly inflation rate hovered below 20 percent, the rate of increase of Treasury Bills discounted was above that of inflation, and the real government debt incurred from buying notes increased (see Graph 1.8). In summer 1921, during the first hyperinflationary wave, however, the real overall value of all Treasury Bills discounted fell and

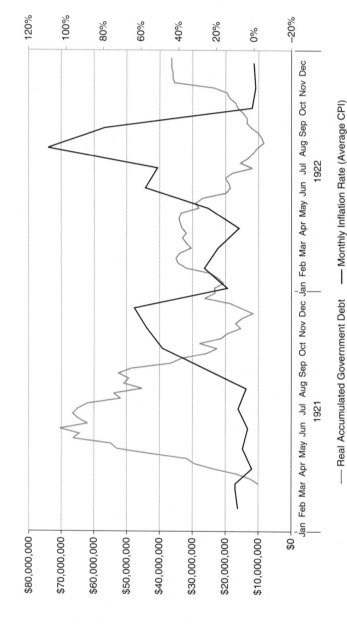

GRAPH 1.8. Total real accumulated Austrian government debt in US$ and monthly inflation rate in percent as measured by Average Consumer Price Index (CPI), March 1921–December 1922. *Source:* Amount of Treasury Bills held by Austrian National Bank from Bank's official balance sheet published in the press, converted at the relevant dollar exchange rate. For average CPI, see Appendix A.

total government debt was reduced to just above $10 million by year's end. Inflation stabilized around 20 percent between January and May 1922 as real accumulated debt from Treasury Bills issued grew anew to around $35 million, until the second hyperinflationary wave reduced that figure back below $10 million by August.

News and rumors about the size and sustainability of present and future government spending changed expectations of inflation and triggered both hyperinflationary episodes in 1921 and 1922. This book's next chapters will discuss the diplomatic negotiations on foreign credits and assistance from the Allied Powers that helped change expectations, for better or worse. Despite several attempts to secure foreign loans for Austria, it was only after hyperinflation struck a second time in 1922, and international developments made intervention by the League of Nations' possible, that Austria could obtain sufficient funds to credibly balance its budget for the predictable future. This changed expectations about government debt and future inflation, allowing for a stabilization of the Austrian currency. For now, in order to better grasp how fiscal expectations and the experience of hyperinflation were entwined with people's more general understanding of the changes occurring around them, the remainder of this chapter will turn to study the social and cultural facets of Austrian hyperinflation through analyzing statistics and caricatures.

The Velocity of Money and the Subjective Sense of Time

Their fears and hopes about the future shaped the way Austrians made sense of the present. They informed their actions as economic agents and helped create the reality of Austrian hyperinflation. The rate of hyperinflation was governed by people's expectations of the future value of money. These estimates rested in turn on the pace of government borrowing and its chances of obtaining a foreign loan. When rates of inflation rose and the crown's exchange value dropped dramatically, it meant that people desired to hold less and less local currency. With a sharp decline in real cash balances came a rising velocity of money, as the speed at which it was spent increased. And as people preferred spending their money to seeing it turn worthless the next day, real goods were bought up in a frenzy. The accelerated velocity of money, the average speed at which it was spent, became visible in people's general haste to obtain goods or seek foreign currency. As this section argues, the increased velocity of activity hastened people's subjective sense of time and this in turn amplified anxieties about their uncertain future.

At the turn of the century, the German sociologist Georg Simmel had famously argued that the growth in money supply and rise of finance in nineteenth-century Europe had accelerated everyone's own temporal experience of existence.[49] In Simmel's mind, the tempo of life was determined by the frequency and intensity of changes individuals experienced. Increased economic activity, rising incomes, and higher prices had brought about dramatic social changes that had accelerated the individual pace of almost everyone's life. Such changes, Simmel argued, were most profound in the case of extreme examples, such as when paper money in circulation grew rapidly while quickly losing value, often making rich people poor and poor people rich in a very short time. Arguably, then, such sensations might have been amplified during Austria's hyperinflation, too. Indeed, van Walré de Bordes eloquently describes how in Vienna a sudden depreciation and the subsequent panic would quicken the tempo of life:

> When prices are rising from week to week, or it may be from day to day, and when it is known that the money received to-day will be worth less a few days hence, it becomes essential to part with it as quickly as possible and to buy in place of it goods which will not lose their value. To hold money meant inevitable loss. . . . The art was to pass on one's money, as a kind of Black Jack, as rapidly as possible, to somebody else, to get rid of it *coûte que coûte*, as an infected thing, and to buy goods before there should be a further rise in prices. . . . On days when there was a sharp rise in prices there would be a run on the shops. Prices would then increase from hour to hour, and the public were content to buy whatever they could lay their hands on.[50]

The accelerating ascent of prices turned cash-holding Austrians into passengers of a quickening carousel from which they could only escape by discarding their money for goods, thereby making the merry-go-round and its passengers turn even faster. Van Walré de Bordes's anecdotal evidence, however, should not be taken as solid proof of hyperinflation's social effects and consequences. In order to study whether hyperinflation increased the pace of life and changed people's perception of time, we need make use of statistics. There is indeed good reason to believe that the pace of economic activity changes individuals' sense of time. A famous study on unemployment in the Austrian town of Marienthal during the Great Depression in 1931 showed that long-term unemployed persons suffering from idleness were unable to experience the "mediate future," which had turned "remote," resulting in a "sterile and hypertrophic present."[51] Unemployed women whose days were filled with child rearing and housework remained less affected, but unemployed men, having nowhere specific to go, experienced time as going by more slowly.[52] Walking at a slower pace and stopping frequently, long-term unemployed men, the study argued, had a distorted sense of time.

What about periods of increased economic activity, such as hyperinflations? In order to establish how individuals experienced the accelerated depreciation and quickened price increases, it might be helpful to use a similar categorization of past, present, and future. Keeping with Eugène Minkowski's "six zones of experienced time," we might expect that in times of hyperinflation some individuals become unable to experience the "mediate future," which has turned "immediate," resulting in a hyperactive present that demands an increased degree of planning and activity (see Table 1.1).[53] As the future draws closer ever quicker, people *rush* to spend their money more frequently. To follow Simmel, changes in personal wealth and status occur more intensely and more often, so that the subjective experience of time is indeed faster. But it is the collapse of the "mediate" into the "immediate future," due to which decisions need to be taken sooner, past choices evaluated at higher frequencies, and opinions about the future reassessed constantly, that makes people restless and experience a distorted sense of time.

TABLE 1.1. Minkowski's six zones of individual time experience

Remote future	Zone of prayer and ethical action
Mediate future	Zone of wish and hope
Immediate future	Zone of expectation and activity
Present	
Immediate past	Zone of the remorse
Mediate past	Zone of the regretted
Remote past	Zone of the obsolete

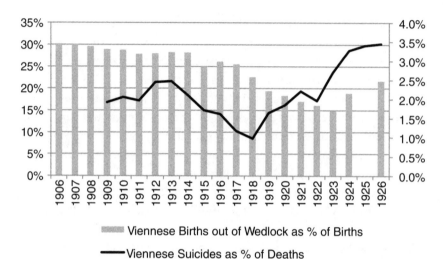

Viennese Births out of Wedlock as % of Births

Viennese Suicides as % of Deaths

GRAPH 1.9. Births in Vienna out of wedlock as a percentage of total Viennese births (gray columns, left axis) and number of suicides as percentage of total deaths in Vienna (black line, right axis), 1906–1926. *Sources: Statistisches Handbuch für die Republik Österreich,* vol. 14 (Vienna, 1933), p. 17; *Statistisches Jahrbuch der Stadt Wien für das Jahr 1908* (Vienna, 1910), p. 58; *Wirtschaftsstatistisches Jahrbuch 1926, herausgegeben von der Kammer für Arbeiter und Angestellte in Wien* (Vienna, 1927), table 63.

Day-to-day managing replaced organized planning, and the acceleration of economic life automatically spilled over into all spheres of individuals' experiences and impacted society as whole. One indicator that indeed decisions could not be postponed for long under such sped-up conditions comes from demographic data. During hyperinflation, pregnant women seem to have had less time to decide whether to keep a baby or to terminate their pregnancy prematurely. The number of births out of wedlock in relation to total deliveries was lower in 1922 than in any other year of the preceding or subsequent decade, suggesting that the number of illegal abortions rose with hyperinflation. Similarly, the number of suicides in Vienna as a share of total deaths reversed its trend unexpectedly in 1922, suggesting that people might have found less time to ponder taking their own lives or could not make up their mind whether the future compelled them to do so (see Graph 1.9).[54]

There is further statistical support for the notion that Viennese during the two periods of hyperinflation experienced time passing more quickly. One possible approach to study their phenomenology of time is to look at the statistics of the Austrian tobacco monopoly. Annual data show that Viennese

TABLE 1.2. Annual tobacco consumption in Vienna, 1920–1924

	Number of cigars (1,000s)	Number of cigarettes (1,000s)
1920	78,985	993,880
1921	96,304	1,314,577
1922	90,365	1,446,577
1923	73,918	1,255,654
1924	88,936	1,650,110

Sources: Statistisches Handbuch für die Republik Österreich, vol. 3 (Vienna, 1923), p. 35; ibid., vol. 4 (Vienna, 1924), p. 39; ibid., vol. 14 (Vienna, 1933), p. 94.

tobacco consumption in 1921 and 1922 was notably higher than in immediately preceding or subsequent years (see Table 1.2). It would seem likely then that hyperinflation led to higher tobacco consumption in Vienna, though it is hazardous to make such a claim based on annual data alone.

To see how hyperinflation affected smoking habits, we must study the monopoly's monthly revenue figures, which allow us to estimate more accurately the changing amount of tobacco bought by consumers, but which cover all of Austria and not just Vienna. Prices of tobacco products in Austria were fixed by law and often lagged behind inflation, so that the amount of tobacco purchased nationwide fluctuated widely as real prices changed from month to month. As other prices rose, the real price of tobacco products fell significantly until a law was passed to adjust prices. Before price hikes, when tobacco products were relatively cheap, cigarettes and cigars were bought in larger amounts, while after price hikes the amount sold to consumers declined (see Graph 1.10).[55]

Nationwide purchases of tobacco products thus rose abruptly in October 1921 during the first wave of hyperinflation. In October 1921 and February and March 1922, tobacco sales rose to record heights and were above the monthly average for 1923. From November 1921 to February 1922, in spite of price adjustments, sales were 25 percent above the 1921–1922 average, while during the second wave of hyperinflation, from July to November 1922, sales were also high, but below the average of 1923. Perhaps, smokers had increased their tobacco consumption during hyperinflation and felt it difficult to curb their smoking once prices had stabilized. In any case, combined with the annual data for Vienna, these figures suggest that the amount of tobacco sold and consumed in the capital rose above average levels during

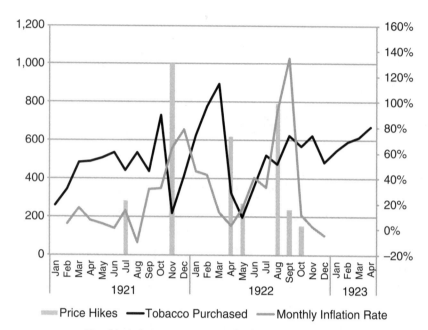

GRAPH 1.10. Monthly inflation rate, estimated tobacco purchases, and tobacco price hikes, 1921–1923 (left axis = tobacco price index and price hikes; right axis = inflation rate). *Sources:* LNA, C 13, Reconstruction financière de l'Autriche 1922–1926: "Statements Monthly Gross Receipts Tobacco" and "Annexe I. Gages Affectés aux Emprunts Autrichien, Dépenses et Recettes du Monopole des Tabacs en 1921–1922–1923 (Rendement net)." Tobacco purchases are given as a relative figure: January 1921 = 262. Price adjustments are shown relative to the largest one of November 1921, which was 258 percent. Information on the adjustments was gathered from relevant issues of the Austrian *Bundesgesetzblatt*.

the first and second waves of hyperinflation, indicating perhaps a period of heightened personal activity and anxiety.

The increase of tobacco sales might indeed reflect a quickened rate of cigarette consumption, but it might also just be indicative of hoarding, though most likely it is both. Ultimately, however, a heightened sensitivity to time is clearly reflected in the statistics of the Viennese (electric) tramway corporation. At a time of rapidly increasing prices, the tramway company did not fail to raise its fares. Whereas cigarettes could be hoarded, though, tram tickets lost their use after each price increase and—similar to depreciating money—were better spent than stored. Fortuitously, the tramway company changed its accounting practices in 1921, with the result that we have statistics specifically for the second half of that year, coinciding with the first wave

TABLE 1.3. Average number of passengers using the Viennese electric tramway, 1915–1924

	Per day and kilometer
1 July 1915–30 June 1916	4,392
1 July 1916–30 June 1917	5,303
1 July 1917–30 June 1918	6,063
1 July 1918–30 June 1919	6,099
1 July 1919–30 June 1920	5,474
1 July 1920–30 June 1921	5,361
1 July 1921–31 December 1921	5,720
1 January 1922–31 December 1922	4,551
1 January 1923–31 December 1923	4,629
1 January 1924–31 December 1924	5,515

Sources: *Verwaltungsbericht der Gemeinde Wien—städtische Strassenbahnen für das Jahr 1923 unter Berücksichtigung des II. Halbjahres 1921 und des Jahres 1922* (Vienna, 1924); *Verwaltungsbericht der Gemeinde Wien—städtische Strassenbahnen für das Jahr 1924* (Vienna, 1925).

of hyperinflation. From the data it emerges that the number of passengers riding the tramway during the second half of 1921 was significantly higher than in 1919–1920, and around 25 percent above the averages of 1922 and 1923 (see Table 1.3).

There is thus also statistical support for the claim that the haste to exchange one's money for goods incurred an accelerated mobility and a distorted sense of time. Individuals whose "mediate future" had turned "immediate" experienced a compressed and rapidly changing present, forcing them to make quick decisions more frequently. Simultaneously, the distant future turned even more remote, and chances of realizing legitimate plans or dreams were put into question. For many, perhaps, the haste and anxiety accompanying decisions to run and exchange or spend one's money went hand-in-hand with more frequent tobacco consumption. People felt as if they had less time on their hands, which resulted in heightened activity while changes in wealth and status around them occurred more frequently and more intensely. A hyperactive present and images of a dystopian or unhappy future thus formed an important part of the distressing experience of hyperinflation. It is by studying cultural sources, in this case caricatures, that we might reveal categories of anxieties beyond the fear of pecuniary loss that made living through hyperinflation so traumatic.

The Depiction of Inflation in Caricatures

In his cultural history of Weimar inflation, Bernd Widdig argued that German society experienced inflation as a period of crisis and loss, of declining bourgeois family values, during which people lost their sense of security and trust in each other and the future.[56] Austrians encountered hyperinflation a year earlier than their German neighbors, faced politically more uncertain prospects, and were arguably the first contemporary country to experience modern hyperinflation. The failure of economists to explain hyperinflation, much less provide a practical remedy for the traumatic rise of prices, could only increase such feelings of vulnerability. And the raced pace of change during hyperinflation reinforced an already existing sense of confusion and helplessness among the populace. How, then, can we uncover the particular anxieties of Austrians that Widdig has shown for Germany? Germans' popular understanding of Weimar inflation was gendered and depicted as male order, thrift, and sense, versus female chaos, spending, and conspicuous consumption.[57] In Austria the experience of inflation was similarly gendered, but also understood according to racial stereotypes. This section will analyze Austrian press caricatures about inflation from 1921 and 1922 to reveal the fears popularly linked with experiencing hyperinflation. Humoristic caricatures are a particularly well-suited cultural source for studying widespread sentiments because they communicate recognizable ideas widely and simply. The specific form of the genre usually requires the artist to choose a single message and to convey it unambiguously, making it easy to decode. The humoristic nature of the caricature moreover makes it a useful source for identifying pressing and deep-seated anxieties because of the way that jokes and humor work.

As Freud pointed out in his almost contemporary study of *Witz*, verbal and visual jokes have the ability to reveal hidden wishes and worries because, in order to be funny, they either satisfy unseeming desires that are suppressed or release individuals of their innate fears.[58] Jokes that are distributed widely often work best when they evoke the repressed wants or deep-seated anxieties members of society are most likely to experience. It is no surprise, then, that inflation itself figured prominently among caricatures in postwar Austria, though they were more about subconscious fears than ravenous longings. Not only were continued inflation and depreciation a cause of anxiety for all Austrians, the failure of experts to provide a remedy and the experienced acceleration of time both served to further exacerbate overwhelming feelings of helplessness and despair. Identifying the source and the mechanisms that created such a caricature's humor can therefore tell us a lot about what artists or editors thought were their readers' most common angsts. For a joke or caricature to be funny, it often suffices to relate a familiar scene to the anxiety-ridden context and then evoke paradoxes, juxtaposition, or absurdity to release that anxiety. The gendered conception of inflation, by associating its perceived negative effects with femininity, allows us to further specify Austrian anxieties related to the rapid changes and undesirable results inflation was generating to their minds.

One recurring theme among inflation-related caricatures was the destabilizing impact inflation had on relationships. As the stability and value of currencies fell apart, the loss of financial stability evoked fear among men that the traditional permanence of romantic bonds was in danger, too. The satirical magazine *Die Bombe,* which catered to an educated, bourgeois, male readership, published several such caricatures in 1921 and 1922. The initial mechanism applied to create humor and thereby release tension and anxiety lay in the juxtaposition of the caricature's titles and the scenes described. Thus the setting of "Secrets" (see Figure 1.1) shows a group of young, slightly clad *variété* dancers, discussing their most private feelings: "What were your thoughts when your banker lost his fortune?" asks one, receiving the unmysterious reply: "I thought: Strange how quickly love fades!"[59] In what will emerge as a recurring theme, the women were characterized as callously materialistic, calculating, and immune to naïve romance. The female protagonist has quickly adapted to her new circumstances, created by financial dissolution, deserting her former lover in his predicament. Men are associated with a past world of affluence that has disappeared and the caricature links male fears about losing one's livelihood to inflation with that of vanishing feminine affection, presented as a sentimental luxury during times of economic hardship.

The negative impact of inflation on amorous relationships between married men and their mistresses is also the idea behind the caricature titled "Marks of Time" (see Figure 1.2), showing two ballet dancers in tranquil conversation: "You know Lizzi, business must be really miserable: All the

FIGURE 1.1. "Secrets." The figure shows a group of young, scantily clad *variété* dancers, discussing their private feelings: "What were your thoughts when your banker lost his fortune?" asks one, receiving the unexpected reply: "I thought: Strange how quickly love fades!" *Source: Die Bombe,* 15 October 1921, p. 4. ANNO Austrian National Library.

FIGURE 1.2. "Marks of Time." Two ballet dancers engage in tranquil conversation: "You know, Lizzi, business must be really miserable: All husbands I know have fallen in love again with their wives." *Source: Die Bombe,* 15 December 1922, p. 8. ANNO Austrian National Library.

husbands I know have fallen in love again with their wives."[60] This caricature creates humor by defining marital love as an unusual occurrence and
plays on the same related fears: the loss of men's livelihood to inflation and
the increasingly unsentimental disposition of women. In both cases the hu-
morous juxtaposition between the display and its title is strengthened by a
seemingly nonsensical linkage of romance and money, a connection that
many among the middle-class male readership of *Die Bombe* might have
known to be all too real. As in Weimar Germany, popular understanding of
inflation gendered the avidity for material well-being that comes with poverty as negative and feminine, while associating the experience of material
hardship through economic loss with masculinity and virtue. In a gendered
understanding of the world women are supposed to be sentimental and
caring, and the experience of inflation thus seems to have increased anxieties about the world becoming more materialistic and providing less room
to experience romantic love and partnership.

Depicting women as immoral, emotionally detached materialists also addressed deep-seated male fears of worthlessness and loss of masculinity. Added
to the uncertainty about being able to provide economically for one's family
came the shame of having failed as defenders of home and country. In the
caricature "Welcome" (see Figure 1.3), a maid informs a high-class courtesan,
about to take a bath, that an unknown customer wishes to see her: "He calls
himself Mr. Dollar," the maid announces the client. "So let him in, the name is
promising," the courtesan replies.[61] With foreign money the new object of female desire, the depreciation of the Austrian crown undercuts Austrian men's
virility, depriving them of access to potential partners. To attract women a
man needs hard, foreign currency. Similarly, the caricature "Hallmark" shows
a young woman in her underwear, unwrapping a dress delivered from a new
admirer (see Figure 1.4). Asked by her maid to remind her of the particular
gentleman's name, she replies: "I only know he has a totally new foreign currency."[62] In these two caricatures, the two women are depicted as doubly de-
praved, both for shedding bourgeois morals in the interest of material gain
and for slighting what their Austrian men present, preferring the purchase of
anonymous foreigners. In popular understanding, inflation thus threatens to
weaken domestic vigor, leaving Austria defenseless to foreign biddings.

In the above examples, females were depicted as calculating materialistic
women, interested in money and unsentimental, who diminish men into

Willkommen.

— Er nennt sich Mister Dollar.
= Dann lassen Sie ihn vor — der Name ist verheißend.

FIGURE 1.3. "Welcome." A maid informs a high-class prostitute, about to take a bath, that an unknown customer wishes to see her: "He calls himself Mr. Dollar," the maid announces the client. "So let him in, the name is promising." *Source: Die Bombe,* 1 June 1921, p. 5. ANNO Austrian National Library.

FIGURE 1.4. "Hallmark." A young woman in her underwear unwraps a dress delivered from a new admirer. Asked by her maid to remind her of the gentleman's name she replies: "I only know he has totally new foreign currency." *Source: Die Bombe,* 15 January 1921, p. 5. ANNO Austrian National Library.

providers of material goods or foreign currency. The caricatures echoed male fears of women losing interest in romance and becoming immune to love, preferring the material well-being of strangers to the courtship of Austrian associates. In such a daunting world, the romantic desires and future plans of young Austrian men were made futile by the pecuniary prowess of foreigners. Precisely such fears are exposed in "Worried" (see Figure 1.5), where two upper-class friends enjoy a familiar conversation while horseback riding. The male equestrian warns his female companion not to trust her new foreign admirer: "Alice, don't you let yourself in with the American, all about him is fake." To which she sarcastically retorts: "Horrible, also his dollar checks at the end?"[63] Alice's cold-hearted mockery of her companion's concern betrays a lack of empathy for her escort. In search of foreign fortune she is prepared to associate herself with dubious characters. The experience of inflation and the rapid transformations it produced thus incurred fears about Austrians becoming selfish, insensitive to their compatriots, lacking integrity and honor, and selling out to foreigners.

If women were invariably portrayed as reacting to inflation by sacrificing bourgeois morals on the altar of present-day and future material well-being, *Die Bombe*'s men were consistently associated with former and vanishing wealth, stability, and order. Drawn as mature, well off, and able to afford the luxury of entertaining mistresses or visiting prostitutes, they regularly express worries about their own financial position. Thus a caricature that appeared alongside the one with our two riders, and tellingly titled "Business Cycle," shows an elderly man scratching his head, complaining to his young mistress about the price of her new stockings (see Figure 1.6): "Oh Lizzi, the price of all women's wear is going up." To which the half-clad woman happily replies: "Consequently women's cost, too."[64] Similarly the caricature "One Satisfied" shows a wealthy, middle-aged man attentively listening to a seductive courtesan complaining nonchalantly how women will be left without anything to wear (see Figure 1.7), and drily commenting: "Which is still the best part of present-day circumstances."[65] Thus the understanding of inflation and its consequences reflected in these caricatures also gendered apprehension about the decline of former wealth and values as male, and the opportunistic materialism this provoked as female. Overall femininity was unfavorably associated with visions of a dystopian Austria where values of honor, loyalty, trust, or faithfulness appeared utterly antiquated, while

Besorgt.

— Alice, lassen Sie sich nicht mit dem Amerikaner ein, alles an ihm ist falsch.
— Schrecklich, am Ende auch die Dollar-Schecks?

FIGURE 1.5. "Worried." Two upper-class friends enjoy a familiar conversation while horseback riding. The male equestrian warns his female companion not to trust her new foreign acquaintance: "Alice, don't you let yourself in with the American, all about him is fake." To which she sarcastically retorts: "Horrible, also his dollar checks at the end?"
Source: Die Bombe, 15 April 1921, p. 8. ANNO Austrian National Library.

Konjunktur.

— Ach, Lizzie, alle Frauenartikel steigen jetzt im Preise.
— Folglich die Frauen selbst auch.

FIGURE 1.6. "Business Cycle." An elderly man scratches his head, complaining to his young mistress about the price of her new stockings: "Oh Lizzi, the price of all women's wear is going up." To which the half-clad woman happily replies: "Consequently women's cost, too." *Source: Die Bombe,* 15 April 1921, p. 4. ANNO Austrian National Library.

FIGURE 1.7. "One Satisfied." A wealthy, middle-aged man attentively listens to a seductive courtesan complaining nonchalantly how women will be left without anything to wear, and drily commenting: "Which is still the best part of present-day circumstances." *Source: Die Bombe*, 1 October 1922, p. 4. ANNO Austrian National Library.

masculinity was associated with society's positive but lost attributes of prosperity, stability, and order. In this way, inflation-themed caricatures addressed, and helped release, male (but probably not just male) fears about a loveless future brought about by inflation, mired by poverty and governed by confusion and uncertainty, in which a new, alien form of selfishness and materialism replaced traditional values of solidarity and rectitude.

Vienna was home to vocal anti-Semitism, and although there was little consensus on what it should mean to be Austrian in interwar Austria, ethnic, cultural, and social categories of self-understanding defined Jews as non-Austrian and Austrians as non-Jewish. Jews figured frequently as the allegorical other in all spheres of life and in inflation-themed caricatures as well. In the popular imagination, the gender attributes of Jews and other minorities are often reversed, with men appearing effeminate and women manly. In relation to inflation, it was Jewish men that were thus associated with the unfavorable attributes of greed, materialism, and lack of integrity.[66] Jews invariably served as icons for currency speculators, and a popular identity existed between sinister Jews and the speculative forces believed to fuel currency depreciation. In a series of propagandist caricatures printed by the Christian-Social *Reichspost* in 1922, Jews were associated with the negative values of avarice and exposed as prone to hysteria once the currency stabilized (Figures 1.8 and 1.9).[67] But unlike in *Die Bombe*'s caricatures, where anxieties were treated with kind humor, the *Reichspost*'s racialized schematization is callous and crude. Designed to convey the impression that the government is successfully stabilizing the currency, Jews are shown to react with disorderly panic to news that the fall of the crown has been halted. But by associating depreciation with Jewish speculators, the government was also defining inflation as originating from a foreign, and ultimately non-Austrian problem. By ending depreciation, the government was punishing and banishing Jews for their immoral activity, by which they had risked Austria's future for their own financial benefit.

Two final examples of anti-Semitic caricatures associated with inflation illustrate particularly well the reversal of gender attributes. Published on the front page of the *Reichspost,* they are outspoken, if rare examples of visual incitement against Jews by the Christian-Social newspaper. In the first, from August 1922, the time of the second wave of hyperinflation, two distraught Jewish women debate what to do if the crown depreciates further and they

FIGURE 1.8. "Fall." A Jewish acrobat falls down Jacob's ladder as Jewish speculators run away in panic: "It is also ensured that the exchange rate does not go up into the sky." *Source: Reichspost*, 27 February 1922, p. 1. ANNO Austrian National Library.

Von der Woche.

FIGURE 1.9. Center panel: "Following Dr. Seipel's success in Geneva." Distraught Jewish speculators who bet on the crown's collapse leave the Vienna Stock Exchange in shock: "We are now being saved, so everyone save himself if he can!" *Source: Reichspost,* 8 October 1922, p. 7. ANNO Austrian National Library.

can no longer afford imported perfume from Paris (see Figure 1.10).[68] The second, from April 1922, shows a Jewish man relaxing on the sun terrace of a hotel at the Semmering resort studying a newspaper (see Figure 1.11). Upon reading that Austria had supposedly 60,000 unemployed, he asks his Jewish friend in jest whether he thought they had been counted among that number.[69] The two caricatures play upon fears of foreign, sinister elements ravaging and exploiting the financial markets and destroying Austria for their own benefit. At the same time, they create humor through presenting the absurd idea of suffering from lack of French perfume at a time of hyper-inflation, or being unemployed while affording the luxury of a hotel. In all the anti-Semitic caricatures Jews are shown to be immune to, and even prof-iting from, the hardship regularly experienced by Austrians. As opposed to the caricatures in *Die Bombe*, the jokes are alienating and the scenes provide no point of identification to readers.

For our purposes, it is particularly interesting to see how the gender at-tributes associated with inflation in *Die Bombe*'s caricatures are reversed in

Die größte Sorge.
Zeichnung von Theo Zasche.

FIGURE 1.10. "The biggest worry." Two unsightly Jewish women exchange their problems in the street: "If the Austrian crown drops any further, and we can no longer buy perfume from Paris—what shall we do then?!" *Source: Reichspost,* 7 August 1922, p. 1. ANNO Austrian National Library.

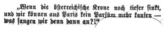

„Wenn die österreichische Krone noch tiefer sinkt, und wir können aus Paris kein Parfüm mehr kaufen — was fangen wir denn dann an?!"

Am Semmering.
Zeichnung von Fritz Schönpflug.

FIGURE 1.11. "At the Semmering." Two Jewish men converse on a hotel terrace at the Semmering resort not far from Vienna: "I just read there are 60,000 unemployed in Austria. You think they counted us in, Sami?" *Source: Reichspost,* 18 April 1922, p. 1. ANNO Austrian National Library.

„Da les' i grad, daß es jetzt in Oesterreich 60.000 Arbeitslose geben soll. Ob sie uns zwei mitgezählt haben, Sami?"

these anti-Semitic versions. The men here are given slender, effeminate appearances, while the women are depicted as staunch and manly. Much as Austrian men were elderly and appeared worried about their deteriorating material situation, it is Jewish women who display difficulties adapting their lives to the new and troubling circumstances created by depreciation. Jewish men, on the other hand, much like Austrian women, are young and agile. They show adaptive skill in face of the new challenges and opportunities currency depreciation creates for them. Much like the opportunist Austrian females, they are coldhearted and untroubled by the suffering of others around them. This reverse matching of gender attributes in anti-Semitic caricatures gives weight to the earlier analysis that changes brought about by hyperinflation and depreciation were popularly associated with bringing closer an uncanny future in which honest and good-hearted Austrians would suffer economic and emotional deprivation due to the actions and decisions of others less noble and more selfish than them. In popular imagination, at least, the vanishing of Austrian wealth and power gave way to the emergence of condemnable behavior inspired by selfishness and materialism that was easily categorized as Jewish and feminine, and therefore non-Austrian and weak.

A gender analysis of inflation-themed caricatures reveals popular hopes and fears associated with the forceful changes brought about by hyperinflation and depreciation. Specifically male fears about relationships and their own masculinity during a time of intense economic uncertainty were successfully played upon by caricatures. But they also show how inflation was popularly associated with qualms about Austrians discarding traditional values of concern and affection for a new, foreign, and amoral way of life. Visions of Austria's future also informed the way economic experts thought about inflation. For some, like Federn or Stolper, the idea of a small, independent Austria was unattractive, while others feared the economic power and Prussian character of Germany. But without offering a clear explanation for, or remedy to inflation, economic experts could do little to assuage popular fears. The quickened subjective sense of time and activism resulting from hyperinflation increased already existing anxieties about the future, a future that constantly seemed imminent, uncertain and almost impossible to manage. With inflation rates determined by expectations about the size of the government's growing debt, the course of hyperinflations was thus linked to pessimism and popular despondency about Austria's economic, political, and, not least, everyone's individual prospects, too. To put an end to hyperinflation, to stop the accelerating merry-go-round, Austrians needed to be convinced of the possibility and likelihood of a different future from the one they had come to expect, loathe, and fear.

2

The Road to Geneva

1921–1922

> A Roman who was born under Theodosius and died under
> Romulus Augustulus had seventy years in which to pass
> through the changes which Austria has seen in three.
>
> —G. M. Young to Treasury
> 18 March 1922

COMPARED TO THE INITIAL postwar years, by the beginning of 1921, some kind of normalcy had returned to Vienna. In Istanbul people were starving, in Saint Petersburg the mood was gloomy, and in Budapest the situation was catastrophic. But in Vienna the cafés were full, the opera and theaters were sold out, and the shops were well stocked. The American Relief Administration and the local office of the Reparations Commission were making remarkable efforts to obtain sufficient food for the city's inhabitants and their children. Certainly there were many people struck by poverty, including higher state officials and academics, as well as formerly wealthy individuals who might have lost their fortunes to nationalization in the successor states or their own patriotic, if unwise acquisition of war bonds. But the working class, strengthened by new socialist legislation, received real wages that were better than before the war. Food, especially flour and bread, was heavily subsidized and affordable. Foreign visitors, tourists, and speculators coming to hunt for bargains or information were surprised to find the Inner City inhabitants "looming bright and well off." One even dared conclude, "starving Vienna seems somewhat of a myth."[1]

But this was the proverbial quiet before the storm. We saw in Chapter 1 how hyperinflation in Austria would be a period evoking confusion, anxieties, and uncertainty about the causes, course, and consequences of precipitous depreciation and towering price increases. As a remedy, Austria's politicians put almost all their hopes and efforts into obtaining foreign assistance in the form of a large loan to stabilize the currency and cover expenditures. In 1921, wheat, flour, and other imported food items still remained heavily subsidized and the families of state-paid workers and officials made up at least 10 percent of the country's population. To cover large expenditures and to service its debt, the government resorted to borrowing money from the Austrian section of what was still the Austro-Hungarian Bank. The continuous expansion of government debt and money supply went hand in hand with high rates of inflation and depreciation of the currency.[2]

This chapter covers the events that led to the League of Nations intervention in Austria in October 1922 and the adoption of its reconstruction scheme to stabilize the Austrian currency and budget. It argues that the League was called into action as a means of last resort after Britain, France, and Italy were not able to put aside their national interests in favor of saving Austria. A first rescue scheme under League auspices failed because in 1921 the Austrian government of Chancellor Michael Mayr refused to accept foreign control over pledged revenues and moneys lent. The Austrian government subsequently turned for help to private bankers, but the state was unable to pledge its frozen assets, and the bankers, in any case reluctant to help, demanded some form of foreign financial control. When a second wave of hyperinflation threatened to devastate Austria in 1922, the League was called upon again, and this time a scheme was agreed upon that incurred limitations of Austrian sovereignty. Handing Austria to the League of Nations was a way for the Allies to rid themselves of a problem, but it also provided the impartiality necessary to make foreign control palatable to Austrians by giving it an international character.

As a consequence, Austrian state finances would be under League of Nations oversight from 1923 to 1926. A General Commissioner would reside in Vienna to ensure Austrian compliance with a program of economic reconstruction, budgetary retrenchment, and austerity. A foreign advisor would be installed at the Austrian central bank for even longer, and the government's ability to borrow freely on capital markets would be curtailed. Foreign financial control had hitherto been applied only to economically backward countries, such as Ottoman Turkey and the Khedive's Egypt, in Tunisia, or in the Balkans, and it was the first time a developed European state had to give up certain sovereign prerogatives for a promise of foreign financial assistance.[3] In Austria this created resentment, both from governmental bodies and from the public. As we shall see in subsequent chapters, the way League control evolved in Austria was in effect very different from what its planners intended it to be. In any case, it is important to understand that international control was not something malicious bankers or governments imposed on a helpless country to serve their own narrow interests. Rather, as this chapter aims to demonstrate, it was a measure that all sides came to see as necessary and even beneficial, after alternative routes to raise money had repeatedly proven ineffective.

Foreign efforts to help Austria come to grips with the new postwar realities were motivated by a desire to stabilize the entire region of Eastern Europe. Political conflict in the Balkans had been the source of two wars in the twentieth century even before the conflict between Austria-Hungary and Serbia triggered the First World War, but much of the foreign help provided to Vienna was also motivated by stereotyped assumptions about the civilized and cultured character of Austrians.[4] If Vienna could recover some of its previous importance as a center of finance and commerce, the thinking went, it would serve as a stabilizing factor for the entire region, much of which was still in turmoil. In Hungary, two separate attempts by Karl I to regain his throne, in March and October 1921, almost led to civil war and saw the mobilization of Czechoslovak and Yugoslav troops. Yugoslav troops were engaged in war over territorial disputes with Albania, too, while the Poles had thrown back a Soviet military advance on Warsaw the previous year. Apprehensive governments in both London and Paris feared that an economic collapse of Austria was certain to result in armed conflict between its neighbors, all vying to gain control over Vienna.

But putting Austria back on her feet, as so often said, was made difficult because it required extensive international cooperation. A large foreign loan was generally viewed as the only measure to terminate inflation, through stabilizing the exchange rate and eliminating the budget deficit that was being financed by money printing. Yet foreign governments had financial difficulties of their own following the war, and thus any large loan would have to be subscribed by public investors. However, the Peace Treaty of Saint-Germain-en-Laye had placed a mortgage on all of Austria's assets as a guarantee for payment of reparations, the size of which had been purposefully, but now it appeared unwisely, left undecided. In addition, Austria's debts for food supplies paid with relief credits were identically secured and ranked before reparations (making it unlikely that the latter would ever be paid). Because all Austrian state assets were pledged to secure future relief and reparations payments, the Austrian government could not provide any securities against which to borrow. Without any assets to offer as security, neither private banks nor foreign states were willing to assist the Austrian state with raising sufficient sums from the public to put an end to inflation. Liens incurred from reparations could potentially be lifted by a majority decision, but relief liens needed a unanimous decision of creditor states, making things more complicated politically. Finally, all proposals for a loan to Austria included some form of foreign financial control of pledged revenues and money lent, too, which the Austrian government initially opposed.

An early proposal authored by Sir William Goode, the British delegate and president of the Reparations Commission's Austrian Section in Vienna, suggested that Austria could under no circumstances pay reparations, and that in fact the United Kingdom had to help restore Austria's economic strength by offering an extensive credit of £62.5 million. Goode, born to missionaries in Newfoundland in 1875, was an adventurous journalist stationed in London, where he served as foreign liaison officer for the British Ministry of Food during the war. By 1919 he had been made British director of relief missions before being sent to Vienna as head of the Reparations Commission's Austria Section. His plan foresaw the foundation of a new central bank, an internal loan guaranteed by the Allied Powers, and foreign control over Austria's budget.[5] The British Treasury, however, stood opposed to the plan, not least because, as its Controller of Finance, Basil Blackett, remarked, Goode's scheme was likely to commit Britain indefinitely. Blackett, born in 1882 to British missionaries in India, had joined the Treasury in 1904 and had made a career as a specialist in banking and currency. As Treasury controller, he directly advised the Chancellor of the Exchequer, Austen Chamberlain, and writing to him about Goode's plan, emphasized that

> the time has come to take a definite stand on the ground that the British Govt will not place further burdens on the British taxpayer for the benefit of Austria. There is about £1,000,000 still remaining unallocated of the £10,000,000 relief loan voted this year. This should be finally

earmarked for Austria with an intimation that no further direct assistance will be provided and that indirect assistance in the form of a
British Govt guarantee for an Austrian loan will not be granted.[6]

It was not that Blackett felt that Austria should not be helped; rather, in
his mind the Austrian problem was too large to be tackled by Britain alone
and needed to be solved through international cooperation instead. The
British Cabinet consequently refused Goode's plan and recommended allot-
ting all remaining £1.1 million in relief funds to Austria, while stressing that
further assistance would have to be commenced by France, which had shown
little initiative so far.[7] The French government quickly presented its own
version of the Goode plan in December 1920, proposing the creation of
an Austrian central bank, a five-year loan to Austria from foreign banks
or governments, and conferring extensive powers of control over Austrian
finances and fiscal policy to the Reparations Commission. In its written
response, the British Cabinet suggested that the League of Nations would serve
as a better machinery of control than the politicized Reparations Commission
and asked the French government if it would free Austria's assets from existing
liens so as to help secure a loan when the Allied Supreme Council met in
January 1921.[8]

Weakened by absence of the United States and occasionally eyed suspi-
ciously by the British and French, the League managed to prove its worth in
several spheres of international contestation. The League Covenant had already assigned it the role of overseeing and managing some of the open questions and problems arising from the postwar peace settlements, such as the
rights of national minorities in new nation-states or the fate of former
German colonies and occupied Ottoman lands. An international conference
of bankers and financial experts convened by the League of Nations in
Brussels in September 1920 had proposed the creation of a committee to
coordinate efforts to reestablish international trade and stable currencies.
To prepare the conference, the League Secretariat had previously established an Economic and Financial Section, and after the conference, which
primarily called on governments to balance their budgets, formed an Economic and Financial Committee, made up of formally independent experts.
In the minds of many Austrians the question of Austria's economic viability
had not been sufficiently considered by the Allies when deciding upon its

foundation in Paris. Like with other problems created or left unresolved by the peace settlement, the League and its Financial Committee of international experts would go on to play a pivotal role in assisting in Austria's economic reconstruction and nation building.

Putting large hopes in Goode's scheme, Austria's government had sent the banker Ernst Simon to London to sound out conditions for getting advances on the future loan from bankers. In December 1920, Simon cabled the Austrian Finance Ministry that money was not forthcoming and he recommended to inform the Reparations Commission that, unless some form of credits materialized soon, the government would not guarantee the continuance of Austria's administration.[9] Goode and Simon would go to address the Supreme Council in Paris in January, but he warned that the Powers were preoccupied with Germany and unlikely to find time to discuss lifting the liens on Austria's assets. Therefore, echoing the British Cabinet decision, Simon suggested that Austria appeal for help to the League of Nations, of which it had become a member on 16 December 1920. Writing a few weeks later from Paris, Simon advised that his government inform the Allied Powers that if no help were forthcoming, Austria would request the League to permit its unification with Germany.[10] Goode himself complained at the time that no progress was being made on behalf of Austria. "At the moment" he wrote, "I am, like nearly everybody else concerned with Austria, doing nothing."[11]

The Supreme Council Conference at the Quai d'Orsay's Salon de l'Horloge in January 1921 was indeed dominated by the question of German reparations, but on its second day the French presented their own plan for Austria, drafted by French Minister Louis Loucheur.[12] Loucheur had been Minister of Armaments during the war and Prime Minister Georges Clemenceau's main economic adviser at the Paris Peace Conference, and was now in charge of reintegrating Alsace and Lorraine into France. His plan proposed an immediate loan of $40 million (about £10 million), coupled with control of state finances by the Reparations Commission and a regional conference on Central Europe's economic future. Jacques Seydoux, the French Foreign Ministry's Assistant Secretary for Commercial Affairs, who had organized its Blockade Department during the war, proposed that the funds be made part of the larger scheme authored by Goode and suggested appointment of a separate committee to discuss its details. British Prime Minister David Lloyd George voiced earlier skepticism, commenting that the economic reconstruction of Austria and Central Europe was not a matter for the Reparations Commission but one for bankers and business. The Reparations Commission was too political a body and the British wished to coordinate the recovery of Austria on purely economic lines. He received support from Foreign Secretary George Curzon, who dampened hope of British participation, stating that their government alone had spent £4 million on Austria in 1920, while Italy and France had carelessly done nothing.[13]

Yet the Italians agreed to the committee and the British would not oppose it, so Loucheur chaired a first meeting to discuss the details of his plan that same afternoon.[14] Loucheur identified Austria's uncontrolled printing of money as the basis of its economic problems, and as a start proposed the foundation of a bank, capitalized with £4 to £5 million from the Allies, the United States, and neutrals.[15] Financed by bonds guaranteed through Austrian assets, such a bank would finance Austrian foreign trade and thereby help stop inflation and depreciation. Llewellyn Smith, former head of the British economic section at the Paris Peace Conference and now Chief Economic Advisor to the British government, countered that all of Austria's assets were already pledged to cover reparations and relief claims, so that several states would first have to lift their liens for Loucheur's scheme to work.[16] In a proposal presented a few days later, the committee therefore called for the lifting or deferral of all liens on Austria's assets, the creation of a private international corporation to provide commercial credits, the reduction of the number of Austrian state workers, and the creation of a small control commission of financial advisers to supervise the issue of Austrian currency.[17]

The financial attaché at the Italian embassy in London, who had been present at the conference in Paris, told his Austrian colleague, envoy Georg Franckenstein, that Loucheur's project stood a good chance, that major banks were already on board, and that if results were positive, the crown would appreciate instantly. Franckenstein, a scion of Austrian high aristocracy who, impersonating one of his forefathers, rode with the helm of the Kaiser-Huldigungs-Festzug in 1908, was a career diplomat stationed in London before the war and had been a member of the Austrian delegation to Saint-Germain. The envoy joined Simon's skepticism about the Italians' enthusiasm, not least since the suggested sum (now 200 million French francs, or £4,260,260) was hardly enough to effectively stabilize the Austrian crown, so that further loans would certainly become necessary.[18] Their fears were soon corroborated by news from the Foreign Office that London bankers would not join the scheme and that foreign governmental loans or British guarantees would not materialize either.[19] In fact, as Foreign Secretary Curzon told Franckenstein, the Austrian problem was not on the agenda of the London Conference to be held in March, and only if Austria got Italy and France to actually provide credits would Britain follow with fresh money, too.[20]

The Austrian crown had lost over 60 percent of its already diminished value during the year 1920 alone. Alarmed by the limited attention the Powers were granting the Austrian government, Vienna sent to London the Foreign Ministry's trade expert, Richard Schüller, a jovial and optimistic lawyer born in the Moravian city of Brno in 1870 who had trained in Vienna and later specialized in economics. Schüller and envoy Franckenstein joined forces behind the scenes to put Austria and the Loucheur scheme back on the conference agenda. They managed to get Austrian Chancellor Mayr, who also acted as Foreign Minister, invited to London to address the Supreme Council, and the British Foreign Office to telegraph its ambassadors and inquire which states were actually prepared to lift their liens.[21] Speaking to the assembled statesmen in March, Mayr explained that despite important steps, such as a raise in taxes and a heavy capital levy, his deficit, mainly caused by paying for subsidized food imports, remained uncovered. Austria needed foreign credits and if they were to come through the Loucheur scheme, governmental guarantees would be necessary, because otherwise private banks were not prepared to help raise funds from public investors.[22] In response, British Prime Minister Lloyd George thanked Mayr and assured the Austrian delegation that there was no lack of good will to help Austria, but that the circumstances of overburdened taxpayers all over Europe made foreign governmental guarantees difficult, if not entirely impossible.[23] What Mayr was not told was that Blackett and his French colleagues had already discussed the alternative idea of referring Austria to the League, something Chamberlain had also discussed and probably agreed upon with Loucheur.[24]

An Austrian delegation met with Allied financial experts that afternoon in the Treasury boardroom.[25] Austria sought $55 million (£12 million) in annual loans to cover its trade deficit and to pay for the import of food and coal. Loucheur recalled that Allied money would only be made available against adequate guarantees or securities; beyond that, some form of foreign control over Austria's finances would also be necessary. The Austrians assured Loucheur they had plans to guarantee the payment of interest out of revenues from customs or the tobacco monopoly, but that they stood opposed to their control by private banking interests. Foreign governments would not give guarantees for loans from banks without any foreign control, and Loucheur ventured that direct control by the Allies would be very difficult, too. Chamberlain thereupon retorted that some form of control by the League of Nations appeared to be the only solution. Before passing Austria to the League, however, a further meeting was scheduled for which the Austrians were asked to submit detailed figures on public revenues, food subsidies, and the cost of coal imports.[26]

Chairman Blackett opened the ensuing meeting, telling the Austrian delegation that he wanted to clarify some of their submitted figures. However, Austrian Chancellor Mayr impatiently intervened, demanding that after he and his colleagues had been asked so many questions the time had finally come for them to ask some of their own.[27] When would Loucheur's scheme be carried out, when would Austria obtain its first advances, would banks and investors actually provide funds, and would the Allies really lift their liens to make loans possible? Austrian state workers, unable to keep on living from their devalued salaries, were threatening to strike, he claimed, and the government had only been able to avert conflict until his arrival in Vienna. If he returned without definitive guarantees, the Chancellor warned, the country's administrative apparatus was certain to fall apart. Taken utterly by surprise, Blackett reassuringly promised Mayr that his questions would be submitted to the Allied ministers and that their answers would be communicated back to him as soon as was possible.[28]

Though Chamberlain would inform the Austrian delegation of the Allied decision only on the final day of the conference, Blackett and the committee of financial experts quickly agreed upon all matters after the Austrian delegation left the Treasury. The French ambassador to London quipped sardonically that if the short statement by Mayr had been informative, the Austrians had in fact advanced no further. To provide them something to take home, he suggested a declaration by France, Britain, and Italy that they were indeed prepared to abandon their liens in favor of a loan. If other governments with similar claims followed suit, Austria could perhaps make use of the

League of Nations' Ter Meulen scheme, a plan to co-issue bonds among national governments to be used by merchants as guarantees for their payment of imports.[29] As Chamberlain subsequently told the Austrians, the League's Financial Committee would hold a meeting within a fortnight to assess the value of Austrian assets and present the scheme to foreign bankers.[30] Telegrams were sent for publication in Vienna, announcing that the Allies had agreed to postpone their liens and support a loan under the trusteeship of the League, but since immediate help was to come only in the form of the commercial Ter Meulen plan, the news was not received well.[31]

The Allied Powers had referred Austria to the League of Nations. Their meetings had been overshadowed by the larger question of German reparations, and despite genuine sympathies for Austria's situation, none had been ready to take up its plight. It might have seemed that Mayr's undiplomatic outburst finally provoked the political dignitaries and financial experts to take that decision, no matter how inconclusive it seemed, but it in fact it had been well prepared. The Austrian problem was simply too complicated and at the same time deemed too insignificant to push the Allies into cooperative action. Throughout 1920, mass strikes of workers in France, Italy, and Czechoslovakia had failed to produce socialist revolutions and the Soviet army had been thrown back outside the gates of Warsaw, so the risk of a socialist takeover in Vienna seemed less likely. And Allied disagreements on German reparations meant that a form of control, deemed necessary for any foreign loan, had to be found outside the Reparations Commission. The League had already been assigned other tasks the Allies were unable or unwilling to agree upon, and perhaps it could provide a form of control that Austrians could accept and stimulate the international cooperation needed to solve the question of liens on Austrian assets. If those two problems could be overcome, there was a chance that Austria might obtain a foreign loan large enough to balance its budget and stabilize its currency.

The First League of Nations Scheme

The League of Nations had already dealt with the Austrian problem at its Financial and Economic Committees' first meetings toward the end of November 1920. In fact, an appeal for help from private Austrian bodies, including the Austrian Chamber of Commerce, the Federation of Industry, and the Austrian Banking Federation had been the only nonadministrative matter on its first agenda. At the time the League had decided to await an official decision from the Allied Powers regarding Goode's scheme, but after the Supreme Council's January meeting in Paris had aired the idea of nonpolitical control, League officials had gotten busy considering possible ways to help resolve the Austrian crisis.[32] A memorandum on the matter drafted in February had concluded, "Austria is a rare opportunity for the League to do something positive, but we must act with considerable caution."[33] It carefully warned to avoid any greater responsibility than the League could bear and to endeavor only to "coordinate, bring people together and exhibit methods." But once the Supreme Council decided in March to involve the League through applying its Ter Meulen scheme, League experts started to think more practically about how to step in and salvage the crippling Austrian economy.

According to a plan by Frank H. Nixon, a former British Treasury official and freshly appointed acting director of the League's Economic and Financial Section, the League would intervene through a control commission appointed by its Financial Committee, which would issue a loan in Austrian crowns at a guaranteed exchange rate. Such a step, he believed, would rebuild confidence and stabilize the currency, allowing for an increase in private savings and further borrowing by the state.[34] In what would become a recurring theme, he identified large governmental subsidies on food and high expenditures on state workers' wages and pensions as the basis of the Austrian government deficit and crisis.[35] He observed that printing new notes, causing a steady increase of prices and the continued depreciation of the crown, was the only means used to cover the budgetary shortfall. For a permanently balanced budget to result, it would be necessary to abolish food subsidies, curtail unemployment benefits, and dismiss a large number of state workers. Arthur Salter, Nixon's superior as Director of the League Secretariat's Economic and Financial Section and formerly a Secretary of the Supreme Economic Council in Paris, traveled to Austria before Easter 1921 to gain a personal impression of what stabilization might entail.

Salter, born in Oxford in 1881, had enjoyed an impressive career within the British civil service. During the war he had managed British shipping requirements and coordinated the vital maritime transport with the French and the Americans. When the League of Nations was founded, he was called to head its Financial and Economic Section, where he was to play a key role in the League's efforts toward Austrian and Hungarian financial and economic reconstruction, as well as League-sponsored loans to other countries, reminiscing at a later point in life that "the first League achievement was in Austria."[36] Salter spent five days in Vienna in April 1921, where he reckoned that a half million citizens, mostly middle class or rentiers, were suffering acute distress. To stabilize the currency, he wrote Nixon, it would be necessary to put an end to food subsidies, which would hurt this "best and most deserving part of the Austrian population," while Vienna would need to regain its position as the region's banking and commercial center to make stabilization permanent.[37]

The League's Financial Committee of international experts was thus well acquainted with details of the Austrian predicament when it convened in Paris on Easter Monday to discuss in closed session how to help the country.[38] The committee consisted of delegates from member states who were authorities in matters of finance and were to advise the League Council on financial matters, ostensibly as technical experts and not as representatives of their governments. They agreed that as a first step it was imperative for all interested states to release their liens on Austrian assets for at least twenty years to allow for a foreign loan.[39] The Austrian government, in return, needed to put an end to food subsidies and curtail expenditures to balance its budget and restore its credit. Thereupon the creation of a central bank and the floatation of a *domestic* loan could be followed by a foreign loan secured by certain Austrian assets.[40] Joseph Avenol, the committee's French member, later to become Deputy Secretary General and Secretary General of the League, told the Austrian envoy in Paris that the domestic loan was considered a "conditio sine qua non" for a foreign loan, as it would demonstrate to foreign investors the will of Austria's people to help themselves.[41] The Austrian Finance Minister, however, considered the prerequisite of a domestic loan before an international loan impossible. The sudden end to food subsidies and wage adjustments it required, without providing anything tangible in return, he thought, would surely provoke civil unrest.[42]

Before taking any concrete action, however, the Financial Committee decided to send a small delegation to Vienna, made up of Sir Drummond Fraser, the British banker appointed to head the League's Ter Meulen scheme;

Danish financier Emil Glückstadt; and Joseph Avenol himself.[43] Over a period of eight days in late April, the three financial experts interviewed over two dozen prominent Viennese politicians, civil servants, and bankers to establish whether the limited Ter Meulen scheme was applicable, and whether food subsidies could be abolished to balance the budget. Hermann Schwarzwald, a gifted civil servant who was born in Czernowitz in 1872 and had served in the Austrian Trade Ministry before joining the Finance Ministry in 1917, blamed most of the chaos and inflation on Austria's political situation. Since no party would or could take responsibility for increasing indirect taxation, the best remedy, he thought, was foreign financial control, which the League could provide.[44] Trade expert Richard Schüller believed more optimistically that food subsidies could be abolished gradually over six months, so that food prices would rise, consumption would fall, and production would increase.[45] Regarding the Ter Meulen scheme, several Austrian bank directors stressed the inadequacy of the plan. In their view, not Austrian commerce but the Austrian state needed funds, and the limited League plan, designed to finance cross-border trade, was entirely inadequate. And reiterating the Finance Minister's position, they argued that only a foreign loan to stabilize the exchange rate could create the necessary confidence to float a domestic loan and stabilize budget and currency successfully.[46]

At a meeting held at the offices of the Austrian Finance Ministry, the three League delegates summed up their impressions. Everyone they had interviewed seemed convinced that if the current government failed to balance its budget, there would hardly be another one willing to take responsibility. The Austrian state apparatus would simply collapse. Since everyone had further agreed that the financial crisis was due to the ever-increasing deficit being covered by new notes, the first step to arrest inflation and depreciation was to put an end to this process with the help of a loan, increased taxation, and a cut of expenditures. The Ter Meulen scheme was thus inadequate, but a large loan would have to come from private investors, the delegates explained, so that the Austrian government had to first present a plan to balance the budget and sufficient guarantees for its execution.[47] If the world was to be convinced that Austria was serious, the government as a first step had to reduce the number of officials and cut administrative expenditures, "courageously ignoring internal difficulties, which without a doubt are inevitable."[48] Otherwise, private investors would not lend Austria any money.

Within a fortnight the Austrians had drawn up a plan to balance the budget, suggesting that food subsidies be abolished, no new state workers be hired, and indirect taxation and customs be increased.[49] To convince the delegates of its feasibility, official declarations from all parliamentary parties stating that they agreed with this action were attached; moreover, Austrian Chancellor Mayr and his Finance Minister now confirmed that, in return for a foreign loan, the Austrian government would accept a foreign Commission of Control to administer pledged revenues, too.[50] The Austrian political parties had also approved of foreign subscription of part of the capital of a new central bank and the allocation of revenues from the tobacco monopoly and customs as security for foreign credits.[51] As Avenol reported back to Blackett, while Austria's political parties all accepted these necessary measures, he felt that the Austrian government still lacked the authority to actually guarantee the passage of energetic reforms, so that a foreign authority was needed to take this responsibility from it.[52] The British envoy to Vienna was under the impression that Avenol was "distinctly sanguine" about the plan's success and satisfied that a real step forward had been taken.[53] To make use of the momentum, he urged Foreign Secretary Curzon to proceed quickly with the liberation of liens, so that an advance on the loan through foreign credits could be furnished to start tackling Austrian reforms promptly.

Members of the League's Financial Committee reconvened in London at the end of May 1921 to hear its delegates' report and review how the League could effectively assist in Austrian reconstruction.[54] As its South African delegate, Henry Strakosch, summarized, the Austrian government saw a foreign loan, domestic loan, and budgetary reforms as parts of a whole that could not be achieved separately. Strakosch, born in 1871 to a wealthy sugar manufacturer in the Austrian town of Hohenau, had been educated in Vienna and then England before working for the Anglo-Austrian Bank in London. In 1895, he had joined a South African gold mining company and he became a British citizen in 1907, influencing South African monetary policy after the war as a close confidant of Bank of England (BoE) Governor Montagu Norman.[55] Strakosch argued that time would elapse before a large loan could be organized, and until then an advance to pay for the purchase of imported food was necessary, so the Austrian government needed to be certain that such funds were indeed available before consenting to a larger plan.[56] Avenol and Blackett assured the Financial Committee that the French and

British governments were indeed ready to release their liens on Austrian assets, with Blackett producing a letter from the Treasury expressing British willingness to collaborate in the placement of short-term bonds for Austria.[57] Within a few days, Strakosch had ascertained that the value of pledges from bankers for Austria was about £2.75 million, and the League's Financial Committee decided to recommend advances of up to £5 million.[58] The Danish economist and banker Kristen Riis-Hansen, who had accompanied the delegation to Austria, was appointed the Financial Committee's agent in Vienna, while a subcommittee made up of Emil Glückstadt, Joseph Avenol, Basil Blackett, and the Italian delegate and banker Federico Balzarotti was charged to start work on issuing Ter Meulen bonds as soon as all liens were officially suspended.[59]

Formally, the League's Financial Committee still focused on how to implement the Ter Meulen scheme, but the Austrian press knew to report that discussions had included talks on a larger loan incurring League control of Austria's state finances. Such a step, however, had to await the suspension of liens by all governments with claims on Austrian assets, which proved difficult if not impossible. When the Reparations Commission had discussed the question at the end of March 1921, the French delegate had lacked instructions, while his Italian colleague had stated that Rome was unwilling to play along.[60] Now diplomatic efforts were renewed, with the Austrian government requesting all states with liens to lift them and the British Treasury asking the Foreign Office to instruct its diplomatic representatives to do the same. The matter was put on the agenda of the Allied Ambassadors Conference scheduled for early July 1921, but at that meeting the Italian representative stalled. He declared that his country was suffering from a ministerial crisis, and he was therefore unable to give any undertakings until a new government was formed.[61] Moreover, Italy, eager at increasing its influence over Austria, now declared the League unsuitable as a body of control, as it had not been recognized by the United States. The situation seemed at an impasse. A unanimous decision was necessary to lift the relief liens, and in light of Italian opposition to the League, it was decided to first ask the United States, which had provided relief funds through its Allies, to agree to the suspension before further steps were taken.[62]

Upon arrival in July 1921, the Financial Committee representative in Vienna, Riis-Hansen, complained to the Austrian government that food subsidies had not been reduced according to plan and that no serious attempts at savings had been undertaken, leaving the deficit uncared for.[63] Riis-Hansen, born in 1876, had lectured in economics and served as Danish Minister of Trade before turning to banking. He reassured the Austrian Finance Minister that the League Financial Committee remained optimistic about the realization of its scheme, and that he had reason to know it had telegraphed a statement to Paris and London that advances needed to be ready by mid-August. Austria could thus count on £5 million as soon as the question of liens was settled.[64] In response, the Austrian government provided a report on the budgetary measures already taken, blaming any tardiness on the delay of advances. Regarding League control of the pledged revenues, it now retracted however, arguing that a "Kulturland" like Austria could not accept unnecessary foreign interference. Some form of oversight regarding the service of loans would naturally be accepted, but direct intervention into administrative affairs by a League agent was in fact out of question.[65]

While the currency had appreciated during the second quarter of 1921 in anticipation of League assistance, a strike by state workers in July compelled the government to raise their wages. Expected expenditures and deficits increased and a violent fall of the crown quickly ensued.[66] On 1 June, one U.S. dollar still cost 590 crowns. It was priced a month later at 750 crowns and on 1 August at 955 crowns (see Graph 1.1). The new Austrian Chancellor and Vienna Police Chief, Johann Schober, complained that renewed depreciation had wiped out any progress obtained from savings and taxation. Schober was born in Upper Austria in 1874 and, with a degree in law, had joined the Vienna police, being appointed its Chief by Emperor Karl I in 1918. A monarchist at heart, the bespectacled gentleman with a characteristic mustache was unusually nonpartisan and a key figure in the Austrian republic. In his view, it was urgent to put trust back into the League scheme and indispensable that advances come forward, not least since further bouts of depreciation would strengthen state workers' demands, make a general strike more likely, and result in his government's fall. Similarly, the British envoy wired London that something needed to be done to restore confidence in Vienna, but no advances on a future loan seemed possible before the U.S. Congress passed a bill on the liberation of liens.[67]

In September 1921, unaware of how quickly the situation in Austria would deteriorate, Nixon, Avenol, and Blackett unofficially agreed to keep the

League plan alive and Austria going until all liens were suspended.[68] If the French took the initiative, Blackett would see that the £1 million left over for British relief to Eastern Europe would be earmarked for Austria. But when the Austrian Finance Minister resigned a few weeks later, the U.S. dollar already cost 2,518 Austrian crowns.[69] The first wave of hyperinflation was in full swing and Schüller, now convinced that Austria's currency and finance had completely broken down, thought panic would ensue at any moment.[70] On 17 October, the British envoy confidentially informed Chancellor Schober that despite lack of action from the French a small British advance of £250,000 had been arranged.[71] Meanwhile, there were riots at the Vienna Stock Exchange and a railway strike stopped all train traffic with Hungary, so that the Austrian government secretly informed London that if large advances were not officially announced, it would choose to resign.[72] In December workers became restless and terrorized the streets of Vienna's first district, looting shops and vandalizing hotels and cafés, driving fear into the heart of the city's middle and upper classes.[73] By January 1922, as the Austrian currency dropped to a record low of almost 10,000 crowns per U.S. dollar, food subsidies were finally cut and Chancellor Schober personally appealed to Prime Minister Lloyd George for an advance of £3 million. To help prevent the collapse of his country, Austrian President Michael Hainisch addressed a personal entreaty to King George V himself.[74]

Basil Blackett thought there was a possibility of £2.5 million being advanced from funds that did not require parliamentary approval, but notified Austrian envoy Franckenstein that such an operation would necessarily incur British control of the money.[75] The Austrians, with their backs to the wall, accepted, and within a fortnight Prime Minister Lloyd George announced in February 1922 that the United Kingdom would provide £2 million to Vienna. G. M. Young, a former employee at the British embassy now working at the Anglo-Austrian bank in Vienna, was put in charge of the funds and appointed the Treasury's representative to the Austrian capital.[76] As security, Austria pledged its Gobelins tapestries, an art treasure of presumed international acclaim, and promised to repay the advance from proceeds of the large foreign loan it hoped to obtain once liens were lifted.[77] For the moment, it seemed, the fall of the Austrian crown had been halted, and in expectation of foreign help it even appreciated on the exchanges.[78]

With repayment of British advances now tied to the success of the League plan, activities to get Austrian assets freed and the foreign loan floated pulled ahead with renewed steam. The British Treasury asked the Foreign Office to urge the U.S. government to at least publicly announce its intention to postpone its claims for twenty years.[79] The League Council instructed the Financial Committee to appoint a financial adviser in Vienna and to institute a system of cooperation with the Austrian government to implement reforms, while the Austrian Finance Ministry was requested to send a representative to London to officially ask for such a controller.[80] But addressing the Financial Committee on 1 March in London, Austria's delegate once more reneged on its promise, arguing that the moment for appointing a controller was not opportune. The Austrian government would only welcome a counseling representative of the Financial Committee, to keep it informed and to advise the Austrian government on putting the advances to good use.[81] Perhaps emboldened by the renewed stability of the crown's exchange rate and maybe feeling that the worst was behind them, the Austrian government was, as we shall see, hoping to evade the strictures of foreign control.

Young had been given a supervisory role over the advances to Austria and, with fresh foreign exchange available, Chancellor Schober proposed in early March the creation of a special commission to supervise its management in support of the crown, intervene on the foreign exchange market, and fight speculation.[82] Young wished to see immediate steps toward fiscal reform and informed Schober that, unless assurances were obtained from all parties in support of economies to balance the budget, he would release no funds.[83] Meanwhile, the crown started losing value again and the Pan-Germans, angry at Schober for having signed a treaty with Czechoslovakia, made their cooperation in government conditional on Schober's resignation. To support the Chancellor against what he thought was political blackmail, Young promised to free advances if Schober vouched for the immediate introduction of fiscal measures and remained in office to save Austria.[84] The Pan-Germans relented and promised their cooperation, but Schober unwisely published Young's letter in the press, and the latter was attacked for interfering in Austria's political affairs.[85] The Pan-Germans subsequently withdrew their support anew and Schober remained with a bare majority in parliament, but none on the parliament's financial committee, unable to put through any measures of fiscal reform.[86] Besides embarrassing the Pan-Germans, Schober might have had other intentions when publishing Young's letter, for the subsequent Pan-German attack and polemics against the two made foreign financial control in Austria all but impossible, at least for the moment.

The attempt by the Schober government to stabilize the Austrian crown with the help of the advances provided by Young in early January 1922 was not a futile exercise. Austrian debt had been substantially reduced by hyperinflation and the lessening of food subsidies, which had threatened to consume all government revenue, incurred an important reduction of public expenditures. The monthly increases in Treasury Bills and circulation were falling in the first months of 1922, so there seemed to be a genuine opportunity to quell inflation (see Graph 1.6). The exchange rate was stabilized through intervention, with monthly inflation for the moment indecisively hovering around 20 percent. Had it not been for the Pan-German attack and political infighting, Schober might have been able to pass reforms and take important steps toward balancing the budget. Instead, without further measures to cut the deficit being politically possible, note issue soon increased to pay for government expenditures. Once negative news in April would make clear that liens were not yet being lifted and a foreign loan to cover future deficits therefore would not materialize, inflationary expectations returned by the end of the month and with them depreciation of the exchange rate and inflation (see Graph 1.1).

As Frank Nixon had complained in July 1921, the "Austrian project is battling for its life with political difficulties."[87] These were both international and domestic. The question of the release of liens demonstrated to bureaucrats at the League of Nations how much their approach and the Austrian problem remained entangled with larger political questions and Allied plans about the future of Central Europe. Italy remained obstructionist, hoping to eventually increase its influence over Austria. France was interested in a successful League scheme as guarantor against Austro-German unification, but generally favored strengthening its Czech ally over assisting Vienna.[88] Meanwhile, British concerns were to prevent the scheme from becoming an instrument of French or Italian policy and to normalize the economic situation in all of Central Europe.[89] But with the Austrian government unwilling to accept any form of foreign or League control over money lent and revenues pledged, the League scheme remained inconsequential and was in fact of no effect.

The first League scheme above all failed because a quick release of liens could not be obtained once the United States had left the Reparations Commission. Nixon had suggested that the other obstacles could have been tackled through international control, something Blackett and Avenol had both agreed to.[90] But in the end the Austrians, after earlier assurances to the contrary, had straight out refused foreign control, and now it seemed to have become impossible. Even with liens freed, foreign governments would have felt hard pressed to sell a loan to private investors without offering some control over the use of loan funds and the administration of revenue streams pledged as securities. However, underlying Austria's rejection of foreign intervention were neither suicidal brinkmanship nor impulsive patriotism, but the prospect of a workable alternative by means of a loan coming directly from private bankers in London and New York without international, foreign, or political control of Austrian finances.

Between Two League Schemes: The Possibility of a Bank Loan

By March 1922, as the Austrians refused League control a second time, passage of American legislation on Austrian debt appeared increasingly likely, so that Sir William Goode sailed for New York to personally try to convince the partners of J. P. Morgan to help issue a loan for Austria.[91] Goode told J. P. Morgan that he was empowered by the Austrian government to negotiate a direct loan of £5 million, and Thomas Lamont, one of its partners, agreed to discuss further details in Paris in April.[92] In return, their partners at the London banking house Morgan, Grenfell & Co. informed Austrian envoy Franckenstein that they were now prepared to investigate the situation in Austria. Unbeknown to him, they secretly cabled New York that in fact the business was too much trouble because the release of liens remained uncertain.[93] But the bankers were well aware of the profits accruing potentially from issuing future loans for European governments and businesses, and presently turning Austria away could have meant losing that prospective business, too. It was better to make an honest effort on behalf of Austria and demonstrate goodwill, thereby making sure to be Vienna's first choice once conditions improved. But more importantly, perhaps, they were also following the implicit directives of the Governor of the BoE, Montagu Norman.

Norman, a distinguished yet eccentric bachelor until the age of fifty, governed the BoE from 1920 to 1944. Born in 1871 into a dynasty of bankers, he began his career working for family firms before becoming a director of the BoE in 1907 and its Deputy Governor in 1917. Energetic and charming yet mentally unstable, he had grand plans to refashion the business of central banking in all of postwar Europe. Acutely aware of the challenges posed by the rise of labor and nationalism to the interests of his class, Norman wanted to separate the power over monetary policy from politics by creating a network of independent and cooperating central banks across the continent, all of which would naturally look to London for his leadership. Norman had good relations with Governor Benjamin Strong of the New York Federal Reserve, and together they planned and put into practice the postwar restoration of the gold standard. As Governor, Norman also had large sway over the British capital market and the London City, and he was further particularly close with Henry Strakosch, South Africa's delegate on the League Financial Committee. In 1921, Norman hoped to use these influences toward a realization of his plan by establishing an independent central bank in Austria and stabilizing its currency through launching a system of cooperation among Europe's larger central banks, possibly even getting the New York Federal Reserve and American money involved.

In October 1921, Norman had already agreed with Gerald Vissering, Governor of the Dutch National Bank, and Pierre Jay, Chairman at the New York Fed, that a consortium of central banks led by the Federal Reserve should work toward the rehabilitation of Austria and Central Europe on "purely economic lines."[94] Norman had felt that Loucheur's plan promoted by the French was too politically motivated and had lobbied for a project led by neutral countries or the League of Nations to take the matter out of the hands of statesmen. The League had accepted the responsibility, and toward the end of 1921, Norman had approached Morgan, Grenfell about a £2.5 million advance against Austria's Gobelins tapestries. But their American partners at J. P. Morgan in New York had found the business impractical without an explicit request from Allied authorities, and before passage of the planned refunding bill allowed the U.S. Treasury to extend the time of payment of debt owed it by foreign governments. Norman and Blackett had informed envoy Franckenstein before the end of the year that Morgan, Grenfell had definitely declined the business, and in early 1922 J. P. Morgan had still told the Austrian Chargé d'Affaires in New York that any loan, no matter what its collateral, remained unfeasible.[95]

But in February, Congress established a Foreign Debt Commission to settle the question of Allied and postwar loans, and a special resolution passed by Congress came into law in early April, specifically allowing the United States to postpone Austrian relief debt and lift its liens for up to twenty years. Now Morgan, Grenfell relented to pressure from Norman, and its partner, Charles F. Whigham, informed envoy Franckenstein that they would in fact handle the business after the complete release of Austrian assets.[96] An international economic conference in Genoa taking place toward the end of the month offered the ideal opportunity to get all countries with liens to release Austrian assets in unison. The Austrian government, the League of Nations, and the Reparations Commission all hoped that an agreement on lifting the liens would be reached there to clear the road for advances and a future loan.[97]

The Genoa conference from 19 April to 10 May 1922 was organized with the aim to settle remaining questions between the Allied Powers and other countries in Europe.[98] One of the most important was the relationship with Soviet Russia, but these talks collapsed when France insisted on repayment of Czarist debts. Other discussions focused on Germany and reparations, but also on questions of monetary policy and central bank cooperation. Eventually, Italian Foreign Minister Carlo Schanzer chaired a meeting on Austria, at which all concerned countries seemed in favor of lifting their liens except for Romania and Yugoslavia, which demanded postponement in return of their own "liberation bonds" (debt incurred to the Reparations Commission as price of their liberation).[99] Blackett saw no reason to object, but France and Italy feared a reduction of their reparation claims on these and possibly other countries, so liens on Austrian assets remained in force.[100] The League's unofficial observers present in Genoa all agreed that for Austria the result after three weeks of waiting had been a heavy blow.[101] The new British envoy to Vienna, Aretas Akers-Douglas, had earlier warned that without some sort of achievement in Genoa, a new political crisis would ensue.[102] Indeed, before even returning from Italy, Chancellor Johann Schober was finally toppled by the Pan-Germans and resigned.

Albeit its secret misgivings, the Morgan group had already agreed to discuss the loan for Austria, and despite the failure in Genoa, negotiations in London began between Thomas Lamont and Wilhelm Rosenberg, the noted attorney and financial expert advising the Austrian Treasury.[103] Pending the lifting of the liens, Rosenberg suggested a loan of £8–10 million secured by customs revenues, to which Lamont wanted the tobacco monopoly added as further collateral.[104] But he cabled New York that it seemed to him barely possible to place such a sum in Europe and the United States for Austria.[105] J. P. Morgan wanted a complete investigation before reaching a negative decision, and cabling from the United States its partner Dwight W. Murrow recalled why they had agreed to consider the loan:

> The improved situation in Austria seems to us truly remarkable. The question is whether improvement is to go on or whether by a failure of the lending countries of the world Austria is to be abandoned. . . . This is the first real step taken in the reconstruction of the world by united action. France and England and Italy and Czechoslovakia disagree as to the treatment of Germany. They are all united with reference to the Austria plan. Nine years ago the war started in Austria. If Austria's former enemies can help put her on her feet by a legitimate business investment it may well be that the first real step in reconstructing a new world will have been taken in Austria.[106]

Austria was naturally perceived as a lynchpin of Eastern European affairs, and Morgan, Grenfell, together with other London houses potentially interested in issuing the loan (Barings, Rothschild, and Schröder's), sent G. M. Young back to Austria to investigate this time on their behalf. Young was instructed to assess the minimum amount of funds needed to terminate inflation, to examine the sources of revenue to be pledged as security, and to report on the state of the suspension of liens. To assess the feasibility of stabilization, he was to evaluate the extent of the Austrian budget deficit, the trade deficit and the possibility of ending the printing of notes.[107]

Young arrived again in Vienna in June 1922 and explained to Austria's new Christian-Social Chancellor, Ignaz Seipel, that if he wished for a private loan from New York and London banks to materialize, he had to act and get Romania and Yugoslavia to the release their liens to allow for securities.[108]

Seipel, born in Vienna in 1876, was a stern theologian and a Roman Catholic prelate who had served in the Austrian government during the war and as its last Minister for Public Works and Social Affairs in 1918. He had been a member of Austria's first constituent assembly, had helped draft its constitution, and stood at the helm of its clerical, conservative Christian-Social party from 1921 to 1930. From simple means but rabidly anti-Socialist and prone to intrigue, he fancied himself a Kathechon, fighting to restrain the Bolshevik enemies of Christ while pursuing a reactionary and increasingly illiberal program. Formerly teaching at the University of Salzburg, he was Austria's most prominent statesman of the 1920s, serving twice as Chancellor but doing little to rein in the rising antidemocratic forces to his right nor the virulent anti-Semitism coming from some of his own party members. With an authoritarian streak, tireless and determined to lead, he was admired by Austria's conservative bourgeoisie for his perceived steadfastness and courage.

Young's return to Vienna in early June as representative of the American-British Morgan group coincided with the Austrian crown dropping to record lows and was widely announced in the Austrian press.[109] To study the nature of Austria's deficit, Young dove into a long series of investigative meetings with Austrian experts on agricultural production, the budget, the state railways, and the trade balance.[110] His impression was that the crown could be stabilized at around £1 / 50,000, resulting in an annual budget deficit of £16 million, which included the £6 million in losses run by state enterprises, primarily the railways. State enterprises might be made profitable, he thought, and raising £10 million through taxation and savings to cover the next twelve months would not be too difficult once the currency was stable. Young's report to London banks from the end of June 1922 identified the continuous increase of indexed state wages as the main force behind note printing and the budget deficit, and he suggested that taxation on property, income, and production be significantly increased. To balance the budget, Austria would have to raise the charges for tobacco, postal service, and telegraph, and since the deficit was now mainly due to the many state workers, he suggested the dismissal of a large number of them without compensation. But plans for a new central bank, he thought, were the best insurance against inflation and depreciation, as law would make it independent from Austria's government and prohibit the undue printing of fresh notes.[111]

But, as Young observed, the failure of the Genoa conference and Schober's ousting had created a "crisis of despair such as this country is liable to and the crown has taken a violent plunge downwards."[112] Whether or not the London banks actually organized a loan, Austria's future, in Young's mind, remained extremely bleak and to Whigham at Morgan, Grenfell, he wrote that the situation was "very grave indeed, and one which requires the intervention of our Governments."[113] Thus, without a foreign government's guarantee, the banks concluded unanimously in early July, "financial conditions in Austria are so unstable that there is at the present time no basis which would justify a public loan."[114]

Anticipating the negative result of Young's mission, Lord Arthur Balfour, the British delegate to the League of Nations, BoE Governor Montagu Norman, G. M. Young, Under-Secretary of State Eyre Crowe, the Treasury's Basil Blackett, and Chancellor of the Exchequer Robert Horne had discussed the Austrian situation a few days earlier at the Foreign Office. All had been in agreement that Austria was at a breaking point, but that further financial assistance was only possible and useful if somehow the Austrian government accepted foreign control of its fiscal and monetary policy. The British Cabinet thereupon let the Austrian government know that it thought it futile to advance credits, which would merely postpone a catastrophe that appeared inevitable as long as no far-reaching decisions were taken in Vienna.[115] The Austrian crown had already weakened following the failure to suspend liens at Genoa, and with the public miscarriage of Young's mission on behalf of private banks and the British Cabinet decision to advance no further funds, the crown went into free fall on the exchanges. The Austrian government meanwhile put all blame on the empty foreign promises to provide assistance and continued printing money to cover deficit expenditures. One U.S. dollar had cost 7,600 Austrian crowns in early April and 8,200 in early May, but its exchange value had dropped to 21,000 in mid-June and to 42,000 by the end of July. The second wave of Austrian hyperinflation was well under way (see Graph 1.1).

In response to continued pleas from Austria for assistance, Lord Balfour and Lloyd George put the original plan of working through the League onto the agenda of the Supreme Council, scheduled to meet in August 1922.[116] The League plan still required the liberation of Austria's assets, so that British diplomatic efforts to get countries to suspend their liens, already under way since Genoa, intensified.[117] The Italian delegate to the Reparations Commission, however, had already withdrawn consent to release Austrian assets and Yugoslavia and Romania had also gone back on any promises made at Genoa, so Blackett doubted whether the League scheme was still at all suitable.[118] Furthermore, the situation in Austria had meanwhile deteriorated so far that "it is idle to expect that private capital would be forthcoming to help Austria without the guarantee of the British government or some other solvent government for the money lent."[119] It was Lord Balfour who eventually managed to personally convince Italian Foreign Minister Schanzer to drop an Italian counterproposal to the League scheme and fall in line with France and Britain instead. At a secret session on 8 August 1922, shortly before the Supreme Council was to meet in London, the Reparations Commission's Austria section finally decided to recommend the partial liberation of Austria's liens, with the Italian representative voting yes and some states, including Yugoslavia, abstaining.[120] This meant that Austria could finally borrow against state assets, particularly the income from customs duties and the profits of the tobacco monopoly, if it could still find a willing lender.

At the same time, a secret government meeting chaired by Chancellor Seipel in Vienna produced a draft statement for Prime Minister Lloyd George, warning that if Austria received no loan guarantees from the Supreme Council in August, its government would resign. On the night before the opening of the conference, envoy Franckenstein warned Sir Edward Grigg, Lloyd George's secretary, that Seipel was fearless and determined to carry out the threat.[121] It was, however, not until the evening of the last day of the conference that Lloyd George assembled his colleagues to discuss Austria, following another urgent note from Franckenstein, warning of the dangerous consequences to peace if Austria were to collapse.[122] French Prime Minister Raymond Poincaré promised that France would cooperate in any effort the Allies were disposed to make, and Italian Foreign Minister Schanzer confirmed that Rome would also consider granting further assistance. But none of them was ready to commit to any effective help on the spot, and all agreed when Poincaré suggested they ask the League to consider the matter anew.[123]

Lloyd George wrote to envoy Franckenstein that the Allies had decided to provide no further credits, since extensive sums provided in the past had not helped, but that they hoped the League would now propose a program of reconstruction, including a foreign loan, in return for "definite guarantees that further subscriptions would produce substantial improvement and not be thrown away like those made in the past."[124] Such "definite guarantees" were likely to curb Austrian sovereignty, but, as Blackett explained to Franckenstein, the Austrians ought to have no illusions: the British government saw the referral to the League as a formality, and Austria would either prove that it could help itself alone, or collapse to provide the grounds for a new solution.[125] In London, the Austrian question was perceived largely as political and thus the League Financial Committee was expected to achieve little without a prior decision from the League Council or General Assembly.[126] In Austria this view seems to have been shared, and the Allied referral to the League caused disappointment and further despair. British Ambassador Akers Douglas reported that the day after, "disorders are prophesised, and timid Jewish business men are hastening to get their passports in order. The Austrian board of the Anglo-Bank have privately enquired whether in certain eventualities, they might deposit their gold and securities in the Legation."[127]

In spite of Blackett's cautious warning, referral to the League seemed a real opportunity to Chancellor Seipel, however, who, notwithstanding his threats, did not resign after all.[128] Instead, he informed the Entente through their representatives in Vienna that he was leaving the next day to discuss the Austrian problem with the most interested governments, and rode off to Prague and from there to Berlin and Verona.[129] In Prague, Seipel asked Prime Minister Edvard Beneš whether he thought the League would prove capable of helping Austria get a foreign loan and, if not, what he thought about Austria joining Germany, economic cooperation with the Little Entente (the alliance of Czechoslovakia, Romania, and Yugoslavia supported by France), or an Austrian customs union with Italy.[130] Beneš thought the League would do all it could, but that the final outcome depended on the Powers. In his mind the only alternative to a foreign loan for Austria was increased regional cooperation among the successor states, since for Czechoslovakia and France Anschluss meant war, while a customs union with Italy was unrealistic.[131] In Berlin, Reichskanzler Joseph Wirth told Seipel that the League of Nations offered the only venue for a solution; if it failed, Seipel ought to turn to Italy, since the time for Anschluss had not yet come.[132] In Verona, Italian Foreign Minister Schanzer cordially agreed to consider a Customs and Currency Union if Austria's appeal to the League produced no results.[133]

Historians have often claimed that Seipel's whirlwind trip, ostensibly to get a better understanding of the League referral, might have been intended to raise fears among the French and Little Entente that he was set to push for unification with Germany.[134] Certainly, after his personal meeting with Seipel, Schanzer wrote privately to Lloyd George from Oberbozen in South Tyrol about his fears of a war erupting in continental Europe. Germany itself was already sliding down the slippery slope toward hyperinflation, and he argued that "we might have bolshevism not only in Austria but also in Germany and I doubt whether France and Italy would not also be victims of it." Italy would not tolerate Austria joining up with Germany or heading a Danubian Federation. To preserve peace, he argued, it was imperative to sustain Austrian independence and thus guarantee Austrian success at the upcoming League meeting in September.[135] The League was being handed a second chance to prove itself where the Powers and private banks had so sadly failed. This time, with assets freed and European peace at risk, the League was to stand up to the task of saving Austria, but only because Austria by now had no other choice than to accept foreign curtailment of its sovereignty in the form of international financial control.

The Second League Scheme

Already by the time of the Genoa conference in April 1922, Nixon believed that the scheme drafted by the League's first delegation to Vienna one year earlier was no longer practical, but that its principle, pledging Austrian assets to secure a foreign loan, remained valid.[136] In 1921, the League plan had primarily failed because Austria had been unable to offer any security against a loan, but meanwhile the liens had been lifted, offering new hope. A memorandum drafted by Jan van Walré de Bordes for Arthur Salter in early August 1922 recalled that the only way to stabilize the Austrian currency and suppress inflation remained a foreign loan. Even if Austria's budget was miraculously balanced and all note issuing ceased, there would still remain a balance of payments deficit that needed to be covered until Austria improved its terms of trade.[137]

Following the Supreme Council meeting, the British Cabinet had asked the League to discuss the Austrian question, and on 31 August 1922 the

Council instructed the Financial Committee to hear Austrian representatives expected in Geneva for 6 September 1922 and to examine together whether it could help remedy Austria's position.[138] Salter left instantly for Vienna to update himself on the situation and Lord Balfour, acting British member on the League Council, cabled London asking that representatives from the Treasury and the Foreign Office travel to Geneva promptly to advise him on the Austrian question. Salter later remembered to have found Vienna "a tragic scene; its great streets empty of traffic; its shops closed; its people of all classes, including scholars of wide reputation, remnants of the older aristocracy and once prosperous businessmen" visibly starving.[139] British Trade Attaché Owen S. Phillpotts left for Geneva on order from the Foreign Office, and Blackett was forced to interrupt his holiday in Brittany on orders from the Treasury.[140]

In Geneva, Chancellor Seipel, sporting his clerical garb and addressing the League Council in German, with many of the delegates to the League Assembly present, made a moving appeal for financial assistance to his country.[141] Austria's collapse, he warned, would inevitably create unrest in Europe, and he asked the League to help him obtain funds to end currency depreciation and protect his people from hunger and cold. In his address Seipel willingly accepted that a foreign loan also forcefully incurred some form of international control to ensure that reforms were implemented. A subcommittee was appointed by the Council, comprising British, French, Italian, Austrian, and Czechoslovak representatives, to work out a plan and provide a solution.[142] Lord Balfour, who presided over the subcommittee, suggested that all financial and economic questions be referred to the nonpolitical experts of the League's Financial and Economic Committees.[143]

A report submitted by Salter's Financial Section to the Financial Committee identified excess demand for foreign exchange, a general loss of confidence, and speculation as the main reasons behind Austria's currency depreciation.[144] It noted that Austria had important invisible exports and that there had been a considerable increase in the export of manufactured goods from 1921 to 1922, but it saw little chances of success for a public issue of a foreign loan without foreign governmental guarantees.[145] To propose a solution, the Financial Committee members would have to study the Austrian budget, estimate the anticipated deficit, and consider how long it would take to get it balanced. They were to ascertain further what security Austria might offer to private lenders and how to realize the scheme for a new central bank.[146] The Financial Committee concurred with the Secretariat that a credit operation to cover the anticipated deficit of 520 million gold crowns (approximately $110 million) with a foreign loan was impossible without governmental guarantees and that Austria would have to accept certain financial measures and international control to see it through.[147] On the question of securities, the Italian expert Maggiorino Ferraris noted that revenues from the tobacco monopoly would only suffice to guarantee a loan of $66.5 million, though the customs revenue could be considered as a supplementary security.[148]

In Vienna, the Austrian Parliament and its Foreign Affairs Committee discussed the question of control in a heated debate, but eventually gave permission to continue negotiations on the matter.[149] In Geneva, the Austrian Foreign Minister informed the subcommittee that the Austrian government preferred a single Controller to a Commission of Control, and that either was only acceptable if it came together with the provision of advances on the planned loan. To Balfour, the essential difficulty of Austria was that lenders demanded reforms before the provision of funds, while Austria appeared incapable to credibly promise or implement reforms without immediate foreign credits. Control was to solve this problem by giving a foreign controller power over the release of any borrowed funds.[150] In private, Austria's Foreign Minister even told Phillpotts that "control is the main need necessary to the regeneration of Austria, and the credits are a secondary matter." He continued that, "if offered credits without control and credits with control, they [the Austrian Chancellor and Foreign Minister] would choose the latter though they could not say so in public." The Austrian government had come around to view League control as a beneficial tool, one that might assist in the reconstruction of the politically divided country for, in the words of a British lawyer involved in the negotiations, it was "so drastic in character as to amount to a financial dictatorship."[151]

If League control was something the powers could easily agree upon, the necessary loan guarantees from foreign governments were not. At a meeting of the Financial Committee, Strakosch explained to his colleagues why they were essential.[152] If revenues from customs and tobacco proved insufficient to service the loan, the League could approach the guaranteeing governments for payment, which would make marketing the loan to investors a great deal easier and otherwise impossible. The Financial Committee's experts reported back to the Council's subcommittee that Austria's budget could be balanced within two years if the sum of £22 million (about $100 million) was obtained, but that this would require foreign control, full cooperation of the Austrian government on reforms, and the establishment of a new and independent central bank.[153] Foreign governments, it suggested, should at once guarantee the loan and advances; the latter, however, could only be raised by the end of the year. Until then, the reminder of earlier French and Italian credits would cover the Austrian deficit.[154]

Balfour suggested that the Austrian government begin implementing necessary reforms immediately, and in return he and his colleagues on the League Council would ask their respective governments to accord guarantees to Austria for a loan of 520 million gold crowns (about $100 million). Blackett reported to London that the Austrian budget could indeed be balanced with help of a loan if Austria accepted foreign control and began immediate reforms, but he strongly disliked the idea of guarantees from foreign governments and thought Britain should not partake.[155] Balfour urged the Treasury to reconsider Blackett's refusal, since the League's plan offered a real prospect of working, now that Italy, France, and Czechoslovakia were prepared to move forward in unison.[156] If the United Kingdom stood aside, the whole plan would certainly fail, Balfour argued, and within days Chancellor of the Exchequer Sir Robert Horne cabled that the Treasury would ask parliament to give its guarantee.[157]

By the time Chancellor Seipel returned to Geneva in late September to personally attend the final proceedings, Balfour was able to inform him that the British had joined the Czech and French and were ready to guarantee a foreign loan to Austria.[158] In return, Seipel could state that his government had negotiated with all political parties and that they each were prepared to accept League control. Characteristically, the Italian answer on guarantees was still outstanding, but it arrived just on time for the League Assembly to receive a conclusive report before its session was lifted.[159] Negotiations among the assembled statesmen about the size of the loan, the extent of control, and the individual shares of government guarantees had continued to the very last day of the League session. In a closed meeting Seipel expressed his desire that the Controller be given wide powers and that a League delegation be sent to Vienna as soon as possible to assist with the implementation of reforms, which he thought would have a very salutary effect on the mood of the Austrian population.[160] Seipel addressed the Council at its last meeting and praised the League for its help, while Balfour outlined in detail the agreement that had been reached.

The League of Nations' efforts directed by Lord Balfour to save Austria had resulted in three separate protocols, which were ceremoniously signed on 4 October 1922 (see Appendix C in this volume).[161] The first, endorsed by Austria, Great Britain, France, Italy, and Czechoslovakia and open for signature to all countries, declared that the "political independence, the territorial integrity, and the sovereignty of Austria" were inalienable and that none of them sought "special or exclusive economic or financial advantage which would compromise that independence." It was meant to assuage Austrian fears about foreign domination through financial control, but in effect it pandered to France and Czechoslovakia, too, by reaffirming the Austrian pledge not to seek unification with Germany or any other country. The second protocol was signed by France, Italy, Great Britain, and Czechoslovakia as the main guarantors of a 650 million gold crowns (about $130 million) loan to Austria and was open for signature to other states willing to participate in the loan scheme. It outlined the conditions of the international public loan, the obligations of its guarantors, and the powers and duties of a committee of representatives of the guaranteeing governments (the so-called Control Committee). Finally, a third protocol set out the obligations of Austria and the functions of a League of Nations General Commissioner, a foreigner appointed to oversee the execution of a program of reforms to reduce Austrian state expenditure and increase revenues. The proceeds of the international loan would finance the deficit during a transition period of two years until Austria's budget was balanced. By putting an end to the printing of paper money and thus to inflation and depreciation, it would allow for the foundation of a new central bank and the rehabilitation of Austria's currency and economy.

The League of Nations proved the only body capable to help Austria.[162] In 1921, Britain, France, and Italy had been unable to agree upon a common scheme because their national interests in Central Europe were too divergent. Austria, at first unwilling to accept foreign control, had turned to private bankers in a futile attempt to circumvent the Powers, but, bereft of assets to offer as security, had found no rescue without the latter's guarantees.

Ultimately the League provided the mechanism that tamed the national jealousies regarding Austria, which had made cooperation on the Supreme Council or the Reparations Commission so difficult. The League also gave foreign control of pledged revenues a neutral face, making it more palatable to Austrians. Once liens were legally lifted and the foreign guarantor states ratified their loan guarantees, the way was clear for a rescue operation under League leadership to salvage Austria from what appeared to otherwise be inescapable destitution.

The concept of foreign financial control had its origins in foreign lending practices developed during the nineteenth century. Tunisia, the Ottoman Empire, the Khedive of Egypt, Greece, and Serbia all borrowed money from banks or private investors in Europe and then failed to service their foreign debt. When they needed new funds, they approached their creditors, who would only furnish fresh money if they could ensure that their claims were at least partially honored and that the new debt would be regularly serviced. Invariably the solutions found included extending control to foreign creditor representatives over certain tax revenues. In Tunisia, an International Debt Commission took control over major revenues in 1869 to consolidate its foreign liabilities and ensure regular payments, followed by French occupation in 1881. When the Ottoman Empire defaulted in 1875, a foreign-staffed Council of the Administration of the Ottoman Public Debt was given the right to fully administer and collect revenue streams, employing thousands of local officers across the Empire. Serbia, unable to meet foreign debt payments by 1895, obtained a joint loan from several banks for which it pledged state revenues and agreed to establish an Autonomous Monopoly Administration to run them. In Greece, the Commission Financière Internationale de la Grèce, staffed by foreign diplomats, obtained a right to collect revenues in 1897 in return for extending a new loan. Egypt, after declaring a moratorium in 1876, formed its own Caisse de la Dette Publique to regain access to international capital markets, pledging revenues and allowing foreign administration of railways and the Alexandria harbor. Upon foreign pressure, the Khedive eventually agreed to the entire fiscal administration being run by foreigners, causing nationalist resentment and, after violence broke out in 1882, Britain's military intervention and occupation of the country.[163]

In the above examples, the extent of foreign financial control and the limitation on fiscal and political sovereignty varied from case to case. But the financial domination sought by bankers was at times certainly an important tool for Europe's imperial powers seeking to enlarge their economic and military spheres of influence. It is important to acknowledge these colonial origins of foreign financial control, which were cause for Austrian apprehensions about potential foreign incursion. Some of the foreign bankers and politicians probably did envision transforming Austria into a protectorate to be governed and administered in the interest of foreign creditors and governments. Certainly Loucheur's plan to charge the Reparations Commission with control of pledged revenues would have politicized financial control and turned Austria into a likely stomping ground for the Allied Powers. Placing financial control in the hands of the League of Nations was intended precisely to prevent any undue infringements of Austrian sovereignty by creditor nations. International financial control would work to protect the interests of creditors, but the League intended also to safeguard the sovereign rights of Austria as a member state. This point was stressed clearly and explicitly by Balfour in his address to the Council on 4 October 1922:

> The last thing that we desire to do is to interfere in the slightest degree with Austrian independence or Austrian Sovereignty, and we have indeed formally entered into an arrangement . . . that none of us is to extract any separate advantage or interfere in the smallest degree with the series of elaborate transactions which I am endeavouring to describe.[164]

The League of Nations, after all, embodied the Wilsonian ideal of national sovereignty and self-determination. Still, Susan Pedersen has demonstrated how the League Mandate system, for example, served to extend the longevity of imperial and even colonial policies into the interwar period and beyond.[165] For Austria, however, international financial control through the League of Nations, unlike one organized by foreign bankers or the Allied Powers, was acceptable precisely because it promised to be politically more neutral and respectful of national sensitivities about sovereign rights.

It would thus be wrong to argue that League control had been forced on Austria. Austria, after all, had successfully opposed foreign control by bankers or the Reparations Commission. Now Austrian officials, including Chancellor Seipel and his Foreign Minister, stated privately what they could not admit in public: they welcomed the League's presence in Vienna to strengthen their own political position vis-à-vis parliamentary interference. League assistance and a foreign loan were certainly cheered, but its control of the loan funds and pledged revenues was not a bitter pill that had to be swallowed. In fact, the historical record points to a reading according to which the political and economic leadership of Austria was in agreement with foreign politicians, bankers, and financial experts, namely that League intervention *and* control were not just necessary to assuage public investors, but would prove beneficial to Austrian reconstruction and prosperity. Still, the work of reconstruction would necessarily be costly, painful, and politically difficult. The Socialists had agreed to League control following debates in the Austrian parliament's Foreign Affairs Committee, but they would fight the economic reforms desired by the Christian-Social leadership. As we shall see in Chapter 3, for the League of Nations overseeing the implementation of the commitments made by the Austrian Chancellor in Geneva would prove to be an uphill battle.

3

How to Kill a Hyperinflation

1922

> They [the Austrians] are such a weak lot that they always
> seem to start off by taking the easiest way, when this is
> entirely contrary to principles of sound finance.
>
> —Adrianus Pelt, Secretary of the League of
> Nations Financial Committee
> Delegation in Vienna
> 23 October 1922

ON MONDAY AND TUESDAY, 27 and 28 November 1922, violent clashes between Jewish and deutschvölkische students erupted in the center of Vienna.[1] The Pan-German students had declared a strike in demand for a *numerus clausus* to limit the increasing number of Jewish students and faculty and to prohibit Jewish professors from serving as rectors or deans.[2] Fights erupted along the picket lines surrounding the university's main building by the Ringstrasse on Monday, and on Tuesday five thousand right-wing students filed past the monumental building and the University Rector, Professor Karl Diener (who supported their demands), brandishing sticks and turning their heads in paramilitary formation.[3] The protests, which disrupted the daily lives of many ordinary Viennese and students, were ostensibly motivated by the desire to safeguard Austrian higher education from becoming too Jewish. But neither demonstrators nor spectators would have been unaware of the fact that at precisely the same time, just a few hundred meters further up the Ringstrasse, events were taking place that were going to shape the future of Austrian society in more meaningful ways.

During that final week of November 1922, the Austrian parliament was debating and ratifying the last remaining laws pertaining to the three Geneva

Protocols, signed by Chancellor Seipel in Geneva in October. This brought to a close a period of six weeks during which an international delegation of experts sent by the League of Nations Financial Committee had worked tirelessly to assure that the Austrian government lived up the commitments it made by signing the protocols. The delegates restored Austria's credit primarily by insisting on the timely foundation of a new, independent central bank and the public issue of Treasury Bills in Austria to cover the budget deficit until a large foreign loan could be floated. Despite the frustrating inertia of the Austrian government and the antagonism of the Socialist opposition, the delegates also successfully produced a compromise to allow for the ratification of the Geneva Protocols and all its other bylaws, including a reform program that did not mention the installation of a foreign General Commissioner. The delegates had eventually felt obliged to overstep their mandate in order to help convince the Socialist opposition to agree to an arrangement, which finally allowed the disputed Ermächtigungsgesetz, meant to give the government extraordinary powers to implement certain reforms without requiring parliamentary approval, to pass. Bereft of any actual power, the delegation had made sure that by the end of November all legal steps had been taken to allow the League's plan to commence.

The intervention spearheaded by the Financial Committee's delegates was treading novel ground. Bankers and Treasury officials had advised and reformed foreign administrations in the past, but the financial experts in Vienna were not expected to represent the interests of banks or governments. Formally at least they represented the League of Nations and thus the common interests of the international community. It is difficult to imagine how else they might have intervened directly in the country's political process without provoking rejection. Most important, as will be shown in detail, the League's delegation thereby played a decisive and largely unrecognized role in ending inflation and bringing about the permanent stabilization of the Austrian currency. Only through direct mediation and pressure had the delegates been able to facilitate an understanding between the political parties that altered the fiscal expectations of ordinary Austrians and that gave way to renewed confidence in Austria's credit and economic future. The adoption of a reform plan to balance the state budget and the foundation of an independent central bank were at least as important in changing public outlooks. But by bringing about a political compromise toward the end of

November, the delegates created the conditions necessary for the Ermächtigungsgesetz to pass and League control to be implemented, which produced
the relatively late change in people's expectations about Austria's prospects and
created the conditions necessary for the Austrian crown to truly stabilize.

The first part of this chapter analyzes how, during the initial weeks of their
stay, the Financial Committee's delegates made sure that all required laws
were presented to parliament on time and in conformity with the Geneva
Protocols. The minutes and correspondence of the delegation held at the archive of the League of Nations show that they had to painstakingly make
sure that the reconstruction law and reform program would result in a balanced budget and a new central bank. They also had to apply pressure to
convince the Austrian government to stop printing money. Finally, they
had to intervene directly in Austria's political process to ensure that the
Ermächtigungsgesetz, which Seipel had promised in Geneva, was successfully ratified. The delegates thus played a vital and critical role for getting
the League intervention in Vienna off the ground.

The chapter's second part covers the parliamentary debates, reprinted
verbatim in the Vienna press, to show how the often virulent polemic surrounding those sessions masked the secret negotiations toward a compromise, facilitated by the international delegates. This compromise was only
reached after the League's delegates intervened actively in the negotiations
and met with members of the Socialist opposition.

The chapter's final section uses financial data to illustrate that the crown
was not permanently stabilized in August, as many economic historians have
claimed, and that the risk of hyperinflation was not fully eliminated until
early December. Only after the League delegation, by facilitating the compromise between the political parties, created the necessary conditions for
laws to pass and for people to change their expectations about the political,
fiscal, and economic future of Austria did the risk of a return of hyperinflation abate.

The international delegation to Vienna consisted of six men, all of whom
were members of the League of Nations Financial Committee. It was chaired
by the Belgian central banker Albert Janssen and included Joseph Avenol,
the French Treasury official, who had already been to Vienna as a member
of the League delegation in April 1921. The other members were the South
African Henry Strakosch, himself of Austrian descent and a confidant of

Bank of England (BoE) Governor Montagu Norman; the British Treasury official Otto Niemeyer, who had replaced his superior, Basil Blackett, after the latter accepted a position in India; the Czech nationalist lawyer and banker Vilém Pospíšil, later Governor of the National Bank of Czechoslovakia; the Italian politician and League Council representative Maggiorino Ferraris; and the Swiss banker Alfred Sarasin, scion of a patrician family from Basel and later president of the Council of the Swiss National Bank.[4] As members of the League Financial Committee, all of them would continue to remain preoccupied with Austrian reconstruction over the years. Particularly Strakosch, who had Norman's ear, and even more so Niemeyer, the daunting and commandeering Treasury official who would later move to join the BoE itself.

By agreement with the Austrian government, negotiations with the delegates were kept secret and hardly figured in the Vienna daily press. It is this conspicuous absence of the League delegation from the pages of Viennese newspapers that might best explain the scarce attention given to it by historians. Heinrich Benedikt's authoritative study of the First Austrian Republic devotes just a few sentences to the delegation, and Charles Gulick's history of Austrian interwar labor fails to mention it at all.[5] Instead, the historiography generally resorts to a binary description of the events in autumn 1922, focusing on the political debates in parliament between the governing conservative coalition and its Socialist opponents.[6] Karl Ausch's financial history of Austria's interwar years tells the tale of a cunning and mischievous Chancellor Seipel, who managed to outmaneuver the Socialists with help from the League delegation, while Benedikt's account paints the picture of a resilient conservative block that managed to overcome its Socialist foe.[7] In these partisan descriptions, the League delegation remains obscure and faceless, relegated to the background of events.

These two opposing narratives reflect the continuity of an antagonism found already in the contemporary accounts by Socialist leader Otto Bauer and Christian-Social Minister of Finance Victor Kienböck. Bauer polemically described the delegates as a group of bankers in the service of "international finance" who robbed Austria of its independence and best financial assets, only to reconstruct it on the backs of workers, officials, and civil servants.[8] Kienböck's opposed narrative presented the delegates as chivalrous technical experts who helped the conservative coalition overcome Socialist obstructionism to save Austria from collapse.[9] Naturally, a more nuanced approach is needed to do justice to the complexities faced and managed by the international members of the League delegation in 1922. They not only successfully laid the legal and political basis for the League's intervention and its scheme for Austrian reconstruction, but through fostering confidence of Austrians in their state's own future, restored their country's credit, thereby returning stability to its currency's value.

The Work of the League of Nations Financial Committee Delegates

The Geneva Protocols signed by Chancellor Seipel on 4 October 1922 were designed to eliminate those political and fiscal uncertainties pertaining to Austria's future that had hitherto harmed its credit and made foreign banks and governments unwilling to lend to it. By guaranteeing Austria's independence and territorial integrity the Protocols had eliminated the most fundamental uncertainties pertaining to Austria's future existence as a sovereign state. The foundation of a new, independent central bank and the immediate implementation of fiscal reforms were to restore Austria's credit by increasing its future ability to pay and by eliminating the risk that stemmed from a return of note printing and inflation. The League's two-year reconstruction plan ultimately relied on the successful issue of an international loan guaranteed by foreign powers to finance the government's deficit for an intermediary period of two years, by the end of which Austria's budget would, it was hoped, be successfully and permanently balanced.

Together with international control, the measures prescribed and agreed upon were to bring order to the country's fiscal household and to restore foreign investors' confidence in the fledging economy. To prepare investors on world capital markets for the League-tokened Austria loan, a first sale of Treasury Bills via Vienna banks before year's end and thereafter a small international loan on foreign markets were planned. The small international loan would also have to carry foreign government guarantees to serve as a blueprint for the larger one. This process required the ratification of a number of laws and a reform plan, which Seipel was committed to putting before parliament by 4 November 1922, so as to allow the foreign states sufficient time to subsequently ratify their own, critical loan-guarantees before the end of the year.

Charged by the League solely to cooperate with the Austrian government on its program of reforms, the delegates soon found themselves forced to overstep their mandate in order to ensure the timely implementation of all the Protocols' provisions, including foundation of a new independent central bank and the termination of the practice of printing new notes of money. The delegates' function was meant to be advisory, but they discovered that direct involvement was necessary to ensure that the Austrian government kept its side of the bargain. Further, the delegates also had to politically intervene to guarantee the timely ratification of a necessary body of by-laws, foremost among them the Ermächtigungsgesetz. In their decision to extend their activities beyond their mandate, the delegates were mainly motivated by a desire to help Austria and Central Europe return to normalcy, but also by the need to prevent their governments' guarantees for the planned international loan from ever having to be called upon.[10]

The delegates' first task and success was to put an end to the Austrian government's practice of financing its deficit with new notes from the central bank. Currency depreciation on the exchanges had been halted in August and prices were stable in September 1922, but a month later the government was still covering expenditures with freshly printed money. Thus the central bank's balance sheet showed an increase in circulation of 7 percent for the first two weeks of October.[11] At the time, in Geneva, the Financial Committee had recommended covering the Austrian deficit for the time being by selling short-term Treasury Bills to Vienna's private banks instead of the central bank (secured by customs and tobacco revenues and eventually convertible into the long-term loan).[12] Chancellor Seipel had in fact promised to do so, but upon arrival in mid-October the delegates were trapped by Austria's new Finance Minister, August Ségur. Ségur, a lifelong civil servant born in the Moravian city of Brno in 1881, sought their agreement to a bill he planned to present to parliament that same afternoon, which authorized the government to borrow a further 750 billion crowns (about $10 million) in new notes from the central bank.[13] The delegates acceded to the request after they were told that the money was needed to pay salaries coming due at the end of the week, but they haplessly insisted that an agreement with Vienna's banks on the sale of Treasury Bills be reached as soon as possible.

Socialist parliamentarians attacked the new law as a continuation of inflationary practice, to which Ségur sheepishly replied that new ways of funding would soon be found with help of the delegation.[14] Getting the Austrian government to officially announce an end to this practice and instead issue Treasury Bills to the banks and public was thus among the League Delegation's most pressing tasks. To the delegates' surprise, however, they soon learned that the recent law had not covered all outstanding expenditure for the remainder of the year. As Finance Ministry official Herman Schwarzwald told the foreign experts, two further tranches of 750 billion crowns each would be needed for expenses in both November and December. Schwarzwald reassured the delegates that these funds would be obtained from Vienna's banks, with which negotiations on the matter were already under way. But he cautioned that in return the banks demanded to be released from their pledge to contribute 60 million gold crowns (about $12 million) to the capital of the new central bank, thereby delaying its foundation until foreign reserves were obtainable from the international loan.[15] The delegates saw an early foundation of the new central bank as the best guarantee against renewed inflation and therefore insisted that Schwarzwald find a different way to convince the banks to lend.[16]

A few days later Chancellor Seipel and Finance Minister Ségur retracted and explained to the delegates that a loan from Vienna's banks, secured by foreign advances lying dormant at the Austro-Hungarian Bank, could be arranged much more quickly than a sale of Treasury Bills. Moreover, the two argued, unlike issuing Treasury Bills, such a loan would not divert funds from the planned international loan or prejudice the ratification of the Geneva Protocols by pledging Austria's customs and tobacco revenues as security.[17] The delegates, however, remained adamant and insisted on a public issue of Austrian Treasury Bills to scout out and guarantee the future success of the planned foreign loan. Selling Treasury Bills to Viennese banks would help restructure the domestic capital market, signal the restoration of Austria's credit to the world, and make Vienna banks directly interested in the large loan's success. It nevertheless took another week of negotiations until the banks promised the Austrian government to subscribe to 432 billion crowns of Treasury Bills in foreign exchange and place a further 288 billion with the public.[18] But this still left the government in need of 700 to 800 billion crowns, which it hoped to raise through a separate issue of Austrian Treasury Bills abroad. The result was not a complete success, but as a first step the delegates had managed to reduce the risk of further inflation and, by obtaining the banks' agreement to buy and sell Treasury Bills, had taken an important step toward restoring Austria's credit and realizing the long-term loan.

To completely eliminate the government's option of printing notes to cover expenses, the delegates next insisted on the foundation of a new, independent central bank, which would be legally prohibited from lending directly to the government. In return for underwriting the Treasury Bills, the Vienna banks had in fact been released from their pledge to provide most of the new bank's capital, which in itself was welcomed by the delegates, who wished to limit the former's influence on the new central bank. Still Strakosch, who together with his Belgian colleague Janssen studied the bank's draft law and statutes, suspected a ploy by the Finance Ministry in collusion with the Vienna banks to delay the central bank's foundation. He feared that the government aimed at gaining a freer hand in the formulation of the bank's statutes to increase its own influence over its operations, even though in his mind it was obvious to everyone that quickly replacing the "most discredited bank of Europe" was essential to establishing much-needed foreign confidence in Austria.[19]

Upon the Financial Committee's recommendation, the bank's capital had already been reduced from 100 million to 30 million gold crowns (about $6 million) and the delegates insisted that the sum be found without further delay.[20] The British delegate, Otto Niemeyer, let the government know that no one would guarantee Austrian loans "or lend a penny to guaranteed issues" unless the new bank was visibly functioning.[21] He stressed that the ability of the Austrian government to sell 700 billion crowns in Treasury Bills abroad as it planned depended on the successful passage of the guarantee laws by foreign parliaments and the confidence of foreign investors, both of which required a permanent end to inflation and thus the immediate foundation of the bank. Only this action would signal to the world that Austria was serious about stopping inflation. The Austrian government replied that certain changes would first have to be made to the bank's draft statutes, endorsed by the League Financial Committee in August, and which would have required the bank to keep its reserves abroad.[22] Insisting on the foundation of the new bank by no later than 1 December 1922, the delegates repeatedly pressed the Finance Ministry to provide it with a draft of the desired changes, but received little response.[23]

To circumvent Austrian Finance Minister Ségur's foot-dragging, the delegates proposed their own amendments, giving special attention to the central bank's future exchange rate policy. The original draft obliged it to preserve a "normal exchange rate" and the delegates knew that different wording was needed to convey the bank's pledge to keep exchange rates stable, though it was yet too early to decide on an upper bound or on a formula to limit the amount of notes the bank would be allowed to issue.[24] Janssen, a central banker himself, rightly argued that fixed limits to circulation were a principle that could not be applied after a period of hyperinflation, because the real value of circulation (real money balances) had fallen considerably below normal levels and needed to grow back. Instead, Janssen argued, to ensure that circulation did not increase too rapidly and thereby provoke depreciation, the central bank would simply need to be trusted to maintain a healthy ratio between its reserves and the amount of commercial bills it discounted.[25] Ultimately, a limit would be set on the amount of commercial paper the bank could discount without having to pay a special tax, and in order to leave room for a possible appreciation of the crown, for which many Austrians clamored, their draft proscribed only undue depreciation, but not appreciation of the crown's exchange rate.[26]

To raise the bank's capital, the Vienna banks meanwhile agreed to guarantee together with the Austrian government the placement of central bank shares worth 15 million gold crowns (about $3 million) and to sell the other 15 million gold crowns' worth of shares to the public themselves.[27] The delegates granted in return that not all the capital needed to be paid in at once and that 5 million gold crowns could be raised by selling the building and printing machines of the Austro-Hungarian Bank. In the unlikely event that not all shares were sold, the government would provide the remainder.[28] Toward the end of October, the League delegates and Austrian government also reached an agreement regarding the bank's foreign reserves, which could remain in Austria if all of the capital were raised domestically. Just one month after the signing of the Geneva Protocols and two weeks after their arrival in Vienna, the delegates had thus managed to initiate two important steps for putting a permanent end to inflation. The foundation of a new and independent central bank to ensure an end to the printing of money and the public issue of Treasury Bills to finance government spending. If successful, the two measures would make excessive borrowing from the central bank both impossible and unnecessary.

While these were indeed successes, the cornerstone of reconstruction rested on rectifying the source of Austria's problems—its budget deficit—and Chancellor Seipel was committed to presenting parliament with his government's reform program by 4 November 1922. The program was to be drafted with the delegates, and at their first meeting with Seipel and Ségur they had been presented with a confidential draft, which they were astonished to see printed in full in the Vienna press just a few days later.[29] Even more of a surprise than the government's deceitful disclosure was the program itself, which was merely an expanded version of the proposal presented to the Financial Committee in August.[30] Niemeyer, who together with Avenol was charged with reviewing the expenditure's side of the program, expressed his disappointment over what he termed the complete lack of concrete figures and the insufficient reduction of state workers it proposed.[31] Avenol, busy trying to get the banks to agree to the Treasury Bill issue, told his colleagues that he had only skimmed the plan, but agreed with Niemeyer that reducing the deficit had to be achieved by firing state workers and implementing savings, not through increasing revenues.[32]

The Austrian government's plan foresaw a balanced annual budget by the end of 1924 reduced to the level of 237 million gold crowns (about $47 million), still very close to the figure of 234 million recommended by the Financial Committee. It also confirmed administrative reforms, a reduction of state workers, and simplified taxation to reduce expenses, and expected an extensive increase in revenues to double state income.[33] All state enterprises—the railway, phone, and telegraph authorities as well as the salt and tobacco monopolies, and state forests—were expected to return to profit, but only tobacco was presently earning good money, and no details were provided on how the Austrian government intended to turn the others around.

Nor were specific details included about how budgetary retrenchment would be undertaken. Implementing significant savings, however, was deemed necessary by the delegates to ensure the Austrian budget would indeed be balanced within two years, and also to produce confidence abroad without which foreign parliaments would not ratify their vital loan guarantees. Studying the plan, the delegates quickly agreed that a more detailed program was necessary and returned the draft, asking the government for exact and detailed figures of expected expenditure and revenues for every six months until the end of 1924.[34]

A revised plan presented to the delegates toward the end of October provided more detailed figures, but shocked them by proposing to obtain a balanced budget as high as 495 million gold crowns (almost $100 million) by the end of 1924.[35] Current revenues from taxation were to increase by 140 percent, while present expenses were to fall by little more than a quarter. Niemeyer was convinced that the estimates of future receipts and expenses were simply exaggerated and the increase of taxation to 70 gold crowns (about $14) per capita naïve at best.[36] In light of the excessive wage bill, Niemeyer suggested demanding that every state worker below the age of thirty-five be discharged immediately, and that every three months 25,000 more be laid off.[37] In what was turning into a cat-and-mouse game, the delegates informed Finance Minister Ségur that his new program foresaw too much taxation, asking him to pursue more radical savings and present a detailed schedule pertaining to the reduction of state workers.[38] Following Niemeyer's suggestion to adopt a hard-line position, they demanded a stronger effort to curtail expenses, most importantly through shedding 25,000 state workers every six months, producing a total of 100,000 dismissals until the end of 1925.[39]

As only four days remained until 4 November 1922, one month after the signing of the Protocols and the day Seipel was charged to bring his reform program before parliament, the delegates felt they needed a clearer picture of possible economies to face Ségur's final draft with arguments of their own.[40] Interviews with the heads of Austria's civil administration revealed that all of them were reluctant to implement radical reforms and that none of them had any concrete plans to do so.[41] Niemeyer thereupon proposed that the delegation not just oppose Ségur's plans, but demand that the budget be brought down to 350 million gold crowns (about $70 million), commensurate with a more realistic level of taxation of 50 gold crowns per head (about $10). The other delegates were more lenient than Niemeyer and the delegation decided to ask Ségur for a budget balanced at 400 million gold crowns (about $80 million).[42] Meanwhile, Ségur had already submitted a slightly revised draft, balanced below 400 million, cutting thirty million in expenditures and moving eighty million to the budgets of Austria's communes and provinces.

Faced with this trick of accountancy, Avenol and Niemeyer felt compelled to take a tougher position and, in order to obtain a budget of 350 million gold crowns, quoted 300 million (about $60 million) as a starting point. The other delegates, who had been more lenient than Niemeyer and Avenol, decided however to inform Chancellor Seipel that they were ready to compromise and straight-out offered a budget balanced at 350 million gold crowns.[43] To increase pressure on the government, Chairman Janssen told Seipel that in order to leave sufficient time for the guarantor states' parliaments to ratify the guarantee laws before year's end, all laws had to pass by Saturday, 11 November 1922. Any further delay would put the foreign guarantees, and therefore the issue of an international loan and with it the entire League scheme, at risk.[44]

If Austrian brinkmanship did not make the task of the League delegates difficult enough, the Socialist opposition, which had declared publicly that it would not obstruct ratification of the reform program, now swore to oppose the most contentious measure prescribed by the Protocols, the so-called Ermächtigungsgesetz. This empowerment law, once passed by parliament, was meant to authorize any future legal measures the government deemed necessary to take in pursuance of the reform program and a balanced budget, eliminating the need of parliamentary legislation. At their first meeting with the delegates, Seipel and Ségur had cautiously revealed that due to the law's constitutional character, it required a two-thirds majority to pass, and that given Socialist opposition, the government would have to negotiate with them.[45] The Socialists were afraid Seipel would use his new powers to reverse earlier legislation improving workers' rights and strengthen his own party's hold over the country's administration, the army and state enterprises. The delegates had not turned their attention to it until shortly before 4 November 1922, being kept busy with the issue of Treasury Bills, the new central bank and the reform program, but viewed the Ermächtigungsgesetz as a necessary measure for international control to work and restore foreign confidence.

In the eyes of the delegates, the first draft of the Ermächtigungsgesetz did not empower the Austrian government sufficiently, because its preamble

placed too narrowly defined limits on the powers to actually guarantee sufficient reforms.[46] The League delegation also raised the explicit concern that
government actions might be limited by earlier laws and demanded that a
new draft bestow the power to cancel existing legislation if it stood in the way
of savings to balance the budget.[47] Since the Austrian government needed
Socialist support to pass the Ermächtigungsgesetz and time was running
out, the delegates decided to get in touch with the opposition (albeit indirectly) to facilitate a compromise that would guarantee ratification.[48] The
law had been stipulated by the second Geneva Protocols and needed to be
enacted if foreign states were to ratify their guarantees. The compromise that
was eventually reached, however, was far from what some in Geneva had intended it to be.

On 1 November 1922, British commercial attaché Owen S. Phillpotts was
sent to speak to Socialist Party leader Karl Renner, the pragmatic Socialist
who had served as the Republic's first Chancellor from 1918 to 1920 and
would once more lead the country's first government following World War II.[49]
Renner, who had opposed party leader Otto Bauer's decision to choose the
opposition in 1920, now complained that Chancellor Seipel was purposely
keeping the Socialists out of his coalition and gaining too much political
capital out of the reconstruction scheme. Once given the extraordinary
powers envisioned by the Ermächtigungsgesetz, Renner feared, Seipel would
purge the administration of Socialists, undo their legislative achievements,
and impose forms of taxation that would disproportionality hurt the working
class and its cooperative societies.[50] Since Socialists lacked a feasible alternative to Seipel's plans, however, Renner declared that they were willing to support the Chancellor, albeit not at any price. Because the Socialists could not
risk wrecking the League scheme, which they acknowledged was Austria's
best, only, and possibly last chance of salvation, Renner would change his
party's pronounced opposition to a transformed empowerment law.[51] With
help from Phillpotts and the League delegation, the Chancellor and the Socialists agreed to work toward the creation of an Ausserordentlicher Kabinettsrat, in which all parties would be represented in proportion to their
seats in the Nationalrat, and which would be consulted each time the government wished to evoke the reconstruction law.

Creation of the Ausserordentliche Kabinettsrat was eventually included in
the Ermächtigungsgesetz. It would consist of the Chancellor, Vice-Chancellor,

all government ministers, and twenty-six elected members of parliament and would take decisions by simple majority. Convened by the Chancellor to debate and decide upon future reform measures that had not been sufficiently outlined in the reconstruction law, it had no legislative authority. If it failed to reach a decision after no less than three meetings, the government had the right to issue a decree on the matter. It was neither an enlarged coalition government, nor a slimmed-down legislature, but rather a debating circle, with no particular powers.[52] If it functioned well, it could make governing easier, but in practice the Ausserordentliche Kabinettsrat hardly met. Although prominently cited in Geneva as a precondition for control to work, the empowerment law was not going to silence or even curtail sovereignty of the Austrian parliament, nor bestow any extraordinary powers on Chancellor Seipel.[53] Passage of Austria's budget and any legislative reforms would still need parliamentary approval, but the debates that ensued in parliament the next day did not reveal any sense of willingness among Austria's largest political parties for cooperation.

The Debates in Parliament

When the Ermächtigungsgesetz, the Geneva Protocols, the reconstruction law (including the reform plan), and the laws and statutes pertaining to the foundation of the new central bank were presented together to the Nationalrat on 4 November 1922, pandemonium ensued.[54] The parliamentary debates were reprinted verbatim by the press and offered the Austrian population a first glimpse as to how things stood with the League intervention and reconstruction of their country. As Seipel had forewarned Janssen and Avenol the previous day, the laws were strongly opposed not only by Socialists, but also by members of his own party and its Pan-German coalition partner.[55]

Chancellor Seipel opened the session in parliament with a call not to delay the passage of his proposals, so as to allow for foreign governments to ratify their guarantee laws before year's end. Infuriated by interruptions from the Socialist benches, Seipel directly addressed accusations that he planned to usurp power by means of the Ermächtigungsgesetz. The Chancellor stressed that it was not his intention to silence parliament or to reduce their powers any more than he was forced to by the Geneva Protocols, and claimed that the Ermächtigungsgesetz had not been his idea, but rather represented a generally accepted practice. Seipel offered to discuss ways to allow parliament to control its implementation, a hint at the negotiations that were going on between his party and the Socialist opposition.[56]

In fact, the Socialists primarily demanded that the reform program be changed in return for their support in passing the Ermächtigungsgesetz. To protect workers, they desired guarantees that import taxes on food and coal be suspended, against calls from Austrian farmers desiring the contrary, and they opposed the government's plan to tax electricity and gas. Furthermore, they opposed the planned division of tax revenues between federal and local authorities, most importantly of the luxury tax, which was an important source of revenue for the Socialist City of Vienna, and demanded the insertion of a paragraph in the reconstruction law to prohibit the sale of state enterprises without the Kabinettsrat's agreement.[57] Replying to Seipel in parliament, Socialist speaker Karl Dannenberg accused the government of planning to reconstruct Austria on the back of its industry, urban population, and working class, while sparing agrarians. Looking at the reform program, he deplored the fact that Austria's tax burden would reach harmfully high levels, while taxation of the rich was not sufficiently exploited.[58] Defending the interests of city workers, he harshly attacked the program:

> What we have here is no financial program, it is a mockery that lacks fire. It is the sorry effort of ignorant bureaucrats, resulting from agrarian arrogance, bourgeois tax-evasion, from guile against cities and industry, and from an infernal hate against workers. If nobody in Austria will stand up for the development and future of industry, for the fate of our towns—then workers and employees are prepared to take up the fight for a real reform program.[59]

Dannenberg's words were exemplary of the first day's charged debate, and his insulting rhetoric and purposefully implied yet ambiguous threat of revolt did not indicate willingness for compromise.

Speaking the next day, Karl Renner declared his party not opposed the League's loan plan, but vowed that the Socialists would not accept the humiliating foreign control it incurred. In his speech, Renner further claimed that Seipel had in fact explicitly asked Arthur Balfour for the extraordinary powers in August, a claim the Chancellor loudly decried as an invention. Renner then jokingly agreed, adding that he believed to know the Chancellor had spent most of his time in the resort of Chamonix instead of negotiating, a claim that provoked Seipel to lash out and call him a liar in return.[60] To prevent further degrading scenes, the party leaders then agreed that on the third and final day of debates, parliamentarians would no longer meet in full plenum, but separately and would speak in front of their own party colleagues only. The first reading of the laws was thereupon completed without further interruptions the next evening (Wednesday, 8 November 1922), and the reconstruction law, reform program and bank statutes passed by simple majority for discussion to the Finanzausschuss.[61]

Discussions in the Finanzausschuss resulted in the creation of a subcommittee charged with negotiating the division of tax revenues. Since the guarantor states, about to meet to prepare the uniform guarantee law for their parliaments, would not proceed without the Ermächtigungsgesetz, Janssen warned Seipel that if he did not soon settle his differences with the opposition, the delegates would initiate direct talks with the Socialists to facilitate an agreement.[62] In a joint letter to Seipel, the delegates warned again that negotiations had to be concluded before 26 November 1922 in order to allow for the foreign parliaments to ratify their guarantees before year's end.[63] Janssen urged Seipel to publish the letter to put pressure on the Socialists, and the Chancellor, in a sudden turn of face, not only agreed but asked the delegates to meet with the opposition and help bring about an understanding.[64]

The League delegation thereupon secretly sent its secretary to the chief editor of the *Arbeiterzeitung* with a request to meet directly with leaders of the Socialist Party.[65] Clandestinely assembled at the apartment of Karl Seitz, the Vienna Mayor and Socialist Party President, delegates Avenol and Ferraris were told by the Socialists that they would help pass the laws if the reform program were made less favorable to agrarian interests and more advantageous to Austria's industrial and urban working class.[66] In particular, this related to splitting tax revenue between federal and local authorities and the favoring of other provinces over Vienna in matters of taxation. If those problems were solved, the Socialists would abstain or even vote with the government to allow all laws, including the Ermächtigungsgesetz, to pass. Otherwise, they would oppose it and therewith stall the whole reconstruction scheme in order to rescue Austria, as they termed it, from reverting to an agricultural state.[67]

The delegation's secretary described the conversation as friendly and surprisingly apolitical, and the delegates returned to the Hotel Imperial convinced that the reform program was too one-sided in the favor of agrarian interests. The next day, Avenol asked Foreign Minister Alfred Grünberger to grant a larger proportion of tax revenues to the City of Vienna and indeed, the following day the Finanzausschuss terminated its debates with the Socialist Party, declaring itself in favor of the empowerment law.[68] The Socialists now pacified, the Nationalrat passed the Geneva Protocols in the second reading, 103 votes to 68, and began discussing the reconstruction law and reform program until late Saturday night.[69] On Sunday afternoon, before the vote on the Ermächtigungsgesetz, there was a final public exchange of insults when Seitz accused Seipel repeatedly of high treason and of selling Austria out to the interests of international finance. Chancellor Seipel, who was welcomed to the plenum with a loud wave of both applause and insults, spoke in an unusually strong tone and resorted to anti-Semitic imagery by referring to Austrians as the "authochthonal German-Christian inhabitants of the state."[70] But the debate, after all, was just a smokescreen, as a compromise had already secretly been reached. Indeed, following Seipel's speech the Socialist parliamentarians simply quit the hall to allow the Ermächtigungsgesetz to pass its second and third readings with the required two-thirds of the votes present. The third readings of the reconstruction law and the reform program then passed on Monday morning, 98 votes to 60.[71]

An unexpected hurdle to the final ratification arose the next day in the second chamber, the Bundesrat, where government parties and opposition held almost the same number of seats.[72] The Socialists flexed their muscles and at first Seipel threatened to resign, but he then gave a conciliatory speech in the Chamber asking the opposition to cooperate once more.[73] A familiar solution was found: this time it was the Christian Social and Pan-German members who left the assembly, which allowed all of the laws to be rejected by the remaining Socialists, which automatically returned them to the Nationalrat.[74] There they passed a further three readings before being finally ratified and signed into law by the President on 8 December 1922. The Ermächtigungsgesetz, however, probably because time was now very scarce indeed, was directly and unanimously voted into law by the Bundesrat.

One final step was necessary to eliminate the risk of inflation once and for all.[75] Shortly before the delegates decided to issue a final ultimatum to the political parties and to talk to the Socialists directly, Chairman Janssen had reprimanded Foreign Minister Grünberger that no formal decision to stop the borrowing from the central bank had yet been taken.[76] Although the Austrian government had entered an agreement with Vienna's private banks on the issue of Treasury Bills, it still had not committed itself publicly and officially to terminate its practice of borrowing new notes. Upon heavy pressure from the delegates, the new Finance Minister, Victor Kienböck, relented, promising in writing that his government would demand no further advances from the central bank, with an official declaration to that end appearing in the press shortly thereafter.[77]

Following the successful completion of parliament's work and the government's pledge no longer to borrow from the Austro-Hungarian Bank, the Finance Ministry could announce that subscription for Treasury Bills and the new central bank shares would commence Monday, 4 December 1922.[78] The banks were initially unsure whether they could place all Treasury Bills with the public, but as the date of issue approached, they found the market receptive.[79] Treasury Bills sold between the 4th and the 14th were convertible into shares of the new central bank and thus did not reach the state's coffers, but from the 14th to the 19th public subscription totaled 115 billion crowns (about $1.5 million), enough to last the government until the end of the year.[80] We have data of daily subscriptions of the Austrian 8 percent loan through the Österreichische Postsparkasse, starting 15 December 1922, once the sale of the convertible issue was over. The figures show that these uncovertible bills sold well from the start and that demand for them stayed high until the last day of 1922. In 1923, people continued to buy the bills, so that by the middle of January, Austrians had lent the government over 280 billion crowns (about $3.8 million) in fresh funds, enough to cover its deficit until the middle of February.[81]

The success of public subscriptions of Treasury Bills was an enormous achievement for everyone involved in Austrian reconstruction. Of course, the case could be made that the Bills were a good investment. They were indexed to the American dollar and secured by pledged revenues, and some were convertible into new central bank shares. At an interest rate of 8 percent, they seemed a lucrative and risk-free investment. But the readiness of Austrian investors to buy any financial paper that had the name of the Austrian government on it was a remarkable sign of confidence in their state's future and in the League's intervention that promised to make it better.

If the months of hyperinflation had been characterized by deteriorating expectations of Austria's fiscal and thus economic and even political and social future, the successful floatation of Treasury Bills demonstrates that the months following the signature of the Geneva Protocols were characterized by a gradual return of confidence. The League delegates played a crucial role in this restoration of Austria's credit, getting the government to end its practice of printing money. In their discussions with the Austrian government they had at times been firm but also willing to compromise on budgetary figures or the creation of the Ausserordentliche Kabinettsrat. By giving their blessing to the reconstruction and reform laws, the Ermächtigungsgesetz, and the law and statutes of the new Austrian National Bank, the delegates had helped establish the foundation for the League scheme to commence. By facilitating the vital compromise between the political parties on the controversial Ermächtigungsgesetz and the reform program, they had also helped create the conditions necessary for the small and later large international loans for Austria. The League delegates were banking and financial experts, not diplomats, but they had made sure that the Austrian government upheld the international agreements Seipel had committed his country to in Geneva, thereby materially changing the economic prospects of Austria.

At the end of 1922, Henry Strakosch was able to write to Montagu Norman that in Austria, "confidence generally seems to be returning."[82] His positive assessment echoed the analysis of Michael Spencer-Smith, head of the Anglo-Austrian Bank, who had visited Vienna from London a few weeks earlier and who had been able to inform Norman that

> the only thing I would like to say is this: that for the first time I really do see the beginning of a different spirit here. There seems to be a genuine desire on the part of everybody one meets to face fact, and there is a distinct recovery of confidence, which is shown by the increase in the banks' deposits and especially in the deposits of the Savings-Banks.[83]

In the eyes of foreign bankers the League of Nations scheme had so far proved a success. It had bestowed credibility to the Austrian government's pledge to balance the budget within two years, which had increased confidence among Austrians in the future value of their currency. While depreciation had halted since August and prices were stable in September, it had only been through the important work of the League's delegates present in Vienna that confidence was reestablished toward the end of the year. Though many credited Chancellor Seipel and his whirlwind tour in August with stabilizing the exchange rate, the following section will show that it probably took longer to change expectations and that the risk of a return to inflation had only been banished effectively toward the end of November and was in no small part due to the intervention of the League of Nations delegation of financial experts.

When, Why, and How Did Stabilization Occur?

Chapter 1 discussed how hyperinflation had resulted from people's expectations that for the foreseeable future the Austrian government would finance the budget deficit by exchanging Treasury Bills for ever more newly printed notes, thus creating fresh debt it would not be able to redeem. And despite the fact that the central bank continued to print new notes until the end of November 1922, the Austrian exchange rate and prices had steadied in August and September, respectively. How is this to be explained in light of the uncertainty that surrounded the ratification of the laws pertaining to the League scheme and the secrecy surrounding the League delegation's activities described in the first two sections of this chapter? Certainly nobody in August or September was willing to bet money on the League scheme's success? Did Austrians really believe that their government had stopped borrowing from the national bank for good?

Most historians fail to mention any specific mechanism behind the stabilization of Austrian exchange rates, which was undertaken following the League meetings in August 1922.[84] Brendan Brown writes that stabilization occurred in August in anticipation of the measures to be implemented following the signature of the Geneva Protocols in October, while most political historians do not offer any explanation for stabilization at all.[85] Brown follows economist Thomas Sargent, who in his seminal work on hyperinflations argued that the abrupt stabilization of exchanges in August and the end of price rises in September were due to the formal intervention of the League and the Austrian government's commitment to change its policies.[86] Sargent assumed, somewhat precariously, that even though the exact details of the agreements were not publicly announced, the serious deliberations of the League Council in August had been sufficient to change expectations among the Austrian public. Once Austrians were sure that the government would abandon the practice of printing new notes and instead cover its deficit by borrowing from the Vienna banks, inflation ended and exchange rates stabilized. Continued increases in circulation thus failed to cause further inflation, because the public had become convinced that the new Treasury Bills would eventually be retired with funds from taxation or loans.[87] Impressed by the League's preoccupation with Austria in August, according to Sargent's view, the public believed that a new central bank would be founded, which would no longer bankroll the government.

Sargent based his thesis partly on Leo Pasvolsky, a Russian-born economist who in 1928 explained the League's role in stabilizing the Austrian crown as follows:

> The Austrian crisis was checked by the action of the League of Nations. The moment the Council of the League decided to take up in earnest the question of Austrian reconstruction, there was immediately a widespread conviction that the solution of the problem was at hand. This conviction communicated itself first of all to that delicately adjusted mechanism, the international exchange market. Nearly two weeks before Chancellor Seipel officially laid the Austrian question before the Council of the League, on August 25, the foreign exchange rate ceased to soar and began to decline, the internal price level following suit three weeks later. The printing presses were still grinding out new currency; the various Ministries were still dispersing this new currency through the country by means of continuing budgetary deficits. Yet the rate of exchange was slowly declining. The crisis was checked.[88]

For Sargent and Pasvolsky, it was thus the perceived commitment of the League to help reconstruct Austria in August 1922 that had created a change in expectations among Austrians to bring about an end to hyperinflation and currency depreciation.[89] This has become the predominant view repeated across the financial literature, too.[90] More recently, however, economists have argued that a stabilization of exchange rates does not signify the end of hyperinflation, but is merely a precondition, which helps put an end to price increases if followed by fiscal reforms. If deficits continue, inflation inevitably returns.[91] Sargent and Pasvolsky in fact ignored earlier works by Jan van Walré de Bordes and Eduard März, which showed that the sudden stabilization of the crown's exchange rate in August did not occur "naturally," but had actually been manufactured by the Austrian Devisen Zentrale (DZ).[92] Rather, from what follows in this section, true stabilization of the Austrian crown was only achieved toward the end of November, when expectations changed due to the critical interventions taken by members of the League's delegation.

The DZ, founded during the war in 1916, had since been placed under the Ministry of Finance and served as a regulator of the exchange rate by intervening on the exchanges. A decree of 27 July 1922 required that all foreign exchange received in return for exports needed to be delivered to the DZ, which was the only place through which foreign exchange could be legally obtained. Vienna's banks and exporters were required to deliver all foreign exchange they received, and merchants had to apply to the DZ to obtain foreign currency for imports. Available data from DZ at the archive of the League of Nations only covers the period after 15 October 1922, which coincides exactly with the period of the League delegation's activities in Vienna and the scope of this chapter. A careful analysis of these records reveals that events in late November had a strong impact on public expectations.

According to van Walré de Bordes and März, favorable reports from Geneva at the end of August caused speculators to bet on an appreciation of the crown, of which the DZ knew to take advantage.[93] The changed outlook among speculators allowed the DZ to mobilize its foreign exchange reserves and clandestinely stabilize the exchange rate. This artificial stabilization was, however, still very fragile.[94] As pointed out by van Walré de Bordes, demand and supply for foreign exchange fluctuated in Vienna between August and December, and while the delegates were engaged in trying negotiations with the Austrian government, the DZ had in fact to intervene to keep the crown from depreciating. While in September, supply of foreign exchange exceeded public demand and the DZ witnessed an inflow of foreign currencies, in October and November the DZ had to provide foreign exchange out of its reserves to satisfy the public. Van Walré de Bordes relates how publication of the Geneva Protocols in October actually led to new hoarding of foreign exchange by a fearful public, disappointed by news that foreign loans were not immediately forthcoming. Hoarding only ceased in November, he writes, after the government publicly announced it had permanently ended its practice of borrowing new notes.[95]

Van Walré de Bordes's observations were based on the available *net* flows of the DZ. These, however, represent only a fraction of the funds demanded and supplied. The total amount of foreign exchange applied for by financial institutions is far more informative (see Graph 3.1). The data illustrate how demand for foreign exchange only started to decline consistently toward the end of November. Since the arrival of the League's delegates on 16 October 1922, demand for foreign exchange had fluctuated around £400,000 per day (about $1.8 million), which was double or triple the amount of foreign exchange delivered to the DZ through banks and public Wechselstuben (exchange offices). Similarly, foreign exchange supplied to the DZ rose only by the second half of November, but thereafter remained high until the end of the year (see Graph 3.2).

During October and the first half of November 1922, the amount of foreign exchange delivered by the public through Wechselstuben had been significantly below £50,000 per day (about $270,000), but it reached a record £110,000 (about $650,000) on 18 December. In fact, from 22 November 1922 onward, there appears to have been a marked change of expectations regarding currency depreciation among the public in Vienna, reflected in the increased supply of foreign exchange to the DZ from Wechselstuben and banks (as well as the continuous drop in applications for foreign currencies from financial institutions).[96] It would appear that on or shortly after 22 November, Austrians no longer feared that depreciation might return, therefore changing their hoarded foreign currencies back into Austrian crowns to increase their cash holdings.

The first and second part of this chapter related three events that coincided on the day before 22 November. First, the Austrian government published a formal declaration no longer to borrow from the Austro-Hungarian Bank. Second, the press published a letter by the League delegation, in which it set a definite deadline for negotiations with the opposition, demanding the laws be ratified by 26 November. And finally, newspapers reported that the

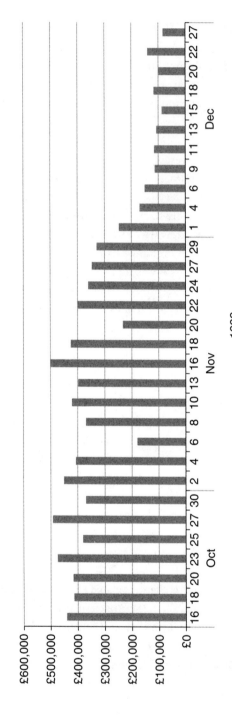

GRAPH 3.1. Amount of foreign exchange applied for by Austrian merchants, banks, and the government in UK£, 16 October–27 December 1922. *Source:* LNA, C 28. Position financière de la Devisen Zentrale.

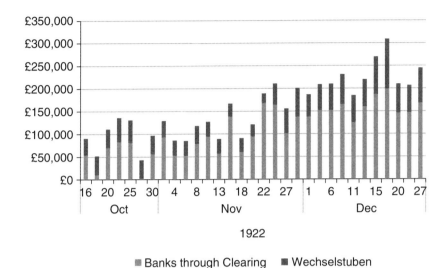

GRAPH 3.2. Foreign exchange offered by banks and Wechselstuben to the Devisen Zentrale in UK£, 16 October–17 December 1922. *Source:* LNA, C 28, Position financière de la Devisen Zentrale.

government and Socialist leaders were about to reach a compromise agreement.[97] These reports occurred only because the delegates had put heavy pressure on the Austrian government, and their announcement seems to have affected people's expectations. If their fears of depreciation and inflation abated, it was because they felt convinced that the League's intervention scheme was about to be implemented successfully.

While debates commenced in the Austrian parliament, indicating little chances of compromise between the parties, the public sensed that ratification was a forgone conclusion. The League delegation, by facilitating negotiations with the Socialists, setting a final ultimatum for ratification, and getting the government formally to declare its decision to silence the printing press, had changed the public's expectations about Austria's economic and political future.

It was thus not until the end of November 1922 that Austrians really began to trust in the League scheme. Thomas Sargent and other scholars are right to claim that stabilization occurred once people's expectations changed, but wrong to pinpoint the League's preoccupation with Austria in August 1922 as the point in time the change took place. The events in August only allowed the DZ to try to stabilize the crown artificially through secret interventions. Neither Seipel, the so-called Saviour of Geneva, nor Balfour and his French colleague Gabriel Hanotaux, the courageous godfathers of League intervention, deserve credit for bringing hyperinflation to a sudden halt. Rather, it was the energetic steps taken by the financial experts of the League delegation in late November 1922 that really changed people's expectations and bestowed new credibility on the Austrian government's present and future policies.

It is perhaps not surprising that the League delegates failed to be given the attention they deserved by historians, precisely because of these achievements. As we shall see in subsequent chapters, the Austrian public and press generally considered the League intervention in Austria a foreign imposition that did more harm than good to the Austrian economy. Governing politicians and Socialist opposition alike felt comfortable blaming unpleasant reforms and painful adjustments on the League intervention. This view was widely adopted by historians writing about the Austrian First Republic. Appraising the League delegates for their achievements would have disturbed such a clear-cut narrative. Credit for stabilizing the currency and completing the difficult process of ratifying the contentious reconstruction laws was to be given to Austrian politicians alone, not to mysterious bankers and financial experts acting in their shadows.

If future uncertainty and expectations had shaped the way people made sense of hyperinflation, steps taken in late November 1922 provided sudden clarity: The League scheme would proceed, there was no turning back, and Austria would undergo a painful process of economic reconstruction under League control. This fact overturned long-lingering fears of financial collapse, but it also destroyed some of the unrealistic hopes harbored by Pan-German members of the middle class and university graduates. There was no hope of Anschluss with Germany, which deutschvölkische students so desired. Austrians for whom the chaos of hyperinflation had harbored visions of a grander future were now awakened to an outlandish reality into which most others seem to have settled with relief. The outbreaks of anti-Semitic violence at Vienna University, described at the outset of this chapter, began on the very same Wednesday, 22 November 1922, for which the DZ data indicate a change of expectations about Austria's future. On the following Monday, after the Ermächtigungsgesetz had been approved, the

Nationalrat successfully passed the reform program in its final reading and the 5,000 right-wing students marched on the Ringstrasse demanding a *numerus clausus,* while others exchanged their foreign currency back into Austrian crowns.

Calls for an anti-Jewish *numerus clausus* had already existed before the war, and Hungary had restricted Jews' access to higher education since 1920, but the timing of anti-Semitic violence in Vienna is supportive of the thesis that however Austria's future was being imagined, it was widely understood that its attributes and makeup would be discernible as non-Jewish. For some, such as Pan-German students, stabilization meant the crystallization of a status quo in Austria that they disliked and vehemently opposed, an unwanted state of affairs that Jewish students made visible to their eyes. The members of the League of Nations Financial Committee's delegation had played a crucial role in bringing about this new state. Insisting on the timely ratification of the Geneva Protocols and of all their bylaws, facilitating a compromise with the Socialist opposition, and eliminating the risk of inflation by means of a new central bank had created a successful start to League intervention that changed people's expectations. No one, however, knew precisely what to expect of the League intervention itself. Austria was to remain for two years under the financial control of a foreign League of Nations General Commissioner. The recalcitrance of Seipel and his government to work constructively with the League's delegation of financial experts did not bode well.

II
Control

4

The Inception of Control

1923–1924

> Vienna is at the present moment, a place which I should
> like to call the League of Nations' International
> Reconstruction Laboratory.
>
> —League of Nations General Commissioner
> Alfred Rudolph Zimmerman
> 29 March 1923

ARRIVING IN VIENNA ON LATE FRIDAY, 15 December 1922, League of
Nations General Commissioner Alfred Rudolph Zimmerman showed little
optimism about the prospects of Austria and scarce enthusiasm for his new
job.[1] Stepping from the train onto the station's freezing platform, he told Arthur Salter, head of the Financial and Economic Section of the League's
Secretariat, that he had accepted the position only temporarily and under
significant pressure. He was skeptical, had little hope the scheme would actually work, and was fully determined to return home to Rotterdam within a
couple of months.[2] Little did he know he would end up staying in Vienna for
the next three years.

Born in 1869 to a family of Amsterdam merchants, Zimmerman had
studied law at Leiden before embarking on a career with the Dutch civil service. As Burgomaster (mayor) of Rotterdam, he had acquired a reputation as
an ardent anti-socialist, which was probably the reason that the position was
offered to him after an American candidate had turned it down.[3] But the fact
that he spoke German, was known to bankers, and had worked in Austria
before was also relevant. The Dutch had been uninvolved in the war, which
lent them a sense of neutrality and made Zimmerman, like his Swiss or Scan-
dinavian colleagues, particularly well suited for playing important roles within

the multivariate bodies of the League. Yet Zimmerman's initial remarks, outspoken, prejudiced, and undiplomatic, were characteristic of the Dutchman, who would henceforth become known in Vienna for his notorious candor and a lack of tact.

The Geneva Protocols themselves did not bestow any far-reaching powers on the General Commissioner. They relied on the Austrian government passing an empowerment law through parliament, which would entitle it to pursue all necessary measures of a reform program over a period of two years. International financial control through the League of Nations was explicitly confined to Austrian borrowing. The General Commissioner had full control over the loan proceeds and decided upon their release for covering the deficit. Further, he had to approve any measures that might affect the tobacco and customs revenues pledged to service Austria's loans. Finally, his authorization was needed if the Austrian state wished to borrow any more foreign funds during reconstruction. Beyond that Zimmerman had the authority to demand all information and figures necessary to report regularly on whether Austria was adhering to the pace of the reform program that had been drafted in Geneva and passed by parliament. The General Commissioner was of course to advise the Austrian government on its policies, but he had no explicit mandate to dictate decisions and would have to use his control of loan funds and the moral authority bestowed on him by the League of Nations to direct the course of reconstruction.[4] The Austrian reconstruction and empowerment laws did not mention the office of the General Commissioner at all.[5]

The League's scheme for Austria, outlined in the Geneva Protocols and finalized with the League Financial Committee's delegates in Vienna, was a program of fiscal reform in return for floating a foreign loan to attract fresh capital. Hyperinflation had been the consequence of large budgetary deficits. By cutting expenditures to balance the budget permanently, it was thought, the risk of inflation would be removed. Eliminating the risk of inflation would then allow the Austrian government to borrow both at home and abroad, while Austrian firms could seek foreign capital to increase productivity through modernization. Balancing the budget permanently was the first and most important part of the League scheme, the linchpin upon which stable prices, fixed exchange rates, and foreign confidence rested.[6] What was needed for the scheme to succeed was a form of assurance that the Austrian government's fiscal policy was credible—that it would not simply renege on its pledge to balance the budget once a foreign loan was obtained but would follow Zimmerman's advice. Control by the League was intended to provide such vital credibility.

Stabilizing the Austrian currency in 1922 rested on renewed credibility of Austrian fiscal policy and a return of confidence in the country's political and economic future. Consolidating these immediate achievements to restore Vienna's position as a regional center for commerce and finance would require three conditions to be fulfilled: Fiscal policy would have to result in a sustainable and balanced budget, the new central bank needed to prove itself able to safeguard a stable exchange rate, and the two had to result in an inflow of foreign capital. The League's central role was to give credibility to Austrian fiscal policy through control over its budget. The General Commissioner's power to withhold the proceeds of the planned League loan guaranteed investors and citizens that the Austrian government would aim at balancing its budget and not return to a policy of growing deficits and inflation. If the new Austrian National Bank (ANB) proved capable of upholding a system of fixed exchange rates, foreign loans could be floated to attract fresh capital to cover the temporary budget deficit during the period of reconstruction, pay for imports, and finance the investments and modernizations required to make Austrian industry competitive on world markets.

The authority bestowed on the General Commissioner to withhold funds raised with the League's assistance, it was thought, would be sufficient to guarantee the implementation of the administrative and budgetary reforms the Austrian government had pledged to implement. But, as will be shown in further detail, this "credibility technology" failed to operate as planned. First, Zimmerman was unlikely to carry out his threat initially, because he considered it detrimental to foreign confidence and to the League's reputation, and thus a risk to the success of floating the large and vital loan.[7] Second, the return of credibility and confidence quickly resulted in unexpected revenues that allowed the Austrian government to balance the budget within just six months, thus rendering Zimmerman's threat to withhold funds less effective much sooner than planned.[8] And finally, since eliminating the budget deficit was the primary focus of the scheme and the main indicator foreign investors looked for, allowing the Austrian government to balance its budget at a considerably higher level than agreed upon and thereby to dodge reforms it deemed politically too costly, did not threaten the loan's success.

The fact that the Austrian government balanced its budget not through austerity but with the help of increased revenues from taxation was largely swept under the carpet. In order to promote the scheme to foreign bankers, the League's General Commissioner presented the quick balancing of the budget as a success, and over time made peace with the high level of expenditure and revenues it rested upon. While the Austrian government did not uphold its pledge to lower its budget, the League did not widely publicize this fact, thereby not only failing in its duty to provide accurate surveillance, but also fostering undue optimism. The League's Information Section dispatched a public relations officer to put a positive spin on the slow progress of reforms and good news from Austria was advertised widely, while the problem of insufficient reforms was not given enough exposure.[9] The young League of Nations was in dire need of a success, and good press on Austrian reconstruction provided welcome publicity. The League's public emphasis on Austrian achievements allowed the Austrian government in turn to further avoid measures it considered politically unwise without risk of sanction.

With the determined help of Governor Montagu Norman at the Bank of England (BoE) and Otto Niemeyer at the British Treasury, Austria successfully raised $160 million on the world's capital markets in 1923. Niemeyer, born in 1883 to a German banker in London, served as the British member of the League Financial Committee and was also the British delegate on the Control Committee of Guarantor States. In 1906 he entered the Treasury, where he worked until leaving for the BoE in 1927. He had been a member of the League's delegation of financial experts to Vienna in October 1922 and remained heavily involved in Austrian reconstruction throughout the decade, dominating many of the League meetings. Norman and Niemeyer's success was a sign of investor confidence, both in the League scheme and in the Austrian government's pledge to balance its budget and service the loan. The loan could not have been floated without the positive reports sent around the world by the League's General Commissioner from Vienna. Without the foreign loan, however, reconstruction would have been impossible. Although Austrian reconstruction was widely acclaimed as a success for the League of Nations, its scheme was born in sin.

Control and Credibility

The fact that the Austrian government was not ready to take orders from abroad became clear as early as the end of November 1922. Before the end of the year, Austria needed to choose who would head its new National Bank, which had the important tasks of watching over a stable exchange rate and conducting a monetary policy that would foster financial stability. Montagu Norman and Otto Niemeyer both considered it vital that the first President of the new Central Bank be a foreigner to secure his independence from Austrian banks and the government.[10] But this demand was not included in the Geneva Protocols and it was widely opposed by Austrians. Norman himself had cited the appointment of a foreign President as a precondition for his assistance in floating the loan for Austria. Both Salter and Zimmerman insisted on a foreigner, and even the Austrian Finance Minister initially welcomed the idea, for it would strongly indicate the radical change in monetary policy and thus make issuing the foreign loan easier. In November 1922, Chancellor Seipel still told Salter that he was evaluating the appointment of the Belgian central banker Albert Janssen, who headed the League delegation in Vienna since late October.[11] In a letter to Léon van der Rest, Governor of the Belgian National Bank, Norman stressed that even if not everyone in Austria favored the appointment of a foreigner, both the Austrian Chancellor and his government had agreed that foreign salvation could only come with efficient and effective foreign control:

> In my opinion it is essential not only that foreign control shall be established but that it shall extend to both the administrative and financial spheres, and this can only be satisfactorily secured by the appointment of eminent foreigners to the positions of Commissioner General and President of the new Bank. . . . Immediate establishment of an effective dual foreign control appears to us to be an essential and fundamental condition to the intervention of the League of Nations with any hope to achieving success.[12]

Norman's cooperation was vital to getting an international loan for Austria issued, but officially he was not involved with the League operation and therefore pressured the Austrians more subtly. Writing to envoy Georg

Franckenstein, he noted that he thought charging an Austrian with running the new bank was not contrary to the protocols, but it was certainly in contradiction with what people involved had told him so far and therefore would undoubtedly "affect the rehabilitation of Austria."[13] In Vienna, the British embassy diplomatically highlighted the advantages of appointing a foreigner, conveying to Chancellor Seipel the important view of British creditors, who thought that such a step would keep the ANB free of politics and achieve a clear break with the old traditions of inflation.

There was, however, considerable opposition to the idea of a foreign ANB president in Austria. The *Neue Freie Presse* pronounced that the appointment of a foreigner was so unwelcome that it would risk cooperation with the League and destroy the entire scheme.[14] Two directors of the Viennese Boden-Kredit Anstalt (BKA) were sent to London in December by its unscrupulous President, Rudolf Sieghart, to ask Norman to actually prevent the appointment of a foreigner.[15] Norman, quite naturally, suspected that Austrian bankers wished to have one of their own at the helm of the central bank to ensure them easy access to credit. He was almost certainly right. Despite pressure from the League, the Foreign Office, and the BoE, Richard Reisch, a director of the BKA and a close associate of President Sieghart, was appointed to head the new central bank. With his own protégé in place, Sieghart through the BKA would singlehandedly manage to do a great deal of damage to the Austrian economy within just a few years.

Urgent telegrams to Vienna from the Foreign Office and envoy Franckenstein in London not to appoint an Austrian and incur "disastrous results" for the loan arrived too late to have an effect, but it is unlikely that they would have mattered.[16] Chancellor Seipel was bound to assert his freedom if he could. Officially, Seipel blamed Mussolini, who threatened not to ratify Italy's guarantee law if a foreigner who was not an Italian were selected. Since the French opposed an Italian, Seipel argued, he had been left with no other option than to choose one of his own. Of course, he reassured the British ambassador, a foreign adviser to the bank, embodied with extensive powers, could still be appointed to calm worries in London.[17] Trying to calm tensions between London and Vienna, Salter argued that Austria had ratified the protocols but that the Allied Powers had done little yet to help the Austrian government place short-term bills abroad. Defending the Austrian decision, he argued that Chancellor Seipel was in fact right to conclude that he had simply more to gain from nominating an Austrian than from listening to London.[18] Niemeyer was furious and in a long letter to Salter wrote that it was "absurd of the Austrians to pretend that they themselves have behaved heroical and very dangerous to let them lay this unction to their souls." He continued that

> the Austrian have done nothing except, after very considerable delays, pass a paper programme. . . . The Austrians' dilatoriness on the above makes their recent Bank of issue appointment not merely exasperating but rank folly. By this single piece of idiocy, they have put back any possible loans for many months. Nor is this only MY impression. . . . Everyone here knows why the Austrian Banks (who are at the back of all this) want one of themselves. The Boden Credit actually sent people here to explain that they must have someone "who would understand the needs of austrian banking" . . . the Vienna Jews in their own interest have secured that the bad old traditions of inflated credits will go on . . . and that there will be no sound monetary policy. This of course is fatal for foreign interest in Austrian finance.[19]

In Niemeyer's opinion the matter was not primarily one of foreign control, but foremost of whether Austria would be able to raise money abroad. Having a foreigner in charge at the national bank would have made placing a loan for Austria easier. By refusing the British advice, Niemeyer thought, Austria had "wantonly thrown away her chance."

Niemeyer was prone to exaggerations in his correspondence and probably relished his own characteristic outbursts of anger. Despite the importance London attached to a foreign president, the scheme was not abandoned, neither by the League nor by the British. Discussing the nomination at the BoE, Niemeyer, Strakosch, Janssen, and Salter all agreed with the Deputy Governor (Norman was in the United States) to make the best of the disappointing decision and accept the appointment of a foreign adviser to the newly founded ANB instead. The acceptance of such a foreign Conseiller would now be made a condition for the issue of a loan in London and Niemeyer suggested that the adviser be fitted with powers equal to those of ANB President Reisch.[20] By the time the Swiss banker Charles Schnyder von Wartensee took up the position in June 1923, however, he had mainly been given an advisory function and President Reisch with his directors remained fully in charge of the bank.[21]

Although appointing a foreigner to head the ANB had been considered "vital" and the failure to do so had been "fatal," neither the British nor the League were ready to abandon the scheme.[22] The League was too committed in Austria, needed a success, and hoped its intervention would prove a stepping stone toward further important achievements in Europe. The BoE similarly considered the fruits of possible success too great to abandon the scheme prematurely. Norman had larger plans, working toward the gradual return of Europe to the gold standard under London's leadership and the creation of a network of independent European central banks with strong ties to Threadneedle Street.[23] The participation of private banks in floating the loans also offered a way to engage U.S. capital in European reconstruction. And, finally, a success in Austria would possibly pave the way for solving the larger problem of Germany, which was beginning to experience hyperinflation itself. Ultimately, despite all the talk, a foreign president was technically not really vital, since after all the sine qua non of League intervention was to eliminate the deficit and permanently balance Austria's budget with the help of an international loan.

Because it remained crucial to create confidence among foreign banks as negotiations with them on issuing the League sponsored-loan were under way, Zimmerman urged the Austrian government to pursue reforms right away. Immediately upon arriving in Vienna, he demanded a cutback in state workers' wages, quick dismissals, and reduction of the budget to levels foreseen in the reform plan, but Seipel stalled. The Austrian government focused exclusively on balancing the budget, dodging any reforms it deemed politically too costly. By increasing taxation and taking advantage of the stabilized exchange rate, the government managed to almost eliminate the deficit within the first few months of 1923. A quick dismissal of state workers or cutting of wages and pensions would have slashed expenditures, but it would also have reduced the popularity among voters of the Christian-Social and Pan-German coalition parties forming the government. Had the budget not been balanced, Zimmerman might have complained vocally and publicly, thereby risking a premature end of the intervention. But with rising revenues eliminating the budget deficit, the Austrian government powerfully asserted its independence, conscious that its actions were unlikely to provoke a collapse of foreign confidence or the withdrawal of the League. As with the appointment of an Austrian ANB President, Chancellor Seipel successfully resisted foreign demands if they entailed too high a political cost in his view.

Since the deficit was being reduced, albeit with the budget at a higher level, and a loan issued to foreign investors seemed therefore possible, Zimmerman only mildly criticized the government in public. While the League's Information Section disseminated weekly progress reports to foreign ministries and major newspapers around the world, the General Commissioner chose to order reforms privately.[24] During an early conversation with Chancellor Seipel in January 1923, the General Commissioner insisted that government ministries be reduced and administrative reforms accelerated.[25] Zimmerman wanted the Austrian government to produce quick results so that he could present them to bankers at an upcoming League meeting in Paris.[26] However, despite initial promises, Seipel decided to postpone the reduction of ministries, citing strong opposition from the Socialist and Pan-German parties. When Zimmerman complained that almost nothing had been done to address the large budgetary expenditures on administration, the army, or the railways, Seipel argued that he could not risk a political crisis.[27] In one of his first letters to Zimmerman, he made very clear that he was determined to undertake reconstruction on his own terms and not on those of the League's General Commissioner: "[If I] were obliged to put into force any measure which is not included in the Geneva Protocols nor in the Reconstruction Law," he wrote,

> or in the scheme for financial reform drawn up jointly with the League of Nations, at a time when I cannot possibly put it into force with success, I should then no longer be the Federal Chancellor and trusted with the highest responsibilities towards his country, but merely the executive agent of a foreign will. . . . I regret that Your Excellency has not taken into account any of my arguments, and more especially the seventh, which was, however, the strongest argument of all, and involved the most delicate points . . . namely the question of political coalition which is essential to the radical reform which our country requires.[28]

For Seipel, international control of a sovereign state by the League of Nations could not mean complete submission to the latter's will. But none of the London banks were yet definitely on board, nor had foreign governments ratified their guarantees yet, so that Salter, who was still in Vienna at the time, hoped at least to foster foreign confidence with public declarations from Seipel. But the Austrian Chancellor would not do this either. Making statements about the planned dismissal of state workers, specific reductions of expenditures, or the functioning of the Ausserordentliche Kabinettsrat, risked antagonizing his own electorate or provoking the opposition.[29] General Commissioner Zimmerman reluctantly conceded, fearing both the strength of the Socialists and the negative impact of a public dispute on bankers currently contemplating the planned loans' success.

Two committees convened in the French capital at the end of January 1923. The Control Committee of Guarantor States held sessions over three days, interviewing both Zimmerman and an Austrian delegation. Its main concern was to discuss and agree on the technicalities of guaranteeing the small Austrian Treasury loan, which was to be floated as a model for the larger loan foreign governments had promised to guarantee. The Committee consisted of bankers and Treasury officials and was chaired by the Italian laissez-faire economist and Fascist sympathizer Maffeo Pantaleoni. Its members listened to Zimmerman's report and voiced concern about the slow pace of administrative reforms, pointed out the disastrous state of the railways, but praised the Austrian government for no longer borrowing from the central bank. Representing their governments, it was not their job to criticize Austrian policy, but only to protect the rights and interests of their respective, guaranteeing states. The service of the smaller and larger loans would in any case be secured through the pledge of tobacco and customs revenues, while it was up to the League to ensure that Austria stuck to the reform program. Arthur Salter and his staff at the League Secretariat were asked to take care of the Committee's administrative duties before it proceeded to officially authorize the Austrian government to issue £3.5 million (up to $16 million) of Austrian Treasury Bills, denominated in Austrian crowns, under foreign state guarantees.[30]

In his address before the League Council's Sub-Committee on Austria, which also convened in Paris the next day, Zimmerman, however, expressed deep dissatisfaction over the slackness of reforms and the postponed amalgamation of ministries. Chancellor Seipel haughtily explained that political difficulties prevented him from reducing the number of ministries and that his government could not simply listen to foreign wishes, but had to take into account domestic unemployment, uneasiness about the curtailment of Austrian sovereignty, and Socialist agitation against planned reforms.[31] Only he as Chancellor could decide when and how to initiate reconstruction, Seipel argued, and the League would have to trust him. The Sub-Committee members were worried. They considered reducing administrative expenses important, as well as containing Socialist influences in the army, but they also knew that success of the smaller and larger loans hinged primarily on balancing the budget. A foreign loan for Austria was still considered vital, and if the meeting failed to announce significant progress, a new crisis would surely put an end to the crown's recent and fragile stability.[32] In order to create confidence among foreign investors, Arthur Salter made sure, therefore, that the Council's public declaration included just a "measured homily."[33] Authorizing the issue of the small loan, its official statement therefore praised Austria and its people for the impressive progress it had achieved and merely called upon all Austrian political parties, by which they meant the Socialists, to refrain from delaying reforms and to comply with all of Zimmerman's proposals and requests.[34]

Negotiations with London bankers issuing the relatively small loan were concluded shortly thereafter, and it was successfully floated within just a few weeks. Meanwhile, in Vienna, Zimmerman unsuccessfully continued to push for measures to reduce expenditure.[35] The General Commissioner grew increasingly worried about the slow pace of reforms and his second report in mid-January called upon the Austrian government to use its extraordinary powers for "drastic action," even if they ran counter to the interests of certain sectors of the population.[36] At a meeting with Pan-German Interior Minister Felix Frank in February, Zimmerman complained about changes to the planned law on administrative dismissals, which now offered increased indemnities and granted state worker representatives the right to veto each individual discharge.[37] Moreover, in view of the Chancellor's continued reluctance to merge the War and Interior Ministries, Zimmerman even threatened to oppose issuing the long-term loan as long as Austria retained its "superfluous" army of 23,000 men.[38] Constant compromises with the Socialist opposition were watering down reforms, he felt, and according to a member of Zimmerman's staff, political difficulties remained "the kernel of the whole reconstruction problem."[39]

Due to unexpectedly high revenues from taxation, monthly deficits were continuously lower than expected, further making a drastic cut in expenses

appear somewhat unnecessary. And in light of the importance of foreign
confidence for a successful issue of the loan, a public confrontation seemed
unwise.[40] These particular circumstances and the fact that investors' eyes
were focused mostly on the balancing of the budget allowed Seipel to further
renege on his promises. In February, the Austrian Chancellor had agreed that
reducing the army by 10,000 men was realistic, but then reduced the figure to
7,000, citing opposition from party colleagues in the provinces.[41] One week
later, Zimmerman was told that getting the various parties to agree on the release of 7,000 soldiers was difficult and that only 4,000 men would be dismissed.[42] A livid Zimmerman reminded the Chancellor that he had originally
been promised the dismissal of 10,000 soldiers, but Seipel flatly denied this.
They had discussed the regular release of 3,000 plus an additional discharge of
4,000 soldiers only, he claimed.[43] Furthermore, he posited, reducing the army
was in fact not explicitly mentioned in the Protocols and therefore not among
Zimmerman's concerns. Angrily, Zimmerman ventured that any measures
required to balance the budget fell under his authority and that the Protocols
explicitly called for halving the defense budget. Seipel responded using an
even more confrontational and at times belligerent tone, upon which Zimmerman decided to drop the matter, leaving Seipel's "note" unanswered.[44]

Three months into office, Zimmerman was weakened, frustrated, and particularly angry with Chancellor Seipel for refusing to close the Ministry of
War and reduce the army.[45] Seipel had repeatedly shown Zimmerman that
he rejected his authority, remained powerful, and could outwit the League's
representative. Addressing the Control Committee in Geneva in April, Zimmerman thus requested to make approval of the larger long-term loan conditional on the Austrian government's willingness to execute his demands.[46]
He favorably noted a fall in unemployment, the stability of the crown, and
rising revenues from tobacco and customs, but voiced dissatisfaction about
the pace of reforms, blaming the delay on concessions being made to the
Socialists. Before the Council's Sub-Committee, he repeated his positive assessment of Austria's economic situation, but once more bemoaned the
political concessions that hitherto made serious measures impossible.[47] The
Sub-Committee authorized the long-term loan, but in a nod to the General
Commissioner, demanded slimming down the railway administration and
a faster dismissal of state workers. In his concluding statement Zimmerman
threatened to not shy away from withholding funds if reforms were not im-

mediately implemented. A conciliatory Chancellor Seipel ambiguously promised those present to collaborate "in every possible respect" and to "proceed
with the prompt execution of all the measures of reform and reconstruction" agreed upon.[48]

The international long-term loan was successfully issued on the world's
capital markets in June 1923 and the proceeds added to those of the small
loan under Zimmerman's control. But since parliamentary elections were
being held in October, forcing the realization of reforms became even more
difficult. A central point of contention between the General Commissioner
and the Austrian government pertained to the dismissals of state workers and
the latter's demands for wage increases.[49] Wages of state workers had been
frozen in March, but prices had continued to rise, thereby substantiating
their demands.[50] Since payments to state workers were the largest budgetary
expenditure, Zimmerman feared the impact a wage increase would have on the
effect of reforms. But refusing state workers' demands was sure to make the
League intervention unpopular and to increase the share of votes going to
the Socialists in October. Zimmerman therefore counted on the cooperation
of the Austrian government and continued to state his demands privately,
voicing his concerns before the League of Nations in closed sessions while
issuing overall positive reports to the public.

Negotiating with state workers in May, Finance Minister Victor Kienböck
proposed increasing salaries by 20 percent (at an annual cost of 400 billion
crowns, or $5.6 million) if they would agree to eliminate the wage index.[51]
Kienböck, born in Vienna in 1873, had trained and worked as a lawyer before entering politics and served twice as Seipel's Minister of Finance. Zimmerman, who had long argued against the index apparatus because it made
accurate budgeting impossible, would accept Kienböck's proposal if it were
to cost no more than 500 billion crowns ($7 million).[52] Prolonged negotia-
tions resulted in an agreement by July, raising wages at an annual cost of 480
billion ($6.9 million), but only suspending the index-linkage until No-
vember.[53] The agreement was publicly announced without obtaining Zimmerman's prior approval and the snubbed General Commissioner, no less
angry about the fact that a chance for abolishing the index had been squandered, too, warned Finance Minister Kienböck that, should the index have
risen further come November, he would refuse funds to pay for even higher
wages (see Graph 4.1).[54]

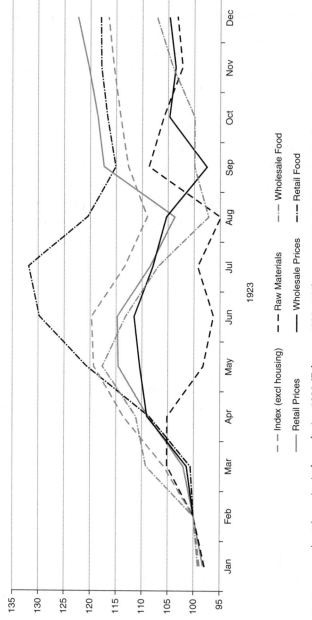

GRAPH 4.1. Austrian price indexes during 1923 (February 1923 = 100). *Source:* LNA, C 4, Reconstruction financière de l'Autriche 1922–1926, "Index" (Index [excluding the cost of housing] is what state workers' wages and pensions could be adjusted to).

The fact that the index had risen 20 percent during the first six months of 1923 reinforced Zimmerman's concerns about insufficient expenditure cuts and the slow reduction of state workers. Of the 25,000 discharges scheduled for the first half of 1923, only 15,542 had been carried out and Zimmerman notified the Austrian government that this backlog would be added to the 25,000 fresh notices scheduled for the second half of the year.[55] Despite these serious concerns, Zimmerman chose not to alarm the public. His fourth report, published in July 1923, one month after the large loan had been successfully floated, highlighted that the budget deficit was being reduced continuously and that the monthly deficits were consistently lower than expected.[56] Further positive news pointed to the fact that the railways had been transformed into an autonomous enterprise, that its fares had been increased, that the privileges of state workers had been reduced, and that the number of Federal Ministries had been slashed to seven. As the budget continued to remain far above the one prescribed by agreement with the Financial Committee's delegates in 1922, his positive assessment was tempered by a comment that the improved budgetary situation was due not to a reduction in expenditures, but to an increase in revenues from new taxation. But it remained just a comment. To ensure the effective reduction of expenditure on wages, he privately warned the Chancellor that he would not hesitate to withhold monthly transfers to enforce a timely dismissal of state workers as long as the high level of expenditures persisted.[57]

After the October elections returned Chancellor Seipel's governing coalition to power, Kienböck set out to draft the budget for 1924. It aimed at permanently eliminating the deficit, but within a budget higher than prescribed by the reform plan. When in November the index returned to force, Kienböck entered into fresh negotiations with state workers' representatives on a wage increase. Worried about the high level of the budget, Zimmerman insisted that higher wages be covered by a change in the partition of Ertragsanteile (the transfer of tax revenues to provinces and municipalities) and not come from new taxation. Kienböck argued that the League delegates had established the figures Zimmerman was so unfailingly demanding at a time when nobody could have realistically assessed the strength of the Austrian economy. If Zimmerman continued to insist on these outdated numbers, Kienböck threatened, he would see no other alternative than to resign.[58]

Kienböck's preliminary budget of roughly 8,000 trillion crowns in expenditures (about $110 million) showed a deficit of 836.7 billion crowns ($11.7 million or 13.5 percent of revenues), far less than the total 2.7-trillion-crown deficit for 1923, but still more than five times the 146.7 billion considered sustainable by the League's delegates in October 1922. Total expenditures were 30 percent less than in 1923, but still higher then what the League delegation had planned. Extra expenditures would mainly go to the federal railways, partly to pay for its initial electrification, be transferred as Ertragsanteile to the provinces, or pay for greater pensions and unemployment benefits.[59] To nevertheless reach a balanced budget by the end of the year, revenues from customs, income tax, and commercial transactions *(Warenumsatzsteuer)* would have to be raised beyond what the League's delegates had recommended at the time of stabilization.[60] The budget presented to parliament on 26 November 1923 also included salary increases for state workers ranging from 20 to 50 percent (at a cost of 690 billion crowns, $8.4 million) in return for a suspension of the index-linkage until 31 May 1924.[61] With post and telegraph workers going on strike in December, Zimmerman backtracked on earlier threats, deciding not to intervene in negotiations accompanying the budget as long as a law was attached that required the deficit to be no larger than 146.7 billion crowns once the books were closed for 1924.[62]

News that the Austrians were passing a budget for 1924 that would be far larger than what the League Financial Committee's delegates had initially thought prudent caused large consternation in London. Niemeyer was "greatly disturbed" and Norman "seriously discomposed."[63] As the Governor of the BoE put it to Zimmerman, the fact that the budget might still be balanced throughout the year did not relieve his worries about the high level of expenditure. Zimmerman, between hammer and anvil, defensively reassured Norman that there existed "not the slightest reason for uneasiness," since the government had legally obliged itself to reduce the deficit. Possibly worried about his own reputation, Zimmerman, who had not spared Kienböck with reproach, actually defended the Austrian government. Arguing that the attached law was sufficient proof of its goodwill, he reassured the Governor that there was "no reason whatever to doubt" that the budget would finally be balanced.[64] Meeting in December, the Control Committee echoed Norman's concerns when its Chairman, Pantaleoni, specifically in-

sisted on reducing the 500 billion crowns ($7 million) earmarked for the
army, although it did not really have authority to advise Austrian policy. But
as a large budget was more prone to develop a deficit, which increased the
risk of foreign government guarantees being called upon to service the international loan, French delegate Jacques Seydoux, now resident economic
expert at the Quay d'Orsay, pointed to the considerable deficit of the railways, and Otto Niemeyer insisted that Austria was duty bound to reduce expenditures to the level agreed upon in November 1922. In conclusion, the
Control Committee endorsed an accelerated pace of administrative reforms
and dismissals, urged further reductions in expenditure and encouraged
General Commissioner Zimmerman to veto any new expense that risked
widening the deficit.[65]

Emboldened by the Control Committee's support, a resolute Zimmerman
returned to Vienna in early 1924, determined to get the Austrian government
to see the danger and folly behind its high levels of expenditure. Addressing
Finance Minister Kienböck and Chancellor Seipel in writing, Zimmerman
warned that the budget was being balanced thanks to unexpectedly high
revenues and that nobody knew when they might fall back to what might be
considered normal levels.[66] To prepare for that eventuality, Zimmerman advised, a drastic reduction in the number of state workers was necessary. To
diminish the risk to stability inherent in their large budget, he would not
approve of any further raise in state workers' wages before the law on transfers *(Ertragsanteile)* was passed, and he would certainly not allow a further
increase in taxation.[67] But these were little more than empty threats. Zimmerman had so far refrained from making the extent of his disputes with
the Austrian government public. The Austrian government was requiring
fewer transfers from the loan proceeds than expected. And by the end of
1924, League intervention was scheduled to expire anyway.

It should not surprise us by now that Zimmerman's requests fell on deaf
ears. Finance Minister Kienböck went yet again behind the back of the General Commissioner, publicly presenting a new wage proposal to Austrian
state workers.[68] Zimmerman had been definite and resolute in his demands
and yet had been disregarded once more. He decided that the time had come
for a final, unprecedented step. Calling for a meeting of the entire Austrian
cabinet, the League's General Commissioner addressed the government *in
corpore.* Standing before the assembled ministers, he appealed to their honor,

accusing them of breaking their word by running higher expenses than what they were allowed. In a schoolmasterly fashion, he voiced concern about the speed of reforms, the increase in expenditure, and the failure to amalgamate federal and provincial administrations. If reforms were not implemented faster, he warned, a balanced budget would not fool anyone into thinking that the state's finances were sound. In threatening tones, he warned that if matters in Austria did not change, if the budget were not reduced, Austria's foreign creditors would demand the prolongation of control beyond 1924.[69] It is difficult to imagine the Austrian ministers taking Zimmerman's performance seriously. Given that his authority of control had, de facto, been reduced to administering the earmarked revenues that serviced the League loan, his words were unlikely to strike fear into anyone present.

The French historian Nicole Piétri, who wrote a magisterial dissertation on the League intervention in Austria, pointed out that from the start relations between Zimmerman and Seipel were "malaisée."[70] The stern, straightforward Protestant Dutch and the confident, crafty Catholic Austrian certainly did not get along. But Piétri's view that Zimmerman was mainly upset about the Chancellor's decision to renege on his promise to merge the Ministries of War and Interior obfuscates larger issues. The Austrian Chancellor and his ministers, primarily Finance Minister Kienböck, spared no effort to impress on Zimmerman that they did not acknowledge his authority. It is impossible to disentangle the separate motives behind the ministers' refusal to follow all of Zimmerman's demands, but beyond political considerations, they were certainly motived to no small degree by a desire to demonstrate that they remained in charge. Zimmerman *had* to take their actions personally.

By giving priority to balancing the budget over the reduction of its size, Zimmerman aimed to fulfill his role as League General Commissioner without destroying foreign investor confidence in Austria. Focusing on the deficit allowed him to report certain progress without having to declare that the Austrian government was reneging on its pledge to follow through on reforms. The Austrian government, by focusing on the deficit, was itself able to ignore foreign demands to reduce expenditure, which would be politically costly. What supported this unholy alliance was the fact that during its first sixth months, League intervention in Austria stood on very shaky grounds. In spite of Zimmerman's positive reports and the government's success in reducing the deficit, getting foreign banks to sign up and issue an international loan for Austria was not an easy feat. If it ended up a success, this was not due to Austrian reforms, but to the unwavering energies put into the scheme by Norman, Niemeyer, and others. Still, the smaller, short-term loan was just barely a success and the larger, long-term loan could only be floated after prolonged negotiations had made sure it brought with it the participation of American capital in the reconstruction of Europe.

Control or Confidence: Foreign Loans for Austria

Governor Montagu Norman at the BoE had already once tried to facilitate a loan for Austria from private bankers. In early 1922 he had failed because of the unstable political conditions in Austria, the lack of securities or guarantees, and the question of control. The Geneva Protocols resolved all three problems and foresaw a large international loan issued through banks to foreign investors on the world capital markets. Norman took a leading role in coordinating the issue for three main reasons. First, he planned to use Austrian reconstruction to further the spread of the gold exchange standard and the formation of central bank cooperation that he hoped it would entail. Second, he believed that a successful operation in Austria could serve as a basis for Hungary and for solving the German problem (as eventually it did through introducing the League to Hungary and adaptation of the Dawes plan for Germany). Finally, Norman hoped to engage American banks, which had hitherto stayed out of Europe and would be needed to finance a larger German settlement and the general reconstruction of Europe's war-ravaged economies.

In his plans Norman was readily supported by Otto Niemeyer at the British Treasury and by Henry Strakosch, both of whom wanted the League intervention carried out because the "political consequences of failure" were "too serious to be risked."[71] If Austria fell back into hyperinflation and political chaos, renewed war in Central Europe was considered a realistic possibility as Austria's neighbors enviously watched over their territorial interests. And if the Austrian problem could not be solved, how could one have any hope of resolving the larger problem of German hyperinflation and French occupation of the Ruhr? Having these larger questions in mind, Norman and the League wanted to outflank the slow and hampered political process of European reconciliation through mobilizing private capital with the help of private bankers. If independent central banks could be trusted to keep exchange rates fixed and prices stable, private capital would seek lucrative investment opportunities. Solving the continent's most pressing economic and financial problems would then facilitate a quick return to economic growth and international trade not just in Europe, but worldwide, making it easier to resolve the remaining political difficulties.

In January 1923, the heads of the same banks that had turned Austria away in 1922 were invited to the BoE to discuss the idea of issuing the Austrian loans in London and elsewhere.[72] The Geneva Protocols foresaw first issuing a smaller, immediate, interim loan to help Austria straightaway. The loan would also serve as a trial for the larger reconstruction loan, which would be floated, under similar conditions, by the same banks at a later point during the year. But the bankers of N. M. Rothschild, Morgan, Grenfell & Co., J. H. Schröder's, and Baring Brothers were still reserved about raising money for Austria. The fact that the bonds of the interim loan would be convertible into the later long-term bonds, to be secured by tobacco and customs revenues did not provide them with sufficient security.[73] In an effort to change their minds, Strakosch optimistically demonstrated that revenues from the pledged tobacco and customs monopolies were already higher than expected. Niemeyer then warned that League intervention had reached a stage at which it had to proceed or break down, because any delays would destroy confidence and endanger the yet feeble stability of the Austrian currency.[74] What everyone agreed upon was that the loans presented an excellent opportunity to get U.S. bankers involved in European reconstruction. Eager to end American isolationism, the London bankers agreed to raise £1 million ($4.6 million) for Austria under the condition that the same be done on Wall Street.[75] Morgan, Grenfell immediately cabled their American partners at J. P. Morgan with the meeting's results, calling to their attention that any further delays to the League scheme entailed grave dangers.[76]

The Control Committee and the Council's Sub-Committee meeting in Paris in January 1923 were aware of the importance of mobilizing foreign capital quickly.[77] As already noted, recognizing that Austrian confidence and fiscal expectations still depended mainly on the ready availability of loans, the Control Committee authorized Austria to negotiate an interim loan of

up to £3.5 million ($16 million) despite the slow pace of administrative re-
forms.[78] Neither was the Council's Sub-Committee discouraged by Zimmerman's complaints, nor by Seipel's plea to just trust Austria to do what only
he knew best.[79] The imperative of obtaining agreement from bankers to collaborate on helping Austria borrow abroad was clear to all involved. In his
concluding address to the Council, Chancellor Seipel appealed to all concerned countries to assist in the provision of foreign capital so that Vienna could
remain "a center of peace and order in the heart of Europe."[80]

In February 1923, leaving the League conference in Paris, Finance Minister Kienböck and ANB President Reisch traveled to London to begin negotiations on the smaller interim loan.[81] Niemeyer envisioned twelve-month
Treasury Bills, divided among different countries, guaranteed by their respective governments, and issued in their national currencies on their financial markets. The London bankers had conditioned their participation on
that of New York, but J. P. Morgan considered lending money to Austria all
but impossible, not least because of the deteriorating situation in Germany
and the French occupation of the Ruhr.[82] In order to overcome continental
bankers' reluctance to lend funds to Austria, Norman promised Kienböck
that if worse came to worst, the BoE would pick up the entire London tranche
of £1.8 million ($8.5 million) itself as long as the Austrians got firm commit-
ments for the remainder elsewhere.[83] To coordinate discussions across Europe,
Norman proposed that Russian émigré and banker Peter Bark, who had
served as the last Finance Minister of the Russian Empire, conduct all negotiations on behalf of the Austrian government.

Agreements were reached surprisingly quickly, not least because of the
preparatory work done by Norman and Niemeyer.[84] In Paris, the head of the
Banque de Paris et des Pays Bas (Paribas) promised to underwrite £800,000
($3.7 million) together with a small syndicate of French banks.[85] With the
explicit commitment of the BoE in hand, Strakosch and Kienböck obtained
firm agreements in Brussels and Amsterdam. Zimmerman's Austrian aide
Hans Patzauer got pledges from banks in Stockholm and Copenhagen,
while in Geneva, Reisch and Bark convinced initially reticent Swiss bankers to
take a share in the interim loan, too. Within a fortnight of negotiations it
appeared that the entire £3.5 million ($16 million) were obtained.[86] Just to
be sure, Norman promised that if subscription on the continent produced

less than their share of £1.7 million ($7.8 million), the BoE would increase its own share by another £200,000 ($916,000).[87]

The London tranche of £1.8 million ($8.2 million) was issued during the final days of February 1923 and proved a success, but outside England the results were less favorable.[88] In the Netherlands, the public only took up 34 percent of the issue and the Dutch banking syndicate was forced to secretly take up the reminder, while in Sweden all 1.8 million Swedish kroners ($478,000) had to be put up by banks. The mixed success was a clear sign that floating a larger loan would require long preparations and a strengthening of investor confidence, especially as the unfolding Ruhr crisis and the German descent into hyperinflation worried investors.[89]

Peter Bark coordinated the difficult negotiations for the larger long-term loan, which was approved by the Control Committee and the League Council in April.[90] Bark, Georg Franckenstein, and F. H. Nixon, still on Salter's staff, set out for the capitals of Europe.[91] In Paris, the French Finance Minister Charles de Lasteyrie explained that, given the large number of French emissions expected for May and June, no more than 100 million French francs ($6 million), less than half the desired sum, could be reserved for Austria. In Belgium, a public issue was opposed because the country planned its own reconstruction loan, although the Belgian Société Générale would take £200,000 ($916,000) on its own account. In Amsterdam, C. E. Ter Meulen of Hope & Co. pointed to the disappointing results of the interim loan. He no longer believed in the success of the League intervention, and Dutch bankers would only participate if significant American participation was certain. When Swiss bankers, still contemplating a tranche of 100 million Swiss francs ($18 million) got wind of troubles in Amsterdam and Paris, they had to be persuaded to take even as much as a quarter of the sum.[92]

U.S. participation in the large loan crystalized as essential for its success. Assembled at the BoE in April 1923, Whigham of Morgan, Grenfell told Austrian envoy Franckenstein that while a tentative syndicate had been formed in New York, Morgan's still felt all capital would be needed to finance growth on Wall Street.[93] Governor Norman promised to send a telegram to J. P. Morgan immediately, stating that placement of some part of the loan in the United States was essential.[94] In their response to the Governor, Morgan's explained that in spite of skepticism about the economic

future of Central Europe, they were in fact prepared to do everything necessary to assist him and the League. They acknowledged that the Austrian
project was not just a business transaction and so long as the Ruhr situation did not deteriorate any further, they were in fact ready to commit $10
to $25 million (£2.2–5.5 million).[95] For final negotiations, they cabled, it
would once again be best to await the arrival of their partner Thomas Lamont
in Paris.[96]

Talks between Peter Bark and Thomas Lamont in May revealed that a New
York syndicate would issue $25 million, but that the bonds would not be sold
on to private investors.[97] Precipitously Paris put up new conditions, and to
pressure the French, Bark and Lamont agreed that the American syndicate
would pull back if the French failed to issue on time. Meanwhile the BoE
promised confidentially to increase its own share if necessary.[98] Dutch
bankers, who had initially refused to participate, now agreed to take some
part of the loan, the Vienna banks agreed to a tranche of $13 million
(£2.8 million), and the Swedish considered taking £540,000 ($2.5 million).[99]
Nothing could be raised in Norway or Denmark, and meanwhile final negotiations with French and Italian bankers dallied so that their issues were
postponed to as late as August. The British tranche had to be increased from
£6 million to £10 and then £14 million ($64 million) to make sure the whole
sum was raised in June.[100] The involvement of Norman, appealing personally to his counterparts on the continent to convince their country's bankers
to partake in the operation, certainly played no small part in the successful
outcome of the negotiations. But even more important to private bankers was
that the international loan promised to engage America's most prominent
banking group in European reconstruction.

Speaking to a crowd of American journalists on the eve of the London
issue in early June, General Commissioner Zimmerman described the
League intervention as an unprecedented success in international collaboration and "perhaps even the starting point of a still wider stabilization and
reconstruction."[101] The investing public certainly believed so. Within two
days, not only was the British tranche fully underwritten, but so were all the
other issues.[102] The Swedish tranche was covered in less than an hour and
oversubscribed several times.[103] The New York syndicate of banks oversubscribed the American tranche within fifteen minutes.[104] Even the Dutch issue

was oversubscribed, with offers coming from Sweden and England so high that the pessimistic Ter Meulen considered them simply fantastic.[105] The most encouraging news came from Switzerland, where the down-sized tranche of 25 million Swiss francs ($4.5 million) was oversubscribed to the incredible extent of CHFr. 30 billion ($5.4 billion), an indicator of the massive amount of Austrian flight capital that had found rescue in Zurich and Geneva.[106] Finally, in Vienna itself, the Austrian tranche of $13 million (£2.8 million) was presented to new subscribers and holders of earlier loans wishing to convert. While at first the loan mainly attracted holders of the interim loan and of the Treasury Bills that had been issued to Austrians in December 1922, new subscriptions rose over the following weeks. By mid-July the Austrian government had managed to raise more than $4 million of new funds from Austrian investors (see Graph 4.2).

Prioritizing the balancing of the Austrian budget over reducing its size thus paid off for both the League and the Austrian government. Credibility bestowed upon Austria's fiscal policy by the General Commissioner and his reports during the first six months of reconstruction had generated significant confidence among foreign banks and investors in the Austrian government's ability to service the loans. Although the budget was not being reduced significantly, eliminating the deficit had been enough of an improvement in investors' eyes. Confidence in the League intervention had translated into the quick subscription of its loan all over Europe. Even if initially bankers were reluctant to underwrite the loan, ordinary investors were confident about Austria's future and Austrian citizens willing to lend fresh money to the state. At the end of the day, Austria had issued bonds worth £34 million ($160 million) on global capital markets to cover its debt and to finance the budget deficit as it continued down the difficult path of reconstructing its administration and economy. An investing public had demonstrated its confidence in the League intervention and in the Austrian government's pledge to balance the budget and service the debt. Within a few days the Dutch tranche was quoted at a premium, and over the following months most of the other bonds were quoted higher as well. In Vienna and Geneva, Salter, Zimmerman, and their teams could be satisfied. They had shown that the League of Nations, through fostering international collaboration and providing international control, was able to succeed where governments and banks alone had previously failed.

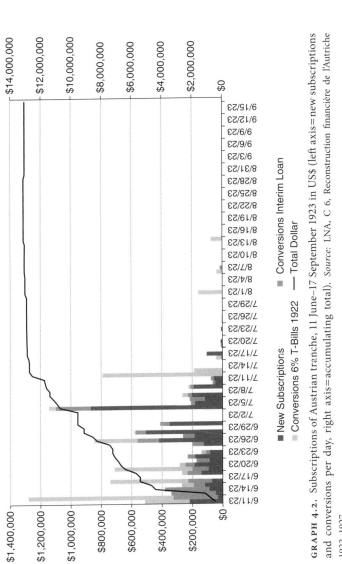

GRAPH 4.2. Subscriptions of Austrian tranche, 11 June–17 September 1923 in US$ (left axis=new subscriptions and conversions per day, right axis=accumulating total). *Source:* LNA, C 6, Reconstruction financière de l'Autriche 1922–1927.

Legend:
- New Subscriptions
- Conversions Interim Loan
- Conversions 6% T-Bills 1922
- Total Dollar

From Confidence to Hubris

The credibility bestowed upon the fiscal future of Austria through the League's intervention and General Commissioner Zimmerman's control, coupled with the successful floatation of the loans in June 1923, could not but make Austria appear attractive to investors. What followed, therefore, was the hoped for and unprecedented inflow of capital. Despite failure of the Austrian government to reduce its budget, eliminating the deficit was enough to make the League's credibility mechanism work and to create confidence among Austrians and foreign investors. Encouraged further by the prolonged stability of the currency, foreign and repatriated capital flowed into Austria, where share prices on the Vienna Stock Exchange (VSE) had already started to rise in March 1923. After the successful floatation of the loan, the inflow of capital financed a speculative bull run. Quick profits obtained through speculation in Austrian shares further financed an expansion of the Austrian banking sector, reflected in the foundation of eighty new banks and many more Winkelbanken operating without authorization. Consumption by happy speculators further helped produce a rise in state revenues from indirect taxation and import duties (see Graph 4.3).[107]

The volume of shares traded on the VSE best illustrates the effect of capital inflows and the course of the speculative bubble. After stabilization in 1922 the monthly number of shares that changed hands fell, but from March 1923 onward, as prices on the VSE began to rise, the monthly figures of traded shares rose to levels that would later appear extreme in hindsight (see Graph 4.4). Following the issue of the League loans in June, the number of shares traded attained its highest level, just as the rally reached its zenith and prices seemed to go through the ceiling. And trading remained exceptionally high over the following months. Investors and speculators who bought stocks in March saw their value double by July and triple by October 1923, when a first correction took place and investors realized profits.[108]

It is difficult to come by data on cross-border capital flows for the 1920s and even more difficult to obtain figures for Austria specifically, but data of the Devisenzentrale provided to the League in Geneva give some indication

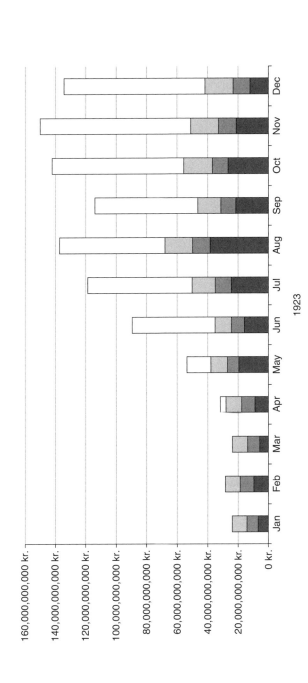

GRAPH 4.3. Revenue from turnover taxes in 1923 in Austrian crowns. *Source*: LNA, C 17, Reconstruction financière de l'Autriche 1922–1928, closed accounts—taxes and monopolies.

Legend:
- ■ Financial Securities Exchange Tax
- ■ Foreign Currency Exchange Tax
- ▨ Bank-transactions Tax
- □ Commercial Turnover Tax

1923

Y-axis:
160,000,000,000 kr.
140,000,000,000 kr.
120,000,000,000 kr.
100,000,000,000 kr.
80,000,000,000 kr.
60,000,000,000 kr.
40,000,000,000 kr.
20,000,000,000 kr.
0 kr.

X-axis: Jan Feb Mar Apr May Jun Jul Aug Sep Oct Nov Dec

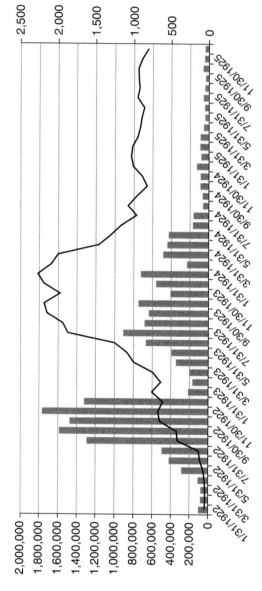

GRAPH 4.4. Vienna Stock Exchange, number of stocks traded (gray columns, left axis) and Monthly Index (black line, right axis), 1914=100), 1922–1925. *Sources:* Wiener Börsenkammer Index and global financial data.

■ Stocks Traded ⎯ VSE Index

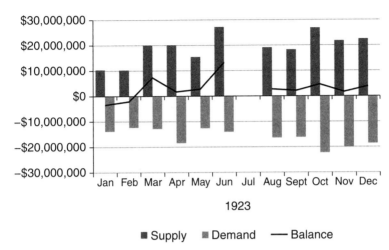

GRAPH 4.5. Monthly clearing of foreign exchange supply and demand at the Austrian Devisen Zentrale in US$ (includes government demand and supply), 1923. *Source:* LNA, C 28, Position financière de la Devisen Zentrale.

of the state of Austria's balance of payments.[109] Generally, demand for crowns outstripped their supply in 1923 (see Graph 4.5). Even though in January and February, before flotation of the smaller interim loan, the Devisenzentrale lost foreign reserves defending the crown, after the successful issue of the smaller loan the supply of foreign currencies was consistently larger than market demand (data for July 1923 were lacking in the archives). Despite a growing trade balance deficit, Austria's balance of payments probably remained positive, due to a large inflow of foreign capital attracted by high interest rates and the rally on the VSE. The freshly appointed foreign adviser to the ANB, the Swiss central banker Conseiller Charles Schnyder von Wartensee, wrote in July that the Austrian trade deficit was being covered by the acquisition of crowns from foreigners showing confidence in Austria and seeking to invest in the country.[110]

Because the ANB needed to accumulate foreign exchange in order to make its promise to defend the fixed exchange rate regime credible, it further encouraged the inflow of foreign capital through holding its discount rate at a comparatively high rate of 9 percent.[111] The inflow bolstered the ANB's foreign reserves, which grew by 185 million gold crowns (about $37 million), two-thirds of which came from the exchange of loan funds by the Austrian

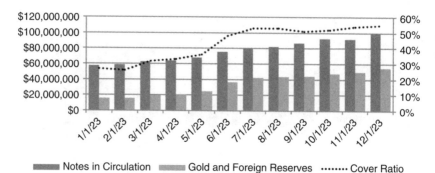

GRAPH 4.6. Austrian National Bank reserves and note circulation in US$ and cover ratio in percent, 1923. *Source:* ANB balance sheets as reported in *Neue Freie Presse.*

government, but one third of which came from private capital flows (see Graph 4.6).[112] Through steadily accumulating foreign currencies it managed to double its cover ratio, which by the end of year stood at over 50 percent.

Confidence in the monetary policy of the ANB was put to a first test in December 1923, when state post and telegraph workers went on strike to demand higher wages for 1924. Regular means of communication went silent, and the ANB had to cable the BoE from nearby Bratislava to ask it to intervene on important markets if the crown should fall. However, despite a decline of prices on the VSE, the BoE was not required to take action as the ANB's pledge to defend the crown's exchange rate proved credible enough to deter most speculators from attacking the currency. The Anglo-Austrian Bank in London, the main dealer of crowns in the city, continued to accept the stabilization rate as a basis for transactions, "de facto stabilizing the crown" while "simply following their own interest" and making a handsome profit on commissions.[113]

The real risk to stability lay in the euphoric rise of share prices on the VSE. In his second report to Zimmerman, submitted in August, Conseiller Schnyder von Wartensee wrote that the successful issue of the League loan had led to further speculation in Austrian shares, also increasingly attracting "simple people, former civil servants," and the general strata of the population that should not engage in hazardous "stock market games."[114] Schnyder von Wartensee believed that much of the foreign currency that flowed into Austria went into speculation instead of being put to productive use in commerce and industry. Because he considered it impossible that Austrian industry would ever pay the sort of dividends investors had been accustomed to before the war, an inevitable correction had to occur and would particularly hurt those who speculated on credit as well as small investors who were likely to lose their hard-earned savings.[115]

The inevitable correction came in March 1924, when French banks, led by Lazard Frères and the Banque de France, intervened on international markets to stop the depreciation of the French franc. The continued fall of the franc had largely been caused by speculation, inspired by the French government's budget deficit. All over Europe, speculators had driven down its price, by more than one-third since December, expecting France to follow the Austrian and German precedents.[116] Against the gold reserves of the French national bank, J. P. Morgan lent $100 million to prevent this from happening. Widely announcing the help of U.S. capital, a French syndicate then began buying up francs all over Europe, driving up the franc's value in Berlin, Amsterdam, Vienna, and Zurich, and teaching speculators a lesson.[117] Once the franc had appreciated continuously for several days, panic set in among the many speculators engaged in forward contracts, who now looked to buy francs, afraid that further appreciation would incur substantial losses. The syndicate, no longer forced to intervene, watched as speculators bought francs and the currency appreciated on the exchanges. In Vienna, where speculators from all over Central Europe had congregated, the VSE went into a tailspin. Speculators, facing losses in francs, massively offloaded their shares in order to cover their speculative engagements. As French franc debts matured in April, May, and June of 1924, financial institutions closed in Holland, in Germany, and in Austria.[118] The ANB and the Austrian government, which had so confidently watched Austria's progress during the first year of reconstruction, suddenly had a financial and fiscal twin crisis on their hands.

Looking back on his first year in office, Zimmerman considered it a cardinal mistake that extraordinary powers for the government had not been established in 1922. The Extraordinary Cabinet, or Ausserordentlicher Kabinettsrat, agreed upon in its stead had stopped meeting after just a few months. Only a fully empowered government could have carried out the necessary reforms, he thought, and "the fact that this most essential paragraph of the Geneva Treaty had been allowed to remain practically a dead letter" in his view proved fatal to the League scheme's success.[119] However, even though Chancellor Seipel did continuously cite political considerations for ignoring much of the reform plan, what really allowed for the disregard of Zimmerman's commands was the priority foreign observers placed on balanced budgets over reduced ones. Only because the budget was gradually being balanced was Seipel able to disregard reforms he considered politically costly. Only this allowed him to refuse the reduction of the army, dismissing the full number of state workers, or cutting budgetary expenditures, without undermining foreign confidence and risking the League and Zimmerman turning their back on him. In a way, Seipel and Kienböck had managed to both have their cake and eat it.

Zimmerman's position had been particularly difficult in 1923 because the loans for Austria had not yet been raised. Therefore, the General Commissioner had felt compelled to present Austria in a good light to not undermine investor confidence.[120] Zimmerman, however, remained powerless mainly because the Austrian government was able to do without extra funds. The inflow of capital, which fueled a bubble on the VSE, financed excessive consumption, reflected in growing imports and higher revenue from luxury taxation. This flushed the treasury with cash, but once the bubble burst, revenues expectedly dropped. Worried about the deteriorating situation in Austria, the League of Nations Financial Committee would start sounding a tougher tone in its dealings with Seipel and Kienböck. The BoE, viewing monetary developments with concern, would try pressure the ANB to pursue a more restrictive policy. This would strengthen the position of Zimmerman but also would draw public attention to the emerging conflict between the Austrian government and the ANB on the one side, and with the League and foreign creditors on the other. International financial oversight and control by the League and its General Commissioner in Vienna was to face its largest challenge yet.

5

Reconstructions at the Crossroad

1924

You will, I know, believe me when I say that the criticisms which I do make are inspired solely by a sincere desire to see that the scheme for Austrian reconstruction should produce effective and lasting benefits to Austria herself. I am afraid that the Bankers at Vienna are not one of the strongest points in Austria's health.

—Letter from Otto Niemeyer to Georg Franckenstein
7 November 1924

ON THE FIRST DAY OF THE YEAR 1924, the First Vienna Football Club played the Paris Red Stars in the French capital. The eighth Olympic Games were scheduled to take place there that summer, but German teams had been banned from attending, inciting calls in Austria to boycott the games in solidarity. Enmity over reparations and the occupation of the Ruhr not only soured sporting relations between France and Germany, but bestowed diplomatic significance on the Austrian footballers' visit to Paris. In the name of French President Alexandre Millerand, the Austrian players were cordially received at the Quai d'Orsay, and Viennese papers noted how Austria might serve as a role model for Germany's reentry into the global arena of international sports. But despite celebrating the surprisingly amiable tone of official speeches, press dispatches from the game itself were couched in bellicose language. The Viennese *Sporttagblatt* described the match as a "big battle" for which the French Red Stars had "mobilized all their canons," resulting in a final score of 2–2 that left neither team "defeated" on the "battle-ground."[1] According to one report the Austrians would have actually won had not the referee "dictated" a penalty kick.[2] The team's performance was celebrated back home, but despite Germany being invited to rejoin the Olympic Committee before the games commenced, Austria's footballers were prevented from attending the Paris Olympics for financial reasons.

What the above episode illustrates effectively is how the international arena of sports, much like that of politics, not only fostered peaceful collaboration among former enemies, but also allowed Austria to contest its status as a defeated nation and aggressively challenge the victors on even grounds. As we shall see, the relationship between Austria and the League of Nations in 1924 experienced marked transformations. The League, no longer shackled by the need to sustain foreign confidence in an upcoming loan, and itself now heavily invested in the Austrian project (as well as in Hungarian reconstruction), took off its gloves and gave a harder punch. The Austrian government, keen on seeing control terminated on schedule at the end of 1924, adopted a more cooperative attitude toward the League but demanded that its terms be amended in Austria's favor. Finally, Alfred Rudolph Zimmerman, who had by then developed a better understanding of the Austrian situation and of the services his office could render, emerged as an unlikely defender of Austrian policies vis-à-vis the Financial Committee in Geneva. The evolving financial crisis in Austria questioned the government's ability to uphold a balanced budget, and thus also put in doubt the scheduled termination of League intervention at the end of 1924. Markets could interpret the League's timely departure as a sign of confidence, or lingering doubts about Austrian currency stability might resurface. Resolved to uphold the reputation of its intervention, the League would not release Austria in a state of economic uncertainty, and the Austrian government demurred.

One year earlier, at the start of the League's intervention in Austria, the French economist Charles Rist had traveled on a mission from Paris to Vienna to study the country's political and economic conditions.[3] Rist, who would later be appointed Deputy Governor of the Banque de France and serve as foreign adviser to the Romanian central bank and government, returned convinced that Austria largely faced three economic challenges: First, overcoming the impoverishment that had resulted from the war; second, fixing the economic dislocations caused by inflation; third, reestablishing relations between Austrian producers and their lost markets in the Austro-Hungarian successor states. For the moment, Rist felt, Austrians were simply consuming more than they produced, importing more than they exported, and essentially living on savings and capital. Though Austrians were unlikely to return to the levels of prosperity they had been accustomed to before the war, Rist was optimistic that at least the second and third challenges could be grappled with. The gradual return of Central European trade and banking to its former channels, the growth of industrial production and manufacturing in Austria, and the preservation and strengthening of Vienna as the region's commercial and financial center would eventually balance the country's current account. Austrians would need to get used to lower living standards and still reduce consumption by 20 percent, but re-establishing trade among the Austro-Hungarian successor states would make the Austrian economy viable. The League intervention, he recommended, could help bring about the essential reduction in living standards by curtailing government expenditures and wages. By necessity Austria would be poor, but it would live.

Twelve months later, none of Rist's expectations or recommendations had materialized. One year after the beginning of League control, the Austrian budget had been reduced only slightly. Nominal and real wages of state workers had risen, not dropped. Tariff walls surrounding Austria still hampered foreign trade, and the timely disappearance of Habsburg's legacy of national jealousies seemed only a remote possibility. Domestic consumption had surged, but with prices in Austria rising, exporters faced even more difficulties competing for customers abroad. Banks had made handsome profits from commissions of foreign investors, an important form of invisible exports, but sudden stabilization of the French franc in March 1924 and the end it put to currency and stock exchange speculations meant that such revenues were unlikely to return. In short, one year after the beginning of League intervention in Austria, the crux of the country's economic problems, its trade and balance of payment deficit, had not been resolved but had in all likelihood worsened (see Graph 5.1). Was the League intervention in Austria going to work?

The League's plan for Austria focused on reducing and balancing the government budget to establish a stable currency. Valuable time to tackle these issues had been lost during the first year as the Austrian government shirked from or postponed administrative reforms and the League prioritized the issue of foreign loans. If General Commissioner Zimmerman harbored any hopes that his control over the loan funds ensured that they would be

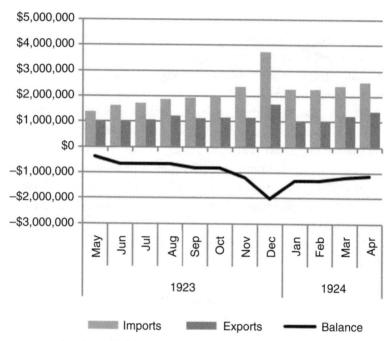

GRAPH 5.1. Austrian trade balance in US$, May 1923–April 1924. *Source:* NA, T 208/88.

undertaken in the second year, he was soon disillusioned. The unexpected stabilization of the franc in March caused panic in Vienna markets. The Vienna Stock Exchange (VSE), already falling since December, went into a tailspin as speculators began massively offloading their shares to cover engagements due in April, May, and June. The financial crisis, through its fiscal effects, then threatened to put the entire League plan at risk. In the face of falling revenues, the Austrian government's claim to permanently balance its budget at a high level suddenly appeared less credible. At the same time, a large outflow of foreign reserves from the Austrian National Bank (ANB) generated doubt about the central bank's ability to uphold the currency's newly fixed exchange rates. With monetary policy at the ANB outside of its purview, the League's Financial Committee concentrated on making sure that Austrian fiscal policy stood on solid grounds.

At the same time that the League intensified its intervention in Austrian affairs, and the Austrian government was forced to accept that the League Council had the last word, the ANB asserted its own international independence more forcefully and successfully. As a consequence, Governor Norman at the Bank of England (BoE) gradually abandoned his close cooperation with the ANB. At the center of his dissatisfaction with the Austrian central bank was the latter's refusal to confront the financial crisis by increasing the discount rate and inducing deflation. In the short run this would have helped "cleanse" the economy of moribund banks and industries. In the long run, falling prices in Austria would have helped reduce public expenditures, diminish the trade deficit by facilitating exports, and increase productivity, bringing reconstruction to a successful end. But ANB President Reisch vehemently opposed a tightening of monetary policy, which would also have incurred a high cost to banks and industry and undoubtedly resulted in a severe recession, lower wages, and a rise in unemployment. In Norman's eyes, Reisch was acting under the sway of what he perceived to be Vienna's reckless bankers. Reisch thought that Norman was being ignorant and dictatorial. Consequently, after working tirelessly to make the League loan for Austria a success, Norman drastically reduced the BoE's involvement in Austrian reconstruction, creating a personal rift between him and Reisch that made continued cooperation between the two central banks impossible.

Austria Back in Crisis

Entering the second year of reconstruction, Austria's government faced a financial crisis. Share prices on the VSE had risen meteorically in 1923 but had begun to fall rapidly after the French franc stabilized in March 1924. Since a crash of the VSE was likely to produce a panic and provoke an outflow of capital large enough to undermine confidence in Austria's fixed exchange rate, General Commissioner Zimmerman agreed to provide emergency support for the market via a syndicate of Viennese banks. Lending funds from the League loan to the ANB, the latter extended aid to the banks with which to intervene in the VSE to shore up share prices and prevent a rout. After Zimmerman had provided 100 billion crowns (about $1.4 million) for three months against ANB guarantees at the end of March, the ANB cabled the BoE in April that the crisis was under control.[4] However, once the first bulk of French franc debts came due in mid-April, the Finance Ministry needed Zimmerman to provide another 200 billion crowns (about

$2.8 million), to which he agreed only reluctantly. Despite almost £1 million (about $4.2 million) in total funds from Zimmerman and another £3.85 million (about $16 million) from the ANB itself, the banking syndicate was unable to stabilize falling stock prices (see Graph 4.4). When in May the large Depositenbank announced serious losses, putting further downward pressure on share values, Zimmerman categorically refused to provide any more money. The General Commissioner stressed that he was no longer convinced interventions would end the rout, and he voiced fear about the risk of inflation from further increases in credit and circulation.[5]

While some banks were fighting off runs from worried depositors, smaller ones had already been forced to close completely or needed ANB assistance to survive.[6] The Austrian financial sector had been hit hard, and the publicized bank failures raised suspicions about the health of Vienna's larger banks as well. By the end of May, when Zimmerman insisted on a first repayment of the initial 100 billion crowns (about $1.4 million) advanced to the syndicate, the banks' situation had become too precarious to make the repayment possible. The ANB, which stood as guarantor, argued for its part that it had agreed to the loan conditions under duress and never thought the banks would repay on time.[7] The ANB Directors certainly knew of the extent of difficulties Vienna banks faced, and their claim of having been dishonest when asking for loan funds from the General Commissioner was probably not just a bad excuse. Meanwhile, in order to prevent a worsening of the financial collapse, the ANB freely discounted bills presented by banks and thereby from April to June almost tripled its portfolio, expanding circulation (see Graph 5.2).

At the same time, due to capital flight and the foreign exchange requirements of speculators, the ANB itself lost foreign reserves, so that its coverage, expressed as a ratio of reserves to note circulation, dropped to its lowest level since June 1923 (see Graphs 4.6 and 5.2). To Zimmerman, it seemed that all the hard-earned successes of his first year in office were unraveling before his eyes. It was "incomprehensible" that "these people, who have witnessed all the misery of intense inflation, can be so lighthearted in their banking policy," he wrote to Henry Strakosch, Norman's confidant and an expert on the League Financial Committee.[8] Zimmerman was particularly concerned about the release of new notes into circulation and the impact that might have on prices and expectations. But he acknowledged the need to limit

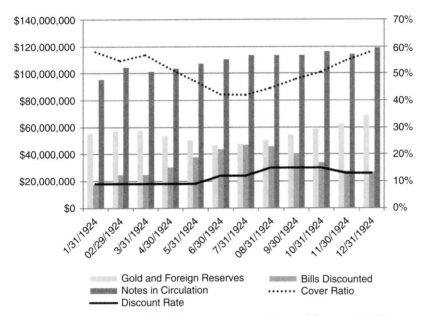

GRAPH 5.2. Austrian National Bank reserves, note circulation and discounts in US$, cover ratio, and discount rate in percent, 1924. *Source:* ANB balance sheets as reported in *Neue Freie Presse.*

damage from the financial crisis and, fully aware of the importance of confidence, could hardly provoke an open rift with the ANB. Zimmerman was thus compelled to reluctantly accept a gradual repayment schedule from the banking syndicate in order to prevent a further worsening of the ANB's balance sheet by calling upon the latter's guarantee.[9]

A scrutiny of the bills discounted by the ANB provides some insight into the severity of difficulties Vienna's larger banks faced. Bills presented by banks can be divided into commercial and financial bills. Commercial bills are self-liquidating; that is, after a certain time, usually within ninety days, a commercial bill is up for payment and the central bank that had discounted the bill is paid, after which the bill disappears from its portfolio. Financial bills, however, are not self-liquidating. They do not result from commercial activity, but are nothing else than promissory notes signed by the borrowing bank. The ANB was only meant to lend against commercial bills, but in times of distress, a bank might approach the central bank and exceptionally borrow money against financial bills to replenish its liquidity. Data provided by the

ANB to the foreign Conseiller show that, following March 1924, all Vienna banks increased their amount of financial bills. The Credit-Anstalt was the largest discounter of financial bills, but smaller banks such as the Merkurbank, Verkehrsbank, and Zentralbank also borrowed considerably against financial paper. According to monthly reports submitted for approval to the foreign Conseiller, the share of financial bills in the ANB's portfolio grew from 28 percent in April 1924 to 41 percent in June and 58 percent in September.[10]

Since the total value of discounted bills during that time rose by only one-third, we can deduce that banks decreased their discounting against commercial bills and replaced them with loans against financial paper. This action indicated the difficult position banks were finding themselves in. The ANB preferred commercial paper and discounting financial paper was a sign of distress. Either the banks had less commercial paper available, as the domestic economy headed for a recession, or they were hoarding commercial paper to present it once the ANB refused to discount any more financial bills. Graph 5.3 is based on data from those largest banks where more than 30 percent of their discounted bills were financial. Among the general rise of bills presented for discount to the ANB during the second quarter of 1924, they increased their share of financial bills, and though they reduced their

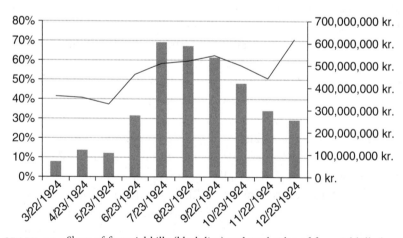

GRAPH 5.3. Share of financial bills (black line) and total value of financial bills (gray bars) of those banks with more than 30 percent financial bills among bills discounted with the Austrian National Bank, March–December 1924. *Source:* ANB, VI / 9: Conseiller Reports.

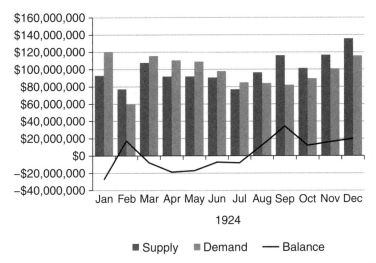

GRAPH 5.4: Demand, supply, and balance of foreign currencies at Devisen Zentrale in US$ (net inflows shown as positive, net outflows as negative), November 1923–September 1924. *Source:* LNA, C 25, Gebarungsumsätze und Saldi der Devisenzentrale.

total discounts after the ANB raised its rates during the second half of the year, the share of financial bills among their discounts rose at year's end. In August 1924, the Financial Committee's delegates would learn from ANB Director Viktor Brauneis that some banks were forced to lend as much as half of their assets in return for liquidity. One bank alone borrowed almost $2 million.[11]

What made this situation so dangerous was that as the discounting of financial bills increased and banks extended liquidity to their customers, the ANB saw over one-fifth of its total reserves vanish. As mentioned above, the ANB steadily lost foreign currency and its reserves dropped from over $54 million in March to slightly over $40 million by August 1924 (see Graph 5.2). The ANB's foreign adviser confirmed that $10–$15 million had been lost by failed speculators, though foreign exchange was also withdrawn by anxious citizens.[12]

Much of the liquidity obtained by discounting financial bills at the ANB was thus used to buy foreign currency that was placed abroad or used to repay foreign debt. Data from the Devisenzentrale show that demand for foreign exchange continuously outstripped supply in Vienna after March 1924. The net-deficit reported by the Devisenzentrale for that period matches the losses of the ANB (see Graph 5.4) quite precisely. The decline in foreign currency reserves of about $14 million also matches the value of increased discounts (ca. 1 trillion crowns) at the ANB over that period. The Vienna banks were thus obtaining liquidity from the ANB through financial bills, with which to pay back foreign loans that were being withdrawn or in order to satisfy withdrawals from customers. Customers and banks then converted their deposits into foreign currencies, out of fear of depreciation or to cover their losses in the French franc speculation. In a time of crisis, it was important that the central bank provide liquidity as lender of last resort, but the drop in reserves and rise in circulation risked undermining fragile foreign and domestic confidence in currency stability.

Falling foreign reserves were a gauge of Austria's deteriorating balance of payments, and the ANB needed to find ways to attract fresh capital from abroad. Ideally, Austrian corporations would have offered profitable investments and obtained long-term loans from foreign banks to be converted at the ANB, increasing the latter's reserves. Indeed, a letter from the Vienna Chamber of Commerce to Georg Franckenstein in July 1924 stressed how important it was to obtain foreign loans to increase productivity in Austria and asked the envoy to introduce Viennese bankers to London and to assist them in their search for foreign capital.[13] Similarly, the director of the Anglo-Austrian bank in Vienna wrote to Norman in May 1924 that the greatest difficulty a revival of Austrian industry faced was "the fact that credits from abroad are only obtainable for short periods."[14] Norman's unofficial embargo on foreign lending by the City in anticipation of sterling's return to gold was not helping Austria to obtain long-term funds. Moreover, historically speaking, foreign capital had always been scarce in the region. But the main reason there had been few long-term foreign loans to Austrian industries was a lack of confidence in the stability of the country's currency, banks, and economic outlook.[15]

Given the extent of the crisis that swept over Austria in 1924, it is not surprising that London bankers were worried about the country's development and prospects. In April, when the city of Graz inquired about the possibility of issuing a municipal loan in London, Franckenstein was told that British bankers were not forthcoming to the idea.[16] In July, Strakosch informed Franckenstein that feelings in the City remained unchanged, and that he thought that "even if it were feasible in existing circumstances to find English capital for Austrian firms I am sure that the capital would only go to the banks in relief of advances which they have made and now deeply regret."[17] According to Strakosch, the financial crisis that had engulfed Austria had "had a deterrent effect on financial houses in this country extending credit facilities to Austrian enterprises." He did not trust the soundness of Austrian banks and proposed a deflationary contraction instead of fresh capital. The well-informed Baron Schröder similarly told Franckenstein that London houses interested in continental Europe were completely engaged and that further facilities for Austria were unavailable.[18]

According to the informal rules governing the gold exchange standard, the ANB could have been expected to immediately increase its interest rate to attract capital inflows from abroad. Such a move would also have contracted the money supply by forcing banks to reduce the amount of financial bills discounted, thereby further improving the cover ratio. Moreover, it could have signaled the ANB's determined focus on upholding the crown's exchange rate. However, it would also have dampened economic activity and increased unemployment. When Reisch informed Norman in May 1924 that he desired another 200 billion crowns (about $2.8 million) from Zimmerman to prevent a panic without increasing the rate, Norman replied that a higher rate was precisely what was needed. The ANB's new foreign Conseiller, the Dutch economist Anton van Gijn (mostly spelled Gyn in documents), similarly thought that the currency's stability remained threatened as long as the rate was not raised. To counter capital outflows, the ANB finally increased its rate from 9 to 12 percent in July, but Norman still considered this too low. A high rate could signal the bank's determination to act, or it could be interpreted as a desperate attempt to regain control. Thus, when the rate was raised to 15 percent in August, concerned American bankers approached J. P. Morgan to inquire as to whether control of the situation in Vienna was slipping out of the ANB's hands.[19]

With the final outcome of the financial crisis and its consequences for fiscal and monetary policy uncertain, the League and Zimmerman increased pressure on the Austrian government to fully implement reforms and reduce expenditures. The League intervention was originally planned to come to a successful completion by the end of 1924 and the Austrian government hoped to see control lifted at the end of that year according to schedule. Since it had eliminated the budget deficit by increasing revenues and not through reducing expenditures, it submitted an official request to the League Council in March 1924 asking that its agreement with the League be amended. Adjusting the budgetary demands considered sound at the beginning of the intervention to the new realities might have allowed the League's Financial Committee to declare Austria financially and economically stable, to announce an end of control, and to withdraw the Commissioner General from Vienna. But the League could not risk failing in Austria, and with major reforms still outstanding, the current account in deficit, and the effects of the financial crisis uncertain, the General Commissioner's control over the League loan and Austria's pledged securities would eventually be prolonged in return for granting the Austrians an increase in expenditures.

Tightening Control

The relations between the Austrian government and the League of Nations underwent noticeable change in 1924. Chancellor Seipel, keen on bringing control to an end, adopted a friendlier tone in his communications with the General Commissioner. Vis-à-vis the League, the Austrian government still tried to assert its independence, but the Financial Committee, which in 1923 had vacillated between chastening Austria and highlighting its successes, adopted a sterner approach. The League's Financial Secretariat, by now more experienced than in its first year, carefully prepared meetings in advance, profiting from the close cooperation of Arthur Salter and Otto Niemeyer. Both of them thought that it was important for the League's clout and Austria's economic future to discipline profligacy and demonstrate authority. Zimmerman himself had become more sympathetic toward Austria's predicaments, explaining and at times defending the Austrian government's point of view in his correspondence, but generally siding with the Financial Committee's international experts during meetings in Geneva.

As noted above, in early 1924 the Austrian government wanted and expected to see Zimmerman leave and League control cease by the end of that year. Although Chancellor Seipel and his ministers had failed so far to follow through on many of the measures agreed upon, they believed that the enduring stability of the crown, the reduction of the budget deficit, and the unexpectedly high revenues witnessed in 1923 justified amending the terms of Austria's agreement with the League. To test the waters and see whether the Financial Committee was ready for a timely completion of its intervention, the Austrian government decided in early 1924 to request the League Council to raise the budgetary limits on expenditures that had been set by the League's delegates in 1922 and agree to a suspension of the dismissal of state workers prescribed by the Protocols.[20] Sounding out the relevant opinions in London and Geneva revealed that the Austrian idea was not well received, even though it would have allowed the parties to part ways amiably. Niemeyer staunchly opposed the Austrian request, which, he thought, implied nothing less than a complete revision of the international agreement. In his view, Austria's rising cost of living mirrored a risk of returning inflation, requiring less rather than more government spending. Salter agreed that the recent prosperity in Austria had mainly been based on the influx of foreign capital in search of quick profits. This would soon cease, he thought, so that Austria's budget remained too high and the League intervention could not be ended unless expenditures fell.[21]

At the League's March session in Geneva, General Commissioner Zimmerman presented a letter from Austrian Foreign Minister Alfred Grünberger to the League Council in which the Austrian government made two official requests.[22] Grünberger, born in Karlsbad in 1875, had studied law in Prague before entering the Habsburg Trade Ministry and had initially served as Trade Minister after the war. In 1922 he had become Seipel's Foreign Minister, had helped draft the Geneva Protocols, and participated in negotiations with the League Financial Committee's delegation that fall. Since the budget had been balanced on a higher level than expected, he asked in the name of the Austrian government that the limit on expenditures agreed upon in 1922 be raised. Second, the Austrian government wished that the remaining funds from the loan, now no longer needed to cover a deficit, be freed for productive investments, such as the ongoing electrification of the federal railways. The General Commissioner explained to the Council's assembled dignitaries that the Austrian budget had been balanced through an increase in revenues, so that it now stood at a level considerably higher than that originally envisioned in 1922. Thus questions arose as to whether the limit of 350 million gold crowns (about $70 million) on expenses could be lifted and whether the remainder of the loan could be used for other purposes than covering the deficit. Addressing the Council members in person, Foreign Minister Grünberger noted that the agreement reached with the League's delegates in 1922 foresaw in fact the possibility of reexamining the figures. Treading carefully, he explained that the Austrian government did not expect concrete answers immediately, but that it wished to raise the matter so that a procedure could be established on how to evaluate whether and when the financial stability of Austria seemed assured. The written request did not explicitly mention the termination of control, but Grünberger's final remarks directly linked the Austrian requests to the official formula of the Geneva Protocols, which would have to be used to establish the timing of the end of League intervention.[23]

The Council's Sub-Committee on Austria proposed to submit the formal requests for further examination to both General Commissioner Zimmerman and the Financial Committee. Both would draft official reports on the question of terminating control and amending the budgetary limits until their next meetings in June.[24] The Council's official statement immediately dampened any Austrian hopes of a favorable decision, however, toiling the customary line by pointing out that the high level of revenues in Austria was unlikely to continue and that for a termination of control the Sub-Committee deemed more administrative reforms and a reduction of expenditure necessary.[25]

Had the French franc not suddenly stabilized a few days later and the VSE gone into its steep decline, the Austrians might have nevertheless received a positive reply in June. A League delegation would have then visited Vienna, declaring Austria financially and economically stable so that control would have terminated on schedule by the end of 1924. After all, Zimmerman was neither becoming more popular nor effective in Vienna, the loans had been floated, and the model of League intervention was already being successfully applied in Hungary. But Salter and Niemeyer pushed the Financial Committee toward an uncompromising position regarding Austria for two reasons. First, the financial crisis put the entire scheme at risk and it was important to safeguard international trust in the League's "credibility technology." Second, the effects of the French franc crisis on Vienna had already undermined foreign confidence, so that keeping up appearances had become insufficient, and more serious reforms were now necessary to ensure stability of the Austrian currency. Bidding for time, Salter informed Vienna in April that sending a delegation to Austria before the June meetings was impossible. He favored an initial joint report at the next meeting from Zimmerman, the Financial Committee, and the Committee of Control, to be followed by an inquiry into the state of the Austrian economy during the late summer.[26] The secret consensus materializing in Geneva was then to postpone any decision on the termination of control until September and to ascertain meanwhile whether the high Austrian revenues were likely to endure (see Graph 5.5).[27]

Zimmerman had warned in his thirteenth and fourteenth reports (January and April 1924) that elevated government revenues had hitherto been a consequence of the unusually high consumption and living standards, which would not continue permanently.[28] While expenditures and revenues in January 1924 were higher than they had been a year earlier, the deficit had turned into a small surplus, but this was not entirely good news and incurred substantial risks: once the economy inevitably slowed down, some revenue streams would turn out to have been merely temporary and a fiscal deficit would quickly reemerge. This raised concern about the prospects of Austria's currency stability and economy, so that Zimmerman dared to say that Austrian policy even stood diametrically opposed to the League scheme.[29] Instead of leading the Austrian budget toward permanent balance, he warned, the government was postponing necessary adjustments until the situation inevitably become acute once again. To underline his point, a chart was printed in Zimmerman's fifteenth report (May 1924), visualizing how reality had come to be out of touch with the reconstruction plan (see Figure 5.1).

To serve as a basis for discussions with the League in June, Finance Minister Viktor Kienböck began preparing a budget for 1925. His draft budget laid before parliament in April was larger than the one for 1924, but balanced, at 550 million gold crowns ($110 million). Zimmerman immediately voiced his opposition. The sum, 10 percent above the maximal ceiling on revenues considered even possible by the Financial Committee's delegates in 1922, would prove too harmful to the economy, he thought. The financial experts had considered 490 million gold crowns ($98 million) the highest feasible level of taxation, and Zimmerman suggested that the government reduce expenditures correspondingly to at least 475 million gold crowns ($95 million).[30] This, he recommended, would allow cutting corporate taxation and eliminating taxes on foreign exchange and banking transactions, which would help attract foreign investments. In his view, the unfolding crisis in Austria made it more urgent than ever to slim the budget, and he

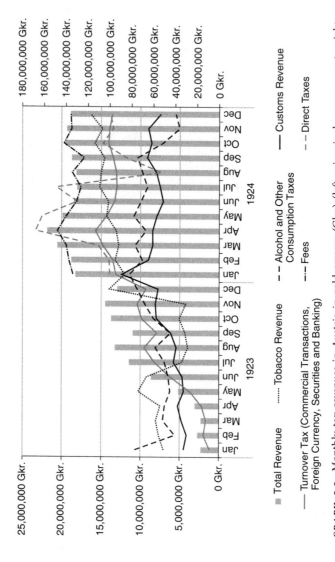

GRAPH 5.5. Monthly tax revenues in Austria in gold crowns (Gkr.) (left axis=single revenue posts, right axis=total revenues), 1923 and 1924. *Sources:* LNA, C 17: Gross revenues of taxes and monopolies; LNA, C 13: Statement Monthly Gross Receipts, Tobacco.

Legend:

■ Total Revenue

— Turnover Tax (Commercial Transactions, Foreign Currency, Securities and Banking)

⋯⋯ Tobacco Revenue

– – Alcohol and Other Consumption Taxes

— Customs Revenue

–·– Fees

– – Direct Taxes

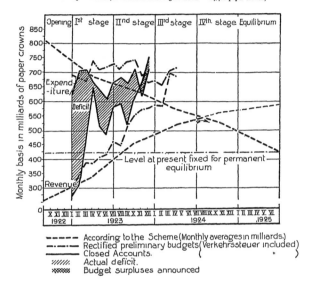

MONTHLY CLOSED ACCOUNTS OF THE AUSTRIAN GOVERNMENT, 1923.

COMPARISON BETWEEN PROVISIONAL FIGURES PUBLISHED, PROGRAMME ESTIMATES AND
PRELIMINARY BUDGETS

(Refund of Taxation to Provinces not shown).

Milliards of Paper Crowns (at stabilised rate: 1 gold crown = 14,400 paper crowns)

The expenditure and revenue figures shown in the Programme and in the closed accounts
will be found in the text (the true expenditure figure will be increased by certain outstanding
payments in respect of the latter months of 1923).

The expenditure and revenue figures of the preliminary budgets were published in the Fourteenth Report.

FIGURE 5.1. Graph from Alfred Rudolph Zimmerman's fourteenth report to the League
Council, comparing the scheme's plan and the actual figures in billions of crowns (ex-
cluding planned reform on Ertragsanteile). *Source:* Alfred Rudolph Zimmerman, "Financial
Reconstruction of Austria (Second Year)—Fifteenth Report by the Commissioner-General of the
League of Nations for Austria. (Period February 15th to March 15th, 1924.—Third Month of the Third
Stage.)" *League of Nations Official Journal* 5 (1924): 785.

advised the Austrian government to demonstrate restraint before the League
met in June.[31] Since the League was likely to take Austria's total level of taxation into consideration, Zimmerman recommended that the government
meanwhile find ways to strengthen its control over the finances of Austria's
provinces and communes as well.[32]

Finance Minister Kienböck faced familiar difficulties trying to pass a reduced budget by June. Representatives of provinces and communes refused to accept a reduction of the Ertragsanteile, the share of revenue they received from federal taxation, as did the Socialists who governed Vienna. The Socialist Party also opposed reducing social welfare or curtailing the army budget, and civil servants, many of whom were still badly paid, demanded that the higher wages granted temporarily until 1 June 1924 be carried into the next year.[33] Zimmerman warned Kienböck that a general pay raise was premature and reminded the Finance Minister not to make any concrete offers without consulting him first. After Kienböck got Zimmerman's approval to increase the particularly low pay of higher officials in 1925 in return for the Pan-German party's support, the majority of state workers, fearing a reduction of their pay, grew impatient, threatening to strike.[34] Chancellor Seipel wished to publicly declare that if the League allowed a larger budget, he would increase state workers' pay, but Zimmerman was adamant that no increase was possible unless the League also approved using some of the loan funds for, say, railway electrification, and thereby actually released funds to pay for higher wages.[35] Addressing state workers' demands, the Chancellor explained that he had to await the League's decision in June, warning Zimmerman that he would not be able delay an increase of state workers' pay much beyond that point.

Facing the risk of mass demonstrations and a nationwide strike, Finance Minister Kienböck, once again without consulting the General Commissioner, published a decree providing a one-time advance of 63 billion crowns (about $880,000) for state workers at the end of May.[36] A budget for 1925, with expenditures reduced to 520 million gold crowns (about $104 million), passed through parliament on the final day of the month, with all parties in agreement on a partition of Ertragsanteile that would pay for the wage increases. The following day, 1 June, Chancellor Seipel was shot twice and severely wounded by an unemployed Austrian worker who confronted him at Vienna's Südbahnhof. The Pan-German Interior Minister and Vice-Chancellor, Felix Frank, took immediate charge of Seipel's office, and when Finance Minister Kienböck and Foreign Minister Grünberger took the budget to Geneva the following week, Chancellor Seipel remained in Vienna, recovering from his wounds.[37]

It is not unusual among historians to speculate in such situations about what might have happened if Seipel had not been hurt and had been able to attend the important meeting. After all, he was much better versed in the game of international diplomacy than his Finance Minister. But the truth is that the consensus reached among officials ahead of the meeting was to further postpone its decision on the Austrian budget and the termination of League control, and though unknown to the Austrians, delay was a foregone conclusion. A memorandum drawn up by Zimmerman's Dutch aide, Adrianus Pelt, summed up the planned procedure for the choreographed June session. There remained still too much uncertainty about the future development of Austrian state revenues, so any decision regarding the budget level or using the loan for expenditures would be postponed to the fall. The League would use the extra months to further pressure the Austrian government into implementing outstanding reforms, particularly abolishing the pension automatism, which determined that retirees automatically benefited from wage increases obtained by those still employed, reaching a favorable agreement with state workers and obtaining passage of a law regarding the permanent partition of Ertragsanteile. Once a sound and balanced budget was thereby secured, Austria could perhaps be granted a higher level of expenditures and permission to use loan funds to electrify its railways, too.[38]

The Belgian Chair of the Financial Committee, the central banker Albert Janssen, had been sent to Vienna ahead of the June 1924 session and returned with a pessimistic report on the financial and monetary outlook of Austria. The inevitable correction of the VSE had been aggravated by the losses of French franc speculators. Money was scarce and market interest rates high. Not only had the central bank been forced to lend massively to Vienna's banks to support their liquidity, General Commissioner Zimmerman had been required to advance money from the League loan in order to keep the market from collapsing. Tax revenues would certainly fall and the return of a budget deficit was hence likely. Given the country's negative balance of payments and trade, this would ultimately put currency stability at risk. In his view, reconstruction had taken a setback by at least one year. Remaining silent on the possible size of the budget, he recommended that no loan funds should be allowed to pay for budgetary expenditures as long as the risk of a returning deficit remained high.[39]

Vis-à-vis Salter, Zimmerman had privately expressed himself in favor of increasing the maximal limit on Austrian expenditures, and he had expressed this view even publicly to the Austrian press.[40] Prior to the meeting in Geneva, he had agreed with Salter to postpone decisions to September but had also suggested that the Financial Committee inform the Council that the budget could indeed be increased.[41] Addressing the Financial Committee in June 1924, he recalled that in late 1922 its international experts had decided to limit public expenditures to 350 million gold crowns, but at the same time had agreed with the Austrian government that this figure could possibly be modified later. It seemed like Zimmerman could not make up his mind. While it was true that the Austrians had not observed this limit, he continued, they had after all eliminated the deficit. The proposed budget of 520 million gold crowns (about $104 million) for 1925 was in fact too high (see Table 5.1) and, including the provinces and communes, constituted a total tax load of 663 million gold crowns, or 121 gold crowns per head (about $24, or in total almost one-seventh of national income). Compared to the financial experts' recommendation of 75 gold crowns per capita in 1922, this constituted a "very heavy burden" for Austria's economy and population, but Zimmerman voiced doubts as to whether the government could actually reduce the budget any further. He carefully explained that the extra expenses were due to a necessary increase in wages, generous pensions to state and railway workers (132 million–142 million gold crowns), and the unexpectedly high cost of electrifying the railways (122 million gold crowns instead of 55 million), but also proposed insisting on more dismissals (at the railways, the tobacco monopoly, the state's salt mines, the gendarmerie, and the agrarian

TABLE 5.1. Budgets presented to the League of Nations in June 1924 (million gold crowns)

	Expenses	Revenues	Balance
Closed accounts of 1923	520.5	402.3	−118.2
Budget *Préalables* for 1924	509.5	428.5	−81.0
League delegation in 1922 for 1925	350.0	489.3	+139.3
Proposed draft budget for 1925	520.2	533.4	+13.2

Source: LNA, F 155: Budget normal révisé 1925, 3 June 1924. See Appendix B for details. Not including Ertragsanteile of 130 million gold crowns and productive investments (electrification of federal railways) of 35 million.

administration) and the amalgamation of the federal administration in the provinces with that of existing local authorities to obtain savings.[42]

The next day, the Financial Committee's international experts interviewed Austrian Finance Minister Viktor Kienböck, Foreign Minister Alfred Grünberger, and Trade Emissary Richard Schüller. Kienböck clarified that if transfers to the provinces and productive investments were included, the overall budget for next year totaled 672 million gold crowns (520 million plus 35 million for electrification and 117 million transferred to the provinces). Kienböck might have expected a more conciliatory reaction: after all, the budget had been balanced, and so the belligerent cross-questioning by members of the Financial Committee took him by surprise. He explained that the elevated level of expenditures was necessary to pay higher salaries and pensions to current and former state workers and to keep Austria's administrative apparatus running. Fully aware that they needed good reasons to justify postponing a decision, Strakosch raised general concerns about Austria's trade deficit and negative balance of accounts, which, he argued, threatened currency stability and thus the permanent balance of Austria's budget.[43] Niemeyer in turn raised doubts as to whether capital inflows would continue once the German currency stabilized. Kienböck dutifully responded to the grilling by answering all questions, but, he explained, he only possessed estimates of accounts in 1924 and had not yet gained support of all parties for details of his 1925 budget, so that he had no precise figures on which to base his replies.

When Kienböck returned before the League Financial Committee a few days later with more details, he went on the offensive and vehemently decried what he perceived as repeated and unjust insinuations that his government had produced no results.[44] He pointed to successful administrative reforms, such as the unification of the postal, telephone, and telegraph authorities as well as the commercialization of the railways, and noted that 67,382 state workers had been dismissed since October 1922.[45] Furthermore, the Finance Minister argued, prices in Austria had risen by 30 percent since 1922, which meant that in real terms the slight increase of expenditure over the previous year was proof of considerable savings. Finally, he explained that much of the gap between his proposed budget and that agreed upon with the League in 1922 was due to higher expenses on wages and pensions (104.3 million gold crowns instead of 62.3 million, and bound to reach 155 million), which were necessary to guarantee the smooth functioning of Austria's administration. His revenues of 533 million gold crowns,were commensurate with a tax load of 84 gold crowns per head (112.8 including taxation of provinces), which Kienböck conceded was a heavy burden, but no heavier than before the war.

Behind closed doors, Niemeyer and Salter were left with convincing the other experts of the Financial Committee to postpone answering the Austrian requests yet again. Salter officially proposed sending a delegation to Vienna for further inquiries and Niemeyer came out supporting the plan, commenting that financial circles in London were worried about Austria and that American lenders had expressed hopes that the League would turn down Austria's requests. Niemeyer further argued that investors looking to the League reports for information would grow more worried if they detected undue optimism, but Zimmerman tried to obtain concessions from the Financial Committee that might help the Austrian government back home.[46] Given the delicate political situation in Vienna, Zimmerman thought it unwise to let the Austrian government face state worker demands empty-handed, and told the Financial Committee that he thought Austrian demands moderate and not entirely exaggerated.[47] Freeing loan funds for electrification, which would allow paying the promised advance to state workers without incurring a deficit, would be of help to the Austrian government.[48] Kienböck, too, stressed how vital it was that the Austrian delegation return to Vienna with some proof of success, but Strakosch and Niemeyer rebuffed the proposal, arguing that investing money from the loan, before the deficit had permanently vanished, would be irresponsible.

The compromise solution that emerged from several debates among experts on the Financial Committee in June was to draft two reports, with only the first made public and intended to calm investors. It made no promises on the Austrian budget, but instead suggested that a new delegation visit Austria to study the state of its economy and reconstruction in August. The second, secret report for the Council raised serious concerns about the Austrian situation, and the Austrian government was given a confidential summary of the latter. There had been no reduction in expenditure, it claimed, nor had there been sufficient progress on administrative reforms in Austria. Furthermore, the reduction of state workers was taking place too slowly, pensions were exceedingly generous, and the government lacked fiscal control over the local authorities.[49] And while the League Financial Committee conceded that in light of Austria's financial and economic development, the League's limit on expenditure might be raised, it expressed doubt on whether Austria could sustain the taxation necessary to carry Kienböck's budget.[50] The ongoing financial crisis made the situation still too unclear to allow the Financial Committee to suggest a concrete figure, while using the loan remainder for anything but the budget deficit contravened the conditions set down in the loan prospectus and would be a "breach of faith with the bondholders."[51] For now the Austrian government would have to stick with the figures agreed upon with the League's financial experts in 1922 and avoid using the loan funds for anything but covering potential deficits. In an unprecedented step, Zimmerman, who had hoped for a more conciliatory Financial Committee, refused to sign the secret report.[52]

Zimmerman had grown increasingly sympathetic to the plight of the Austrian government. From being its adversary, he had become a facilitator between Vienna and Geneva. This was partly because he had grown to appreciate the specificities of Austria's political predicaments and partly because he was better informed about the actual state of Austria's economic and financial development. But he certainly also wished to be relieved of his position and to return to Holland on time. Privately, Zimmerman therefore favored increasing the budget level and reaching a compromise with Austria that would allow for his control to be terminated on schedule. In vain the General Commissioner had pushed the Financial Committee to help the Austrian government by giving it some indication of the future budget level or allowing use of loan funds to pay for electrification of the railways. The General Commissioner's refusal to sign the confidential second report clearly signaled his dissatisfaction to the League Council and Financial Committee over their prevarication. Zimmerman had done their bidding in 1922 and had falsely hoped that the League would listen to him in return. Instead, he was charged with informing the Austrians that their budget remained excessive and that the extraordinary revenues everyone had witnessed in 1923 were very unlikely to return. Privately Zimmerman continued to mediate between Vienna and Geneva, but he stayed loyal to the League and in his communications with Austrian ministers he remained stern. Continuing his efforts to limit any new expenditures by keeping them provisional or by opposing them altogether, his relationship with the Austrian government remained tense and adversarial.[53]

The Delegation to Vienna in August

The Austrian ministers returned to Vienna without achievements. There had been no decision on the budget or on the usage of the loan reminder, nor had there been any indication as to whether control would be lifted in time. Instead, there would be a further League delegation, which would study the state of Austrian reconstruction and recommend its findings to the Council in September.[54] Reacting to the Financial Committee's report, the Socialist *Arbeiterzeitung* declared the Austrian government defeated and Finance Minister Kienböck faced agitated state workers who had hoped an increased budget would pay for permanently higher wages.[55] After negotiations between workers and the Finance Ministry were broken off and the government was presented with an ultimatum in July, Kienböck agreed to increase wages if and once the index was suspended and the pension automatism was abolished.[56] To reach a compromise on the Austrian budget with the upcoming Financial Committee delegates, Zimmerman told Kienböck, it was essential to have detailed figures by August. Negotiations would be much facilitated, too, if Interior Minister Felix Frank immediately adopted the other outstanding reform measures cited by the Financial Committee in June.[57] Writing to Salter, Zimmerman explained that the inbound delegates would need to remind the Austrian government that, if it wished to see international control wound up at any time, it had to cut expenditures and balance the budget at a realistic level.[58]

The members of the Financial Committee started arriving in Vienna during the month of August and as usual settled into the luxurious Hotel Imperial on Vienna's splendid Ringstrasse.[59] The group of international financial experts much resembled the one of October 1922 and consisted of the Belgian banker Albert Janssen, the Dutch banker C. E. Ter Meulen, Otto Niemeyer, the French financial expert Jean Parmentier, the Swiss banker Léopold Dubois, the Czech banker Vilém Pospíšil, and a stand-in for the Italian banker Guiseppe Bianchini. Concerned about the financial crisis' negative effects for the Austrian economy, they first interviewed representatives of Austria's main economic sectors before addressing the budget question.[60]

The delegates discovered that bankers and industrialists were relatively optimistic about Austria's outlook, and that the main challenge they all faced was the scarcity and high cost of capital. Representatives of Austria's Bankenverband, the national banking association, warned that if new long-term loans from abroad were unobtainable, a way would have to be found to raise capital by placing Austrian industrial bonds in foreign markets. Worker representatives from Austria's Arbeiterkammer were also certain that some industries would be forced to vanish and that unemployment would increase if foreign capital did not become more readily available.[61] All appeared convinced that the banking crisis was generally over, and even though industrial production and exports appeared almost unaffected by the crisis, the delegates were of the opinion that its effects could only be known after some time. Much depended on the supply of credit, and especially long-term loans, to replace the foreign funds that had been withdrawn, while prices and the exchange had to be watched carefully.[62]

Based on their interviews and on their inquiries into the Austrian budget, the financial experts agreed that spending could be increased to 480 million gold crowns (about $96 million), and that if expenditure for 1925 and the budget for 1926 remained balanced within these limits, they could discuss terminating control by the end of the following year. This implied that the Austrian government needed to reduce expenditures by a further 35 million gold crowns (by about $7 million) and required it to finally regulate its fiscal relationship with the local authorities once and for all. Finance Minister Kienböck promised a written answer by the time they met again in Geneva on 9 September 1924, as to how he planed to achieve these goals.[63] Niemeyer thought that a compromise along these lines, perhaps even granting the Austrians a balanced budget of 490 million gold crowns (almost $100 million), was likely to result in a mutual agreement. Reporting to the British envoy in Vienna before his departure, Niemeyer explained that eventually League control over the loan funds and pledged revenues would be lightened in appearance, but continue in practice, allowing for the loan remainder to gradually be spent on productive capital expenditures, such as electrification of the railways or road construction.[64]

The League Meeting in September

Chancellor Seipel, against his doctors' advice, traveled to Geneva with Foreign Minister Grünberger and Finance Minister Kienböck to attend the crucial League session in September.[65] Austrian hopes were high that an increased budget would be approved and that a schedule for the termination of control would be agreed upon. However, Kienböck had already warned Zimmerman that despite his earlier promise, he could not accept the responsibility of reducing the budget by as much as 35 million gold crowns, and addressing the League Financial Committee in Geneva, Kienböck straight-away refused to accept its offer to balance the Austrian budget at 480 million gold crowns. Notwithstanding earlier promises, he could not go below 500 million (about $100 million), he argued. Austrian expenditures for 1925 were only marginally higher than in 1924, and he could not accept the responsibility for further reductions in expenditure just because estimates established back in 1922 were lower. Kienböck explained that to reach 500 million he could make a commitment to cut the budget by 15 million gold crowns through increasing tariffs for postage and obtaining savings from the federal railways, but that he could do no more. The Finance Minister pointed out that it was not the continuation of control that he feared, but the danger to Austrian credit and reconstruction if he were forced to adhere to the unrealistic figures they had established in 1922.[66]

In what had become a familiar examination, Strakosch warned that there would be a collapse of foreign confidence if Kienböck failed to take more energetic steps, and Niemeyer threatened that control would continue in its present form if the budget were not reduced. The Swiss, Swedish, and Italian experts took a more conciliatory position, while Zimmerman himself came to Kienböck's defense, explaining that spending less in 1925 than in 1924 posed political challenges to the Austrian government that had to be taken into account. Niemeyer expressed understanding for Kienböck's reluctance to presently make commitments he might not be able to keep, but Austrians would need to understand that this simply meant a new examination would be necessary at a later point in time and control would continue unaltered into 1925. He further warned Kienböck that there was still no agreement on the Ertragsanteile and therefore no guarantee that local authorities, over which the government had no oversight, would not increase taxation to compensate for federal savings. The Financial Committee was ready to relax control, reducing Zimmerman's authority to oversee global figures without right to object to particular taxes or expenditures, but the Austrian government would have to do its part and find a way to obtain and make a commitment to the required budgetary figure.[67]

The Dutch banker C. E. Ter Meulen, who like many of his colleagues on the Financial Committee had been a member of the 1922 delegation and who now chaired its meeting, was visibly disappointed about the proceedings. As he told his colleagues, he felt that the Financial Committee had already made its utmost concession by showing willingness to raise its limit on Austrian expenditures to 480 million gold crowns (about $96 million), and he regretted that Kienböck was unwilling to budge. In his opinion, there was no sense in continuing discussions with the taciturn Finance Minister, and since control now seemed certain to remain in place, he was prepared to offer Austria a budget of 485 million. The Italian delegate Bianchini asked his colleagues why they thought an Austrian budget balanced above 500 million would be so terrible, only to have Ter Meulen remind him that the reason Strakosch, Niemeyer, and Janssen were so strongly opposed to Austria's figure was that they feared the disastrous impression it was bound to make on foreign investors. In fact, the three of them felt that if the Austrians were pressed, they could easily obtain a commitment to obtain the savings Kienböck had mentioned, which would bring the budget at least down to 495 million (almost $100 million).[68]

Zimmerman spoke out in favor of accepting Kienböck's figures as long as the Austrian government promised not to increase taxation without his prior approval. In Kienböck's defense, he reiterated that it was politically difficult for the Austrian government to spend less in 1925 than in 1924 and difficult to fix the country's budget in advance down to the last 20 million. If it accepted Kienböck's proposal, the Financial Committee would agree to a level that was perhaps excessive, but, by limiting increases in taxation, could refuse letting this concession further burden the economy. The Swiss member Léopold Dubois and the Swedish banker Marcus Wallenberg were also inclined to accept Kienböck's figures, but only as long as the Austrian government promised to cut spending to 480 million eventually. Ter Meulen sided with the hard-liners, and following the meeting informed Kienböck that the Financial Committee thought it entirely possible to cut a further 15 million in spending. It thus proposed 495 million as its utmost and final concession if Austria pledged to implement a list of outstanding reforms compiled by the delegation during its visit in August.[69]

Keen on finding an agreement, but no less eager to assert his independence, Finance Minister Kienböck expressed his willingness the next day to accept the figure of 495 million gold crowns, but only if allowed to exclude expenses and fees on universities from the federal budget. This would essentially resolve the issue by an accounting trick, and a debate ensued among the members of the Financial Committee whether it ought to be accepted. The decision was to agree to Kienböck's new proposal but to obtain further assurances of reform from the Austrian government in return. In 1922, the Geneva Protocols had not foreseen that the provinces remained free to impose their own forms of taxation. In August 1924, the Finance Committee had therefore included among its list of demands the definite regulation of the fiscal relationship between the government and provinces. Because it remained politically delicate, the Ertragsanteile had at the time been kept off the final list, but now Chancellor Seipel had to promise Ter Meulen in a confidential letter that he would begin negotiating an agreement with Vienna's socialist municipality on the Ertragsanteile immediately. In return, the Financial Committee promised to relax the Commissioner General's control as soon as this and all other reforms had been passed into law. A final inquiry would then be necessary to officially state that financial stability had been obtained and to recommend the termination of the League's intervention in Austria.[70]

The final joint report by Zimmerman and the Financial Committee for the League of Nations Council on 16 September 1924 did not reflect the nervous horse-trading that had produced it over a period of one week.[71] In a balanced way it noted both Austrian achievements and the continued need for reforms. After shortly describing the major challenges the country had faced in 1922, it laudably stated:

> Any Austrian who recalls this state of affairs, with all its dangers and anxieties must, in September 1924, feel happy at the change which has occurred in the situation within the short space of two years. The intervention of the League of Nations and a remarkable change in public opinion have made it possible to convert Austria, which was on the verge of ruin, into a re-organised State, a State far from perfect, no doubt, but one in which order is assured and calculations may be made for the future. This result has been obtained by sacrifice far less heavy than those thought to be unavoidable in 1922.[72]

Indeed, the crown had remained stable, the ANB enjoyed large foreign reserves, and businesses were, on the whole, no worse off than in other countries. But while important reforms still needed to be carried out, the largest challenge for Austrian producers was a lack of capital. As the report noted, foreign lenders were disenchanted by the banking crisis following failed speculations in stocks and the French franc. The diminution of capital in Austria and the tightness of credit had driven banks and industries to turn to the ANB for liquidity. The ANB, however, had lost $9 million in foreign reserves, while discounts and circulation had increased so that coverage had dropped from 54 to 42 percent between March and August 1924 (see Graph 5.2). The persistent trade deficit implied that Austria would further lose foreign exchange to pay for imports. While much of the Austrian industry still seemed unaffected by the crisis, the report concluded, all depended entirely on whether foreign long-term credits would become obtainable again, which would only happen soon enough if "necessary steps were taken to attract investors."[73]

To facilitate a renewed inflow of capital, the report suggested abolishing the taxes on foreign exchange and banking transactions, which made Austrian capital unnecessarily dear, and further reducing taxation hindering the issue of bonds, such as the high corporate tax. Addressing the budget, the report conceded that the adjustment of officials' salaries, Austria's liberal pension arrangement, and the general increase of world prices, justified an increase from 350 to 495 million gold crowns. Further savings would be obtained by an attached list of reforms, which, once adopted, would allow for a curtailment of the General Commissioner's powers. The policy of the Austrian government to balance the budget at a higher level had retroactively been approved. In return the government of Chancellor Seipel, if it wanted to see control terminated, had to implement all outstanding reforms and reach a compromise on the Ertragsanteile. Until then, General Commissioner Zimmerman was to stay in Vienna.

The Image of General Commissioner Zimmerman in Austria

General Commissioner Alfred Rudolph Zimmerman does not enjoy a favorable appraisal from Austrian historians. Much like the League intervention itself, Zimmerman is invariably described as dictatorial, authoritarian, and arrogant.[74] While these features were probably correct as a personal characterization, they convey a wrong image of his office and position in Vienna. As previous sections showed, institutionally the General Commissioner was rather weak and his office was regularly ignored or circumvented by Chancellor Seipel and his government. Only in the summer of 1924, with Austria depending on the League for a favorable decision on questions pertaining to its budget and the end of control, did Chancellor Seipel voice a more conciliatory tone in his correspondence with the General Commissioner. In return, Zimmerman began defending the Austrian point of view in his correspondence and interviews with the League Financial Committee in Geneva.

Only one monograph deals extensively with the work and person of General Commissioner Zimmerman in Vienna. Written in Dutch by the historian Jac Bosmans, it has remained fairly inaccessible.[75] Bosmans provides a detailed and balanced account of the General Commissioner's work, the history of the League intervention in Austria, and the sessions in Geneva, based on Viennese archives and those of the League of Nations. He concludes that the Socialists vehemently criticized Zimmerman, whereas the government parties (Christian-Social and Pan-German) were less vocal in their reproach. This was due to the fact that the government was forced to work with Zimmerman, and that it soon discovered that his influence and importance were less than initially feared. The Socialists, vilified by Austria's conservatives as a Jewish party set at bolshevizing their country, retorted with anti-Semitic imagery themselves, accusing the Christian-Socials of selling out to the interests of Jewish capital.[76] Caricatures in the socialist press displayed Zimmerman as the personification of foreign intervention, colonizing Austria on behalf of foreign or local capitalists aimed at supporting Seipel's anti-Socialist rhetoric and policies.

Upon Zimmerman's arrival in 1923, reactions in Vienna had not voiced unanimous opposition to the presence of a foreign controller. While there were outcries about infringed sovereignty, both from the Socialist left and the Pan-German right, Zimmerman received a friendly, if reserved, welcome from Austria's industrial and administrative elites. The liberal *Neue Freie Presse*, which hailed him as a "friend of Austria," welcomed him as a guarantor of badly needed good governance:

The General Commissioner will not act like a Tyrant, he will only strengthen the government's backbone, he will give it the moral authority to do what it itself desires to do and what it must do in order to live up to its commitments and prevent a relapse into the economics of stagnation and bankruptcy.[77]

Throughout Zimmerman's stay in Vienna, the bourgeois-friendly *Neue Freie Presse* in fact tried to convey a sympathetic portrait of the General Commissioner, but while he remained largely unmentioned in the Christian-Social *Reichspost*, he was continuously disparaged by the Socialist press.

Austrian historians' negative assessment of Zimmerman might be explained by their reliance on contemporary sources. The General Commissioner did not enjoy much popularity in Vienna and his picture as far as it emerges from the Austrian press is mostly negative, with the exception, as noted, of the *Neue Freie Presse*. While a careful study of archival material such as Bosmans' reveals a more nuanced image, caricatures printed during the second year of Zimmerman's presence in Austria are strikingly similar in their depiction of the General Commissioner. Socialist and socialist-friendly papers alike presented an image of Zimmerman as opportunist and callous, as moralizing yet corrupt, and as the tool of capitalist imperialism.

The caricatures that will be discussed in this section are related to the important League meetings that took place in March, June, and September 1924. These were times when the power of the League over Austria became most visible, with Austrian ministers traveling to the League headquarters for negotiations about the budget ceiling and a possible termination of League intervention. The disappointing deferrals and final refusal in Geneva were widely reported and reviewed by the Vienna press. The reports and decisions by the League Council and Financial Committee had been carefully prepared, most notably by Salter in Geneva and by Niemeyer in London, neither of whom was well known to the Viennese. Zimmerman, who played a minor but rather pro-Austrian role during these proceedings, was, however, well known to Austrians. Thus in some of the caricatures Zimmerman's image is representative of the League of Nations and its intervention in Austria; in others it is he personally, in his function as General Commissioner, that is the subject of the joke. In any case, as we shall see, the characterizations given to the League and to Zimmerman were very much the same. Zimmerman and the League of Nations were portrayed as pitiless oppressors of Austria's working class, destroying the economy in the service of an imperialist capitalist power that had come to force Austria into submission.

Possibly the first caricature (Figure 5.2) featuring Zimmerman in 1924 was published on the cover of the satirical magazine *Der Götz*, though it did not show him at all.[78] It presented the scene of a traditional nativity play, with Chancellor Seipel, Interior Minister Frank, and Finance Minister Kienböck depicted as the three Magi in the forefront. In the background stands the

FIGURE 5.2. "The sanctimonious Magi from the Borrowrient." Chancellor Ignaz Seipel, Interior Minister Felix Frank, and Finance Minister Victor Kienböck, depicted as the Magi, study a map to Geneva. They agree, "This is not the right carpenter (Zimmerman) for us." *Source: Der Götz,* 4 January 1924, p. 1. ANNO Austrian National Library.

stable of Bethlehem, surrounded by angels, in which the Savior has just been born. The joke, related in the caption, is a word play on Joseph's profession, carpentry, and the German meaning of Zimmerman, carpenter. Studying a map showing the way to Geneva, the three Magi agree, "This is not the right carpenter (Zimmerman) for us." This absurd equation of Zimmerman with a deity returns repeatedly, but here the subjects of the joke are the three Austrian ministers. The kernel of its humor is the pun on Zimmerman's name, creating the absurd notion that one might mistake Jesus for Zimmerman. But the message is political. The catholic Chancellor, Prelate and Professor for Theology, looking with his Ministers to find a savior, realize that Christ is not the one they were looking for. Instead they stick to the staunchly anti-Socialist Zimmerman and leave the benevolent son of a carpenter in the den. The juxtaposition of Zimmerman with Christ underlined the "non-Christian" identity of the General Commissioner in a country where "Austrianess" was categorically understood as being Christian or at least "non-Jewish" and therefore presented the theologian Seipel and his colleagues as hypocrites.

Another caricature appearing in the month of January, this time in the bourgeois and Socialist-friendly *Der Morgen,* featured what would have been a familiar scene for Viennese newspaper readers (Figure 5.3).[79] It showed Zimmerman, Seipel, and Kienböck singing on stage and dressed as the protagonists of Johann Nestroy's play *Der böse Geist Lumpazivagabundus.* One of the most popular productions in Vienna, the title and caption paraphrased well-known lines from the magical comedy, which has been interpreted both as a moralist tutorial or a rebellious piece decrying bourgeois values. In it, three good-for-nothing vagabonds are chosen by the Gods to see whether they have the ability to reform their ways. Through divine intervention the three drunkards win the lottery, but only one of them, the tailor, ends up settling down and leading a regular life, while the cobbler and carpenter (Tischler, not Zimmerman in the German original) fail to amend their ways and, inevitably, find themselves penniless again.

The play's moralizing content, commending bourgeois values of industriousness and sincerity, and its simultaneous celebration of frivolousness and joie de vivre, form the basis for this caricature. Critical of Seipel and Kienböck, Zimmerman is assigned the role of the tailor, who eventually ends up leading a rehabilitated life, whereas the two Austrians are given the roles of

FIGURE 5.3. "A poor reformed state I ask you very nicely." Zimmerman, Seipel, and Kienböck singing on stage and dressed up as the protagonists of Johann Nestroy's play *Der böse Geist Lumpazivagabundus*. *Source: Der Morgen, 7 January 1924, p. 14.* ANNO Austrian National Library.

cobbler and carpenter, who will always fail to be reformed. But the rewording of the original lyrics puts the scene at the play's beginning: the three incurable men have all just met and decided to try their luck in town and find an inn to get drunk at. The contrasting paraphrase of the original lyrics replaces the protagonists' desire for alcohol with a desire for economic reforms, and accuses Zimmerman of failing to see the importance of funding science and the arts.

The joke here lies in the absurdity of casting the figures as characters anything like their real personae. If the juxtaposition of the serious politicians with lazy vagabonds creates part of the humor, it is further accentuated by the illogical identity of the protagonists' desire for alcohol and frivolity with the Austrian politicians' and General Commissioner's quest for economic savings. The reforms are equated with an unhealthy dependence, damaging yet to them joyful. Much as the cobbler, carpenter, and tailor cannot be trusted with money because of their alcoholism, Seipel, Kienböck, and Zimmerman must not be given power over Austrian economy and culture, which they will use inevitably to feed their unhealthy and destructive addiction to austerity.

Whereas these critical caricatures in January were as much about the Austrian government as about the General Commissioner, two caricatures published the following month made fun of Zimmerman alone. The first, published on 24 February in the Socialist *Arbeiterzeitung,* featured him as the angry Almighty (Figure 5.4).[80] Titled "Thus Spoke the Lord—Dr Zimmerman," a pun on Nietzsche's famous title *Thus Spoke Zarathustra,* it is a cartoon showing the General Commissioner as an all-knowing and

FIGURE 5.4. "Thus Spoke the Lord—Dr. Zimmerman." A pun on Nietzsche's famous title *Thus Spoke Zarathustra,* the cartoon shows the General Commissioner as an all-knowing and all-seeing God, whose scorn knows no mercy for his people. The caption reads "Jehova, the Zealous God from Rotterdam." *Source: Arbeiterzeitung,* 24 February 1924, p. 7. ANNO Austrian National Library.

all-seeing God whose scorn knows no mercy for his people. In a series of frames, Zimmerman is exposed as pitiless with members of the working class, while generous to industrialists and bankers. Humoristic two-liners demonstrate the absurd policies of Zimmerman, which destroy an entire economy with the sole aim of securing his own salary. The final shot shows Zimmerman on his throne ruling over Austria in splendid isolation. Using the Hebrew terminology for the biblical God of the Israelites, the caption reads *Jehova, the Zealous God from Rotterdam*, categorizing Zimmerman as "Jewish" and thus both foreign and harmful to Austria.

A similarly religious imagery of zealotry is found in another February caricature (Figure 5.5).[81] Published the following day, 25 February, in *Der Morgen*, it displays Zimmerman dressed as a Capuchin monk by his luxury car preaching to the people of Austria. In the caption, a paraphrase of the well-known Kapuzinerpredigt from Friedrich Schiller's play *Wallenstein,* he moralizingly calls on the people to be content with their lot and refrain from evil habits. Laconically, the caption notes that the cleric preaches low wages and parsimony as the way to enter paradise, before instructing the chauffeur in his eight-cylinder limousine to drive him to collect his own "modest monthly remuneration." The original scene in Schiller's drama has a monk encountering drunken soldiers in Wallenstein's camp, provoking his stern lecture. But unlike the religious Capuchin, Zimmerman here is criticized as an opportunist hypocrite who preaches water while drinking wine.

The imagery of Zimmerman as a hypocrite interested in prolonging League control for his own extravagant remuneration enjoyed particular popularity. Following the League's March session, at which the Austrian government had first brought forward its questions regarding budget and control, two almost identical caricatures appeared, one in the Socialist *Arbeiterwille* and the other in the Viennese *Arbeiterzeitung,* though with differing captions. The image showed Seipel and Zimmerman both dressed as Roman augurs walking on the "Forum XII. Novembris" (the First Austrian Republic had been founded on 12 November 1918), while in the background Kienböck can be seen offering a sacrifice to the League of Nations in the form of the loan remainder (the usage of which to electrify the railways had been denied). In the version published by the *Arbeiterwille,* Zimmerman says to Seipel: "Now you know dear Chancellor that you will only get rid of men when I will be guaranteed to receive somewhere else an income as high as I

Rarifatur der Woche.

Generalfommiffär Dr. Zimmerman.

„Was sagt der Prediger? Contenti estote,
Begnügt euch mit eurem Kommißbrote:
Seid zufrieden mit eurer Löhnung
Und verflucht jede böse Angewöhnung!
Laßt euch vom Sparsinn leiten bloß:
So kommt ihr sicher in Abrahams Schoß!"

(Er nimmt bei den letzten Worten in seinem achtzylindrigen
Auto Platz und fährt fort — seine bescheidene Monatslöhnung
zu beheben.)   Frei nach Schiller.

FIGURE 5.5. "Caricature of the Week. General Commissioner Dr. Zimmerman." Zimmerman, dressed as a Capuchin monk, stands next to his luxury car, preaching to the people of Austria. In the caption, he moralizingly calls on the people to be content with their lot and to refrain from evil habits.

"Contenti estote, the preacher said?
Be content with your army bread:
Be happy with your pay
And curse each evil way!
Let savings be your only guide:
And you'll safely enter paradise!"

(And with these words he takes his seat in his eight-cylinder car and drives off to collect his modest monthly remuneration.) Based on Schiller. *Source: Der Morgen*, 25 February 1924, p. 5. ANNO Austrian National Library.

get in Austria."[82] To which the Chancellor replies: "Yes, you are right. But I could not believe that the dear Almighty thinks higher of the mayor of Amsterdam [*sic;* Rotterdam] than of his own Prelate." According to the *Arbeiterzeitung* caption ("Those in the Know," Figure 5.6), Zimmerman and Seipel, both clasping the texts of their speeches, agree "on our final goal—to stay in our positions as long as possible."[83] An aphorism above the two reads: "In ancient Rome there was a saying: When two augurs cross paths, they smile."

The Financial Committee, postponing its answer to the Austrian requests in February, had shown that it was in no rush to leave Austria, which the *Arbeiterwille* blamed on Zimmerman's interest in money. Its title, "Who eats from the Carpenter . . . ," relates the scene to John 6:54 and the Holy

FIGURE 5.6. "Those in the Know." Zimmerman and Seipel, both clasping the texts of their speeches, agree "on our final goal—to stay in our positions as long as possible." An aphorism above the two reads: "In ancient Rome there was a saying: When two augurs cross paths, they smile." Here the Prelate and the General Commissioner are depicted as hypocritical religious authorities, fooling the population in order to secure and perpetuate their own influential positions. *Source: Arbeiterzeitung,* 21 March 1924, p. 7. ANNO Austrian National Library.

Communion, this time contrasting Zimmerman's behavior with that of Christ.[84] The anticlerical caricature also ridicules Seipel's religious ideals, and thereby the Catholic Church, by having him blasphemously equate the Financial Committee with the Lord and his love for members of the clergy. But unlike the true Christ and the Heavenly Father, Zimmerman and the Financial Committee have no attention, mercy, or love to spare for common people. In the version published by the *Arbeiterzeitung,* the Prelate and the General Commissioner are depicted as hypocritical religious authorities, working together and fooling the population in order to secure and perpetuate their own influential positions.

The common characteristics of Zimmerman's depiction in these caricatures, his pompous and moralizing demeanor coupled with a heartless and materialistic personality, reappear alongside similar imagery of the League of Nations. Following the Financial Committee's June session, which had again postponed answering the Austrian requests, sending a delegation to Vienna instead, the Socialist *Arbeiterzeitung* printed a caricature titled "After the Battle of Geneva" (Figure 5.7).[85] The victorious General Zimmerman is granted a triumphant procession into Vienna, his chariot drawn by the Christian-Social Ministers Kienböck and Grünberger, while the "barbarian" Pan-German Ministers Frank, Waber, and Schürff are paraded as prisoners of war. Zimmerman, impersonating the foreign goddess Cybele, is instantaneously ridiculed by the sorry state of his Austrian hostages. The Austrian capitalist class, ailing but secure, grimly looks on. It is a straightforward caricature, meant to portray the absent Socialists as Austria's only remaining sane force. What makes it particularly interesting is the way it presents members of the League's impending delegation. Following upon Zimmerman, its members bear *insignia* of dollar and pound sterling, and their unfriendly demeanors have been orientalized and racialized. The ancient Roman setting associates their imminent arrival with the troops of imperial conquerors, but these troops are crude and non-European. Zimmerman and the League

FIGURE 5.7. "After the Battle of Geneva." The victorious General Zimmerman is granted a triumphant procession into Vienna, his chariot drawn by the Christian-Social ministers Kienböck and Grünberger, while the "barbarian" Pan-German ministers Frank, Waber, and Schürff are paraded as prisoners of war. *Source: Arbeiterzeitung*, 25 June 1924, p. 7. ANNO Austrian National Library.

are cast as the occupying legions of international capital, marching in the service of the country's capitalist class, yet foreign and coarse.

A very similar take on the League of Nations intervention as an imperialist, colonial project appeared two weeks later in *Der Morgen* ("We Shnorrers Greet You," Figure 5.8).[86] Once more, the town of Vienna is transposed to the ancient city of Rome, underscoring the imperialist character of League intervention, or perhaps Austria's own imperial past. Titled "Schnorrituri te Salutant," it shows yet another traditional Roman scene, that of gladiators greeting their Emperor before engaging in mortal combat. The role of the fighters is performed by broke Austrian capitalists and failed speculators, filing past Zimmerman, giving the Roman salute. Legionary insignia and a

FIGURE 5.8. "We Shnorrers Greet You." Once more, the town of Vienna is transposed to the ancient city of Rome, underscoring the imperialist character of League intervention. It shows yet another traditional Roman scene, that of gladiators greeting their emperor before engaging in mortal combat. The role of the fighters is performed by broke Austrian capitalists and failed speculators, filing past Zimmerman and giving the Roman salute. Source: *Der Morgen*, 7 July 1924, p. 16. ANNO Austrian National Library.

helmet further underline the scene's classic character. Zimmerman, draped in a toga atop the steps of the Vienna Stock Exchange, mightily oversees the pitiful procession while reclining on bags containing the loan reminder and his own salary. Flanking the General Commissioner are representatives of the League of Nations and members of the Financial Committee delegation to Vienna. The financial experts, elderly and skeptical, carefully observe the parade, taking notes while contemplating the state of Austrian finance. Yet they remain detached and emotionally unaffected by the sorry picture unfolding before their eyes. Members of the League, seated on Zimmerman's other side, are presented not just as foreign, but once again as oriental and racially diverse. An angry Japanese, a bewildered African, and a figure sporting a turban join four grim European representatives. The colonialist character of Zimmerman and the League is underlined by the figure of Finance Minister Kienböck, kneeling and barely clad, waving a palm branch. Another servant (ANB President Richard Reisch?), ringing the closing bell of the Vienna Stock Exchange, sports a toga and fasces, underscoring the associations of imperialist capital and foreign domination.

Whether the joke was on the Austrian government, on Austrian capitalists, or on the League of Nations and its General Commissioner, the latter was portrayed in the Socialist-friendly press as motivated by greed, serving his own material interests and those of the ruling capitalist classes, as non-Austrian, non-Christian, and quintessentially foreign. Zimmerman and the League are never ridiculed as powerless, never shown as being taken advantage of by Austrians and their government or as trying to genuinely advise or assist. Both are servants of international capital, which self-servingly took advantage of the Austria's plight to the detriment of its working class and economy. Though this image reflected an erroneous or at best partial understanding of the work done by Zimmerman and the Financial Committee, the view of the League and its officials as malevolent proved surprisingly resilient in Austria. It served, after all, to expunge Austrian politicians, both Socialist and conservative, of their failures and responsibilities. Whether as colleagues of Zimmerman or as the League's prisoners, Austrian politicians were presented as bereft of power.

As has been demonstrated, Zimmerman himself complained to the League of being powerless himself, and the Austrian government, neither his slave nor his captive, successfully asserted its freedom during 1923 and 1924.

During the second year of League intervention, Zimmerman in fact defended Austrian points of view and tried to influence the Financial Committee to adopt a more conciliatory position. Describing the General Commissioner as a foreign dictator in accordance with how he was depicted in the above caricatures is thus historically inaccurate. Nor was the League of Nations an instrument of foreign bankers. But perhaps the most compelling case of how Austrians withstood foreign pressures during the years of League intervention was ANB President Reisch's refusal to follow the advice of Norman at the BoE.

Central Bank Cooperation

During 1924, as the League intervention in Austria was being prolonged, cooperation between the BoE and the ANB slowly foundered. In the eyes of Governor Montagu Norman, the financial crisis in Austria made it imperative to increase the ANB's discount rate, but the latter's President, Richard Reisch, was not prepared to stimulate deflation. A continued fall in prices might have facilitated the balancing of fiscal accounts and helped exports, but it would also have provoked more bankruptcies, economic contraction, and heightened unemployment. Zimmerman had hoped that the League delegation visiting Vienna in August would help push the ANB toward a higher discount rate and in his nineteenth report chastised the ANB's lax discounting policy, causing a scandal by publishing excerpts of it in the Austrian press. Reisch reacted by offering to resign and publicly attacking the General Commissioner in return.[87]

What Austria needed most was capital, and a "peripheral" country like Austria was in fact unlikely to attract fresh inflows by increasing the discount rate, even if done drastically.[88] After the rate was raised twice to appease Norman, the League, and potential foreign lenders in mid-1924, it had had little effect on the ANB's balance sheet.[89] Short-term capital was readily available abroad, but Austrian banks were hesitant to borrow because they did not trust the stability of the crown and were not ready to carry the exchange risk. In order to encourage the inflow of capital, therefore, the ANB began as of August 1924 to contractually guarantee the availability of foreign exchange to Vienna banks in return for their foreign deposits. Against a fee they offered them repurchase agreements with a fixed exchange rate. Immediately the amount of foreign currency thus deposited at the ANB in return for crowns, or put into Kost (as was the technical term), increased, and discounts to Vienna banks fell (see Graph 5.2).

Despite the improvement of the ANB's balance sheet, Finance Minister Kienböck reassured Zimmerman in November 1924 that he thought the time for a reduction of the discount rate had not yet come.[90] Niemeyer warned that reducing the rate in November would be "very nearly suicidal," while Norman himself wrote to foreign Conseiller van Gijn that the city regarded a reduction as "unjustified" and would react "with surprise" to such a step.[91] Norman wanted to see deflation, and neither had prices started to fall, nor was an economic contraction under way. General Commissioner Zimmerman agreed with London, but President Reisch thought it impossible to leave the rate unchanged in light of the high economic cost it entailed and in view of the bank's improved balance sheet. The rate was thus lowered from 15 to 13 percent on 5 November 1924, and envoy Franckenstein was instructed to alleviate concerns at the BoE by emphasizing the improved position of the ANB's discount portfolio and foreign currency reserves, which had returned to their April level.[92]

In order to explain the ANB's discount policy and create confidence in London, President Reisch traveled to meet with Governor Norman in December 1924.[93] Conseiller van Gijn had previously been told by Strakosch, who had Norman's ear, that rising prices and the high percentage of financial bills among the ANB's portfolio had spoken against reducing the rate and that what Austria needed was deflation.[94] Norman was indeed worried about prices in Austria and planned on impressing personally on Reisch the "vital point" that there had been "for some time a steady rise in Austrian prices which, if it continues, will endanger the entire reconstruction scheme." Norman, who had wanted to use the League intervention in Austria to start creating a network of independent central banks in Europe, favored deflation as a means to reduce wages globally. He expected that the ANB would cooperate on monetary policy and follow the BoE's lead, but Reisch was not playing along.

In Norman's view, rising prices resulted from the ANB's lax discounting of bills and acceptance of Kostdevisen (foreign deposits put into Kost with ANB by banks), both of which increased circulation without a corresponding raise in the ANB's freely available foreign currency reserves

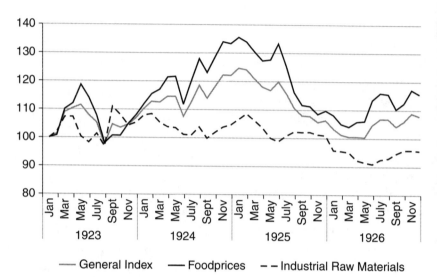

GRAPH 5.6. Austrian price indexes, 1924–1926 (January 1923=100). *Source:* Österreichisches Bundesamt für Statistik.

(see Graphs 5.2 and 5.6).[95] For Norman, higher prices made Austrian exporters less competitive and increased government expenditure, making Austria's balance of payments worse and putting a balanced budget and reconstruction in danger. Norman was convinced that a tight monetary policy would check the rise in prices, but Reisch argued that the Governor was wrong because Austria was not a price-setter and its price-level was fundamentally dependent on the cost of imported goods.[96]

Rather, Reisch stressed, the recent increase in prices was a natural adjustment to world prices and could not be checked by increasing the discount rate or contracting the money supply. He told Norman that Austrian prices were determined by the high cost of raw material imports, so that not only had the reduction of the bank rate to 13 percent been necessary and justified, but further reductions to foster the economy would probably be necessary in the future.[97] Reisch would reduce production costs, but do so by lowering the cost of capital, not prices, while protecting currency stability through making sure the amount of discounted bills remained steady and foreign capital continued to come in via the Kostgeschäft.[98]

Norman was angry that Reisch refused to fall in line and bring on deflation through a high interest rate level. Reisch had wished to discuss the pos-

sibility of issuing an Austrian loan in London to pay for railway electrification, but now Norman cut him short, arguing that foreign loans could only
lead to renewed speculation and inflation.[99] Only a few years earlier, Norman
said, Austria had enjoyed more sympathy in London than any other country,
but now confidence in Austria was shattered. The Governor feared that the
discount rate had been lowered under pressure from Austrian bankers and
industrialists, and if prices rose further, he worried, the Austrian budget would
not remain balanced. A renewed deficit meant a renewed danger of inflation
and put the currency's stability at risk, undermining his and all the League's
efforts on Austria's behalf. Under these circumstances, Norman told Reisch, he
could not support the request for an electrification loan and he would oppose any new borrowing by Austria until the ANB's policy changed.[100]

Reisch himself felt that the Austrian position was not understood in
London and that Norman paid undue attention to the price level because of
its potential effect on the League's reconstruction scheme.[101] Norman's view
that prices depended foremost on the level of money supply was essentially
wrong, Reisch thought, and he was determined to return to London within
several months to convince the Governor of his superior understanding of
economic theory. Norman, on the other hand, had made it clear that accepting his opinion was crucial if Austrians wanted to obtain loans in
London, so that Franckenstein, alarmed about the dangerous lack of understanding between Reisch and Norman, warned Vienna.[102] According to the
Austrian envoy, it was indeed possible that Reisch knew more about central
banking than Norman, but for the good of Austria, Reisch had to swallow
his pride and better carry out Norman's desires:

It might well be that in theoretical knowledge we are more or less superior to the English; . . . The overpowering question is however: Do we
require British sympathy, Anglo-Saxon capital, foreign confidence and
the help of the most powerful financier, our proven and great friend
Mr. Norman? If so, we must shed vanity, sensitivity and suspicion for
the good of our Fatherland and accept the current power-relations with
courage and determination.[103]

Franckenstein suggested that Reisch follow Norman down a deflationary
path for the sake of long-term loans, but the ANB President feared the

consequences such a decision would have for the Austrian economy and refused to change course.[104]

At the center of the disagreement between the two bankers stood the question whether higher prices had been caused by increasing credit. Reisch
knew that an augmented circulation could drive up prices if spent on speculative activity or consumption. However, if used for productive investments
that created growth and jobs, it was entirely beneficial and also less likely to
affect prices immediately. The disagreement between Reisch and Norman
was thus one about whether Austrians were squandering foreign loans, as
they appeared to have done during 1923, and whether foreign funds placed
in Kost were being used productively, whether liquidity provided by the ANB
was used for speculation and to cover speculative losses, or to buy equipment
and machinery. Otto Niemeyer concluded that Austrian monetary policy
was totally unsound and that Reisch did "not even appear to understand the
economic principles involved."[105] Norman's failure to persuade Reisch to
follow "a strong monetary policy" and contain the rise in prices thus made
strengthening League control in the eyes of the Financial Committee's most
dominant member more urgent than ever.

The financial crisis in Austria had put a successful completion of the reconstruction scheme at risk. While in 1923 the League had been willing to
overlook the high budgetary expenses for the sake of investor confidence, it
now insisted that the agreements be more meticulously kept and decided to
postpone ending its control on time. This position was possible, because, as
opposed to 1923, investor confidence was no longer of primary importance.
The League loans had already been floated, and moreover the financial crisis
had previously dampened whatever optimism foreign investors might have
had. Chancellor Seipel, who at the beginning of 1924 still hoped control
would end in December, now had to be satisfied with a promise that an end
of control would be contemplated twelve months thereafter. The fact that the
Financial Committee approved of a budget significantly higher than what
had been foreseen in November 1922, however, proved to the Austrian government that it did not have to accept all Geneva's directives. Finance Minister Kienböck had heroically stood his ground, but the challenging reforms
Chancellor Seipel had agreed to implement in return, above all finalizing the
fiscal and administrative relationship between the Federal government and
provinces, would bring about the fall of his government back in Vienna.

In the end, no Austrian football team had traveled to attend the Olympic Games in France that summer as the Austrian government was unable or unwilling to cover the costs of sending a national delegation. But a private fund-raising campaign managed to support the participation of almost fifty Austrian athletes, who competed in eight out of twenty disciplines.[106] The Viennese *Sportblatt* argued that Vienna's socialist municipality should have found a way to finance Austria's participation because of the Olympic commitment to pacifism and sport's unique ability to unite individuals across all nations.[107] Looking back at the games, however, the Socialist *Arbeiterzeitung* heavily criticized the claim that the "bourgeois" event was fraternizing and committed to promoting peace. Not just the decision to exclude Germany had been questionable, but a general atmosphere of competitive nationalism had reigned in Paris, which belied the claim that the games were not political.[108] For once, the liberal *Neue Freie Presse*, summing up the international happening itself, agreed. More than at preceding sporting events, it commented, nationalism had been palpable at the Paris "battle of nations," and the newspaper found it particularly worrisome that jurors and referees had repeatedly made embarrassing decisions that smacked of blatant favoritism.[109]

Zimmerman was accused of lacking neutrality and the press, particularly Socialist publications, continued to depict him as partial and as an oppressive subjugator of the Austrian economy, too. In fact but probably unknown and despite his difficult personality, he was also a conciliatory factor trying to facilitate a compromise between Vienna and Geneva on more than one occasion. The League was certainly choosing an inflexible position, insisting that the Austrian government fulfill all outstanding reforms and delaying the end of its Austrian intervention. But this in fact revealed the League's weakness, which had no other means to enforce its side of the bargain than to refuse lifting its control. Zimmerman himself sympathized with the Austrian view and considered it vital to find a compromise that would allow him to go home to Rotterdam. But the League's determined behavior was also due to the ANB's decision to follow a policy independent from London. Norman remained disappointed, if not betrayed, by the ANB's refusal to hold rates high enough to bring about deflation to reduce prices and wages, the current account deficit, and public expenditures. The Governor would continue to try and pressure the ANB to bring about those changes, without which, he argued, trade and balance of payment deficits would persist and the League scheme would remain at risk. Unless the Austrian government and central bank proved to be more cooperative, the League intervention, he warned, could not be brought to a happy conclusion. Despite Norman's admonitions, however, the termination of League control would be initiated much sooner, and before the League Financial Committee thought it had been crowned with success.

6

The Politics of Control

1925–1926

There exists in some quarters a certain uneasiness about
the Anschluss movement and there the feeling prevails
that the suppression of the Control might strengthen the
national sentiment and so weaken the movement for the
joining to Germany.

—General Commissioner Alfred Rudolph Zimmerman
28 July 1925

ON THE FIRST DAY OF 1925, Austria introduced a new currency to replace the crown. Ten thousand Austrian crowns were exchanged for one
Austrian schilling (sch.), which itself was broken down into 100 groschen.
The adoption of the new currency incurred not just a visual break with the
Austrian National Bank's (ANB) old monetary system, but signaled the central bank's determination to definitively overcome inflation, too. The design
of the new silver schilling featured the Austrian parliament building and,
like most of the other coins, prominently identified the young Republic as
its emitter. New schilling notes still portrayed idealized heads on their front,
but these were rendered younger than on former notes and also male, with
modern ornamentations, indicating a break with the past and presenting
Austrians with a forward-looking and rejuvenated currency.[1] The ANB immediately switched its accounts to the new denomination, but businesses had
until July 1926 to adapt their accounting practices. Incidentally, this would
also be the time when the League intervention in Austria would come to its
official end.

The financial crisis in 1924 had strengthened the case for League control
in Austria. Instead of being terminated according to schedule, it was now

extended by another year, to last at least until the end of 1925. For the League to eventually declare Austrian reconstruction complete, the Austrian government would not get around implementing the full list of reforms, intended to stabilize the balanced budget and help the country attract foreign capital. Apart from tax reform and administrative measures to obtain economies, it included the politically sensitive curtailing of the fiscal autonomy of local authorities. There also still existed federal administrative offices in the provinces, which had to be closed or united with local services. Chancellor Seipel would resign over the political challenges posed by these reforms and leave it to a successor government to enforce the agreements reached with Financial Committee of the League of Nations. As stipulated by the Geneva Protocols of 1922, for international control to end, the League Council, which relied on the Financial Committee for expert advice, had to assert that permanent financial and economic stability in Austria was obtained. It was paramount to please the Financial Committee if Austria wished to regain full freedom over fiscal policy, spend the loan remainder on productive investments, or issue new foreign loans to raise fresh capital on financial markets.

Upon returning to Vienna from Geneva in September 1924, Finance Minister Viktor Kienböck informed General Commissioner Zimmerman that secret negotiations with the heads of the provinces were under way. At the same time, a draft budget agreed upon with the Financial Committee was presented to parliament in October, including higher wages for state workers. Workers with the autonomous railways, led by Pan-Germans and National Socialists, went on strike demanding similar compensation, and Seipel seized the opportunity of the strike to step down.[2] Ostensibly he blamed the railway workers for his decision, but in fact he was making no progress in his negotiations with representatives of the provincial wing of his party and hoped that his resignation would pressure them into agreement.[3] After another ten days of inconclusive talks Seipel announced that he had exhausted his efforts to form a new government and would not resume office.[4] As Kienböck explained to Zimmerman, the ex-Chancellor would remain at the head of the Christian-Social party and thus still be involved in political affairs, but had chosen to leave the task of completing reconstruction to a new government.[5]

Seipel had stood at the helm of the Austrian government since 1922 and would return to the Chancellery once international control was lifted. Meanwhile the successor cabinet implemented most of the outstanding reforms, so that within less than a year the League Council would recommend ending control and declaring Austria permanently stabilized. However, this chapter argues, it did so against the better judgment of most members of the Financial Committee, who considered Austria's position still precariously unstable. As will be shown, the motives behind the League Council's decision to terminate control were mainly political. For one thing, as we have already seen, General Commissioner Zimmerman and the League scheme had become increasingly unpopular in Austria, and calls for unification with Germany were being voiced more forcefully. To strengthen Austrian nationalism, Italy and France, the two Powers most opposed to Anschluss, were in favor of putting an end to the League's intervention, even if prematurely. Furthermore, with almost all reforms executed, what the League Financial Committee had not achieved so far, it was unlikely to obtain by continuing control. And finally, members of League Financial Secretariat in Geneva thought that if termination was offered to Austria earlier than necessary, then its government might be persuaded to make some valuable concessions that could help minimize the risk of Austria falling back into economic and financial disarray.

The Christian-Social government that inherited reconstruction from Seipel's cabinet in November 1924 was headed by Chancellor Rudolf Ramek, a politician considered "practically unknown" by the British envoy to Vienna.[6] Born in 1881 in Austrian Silesia, Ramek had trained as a lawyer and then practiced in Salzburg before the war. Following the Armistice he had been elected to parliament and from 1919 to 1920 served as Minister of Interior and Justice under Socialist Chancellor Karl Renner. Ramek's choice as Foreign Minister was Heinrich Mataja, a Viennese lawyer born in 1877, who represented the more liberal, Viennese wing of the Christian-Social party. The Finance Ministry fell to Jakob Ahrer, born in 1888, a lawyer by training and deputy head of the province of Styria.[7] Overall, the rejuvenated cabinet represented a power shift away from the Christian-Social party's Vienna block toward its provincial wing, which had successfully resisted Seipel's attempts to curtail the provinces' fiscal autonomy. It fell to this new government to complete reconstruction, which, beyond implementing all outstanding reforms, as agreed upon in September 1924, required keeping the budget for 1925 balanced and no higher than 495 million gold crowns. The task was

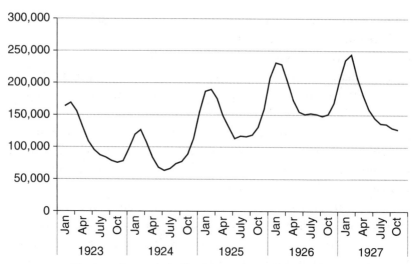

GRAPH 6.1. Number of Austrians officially unemployed, January 1923–October 1927. *Sources:* Zimmerman reports and LNA, R 519, Rapport confidentiel de M. Rost von [*sic*] Tonningen au Comité Financier, 30 November 1927.

particularly difficult because the financial crisis had turned into a fiscal and economic one as well, burdening the budget with social welfare and unemployment payments. In early 1925 the actual number of Austrians out of work surpassed 200,000 and in per capita terms was the highest in the world (see Graph 6.1).[8]

Austria's long-term economic stability, and particularly that of its currency, remained threatened by the country's current account deficit. A negative current account was indicative of a net outflow of capital, which would necessarily cut into the ANB's reserves if it wished to keep exchange rates fixed. What appeared particularly worrisome to observers was that despite the financial crisis and stock-exchange rout in 1924, the gap in Austria's trade balance had widened that year (see Graph 6.2). Before the war, trade among the various parts of the Austro-Hungarian Empire had functioned practically unhindered, but the sovereign states created by the peace treaties had all instituted their own customs and tariffs. The Porto Rosa conference of Successor States in October 1921 had not only fallen short of creating a customs union between Austria, Czechoslovakia, and Hungary as proposed by the Paris Peace Treaties, but the conference resolution to at least drop trade restrictions had not resulted in any effective treaties either. With almost half

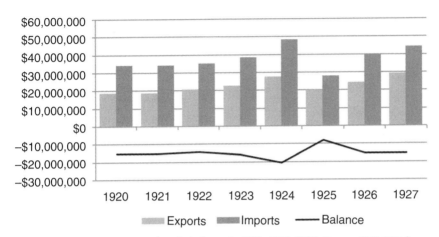

GRAPH 6.2. Austrian annual trade balance in US$, 1920–1927. *Sources:* 1923–1927 from LNA, C 40, Statistics Commerce; 1920–1922 from Nicole Piétri, "La réconstruction économique et financière de l'Autriche par la Société des Nations (1921–1926)" (doctoral thesis, Université de Paris I, 1981), p. 1004.

of its foreign commerce still with Habsburg successor states, Austria continued to promote the idea of free trade in the region, while many of the new countries tried to strengthen their industrial or agricultural sectors with protectionist tariffs and import bans.[9] This hurt Austrian exports, whereas the country still remained dependent on imports for food (grains, fats, sugar, and cattle) and for most primary materials and inputs used by its manufacturers and industry (mainly coal, but also textiles, metals, and rubber).[10] Austrian Trade Emissary Richard Schüller's untiring attempts to pursue bilateral trade agreements with Austria's neighbors were arduous and only crowned with partial success as cross-border trade among the successor states generally declined.

Food imports explained almost all of Austria's trade deficit, but the adverse trade balance in itself did not have to be a problem. It might have signaled the wealth of Austrians and offset their capacity to earn foreign exchange from tourism, foreign investments, or services rendered to foreigners. Such capital inflows, so-called invisible exports, could have been used to pay for extra imports, but Austria's balance of payments, though difficult to estimate, was most likely negative, too.[11] An assessment of capital flows by Zimmerman's Dutch aide, Meinoud Rost van Tonningen, suggested that without funds provided from the League loan and recent

TABLE 6.1. Austrian balance of payments, 1923–1926 in gold crowns (and US$)

	Surplus of foreign supply	Minus League of Nations loan funds given to Austria	Minus capital inflows from corporate loans	Equals ordinary balance of payments
1923	+185,221,660	−254,732,700		−69,511,040
	($37,340,672)	($51,354,092)		($14,013,420)
1924	+24,872,960	−66,054,920	−9,993,600	−51,175,560
	($5,014,387)	($13,316,667)	($2,014,709)	($10,316,989)
1925	+45,269,620	+36,094,940	−83,280,000	−1,915,440
	($9,126,352)	($7,276,737)	($16,789,241)	($386,153)
1926	+62,418,360	−52,785,640	−26,372,000	−16,739,280
	($12,583,536)	($10,641,581)	($5,316,593)	($3,374,638)

Source: JPM, Box 36, Rost van Tonningen, Report on Balance of Payments.

foreign bond issues, neither of which were likely to return, the Austrian balance of payments already showed a substantial deficit (see Table 6.1).[12] In the not-too-distant future, the Austrian government would be forced to pay interest on its foreign debt without recourse to foreign exchange from the loan funds, which posed a serious risk to the long-term stability of the Austrian currency.[13] Without effective measures to ameliorate Austria's current account, either by increasing exports or attracting capital inflows, the ANB would continue to slowly hemorrhage foreign currency reserves, forcing it to either uphold an oppressive discount rate or abandon the gold exchange standard.

Given Austria's recent familiarity with inflation and an almost universal belief in the benefit of holding a currencies' value stable in relation to gold, abandoning fixed exchange rates in favor of depreciation was not an option. Reducing the value of the Austrian currency to curtail imports and stimulate exports would moreover have made servicing foreign debt even more difficult. But a high discount rate, which might have helped attract capital inflows, was certain to dampen economic activity and investments. The ideal way out of this dilemma, a general agreement on lowering tariffs between all the successor states, would have certainly helped Austrian exporters, but whether that could be reached remained at best uncertain.[14] Effectively, Austria and the League of Nations were left with three practical ways to patch up the country's negative current account.[15] First, obtain new capital inflows by attracting foreign money to Austrian banks. Second, float new loans for Austrian private and public enterprises abroad. And third, introduce new measures and reforms to reduce the cost of production, improve productivity, and help exports. The alternative course was less appealing. Lowering Austrian imports and consumption through a further cutback of government expenditures or with the help of a high discount rate to induce economic contraction were unpopular and unlikely.

The British Foreign Office was "anxious and perturbed" about what might happen to Austria if achieving a preferential tariff system for the region proved impossible before the intervention ended. Writing to Niemeyer in February 1925, they asked whether ultimately in such a case the League would still manage to "set Austria on her feet."[16] Niemeyer first lauded Austria's stable currency and balanced budget (though of course on too high a level) but finally confirmed their fears. In his view Austria had missed a "splendid opportunity . . . by sheer levity and want of tenacity."[17] Taxes were too high, it was important to fix the fiscal relationship between government and provinces, and regional tariffs had to fall. In light of the country's perennial current account deficit, he estimated that the loan remainder would only last the country as foreign currency reserve for a few more years. Unless Austria followed League advice and made changes to bring about a more balanced current account, he warned, its financial position and therewith the whole country would inevitably fall back into disarray.[18] Niemeyer did not explicitly state that international control in Austria should continue, but forewarned that without regional tariff reform, Austria's financial position would not hold.

Peter Bark, who had helped float the Austrian loan and was now with the Anglo-Austrian Bank, stated more explicitly that he thought the time to end control had not yet come. In his view the Austrian economy had recovered quickly from the financial crisis of 1924, but everyone he spoke to in Vienna agreed that Austria's private enterprises were "overstaffed, over-taxed, badly managed," and that the banks were unsound and the government remained weak. As he wrote to Norman in July 1925:

Life is stronger than even bad politics. The little man here is prospering; one sees that cheap restaurants, cafés and shops—especially in the suburbs—are very busy, and all these people earn money. The deposits in the banks are increasing—a proof that savings have been started and that the wealth has only shifted from one class of the population to the other. Many new cars are to be seen in the streets, and foreigners are coming to the country in greater numbers, while even the good hotels are doing better business. The general aspect of the town is better. . . . I think one should not lose hope; certainly Austria must be kept under control, and her people must be in constant touch with London, and gradually educated to sound politics, sound finance, sound backing and sound economics. One must have patience but not leave the child alone.[19]

International control in Austria would soon be terminated, however. Not because Austria's economic or financial outlook were particularly encouraging, but because almost nobody could see any benefit in prolonging the League's intervention, and to many it seemed that terminating international control was politically beneficial. The opposing voices were most concerned with Viennese banks' exposure to foreign short-term debt and the immediate risk this posed to the ANB and to currency stability. At the same time, Austria had no working strategy to solve its current account problem. Efforts to engage its neighbors in a coordinated lowering of regional tariffs were not received with enthusiasm. New foreign borrowing by the state or provinces was made difficult by the League and the General Commissioner. And the ANB stood opposed to inducing deflation to lower prices, wages, and imports by means of further economic contractions and higher unemployment.

Deflation: Or the ANB and Bank of England Continued

To counter capital outflows and attract fresh foreign reserves, the ANB could have pursued a policy of high interest rates. In fact, many historians erroneously believe it actually did.[20] But in the eyes of Governor Norman, ANB President Reisch was not deflationary enough. Facing capital outflows and submitting to foreign pressure during the financial crisis in 1924, Reisch had lifted the ANB discount rate over the summer from 9 to 12 and then to 15 percent. In November, against advice from London and the General Commissioner, the rate had been reduced to 13 percent. When Reisch had trav-

eled thereupon to meet Norman in London in December he had encountered
a bad-tempered Governor, unwilling to discuss new loans for Austria as long
as Reisch stayed uncooperative. Envoy Franckenstein had thought it paramount for Austria's interests to please the Governor of the Bank of England
(BoE), but the ANB President remained convinced that Norman was wrong,
that Austria's price level did not primarily depend on the ANB's discount
rate, and that the high cost of capital in Austria harmed producers and
needed to fall further.

In March 1925, Reisch traveled again to London to try to obtain Norman's
approval for a further rate reduction. From earlier conversations with Strakosch he assumed that Norman would probably be opposed, and his plan
was to convince the Governor that the rising price level in Austria did not
result from excessive credit, but was nothing more than an adjustment of
Austrian to world prices.[21] Preparing for the encounter himself, Norman was
in fact willing to support a reduction if the ANB committed to reduce credit
and stabilize prices otherwise. Instead of lifting the discount rate, the ANB
could also curtail Austrian credit and money supply, he thought, by diminishing the amount of Kostdevisen (foreign exchange sold by banks in return
for Austrian currency and to be repurchased at a fixed exchange rate) or by
reducing the quantity of financial bills in its portfolio.[22]

There was willingness to compromise on both sides, but given the personal characters of the two central bankers, it was perhaps inevitable that
they should clash yet again. Norman was authoritarian and not used to being
contradicted, while Reisch was five years his senior and not a person to take
orders either. Moreover, Norman claimed to know what Austrian monetary
policy should be but had never completed his university studies, while Reisch
lectured in financial law at the University of Vienna. The fact that neither of
them spoke the other's language and that they required a translator did not
help. When they met in London in March 1925, their discussions deteriorated into an unseemly quarrel. Reisch pointed out that since December 1924,
circulation had fallen, discounts and the proportion of financial bills among
them had declined, and the emergency advances to the banking syndicate had
been significantly reduced. Reisch had to concede, however, that most financial bills had been replaced by Kostdevisen, so that the aggregate amount
of credit the ANB supplied in Austria had not dropped.[23] Norman replied
that in that case it seemed wise to leave the discount rate untouched and in

fact, since Austrian prices and wages were still too high, to raise the discount rate for three to four months to bring about deflation. Reisch refused the advice outright but offered to stabilize prices in Austria through a simultaneous reduction of discounted bills and Kostdevisen, thereby curtailing ANB credit supply to the economy.[24]

Norman appeared personally injured by Reisch's rejection of his advice and angrily dropped the matter, bringing the meeting to an end. Seemingly oblivious to his counterpart's reaction, Reisch proceeded to raise the sensitive question of emergency support from the BoE in times of crisis. Capital controls in Austria were being lifted upon the League Financial Committee's suggestion, and Reisch desired a pledge of assistance from London if the crown should come under attack.[25] Norman instantly refused to even discuss the matter, lashing out at Reisch, seemingly furious about his lack of cooperation. If Reisch proceeded and reduced the ANB's discount rate, Norman warned, it would result in higher prices, which would make the government's task of keeping the budget within limits very difficult.[26] Franckenstein tried smoothening relations by assuring Norman that Reisch had good intentions and had simply felt misunderstood in the past, but the Governor replied that remaking good ties between the two central banks would take time.[27] When Austria's Finance Minister, Jakob Ahrer, visited Norman in London a few weeks later, the Governor repeated that Austria had to adhere to the budget limits agreed upon with the Financial Committee and that it was therefore best if prices and wages fell.[28]

Because the Austrian government and bankers in Vienna feared a further deterioration of relations with Norman, they urged Reisch upon his return to leave the rate unchanged. Addressing the ANB General Council's meeting on 23 March, Reisch favored postponing a reduction, citing the impending announcement of an end to capital controls, but he declared that the Austrian banks were prepared to unilaterally reduce their conditions for the month of April to lessen the cost of credit to Austrian producers.[29] A counterproposal to presently reduce the rate to 11 percent was voted down 8 to 5 after Director Gustav Thaa pointed out that "foreign circles" capable of impacting on Austria's plans for a new foreign loan were opposed to a reduction.[30] The unilateral cutback by Austrian banks made a future ANB reduction almost a foregone conclusion, and ANB Director Viktor Brauneis, who had been present in March, was sent to London again to see if perhaps on his own he could change Norman's mind.[31] Brauneis argued that to reduce the ANB's rate to 11 percent was justified in light of the steady decline of circulation and the amelioration of the ANB's portfolio. Prices were now actually falling, he argued, and he promised that any reduction of the discount rate would incur a careful monitoring of the economy. Norman considered Brauneis more reasonable than Reisch, but remained steadfastly convinced that the rate in Austria was best left unchanged. But proposing to let misunderstandings be bygones, he encouragingly offered to discuss an agreement on emergency support between the two banks instead. How would the ANB react to this gesture of reconciliation?

Notwithstanding Norman's advice and offer, the ANB General Council on 24 April voted unanimously without debate to reduce its discount rate from 13 to 11 percent.[32] The decision was the proverbial nail in the coffin of Austro-British central banking cooperation. When in June the ANB Directors traveled again to London, Reisch nevertheless took up Norman's offer to Brauneis and asked the Governor whether the BoE could now promise an unsecured emergency credit of, say, up to £5 million ($24 million) in the event that the Austrian currency suffered a speculative attack. Confused and disturbed by such brazen audacity, the Governor refused to make even an unspecified commitment. As Norman informed Reisch shortly thereafter in writing, the BoE no longer desired any close relations with the ANB at all.[33]

In July the ANB General Council unanimously reduced the discount rate to 10 percent and finally, in September 1925, dropped it to the pre-crisis level of 9 percent. By choosing this policy, Reisch was agreeing with the prevailing opinion of members on the bank's General Council, who respectively repre-sented banking, commercial, labor, and industrial interests, but he was at the same time severing his ties with Norman.

Historians have pointed to the deflationary bias of the gold standard, because it tended to reduce global money supply, and accused central bankers of keeping interest rates too high during the 1920s. In fact, President Reisch fought pressure from London to induce deflation in Austria and kept the interest rate as low as possible. Given the risks associated with Austrian monetary policy, the ANB could not reduce its discount rate much further without provoking renewed capital outflows (Poland's discount rate was 10, Hungary's and Germany's 9, Czechoslovakia's and Italy's 7 percent). Foreign banks deposited significant funds in foreign currencies with Viennese banks,

so-called rembourse-credits or renewable loans, for which they were paid a
handsome interest rate. The funds were usually pledged for three months
and regularly renewed, but had the interest rate offered by Austrian banks
fallen below that of competing financial centers, this foreign capital would
have been pulled out and placed elsewhere.[34]

The ANB upheld a level of interest rates high enough to attract and retain
foreign capital, but Reisch would not go higher just to cause deflation and
lower prices. Reisch ignored Norman because he knew that Austrian producers already had difficulties making a profit. The Governor's advice might
have worked at reducing wages and production costs, but it would have
forced a harsh economic recession on a country that was already suffering
from high unemployment. But were there any alternatives? If the ANB
wanted to keep its pledge to uphold fixed exchange rates, Austria had to find
a way to replenish ANB reserves that were being slowly but continuously diminished, yet the League of Nations as well as the Committee of Control
were making it impossible for Austria to borrow fresh money abroad. In
May 1925, the Control Committee of Guarantor States severely criticized
growing Austrian expenditures and the slow pace of reforms, and then
rejected a request for approval of a foreign railway loan of $22 million. The
unnecessarily harsh tone of the resolution angered the Austrians, but the fact
that a body associated with the League itself was preventing Austria from
obtaining direly needed foreign capital seemed absurd.[35] As Governor
Norman complained to Arthur Salter, Director of the League's Financial Secretariat, the League seemed to have difficulties deciding what position to
take on foreign loans in regard to Austria. While the Governor of the BoE
approved and supported policies to prevent indiscriminate borrowing, he
thought everyone knew that the country was in dire need of investments.
Useful projects such as raising money to electrify the railways, Norman argued, ought to have been considered on their own merits.[36]

Alternatively: Provincial Loans or Exports

Apart from ameliorating the country's current account and replenishing ANB
reserves, the Austrian government borrowing fresh long-term capital abroad
might have helped finance productive investments and thereby assisted

Austrian producers and exports. But following the financial crisis of 1924, General Commissioner Zimmerman was, not unreasonably, worried that unchecked public borrowing would be squandered and result in an unserviceable debt level. However, the League only hindered the provision of new long-term loans to Austria's government, since the Geneva Protocols did not bind Austria's provinces or municipalities, and so the General Commissioner belatedly strove to obtain some form of control over how local authorities used funds lent from abroad as well. Positioning himself as a kingpin of public foreign borrowing, would, he hoped, give him further leverage to hasten a lasting agreement between the Austrian government and provinces on taxation and fiscal policy, something he feared would become unattainable if the provinces managed to freely raise foreign capital. Opposing indiscriminate lending and seeking assurances on how funds were spent, the General Commissioner successfully deterred some foreign, mainly U.S., firms from issuing loans for provinces or municipalities.[37]

In October 1924, Zimmerman suggested to William Ford Upson, the U.S. Department of Commerce's trade commissioner in Vienna, that American banks make issuing loans for Austrian provinces contingent on a final agreement between them and the government.[38] The General Commissioner managed to obtain a promise from J. P. Morgan that U.S. banks would act in accordance to this request and not issue any new Austrian loans without his approval.[39] The New York bank of Speyer, too, accepted Zimmerman's conditions and subsequently withdrew from negotiations on a joint loan for Styria, Oberösterreich, and Vienna, though another New York firm, Richard & Co., proceeded to issue a $2.5 million loan for the city of Graz without obtaining Zimmerman's support.[40] If Zimmerman could not completely suppress foreign borrowing by provinces or municipalities, he at least wished to sign agreements with foreign banks to make sure that any funds lent would be controlled. Worried that borrowed money might be used to finance budgetary deficits in the provinces, he suggested that his office be charged with releasing and supervising the usage of such capital raised abroad.[41] Arguably, the General Commissioner's interference deterred some U.S. banks from issuing loans for Austrian public bodies and made it harder for the latter to raise long-term capital abroad.

Opposed to deflation and barred from to raising fresh capital, Austria and its supporters clung to the hope that the country's current account problem might be solved by improving its regional trade position.[42] To reduce Austria's trade deficit, the General Commissioner and Salter at the League of Nations Secretariat supported the idea of a coordinated lowering of regional tariffs, and Niemeyer inquired whether the League's Council might not push more strongly for commercial treaties between Austria and its neighbors.[43] As he warned Salter, if there was no improvement in the conditions for cross-country trade and thus "the Achilles heel of our Austrian plan brings us down, there won't be much left of the League's brightest jewel!"[44] However, merely organizing a regional conference on tariffs and trade, let alone achieving a trade agreement among the region's nation states, proved impossible. In April 1925, Richard Schüller held preliminary discussions with Salter, Niemeyer, and Strakosch but was unable to get Italian or Czechoslovak support for a coordination of policy. Prague demanded that the United Kingdom forfeit its most-favored-nation policy prior to an agreement, a precondition the British Board of Trade expectedly scuttled, leaving Schüller to complain in despair that the British were simply not willing to help Austria balance its current account.[45]

But it was in the very nature of the League of Nations to try and provide guidance and propose solutions where national animosities stood in the way of international cooperation. Treading carefully, League officials suggested that the Austrian government request an inquiry into the progress of its reconstruction, which could then be used to carefully open up a general discussion on the problem of Central European trade.[46] Given the opposition to tariff reductions among Austria's neighbors it was best, however, to gradually prepare the ground for compromise before announcing plans publicly. It is quite possible that Austrian patience with the League was running out, or that announcement of yet another inquiry focused narrowly on the state of Austria's economy would have been used by Pan-Germans and Socialists to topple Ramek's government. Instead of following Geneva's advice, Ramek therefore announced to the press that a League inquiry into the problems of Central European trade was being contemplated for 1925. His cavalier declaration caused consternation in Prague and Rome, so that in June, when the League Council appointed two economists to conduct the inquiry, they were officially charged to study the state of Austrian reconstruction only.[47] Walter Layton, the British editor of the weekly *Economist*, and his French colleague Charles Rist, author of the Carnegie Foundation's 1922 report on Austria, traveled to Vienna that summer and presented their findings to the League in September 1925. Ultimately, the Layton-Rist inquiry would help pave the way for a termination of international control, but it could not do much to bring about a regional return to free trade or a coordinated reduction of tariffs.[48]

The End of Control

Though Austria struggled to find practical ways to solve the challenge posed by its deficits in capital flows and trade in the long run, the new government, headed by Chancellor Ramek, achieved important domestic reforms toward completing the League's reconstruction scheme during its first year in power. At the end of 1924, Zimmerman had voiced concern about monthly expenditures and had opposed a Christmas bonus for state workers. Addressing the new cabinet, he had warned that the economic crisis was steadily commanding higher expenditures on social welfare, requiring renewed and energetic efforts to keep the budget from growing further.[49] During the following months, Finance Minister Ahrer managed to see through most of the measures stipulated by the Financial Committee in September 1924, introducing gold balance sheets, ending capital controls, and reforming the fiscal relationship between local authorities and the federal government.[50] Getting the Austrian budget to remain within stipulated limits, however, was still an elusive endeavor.

Chancellor Ramek tackled the local authorities at a Länderkonferenz in February, where he proposed to merge local federal with provincial offices and place them under control of the latter. If the provinces accepted the authority of the Federal Court of Audit and committed themselves to refrain from new taxation before July 1927, Ramek offered to compensate them with revenues from increased taxation on alcoholic beverages.[51] Negotiations continued into March, and after some changes in favor of the Socialists and local authorities, parliament passed a compromise shortly before rising in July 1925. Zimmerman feared that the agreement did not do enough to strengthen foreign confidence, since it brought about no savings while increasing government expenditure and strengthening the financial position of the socialist municipality of Vienna.[52] But regulating the financial

relationship between the federal government and the provinces and municipalities, and limiting the amount the latter could raise through new taxation, fulfilled an important condition set by the Financial Committee and
rectified a serious lapse of the Geneva Protocols.

The Ramek government effectively implemented most of the other outstanding reforms quietly and efficiently, but it failed to reduce the budget. At
their first meeting with the League Financial Committee in February 1925,
the international experts reminded the Austrians of the need for lifting capital controls to attract foreign inflows and stressed that Austria's budget
needed to remain balanced and below 495 million gold crowns (about $100
million) for control to be lifted.[53] But despite the warning, Austria's foreseeable budget deficit grew to 83 million gold crowns (about $17 million) by
April 1925, so that Zimmerman repeated the need for administrative savings and a continued dismissal of state workers.[54] Eager to complete outstanding reforms, Finance Minister Ahrer promised the quick merger of
the federal administration with that of the provinces as well as a reduction of
ministerial sections and staff to push the annual deficit below 35 million
gold crowns (about $7 million) by the end of the year.[55]

Meeting again in Geneva in June, the General Commissioner presented
the Financial Committee with a list of completed reforms: Capital controls
had been lifted by government decree in March, taxation had been reduced,
and a fiscal accord had been reached with the local authorities.[56] And while
Austria's new government was not keeping expenditures within the limits set
for 1925 and, on an annual basis, was spending 585 instead of 495 million
gold crowns (about $119 instead of $100 million), Zimmerman thought that
current revenues were sufficiently high to keep the budget balanced overall.[57]
As the Council was going to appoint Layton and Rist to study the state of
Austria's economy and budget over the summer, the Financial Committee
redirected its attention away from the budget and to the electrification of
Austria's railways. In May, the Control Committee had refused to allow Austria to issue a foreign loan to pay for electrification, and previously in 1924
the Austrian government had petitioned the Financial Committee unsuccessfully to allow it to use some of the loan remainder for productive investments. Now Finance Minister Ahrer and Austrian Railways Director Georg
Günther traveled to Geneva to ask once more that loan funds be freed to finance the project. The Swiss banker Léopold Dubois, who had previously

worked for the Swiss Federal Railways, studied the plan and reported to his colleagues on the Financial Committee that considerable work would come to Austria's industry from the undertaking.[58] The international experts were skeptical, but significantly more amicable than the Control Committee, and approved a proposal tabled by Niemeyer earmarking 88 million gold crowns (about $18 million) from loan funds for electrification, as long as Austria's budget remained balanced.[59]

In July and August, Walter Layton and Charles Rist worked in Vienna, collecting information and interviewing politicians and representatives from different branches of the Austrian economy. Layton had been instructed by the Foreign Office that neither a Danubian Confederation nor unification with Germany was a possible solution to Austria's economic impasse. Since a preferential tariff system among the successor states was unlikely, too, he had been told to stick to the facts and recommend no specific solution in his report.[60] Rist, on the other hand, later remembered that their study was supposed to bring about a change in the form of League control and possibly the end of Zimmerman's mission to Vienna.[61] Indeed, in July Zimmerman noticed that concern over Austrian calls to join Germany were making it likely that the League would decide to end its Austrian intervention within months, and in August Arthur Salter himself insinuated that he thought the time had come to begin the process of terminating control.[62]

Salter had spearheaded the League intervention into Austria, and under his leadership the Financial Secretariat coordinated the League intervention in Hungary and had gotten involved in Greece and Danzig as well. But if his staff at the League was to take on new work and also start tackling larger questions of global trade and economic growth, they needed to first prove that they could successfully complete a task. Writing to Niemeyer's deputy at the Treasury, Salter argued that the Austrian currency had been stable for three years and the budget almost balanced for eighteen months. Reconstruction had only been planned to last two years, and a continued presence of the General Commissioner in Vienna, he feared, was strengthening the calls for unification with Germany, since "every grievance that is felt by any class in the community is associated with the C-G [General Commissioner] or with the League, and any reaction makes them think of the Anschluss as a sort of Eldorado."[63] Sounding out relevant quarters, Salter directly informed Niemeyer in August that he wished to terminate control, yet at the same time sustain foreign confidence by insisting on a continued presence of the foreign Conseiller at the ANB and the right to reinstate control should Austria regress too far.[64] Niemeyer replied that he was not keen on seeing international control end early, since Austria's economic and financial position were not yet permanently stabilized (a view that, he claimed, was shared by most of his colleagues on the Financial Committee), so it was best not to raise the question at their meeting next month.[65]

As the League of Nations bodies convened for the annual General Assembly in Geneva in September 1925, the two economists, Layton and Rist, presented the Council with their study in which they determined that Austria's economy was not inherently unsound, that the country was viable, and that only a violent crisis could still endanger its stability. Existing unemployment and the trade deficit could be reduced, they observed, through increasing exports, lowering imports, attracting more tourists, and strengthening Vienna's role as a transit and service hub for the Danubian region. Apart from intensifying agricultural production, finding new export markets was the best way to cut the trade deficit and unemployment, but this required putting an end to the high tariffs that surrounded the country.[66] On capital flows, Layton and Rist noted with some concern that Austrian banks had provided loans to replace the working capital of Austrian enterprises, using renewable short-term credits coming in from abroad. The two economists considered the lack of long-term foreign investment responsible for the high interest rate level, exacerbated further by the banks' high fees and commissions, which harmed producers' competitiveness considerably. They concluded, however, that the financial situation was not inherently unstable, if and once short-term loans were replaced with long-term credits, which would further help reduce the cost of capital and make it easier for Austrian producers to face foreign competition.

Salter's confidential plan to use the results of the Layton-Rist inquiry to initiate the termination of control had been favorably received in both Paris and Rome.[67] After hearing their presentation to the League Council, its French member, Prime Minister Paul Painlevé, proposed that international control in Austria might be terminated.[68] His British colleague, Foreign Secretary Austen Chamberlain, suggested that they proceed with caution, lest foreign lenders lose faith in Austria's credit and provoke capital flight. Before reaching any conclusions, the Council thus wished to hear the Financial

Committee's experts on whether in their eyes Austria had attained monetary and budgetary stability.[69] During the subsequent debate on the Financial Committee, the Italian, French, and Czech delegates, not unexpectedly, came out in favor of announcing that control could gradually be terminated. They received support from General Commissioner Zimmerman but were opposed notably by Niemeyer and Strakosch, both of whom thought Austria's financial situation still too precarious to allow control to end at this stage.

After all, notwithstanding its optimistic tone, the Rist-Layton report did state that short-term credits worth 200 million gold crowns (about $40 million) were currently extended to Austria. The Financial Committee's President, the banker Léopold Dubois, pointed out that at any time an unfavorable shock could trigger the general withdrawal of these renewable deposits, thereby endangering the country's currency and stability. Niemeyer and Strakosch were of the view that this posed a grave risk, not least since ANB President Reisch had himself admitted that many such deposits had been used to extend credits to companies that were probably unable to repay them. Strakosch warned his colleagues that in his view the stability of Austria's currency was in fact in danger if League control was lifted too abruptly.[70]

Layton and Rist were invited to discuss with the Financial Committee whether Austria's reliance on short-term loans posed a risk to stability. Charles Rist confirmed that foreign short-term deposits with Austrian banks had increased in 1924, but favored viewing them as a sign of foreign confidence. Moreover, he believed, Viennese banks had substantial reserves deposited abroad with which to face sudden withdrawals if large parts of these renewable short-term loans would be recalled. With the ANB's help the banks would be able to weather this or any other sort of problem, he stated assuredly. In fact, as both he and Layton somewhat precariously argued, exiting Austria would have the effect of strengthening foreign confidence, allowing for short-term credits to be replaced by long-term loans.

The experts on the League Financial Committee were not impressed. Countering Rist's and Layton's testimonies, the Dutch banker C. E. Ter Meulen voiced fear that terminating control would in fact provoke a gradual withdrawal of short-term funds. Strakosch agreed and argued that to maintain stability, the prior transformation of short-term credits into long-term loans was vital. The Swedish banker Marcus Wallenberg concluded that termination of control would at least have to proceed gradually, so as not to provoke a crisis. Bringing Salter's original ideas to the table, he suggested that the Financial Committee tell the League Council that it recommended terminating control at some point in the not-too-distant future, as long as the budget remained balanced. For the sake of foreign confidence, however, terminating control would require granting the League of Nations the right to reestablish control in times of crisis, as well as a continued presence of the Conseiller at the ANB. The Financial Committee thereupon agreed that the Austrian government would first have to accept these conditions before General Commissioner Zimmerman could be removed from Vienna.

The Austrian government had in fact promised the General Commissioner not to ask for a termination of control in Geneva, but since the Council had put the question to the Financial Committee, Finance Minister Ahrer grasped the opportunity. Appearing before the Financial Committee's international experts, he argued that he had completed most reforms and that his budget for 1925 would end with a surplus of 13.5 million gold crowns (about $2.7 million).[71] The Federal Court of Audit now oversaw the government's accounts, local authorities could no longer raise new taxes or borrow without the Finance Ministry's approval, and the administration in the provinces had been amalgamated with that of the federal government. General Commissioner Zimmerman confirmed that most of the reform program had been put into force and that the budgets for 1925 and 1926 were getting balanced at 515 million gold crowns (about $103 million). Although he pointed out that budgetary expenditure on wages and pensions remained very high, that dismissals had not reached the prescribed total figure of 100,000 state workers, and that too much of Austrian money supply was backed by short-term loans, he would not stand in the way of terminating control. Toeing the Financial Committee's majority line, the General Commissioner stated that in his opinion, despite such difficulties, the time had come to gradually wind down control and fix a date for his departure.[72]

The Financial Committee thereupon informed Austrian Chancellor Ramek and Finance Minister Ahrer that it had reached the conclusion that control in Austria could be terminated in June 1926, but only under certain conditions. Since the amount of short-term credits posed a serious danger to currency stability, it was imperative to keep the Conseiller at the ANB for a longer period to help maintain foreign confidence and facilitate assistance

from foreign central banks in times of crisis. Furthermore, if League control
was terminated, the Financial Committee wished to obtain the right to reinstate international control if Austria's situation over the next decade deteriorated so far as to make this seem necessary.[73] The Financial Committee
warned that if the Austrian government did not agree to maintain the Conseiller and accept the possibility of reinstating control, it would suggest that
the Council postpone any decision on the question until June 1926, when
Austria's Court of Audit furnished its report on Austria's closed accounts
for 1925.[74]

Evidently, the Austrians were opposed to any possible future return of
control as much as to the continued presence of a Conseiller at the ANB.
Chancellor Ramek and Finance Minister Ahrer protested emphatically in
front of the Financial Committee and called the conditions unacceptable in
light of the progress made and the favorable study that Layton and Rist had
presented.[75] But in the end the possibility of returning to Vienna with a fixed
date for the end of control was too precious a prospect to pass by. In a move
signaling his willingness to compromise, Chancellor Ramek promised ver-
bally, though not in writing, to obtain the necessary legal measures from
parliament that would allow both the Conseiller to remain at the ANB and
control to be reinstated in Austria during the next ten years if necessary. In
response, the Financial Committee recommended that the League Council
gradually wind down its intervention in Austria. Back in Vienna, Chancellor
Ramek would be allowed to announce that the General Commissioner would
depart the country on 31 December 1925 and his control cease fully by
June 1926, once the Court of Audit had approved the previous year's accounts and an appropriate budget for 1926 had been passed.[76]

The termination of League control within the next six months had almost
become a fait accompli. The League Council expressed satisfaction at the Financial Committee's decision and congratulated Austria on its progress. In
his closing statement, Chancellor Ramek expressed his "heartfelt gratitude"
for General Commissioner Zimmerman, whom he hoped would "give us his
valued friendship in the future."[77] But the festive mood was not contagious,
and some members of the Financial Committee were not pleased with an
unstoppable unwinding of the League's Austrian intervention. Niemeyer and
Ter Meulen repeatedly stated that they thought the Layton-Rist report too
optimistic and that they remained worried about Austria's budget being too

high. Strakosch agreed with their concerns but thought that the compromise reached with Ramek was at least sufficient to prevent the sudden withdrawal of short-term credits, which had been his largest concern.[78] Salter in fact did not think that control would or even could be reestablished in Austria, but believed that the possibility was "a very stiffening element to Austrian finance ministers in power after the termination of control" and would positively effect the country's financial stability as well.[79]

Outside the League, the banks that had participated in issuing the League loan in 1923 had not been consulted. Charles Whigham of Morgan, Grenfell was confidentially informed by Niemeyer in London and reported to Morgan in New York that some Financial Committee members had opposed the decision, but that he thought Layton was too much of an honest character and authority to ignore. Furthermore, Zimmerman's control had been for some time "very limited and in fact has been more apparent than real," which undermined the League's authority and made the General Commissioner's own position "untenable." He reported further that in Geneva, Zimmerman himself had been among the strongest supporters of terminating international control in Austria. Whigham's colleagues in Paris were seriously worried about the stability of Viennese banks and their exposure to foreign short-term loans, but in his view the fact that control over pledged revenues and the budget could be reinstated and that the Conseiller remained at the ANB for a further three years was enough to protect the interest of foreign bondholders.[80]

The Role of the Foreign Conseillers

Chancellor Ramek and Finance Minister Ahrer had strongly protested the continued presence of a foreign Conseiller at the ANB. Historians, too, have viewed the appointments of foreign advisers to the Central Bank of Austria in 1923 and later to Banks of Issue in Hungary, Poland, or Greece, as foreign impositions.[81] According to this view, weak countries that depended on League assistance had little choice but to accept such interference, even if it abrogated their sovereignty over monetary policy.[82] However, the installation of foreign advisers at European central banks in the 1920s represented an entrepreneurial innovation, aimed at supporting, facilitating, and strengthening cooperative relationships between European central banks, not at governing them. The League of Nations actively pursued the foundation of independent central banks across Europe, in line with Governor Montagu Norman's will to initiate a new era of central bank cooperation.[83] A net of independent central banks, Norman imagined, governed by professionals of the highest integrity working together on a basis of collegiality, mutual trust, and perhaps friendship, would be able to help circumvent complicated political stalemates to everyone's benefit. Undoubtedly, his own strong bonds with Federal Reserve Governor Benjamin Strong, a relationship that had proved highly effective in helping Britain return pound sterling's exchange rate to its prewar gold value by 1925, were a model of inspiration. Placing foreign advisers at newly founded central banks in Europe formed part of Norman's vision and correspondence originating with the foreign advisers at the ANB show that Conseillers have been wrongly accused as tools of foreign control.

The first foreign adviser to take up his position at the Austrian central bank was the Swiss Charles Schnyder von Wartensee, who arrived at the ANB in 1923, just as the Austrian loan was being issued on the world's financial markets. Schnyder von Wartensee proved an important and valuable source of information about the monetary and financial developments of the Austrian economy to Zimmerman, and he engaged in regular correspondence with Norman in London, keeping him and others abreast of the situation.[84] In 1923 Schnyder von Wartensee still considered foreign interest in Austrian shares as a sign of confidence, but he soon grew concerned about speculation on the Vienna Stock Exchange (VSE) and worried about capital inflows not going to investments or commerce.[85] Despite his forebodings, Schnyder von Wartensee did not predict the end of French franc speculation, nor the timing of the crash at the VSE. When, following a first drop of share prices, the ANB reported a brief fall in foreign reserves in early 1924, Schnyder von Wartensee even wrote to assuage the General Commissioner's fears of impending capital flight. The loss, he wrote, was no reason for concern, but the consequence of seasonal requirements of merchants and industrialists toward the end of the calendar year.[86]

Schnyder von Wartensee's first annual report submitted to both Zimmerman and Norman at the end of 1923 reflected the Conseiller's positive and sympathetic assessment of work at the ANB.[87] At the time that Reisch was traveling for discussions to London, Schnyder von Wartensee would not confirm Norman's suspicions that the ANB created inflation through supplying too much credit. Schnyder von Wartensee instead supported the ANB position, namely that rising prices in Austria were an adjustment to world price levels.[88] Naturally Schnyder von Wartensee and Reisch did not always see eye to eye, but their main points of contention were not about the essence of policies, but about the timing.[89] Schnyder von Wartensee wanted a quick liberation of the Austrian foreign exchange markets, arguing that it would "show the whole world" that Austria was returning to stability, while Reisch was weary of lifting exchange controls too soon.[90]

Schnyder von Wartensee left Vienna within a year because "in Switzerland nobody could take up the ideas of the working jointly of the central banks."[91] His departure from the ANB coincided with the end of financial speculations against the French franc, and General Commissioner Zimmerman frantically searched for a replacement. A new Conseiller, the Dutch economist Anton van Gijn (sometimes spelled van Gyn) took up the vacant post in June 1924 and remained in Vienna until the end of 1925. Van Gijn, born in Dordrecht in 1866, had first headed the Dutch Treasury and then served as Minister of Finance before teaching economics at the University of Leiden. Like Schnyder von Wartensee, van Gijn regularly sided with the ANB on matters of monetary policy, including the divisive question of setting the discount rate. Writing to Norman, he explained that there was too much distrust in England of the ANB's management and that there was no actual danger to the stability of the Austrian currency.[92] When in November 1924 the rate in Vienna was reduced for the first time after the financial crisis, from 15 to 13 percent, van Gijn informed Norman that in his view the reduction had been unavoidable and was justified.[93]

Van Gijn also sided with the ANB on another matter of importance. The League had retroactively allowed the Austrian government to lend money from the international loan to support Austrian banks.[94] In 1925 the General Commissioner was pushing to suspend this assistance, but van Gijn defended the policy, describing the alternative, where the funds were placed abroad only to be re-lent short-term to Austrian banks as an "action aussi anti-économique."[95] Van Gijn sided with President Reisch against Zimmerman, arguing that these loan funds had to serve the benefit of the Austrian economy and that if the League wished foreign capital to flow to Austria, it could not curtail its own investments in the country.[96] In a report to Niemeyer in September 1925 van

Gijn gave a positive assessment of the ANB Directorate, which in his opinion had "been very well since autumn 1924. Though it is acknowledged that Dr. Reisch was not quite free of the well known Austrian slackness, he is decidedly getting stronger, and Dr. Brauneis takes care, that he is not being influenced too much by the Austrian Finance Minister."[97]

Van Gijn's successor, the Englishman Robert Kay, was a personal acquaintance of Norman who kept in even closer communication with him. Appointed during the final months of control, Kay stayed on in Vienna for three more years, informing London about the state of the Austrian economy, capital flows, short-term debt levels, and probable rate changes.[98] In most of his correspondence Kay, too, explained or defended ANB positions vis-à-vis the Governor. When the ANB reduced its rate from 8 to 7.5 percent in March 1926, Kay wrote that conditions would have justified a reduction of even 1 percent, if not for fear of unsettling gradually increasing saving deposits.[99] Similarly, in a letter to Norman following a rate reduction to 7 percent in August that same year, Kay argued that the low level of discounted bills and economic stagnation justified the decision.[100] Kay also helped alleviate other concerns in London. After the Austrian postal bank got into difficulties and the Austrian government appointed ANB President Reisch himself to manage a salvage operation, Kay relayed information from Chancellor Ramek, explaining the unusual nomination.[101] When an important metal merchant failed in June 1927, Kay quickly informed the BoE of the firms' British creditors and of the amounts they stood to lose.[102] And a month later, after Socialist riots had shaken Vienna, Kay reported that demand for foreign exchange had remained moderate, but that spontaneous and prompt action by the National Bank of Hungary in support of the Austrian currency had been highly appreciated.[103]

Norman certainly valued the correspondence he received from Vienna and wanted Kay to stay on when the appointment came to an end in 1929. Kay was opposed to the idea, even though he felt that the ANB, too, would have seen advantage in him remaining. But public opinion, he thought, would have interpreted him staying as a continuation of foreign control and a confirmation "of the opinion still largely held in uninitiated quarters that the National Bank's policy is controlled by the BoE to the detriment of Austrian economy."[104] Hence Kay formally resigned after three years in office and no new Conseiller was appointed.[105]

To rashly brand this exercise in foreign advising a form of international control would, given the archival record, be folly. Its origins seem to lie with a half-hearted attempt at fostering cooperation among European central banks, after the Austrians had appointed one of their own to head the newly founded ANB. As the correspondence between the three foreign advisers and the BoE shows, the Conseillers at the ANB were not functionaries of the BoE. Rather, they generally sided with views held at the ANB and used their position to clarify misunderstandings and explain decisions and events to London. In fact, whereas the League's General Commissioner often held views diametrically opposed to those of the Austrian government, the foreign advisers seem mostly, though not always, to have agreed with their Austrian counterparts at the ANB. Nevertheless, much like the General Commissioner, the foreign Conseiller in Austria was perceived by the public as being a servant of foreign interests. Naturally, therefore, Ramek and Ahrer were initially opposed to the continuation of this arrangement, but they must have been aware also that the Conseiller served a useful function by facilitating the exchange of information from Vienna to London. This might have compelled Chancellor Ramek and Finance Minister Ahrer to agree and prolong his appointment in the end. Given Norman's distrust of Reisch and Austrian monetary policy, the service provided by the foreign Conseiller was perhaps not one to be slighted.

The Final Months of Control

The termination of international control had acquired irreversible momentum, and news from Vienna soon seemed to corroborate the concerns of those members of the League Financial Committee who had worried about releasing Austria too early. Upon returning from Geneva, Chancellor Ramek prevented a general strike of state workers by agreeing to raise their wages in 1926 with help of a new loan.[106] General Commissioner Zimmerman warned Ramek that foreign loans still required approval from the Control Committee even after he himself had left.[107] In London, Niemeyer expressed disbelief and could not see how the Austrian government would keep its budget within limits if it increased wages.[108] To Salter he wrote that he was "all for bolting if we decently can, but I much fear that in the end political compromise will have led us to the usual economic nemesis."[109] It was now clear to Niemeyer that Austria was unlikely to contain expenditures and "that as soon as the League have declared Austria 'financially stable' the Austrians will proceed to demonstrate the opposite." Writing to the Foreign Office, he complained that he had favored the continuation of control, but instead the League was going to "close its eyes and make itself ridiculous by declaring stability" and making an "undignified and unsatisfactory" retreat.[110]

Zimmerman presented the Financial Committee in Geneva with more disquieting news in December 1925.[111] Unemployment had reached worrying heights, expenditure on social welfare was therefore growing further, and spending on state workers now made up more than half of governmental outlay. In his statement before the Financial Committee, Finance Minister Ahrer tried to reassure the international experts that, thanks to planned savings, his budget for 1926 would remain balanced despite the increase in state workers' pay and pensions.[112] Ahrer then asked for permission to lend some of the loan funds via the ANB to Austrian companies that were in need of capital. The loan remainder could indeed have been freed for use by the Austrian government after the League intervention was completed, but Salter, Niemeyer, and Strakosch had already agreed to keep the funds under foreign control instead.[113] Addressing Ahrer, they argued that the funds needed to be kept liquid to cover possible deficits in the future, a notion Ahrer found absurd in light of Austria's want of capital. In protest Ahrer demanded a definitive decision that at least a certain amount be handed over, but the Financial Committee prudently chose to keep most of the loan remainder under its control, approving only the release of 5 million gold crowns (about $1 million) for 1925 and another 4 million (about $800,000) during the first quarter of 1926, while granting Austria's government the option to apply for up to 10 million gold crowns (about $2 million) in a case of emergency.[114]

Although the Financial Committee refused to be lenient with the loan remainder, it was not going to further postpone the end of League intervention in Austria. Chancellor Ramek had kept his verbal promise on the prolongation of the Conseiller's position and the reinstating of control, and laws to that matter had passed parliament by majority vote. The Socialists, however, who had presented a counterproposal, had declared the laws immaterial because they felt that they touched upon the constitution and should have required a two-thirds majority vote, just as in 1922.[115] Ramek hoped the

Financial Committee would accept the simple-majority vote and view subsequent ratification of the laws by Austria's President as sufficient. To his relief, the Financial Committee no longer wished to fight Austria on legalities and refrained from demanding full parliamentary ratification.

Six months later, in June 1926, Zimmerman appeared for the last time in his role as the League's General Commissioner before the Financial Committee, striking a cautious tone. His final report stated that 122,000 pensioners and 160,000 unemployed now relied on state support so that high expenditure on wages, social welfare, and pensions weighed ever heavily on the Austrian economy. Nor had a solution been found to ameliorate the country's trade deficit or negative balance of accounts, and the amount of foreign short-term credits extended to Austrian banks constituted a permanent danger to its financial stability.[116] Even Salter himself privately agreed that the League was leaving Austria "in an unsatisfactory state," particularly given that the League loan would dry up in just a few years and the country could not easily obtain long-term capital abroad.[117] The end of League intervention and international control did not imply that Austria could freely approach foreign lenders thereafter. As Zimmerman had alerted Ramek, even after he was gone, Austria still needed to seek consent from the Control Committee, the Reparations Commission, and the International Relief Bond Committee to borrow abroad—a fact that pleased Niemeyer, who thought it quite good if it took Austria "a deal of trouble to obtain loans."[118]

The members of the Financial Committee were left with winding up control. The administration of the pledged revenues from tobacco and customs was handed to a body of trustees selected by the banks that had issued the loan, and the Dutch aide of General Commissioner Zimmerman, Rost van Tonningen, was selected as their representative agent in Vienna. Financial Committee President Léopold Dubois was put in charge of the loan remainder, and after Austria's closed and verified accounts of 1925 were deemed satisfactory, the international experts agreed that control could cease. Niemeyer remained worried about Austria and stated one more time for the record that in light of Austria's excessive budget and tendency to increase expenditures further, he would have preferred for control to continue. He had tried to convince Austen Chamberlain that Rist and Layton were being too optimistic, that nobody could tell whether stability would prevail after the League left the Austrians to themselves again, but the final decision was not one for experts but for politicians, and Chamberlain had little patience for Niemeyer's position. The League Council received the Financial Committee's report and determined that nothing prevented a cessation of League control and termination of the General Commissioner's office, congratulating the Financial Committee, General Commissioner Zimmerman, and the Austrian government on the successful completion of Austrian reconstruction.[119]

The League's reconstruction scheme for Austria had certainly been effective in many important ways. Above all, it had stabilized the Austrian currency and terminated inflation, which had been the most pressing of Austria's problems only four years earlier. It had given Austria credibility, allowing it to borrow after nobody would lend it money. Furthermore, it had helped the Austrian government implement reforms to successfully balance its budget, thereby eliminating the risk of renewed inflation. However, extreme unemployment prevailed following the financial crisis of 1924. The cost of capital was high and hurt investments and producers, regional tariffs made exporting difficult and food still needed to be imported to feed Vienna. The ANB, after lending heavily to banks during the crisis, had recalled its loans but allowed banks to amass foreign short-term debt, which now financed much of Austria's economic system. With its trade deficit and negative balance of accounts, the stability of Austria's currency, and thus of its economy and political system, was in fact still precariously in balance.

Outlook

Austria was "free," but its financial situation was neither safe nor sound. The country lacked long-term capital and its banks had taken in short-term loans in the form of renewable deposits instead. ANB President Reisch was aware that a general withdrawal of those funds, which meanwhile totaled about 247 million gold crowns (about $50 million), would put the ANB's free gold and foreign currency reserves of 226 million gold crowns (about $45 million) in danger. A sudden panic or coordinated attack would immediately deplete the central bank's hidden reserves of 11.2 million gold crowns (about $2.3 million), easily prompting a general withdrawal by the public.[120] The 52 million gold crowns ($10 million) of foreign currencies booked under "other activa" were in fact no reserves, as they consisted either of Kostdevisen ($6.7 million), had been lent on to Austrian enterprises (about $2 million), or were denominated in weak currencies (about $400,000). At most 6.2 million gold crowns (about $1.3 million) of these "other activa" could thus be used to defend the currency, providing the ANB with an undisclosed buffer of no more than $12.5 million. This represented about one-quarter of the banks' short-term debt, and any withdrawal beyond that would quickly push down the ANB's official cover ratio and was likely to provoke a self-sustained run on the currency.[121] The ANB had little real ammunition to defend the exchange rate and as long as Norman and Reisch remained at the helm of their respective institutions, the BoE was unlikely to pledge up front support.

Conseiller van Gijn did not think the situation that precarious. According to his calculations, the ANB could first make use of 45 million gold crowns (about $9 million) of loan funds earmarked for times of crisis, the rest of the free loan funds of 47 million (about $9.5 million), and of 49 million gold crowns (about $10 million) of Kostdevisen hidden among "other activa." Put together with the ANB's publicly declared gold and foreign reserves and openly booked Kostdevisen, it meant that the circulation of 596 million gold crowns (about $120) was effectively covered by reserves of 507 million (about $100 million), implying a cover ratio of 85 percent. Even the total withdrawal of all short-term credits would not bring the cover ratio below 50 percent if he was right. Either the Austrian currency was safe and sound, he had written to Zimmerman in December 1925, or one had to lose hope of ever obtaining a solid currency in Austria, or anywhere else for that matter.[122]

According to the report by Layton and Rist, the situation was indeed quite safe for other reasons as well. Based on optimistic figures provided to them by bank managers of the Credit-Anstalt and the Wiener Bankverein, foreign short-term borrowing did not put Austrian commercial banks in danger. The five largest Viennese banks had a total of 950 million gold crowns of creditors (about $190 million), of which 203 million gold crowns (about $41 million) came from foreign banks and another 100 million (about $20 million) from other foreign sources. They only considered the first group prone to sudden withdrawals, but subtracted from it 65 million gold crowns (about $13 million) lent by friendly banks, assuming that these institutions would not recall deposits if that put their Austrian affiliates in danger. In their view only up to 119 million gold crowns (about $24 million) were at risk of withdrawal at any single point in time. Since Vienna's big banks had deposits of up to 112 million gold crowns (about $22 million) abroad, Layton and Rist argued, they had sufficient foreign exchange to face a recall of short-term credits without needing recourse to the ANB at all.[123]

But what if banks actually had deposited fewer funds abroad than they claimed? What if foreign affiliates preferred withdrawing their deposits to saving their associates? What if foreign nonbanking institutions withdrew their deposits, too? What if people panicked? A withdrawal of all $60 million extended short-term to Austrian banks was three times the amount they reportedly held abroad. A sudden withdrawal would thus easily eat up Reisch's buffer of $12.5 million and immediately be detected by the public in the bank's official balance sheet. Once commercial banks' foreign deposits and the ANB buffer were used up, a withdrawal of the remaining $27.5 million of short-term deposits would quickly bring down the ANB cover ratio by half and provoke capital flight and a run by the public.

A look at financial markets indicates, however, that most foreign investors appear to have been unperturbed about the end of international control in Austria. Since reconstruction's start in 1922, the League of Nations' positive reporting on Austria's position had produced a gradual and steady increase in foreign confidence. Following the emission of the League's Austria loan in 1923, the price of its different tranches in London, New York, and Amsterdam had all risen, implying lower perceived risk. In other words, over time, investors in these financial centers were willing to pay more for the League bonds and the fixed annual dividend that they paid. For example, the London tranche traded in June 1923 at a price providing investors with a return of over 7 percent. In May 1926, two months before the end of League control in Austria, the effective yield had dropped to less than 6 percent (see Graph 6.3). The picture is the same for the Amsterdam and New York tranches, though at a consistently higher level for the latter, since U.S. investors generally expected a higher compensation for lending money to Europe.[124]

The positive outlook investors granted Austria might have been justified. The Austrian interwar economy did best during the two or three years following the League's departure. Releasing Austria into freedom had first of

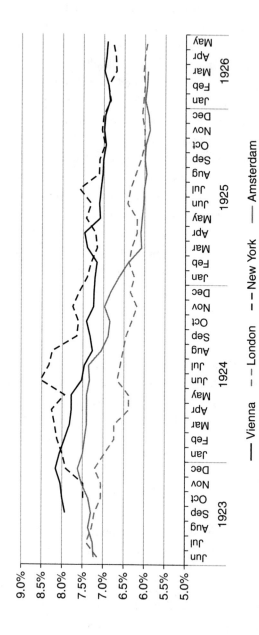

GRAPH 6.3. Yield of the Vienna, London, New York, and Amsterdam tranches of the 1923 League of Nations loan for Austria. *Source:* ANB, VI/9: Conseiller Reports.

all been politically expedient, but it might have been economically wise, too. Either way, accusations of exaggerated foreign control were misplaced. During the first year of League intervention, the Austrian government had succeeded in ignoring the General Commissioner's demands and stabilized the budget at a level deemed too high by him and the Financial Committee's experts. Chancellor Seipel had further refrained from introducing reforms he deemed unnecessary or unwise, thereby asserting the independence of his government and antagonizing the League's representatives in Vienna and Geneva. During the second year of Austrian reconstruction, the League General Commissioner had sided with the Austrian government regarding its requests to amend its spending limits and to free loan funds for productive investments. Finally, the new Austrian government under Chancellor Ramek had managed to bring the League's intervention to an end against the explicit wishes of the most expert members of the Financial Committee and without foreign banks being consulted. At the same time, despite statements to the contrary, the ANB under its President Richard Reisch was decisively pursuing a monetary policy opposed by the BoE, often with approval from the foreign Conseiller. For the three-and-a-half years of international control in Austria, the League, the General Commissioner, and the Conseiller might have been successfully controlling Austrian books and accounts, but not the policies that stood behind them.

It was a warm Monday morning on 5 July 1926 when Zimmerman boarded a train to Rotterdam at the Vienna Westbahnhof.[125] A week before Chancellor Ramek had given a breakfast in his honor, and the liberal *Neue Freie Presse* had commented that those who knew the circumstances and were not tempted by evil slogans of incitement were grateful for Zimmerman's sincere and attentive opposition to budgetary wastefulness and for his insistence on savings, which had been Austria's only possible escape from misery.[126] The day following Zimmerman's departure, the Socialist *Arbeiterzeitung* recalled fighting "foreign rule" of an "agent of foreign financial powers" for over three years. It claimed that the Socialist party had successfully defended the honor and independence of Austria and that the parting General Commissioner left "defeated."[127] Zimmerman, who had been honored by Czechoslovakia with the Order of the White Lion, was seen off by Chancellor Ramek and his Finance Minister, the only members of the government to personally come and wish him farewell, and by Vienna's ubiquitous Police Chief, Johann

Schober. Befitting to the international significance of the General Commissioner's mission, however, almost all members of the diplomatic corps were in attendance, too.[128] When shortly after nine the train pulled out of its station and the crowd dispersed, Zimmerman was undoubtedly not the only one breathing an expectant sigh of relief.

III

Collapse

7

The Precedence of Politics

1927–1929

> The Vienna Rothschilds continue to finance Heimwehr.
>
> —Vienna Embassy to Foreign Office London
> 25 November 1929

IN THE MORNING HOURS OF FRIDAY, 15 July 1927, angry workers at Vienna's electricity plants decided to lay down tools and march on the inner city. The previous day, a jury at a Vienna court had acquitted three young men of murder. The accused claimed to have acted in self-defense at the beginning of the year when they shot at Socialists, killing two of them, after a party reunion in the Burgenland town of Schattendorf. The lengthy court proceedings had been accompanied by intense newspaper coverage, and workers were enraged at what the British Ambassador rightly considered an "appalling verdict."[1] Without electric power, the personnel of Vienna's tramways joined the strike, and workers at the phone and telegraph bureaus walked out as well. Before midday, scores of agitated demonstrators were converging outside Austria's parliament to protest the miscarriage of justice.

Socialist party leaders had not explicitly called for such a strike, though the *Arbeiterzeitung* that morning had carried an inflammatory editorial, and so they were caught unprepared by the large turnout of protesters.[2] The Vienna police had expected disturbances, but not on such a massive scale. When a first group of demonstrators broke through the thin cordon of uniformed guards protecting the parliament building, they were charged aggressively by mounted police. Gathering cobblestones, the protesters reassembled and fought back, pulling officers from their horses and beating some of them severely. Outnumbered and threatened, probably fearing for their own lives, the police opened fire at the unruly demonstrators and retreated into the nearby Justizpalast, home of Austria's Supreme Court.

The police were followed by the enraged crowd, which encircled and then entered the building. While clerks, judges, and the police retreated further into the edifice, people began throwing documents into the street and setting them on fire. Soon parts of the building also stood in flames. A nearby police station was attacked and burned; the editorial offices of the Christian-Social *Reichspost,* also close by, were looted; and the headquarters of the anti-Socialist *Wiener Neue Nachrichten* was scorched. Undeterred by the midday heat, more and more people streamed in from the city's working-class districts. Outside the now blazing Justizpalast, a cheering crowd of demonstrators prevented fire engines from reaching hydrants to put out the flames. Desperate pleadings by Socialist politicians for the protesters to clear away fell on deaf ears, and the police then opened fire, this time using heavy machine guns. The unruly crowd immediately dispersed, but, strengthened with armed reinforcements, the police kept on hunting down individual demonstrators until nightfall.

The chaotic and lethal events of 15 July 1927 deepened the political rift in Austria between Socialists and conservatives and between Vienna and the provinces. Their aftermath quickly deteriorated into a blame game on both sides, and their exact course has since been studied thoroughly by Austrian historians of all political *couleur.*[3] On the one hand, Socialists accused Chancellor Ignaz Seipel, who in October 1926 had returned to the Chancellery, and Johann Schober, Vienna's Chief of Police, of intentional brutality and use of excessive force. On the other hand an internal 113-page police report went to great lengths to collect witness accounts that showed the violence originating from a boisterous working-class mob.[4] The final toll of bloodshed was 85 civilians and 4 policemen dead and more than 1,000 wounded, with 328 civilians and 163 police hospitalized for treatment.

To protest this massacre, the Socialists on Saturday declared a nationwide railway and transport strike for Monday, but they encountered strong opposition in the provinces. Both Socialists and the conservatives had formed paramilitary groups that the other side feared were plotting a takeover of the state. The Styrian Heimwehr, demanding that the strike be canceled, armed 20,000 of its men and threatened to march on the provincial capital of Graz. Caving in to Heimwehr threats and fearing renewed violence and bloodshed if they did not, the Socialist leadership called off the nationwide strike. By Monday life in Vienna had returned almost entirely to normal after public transport throughout the city was shut down on Saturday, with railway, postal, telephone, and telegraph workers still striking on Sunday.[5]

A year earlier, the end of League intervention in June 1926 had been widely celebrated and interpreted as an Austrian coming of age. As the government regained its freedom over fiscal policy without having to listen to the General Commisioner or the League, the country enjoyed the economic fruits of a balanced budget and stable currency. But as the bloodbath on 15 July 1927 painfully demonstrated, in terms of its political legacy, the League's departure had a destabilizing effect, which in turn entailed financial and economic consequences. While international control had still been in force, the Socialists denounced Alfred Rudolph Zimmerman and the League but refrained from attacking the Christian-Socials directly, out of fear of putting reconstruction at risk and being blamed if it failed. The Christian-Socials also had directed most of their scapegoating toward the General Commissioner, albeit less crudely, and had held him personally responsible for the sacking of state workers and other unpopular reforms. With the League's disappearance, however, this safety valve vanished and political rivalries between Austria's socialist and conservative parties turned violent and spilled into the streets. Economically, the young country experienced its best years of growth between 1926 and 1929, recouping ground lost to the economic contraction following the 1924 financial crisis. But Austria's financial stability and economic prosperity depended on domestic and foreign trust in the value of its new currency, the schilling. And as clashes between armed political factions grew more frequent and fears of civil war became more realistic, the risk of a general loss of confidence and a withdrawal of foreign short-term loans provoking broad capital flight became more acute.

From a purely economic perspective, the legacy of the League's intervention was salutary. Under the watchful eyes of the General Commissioner and the League Financial Committee, the Austrian government had balanced its budget and pursued a series of reforms aimed at strengthening financial and economic stability. The official reports and press releases composed by Zimmerman and his staff and disseminated through the Financial Secretariat in Geneva, while never free of criticism, had presented Austrian reconstruction in an overall positive light. Aimed at sustaining foreign confidence, they had helped create the idea of a viable and improving Austrian economy, both abroad and at home. Indeed, by 1926 many Austrians had become accustomed to the new political and economic confines of their country. Before the Financial Committee in Geneva, Chancellor Rudolf Ramek and Finance Minister Jakob Ahrer had vigorously argued that their budget was sustainable, that the economic outlook of their country was good, and that Austria could be released from international tutelage into freedom. One year later, the Viennese Chamber of Commerce and other interest groups, upon request from the Austrian Ministry of Trade, planned and set in motion a "Buy Austrian goods" campaign, to strengthen national production through substitution of imports with Austrian products.[6] The League of Nations and its financial experts had worked all along under the assumption that the country could be made economically viable, and they had managed to convince both Austrians and foreigners that they were right.

As will become clear, however, Austria's weakest link remained people's trust in the stability of its financial system and currency, which in turn were linked to the unsettling climate of its domestic politics. Otto Niemeyer and Henry Strakosch foresaw these problems when they warned their colleagues on the League Financial Committee in 1925 that the extent of foreign short-term loans to Austria posed a potential yet serious risk. According to their assessment, if an unforeseen event provoked the sudden retraction of most short-term loans from Austria and at the same time a customer run turned into capital flight, the Viennese banks and the Austrian currency would require outside assistance to weather the storm. To bolster foreign confidence, the Financial Committee had therefore succeeded in prolonging the Conseiller's term until 1929 and obtained Austrian consent to reinstate international control, if necessary, for the next ten years. The deadly rioting in 1927 did not yet provoke large incidents of capital flight or a run by depositors to exchange bank savings into foreign currency, but as political violence subsequently increased and global money markets tightened, both Austrians and foreign bankers grew nervous about Austria's political and financial stability.[7] As this chapter argues, by 1929 fears of political unrest spiraling out of control became so widespread that pervasive anxieties over civil war provoked capital flight and bank runs, contributing to the closure of Austria's second largest financial institution, the Boden-Kredit Anstalt (BKA) bank. The League of Nations intervention and international control had managed to instill confidence among Austrians in the viability of their economy, but not in the stability of the republican parliamentary system, and Austria was only as economically and financially stable as its domestic politics allowed.

Institut für Konjunkturforschung: Visualizing the Austrian Economy

If in 1922 few people could picture something akin to the Austrian economy, by the time that General Commissioner Zimmerman left Vienna the new nation-state had become a plausible reality to many economic practitioners. From 1922 to 1926 the League of Nations had helped uphold the postwar settlement that created Austria against its will, first affirming and ultimately confirming that Austria's economy was viable. Right after the war people had no clear understanding yet of what the terms "Austria" or "Austrian" might exactly signify, but a series of six new schilling notes issued in 1927 provided a visualization of potential answers. This second series of schilling bills celebrated the labor of workers and farmers by prominently displaying Austrian mining and agricultural activities, the country's primary sectors of employment, on the five- and ten-schilling notes. Austria's scientific and cultural potential were emphasized by depicting the building of the Academy of Sciences on the 100-schilling note and the town of Salzburg, home to the famous Festspiele, on the 1,000-schilling note. Austria was also represented as a country of regions, with Vienna figuring on two notes, and the town of Salzburg, the Salzkammergut, Styria, and the Wachau on one each. Finally, just like the first schilling notes issued in 1925, the new series showed hopeful portraits of young and expectant men and women. Austria was presented as a country that could produce, a country with its own geography, culture, and scientific achievements—in short, a country that indeed had a promising future. One of the clearest testimonies that what had formerly been an outlandish idea had become a familiar reality, was the foundation and work of the Österreichische Institut für Konjunkturforschung, the Austrian Institute for Business-Cycle Research.

Established in Vienna in January 1927, the Institute followed upon the creation of similar research bodies around the world, including the Berlin

Institut für Konjunkturforschung in 1925 and the older Harvard University Committee on Economic Research in 1917.[8] Much like its sister institutions, the Institute concentrated on collecting, analyzing, and distributing up-to-date statistics on the input and output of specific industries, overall energy and raw material requirements, and commodity and other price developments in Austria. Its self-proclaimed neutrality, free from governmental influence, was underlined by fashioning it as a cooperative project of all the country's major interest groups. The Vienna Chamber of Commerce was its initiator, but it counted the Federation of Industry, the Vienna Chamber of Labor, the Austrian National Bank (ANB), the federal railways, and important associations from Austrian banking and trade among its founders. Its independence and methodical approach bestowed the Institute with a claim of objectivity, which gave it access to reliable figures on monthly outputs, employment, and wages directly from trade associations of major industries, to the latest data on cross-border trade and national unemployment from government offices, and to up-to-date freight statistics from the federal railways.[9]

Its young directors, twenty-eight-year-old Friedrich Hayek and twenty-six-year-old Oskar Morgenstern, did not think that exact quantitative forecasts and management of economic performance were possible. Much like the League Financial Committee's international experts, they believed that markets were best left to themselves and governments should refrain from all too intensive interfering in the allocation of resources. But collecting and studying economic data, they thought, could produce not just useful analyses of present economic states, but might even allow for qualitative and carefully worded prognoses about the likelihood of future economic conditions. In his introduction to its first report in June 1927, Hayek explained the Institute's new approach to business cycle studies, including statistical measures to help account for seasonal variations, the calculation of trends, and the introduction of logarithmic scales in graphic representations. Out of its offices at the Vienna Chamber of Commerce, Hayek and Morgenstern composed, published, and distributed the Institute's monthly analyses of the current state of the Austrian and global economy. All this, of course, presupposed the existence of such an entity as an Austrian economy, one that could be studied, understood, and presented.

The reports thus not only provided a data-driven, wide-ranging analysis of the country's economic position and progress, but were in themselves testimony to and affirmation of the existence of an Austrian economy.[10] Their three sections—a monthly qualitative examination of Austria's economic position, a quantitative section devoted to economic and financial statistics, and a final roundup of foreign economic developments—delineated the Austrian economy within a national, regional, and global framework. All reports were amply illustrated with graphic curves representing economic developments over time, thus visualizing and asserting the developing reality of national economic performance.[11] In fact, in his introduction, Hayek announced that one of the Institute's main ambitions was to show how Austrian business cycles differed from those in larger economies like Germany or the United States.[12]

In their presentation of data, Hayek and Morgenstern were certainly limited by what was made accessible to them. Yet their selection of categories helps reveal how they chose to imagine, conceptualize, and represent Austria's national economy. As their German or U.S. counterparts, they understood industrial output and the export of finished goods to be the economy's fundamental motor of growth. The rising importance of Austria's service industry, responsible for significant invisible exports, did not figure notably in their reports, apart perhaps from tourism. Neither was agrarian production frequently discussed, nor much importance given to aggregate demand. There were attempts at tracking the latter through studying seasonally adjusted shoe sales or tobacco consumption, but unemployment, a persistent problem in Austria, was given a positive spin. As the reports took care to explain all too often, rising unemployment figures could be due to rationalization and modernization, which allowed firms to make do with fewer employees. The large iron and metal industries, as well as machine, locomotive, and wagon producers, had expanded during the war and their operations were outdated and overstaffed so that much unemployment originated there. If workers could find employment elsewhere, modernization meant more income for everyone, but new industrial sectors were slow to emerge and required capital for investment that was expensive to borrow. Providing for full employment was not a government responsibility, according to the Institute, and unemployment was seen as a problem that would be solved by market forces once tariffs disappeared and more foreign capital got invested in Austria.

The historical yet artificial dichotomy separating affluent Vienna from the poorer provinces was emphasized by two separate series of unemployment records. Similarly, even though more than a third of all employed Austrians earned their living from working the land, statistics on agrarian production were rarely reported while financial data was deemed fundamentally important and updated continuously. Prices were considered the means by which economies adjust, and variations in commodity prices or raw materials costs were understood as reactions to industrial demand, not global supply, and as reflective of economic activism. Industrial growth and increased export production were considered crucial for Austrian prosperity but deemed largely dependent on the availability of foreign credit to finance investments and modernizations. In contrast to Germany or the United States, the Austrian economy was understood as one highly dependent on the state of foreign capital markets and on export demand in neighboring countries and beyond.

A principal recurring image of the Austrian economy, first developed by the Harvard University Committee on Economic Research for the United States, was the "three-curve barometer," a triptych of indexes produced from (1) stock market statistics (the security market curve); (2) production indexes, wholesale commodity prices, and unemployment figures (the commodity market curve); and (3) discount rate and deposits data (the money market curve) (see Figure 7.1). Hayek elucidated in the Institute's first report how reading this barometer could help economists determine the momentum of Austria's business cycle. He explained that the end of a recession would first be detectable in rising stock exchange quotations, as knowledgeable investors would buy shares in anticipation of profits (security market curve). Thereafter, wholesale prices and industrial output would pick up (commodity market curve), and at a further stage money markets would start tightening in face of high credit demand. Finally the apex of activity on the stock exchange, with output still rising and money markets tightening, would signal the impending turnaround from growth to recession. In the United States the three curves had shown such correlations in the past, but, as would become clear, this logic did not apply to a small, open economy such as Austria's in the late 1920s. Although the stock exchange remained entirely lackluster, some sectors of Austria's economy experienced strong export-driven growth and others stagnated, while the liquidity of Vienna's capital market remained largely dependent on decisions taken in New York, London, or Berlin.

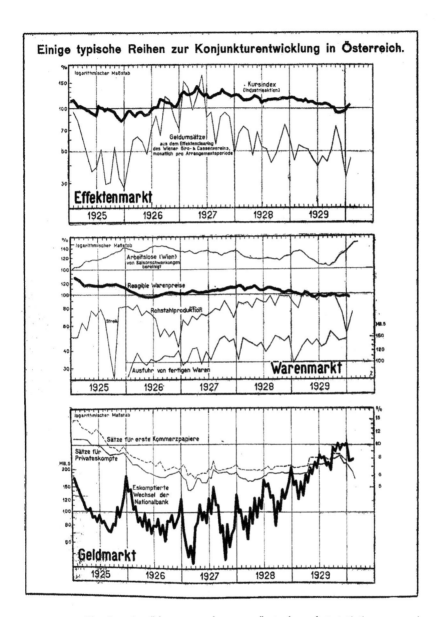

FIGURE 7.1. The Austrian "three-curve barometer": stock-market statistics, economic indexes, and financial data, 1925–1929. *Source: Monatsberichte des österreichischen Institutes für Konjunkturforschung* 4, no. 2 (1930): 23. WIFO Austrian Institute of Economic Research.

Foreign investors, but also Austrian policy makers in government or at the ANB seeking to obtain a clearer view of the state of Austria's economy, could turn to the Institute's publications, which filled the lacuna created after the General Commissioner's reports had ceased. Unlike the League's publications and in line with a view that deemed state policies to be largely extraneous to economic performance, the Institute did not discuss budgetary figures in its reports. But the economic data it collected shows that from 1926 to 1929 Austria experienced its best years of interwar economic growth, even though output of most producing sectors in 1929 still hardly managed to surpass prewar levels (see Graph 7.1). The best-performing segments were highly dependent on investments and exports, such as paper fabrication, agricultural machinery production, or the output from electrical industries, which grew impressively. But the large textile and construction sectors suffered from large overcapacities that were never fully occupied so that, overall, Austria continued to experience high unemployment and only moderate economic improvement.

The Institute's first reports, published during the third and fourth quarters of 1927, began rather upbeat as the recession that had followed the crash of 1924 seemed largely overcome. All industries had still reported falling production in 1925, but by 1926 the output of iron producers and cotton spinning had already returned to pre-crisis levels, and so had the coal consumption of Austria's leather industry. Wholesale commodity prices, in line with global developments, were rising during the third quarter, which, together with strong freight movements reported by the federal railways, strong export demand from Germany, Czechoslovakia, and Hungary, greater cashless payments, and growing raw material imports was interpreted as indicative of economic growth. Although chemical and rubber industries were still consuming less coal than in early 1924 and employment, even if above trend, was hardly picking up, the Institute estimated that Austria's economic upswing would continue. Iron and steel producers reported larger orders, the supply of foreign credits remained strong, and a reduction of rates in New York allowed the ANB, which after 15 July had raised its rate, to lower it back to 6.5 percent in the fall.[13]

Unemployment figures were considered unusually high in 1928, with workers in construction and agriculture suffering most (see Graph 7.2).[14] Liquidity was ample after the ANB had again reduced its discount rate from

6.5 to 6 percent at the end of January, and the continued rises of cashless transactions and railway cargo were seen as signs of growing turnover. However, industrial data began showing a mixed picture: coal consumption was unusually high and the paper industry and automobile producers were doing rather well, but export figures disappointed and seasonally adjusted wholesale commodity prices were falling and would continue to do so, indicating a slowing economy. Production data showed a drop in output across almost all major industries, but if recent increases in the discount rates of the Bank of England (BoE) and the Reichsbank were not to disrupt capital inflows to finance investments, the Institute deemed the immediate outlook "not unfavorable," with spring expected to bring more employment.[15] Austria's rising exports in 1927 were testimony to the fact that its economic performance relied on positive developments in other countries, so that the Institute's modestly positive outlook was made conditional on external developments, largely in Germany.[16]

An unexpected drop in unemployment in spring 1928 was cause for some optimism, but by June the Institute expected a standstill, as important impulses from foreign countries were disappearing. Industrial output was still mixed, with good production and employment figures reported by the iron and paper industry and automobile and machine manufacturers. Continued growth in freight traffic and cashless transactions indicated some further rise in economic activity as well. But even if, for Vienna, seasonally adjusted unemployment dropped below expectations, it remained high in the provinces, and on an annual basis the export of finished goods and import of raw materials was in fact declining. Since investments financed with foreign credits had supported the upswing since 1926, the Institute claimed, a further revival would depend on the development of capital markets and the availability of foreign credits come fall.[17]

But global money markets tightened over the summer of 1928, with New York dominated by its bull market on Wall Street. A slow but steady rise in the cost for money thereafter was blamed for much of Austria's economic stagnation, which the Institute predicted would continue until a global upswing revived the world economy. In early fall, seasonally adjusted unemployment was still too high, especially among textile and construction workers, and as the year came to an end, the Institute perceived a real danger that the high cost of foreign capital might tip Austria into recession. During the fall, chemicals, wood, metal, and machine producers had done better year-on-year, and paper, cardboard, and automobile producers had also increased their output, but most of the other sectors languished. Exports of finished goods and the import of raw materials kept falling, imports were lower, and cargo traffic was waning, as were cashless transactions. In light of the economic downswing in neighboring states, the Institute deemed it remarkable that Austria was not starting to experience a recession itself, a fact it interpreted as proof that Austria's economy was strong and consolidated.[18]

The winter of 1928–1929 was extraordinarily severe and large stretches of the Danube froze over, pushing seasonally adjusted unemployment to new records.[19] By March warmer weather returned, and with it a rise in Viennese employment, though there was less marked improvement in the provinces. Production had suffered from the cold, and even though the iron industry still reported good orders, the overall export of finished goods and import of raw materials was lower than in previous years. Year-on-year, seasonally adjusted cashless transactions at first appeared higher, but eventually they declined too, as did freight traffic and wholesale commodity prices.[20] Global money markets, led by the United States, kept tightening, making new foreign loans to Austria unlikely and the ANB felt forced to react to a large increase of discounts by raising its own rate in April.[21]

The second quarter of 1929 brought record employment for Vienna, but the agrarian sector in the provinces was still shedding jobs. Exports were dropping all around, wholesale prices kept falling, and the iron and steel industry now reported declining orders. Despite paper producers, agricultural machinery, and electrical industries reporting satisfactory output, and leather and textile industries showing improvement, the Institute now deemed the general prospects for growth explicitly unfavorable. Rates on the Vienna money market remained unchanged, while discounts with the ANB rose further, and a drop in its foreign reserves implied that foreign capital was in fact being withdrawn. The Institute reiterated that Austrian stagnation despite downswings in neighbor countries and tight credit markets was a positive sign, but that the ongoing rally on the New York Stock Exchange meant there was still no hope for new credits. Its report warned therefore that a worldwide, U.S.-induced recession was likely before an upswing could occur.[22]

The BoE's decision in June to follow New York and increase its discount rate risked suffocating any chances of growth but showed no effect of tampering speculation on Wall Street. In Austria, ANB discounts remained high as a tight money environment squeezed liquidity. Until the U.S. economy turned around, the Institute remarked in September 1929, stagnation was the best Austria could hope for. Seasonally adjusted unemployment had improved remarkably over the summer of 1929, thanks mainly to tourism and active construction, and, on an annual basis, coal and electricity production were now stable. Moreover, the iron and steel industry reported high output and orders, and freight figures reached a new high. But prices kept falling and exports were down further, so that despite good sales of machines and cars as well as positive reports from the electronics, paper, cardboard, and wood industries, the country's general production index was still underperforming (see Graph 7.1).[23]

The Institute had predicted correctly that things had to turn worse in the United States and the rest of the world before they could get any better. In late October 1929, after stock quotations had risen for over half a decade, shares on Wall Street tumbled and panic set in among investors. Within just three weeks the Dow Jones Industrial Average lost almost half its value. Speculators who had invested with borrowed money were completely impoverished. Making matters worse, the Federal Reserve induced deflation to "cleanse" the economy instead of providing liquidity, which reduced investments, caused problems for borrowers and banks, and resulted in mass unemployment. The U.S. economy entered what would become known as the Great Depression, which—inter alia—put an end to three years of Austrian economic growth. But in Austria growth had merely been a recovery from the financial crisis of 1924, so that in 1929 the country still barely produced more than it had in 1913 (albeit with fewer workers, and with important variations across sectors).

As the Institute's reports make clear, interwar Austria's best couple of years in terms of economic growth were not the product of uniform performance. Overall, modern, export-oriented industries had done best, but traditional sectors had faced strong international competition and global overproduction while lacking resources to pay for indispensable modernizations. Paper, iron, and steel producers and the manufacturers of automobiles, chemicals, or electronic goods had done well, as had agricultural productivity and output, with paper production benefiting from domestic wood supply and the chemical industry from advanced human capital. But larger metal and machine factories, producers of furniture, cement, and bricks, or Austria's textiles, cotton, and wool-spinning industries suffered from overcapacities or were hampered by foreign competition and protective tariffs.[24] The economy's fastest-growing sectors lay in industry, where output had grown by almost 40 percent since 1926, reflecting a successful adjustment to foreign and domestic demand, though growth there was strongest in metal and paper industries, which had previously suffered most from the recession. Growing electricity production and freight transport, benefiting from new hydroelectricity projects and state-funded electrification of the federal railways, also indicated continued economic growth, but Austria's general production index, having still risen impressively in 1927, seemed to stagnate thereafter (see Graph 7.1). Austria's weaker sectors were producing less than before the war, and where there had been growth of industrial or agricultural output, it had been mainly achieved through investments in technology and electrification or new forms of management and assembly lines, which undoubtedly increased unemployment.

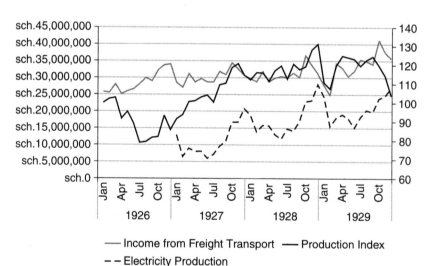

GRAPH 7.1. Austrian economic indicators, 1926–1929 (income to Austrian railways from freight transport in Austrian schillings on left axis, production index [January 1926=100] and electricity production in million KwH on right axis). *Source: Monatsberichte des österreichischen Institutes für Konjunkturforschung.*

Following a strong increase of jobless numbers in 1925 and 1926, the employment situation had improved somewhat in 1927 and 1928. But new work was mainly to be found in Vienna, where the Socialist municipality used high taxation to finance important public ventures, above all the construction of working-class housing. In the provinces, though, unemployment remained high, due to modernizations in heavy industry, manufacturing, and agriculture. Austrian workers, particularly in the steel and iron industries, produced up to twice as much per hour in 1927 as in 1922, thereby earning significantly higher wages, while costing industries less per unit of output. Thus iron and metal workers, but also textile manufacturers and cotton spinners, suffered disproportionately from unemployment.[25] Toward the end of 1929, however, seasonally adjusted unemployment grew also in Vienna, pushing national unemployment figures to new records by 1930. Toward the end of 1929 there were over 225,000 men and women officially unemployed in Austria, less than 10 percent of the national workforce but more than 10 percent of the 2 million Austrian employees drawing a salary (see Graph 7.2).[26]

The wealthy class of Austrian rentiers had completely disappeared, and higher state officials or the free professions had all gotten used to lower living

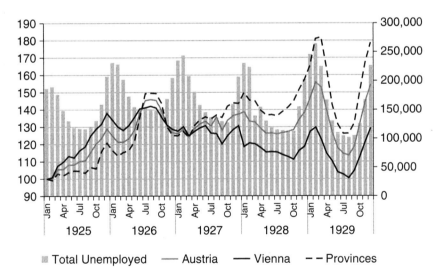

GRAPH 7.2. Unemployment in Vienna, the Austrian provinces, and overall in Austria, 1925–1929 (Austria, Vienna, and the provinces indexed [January 1925=100] and seasonally adjusted, on left axis; total number of unemployed in Austria, seasonally adjusted, on right axis). *Source: Monatsberichte des österreichischen Institutes für Konjunkturforschung.*

standards, too. Workers and simple employees were generally doing better than before the war, largely because rents were frozen, but in terms of food or clothing costs, their real wages were probably lower, which fueled demands for wage increases.[27] For employers, in turn, socialist legislation had increased the cost of labor by shortening the working day, introducing workers' vacations, and making unemployment insurance obligatory. Municipal taxation in socialist Vienna included several charges placed specifically on banks, which made credit more expensive, and extra taxes on wealth and consumption of the middle and upper classes. Industrialists and employers blamed unemployment on taxation and legislation making production more expensive. Labor leaders argued that unemployment might be remedied temporarily by further shortening the workday, but they also understood that more well-paying employment opportunities had to be newly created, which required economic growth and investments. During the League years, the Socialists had resigned themselves to defending the fiscal interests of the Vienna municipality and the social achievements of earlier legislation. But with its focus limited to budgetary retrenchment, the League had left the problem of production and unemployment unattended and industrial workers now demanded better workplace conditions and higher salaries.

The publications of the Austrian Institute for Business-Cycle Research steered clear from politics but noted and even celebrated the country's economic performance. To the editors, there was no question as to Austria's economic viability, with agriculture producing significantly more in 1929 than in 1913 and the important rise in domestic energy production and tourism improving the country's balance of payments. They acknowledged that to prosper Austria required further growth in exports and capital imports, and praised its economic resilience in the face of regional slumps and tightening money markets. Its early reports were couched in optimism, though the Institute did expect and forecast the momentous correction that shocked the United States toward the end of October 1929. With their eyes strictly fixated on economic statistics, however, they failed to predict or even foresee the unrelated collapse of Austria's second-largest bank one month earlier. The League had successfully helped to stabilize Austria's budget and currency, and convinced Austrians of the viability of their economy, but not of its political system, which was gradually breaking apart along class lines. On Wall

Street it was falling company profits and the correction of British share prices that triggered the panic, but in Austria, financial instability was the consequence of political turmoil.

The Rise of Heimwehr

On 30 June 1926, the day League control in Austria ended, the Socialist newspaper *Der Abend* disclosed difficulties at the Zentralbank, the clearing bank for Austria's savings banks that held many of their deposits. The news provoked heavy withdrawals and developed into a political scandal for the government party. Known as a Christian-Social party bank, the Zentralbank had assisted provincial banks in Styria and Lower Austria, where some Christian-Social politicians had corrupted the financial management of public affairs and accumulated large debts.[28] The Austrian government guaranteed the Zentralbank's sch.100 million (about $14 million) of savings deposits and granted a temporary moratorium on the bank's liabilities of sch.120–150 million, mobilizing Treasury reserves (50 million), advances from the ANB (10 million), and funds from the League loan remainder (14.4 million).[29] Otto Niemeyer, who thought only banks and the ANB should have taken action, considered the Austrian government's intervention a "mixture of politics and folly," ruling out advancing any further resources from the League loan.[30] The British embassy in Vienna observed widespread anxiety about the financial dangers the scandal incurred and general suspicion against Austrian government Ministers, some of whom had been deeply involved in the financial scandals.[31]

The Socialists demanded a parliamentary inquiry into the outrageous affair, which revealed that, in return for assisting failed provincial banks, the Zentralbank had received funds from the ANB and the public Postsparkasse, the latter of which had meanwhile similarly accumulated enormous losses.[32] Chancellor Rudolf Ramek and the entire Christian-Social party came under heavy attack from the Socialist opposition over the summer. When in the fall state workers demanded to raise their wages by 23 percent or face a national strike, with railway workers also likely to voice new wage demands, Chancellor Ramek followed Seipel's precedent.[33] On 15 October 1926, his cabinet resigned over the financial scandals his party ministers had been involved in, but publicly blamed the risk of an impending national strike. Seipel returned to the Chancellery four days later to form a new government, promising to rid the party of corruption.[34]

Chancellor for a second time, Seipel successfully negotiated with state workers, reaching a quick agreement to raise their wages by 12.5 percent, thereby avoiding a national strike.[35] As budget debates proceeded in parliament, Seipel rapidly obtained an understanding with the Socialists, promising a revision of handicapped and elderly insurance in return for the opposition's support in passing a budget, and probably its cessation of their attacks connected to the banking scandal as well.[36] The truce naturally proved short-lived, and by February 1927 the Socialists demanded new national elections, for which a date was set in April. The Christian-Socials and Pan-Germans formed an anti-Socialist bloc, which further incorporated the National Socialists, campaigning against the "Austro-Bolshevik" overtaxation of Vienna's municipality, while the Socialist counter-campaign concentrated on the banking scandals and the corruption of the Christian-Social party.[37]

In the last elections in late 1923, the Socialists had received 39.6 percent of the vote and the Christian-Socials 45 percent, relying on the Pan-German party to sustain a parliamentary majority. Now the Socialist party leadership appeared hopeful that the contested elections on 24 April 1927 provided a real chance at gaining more seats in the National Assembly, perhaps even close to half.[38] But despite a high voter turnout, the elections produced little, though perhaps portentous change. The Socialists obtained 42 percent of all votes and increased their number of seats from 68 to 71. The unity list, including Christian-Socials and Pan-Germans, obtained 48.2 percent of the vote and secured 85 seats in parliament. As Chancellor Seipel had been forced to make generous promises to the Pan-Germans in order for them to join his list, the Christian-Socials ended up with only 72 seats, one more than the Socialists, while 12 went to the Pan-Germans and the remaining 9 to the conservative Agrarian League.[39]

Three months later the unrest of Friday, 15 July 1927, was brutally put down by Chancellor Seipel and Police Chief Schober, before order was quickly restored with the help of Vienna's Socialist administration.[40] Envoy Franckenstein feared that foreign investors might question Austrian stability, but discovered that in the London City observers actually admired the Chancel-

lor's strong-willed action to suppress the disturbance.[41] The ANB also officially reported that the riots had provoked no withdrawal of foreign short-term
loans, though Conseiller Robert Kay wrote to Norman that capital to the
amount of $10 million, equaling 10 percent of central bank reserves, had in
fact fled the country.[42] Moreover, the ANB had given banks abroad instructions to intervene in support of Austrian currency, and its Director, Viktor
Brauneis, had presciently noted how Austrians were "satisfied that in normal
times the exchange is safe, but they do not trust it in a crisis."[43]

The Socialists had gained in the elections and were perceived as a threat
by Chancellor Seipel and those economic forces interested in keeping labor
down. There was a real fear on the right that the Socialists were cover for
Bolshevik actors plotting a communist revolution. Even liberal conservatives
and industrialists supported the strengthening Heimwehr, a reactionary, fascist force bent on fighting socialism, but also on replacing parliamentary
democracy with a dictatorship. With Chancellor Seipel's blessing and, unbeknown to him, clandestine Italian support, the Heimwehr transformed itself into the country's most vocal political movement, uniting almost all
"anti-Marxist" groups, from right-wing student organizations and Pan-
German Turners, to anticapitalist farmers and industrial monarchists.[44]
Led by the Innsbruck lawyer Richard Steidle and the murderer of Rosa Lux-
emburg and Karl Liebknecht, the German Major Waldemar Pabst, it became
increasingly more outspoken in its political demands for constitutional reform and opposition to organized labor, threatening to establish a fascist dictatorship by force. In 1927 and 1928 the Heimwehr held public marches
throughout the country and was regularly confronted by Socialist counter-
marchers. After the massacre of 1927 the Socialists had further developed
their own paramilitary organization, the Republican Schutzbund, to defend
democracy, but conservative politicians suspected that it was to be used to
prepare and then sustain a workers' revolution.

Conflict between the armed Heimwehr and Socialist Schutzbund for the
first time threatened to became acute in the fall of 1928. The Styrian Heimwehr announced a march in the largely Socialist industrial town of Wiener
Neustadt in Lower Austria. The Socialists called for a counter-manifestation,
risking a violent clash that many feared could result in civil war, revolution,
or a coup d'état. Socialist appeals to Seipel to ban both manifestations were
ignored by the Chancellor. Instead, on Sunday, 7 October 1928, the two

factions, under pouring rain, marched separately through the empty town, with a heavy military presence in place to prevent any clashes. Despite all trepidation, the manifestations passed peacefully and without any violence.[45] But to some extent Seipel had proven that it was he alone who was maintaining the peace in Austria and keeping the two factions from attacking each other.

In November 1928, shortly before parliament was scheduled to elect a new Austrian President, Chancellor Seipel publicly announced his own views on constitutional reform.[46] Pandering to the Heimwehr and the right, he proposed strengthening the President's executive powers in times of emergency, granting him the right to appoint cabinets and dissolve the legislature, and to let the general electorate vote him into office. Seipel's plans were paramount to weakening the legislature and, though they were largely unfeasible, they understandably provoked Socialist outrage. In April 1929 Seipel then surprisingly stepped down.[47] Historians have debated whether his resignation was wholehearted or motivated by a desire to create conditions for yet another return as Austria's savior at a later date.[48] As will be shown, this might have indeed been his plan, since his resignation triggered an escalation of political and financial uncertainty in Austria. The League of Nations control had not only contributed to Austrian economic and financial stability through providing a credibility mechanism and foreign funds, it had also created political stability, which was now gradually unraveling. After the League had left, Chancellor Seipel was perceived by many to be a strongman who could keep the country from descending into civil war, but his replacements inspired less confidence.

Seipel's successor in 1929, the industrialist Ernst Streeruwitz, a former nobleman and one of three Christian-Social parliamentarians who had marched with the Heimwehr through Wiener Neustadt in 1928, outlawed all uniformed demonstrations in Austria for six months. The Heimwehr put heavy pressure on Streeruwitz and, ignoring the order, continued uniformed manifestations disguised as religious *Fahnenweihen* (banner blessings), calling for a coup d'état if constitutional reform was postponed much longer. The Socialists reacted with yet another uniformed march through Wiener Neustadt, upon which the Heimwehr announced a march on Vienna as soon as the ban by Streeruwitz expired in the fall. In August, a heavy exchange of fire between the Heimwehr and the Schutzbund in the Styrian industrial town of St. Lorenzen left three dead and two hundred wounded, once more rekindling fears of a civil war among many concerned Austrians. Finally, Streeruwitz was forced by Christian-Social politicians who sympathized with the Heimwehr to resign on 26 September, three days before their scheduled march on Vienna.[49] Streeruwitz's successor was no other than Johann Schober, the Vienna Police Chief whose men had helped put down Socialist protests outside the Justizpalast in 1927.[50] Could Schober be trusted to resist the Heimwehr and its demand for constitutional reform if it marched on the Austrian capital to take over the government? We shall see that Schober let down the Heimwehr, which until then he had actively supported, but first we must turn to the financial fallout of the tense atmosphere stirred up by the marching columns of Heimwehr and Schutzund.

The Collapse of the Boden-Kredit Anstalt

The crisis surrounding the Boden-Kredit Anstalt (BKA) bank in Vienna in early October 1929, right after the Heimwehr's march on the capital, is a pivotal moment in Austria's interwar history.[51] For the historian Charles Gulick, the BKA crisis was a "political event of the first importance," directly related to the rumors and polemics surrounding the Heimwehr's belligerent behavior.[52] Fears of a coup d'état and civil war provoked a run on the banks and capital flight, Gulick argued, which forced the BKA to announce its problems, seek assistance, and eventually close.[53] The bank's sudden demise widely signaled the precariousness of Austrian financial and political stability, revealed gross mismanagement at the country's largest enterprises, and drew attention to the tenuousness of its banking sector. As we shall see in Chapter 8, the hurried merger of the BKA with the Credit-Anstalt bank (CA), Austria's largest bank, directly contributed to the collapse of the latter in 1931, and thereby to the country's economic and political difficulties during the Great Depression. Based on a detailed analysis of financial data, we will see that the BKA's collapse was not just due to mismanagement and fraud, nor uniquely related to the Heimwehr's march on Vienna, but that it was the consequence of a prolonged period of financial and political uncertainty, triggered by the unexpected resignation of Chancellor Seipel in April 1929.

Before the war the BKA had been banker to the Habsburgs and Vienna's aristocracy, and like other Vienna banks, it was cut off from most of its industrial investments in the successor states following the armistice. Under the leadership of Rudolf Sieghart, its ambitious and extremely charismatic (if highly dubious) director, the bank pursued an expansionary policy throughout the 1920s. After a series of smaller mergers, it swallowed both the midsized Allgemeine Verkehrsbank and the Unionbank, together with their industrial conglomerates, in 1926.[54] By 1929 the BKA had assembled a large portfolio of ill-performing industrial shares and held controlling interests in over a hundred industrial enterprises, many of them loss-making, but could not sell its assets on the lackluster Vienna Stock Exchange without booking a loss.[55] Sieghart irresponsibly gambled on a more prosperous future, extending working capital to companies that barely produced enough revenue to cover their costs or were unprofitable, demanding that they pay dividends from still reserves and support share prices in expectation of future earnings.[56] Like other Austrian banks, the BKA sought foreign credits to finance its industrial concerns and expand beyond Austria's borders, but it falsified balances, reported unwarranted profits, and continued to pay exorbitant dividends from its own still reserves to uphold a favorable standing in the eyes of foreign creditors (it still paid 15 percent in 1928). The bank also relied heavily on the ANB for vital liquidity, and extensive discounting of financial bills supported much of this fraudulent activity.[57] In 1928 the BKA had surpassed its discounting limit of sch.60 million (about $8.5 million) with the ANB, and during the two weeks from 15 to 30 September 1929 its discounts rose further to reach sch.121 million (about $17 million).[58] According to ANB Director Viktor Brauneis, the situation came to a head because, after a prolonged summer of "general insecurity and discontent," Viennese banks experienced a run by the public and the ANB refused to provide further liquidity to the BKA, forcing it to choose between merger or liquidation.[59]

Whereas the first, fundamental cause of the bank's demise is well documented, the second, linking the timing of events to a run on the banks, remains largely based on anecdotal evidence.[60] Nevertheless, the twofold explanation, that is, continued mismanagement and a sudden bank run, has been repeated by many historians.[61] The ANB's monetary history by Wolfgang Zipser argues that a political crisis coupled with rumors about the bank's difficulties in September 1929 provoked widespread withdrawals, capital flight, and a recall of foreign loans.[62] Rudolf Nötel explains that at times of political crisis the BKA was a most likely victim of depositors' distrust because of its well-known links with the fascist Heimwehr.[63] Fritz Weber writes that political panic in the fall resulted in a run on banks by foreign creditors and domestic depositors, eager to transfer their money abroad.[64] Few primary sources are available to scrutinize these claims, but financial data have not been sufficiently analyzed by historians in this regard. As will be shown, political turmoil might have indeed provoked a run on Viennese banks in September 1929, but the panic should not have come as a surprise to bankers and financiers.

Both Heimwehr and the Schutzbund marched around Vienna on Sunday, 29 September 1929, but their powerful manifestations of force passed peacefully. Fears of civil war proved unfounded, and none of the demonstrations turned violent. Soon enough, Chancellor Johann Schober disappointed Heimwehr agitators by insisting that what both of them considered legitimate constitutional demands be obtained exclusively through legal means and parliamentary compromise. Still, given the politically tense atmosphere, it is perhaps not surprising that nervous citizens hurried to withdraw savings and acquire foreign currency throughout September. Austrian banks paid out sch.44 million (about $6 million) that month and a further sch.40 million (about $5.5 million) in October, while the ANB itself, from 15 September to 15 November, reported the almost equivalent loss of sch.78 million in foreign reserves (about $11 million). The BKA, which probably suffered more than a third of these withdrawals, sought emergency liquidity from the ANB, and after the latter refused, finally presented Chancellor Schober with the bank's untenable situation on Saturday, 5 October 1929. From 15 to 30 September 1929 alone BKA discounts had risen from sch.85 to 121 million (about $12 to $17 million) (see Graph 7.3). Further supporting the BKA with liquidity risked endangering the ANB's own ability to defend the schilling.[65]

The National Bank expected a catastrophe if the BKA was not merged with the CA, citing the risk of a run on the currency if panic broke out. Louis Rothschild, large shareholder and President of the CA, was approached on Sunday, 6 October, and by Tuesday a secret deal to seal the merger was being negotiated between ANB Director Brauneis and the CA's directors. The CA

committed to successively reduce more than half of the sch.132 million
(about $18.5 million) of the mainly financial discounts it would inherit from
the BKA. In return, the ANB, via foreign banks, would covertly (and illic-
itly) provide the CA with up to $15 million of foreign currency deposits.[66]
As Finance Minister Otto Juch explained before the Nationalrat several
weeks later, the Austrian government had encouraged the successful merger
to prevent the BKA and its industrial conglomerates from closing their doors;
and by agreeing, he thought the CA's directors had prevented a crisis of the
first magnitude. The merger might have indeed prevented a larger panic and
saved thousands of jobs, but its announcement still caused general consternation in Vienna, especially among shareholders, many of whom lost a large
portion of their capital in return for new CA shares.[67]

The deteriorating position of the BKA throughout 1929 is well illustrated
by the high percentage of financial bills among the paper it presented to the
ANB for discount (see Graph 7.3). As the Austrian economy slowed down in
1928 and its industrial concerns turned to it for liquidity, the BKA resorted
to discounting financial bills with the ANB to obtain cash. The bulk of
the BKA's demands stemmed from just a few of its principal participations,
and half of its discounted bills were in the names of only three large concerns: the car manufacturer Steyr, the oil producer Fanto, and the textile
conglomerate Mauthner. The BKA had consistently wound down its discounts with the ANB after the 1924 crisis, and its liabilities to the ANB had
been reduced to nil by 1927, but after it acquired the Allgemeine Verkehrsbank and the Unionbank, its discounts with the ANB had grown to excessive levels. The BKA used foreign deposits and ANB discounts to finance its
ailing industrial concerns, and by 1929 the outstanding debt owed to it by
the car producing Steyr conglomorate alone amounted to sch.106 million
(about $15 million), or almost 120 percent of BKA's own share capital, but
the bank still required that Steyr pay a 5 percent dividend that year.[68] One
reason the BKA could continue to borrow extensively for so long was that
ANB President Richard Reisch, one of the BKA's directors until 1922, was
under Sieghart's spell, but eventually the ANB had to put a stop to the latter's high-risk gamble.[69]

This account is substantiated by a look at the ANB's official balance sheets.
According to its figures, the ANB lost no significant amount of foreign
currency during the first three quarters of 1929, but faced a significant drain

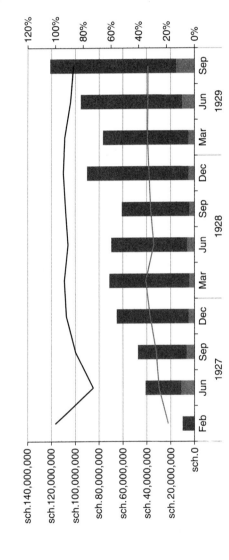

GRAPH 7.3. Discount movements of Boden-Kredit Anstalt with the Austrian National Bank, February 1927–September 1929. *Source:* ANB 1256/1929: *Eskontbewegungen der Boden-Kredit Anstalt.*

■ Financial Discounts —— Percent of Financial Paper among BKA Discounts
■ Commercial Discounts —— Percent of ANB's Portfolio consisting of BKA Discounts

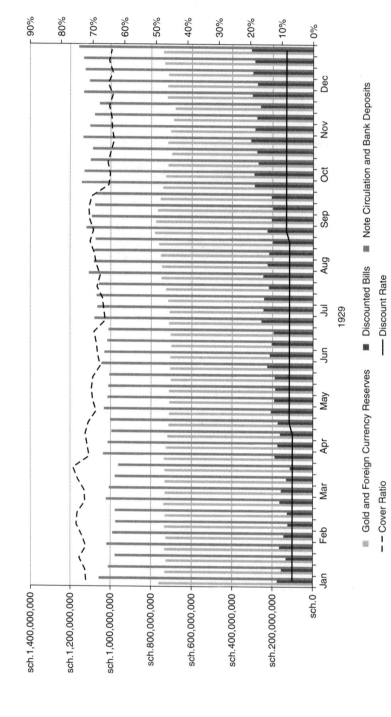

GRAPH 7.4. Weekly figures published by the Austrian National Bank, January–December 1929. *Source: Neue Freie Presse.*

Legend:
- Gold and Foreign Currency Reserves
- Discounted Bills
- Note Circulation and Bank Deposits
- – – Cover Ratio
- —— Discount Rate

1929

on its foreign reserves at the end of the summer (see Graph 7.4). From mid-September to the end of October 1929, the ANB reported a drop of sch.83.5 million (about $12 million) in foreign reserves. At the same time the disclosed amount of discounts by banks increased dramatically, leaving the central bank no choice but to report a drop in the cover ratio from 71 percent in mid-September to 63 percent in late October. These data thus give credence to the explanation that a bank run and capital flight preceding the Heimwehr march on 29 September 1929 were partially responsible for the timing of BKA's unsurmountable problems. But central banks' balance sheets were regularly manipulated to influence public opinion and are not always a reliable historical source.[70]

In order to establish whether political turmoil provoked a panic that timed the bank's demise, we must use financial data that are not as easily and regularly manipulated: data produced by the markets. Three different sets of data will be used for this purpose. The first set compares interest rates to estimate the change in foreign bankers' risk assessment of Austria in 1929. The second set looks at the yield spread between two Austrian bonds to evaluate Austrian investors' perceived probability of a financial crisis and government default. Finally, a third set of data uses exchange rate differentials to measure short-term expectations of currency depreciation in Austria. Together, the three sets of data reveal that there was nothing sudden about the panic in September 1929 and that intensifying financial apprehension during the summer had probably been triggered by Chancellor Seipel's resignation in April of that year.

The Foreign Bankers

Historians tend to agree that the announced Heimwehr march on Vienna provoked a bank run and flight of capital, forcing the BKA to reveal its untenable position. To discern the actual impact of Heimwehr polemics on financial stability, we first look at the minutes of the directors' meetings of the Vienna Bankverein (WBV), one of Austria's largest and best-managed banks at the time. They are kept at the Credit-Anstalt archive in Vienna and uniquely contain bimonthly lists of foreign banks' deposits. Foreign short-term borrowing was an important source of capital for Austrian banks during the interwar period and usually consisted of three-month renewable deposits, so-called rembourse credits, mostly denominated in U.S. dollars or pounds sterling. The total amounts of U.S. dollars and pounds sterling deposited by foreign banks with the Vienna Bankverein from 1925 to 1931 are reproduced in Graph 7.5.

A careful analysis of these figures helps reveal how foreign financiers perceived Austrian risk. Following the end of reconstruction in 1926 (Graph 7.5, column A) WBV expanded its business with foreign deposits, which grew quickly during 1927. There was a sharp yet unexplained drop in foreign deposits at the beginning of 1928, but they recovered during the year and, following the peaceful outcome of the Wiener Neustadt demonstration on 7 October 1928 (Graph 7.5, column F), foreign borrowing, in both dollars and pounds, rose to new heights. Shortly after the resignation of Chancellor Seipel on 3 April 1929 (Graph 7.5, column G), however, the amount of foreign deposits peaked and began to decline. An analysis of these data by Philip Cottrell with C. J. Stone shows that there was no correlation between the amount of deposits and the interest rate demanded by lenders, and it might be reasonable to assume that foreign banks looked to political developments when deciding about their lending policies.[71]

The rate of interest paid for these foreign deposits is in fact instructive. Comparing it with the rate charged for similar deposits in London or New York, it allows us to deduce the risk premium foreign bankers demanded for placing their funds with WBV in Vienna. This spread in interest rates is shown in Graph 7.5 as a black line for dollar deposits and a gray line for deposits in pounds sterling. Referring to the right axis, the lines indicate the difference in percentage points between the interest rates paid in New York or London for a three-month deposit and the mean of the corresponding rates paid by WBV at the time. The Vienna riots of July 1927 provoked a sudden rise in the spread for dollar deposits, but despite the blood spilled in Vienna's streets there was little change in pound spreads (Graph 7.5, column E), and dollar spreads soon fell back as well. Before and after the Wiener Neustadt demonstration on 7 October 1928 (Graph 7.5, column F) the dollar rate rose and then fell, but from March 1929 onward, as Heimwehr agitation became more threatening and vocal, the risk premium on dollar deposits increased steadily. Strikingly, it seems like the resignation of Chancellor Seipel in April (Graph 7.5, column G) heralded the climb of the dollar premium,

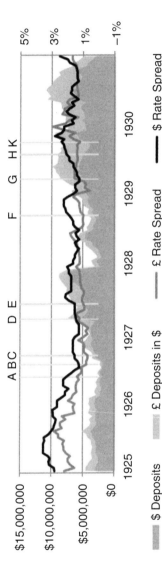

GRAPH 7.5. Foreign dollar and sterling deposits with Wiener Bankverein (both in US$), February 1925–November 1931 and rate differential (risk premium) between their median interest rate and the relevant rates in New York and London. *Legend*: A: Termination of control, 30 June 1926 and Zentralbank-Affair. B: Publication of the Zentralbank inquiry and problems at PSK, 15 September 1926. C: Seipel returns to Chancellery, 30 October 1926. D: General elections, 24 April 1927. E: Wiener-Neustadt demonstrations, 15 July 1927. F: Wiener-Neustadt demonstrations, 7 October 1928. G: Seipel resignation, 7 April 1929. H: Fatal clash in St. Lorenzen, Styria, 18 August 1929. K: BKA crisis, 8–15 October 1929. *Sources*: CA, Wiener Bankverein Protokollbücher, 1925–1931. Bankers and acceptance rates from Board of Governors of the Federal Reserve System, *Annual Statistical Digest: Banking and Monetary Statistics 1941–1970*, "Banking and Monetary Statistics 1914–1941" (1970), pp. 444–445, 656–657.

and notably the amount of dollar deposits also decreased at that time. This suggests that during the summer of 1929, as the Heimwehr ignored Streeruwitz's prohibition of uniformed demonstrations, threatened a coup d'état, and announced that it would march on Vienna, foreign creditors extending U.S. dollars to WBV viewed events in Austria with concern, demanding higher compensation for their risk and sometimes even refusing to renew their deposits.

The Austrian Investor

It seems that there is reason to believe that foreign bankers grew concerned about Austrian stability during 1929, so what about Austrians themselves? One possible source of financial data that can help answer this question comes from sovereign bond prices. Bond prices are established by markets and are reported in daily newspapers, making them reliable and relatively free from bias. Since the amount of interest paid on a bond is fixed, a change in its price results in a new rate of return, that is, a change in the bond's yield. Mostly the price changes in accordance with the perceived risk of currency depreciation or a sovereign default. If a bond is deemed risky, its price will fall, resulting in a higher yield, and vice versa. In order to assess the perceived risk of Austrian default or devaluation, we compare the yields of the Austrian tranche of the League loan of 1923 with that of the Austrian 1922 Federal loan. The Federal loan differed from the League loan in respect to the fact that its annual payments were not guaranteed by foreign states, and that its interest payments were denominated in Austrian currency (as opposed to the League loan, which was payable in dollars). Comparing the change in yields therefore leaves us with a good estimate of how investors evaluated the combined risk of Austrian default and devaluation. A large spread in yields indicates that investors demanded much compensation for choosing the riskier Federal bond over the League bond. A small yield spread indicates that investors did not consider the risk of Austrian default or currency depreciation excessive and were ready to accept the Austrian Federal bond at a yield similar to that of the guaranteed loan denominated in dollars.

The spread of the Federal over the League yield is plotted in Graph 7.6 and provides data for further analysis. The yield spread remained fairly stable after the lethal unrest on 15 July 1927 (Graph 7.6, column E). It moved

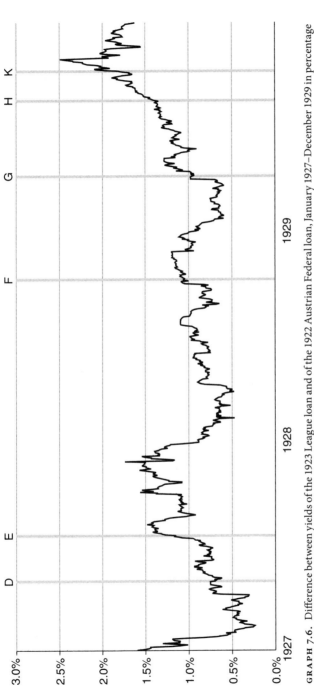

GRAPH 7.6. Difference between yields of the 1923 League loan and of the 1922 Austrian Federal loan, January 1927–December 1929 in percentage points. *Legend:* D: General elections, 24 April 1927. E: Vienna riots, 15 July 1927. F: Wiener-Neustadt demonstrations, 7 October 1928. G: Seipel resignation, 3 April 1929. H: Fatal clash in St. Lorenzen, Styria, 18 August 1929. K: BKA crisis, 7 October 1929. *Source: Neue Freie Presse.*

between 1 and 1.5 percent until almost the end of the year and then dropped below 1 percent in 1928, confirming once more that the riots probably provoked no rise in investor anxiety. However, from around the time of Seipel's sudden resignation in April 1929 (Graph 7.6, column G) until early October, when the BKA merger with the CA was announced (Graph 7.6, column K), the yield spread doubled to more than 2 percent, accelerating after the deadly clashes in St. Lorenzen on 18 August (Graph 7.6, column H). The yield differential represents an increase in the perceived risk of depreciation or an Austrian default on its sovereign debt over the summer of 1929. Austrian buyers of the 1922 Federal loan increasingly demanded a higher compensation than the buyers of the Austrian tranche of the guaranteed League loan because Heimwehr agitation in 1929 and the rising probability of a coup d'état and civil war made either a sovereign default, currency depreciation, or both become more likely in their eyes.

The Foreign Exchange Markets

Foreign bankers and Austrian investors grew concerned about Austrian political and financial stability following Seipel's decision to step down as Chancellor in April 1929. This would not have been enough, however, to trigger a run by depositors on Austrian banks and the currency. To see whether Austrian depositors also grew anxious about the safety and value of their savings we turn to the foreign exchange market, more specifically to the U.S. dollar / schilling exchange rate. The Austrian daily press provided two rates, the Valuta-rate and the Devisen-rate. The Valuta-rate was used when customers wished to obtain dollars in cash; the Devisen-rate applied to customers who bought dollars that got credited to their accounts. The Valuta- and Devisen-rates differed because depositing money in one's account could take several days. At times when the exchange rate was stable, customers were expected to pay a small premium for getting their dollars in cash, so that the Valuta-rate would be above the Devisen-rate. At other times, particularly when the dollar was expected to appreciate (or the schilling was expected to depreciate), the Valuta-rate could fall below the Devisen-rate. A positive spread of 0.2 percent of the exchange rate seems to have been the regularly accepted premium to be paid for cash exchanges (see Graph 7.7),

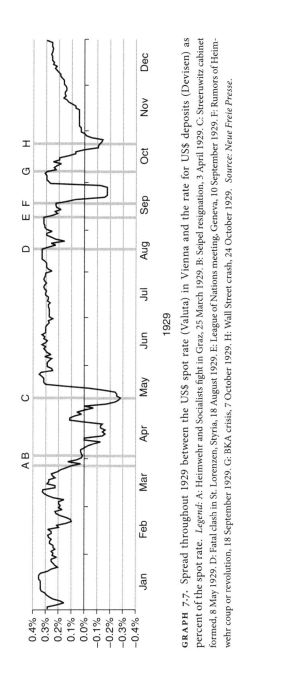

GRAPH 7.7. Spread throughout 1929 between the US$ spot rate (Valuta) in Vienna and the rate for US$ deposits (Devisen) as percent of the spot rate. *Legend:* A: Heimwehr and Socialists fight in Graz, 25 March 1929. B: Seipel resignation, 3 April 1929. C: Streeruwitz cabinet formed, 8 May 1929. D: Fatal clash in St. Lorenzen, Styria, 18 August 1929. E: League of Nations meeting, Geneva, 10 September 1929. F: Rumors of Heimwehr coup or revolution, 18 September 1929. G: BKA crisis, 7 October 1929. H: Wall Street crash, 24 October 1929. *Source: Neue Freie Presse.*

but over time this spread could vary considerably (from −0.4 to 0.3 percent of the exchange rate).

Changes in the spread reflect changes in expectations of Austrian depositors about the stability of the Austrian currency, and hence they help us discern what events caused anxiety among Austrian savers in 1929. When the spread between the two rates turned negative, that is, when the Devisen-rate rose above the Valuta-rate, it could have two related reasons. First, if the demand for dollar notes was so large as to deplete the actual notes from Viennese banks and Wechselstuben, then banks would charge more for the Valuta-exchange, that is, for the immediate provision of dollar notes. If at the same time depositors expected the schilling to depreciate, they would be further willing to pay more than usual for a Valuta transaction. A negative spread thus indicates periods of uncertainty, increased popular demand for dollar notes, and short-term expectations of depreciation.

There are three distinct periods during which the spread dipped significantly (Graph 7.7, columns C, F, and H) into negative territory. In the spring of 1929, the resignation of Chancellor Seipel inaugurated a period of uncertainty and the spread fell below zero (Graph 7.7, column B). There was much speculation about the formation of the new government and the spread reached its nadir when Chancellor Ernst Streeruwitz presented his cabinet in May (Graph 7.7, column C). Demand for dollar notes and the spread then very quickly returned to normal and remained positive throughout the summer. But rumors of a fascist coup in anticipation of the Heimwehr march on Vienna pushed the spread back into negative territory in September, and it reached its nadir during the week before the actual demonstrations. By 30 September 1929, the day following the marches, the spread was back in positive territory. It was the official announcement of trouble by the BKA that pushed the spread down and eventually below zero for a third time, where it remained for several weeks thereafter (Graph 7.7, column G). The data indicate that Austrian depositors' desire for immediate dollars was stronger and more prolonged after Seipel's resignation than during the week leading up to Heimwehr's march on Vienna.

It is doubtful, therefore, that the Socialist and Heimwehr manifestations on 29 September primarily timed the BKA's demise. Rather, it would appear that two separate yet linked developments roughly coincided. The financial data analyzed in this section point to the resignation of Chancellor Seipel in

April as the starting point for growing political and financial anxiety during the summer of 1929. Tightening money markets and economic slowdown were also responsible for the BKA's discounts reaching disquieting levels already in June. If data from WBV are representative of general developments, Vienna banks at the time faced withdrawals of foreign short-term deposits and had to pay higher interests on those that they were able to renew. Finally, political uncertainty and Heimwehr agitation in the fall provoked further withdrawals by customers and a renewed demand for U.S. dollars, increasing the BKA's liquidity requirements even more. If anxious depositors did indeed contribute to the problems of the BKA, these were its wealthy and aristocratic customers, not so much worried about a Heimwehr coup but rather about a Socialist takeover. What appears certain is that political agitation and uncertainty throughout the summer contributed to financial anxieties about Austria both inside and outside the country, and that under such circumstances the ANB could not risk further undermining the country's currency stability to support a failing bank.

The merger of the BKA and the CA in October 1929, and the crash on Wall Street that same month, were painfully felt by the Austrian economy. After the extremely cold weather during the beginning of the year, production had swung back quickly, but the ANB had been forced to increase its discount rate in order to keep up with the tightening of global money markets in the spring.[72] The inflow of new credits dropped and renewal of existing credits became increasingly expensive as political uncertainty gripped the country over the summer. The Institute noted that political unrest and the BKA crisis had caused large withdrawals of savings, and that compared to previous years the ANB had lost double the amount of foreign reserves in September 1929. Yet by the end of October the ANB balance sheet seemed repaired, with the reported coverage ratio still relatively safe at 65.2 percent (see Graph 7.4). But even if capital flight had stopped completely, its negative consequences were immediately apparent. The Institute's general production index for Austria went into steep decline, while orders in the steel industry dropped to their lowest level in sixteen months so that toward the end of the year it seemed clear that the country's economy had entered a recession. Unemployment in Vienna and the provinces was up far more than seasonally expected, the VSE reported large turnovers amid falling prices, and there was a worrisome drop in savings deposits. According to the Institute,

political developments were now central for Austria's future economic prosperity, which largely depended on the availability of fresh capital and foreign credits. The Austrian government's decision to reduce expenditures by
12 percent would possibly contribute to foreign confidence and its ability to
service Austria's foreign debt, but also make the unfolding recession worse.
Nevertheless, the Institute could not do without reserved optimism, arguing
that an end to U.S. speculation might see a return of foreign credits as capital markets relaxed.[73]

While the economy had thus proved surprisingly resilient, political and
financial stability had shown themselves to be fragile. The events around the
July 1927 riots had been a reminder that foreign short-term exposure of Austrian banks posed a serious risk to stability in the event of sudden withdrawals. In early 1927, Conseiller Kay had estimated that short-term foreign
debt in Austria amounted to $147 million.[74] ANB Director Brauneis had
cited a similar amount during a visit to the BoE in October that year, with
more than half of it incurred by the CA and the BKA.[75] In view of the fact
that the ANB declared $118 million of own foreign currency holdings, much
of which was not eligible as official reserves, Norman considered the situation precarious.[76] The British Trade Attaché in Vienna estimated that in 1928
short-term credits had declined to possibly as little as $80 million, but even
that was still a considerable figure.[77] Strictly speaking, the ANB's free gold
and foreign currency reserves stood at only $54 million, and even if all other
foreign assets, including Kostdevisen and money in unstable denominations
were included, the central bank held hardly more than $100 million in for-
eign funds.[78] Comparing the events of 1927 and 1929, it seemed that confidence had waned and Austria had become less financially stable. Chancellor
Seipel, who had restored order brutally in July 1927, instrumentally contributed to the general uneasiness by stepping down unexplainably in April 1929.
But if his plan had been to provoke a regime change and hurt the Socialists,
it had failed. Johann Schober, though widely viewed as a Heimwehr-man, had
once more fashioned himself the true savior of the First Austrian Republic
and a defender of its democratic status quo.

The declining confidence of foreign bankers and the unstable nature of
short-term foreign deposits made it obvious once more how important it was
for Austria to obtain long-term loans from abroad. After the General Commissioner's departure, Director Brauneis and the Financial Committee's new

representative in Vienna, the Dutch Meinoud Rost van Tonningen, had agreed that a new long-term loan would help consolidate the ANB's position.[79] Fresh foreign funds would be exchanged into schillings and thereby help to permanently increase the ANB's foreign reserves, but even before the end of control, there had been strong doubts as to whether a new loan for Austria could be raised abroad any time soon.[80] The Austrian government was negotiating a foreign loan with which to pay for productive investments, but political problems with Italy over South Tyrol and the reluctance of foreign bankers to get further involved in Austria made the loan quite impossible. When the Control Committee of Guarantor States discussed the matter of short-term loans to Austria in March 1929, Niemeyer stressed the importance of getting Austria a new long-term loan as soon as possible, but the so-called Investment loan would not be issued on foreign markets until Schober finally solved Austria's political problems with Italy in 1930.[81]

Aware of the dangerous situation, the ANB Directors had hoped that perhaps the BoE would promise to step in and help defend the schilling if it came under attack. In early 1926, anticipating the end of League control, Governor Norman had unexpectedly informed President Reisch that he was anxious to reenter into close cooperation and wished to discuss mutual assistance during times of crisis.[82] Reisch hoped the ANB would be offered a clean overdraft credit against no security, to face off an attack with sufficient liquidity, but instead Norman only promised to carefully consider any appeal for temporary support the ANB might make during an eventual future crisis.[83] When Director Brauneis again raised the matter of potential emergency assistance in 1927, the BoE replied that it was not ready to pledge specific forms of support, but would naturally consider any proposal Brauneis wished to make.[84] What other option did President Reisch have than to tell the BoE in March 1929 that he thought the ANB's position satisfactory, and that he was convinced it could face any sort of capital outflow by simply adjusting its interest rate accordingly?[85]

Does it matter whether it was political instability going back to Seipel's resignation in April 1929, or just the sharp rise in political tensions that autumn, that was responsible for the timing of the BKA collapse? The League of Nations had successfully stabilized the Austrian economy and convinced Austrians of its viability, but it had not been able to create enduring political stability. Seipel was seen as a strongman capable of containing Heimwehr violence, and thus his resignation, even if motivated entirely for private reasons, must be seen as irresponsible, at least with the benefit of hindsight. If we were to consider the financial fallout of tensions between Heimwehr and Schutzbund due solely to their marches around Vienna in September 1929, then the collapse of the BKA would be but a surprising, unfortunate, and unforeseeable consequence of a short weekend of political turmoil. But by tracing foreign and Austrian financial anxieties back to Seipel's resignation in April 1929, we can see that the BKA collapse, with all its ill-fated consequences for Austria, was not due to a momentary confluence of events, but rather the outcome of a risky policy of escalating threats and shows of force between the armed wings of Austria's main political camps and leaders. Nobody could foresee with certainty in April that this would provoke the sudden collapse of Austria's second-largest bank, requiring a hurried and ill-fated merger with the larger CA, but careful observers of financial markets would have realized that Seipel's recluse and the ongoing and intensifying political tensions that followed it posed a growing threat to financial stability in Austria.

In October 1929, just as in the fall of 1922, hopes of a right-wing regime change in Austria had been shattered, and in much the same way the frustration materialized most brutally on the grounds of the University of Vienna. Three weeks after the BKA's collapse, on 29 October 1929, a group made up of Heimwehr, Nazi, and Pan-German students, enraged about a series of anti-Heimwehr posters put up by Socialist colleagues across the street from the Technological Institute, stormed lectures and the library, expelling Jews and Socialists.[86] The police were called around noon and the Institute was closed for the rest of the day. The rowdy students then marched onto the main University building, where they interrupted lectures, shouting "Juden Hinaus!" Socialist and Jewish students, the Neue Freie Presse reported, were then beaten out onto the Ringstrasse, through a cordon of the völkisch hooligans.[87] The next week, a large group of Heimwehr students blocked the entrance to the University and attacked anyone without proof of belonging to one of the anti-Semitic Student Unions. Clashes became more violent, with further invasion of lectures, shouting, and maltreatment of Jewish and Socialist students, many of them women, who were beaten with sticks and belts or got pushed down the grand staircase. When the University rector expressed his sympathy for the German students but called upon them, in the interest of their own cause, not to pursue further violence, they took his speech as veiled encouragement and the rampaging continued. The liberal *Neue Freie Presse* called for measures to contain the violence, and in a front page article argued that during a time when Austria was being watched from abroad with augurs' eyes, such violence did exceptional harm to the country.[88] Three days later, the entire Vienna University had to be shut until further notice.[89]

8

The Credit-Anstalt Crisis and the Collapse of the Gold Exchange Standard

1930–1931

I am afraid the world has gone very mad, and will only
return to sanity when madness has become so general as to
be intolerable. Meantime no one in the lunatic asylum can
afford to appear entirely sane.

—Otto Niemeyer to Julius Meinl, 25 November 1931

ON SUNDAY, 7 JUNE 1931, Chancellor Heinrich Brüning and German Foreign Minister Julius Curtius held talks with British Prime Minister Ramsay MacDonald and Foreign Secretary Arthur Henderson at Chequers, when Governor Montagu Norman of the Bank of England (BoE) suddenly burst into the room. Norman, who was furious about Brüning's populist manifesto, in which the German Chancellor had very recently promised to put an end to German reparations payments, reported that he had been in constant telephone communication with Vienna and that the situation there was exceedingly critical. Unless central banks and governments could cooperate on saving Austria over the next two weeks, the financial catastrophe would spread across the continent and make the German reparations question obsolete. Norman was prone to dramatic exaggerations, but the subsequent unfolding of events proved him right in the eyes of future observers. As Austrians struggled to contain the fallout of yet another Viennese financial disaster, Germany got itself engulfed in a banking and currency crisis of its own. And by the end of the summer, the pound sterling itself was under attack and Britain was forced to abandon the gold exchange standard. The German translator present at Chequers later remembered Norman eccentrically gesticulating and shouting: "South-Eastern Europe is in flames! The Credit-Anstalt in Vienna just closed its doors!"[1]

The Austrian financial crisis of 1931 was triggered when on Monday, 11 May, the Viennese Credit-Anstalt (CA) publicly announced that it faced unprecedented losses. The shocking news was followed by a government proposal to bail out the bank with help from the Austrian National Bank (ANB) and the Vienna Rothschilds. The bailout was ratified by parliament on Wednesday, but a run on CA had ensued and within a few days a quarter of all its deposits had been withdrawn. Because Austrians exchanged their cash holdings into foreign currency, the bank run soon posed a danger to the stability of the Austrian schilling as well. The ANB, in an attempt to uphold the schilling's fixed exchange value, quickly ran down its reserves of foreign exchange to satisfy worried customers. Two months later, in mid-July 1931, the German banking system went into crisis when large deposit withdrawals at Germany's major banks similarly threatened the Reichsbank's foreign exchange and gold reserves. After the German cover ratio fell below the 40 percent statutory requirement, Germany decided to abandon the gold standard. Pressure on the British pound began as soon as the German capital controls were introduced on 20 July, and finally the BoE decided to go off gold on 20 September 1931.

It is commonplace to assume that the collapse of the CA in May 1931 played an important role in that year's Europe-wide financial crisis. Eyewitnesses and historians both tend to relate to events that summer as a snowballing effect that had its origins in Vienna and spread from there to Germany and then Britain.[2] The Hungarian economist Melchior Palyi, for example, who in 1931 was Director at Deutsche Bank and later lectured in the United States, would tell his students that the CA's collapse brought about the end of the interwar gold standard.[3] The financial historian Charles Kindleberger, who as a twenty-year old traveled through Europe during that fateful summer of 1931, writes that CA's collapse led to bank runs not just in the successor states, but also in Germany.[4] Austrian historians Goldinger and Binder place the account of Norman's outburst in June 1931 at the beginning of their own to stress the linkages that presumably existed between the collapse of the CA in May and the German and British financial crises that followed.[5] Similarly, Karl Ausch writes that the CA's collapse stood at the beginning of that year's fateful chain of events, and economic historian Rudolf Nötel also traces the German and British crises back to the CA collapse.[6] Finally, Barry Eichengreen suggests that the CA crisis produced immediate withdrawals in Berlin because the Austrian and German banking systems resembled each other so much that foreign depositors simultaneously repatriated funds from both countries.[7] Following these lines of thought, Liaquat Ahamed's bestselling study of interwar central bankers cites British historian Arnold Toynbee's comparison that much like the assassination of Archduke Franz Ferdinand in 1914, the CA crisis "set in train a cascade that plunged out of all control and brought down an entire world order."[8]

But some historians have been more cautious linking the Austrian and German crises. Charles H. Feinstein, Peter Temin, and Gianni Toniolo blame the German crisis on heavy involvement of its banks in Austria, but remain on the fence as to whether Germany's problems in 1931 actually originated in Vienna.[9] Earlier, Temin himself had identified the temporal delay between the Austrian collapse and German withdrawals as an indication that the two might have been completely unrelated.[10] Harold James, too, has come out against linking the German and Austrian crises on several occasions, pointing out that German banks held only minimal deposits in Austria.[11] Most recently, Fritz Weber writes that if the CA had only waited a few months more before asking for governmental assistance, it would have never been blamed for triggering the avalanche and that sooner or later latent panic in Central Europe would have translated into an international financial crisis anyway.[12]

In this chapter I argue that the German and Austrian crises were related, but in a way so far not considered by historians. Rather than setting off a series of fateful events in Vienna that triggered the Great Depression in Europe and led to Britain exiting the gold standard system, the CA's collapse had more limited effects on European financial markets. News of its difficulties in May triggered a well-coordinated international rescue mission that eventually helped calm both Austrian depositors and Austrian banks' foreign creditors, and which successfully supported the ANB to keep the Austrian schilling stable until confidence had been restored by mid-June. However, the crisis that erupted in Germany following the closure of the Darmstädter und Nationalbank in mid-July revealed how precarious the stability achieved in Austria really was. Fearing the introduction of a moratorium on foreign debt in their own country after foreign credits to Germany and Hungary had been temporarily frozen on 20 July, Austrians resumed the run on their own currency. The ANB, which had just successfully weathered a storm with the help of foreign central banks and doctored statements, was not able to stem a renewed panic, so that in August, capital controls had to be introduced to preserve the schilling's official exchange value.

The CA's collapse was not the cause of the 1931 financial crisis in Europe, nor was it its beginning. Had the German situation been safe and sound at the time, the ANB might never have suspended gold payment at all. Testimony to this assertion comes mainly from the correspondence between the financial experts who managed the aftermath of the CA's collapse in Vienna during the summer of 1931, the staff at the Bank for International Settlements (BIS) in Basel coordinating international efforts to help Austria weather the storm, and documents gathered from other historical archives. The correspondence at the BIS has previously not been scrutinized by historians in detail, and it provides insights into the unfolding crisis on a daily basis. Figures on withdrawals by depositors and the cancellation and risk premiums for foreign credits, as well as data on bond yields and short-term interest rates in European financial centers presented in the final part of this chapter, further corroborate this.

Political Development

For Austrian Chancellor Johann Schober, the year 1930 had started with a success. After surmounting the political and financial crisis in autumn 1929, he had quickly reached a parliamentary compromise with the Socialists on constitutional reform. In January 1930 the second conference on reparations in The Hague put into effect the Young plan, which reduced German reparations payments and charged the newly founded Bank for International Settlements with facilitating these transfers and acting as trustee for a new international loan to Germany.[13] Schober had patched up relations with Italy, so the conference also resulted in the complete cancellation of all reparations claims on Austria. Actually, nobody had ever expected Austria to pay reparations and Schober's main achievement lay in the fact that officially wiping out these claims lifted all reparations liens on Austrian assets. On the sidelines of the conference, Schober also obtained Italian endorsement of a repayment proposal for Austria's postwar relief debt so that nothing stood in the way of completing negotiations on a long-awaited new international loan for Austria.[14]

Floating the so-called Austrian Investment loan had to be postponed until after the $300 million German Young loan was issued in early June 1930, but the German loan was not much of a success and the size of the Austrian loan was consequently reduced from an initial $105 million to $60 million.[15] The French had requested that their holders of certain Austrian bonds that had been issued before the war receive compensation for losses incurred through depreciation of the crown, but the Austrians had refused the demand.[16] Paris thus did not participate in the issue, and even if the Vienna tranche of the loan was oversubscribed, the larger New York offering was only sold to bond dealers, and in London underwriters ended up with almost two-thirds of the loan on their hands.[17] After Schober deported Heimwehr leader Waldemar Pabst in June 1930, his Christian-Social Vice Chancellor and Heimwehr sympathizer Karl Vaugoin resigned in September, bringing down the government, and national elections in November took place amid renewed rumors of a Heimwehr coup. The Socialist opposition garnered 41.1 percent of the vote, gaining a further seat in parliament; its 71 delegates made it Austria's strongest legislative party for the first time. The Christian-Socials received only 35.7 percent of all votes and dropped from 73 to 66 mandates, while the Pan-Germans and Agrarian League, running on a joint list, got 11.6 percent, fielding 19 representatives. For the first time, the Heimwehr ran independently and received 6.2 percent of the vote, or 8 seats. A new government, headed by the Christian-Social Governor of the province of Vorarlberg, Otto Ender, with Johann Schober as Vice-Chancellor, took office on 4 December 1930.

The Investment loan increased the ANB's foreign currency reserves and thereby strengthened the central bank's capacity to deal with challenges stemming from Austria's current account deficit. Austria's need for new long-term capital had been given much attention by Layton and Rist in their 1926 report, but they had deemed a regional reduction of tariffs even more important for Austria's economic and financial stability. Fresh foreign loans could temporarily finance Austria's trade deficit, but it was best to make the latter disappear through increasing exports. Bilateral negotiations between Austria and her neighbors did little to bring down protectionist tariffs in the region, and in 1930 Vienna intensified its secret talks over a customs union with Germany. The Treaty of Versailles obligated Germany to respect Austrian's independence, and both the Treaty of Saint-Germain-en-Laye and the Geneva Protocols banned Austria from taking any further steps that might curtail its independence, though they also guaranteed the country's full freedom in matters of tariffs and trade.[18] In March 1931, following reports in the Austrian and German press, the two countries announced their plan to negotiate a customs union, stirring up strong protests both in France and Czechoslovakia.[19] Austrian envoy Georg Franckenstein presented the plan in London, carefully explaining that other countries would be free to join the union and that nothing about it questioned Austria's independence or sovereignty.[20] The British Foreign Office was in fact sympathetic to the idea, and bankers in London and New York agreed that Austria's economic problems left it little choice other than to seek German support, and even hoped the plan might actually trigger the much-desired reduction of European tariffs.[21]

As planned, a customs union project was presented to the League's Commission of Enquiry for European Union, which met for its second time in May 1931, and eventually the League Council asked the Permanent Court of International Justice in The Hague to give an advisory opinion on the project's legal compatibility with the first Geneva Protocol and the Treaty of Saint-German-en-Laye (see Appendix C). The proposed customs union, which would have extended Germany's commercial reach to the Italian border, would have dominated the headlines of European newspapers that month had not the CA revealed unexpected losses and an appeal for government help on 11 May. In June, a British creditor representative would express disbelief upon learning of the extent of mismanagement at the CA. The bank had been run so unprofessionally, he thought, that even without its fusion with the Boden-Kredit Anstalt (BKA) bank in 1929 it would have been financially unsound.[22] ANB President Richard Reisch later admitted that the CA had already been ailing at the time of the BKA crisis, and that it had been able to continue only thanks to the popularity and good credit its President Louis Rothschild enjoyed abroad.[23] That was not entirely true, as the ANB itself had clandestinely advanced substantial sums of foreign currency to the CA to facilitate the merger.[24]

Newspapers in Vienna announced that the loss would be covered through writing down capital, mobilizing reserves, and with fresh funds from the

Austrian government, the ANB, and S. M. Rothschild. On Tuesday, 12 May 1931, N. M. Rothschild in London were told by the Austrian press office that the measures taken put the CA back into a sound position, while the bank's directors cabled that all losses had been completely covered.[25] But over the subsequent five weeks Vienna's banks experienced a run of unprecedented proportions, with the CA hit worst. Austrians massively withdrew deposits and exchanged them into foreign currency, which reduced the ANB's cover ratio and trust in the stability of the schilling's exchange rate. To prevent the crisis from spreading across the region, a number of central banks, led by the BIS and the BoE, provided the ANB with emergency credits, which allowed it to keep disbursing foreign currency to Austrians while at the same time lending to the CA so that it might keep its doors and tellers open. No capital controls had to be introduced, and the continued satisfaction of withdrawals and foreign currency purchases eventually calmed the panic after five weeks. One month later, in mid-July, when Germany faced a similar combination of bank runs and capital flight, Austria was pulled into its maelstrom, but this time foreign central banks could no longer come to its rescue, and with its effective reserves largely depleted, the ANB vainly continued to pay out foreign exchange until capital controls had to be declared in October.

The Collapse of the Credit-Anstalt

The CA secretly informed the Austrian government of its difficulties on Friday, 8 May 1931, asking for help.[26] Austria's largest and most famous bank faced a massive loss of sch.140 million (almost $20 million) for 1930, stemming mainly from bad loans and a drop in the price of shares held as assets, wiping out at least four-fifths of the banks' own capital base. The ongoing recession had reduced cash flows coming from the bank's own industrial conglomerates and the cost of foreign capital had risen, possibly rendering indebted conglomerates and the bank illiquid. The CA directors blamed the loss of sch.60 million alone on the ill-conceived and hasty merger with the BKA in 1929, which had brought in large participations of moribund companies such as Steyr Automobil, Fanto Oil, and Mauthner Textil. Indeed, the previous three were its largest borrowers and together made up almost half of its ten biggest debtors.[27] Given the CA's size and its importance to the Austrian economy, as a direct and indirect employer and as a provider of credit to industry, the government convened an emergency meeting on Sunday, 10 May 1931, at which it decided to save the bank.

Newspapers in Vienna revealed the crisis on Tuesday and published the official plans to cover the bank's loss by writing down its capital, mobilizing hidden reserves, and infusing new funds from the government, the ANB, and the bank of S. M. Rothschild. But the measures did not reassure the public, and until the end of the week Austrian and foreign depositors withdrew over sch.300 million (about $42 million) from the CA, 75 percent of which were converted into foreign exchange (see Graph 8.1). Much like the BKA in 1929, the CA obtained liquidity from the ANB against discounts, while the central bank itself faced a large demand for foreign exchange from depositors of all Viennese banks.[28] Whereas in 1929 the central bank could put an end to this practice, refusing to lend further to the BKA and forcing its merger with the CA, now there was no larger bank left to bail out the latter. To save the CA from bankruptcy, the ANB had to help it satisfy the withdrawals of its worried customers, but with many of these withdrawals being converted into foreign currency, the ANB itself would face a crisis before long.

The ANB realized that the situation was bound to become critical and asked the BIS in Basel for assistance. In the early 1920s, the BoE had still aimed to coordinate international efforts towards central bank cooperation of monetary policy itself, but at the end of the decade Norman had given up on his idea. The task was instead handed to the BIS, which, although established primarily to assist Germany with finding the foreign currency to pay reparations, was also charged to help strengthen global capital markets and stabilize international exchange rates.[29] The bank was owned by twenty-two shareholding central banks, including founding members Belgium, Great Britain, France, Germany, Italy, and Japan, as well as a consortium of U.S. banks led by J. P. Morgan, after the U.S. Congress had prohibited the Federal Reserve from joining. To preserve financial stability and facilitate cooperation, the BIS could commit funds short-term, but of its already small capital base of $100 million, no more than $21 million had been paid in.[30] And although in May 1931 the BIS already had $412 million in assets, only a minor proportion of this sum was available for emergency operations.[31] Much like

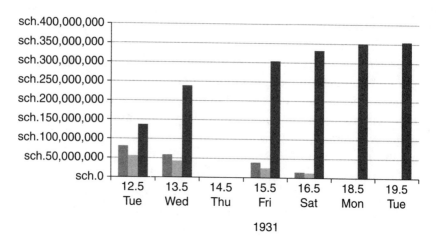

GRAPH 8.1. Withdrawals of schillings and of foreign currencies from Credit-Anstalt in Austrian schillings, 12–19 May 1931. *Source:* BEA, OV 28/3, "Austria": Letter from Bark to Harvey, 21 May 1931.

the League in 1922, the BIS appreciated the Austrian crisis as an opportunity to prove its worth as a new multilateral body aimed at facilitating international cooperation. What stood at stake was Austria's membership in the gold exchange standard system and possibly the stability of the monetary order itself. If Austria suspended convertibility or announced a moratorium on foreign debt, weaker countries could also come under attack and the crisis would spread throughout Europe.

BIS Manager Francis Rodd rushed to Vienna on 11 May to get a firsthand view of the unfolding crisis. Rodd, a privileged young man, was born in 1895, had received his education at Eton, and in September 1914 quit Balliol to join the war. After the armistice he had entered the Foreign Office but eventually moved to the BoE, which posted him to Basel.[32] After moving into Vienna's Sacher Hotel, Rodd monitored the ANB's discounting of paper to help Vienna banks satisfy withdrawals from depositors, of which the CA made particularly strong use. He also kept track of the day-to-day demands for foreign exchange, which he at first considered "moderate and satisfactory," given that the ANB's reserves were more than enough "to take care of any emergency even if there were a considerable demand."[33] The ANB's most recent official statement had listed its portfolio at sch.90 million, but the true figure had been 135 million, and by the morning of Tuesday, 12 May, this sum had risen to 252 million (about $35 million), of which 197 million was on the CA account.[34] According to Rodd, continued discounting by Viennese banks and particularly by the CA would pose the largest risk to the ANB and currency stability. Yet upon arrival he considered the foreign exchange situation to be manageable and the ANB's official position exceedingly strong, with gold and foreign reserves close to sch.1 trillion (about $140 million) and a cover ratio above 90 percent.

The ANB was meeting demands in full, discounting bills from commercial banks to keep them liquid and exchanging schillings freely into foreign currency, though thereby weakening its own capital base. On Sunday, 17 May, the eve of the second week of the crisis, the world's central bankers, convening at the BIS in Basel for its first general meeting, heard an appeal for help from the ANB President.[35] Addressing his colleagues, Richard Reisch explained that to save the CA and its associated conglomerates, the ANB had been forced to discount large sums of financial paper, which was prone to undermine public confidence. Due to the increased discounting of banks, mainly from the CA, the ANB's portfolio had grown by almost sch.400 million (about $56 million) over the week, so that a rise from the previously 60 million to at least 300 million (about $42 million) in discounted paper would have to be admitted in the bank's official balance sheet, due to be published as early as the following Friday.[36] Reisch was fearful that continuing support of the CA might call into question the ANB's ability to uphold fixed exchange rates and provoke capital flight and a run on the schilling. In his view, there was still a bit of time, as discounts could be allowed to increase by another sch.50 million (about $7 million), and the cover ratio drop by up to 20 percent if necessary, before causing consternation among Austrian savers. But thereafter the ANB would require central bank assistance to keep the CA going without causing a panic.

Rodd explained to the present central bankers that the ANB was not seeking their assistance to uphold the cover ratio or reduce the amount of discounted paper in its portfolio. What Reisch wanted was simply enough money to be able to doctor his balance sheets and control the psychological effects of the ANB's continued discounting, for which he thought the sum of sch.100 million was enough.[37] The central bankers agreed the following day to help the BIS arrange a foreign currency credit for the ANB of up to sch.100 million (about $14 million) against its gold and discounted paper. The BIS would provide 40 percent of the money and the rest would come from the Federal Reserve Bank of New York, the Banque de France, the BoE, the German Reichsbank, and the Banca d'Italia.[38] A first one-week advance of sch.30 million (about $4.2 million) could arrive in Vienna by 22 May 1931 and would help the ANB to sustain confidence in the Austrian schilling by paying out without having to show a drop in foreign currency reserves.

Coordinating the international rescue mission from Basel, the BIS informed participating central banks on Monday, 18 May that the situation in Vienna was "relatively calm."[39] Indeed, during the week that followed, the second since news of the CA's problems had reached the public, some depositors even returned funds to banks before they closed on Wednesday for Pentecost. The Austrian Finance Ministry and the CA cabled foreign bankers on 18 and 19 May, asking them not to withdraw their deposits and informing them that depositor "withdrawals in Vienna which have been considerable in the first day after publication have entirely ceased."[40] To sustain the fragile confidence, the ANB carefully doctored its statement, published on Wednesday, 20 May for Friday, 15 May. It showed the full rise of discounts from sch.69 million to 297 million (about $42 million, though the actual level was already sch.384 million), almost 90 percent on account of CA. It further underreported the loss of sch.63 million (about $9 million) in foreign reserves by more than half, admitting only a drop of 29 million through mobilizing hidden reserves.[41] This nevertheless implied that the reported cover ratio had dropped from 83 percent to 68 percent, so that the ANB expected a renewed run on the CA when banks reopened after the holy day on Tuesday, 26 May. Following Pentecost, ANB General Director Viktor Brauneis called the BoE and warned that the Austrian central bank would have to stop lending to the CA unless other central banks provided guarantees to help defend the schilling if it came under sustained attack.[42]

The continued discounting by the CA to pay withdrawing depositors and public flight from the schilling were not the sum total of the ANB's worries. On the horizon loomed the possible withdrawals of deposits, credits, and advances made to the CA and other Viennese banks from abroad. The CA had at least $44 million in foreign deposits or credits. Writing to the BIS at the beginning of the crisis's second week, the ANB reported that foreign credits to the amount of $9.8 million had already been withdrawn or had failed to be renewed, most of them due the end of the month. Despite new foreign deposits of $2 million and the renewal of foreign credits of over $4.75 million, the ANB wrote, further withdrawals were very undesirable and could result in serious complications.[43] Being witnesses to Austrians withdrawing deposits and converting them into foreign currency, foreign banks were naturally hesitant about renewing their own commitments and some removed deposits and canceled credits, or at least reduced them.[44] To dissuade foreign creditors from joining the run, the Austrian Finance Ministry and the CA asked foreign bankers to arrange syndicates to coordinate the renewal for six months of the CA's foreign debts.[45] A foreign creditors' committee was set up under Lionel Rothschild's chairmanship in London and J. P. Morgan's in New York, with similar committees in Germany, the Netherlands, and Switzerland, but in Paris, Edouard de Rothschild refused to rally the French banks without clearer figures on the CA's position.[46] Lionel Rothschild informed his Austrian cousins that any joint promise by foreign creditors to prolong facilities to CA required some form of guarantees from Austria's government in return, a measure the BIS and other creditors had also been pushing for in return for their help.[47]

As ANB directors had assembled over the Pentecost holiday, they had seriously considered proposing a moratorium on Austria's external debt and outlawing foreign withdrawals. For two weeks the ANB had continuously increased circulation by financing the CA and simultaneously lost foreign exchange to capital flight, driving down the cover ratio. Since the beginning of the crisis the ANB had lost sch.30–40 million (about $4.2–5.6 million) in foreign exchange per day, and given Austrians' experiences with hyperinflation, fully disclosing the ANB's loss of foreign reserves could in itself have triggered a panic. Banks reopened on Tuesday, 26 May, and on 28 May ANB Vice President Gustav Thaa phone called the BIS with an urgent appeal for help. The increase in circulation, which would soon have to be admitted fully, would produce a run on the currency that threatened to deplete the ANB's foreign reserves. If the Austrian central bank was to continue to pay out, it needed the BIS to promise its assistance should the currency come under sustained attack. Once capital flight took on larger proportions, it would be impossible to stop, Thaa warned, and he foresaw the entire collapse of the schilling unless support was provided quickly.[48]

The BIS and its associated central banks wanted to avert an Austrian moratorium on foreign debt, fearing the consequences for financial stability beyond Austria. The BIS was therefore ready to publicly declare that it would work together with central banks to defend the schilling's exchange rate, but only if the Austrian government provided guarantees and the ANB stopped acting as the CA's de facto guarantor.[49] To stem the capital outflow and bring in new funds, the BIS recommended that the Austrian government provide guarantees to all CA depositors and creditors, old and new, domestic and foreign. The CA would also have to receive a foreign controller and the ANB accept the return of a foreign advisor.[50] The ANB supported a government guarantee for CA and parliament indeed passed a law on Thursday, 28 May, by which it authorized the Austrian government to guarantee deposits and credits extended to the CA, though the guarantee itself did not follow. But recognizing the law as a first step in the right direction, the BIS responded with an announcement to the press that, together with ten of the world's largest central banks, it had extended sch.100 million (about $14 million) to the ANB and was ready to deliver further amounts as might be required, expressing confidence that with such assistance the ANB would successfully maintain the full and continued convertibility of the Austrian schilling.[51]

Meanwhile, Rodd had been joined by a group of foreigners arriving in Vienna to help him coordinate the international rescue efforts aimed at stabilizing CA, supporting the schilling and preventing the Austrian government from declaring a moratorium. The ANB and the Austrian government had invited the Dutch banker Adrianus van Hengel to come and reorganize the CA, and shortly thereafter the Foreign Creditors' Committee in London appointed him as its representative in Vienna. The forty-five-year-old had trained as a lawyer in Leiden before embarking on a career with the Amsterdamsche Bank, reorganizing the failed Rotterdamsche Bankvereeniging (Robaver) from 1924 to 1927.[52] The BIS sent the forty-eight-year-old Rotterdam economist Gijsbert Bruins, who had been present at the Brussels and Genoa conferences and had overseen note issue at the German Reichsbank under the former Dawes plan from 1924 to 1930, as foreign adviser to the ANB.[53] Finally, the French economist Charles Rist, coauthor of the 1925 Layton-Rist report and since 1926 Deputy Governor of the Banque de France, arrived to prepare an Austrian Treasury Bills issue in Paris, through which the Austrian government hoped to raise the sch.150 million (about $21 million) needed to finance its bailout of the CA.

Even by its most optimistic accounts, the ANB's reserves had dropped 25 percent in three weeks, from sch.966 million to sch.721 million (from about $136 million to $102 million), but these worrisome figures were being kept from the public. The bank's official balance sheet, dated 23 May, admitted a loss of only sch.70 million of foreign currency reserves since the beginning of the crisis (just $10 million), and since new discounts had increased only by another sch.50 million (about $7 million) during the second week, the official cover ratio dropped just 4 percent lower (see Graph 8.2). But the ANB balance sheet for 31 May, published on 4 June, revealed another jump in discounted paper of almost sch.100 million (about $14 million) and a further drop of sch.45 million in foreign reserves (about $6.3 million), using half of the $14 million BIS credit to cover the undisclosed shortfall. Even such heavily doctored figures left the ANB no choice but to publicly report its official cover ratio at 57 percent for the last day of May, compared to 80 percent before the crisis.[54] Some of the foreign currency losses were due to withdrawals by foreign banks, others to demands from a public fleeing the schilling.[55] The ANB had already lost sch.135 million (about $19 million) of foreign currency reserves and on Friday, 29 May alone, it lost another sch.40 million (about $5.6 million) and sch.12 million (about $1.7 million) on Saturday.

The ANB continued to lose foreign reserves. At the beginning of the fourth week, on Monday, 1 June, it paid out the amount of sch.25 million (about $3.5 million), and the bad news it officially disclosed on Thursday, 4 June, further intensified demand for foreign exchange. During the period from Monday, 1 June to Saturday, 6 June, the ANB lost sch.87 million in foreign currencies (about $12.3 million), and in the following week, from Monday, 8 June to Thursday, 11 June, another $8.8 million.[56] The ANB had used the remaining sch.40 million of cash from the BIS to doctor its balance sheet dated 8 June 1931 (about $5.6 million) and asked Basel to prepare a new credit of yet another sch.100 million (about $14 million). As the persistent discounting of the CA increased circulation and put further downward pressure on the cover ratio, the ANB continued to try and calm public fears by manipulating its next balance sheet. Published on Thursday, 11 June, one month into the crisis, it showed that from 1 to 6 June the central bank had only discounted

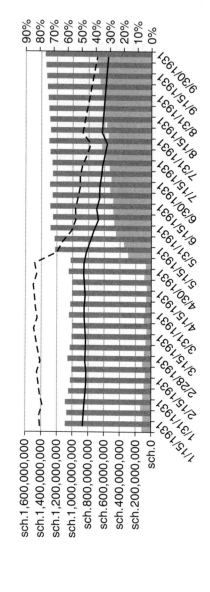

GRAPH 8.2. Published 1931 Austrian National Bank balance sheet data: foreign reserves, discounted bills, money supply (in Austrian schillings), and the cover ratio in percent. *Source: ANB balances in Neue Freie Presse.*

sch.24 million of new paper (about $3.4 million), far less than during previous weeks, and it admitted a decrease of just $7.8 million of foreign currency reserves (two-thirds of the actual outflow that week). Neither the doctored balance sheet, nor increasing the bank rate from 5 to 6 percent on 8 June and to 7.5 percent on 15 June, put a stop to capital flight, however.[57] Officially the ANB's foreign reserves had now dropped from sch.860 million to sch.677 million ($121 to $95 million), but in truth the loss was close to $40 million.[58]

As Norman in Chequers at the time knew all too well, the reason the ANB could not really stem the capital flight was that the underlying cause for distrust lay not so much with the central bank but with the CA. Bruins wrote angrily to Austrian Finance Minister Otto Juch that if the government would have agreed to guarantee deposits at the CA, as both the ANB and BIS had demanded, the situation would not have gotten so far out of hand.[59] Together the ANB and the BIS were pressuring the Austrian government to announce actual guarantees for depositors and foreign creditors, but political problems and not least the country's budgetary position made such a commitment difficult so that the government wavered, wanting to see the foreign Treasury Bill issue and an agreement with foreign creditors secured first.[60] Robert Kindersley, a director of the BoE and chairman of Lazard, Frères, together with James Gannon of the Chase National Bank, came to Vienna on 14 June representing the CA's British and U.S. creditors to put further pressure on the government to guarantee CA's foreign debts, in return for which they would arrange a prolonged extension of the CA's foreign credits. To provoke the government into action, ANB President Reisch and General Director Brauneis even threatened to resign unless the Austrian government announced guarantees soon or if it should dare to declare a moratorium instead.[61]

Negotiations in Paris on the planned Treasury Bill issue had begun with Rist's return on 4 June 1931 but were slowed down by French bankers' demands. The French tried to gain a controlling share of CA in return for their help and the Austrians prevaricated in the hope for an alternative to the French in Germany or Britain.[62] Eventually the French presented political conditions, demanding that Austria officially renounce the customs union project and accept a League inquiry and the recommendations that would result from it.[63] The French hoped to use the Damocles sword of a looming moratorium to pressure the Austrians into concessions, and finally presented their demands on Tuesday, 16 June as a twenty-four-hour ultimatum. In Vienna, meanwhile, the situation had reached a turning point, with withdrawals spreading from Vienna's large financial institutions to savings banks, sapping the ANB's power to maintain fixed exchange rates if the run intensified. Putting further pressure on the Austrians, the French-controlled Länderbank and the Czech Živnostenská Banka exchanged extensive amounts of schillings into dollars at the ANB.[64] The Länderbank, which had withdrawn sch.50.5 million (about $7.1 million) up to 8 June, withdrew another sch.17.5 million (about $2.5 million) the following week, and Živnostenská, which had withdrawn sch.5 million (about $700,000), withdrew another sch.9 million (about $1.3 million).[65] The ANB lost a further sch.58 million (about $8.2 million) from Tuesday, 16 June to Thursday, 18 June alone, as the Länderbank continued its attempt at undermining the ANB's position. The Länderbank and the Czech Živnostenská Banka were responsible for over 25 percent of withdrawals during these few days, but by Friday they gave up, and shortly thereafter the reported rate of withdrawals and discounting dropped markedly (see Graph 8.2).[66]

Why had the tide turned? The Austrian government and the ANB, faced with an impending French ultimatum, had debated a moratorium on foreign debt payments on 15 June.[67] Working to prevent such a moratorium in Austria, Governor Norman had obtained a letter from the Chancellor of the Exchequer, stating that the British government saw great importance in "providing financial assistance for Austria without delay." With the Treasury's endorsement Norman promised a renewable seven-day advance of sch.150 million (about $21 million) through the BIS, secured by the ANB's gold reserves in London and to be repaid by the planned Treasury Bill issue, if the Austrian government finally declared its guarantee of the CA's foreign liabilities.[68] Under strong pressure from Bruins, Rodd, and Kindersley, Austrian Finance Minister Juch announced such a two-year guarantee on 16 June and then, knowing that the CA's losses were much greater than the bank admitted, immediately resigned, a step followed by yet another minister the same day, bringing down the Austrian government.[69] At the last hour a moratorium in Austria had been averted with the help of Norman and the British Treasury. Without Norman's credit the ANB would have had been forced to admit a foreign currency loss of sch.100 million in its next statement (about $14 million), which, he was certain, would have caused a panic and made the moratorium inevitable, leading to financial collapse in Austria and possibly beyond.

In the eyes of the ANB's foreign adviser, Bruins, the matter was under control soon after. The CA's foreign creditors pledged to end all withdrawals, public flight from the schilling slowly ceased, and after several days Viennese financial institutions even saw new deposits coming in. Indeed, from 27 June onward, after a new Austrian government had reaffirmed the guarantee, the ANB enjoyed an influx of foreign notes as rediscounting and foreign withdrawals gradually slowed down too. The official ANB balance sheet for the week of 15 June, published on Friday, 19 June, had even reported, for the first time, a rise in foreign reserves, thanks to private advances Bruins was able to obtain abroad.[70] The ANB's return for 23 June, published on 27 June, showed a slight reduction of just sch.3 million in foreign currencies (about $420,000) and an increase of discounts of only sch.2 million (about $315,000). Taking advantage of the improved situation, the balance sheet for 30 June, published on Saturday, 4 July 1931, reported a rise in discounts from sch.490 million to sch.528 million (about $74 million), even though they had actually dropped from sch.691 million to sch.659 million (about $93 million).[71] Bruins, satisfied with the ANB's position, arranged for a further advance of $1 million from a Dutch bank and felt that the second planned BIS advance of sch.100 million (about $14 million) would not be needed after all.[72]

The Collapse of Amstelbank

Peter Temin was the first to suggest that not just the pervasive gold standard ideology, which led countries to choose contractionary deflation over devaluation, but to a lesser extent also international contagion of financial crises might have been an important transmission channel of the Great Depression.[73] Indeed, Ben Bernanke and Harold James, focusing on deflation's disruptive effect on financial systems, showed that during the 1930s, countries experiencing banking panics suffered more economic contraction.[74] Temin argued that economists knew little about the international transmission of financial panics, but that the temporal delay between the Austrian and German crises indicated that they might have been completely unrelated, while the proximity between the German and British crises possibly suggested a psychological "contagion of fear." Olivier Accominotti has shown meanwhile that Britain's departure from the gold standard in September 1931 might have indeed been related to liquidity problems of London merchant banks exposed to the German crisis.[75] If we wish to address claims about the role of the CA collapse in propagating the panic of 1931 and ultimately the Great Depression, we therefore need to ask about contagion from Vienna.

In June there was a run on Warsaw banks, including the Warsaw Discount Bank connected with the CA, and in July a run on the General Credit Bank of Budapest, another CA associate, but exceptional withdrawals in both Poland and Hungary had already commenced in April, before the CA revealed its problems. The only case where contagion from the CA collapse can be established with certainty concerns the associated Amstelbank in Amsterdam, which on 20 June 1931 suspended payment.[76] Amstelbank, founded in 1920 by the Austrian banking house S. M. Rothschild and its Dutch partners to access western capital, had lent to industries all over Central Europe, but mainly to Poland.[77] On 11 June 1931, Louis Rothschild in Vienna cabled Lionel Rothschild in London informing him that the Amstelbank was satisfying all withdrawals but would not be able to do so much longer, asking him to organize an extension of its foreign credits, which were jointly guaranteed by the CA and by S. M. Rothschild.[78] A week later Louis cabled that Amstelbank needed new credits to satisfy withdrawing depositors, since his bank was fully engaged in keeping the CA afloat.[79] The International Creditors Committee in London was not willing to furnish new funds, so Louis conceded "to apply for a moratorium in spite all its disadvantageous consequences" and obtain an agreement with Amstelbank's creditors that would allow small customers to be paid in full first.[80]

Most Dutch banks weathered the financial storms of 1931 quite successfully, since they had generally refrained from offering credits to industrial enterprises.[81] Amstelbank, however, was a universal bank providing credit to industrial and commercial undertakings, and offering banking services to private and institutional customers. Effectively run by the CA from Vienna (one of its three managing directors was the Hungarian Zoltán Hajdú, who had provoked the CA collapse by refusing to sign its balance sheet for 1930), activities had expanded steadily during the 1920s.[82] Its balance sheet had grown from 29 million guilders in 1922 to 78 million guilders in 1926, and to as many as 146 million guilders by the end of 1930 (respectively about $11 million, $31 million, and $59 million). On its liabilities side it had 127 million guilders in deposits, mostly from foreign banks (about $51 million), whereas its assets side listed $32 million of extended credits, one-third of which had gone to Poland.[83] The bank's paid-in capital and liquid reserves amounted to 10.35 million guilders (about $4.2 million), its cash holdings were 3.5 million guilders (about $1.4 million), and it owned up to 12 million guilders' worth of bills and shares (about $4.8 million). The bank had thus maneuvered itself into a precarious liquidity position, unable to withstand a run by its depositors. Auditors had repeatedly pointed out that Amstelbank's liquidity ratio was dropping and that much of its lending was secured by illiquid assets or none at all.[84] In 1930, the bank's liquidity position had deteriorated further as long-term deposits, which had still grown by more than 13 million guilders in 1929 (about $5.2 million), fell by almost 30 million (about $12 million) without a parallel reduction of the sum of loans the bank extended.

The end of Amstelbank was directly linked to the collapse of CA through a psychological "contagion of fear." Not later than a week after Credit-Anstalt announced its problems, on Monday, 10 May, depositors began withdrawing funds from Amstelbank. The overwhelming majority were private customers, many of whom lived in Vienna, and of the more than one hundred withdrawals recorded from 18 May to 9 June 1931, only eleven were made by corporations. However, the six largest corporate withdrawals constituted more than half of the total of $1.9 million that Amstelbank paid out.[85] Given that Amstelbank's liquid assets were not much more than $2 million, the bank had to find fresh funds or apply for a moratorium.[86] Private depositors of Amstelbank rightly believed that the bank might run out of cash and rushed to withdraw money before others did. A run on the bank occurred, and though there may have been good reasons for the running depositors to worry about the bank's safety, it is reasonable that the run occurred precisely because depositors believed a run was likely.[87] Transmitted by a "contagion of fear," the financial instability that originated with Credit-Anstalt in Austria had thus spread to Holland and closed down a Dutch subsidiary within less than six weeks. After the moratorium was declared, Amstelbank's creditors agreed to extend their funds to allow for an orderly liquidation and the payment in full to smaller creditors and depositors.[88]

Three weeks earlier, on 26 May 1931, Governor George Harrison of the
New York Federal Reserve had ascribed a sudden drop of the German exchange to difficulties in Vienna, but cabled BIS Chairman Gates McGarrah
about alternative rumors that Germany would postpone reparations
payments.[89] McGarrah explained that the high yield on German bonds was
likely due to international currency speculators turning on the Reichsmark.[90]
Two weeks later, on 11 June 1931, van Hengel showed McGarrah a letter to
Norman in which he warned that U.S. banks were not renewing short-term
deposits in Germany and that other banks were following suit.[91] But overall,
the correspondence analyzed here between the various bankers involved in
managing the crisis from Vienna, Basel, and London did not mention the
crisis spreading beyond Austria. There were certainly fears that a moratorium would cause panic beyond Austria's borders, but that was the reason
the BoE stepped in so chivalrously to avoid it. Hungary was facing a withdrawal of foreign exchange and its central bank had taken recourse to a BIS
credit too, but its crisis had originated earlier.[92] Finally, the Greek National
Bank had wished to insure its participation in the Austrian credit against
exchange rate risk, fearing that Austria might not be able to maintain a fixed
exchange rate, but such fears were rational and not a sign of contagion.[93]

There seems to be no indication, therefore, to assume that during the five
weeks from 12 May to 16 June 1931 the Austrian crisis had spread to German
banks. Documents of the discussions held among the German Cabinet on
how to react to the Austrian crisis contain no indication that they were worried about being affected; rather, they were preoccupied with the French
gaining influence in Vienna.[94] While Norman, McGarrah, Bruins, and Rodd
were certainly worried about international contagion should the ANB ran
out of money or Austria declare a moratorium, precisely the fact that this
scenario did not occur kept the crisis from spreading. By mid-June the consensus was that Bruins had successfully managed to control the situation in
Vienna, as withdrawals from the CA were reduced to a trickle and capital
outflows ceased almost entirely. However, the decision to keep paying out at
all costs in order to safeguard the financial stability of not just Austria but
all of Central Europe had weakened the ANB critically. As Germany developed its own, unrelated problems in June and July, rekindling nervousness
among Austrian depositors, the ANB could not stem the returning tide a
second time.

The Credit-Anstalt Collapse and the German Financial Crisis

On 5 June 1931, shortly before heading to England for talks with British Prime Minister Ramsay MacDonald, German Chancellor Heinrich Brüning announced austerity measures for Germany, which included some populist comments on reparations. Germany's communists, socialists, and center parties all stood opposed to Brüning's austerity plan, stoking latent fears about political instability. Capital flight ensued and the Reichsbank lost a first $100 million in gold and foreign currencies over a period of one week, increasing its discount rate from 5 to 7 percent on 13 June 1931.[95] To stem the continuing withdrawals from Germany, U.S. President Herbert Hoover announced plans for a one-year moratorium on all war debt and reparations on 20 June 1931. The Reichsbank thereafter lost yet another $21 million in foreign reserves and only kept its cover ratio above 40 percent with the help of a $100 million emergency credit provided by the BIS together with the BoE, the Federal Reserve Bank of New York, and the Banque de France. Withdrawals continued until finally the French, who had vehemently opposed Hoover's proposal, agreed to it so that the moratorium could take effect on Monday, 6 July 1931.[96]

At the same time in Vienna, actions undertaken by Bruins in late June and early July alleviated the Austrian crisis. The BIS was arranging a credit for Hungary, Yugoslavia and Latvia were experiencing extraordinary outflows, Norway and Finland were having economic problems, and there were withdrawals at the Wiener Bankverein on the account of Germany. But Kindersley wrote to Rodd that in Vienna the "situation is calm and well in hand," while McGarrah informed Harrison that the outflow of foreign exchange from the ANB was shrinking daily and that there were new inflows.[97] The first week in July, Chase National Bank deposited $4 million and Dutch banks $3 million with the CA, each for one week, and officially discounts fell by sch.25 million (about $3.5 million).[98] On Friday, 3 July, Bruins still called Basel to say "the position is generally speaking calm and satisfactory," though by Monday, 6 July, while still "fairly quiet," he admitted to the BIS that "considerable uneasiness is being shown in the market regarding developments in Berlin."[99] With Hoover's reparations moratorium in effect, Berlin and Warsaw reported a premium on dollar notes and, although foreign bank notes were still flowing into the ANB, there was a resurging demand for dollars in Vienna as well.[100]

On Monday, 13 July 1931, the BIS held an emergency meeting to discuss the
unfolding crisis in Germany, but the next day, after the closure of the large
Darmstädter und Nationalbank, capital flight from German (and Hungary)
ensued in full force and a bank holiday was declared in both countries.[101] In
Vienna the run on the schilling resumed, since Austrians now feared that
similar measures might also be announced by their government.[102] The ANB,
which for the previous two weeks had faced an average daily loss of just
$280,000–420,000 (about sch.2–3 million), now lost $840,000 on Monday,
$1.1 million on Tuesday, gained $700,000 on Wednesday, lost another $700,000
on Thursday, and lost $1 million each on Friday and Saturday, 17 and 18
July.[103] Discounts jumped by another sch.100 million ($14 million) as banks
obtained liquidity to satisfy withdrawals, and since the ANB thereby broad-
ened the money supply, the reported cover ratio dropped below the psychologically important 50 percent line for the first time.[104]

On Tuesday, 14 July, McGarrah had cabled Harrison in New York that the
position in Vienna was "reasonably calm," but by the end of the week Bruins's view had changed. He considered the situation "extremely serious," and
ANB Director Brauneis examined the introduction of capital controls.[105]
Still, as Berlin went on to suspend the free convertibility of the Reichsmark,
nobody considered Germany's problems as Austrian in origin. Writing to
former Finance Minister Otto Juch, a BIS official stated that "Austria too will
feel the repercussion of what is happening in Germany."[106] McGarrah, worried about the ANB losing foreign exchange as neighboring countries declared bank holidays and partial moratoria, inquired as to what steps were
being taken to insulate Vienna.[107] Bruins urged the Austrian government to
declare a bank holiday and await developments, or to consider other measures to curb withdrawals and rediscounting, but the Austrian government
failed to agree on any immediate steps.[108] News from London on 20 July that
a standstill agreement had been reached with German banks exacerbated
Austrian capital flight, and Bruins expected that the ANB would need its
second BIS credit after all, by Monday, 27 July.[109] Of the ANB's remaining
sch.613 million (about $86 million) in foreign reserves, no less than sch.302
(about $42.5 million) was borrowed at short notice and the CA was still dis-
counting new bills and increasing money supply at a rate of sch.2–3 million
($280,000–420,000) per day.[110] On 23 July the ANB raised its discount rate
to 10 percent, but the central bank kept losing foreign exchange.[111] Official

reserves dropped to sch.546 million (about $77 million) by the first week of
August and the cover ratio had to be reported as 43.6 percent.[112]

On 13 July, publication of the Macmillan report had revealed that short-
term liabilities of British banks far exceeded the reserves at the BoE.[113] As
capital in Germany and Austria took flight soon thereafter, the BoE was forced
to intervene on the foreign exchange market to prop up the value of the
pound sterling, which had momentarily dropped in Paris and New York.[114]
There was little public awareness of the sudden flight from the pound as the
world focused on the unraveling situation in Germany, but loans of over £25
million (about $113 million) were arranged each by the Federal Reserve and
the Banque de France to allow intervention on the exchange markets. An
increase of the Bank Rate from 2.5 to 3.5 percent on 23 July by the BoE had
little effect, and publication of the May report at the end of July, which revealed that Britain might face a budget deficit of as much as £120 million
(about $544 million), added more fuel to the fire. The BoE sold $200 million in
gold and foreign currency during the second half of July, possibly half of its
reserves, and continued to intervene in August.[115] The Bank Rate was raised
to 3.5 percent on 23 July and to 4.5 percent one week later, and the New York
and Paris loans were publicly announced on 1 August 1931.

As Britain's political parties discussed austerity measures to reduce the expected budget deficit, the BoE continued to prop up the pound using its own
reserves and French and U.S. credits. Lack of progress on the budget question and rumors about the BoE's gold losses provoked new speculation
against the pound, and since fresh foreign credits were preconditioned on
drastic budgetary measures opposed by many of his party colleagues, Prime
Minister MacDonald "gave himself over to the Conservatives" to form a national government.[116] The pound rallied, and by the end of August a further
$200 million in loans from France and the United States were announced.[117]
Macdonald presented an austerity budget on 10 September, and on 18 September called for a general election. In order to influence the vote, the BoE
chose to announce the suspension of gold payments six days prior to the election. The BoE was still losing foreign reserves, but it still had assets; it could
have increased Bank Rate further and the French were willing to extent additional credit. Norman had been away all summer and the decision had
been taken in his absence by the Deputy Governor to strengthen the Conservatives and hurt Labour.[118] Labour was indeed defeated at the polls, and

everyone believed that British suspension of the gold exchange standard was just a temporary measure, but in fact the British Treasury and policy makers soon discovered the benefits of a managed float.

With the holiday season in full swing and Austrian officials keen for a vacation, the government in Vienna finally turned to the League of Nations. On 11 August it publicly announced that in September it would ask the League to investigate and report on the financial and economic situation in Austria.[119] By the time the League delegation arrived, the ANB reported an overall loss of sch.418 million in foreign reserves (about $59 million, or 50 percent) since May, but its real losses were much higher, and further maintaining gold convertibility appeared impossible because official note cover had dropped from 48.7 percent on 1 August to just 33 percent by the end of September. Finally, on 9 October, capital controls were made permanent and Austria's currency, no longer quoted on most exchanges, was henceforth maintained artificially at its fixed rate to the dollar. But on the black market the depreciated schilling was already being quoted at a 20 percent discount.[120]

The Austrian Crisis and Financial Data

To explain the causes that produced a run on the Austrian schilling and drove the country off gold in 1931, Aurel Schubert focuses on the expectations of Austrians.[121] He argues that it was the sharp increase of discounts due to the CA's troubles from 12 May 1931 onward that inflamed inflationary fears among the population. Austrians were well accustomed to tracking note issue and cover ratios after going through months of hyperinflation. The rising amount of discounts at the ANB and the loss of foreign currency reserves strengthened expectations about a possible devaluation, given the disconcerting budget deficits for 1930 and 1931 (see Graph 8.2). The government's pledge to help bail out the CA with sch.100 million (about $14 million), and the guarantees it later extended to creditors, Schubert argues, added liabilities of unprecedented and unknown proportions. The people had to fear that the Austrian government might eventually print money and create inflation, so they sought safer assets and capital flight ensued. Schubert argues that by discounting freely, guaranteeing deposits, and offering foreign exchange, Austrian institutions only created more anxiety. In his view, the ANB's efforts were not just in vain, but in fact counterproductive.

Schubert claims that from 15 May 1931 onward the public expected Austria's fixed exchange rate regime to collapse. To illustrate his point, Schubert compared the yield spread between the guaranteed 1923 League loan and the 1930 Austrian Investment loan, but his data set only runs from May to June, conveniently leaving out July and August, which, as we shall see, is problematic.[122] Schubert then writes that the rising level of discounts at the ANB, which rose because of the CA's liquidity needs to satisfy withdrawals, provoked fears among Austrians about their currency's future purchasing power. But, the highest level of discounts reached in 1931 was lower than corresponding figures during the financial crisis of 1924 (see Graphs 5.2 and 8.2). Furthermore, at the outset, the ANB's official coverage ratio was among the highest in all of Europe and far above what it had been when the Vienna Stock Exchange crashed in early 1924. Schubert notes that there was a jump in the yield spread right after the CA announced its troubles, but in fact the initial spread is quite small, and since the League loan was payable in dollars and the Investment loan in *gold* schillings, the differential does not reflect the perceived risk of the purchasing power of the Austrian schilling.[123] In order to discern what drove Austrians to convert their savings into foreign currency and how this is connected to the German crisis, we shall make use of other financial data to illuminate the chronology of events one more time.

We are already familiar with the data of foreign deposits at the Vienna Bankverein (WBV) and the risk premium earned by bankers in New York and London for placing those funds in Austria from Chapter 7. We can estimate the risk premium by comparing the mean interest rate paid by WBV with the rate for three-month interbank funds in London and New York around the same time (see Graph 8.3).

Looking first at the total volume of dollar and pound deposits, we can clearly discern the drop of short-term lending in dollars and pounds following their peak in June and July 1930. Overall U.S. lending to Europe and financial flows from Western to Eastern Europe had peaked in 1928 or earlier, and by 1930 Germany, Austria, and most other successor states experienced net currency outflows. By the time of the CA crisis in May 1931, dollar deposits at WBV had already dropped by over one-third and pound deposits by almost one-half. Following the announcement of the CA's reconstruction

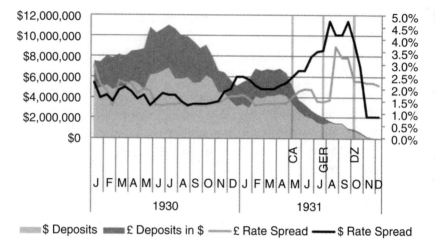

GRAPH 8.3. Wiener Bankverein's foreign US$ and UK£ deposits in US$ and their rate spread, 1930–1931. *Legend:* CA: Credit-Anstalt Crisis, 15 May 1931. GER: London Conference results in German standstill agreement, 23 July 1931. DZ: Austria makes capital controls permanent, 9 October 1931. *Source:* CA, Protokollbücher Wiener Bankverein.

plans, the drop in deposits at WBV accelerated. Sterling deposits almost disappeared over the summer, and only a small amount of dollar deposits had been renewed by the time capital controls went into force in October. Deposits seem to have stabilized in March 1931, and only the news of the CA's problems caused a renewed wave of withdrawals from May onward. This occurred even though WBV was in no particular way associated with the CA, but foreign lenders were frightened not just about the latter, but about the entire Austrian financial system. Increasingly, WBV thus also had to pay a higher risk premium to maintain its foreign deposits.

Risk premiums on both dollar and pound deposits had fallen since the BKA's collapse in 1929, when they had peaked at almost 3 percent (see Graph 7.5). They remained fairly stable during the second half of 1930, but the dollar premium rose to 2.5 percent toward the end of the year. It rose again in April, probably in connection with the announcement concerning the Austro-German customs union in March. A more significant increase in the dollar premium occurred in May, when a rise of the pound premium can also be discerned. At the same time that foreign deposits were withdrawn, the risk premium paid for the renewal of dollar deposits rose gradually at first and then more suddenly to an all-time high of 4.75 percent in August. This aggregate data is too weak to draw any accurate conclusions about how events and decisions contributed to the crisis, but the German standstill agreement signed on 20 July in London is probably the reason for the sharp jump in the risk premium for dollar deposits (the pound premium rose only in early August, see Graph 8.3, column GER).

The dollar spread shows the rise of the risk premium more accurately than does the pound spread, because in contrast to sterling deposits, which were almost all withdrawn from WBV, some dollar deposits were renewed, so there are running data on the interest rate paid for dollars. It should be noted further that there is a tendency for the premium to be shown as too low, because taking into account deposits received up to three months earlier naturally biases the median interest rate paid toward the past. Taking this into account, and looking at the rates of individual deposits, it emerges indeed that a sharp rise of risk premiums for dollar and pound deposits occurred in late July. But this was six weeks into the Austrian crisis and after the CA had announced the problems that provoked the original run of depositors on Vienna banks. So is it possible that the German crisis provoked this sudden jump of Austrian risk premiums?

We might be able to answer this question by looking at more high-frequency data, such as the daily quotations of the Austrian tranche of the guaranteed 1923 League loan and the Austrian Federal loan from 1922. Comparing the prices will allow us to calculate the yield spread between the two bonds, which will shed light on exactly what caused a change of risk assessment among lenders in July 1931. We are already familiar with these two series from Chapter 7. Aurel Schubert presented a similar approach, but he compared yields between the League loan and Austria's 1930 International Investment loan, which are rather similar. Schubert wrongly claims that whereas the 1923 League loan was payable in U.S. dollars, the 1930 International Investment loan was not, and that their yield spread thus mainly represented fears of devaluation. However, the 1930 Investment loan was payable in *gold* schillings, and as an international loan it ranked second, right after the League loan. Further, the BIS was given trusteeship and the loan was serviced from the same tobacco and customs revenues pledged for the guaranteed League loan. The 1923 Federal loan was not payable in gold, and since it was not an international loan it was more likely to be defaulted upon as well. Using the 1922 Federal loan improves the analysis because the spread is a better gauge of Austrian default purchasing power risk. Further, we can compare our findings with those of Chapter 7. Finally, unlike Schubert, the analysis of financial data is presented all the way to September 1931 to include the German and British crises.[124]

The beginning of the CA crisis is clearly discernable if we look at the price of the guaranteed League loan before and after 15 May 1931 (Graph 8.4, α). After the announcement of the bank's losses and the government's decision to participate in its reconstruction, demand for the loan rose steeply. Its price rose further after a guarantee law was passed by parliament, giving the government the option to guarantee the CA's liabilities (Graph 8.4, β). A flight into gold and safety was under way, which was not abated by the BIS announcement on 28 May that it would help the ANB (Graph 8.4, β).

Prices peaked in early June and then continued to fall back again. The resignation of the Austrian government after declaring a guarantee for the CA's foreign creditors on 16 June seems to have worried investors once more as the price rose sharply thereupon (Graph 8.4, γ), but the eventual installation of a new government under the Christian-Social Karl Buresch and, most importantly, U.S. President Hoover's widely advertised proposal for a complete moratorium on all international war debt, calmed investors' nerves and brought some respite. After Hoover's announcement on 20 June, prices for the League loan stabilized, even if only for a short while (Graph 8.4, δ). The new government's confirmation on 26 June that its guarantees included all CA domestic and foreign liabilities led to another sharp jump in the price of the loan, but thereafter prices remained stable and actually fell back again in early July (Graph 8.4, ε). As Bruins was reporting to the BIS in Basel, he had gotten the situation under control. It was only three weeks later that havoc broke loose once more, following discerning news from Germany on Monday, 13 July (Graph 8.4, ζ). Within a few days, prices rose again to the level of early June. They peaked on 17 July and fell back again, only to jump once more on 30 July. Prices then fell and remained fairly stable for the rest of the period under analysis, but at a considerably higher level than they had been before the outbreak of the crisis.

It is to the yield spreads between the guaranteed 1923 League loan, the 1930 International Investment loan, and the 1922 Federal loan that we must turn our attention now, to make this price behavior intelligible (Graph 8.5).

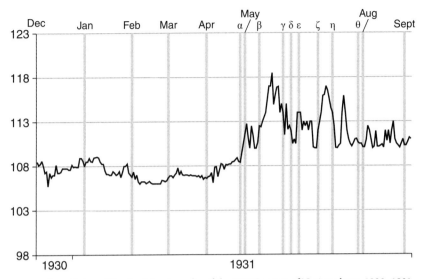

GRAPH 8.4. Price of the Austrian tranche of the 1923 League of Nations loan, 1930–1931. *Legend:* α: Announcement of Credit-Anstalt's losses, 11 May 1931. β: Passage of guarantee law and BIS announcement, 27 and 29 May 1931. γ: Bank of England Loan, Austrian government guarantee to foreign creditors and Austrian government crisis, 16 June 1931. δ: Buresch government and Hoover's proposal of a moratorium, 20 June 1931. ε: Second announcement of Austrian government guarantees, 27 June 1931. ζ: News of capital flight from Germany, 14 July 1931. η: London conference results in standstill agreement with Germany, 24 July 1931. θ: News of impending arrival of League Delegation and inquiry, 11 August 1931. *Source: Neue Freie Presse.*

The first observation is already striking. There was only a relatively slight increase in the yield spread following the announcement that the CA was being bailed out by the Austrian government (Graph 8.5, α). While there was a rush for safe assets, as indicated by the rise in the price paid for the League loan, expectations of devaluation or default remained relatively low. Investors bid up bond prices and accepted a lower yield overall, but they do not seem to have considered the Austrian government's pledge to participate with sch.100 million in the reconstruction of the CA as particularly dangerous for currency stability or sovereign solvency.

Nor was the passage of a law on 28 May allowing the government to grant guarantees to the CA's creditors a cause for serious apprehension about fiscal stability or purchasing power (Graph 8.5, β). Following the legislative decision, there was only a modest increase in expected default risk, and it was soon

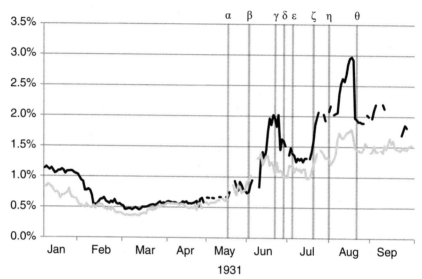

GRAPH 8.5. 1931 Yield spreads between 1923 League of Nations loan and 1922 Austrian Federal loan (black line) and 1930 Austrian International Investment loan (gray line). *Legend:* α: Announcement of Credit-Anstalt's losses, 11 May 1931. β: Passage of Guarantee Law and BIS announcement, 27 and 29 May 1931. γ: Bank of England loan, Austrian government guarantee to foreign creditors and Austrian government crisis, 16 June 1931. δ: Buresch government and Hoover's proposal of a moratorium, 20 June 1931. ε: Second announcement of Austrian government guarantees, 27 June 1931. ζ: News of capital flight from Germany, 14 July 1931. η: London Conference results in standstill agreement with Germany, 24 July 1931. θ: News of impending arrival of League delegation and inquiry, 11 August 1931. *Source: Neue Freie Presse.*

reverted. The real jump in the yield spread occurred only on Thursday, 4 June 1931, when the ANB balance sheet reported a large jump in discounted paper and a fall in the cover ratio from 63.8 percent to 57.1 percent. As Schubert correctly observed, the high level of discounts had a disconcerting effect. The yield spreads between the Austrian Investment loan and Federal loan widened, indicating heightened purchasing power risk, which peaked on 15 June 1931 (Graph 8.5, γ). Shortly thereafter, the announcement of the BoE loan and the government guarantee for the CA's foreign creditors seem to have had a calming effect. Thereupon the spreads continuously declined and their gap narrowed, encouraged by Hoover's proposal and unperturbed by, or possibly even confident about, the government's second declaration to guarantee all creditors (20 and 27 June; see Graph 8.5, δ and ε). From mid-June to mid-July, yield spreads remained at a level not significantly higher than what they had been in January 1931 and purchasing power risk, reflected in the yield differential between the Federal and Investment loans, diminished.

Once news of capital flight in Berlin reached Vienna on 13 July, anxiety among investors about an Austrian default and currency depreciation grew anew (Graph 8.5, ζ). The yield spreads rose continuously thereafter and default risk grew to unprecedented levels. News from London about reaching a standstill agreement on German foreign debt on 23 July had no calming effect on the yield spreads (Graph 8.5, η), which continued to rise until the Austrian government announced the League inquiry on 11 August (Graph 8.5, θ). Further the yield differential between Federal and Investment loan had widened dramatically, indicating serious apprehensions about the schilling's future purchasing power. Thereafter the yield spreads immediately dropped, as it was clear to everyone that a new League investigation might lead to renewed control and a new foreign loan. This reduced the likelihood of the Austrian government defaulting on its debt or devaluing the currency and the differential between the Investment and Federal loan narrowed again, indicating a decline in the perceived risk of the schilling's future purchasing power.

A comparison of the guaranteed 1923 League loan and the Austrian 1922 Federal loan thus confirms claims made earlier in this chapter. As already indicated by the risk premium paid by WBV for dollar deposits, the panic in Vienna abated after 22 June (Graph 8.4, δ) and the atmosphere might have been indeed quite calm until 13 July. International central bank cooperation through the BIS had worked. Providing credits to the ANB, foreign central banks had helped it weather the storm successfully by paying out to maintain the fixed schilling's exchange rate and keeping the CA open. Thus Bruins reports to Basel in late June and early July were hardly overoptimistic, but most likely a truthful account of events as they appeared to him on the ground.

We might still turn to one final set of financial data, namely short-term interest rates in European financial centers, to look for signs of banking distress across the continent during the European financial crisis of 1931 (see Graph 8.6). The short-term interest rate is the rate at which banks lend to each other, and when banks face uncertainty about their future liquidity or about that of their partners, the interest rate at which they are ready to lend and are prepared to borrow rises.

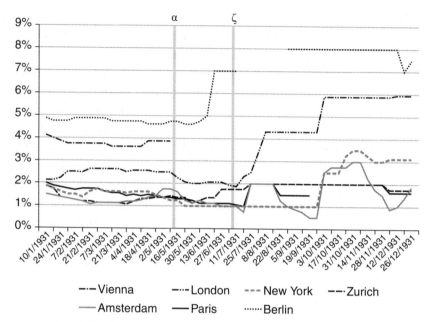

GRAPH 8.6. 1931 Short-term interbank lending rates in European financial centers. *Legend:* α: Announcement of Credit-Anstalt's losses, 11 May 1931. ζ: News of capital flight from Germany, 14 July 1931. *Source: Österreichischer Volkswirt.*

There is no indication that credit markets dried up immediately following the CA crisis. In London, Amsterdam, New York, Paris, and Zurich, short-term interest rates fell until mid-June, when the first problems appeared in Germany. The decision of the Reichsbank to stem the German outflow by an increase in its rate might be reflected by the earlier tightening in Zurich, but only after mid-July, when the German crisis entered its critical stage and general moratoria and capital controls were declared, do we see a more widespread tightening of liquidity across European financial centers.

Older accounts, which present the German crisis and *inter alia* the British one as a consequence of the CA collapse, are wrong. However, it appears that the German crisis did cause the crisis that would force Austria to declare capital controls. Austrian policy, in cooperation with foreign central banks, was to sustain the gold exchange standard system in Central Europe and maintain the CA and its industrial employers. This it did, and it was in fact the German crisis, which itself was due to a lack of confidence about Germany's fiscal stability, that spilled over to Austria and provoked a panic that was further aggravated by the London standstill agreement of 23 July 1931. Schubert is mistaken when he argues that Austrian policy inevitably lead to devaluation, and the question is not whether greater international cooperation could have stopped the CA crisis or whether providing more funds to the ANB would have saved the Austrian currency. The real run on the Austrian schilling was a consequence of the run on the German currency; the CA neither caused the German crisis, nor was it the first step in a series of crises that led to the Germany's problems or the gold standard's demise. If anything, the CA crisis was an example of international central bank cooperation in difficult times, a successfully coordinated attempt at stemming and insulating a crisis from spreading internationally. It was in Germany that Austria's final troubles originated, not the other way around.

Barry Eichengreen prominently argued that interwar central banks lacked the willingness to cooperate and uphold international stability. According to his account, it was the lack of central bank cooperation that allowed the financial crisis in 1931 to spread.[125] The above analysis relativizes his claim. In the Austrian case there was cooperation. Central bankers were willing to assist and agreed on the importance of helping the Austrian National Bank sustain the fixed exchange rates of Austria's currency. The French were certainly trying to obtain political concessions and Norman had to intervene to halt such financial blackmail. But Reisch had asked the BIS in Basel for $14 million and been given it. If this sum turned out to be not enough, should this represent a lack of willingness to help, as claimed by Charles Kindleberger?[126] Kindleberger also famously argued that an important reason for the propagation of the 1931 crisis was that the United States was not yet willing, and the United Kingdom no longer able to act as the world's financial hegemon. In relation to the German crisis, when Britain itself felt the drain of gold, this might be true. But in the case of the Austrian Credit-Anstalt collapse, Norman acted as the dutiful lender of last resort, providing funds at the last minute to prevent an Austrian moratorium.

Aftermath

In the night of 12 to 13 September 1931, the Heimwehr in Styria and Upper Austria occupied strategic positions as their leaders proclaimed an end to the

Austrian Republic. Chancellor Karl Buresch ordered the mobilization of troops, which moved from their garrisons in Graz into the upper regions of Styria, but they gave the Heimwehr men enough time to return safely to their homes. The putsch having failed, Heimwehr leader Walter Pfrimer fled to Yugoslavia.

Chancellor Buresch obtained approval to issue a second tranche of Austria's International Investment loan, and in return he accepted an investigation and the reinstatement of League control over Austria's budget as Foreign Minister Johann Schober officially renounced the end to the customs union project. A delegation of the Financial Committee, including once more the Dutch banker Ter Meulen and Otto Niemeyer, visited Austria in late October.[127] Conversations with Chancellor Buresch and his Finance Minister revealed that the Treasury's situation was weak.[128] The ANB was still paying out sch.1.5 million in foreign exchange per day (about $210,000). The CA, which was kept running at an annual loss of sch.60 million per year (about $8.5 million), had accumulated discounts totaling a staggering sch.580 million (about $82 million). Van Hengel, who was now the CA's new General Manager, felt the situation was hopeless and wished nothing more than to return to Holland.[129] Backed by the League, the Chancellor successfully negotiated an austerity package with his coalition and the opposition parties, which included wage reductions for state workers, reform of the federal railways, administrative savings, and increased taxation.[130] Even the Socialists voted for the new budget reconstruction law on 3 October 1931. Eliminating the budget deficit after a financial crisis and amid a recession came at a price and over the course of the year, unemployment rose from 15 to 22 percent.[131]

In Geneva, the Belgian central banker and Financial Committee member Albert Janssen still claimed that "the maintenance of the currency at the gold parity rate [in Austria and Hungary] is an essential requirement to which everything else must be subordinated."[132] Niemeyer was, however, convinced that the schilling would collapse before Christmas unless the French put forward new funds.[133] In November there were rumors in London that Austria might default on its foreign debt and that the British guarantee for the 1923 League loan would be evoked.[134] Niemeyer was worried about the capital controls in Austria, which hurt trade, but in his opinion default was not immediate because Austria still had significant invisible exports and could keep servicing its foreign debt for some time.[135] Although he considered an Austrian default unlikely, he wanted measures taken by the underwriters to protect bondholders should he be proven wrong.[136] Partners at J. P. Morgan expressed profound shock at the suggestion of an Austrian default, which would be a "fatal blow to international credit." Revealing the shift of priorities of Austria's foreign creditors, they even advised that it would be better to opt for inflation and to keep paying than to risk trade and credit by holding up the gold standard in Austria.[137]

As the year 1931 came to an end, Bruins at the ANB noted that foreign exchange controls were ineffective, that the amount of foreign exchange entering the bank was insufficient and that the ANB was still paying out too much foreign exchange.[138] Instead of introducing energetic measures, the Austrians were stalling in the hope of obtaining a moratorium on all foreign debt.[139] Indeed, in January 1932 the ANB announced that new negotiations with Austria's short-term creditors were necessary because it could no longer allocate enough foreign exchange for payment.[140] In the end, renewed League control helped not only to restore credibility and confidence but also allowed Austria to float new foreign loans in 1932 and 1933, with the help of which Austrian banks gradually reduced their frozen liabilities, until in 1935 they were "practically repaid in toto."[141]

In May 1932 the thirty-nine-year-old Christian-Social Engelbert Dollfuss was appointed Chancellor over a right-wing coalition government, which for the first time included the Heimwehr but enjoyed only a slim majority in parliament. In October, Justice Minister Kurt Schuschnigg made use of an imperial law from 1917 to circumvent parliament and decree the liability of CA directors for the financial damage caused by their bank's collapse. Industrialists welcomed the curtailment of parliamentary prerogatives and the Socialist opposition, still parliament's strongest party, protested in vain. On 4 March 1933 Dollfuss took advantage of a parliamentary crisis to suspend legislative powers and began governing entirely by decree. Over the subsequent months his government set out to dismantle Austria's democratic institutions and to fight Austrian labor. In February 1934, after the Heimwehr searched a Hotel in Linz that was owned by the Socialist Party, clashes between the outlawed Socialist Schutzbund and right-wing forces erupted into a civil war that lasted for over two weeks. Fights broke out in Vienna and other Austrian towns, leaving hundreds dead and thousands wounded. Dollfuss thereupon outlawed the Socialist Party and trade unions, imprisoned Socialist leaders, or forced them into exile. Austria had ceased being a parliamentary democracy and joined the growing number of corporatist, fascist states.

Conclusion

> I came to Berlin in the late summer of 1931, as the world
> economy collapsed. . . . [It was] the historic moment that
> decided the shape both of the twentieth century and of
> my life.
>
> —Eric Hobsbawm, *Interesting Times*

ON 1 APRIL 2000, the newly elected Austrian Minister President gave his inaugural address in the presence of the Soviet, French, British, and U.S. High Commissioners in Vienna. He observed that for the last fifty-three years, despite promises of freedom and independence, tiny Austria remained under Allied occupation. In the name of his people and government he declared the Allied control treaty null and void, and Austria henceforth free and independent. The sensational news, broadcast across the world by radio and television, risked provoking a world war; the Global Security Commission instantly sent rockets with an international delegation and death-ray-carrying policemen to investigate.

An international tribunal assembling in Vienna that same day accused Austrians of endangering world peace and termed the government's unilateral decision an attack on the victorious Allies. Having proven themselves an aggressive and bellicose people, Austrians would be forcefully relocated to the Middle East and the territory depopulated for the next 200 years. After all, it was argued, Austria's national colors originated with Duke Leopold V bloodily conquering Acre in 1191. Austria's Minister President countered with proof in the form of an educational film that showcased 500 years of nonviolent Austrian history, starting with the peaceful unification of Austria and Hungary at the famous double wedding of 1515, praising Habsburg Emperor Charles V for retiring to a peaceful monastic life in 1556, and recalling how Vienna had twice guaranteed Europe's tranquility by putting a halt to Turkish aggression. After watching Empress Maria Theresia and her sixteen children listening serenely to the young Mozart at the cembalo, the foreign judges agreed on leniency and voted to transform Austria into a large historic museum instead. The Minister President protested, demanding equal rights for all, and after the judges postponed their final verdict to the next day, called for peaceful demonstrations across the country.

The following day protestors, donning traditional costumes and sporting historic flags, marched in all of Austria's towns and villages to demand equal rights, not just for the sake of Austria, but for the sake of a better world order. The Viennese procession, ending on the Prater Hauptallee, was finally joined by the waiting judges who got swept along by an enthusiastic crowd and the rousing tunes of Austria's Radetzky March. In a final appeal, the Minister President argued that Austria could not have endangered a peace that was promised fifty-seven years ago without ever being realized. Convinced by the historic arguments, the judges decided to acquit Austria, and, recalling that Stalin, Roosevelt, and Churchill had promised Austria independence in 1943, announced the immediate withdrawal of all occupation forces.

Of course, the above events are fictitious. They are the plot of an Austrian movie, *1. April 2000,* commissioned and paid for by the Second Austrian Republic in 1952. The movie is a satirical comedy aimed at demonstrating the beauties and achievements of Austria to Austrians and the rest of the world.[1] At the time Austria was indeed occupied by the Allied Powers and keen on gaining independence. The plot pits the small Austrian state against the world, presenting Austrians in the year 2000 as the victims of a new global order. Unlike Orson Welles's *The Third Man* (1949), which prominently featured black market racketeers and postwar destitution, *1. April 2000* ignored Austria's problematic and recent history as perpetrators of Nazi crimes. The fictitious presentation of a series of historical *tableaux vivants,* followed by a procession of Austrian villagers and townsfolk in traditional costumes, eerily recalled the Kaiser-Huldigungs-Festzug of 1908, which we encountered in the Prologue. The double wedding (scene 5), Charles V and the siege of Vienna (scene 6), Prince Eugen (scene 10), Maria Theresia (scene 11), and the Radetzky March (scene 19) had all figured in the procession honoring Emperor Franz Joseph, too. In a subtle wink to the historical precedent, the Minister President sends home the two actors impersonating the Emperor and Vienna Mayor Karl Lueger after the court proceedings' first day. The pair complains that they have been waiting for four hours. In 1908, the original pair had been standing side by side under the baldachin, viewing the procession together for a period of about the same duration.

If the original procession in 1908 had still celebrated Austria as a martial power boasting a history of successful battles and military victories, the new version, accompanied by the tunes of Mozart and Beethoven, presented Austrians as a peaceful nation committed to music and the arts. In 1908 Austria had been portrayed as a harmonious, multinational monarchy, consciously ignoring the problems of national oppression and minority aspirations that plagued it. In 1952 Austria was depicted as the tiny victim of the powerful occupying Allies, ignoring the country's role in two world wars, and the difficult history of the First Republic, the right-wing Ständestaat, and the Anschluss that lay in between. The claim that Austria was the first victim of Nazi aggression, cited at the movie's end to justify the country's right to independence, enjoyed popular currency among Austria's postwar generation. Unlike Germany, where during the 1980s public debates about the Holocaust resulted in a widely accepted ideology of contrition that stood opposed to revisionist normalization and that embraced a critical examination of Germany's Nazi past as an essential element of its political discourse, the Austrian Waldheim affair of 1986 had a markedly different effect. Apologetic revisionism of Austria's own Nazi past was widely adopted not only by right-wing Austrians, dividing the political spectrum over the role of Austrians in the horrors of the Holocaust. Anti-Semitic statements, right-wing ideology, xenophobia, and even positive statements about Austria's Nazi past were attacked by Socialists, the Left, and much of the media, but adopted by members of Austria's right-wing Freedom party with impunity and without provoking the same widespread political outcry and rejection that in Germany made right-wing parties and their polemics inacceptable.[2]

While Austrian historians, like their German colleagues, have tackled, studied, and written about the painful history of Austria's fascist past and the complicity of Austrians in the horrors committed in the name of the German people, the Austrian victim narrative remains present and powerful. And while no Austrian historian today would debate the claim that many Austrians (though certainly not all) welcomed the Anschluss in 1938 and enthusiastically joined the National-Socialist party, much of the existing historical narrative about Austrian interwar history in the 1920s still betrays a tendency for self-victimization.[3] Certainly, the First Austrian Republic was created without consulting the wishes of the Austrian people, its borders were drawn against the will of the German speaking population of the late Austro-Hungarian Empire, and the Treaty of Saint-Germain-en-Laye was presented in 1920 without leaving much room for negotiation. But to extrapolate that interwar Austria was for the most part a helpless victim of the new order that reshaped Europe after the Great War contributes to an erroneous and dangerous national narrative. As this book has tried to show, Austria's interwar politicians retained much agency over, and thus responsibility for, the political and economic trajectory of their country, both domestically and internationally.

Austria's interwar version of the victimization narrative comes most obviously to the fore in relation to the League of Nations intervention from 1922 to 1926. With few exceptions, Austrian historians have viewed this episode as one of foreign domination and control. According to them, faced with the destructive forces of hyperinflation, Austrian politicians had to accept the harsh austerity measures concocted by the League of Nations in Geneva. Accounts stress the League's power over fiscal policy, the deflationary monetary policy enforced by the Bank of England (BoE) or the foreign advisor at Austria's National Bank, and, above all, the merciless dictates of the League's authoritarian General Commissioner. In this they present an uncritical reflection of contemporary views aired by politicians of all *couleur* and much of the contemporaneous press. As demonstrated in Part II of this book, Austrian governments did not adhere to the agreed-upon austerity budget, but instead balanced expenditures and revenues at a level considered dangerously high by the financial experts who debated the state of Austrian reconstruction during meetings of the League's Financial Committee in Geneva. The General Commissioner, while perhaps an authoritarian figure lacking political tact, was largely helpless vis-à-vis the Austrian government's infringement of its international commitments and actively tried to bridge the divergent views between Vienna and Geneva on more than one occasion. And finally, the succession of foreign advisers at the Austrian National Bank acted as overall passive, yet helpful observers of Austrian monetary policy, often defending controversial interest-rate decisions against the suspicious criticism harbored at the powerful BoE.

And when Austrian histories do claim Austrian agency, as in the case of Chancellor Ignaz Seipel's European tour in August 1922 or the fallout of the Credit-Anstalt (CA) crisis in 1931, they have been similarly mistaken. Seipel's trip is often seen as having single-handedly led to the League's preoccupation with Austria and to have put an end to hyperinflation. As Part I of this book demonstrated, the international community was seriously preoccupied with Austria long before Seipel's chancellorship. Austrian reluctance to accept foreign financial control and domestic political strife also help to explain why it took until August 1922 to organize an international rescue operation for Austria. More importantly, perhaps, inflation did not cease in August 1922, and it took the untiring efforts of a League delegation made up of international financial experts to ensure that the Austrian parliament ratified all laws necessary to float a foreign loan large enough to change the economic and political outlook of Austrians.

Finally, there is hardly a book in any language on the interwar period that will not relate to the CA crisis as the trigger of the financial avalanche that rolled over Europe that summer. While intuitively such a view makes chronological sense and has been repeated manifold over the decades, Chapter 8 has shown that it gives the Austrian financial crisis too much clout. The Austrian problems might have aggravated preexisting anxieties about financial stability across Europe, which were strongly related to the emergence of budget deficits due to the ongoing global cooldown and the collapse of agricultural prices since the late 1920s. While it can be shown that the CA collapse brought down the Amstelbank in Amsterdam, there is little reason to believe that it directly caused any troubles elsewhere. In Hungary and Poland, financial anxieties were present before the CA announced its losses, and the crises in Germany and Britain are simply too far removed chronologically and much better explained by their domestic budgetary problems and mistakes of monetary policy.

The reason that the CA myth has proven so long lasting is related to the way that we think about large and destructive financial crises. Many people still believe that in 1929 scores of ruined U.S. bankers jumped to their deaths from their high-rise offices on Wall Street, but there is no evidence that such suicides actually occurred. The erroneous belief might go back to the sketch of a stand-up comedian, who joked that failed bankers were lining up to get to the window. Similarly, in Germany people commonly believe that at the height of hyperinflation in 1923, workers returned home with their daily salary piled up in wheelbarrows. But apart from a staged picture of a well-dressed man presenting a pile of banknotes in a wheelbarrow, there is little proof or testimony of this actually happening. One reason for the longevity of such legends is their ability to depict and explain the world we live in. They help create solidarity and social cohesion, and provide legitimacy to social institutions and practices. Because financial crises are by their very nature esoteric, although they have a very real and direct impact on the life of almost everyone, they are prone to generate multiple explanatory accounts. Trying to make sense of what is happening around them, people are less interested in discovering the truth and more interested in finding an explanation that will give legitimacy to their own personal views and choices. The chronological sequence of events, from the CA collapse in May to the end of the gold standard in September, gave rise to the legend that the Austrian crisis had set off the economic calamity of the 1930s. The CA collapse was the result of a series of failed political and economic decisions taken by Austrian bankers and politicians, but by giving it international importance and the ability to ruin Germany and force Britain off gold, it becomes a problem of international dimensions and hence one that would have been up to the international community to prevent and deal with. Given the commonly accepted view that Austria had been oppressed and constrained by the interests of foreign financial elites during the 1920s, there is more than just a little schadenfreude in such accounts.

The spillover from popular lore into historiography is only possible because such legends were considered true by contemporaries, who plotted them down all over diaries, memoirs, diplomatic correspondence, and the press. Rigorous historical research may prove them wrong, but the legends will live on because they are not merely historiographical mishaps, but in fact support a narrative some wanted to and continue to want to believe in. The modern-day misconception of the Austrian interwar reiterates contemporaries' fixation on France and Britain as the powerful victors. Thus, "International aid to end hyperinflation could only be mobilized by threatening France with Anschluss"; "The BoE suffocated the Austrian economy through a credit embargo and enforced deflation"; "The Credit-Anstalt collapse triggered the European Depression because France and Britain offered insufficient help." Such a narrative preserves tiny Austria's position of importance on the stage of world affairs, while at the same time depicting it as the powerless victim of Europe's mighty victors. Dissected to its core, it blames the Allies for having ignored Austria's global importance at their own peril, and the history of Austrian independence really only begins following the Second World War—after 1938 Austria became the victim of Nazi aggression; before it had been the victim of the victorious Powers and their imposed policies and treaties.

There are important lessons to be drawn from interwar Austria's financial history for the problems facing Europe at the beginning of the twenty-first century. At the center of the European financial crisis has been the Greek republic, which, much like interwar Austria, teetered on the brink of bankruptcy under a fixed exchange rate regime. In April 2010, following years of heavy borrowing and economic growth, Greek sovereign bonds were downgraded and the country faced a sudden credit stop. Its ratio of sovereign debt to GDP was among the highest in the world, and the global economic contraction severely hit Greek tourism and shipping. Like Austria, Greece suffered a painful economic contraction, high unemployment, a high trade and budget deficit, and large foreign debt. Greece could have left the Eurozone choosing depreciation and inflation, but this would have made servicing its foreign debt more difficult and raising new debt more expensive. Instead, a series of Greek governments chose to reform the economy with the help of foreign credits and loans, provided through the so-called Troika, made up of the European Commission, the International Monetary Fund (IMF), and the European Central Bank. Much as with Austria in 1931, these three institutions oppose a Greek exit from the fixed exchange rate regime because they are scared that other countries might follow its example.[4]

But this is not where the parallels end. Much like in 1920s Austria, unpopular reforms in Greece triggered protests, general strikes, and violent clashes between demonstrators and the police as the Greek government successively raised direct and indirect taxes and reduced state expenditures, particularly on social welfare. Still, several more aid packages from the Troika were needed, banks had to be bailed out, and bondholders brought to agree to a haircut. Austerity measures eventually eliminated the deficit, but unlike in 1920s Austria, a left-wing government was voted into power in January 2015 with the mandate to resist foreign pressures for continued austerity. The government's collision politics sent Greek financial markets into disarray as investors feared sovereign default, bank collapses, and the imposition of capital controls. Led by Greek Prime Minister Alexis Tsipras and his left-wing Syriza party, the Greek people in a national referendum on 5 July 2015 rejected a set of softened conditions and austerity measures demanded by the Troika in return for another aid package. Following the referendum, Tsipras quickly set at renegotiating the agreement, and in return for up to €85 billion in financial aid and investments, agreed to implement a long list of austerity measures and welfare reforms. Critics argued that these were no different than the ones rejected in the referendum, and in fact even more severe, arguing that Tsipras had been forced by the Troika to ignore the sovereign will of the Greek people. The privatization of state assets, pension cuts, and tax increases were subsequently ratified by parliament, and shortly thereafter Tispras's government fell, though the consequent snap election in September returned him to power. Further austerity measures, cutting pensions and introducing various tax hikes, were passed in 2016 and 2017, each time accompanied by heavy public protests. In July 2017 the IMF agreed to a new conditional €1.6 billion loan to Greece, two years after the republic had defaulted on one of its payments, if European lenders helped reduce Greek debt to sustainable levels. In mid-2017 Tsipras appeared optimistic, and there were even talks of Greece returning to borrow on international capital markets.[5]

Public reactions to the Greek bailout agreed upon between Tsipras and the Troika were largely negative. With unemployment, homelessness, and bankruptcies visibly rising across the country, poverty affected a growing part of the population. At the same time, welfare spending was severely curtailed and the lowering of wages was promoted as a necessary measure to return growth to the Greek economy. The budget was balanced, sovereign debt reduced, and timid economic growth briefly returned to the Greek economy in 2015, but many observing the Greek bailout discerned continuities going back to nineteenth-century gunboat diplomacy.[6] Greeks blamed the European Commission, and more specifically Germany, for the economic misery incurred by austerity.[7] The fact that Tsipras accepted harsh bailout conditions despite the popular referendum was interpreted by many as a coup organized by the capitalist forces in charge of international finance.[8]

But (most) sovereign states are never completely free to do as they please; nor does it seem entirely unreasonable that creditors of bankrupt states link the supply of fresh capital and debt restructuring to certain conditions, particularly if public funds or state guarantees are necessary. The fact is that at any time Greece could have cancelled its agreements and left the Eurozone. It is because Greek voters did not wish to abandon the Euro or the European Union that the Troika was able to force its view on Greek reconstruction. Betting on European leaders not wishing to see Greece leave and undermine European stability, Tsipras had called the referendum to strengthen his bargaining position. But the Troika was not to be bullied by brinkmanship, and despite French and Italian worries, Germany and its allies stared down the Greeks, who quickly turned their ship around. Tispras's collision politics came at a price: financial panic, a run on banks, and the default on an IMF payment worsened Greece's fiscal position and arguable made austerity even more necessary than before if Greece wished to remain a member of the Eurozone.[9]

Austrians, both contemporaries and later historians, accused the League of Nations of installing a "dictatorship" in interwar Austria too. But much like in Greece, decisions about how to implement austerity were taken by a democratically elected government and ratified by parliament. In the Austrian case, the international agreements even required two-thirds majorities to pass. It is certainly true that the agreements negotiated and agreed upon between foreign creditors and national governments intended to limit the economic sovereignty of nations threatened with default, but in some ways these are self-limitations of sovereignty. Chancellor Seipel had himself pushed for the idea. Local elites welcomed the League and its measures not just as a bastion against socialism, but also as a guarantor for what they considered sound economic policy and change. Austria was indeed constrained in its freedom to access foreign capital markets. The League system did not allow it to borrow more money freely without consent from Geneva until 1926, after which it still needed approval from the Committee of Control of Guarantor States. But this was a condition of foreign creditors, without which they would not have lent. General Commissioner Alfred Rudolph Zimmerman did intend to oversee the dismissal of 100,000 state workers and officials and other budgetary measures, but nobody in Austria would have argued that this was unnecessary, and the magical figure was never reached.

It would be simply wrong to argue that Austria had lost all or even most of its sovereignty over economic and monetary policy. Whenever the Austrian government or the Austrian National Bank did not see eye-to-eye with wishes coming from London or Geneva, they simply ignored them.

The League's involvement provided the government with a tool to overcome a disastrous political and budgetary stalemate and, more importantly, with a scapegoat to blame for unpopular measures and thereby safeguard political peace in the country. Much like Greece, Austria's economy was in dire need of hugely unpopular reforms, but the country's political parties were too divided or lacked the necessary trust to find common ground and agree on changes. While politicians believed cutbacks were necessary, they were unwilling to take the blame and pay the political cost of implementing them. Meanwhile, industrialists and bankers knew that only foreign loans could help rebuild the Austrian economy. The most important contribution of the League was hence to give the government *and* the opposition the necessary moral and political cover to implement unpopular but necessary changes, while blaming the cost in unemployment on Zimmerman, foreign financial interests, the League of Nations in Geneva, or even the BoE. The result was a balanced budget, a stable currency, and economic recovery, but also aversion and prejudice about internationalism, toward financial elites and of course against Jews.

The Greek crisis and the hardship the measures chosen for reconstruction of its economy and finances imposed on the weaker strata of the Greek population supported the rise of the ultra-nationalist Golden Dawn party. The racist neo-Nazi group registered as a political party in 1993, but it was only during elections in 2012 that it could enter Greece's national parliament, obtaining twenty-one seats. Its election campaigns featured the burning of Israeli and U.S. flags, and party supporters committed a series of violent hate crimes against foreigners, homosexuals, and political opponents. On 23 October 2012, one of its members of parliament, Illias Kasidaiaris, quoted *The Protocols of the Elders of Zion* in parliament, and during a debate on 6 June 2013 implied that he was a Holocaust denier.[10] His party colleague and fellow parliament member Illias Pnagiotaros described Adolf Hitler as a "great personality, like Stalin," and party founder Nikolaos Michaloliakos is reported to have said on television in 2012: "There were no ovens—it's a lie. I believe it's a lie. There were no gas chambers either."[11] The party is generally homophobic, Eurosceptic, anti-American, and wholeheartedly embraces all forms of political incorrectness. But it is particularly in relation to the financial crisis that anti-Semitic stereotypes have been evoked. Representative surveys established that 85 percent of Greeks believe that Jews hold disproportionate power in the world.[12]

Austria, with its own narrative of victimization, is another European country that has seen a resurgence of far-right politics. The xenophobic Freedom party almost managed to get Norbert Hofer elected president in 2016. The party, which historically attracted former Austrian Nazis and SS members, then joined a coalition government after garnering 26 percent of the vote at national elections held on 15 October 2017.[13] According to Austria's daily *Der Standard,* half of the Freedom party's parliamentary representatives publicly ascribed to a Pan-German ideology. A study published by the Anti-Defamation League in 2015, revealed that over 50 percent of adult Austrians believed that Jews talked too much about the Holocaust, and over 40 percent thought that Jews held too much financial power in international capital markets.[14] Compared with contemporary Germany, these are incredible figures. The prevalence of such views relies on the continuity of the long-held *Opfermythos,* arguing that Austria was a victim of Nazi Germany from 1938 to 1945, an idea adopted and propagated by Austria's postwar politicians, as in *1. April 2000.* Extending this narrative backwards and making Austria a perennial victim bereft of agency—from Saint-Germain to 1945— is supportive of this falsification or simplification of historical facts. Austria remains a politically split country, with a surging far Right and powerful xenophobic party. This is also a consequence of Austrian refusal or inability to honestly face its own (Nazi) past. It also has to do with historians falsely accusing international financial elites at the League of Nations or the BoE for Austria's economic woes in the 1920s, which for many nonhistorians might come down to the same as blaming "das internationale Finanzjudentum."

According to the "Iron Law of Oligarchy," bad systems endure because even after regimes change, the country's new elites prefer to engage in traditional ways of doing business. Foreign interventions are rarely enough to correct deeply rooted problems. Modern Greece had already defaulted five times on its foreign sovereign debt before being hit by the Euro crisis, four times in the nineteenth century and once during the Great Depression in 1932.[15] In interwar Austria, the economic fruits of League intervention were squandered by corrupt financial and political elites, in cahoots to enrich themselves and remain in power. When I first visited Vienna in 2006 to begin research on the CA crisis, the country's national elections were dominated by the BAWAG scandal, which revealed that directors of the Socialist trade union bank had "lost" over €1 billion, requiring the Austrian government to proclaim a state guarantee.[16] In 2009 the politician Karl-Heinz Grasser was accused of pocketing €800,000 during his tenure as finance minister in return for revealing insider information about the ongoing privatization of federal housing projects.[17] That same year, the Hypo Alpe Adria bank, which had received public guarantees exceeding €20 billion from the province of Carinthia governed by Jörg Haider, revealed a hole of €1.5 billion in its balance sheet. The fallout of its criminal transactions cost the Austrian taxpayer more than €5 billion.[18]

In short, historical amnesia has a price and it comes at a real cost. As Lenin said, let us face the truth squarely. In politics that is always the best and the only correct attitude.[19] Or to quote Thomas Huxley, it is our human duty to "learn what is true in order to do what is right."[20]

Appendix A

Austrian Consumer Price Indexes for 1921 and 1922

Index Numbers of the Mixed Commission[1]

	Food	Clothing	Rent	Light and fuel	Official CPI	Official CPI (excluding housing)	Retail prices	CPI
1921								
January	100	100	100	100	100	100	100	100
February	102.8545	125.5	100	114.242	107.956	108.01	114	108.
March	119.0492	125.5	125	125.802	121.239	121.22	122	121.
April	116.1492	133.5	125	125.643	120.805	120.79	116	120.
May	125.3156	141.5	125	128.692	128.87	128.88	121	128.
June	127.9427	135.9	125	124.737	129.019	129.04	150	129.
July	126.4756	167.9	125	132.035	135.159	135.24	143	135.
August	133.9133	161.5	125	163.679	133.939	134	167	134.
September	151.1202	205.7	150	163.679	163.283	163.39	215	163.
October	232.6737	348.1	150	254.347	257.319	257.93	333	258.
November	415.3417	389.1	250	384.864	405.245	406.13	566	406.
December	654.7367	936.4	203.5	714.977	714.286	717.08	942	717.
1922								
January	850.6767				897.262	900.41	1,142	900.
February	990.5607				1,058.55	1,063.1	1,428	1,126.
March	1,028.091	1,149	700	1,053.15	1,070.75	1,072.9	1,457	1,149.
April	1,186.171	1,249	850	1,119.28	1,179.18	1,181.4	1,619	1,277.
May	1,562.607	1,338	900	1,291.94	1,476.01	1,479.7	2,028	1,599.
June	2,753.327	2,183	1,050	2,045.06	2,529.14	2,537.4	3,431	2,706.
July	3,732.515	3,635	1,050	2,905.95	3,574.14	3,588.6	4,830	3,810.
August	8,215.626	8,661	1,650	6,590.74	8,015.72	8,051.6	11,046	8,713.
September	15,388.38	15,418	1,650	15,390.6	15,276.5	15,354	20,090	15,848.

1. Jan van Walré de Bordes, *The Austrian Crown: Its Depreciation and Stabilization* (London, 1924), p. 83; Bundesamt für Statistik, *Wirtschaftsstatistisches Jahrbuch 1925*, Herausgegeben von der Kammer für Arbeit und Angestellte in Wien (Vienna, 1926).

2. Van Walré de Bordes, *The Austrian Crown*, pp. 88–89.

3. Housing excluded.

4. Van Walré de Bordes, *The Austrian Crown*, p. 91.

5. Ibid., p. 93.

6. Ibid., p. 95.

of Volkswirt[2]

	II[3]	Consumer Price Index of the Reparations Commission[4]	Index of cost of minimum diet[5]	Index of cost of average pre–WWI diet[6]	Austrian retail prices	Average
0	100	100	100	100	100	100
0.24	104.58	108.7	113.442	102.98	107.018	108.312
3.96	122.22	121.7	122.766	113.13	101.754	118.8701
0.62	130.82	128.3	114.996	114.84	106.14	119.9529
0	136.59	137	121.212	110.83	131.579	126.9765
4.31	137.36	139.1	150.738	112.39	125.439	130.9142
0.38	157.85	167.4	142.968	109.52	146.491	141.5864
6.92	141.76	147.8	166.278	113.45	188.596	147.1933
1.23	186.61	200	214.452	149.89	292.105	185.8823
2.37	247.67	241.3	332.556	240.58	496.491	276.0167
0.36	406.67	391.3	565.657	424.6	826.316	432.7181
4.1	725.04	669.6	941.725	719.25	1,001.75	707.1831
9.97	1,055.3	934.8	1,142.19	921.54	1,252.63	806.0485
4.4	1,508	1,417	1,428.13	1,107.5	1,278.07	1,017.408
72.7	1,714.2	1,639	1,457.65	1,110.5	1,420.18	1,210.384
26.1	1,760.9		1,619.27	1,262.8	1,778.95	1,305.515
38.5	2,044.5		2,027.97	1,465.1	3,009.65	1,622.899
26.7	2,882.2		3,431.24	2,568.5	4,236.84	2,558.338
71.9	3,840.8		4,829.84	3,589.1	9,689.47	3,867.069
32.5	7,390		11,045.8	7,256.8	17,622.8	8,105.149
50	17,321		20,090.1	14,639	16,286.8	14,528.89

Appendix B

The "Normal" Budget as Presented in Millions of Gold
Crowns to the Financial Committee in May 1924,
Excluding Ertragsanteile

	1923		1924	Provisory Delegation estimate for 1925	1925			Expected changes					
Expenditures	Budgeted	Effective			Recurrent	Nonrecurrent	Total	1926	1927	1928	1929	1930 or after	Add indeterminate dates
Debt service													
a) League of Nations debt	55.5	35.3	71.1	100.5	69.9		69.9	5.78					
b) Other debts (net)			19.4		19.7	-4.8	14.9	5.86	-0.02	-0.02	-0.04	-0.47	-0.54
Pensions													
a) Pensions indemnity (net)	49.3	66.8	74.1	62.3	41.4	40.7	82.1	-0.14					
b) Former pensions of Südbahn and Railways (net)		3.3	13.9		22.2		22.2					-40.51	
c) Increase in pensions					15		15						
Army	45.9	43.1	38.2	26.2	41.2		41.1						
Social service (net)	40.1	47.2	29.1	26	10.5	21.2	31.7	8.61	0.5	-0.02	0.98	0.97	-24.8
Administrative services	135.1	164.6	143.5	135	153.4	16.6	170	-2	-11.41	-1.48	-0.8	-0.46	-0.43
Reform of salaries					47		47						
Assistance to autonomous bodies:													
a) Advances for officials	25.8	35.3	16.6										
b) Other advances	6.2	2.7	3.4		4.6		4.6						
Railways													
a) State railways (subsidy)	86.5	86.6	33.5		7	0.8	7.8	-0.83					
b) Südbahn (subsidy)	21.5		16		2.3	2.9	5.2	-1.07					
c) Other railways	8.9		9.5		3.4		3.4		-0.87				
Other undertakings with deficits (subsidy)	11.4	35	6.4	0						-0.07			
Monopolies (subsidy)		0.6											
Total expenditure	486.2	520.5	474.7	350	437.6	77.4	514.9	16.21	-11.8	-1.49	0.14	-40.47	-25.77

Revenues												
Customs	78.6	69	86	100	100		100					-4.58
Import and export duties	7.8	7	6.3	7.05		4.6	4.6					
Consumption taxes	31.2	46.7	38.6	31.966	49.2		49.2					
Direct taxes	47.2	112.3	112.3	65.4	173.6		173.6					
Taxes on railway transport	1.3	1.2	1.7	76	17.5		17.5					
Dues (excl. tax on railway transport)	76.7	124.6	154.1	114	183.8	12	195.8					-12.05
TOTAL	242.8	360.8	399	394.416	524.1	16.6	540.7					-16.63
Deduct share of provinces and communes in the common expenditure	-45.2	-74.3	-104	-68.64	-117.3		-117.3					
Remainder	197.6	286.5	295	325.776	406.8	16.6	423.4					-16.63
Other administrative receipts	37.3	43.6	39.4	27.4	16.8	8.1	24.9	17.98	15.65	-4.71	-0.01	-4.19
Monopolies												
Tobacco	55.4	63.3	81.9	116.6	92.4	-1.8	90.6	0.02	0.04		1.78	
Salt	5.7	4.6	7.3	10	9	1.9	7.1	0.02		0.07	1.78	0.01
Other monopolies	0.8		1.1		1.9		1.9					
State railways								5.56	5.56			6.94
Undertakings showing a surplus	4.4	4.3	3.8	9.5	2.8	-0.01	2.8					
Total receipts	**301.2**	**402.3**	**428.5**	**489.276**	**529.7**	**21**	**550.7**	**23.56**	**-10.05**	**-4.64**	**3.55**	**-1.48**
Total expenditures	**486.2**	**520.5**	**474.7**	**350**	**437.6**	**77.4**	**515**	**-11.8**	**4.97**	**0.14**	**-40.47**	**-25.77**
Budget balance	-185	-118.2	-46.2	139.27	92.1	-56.4	35.7	35.4	-15.02	-4.8	44	24.3

Sources: LNA, F. 153: Preliminary Draft Budget prepared by the Austrian Government. Forwarded at the request of Dr. Zimmerman to the members of the Financial Committee on 28 May 1924.

Appendix C

The Geneva Protocols (1922) I, II, and III
and Further Documents

Protocol no. I.

DECLARATION.

The Government of His Britannic Majesty, the Government of the French Republic, the Government of His Majesty the King of Italy, AND THE Government of the Czechoslovak Republic,

Of the one part,

At the moment of undertaking to assist Austria in her works of economic and financial reconstruction.

Acting solely in the interests of Austria and of the general peace, and in accordance with the obligations which they assumed when they agreed to become Members of the League of Nations,

Solemnly declare:

That they will respect the political independence, the territorial integrity and the sovereignty of Austria;

That they will not seek to obtain any special or exclusive economic or financial advantage calculated directly or indirectly to compromise that independence;

That they will abstain from any act which might be contrary to the spirit of the conventions which will be drawn up in common with a view to effecting the economic and financial reconstruction of Austria, or which might prejudicially affect the guarantees demanded by the Powers for the protection of the interests of the creditors and of the guarantor States;

And that, with a view to ensuring the respect of these principles by all nations, they will, should occasion arise, appeal, in accordance with the regulations contained in the Covenant of the League of Nations, either individually or collectively, to the Council of the League, in order that the latter may consider what measures should be taken, and that they will conform to the decisions of the said Council;

The Government of the Federal Republic of Austria,
Of the other part.

Undertakes, in accordance with the terms of Article 88 of the Treaty of St. Germain, not to alienate its independence; it will abstain from any negotiations or from any economic or financial engagement calculated directly or indirectly to compromise this independence.

This undertaking shall not prevent Austria from maintaining, subject to the provisions of the Treaty of St. Germain, her freedom in the matter of customs tariffs and commercial or financial agreements, and, in general, in all matters relating to her economic regime or her commercial relations, provided always that she shall not violate her economic independence by granting to any State a special regime or exclusive advantages calculated to threaten this independence.

The present protocol shall remain open for signature by all the States which desire to adhere to it. In witness whereof the undersigned, duly authorised for this purpose, have signed the present Declaration (Protocol I). Done at Geneva in a single copy, which shall be deposited with the Secretariat of the League of Nations and shall be registered by it without delay, on the fourth day of October, one thousand nine hundred and twenty-two.

(Signed) BALFOUR. (Signed) SEIPEL.
G. HANOTAUX.
IMPERIALI.
KRČMÁŘ.
POSPÍŠIL.

Protocol no. II.

With the object of assisting Austria in the work of her economic and financial restoration, the British, French, Italian, Czechoslovak and Austrian Governments have by common consent drawn up the following provisions:

Article 1. The Austrian Government may create, under the guarantee resulting from the present Convention, the amount of securities necessary to yield an effective sum equivalent to not more than 650 millions of gold crowns. The capital and interest of the securities so issued shall be free from all taxes, dues or charges for the benefit of the Austrian State.

Article 2. The expenses of issue, of negotiation and of delivery, shall be added to the capital of the loan as fixed under the preceding article.

Article 3. The service of the interest and amortisation of the loan shall be assured by means of an annuity provided by the revenues assigned as security for this loan in accordance with the provisions contained in Protocol No. III.

Article 4. The yield of the loan may not be employed except under the authority of the Commissioner-General appointed by the Council of the League of Nations and in accordance with the obligations contracted by the Austrian Government and set out in Protocol No. III.

Article 5. The British, French, Italian and Czechoslovak Governments, without prejudice to action by other Governments which may accede to the present Convention, undertake to ask without delay from their Parliaments authority to guarantee (subject always to the approval by the Austrian Parliament of Protocol No. Ill, and to the voting by that Parliament of the law contemplated in Article 3 of the said Protocol) the service of the annuity of this loan, up to a maximum of 84 per cent., to be shared under special arrangements between the parties concerned.

Article 6. Each of the four Governments shall have power to appoint a representative on the Committee of Control, the functions of which are determined by the provisions set out below. Each such representative shall have twenty votes. Those Governments which may agree to guarantee the remainder of the annuity which is not covered by the guarantee of the British, French, Italian and Czechoslovak Governments, shall in like manner have power either to appoint one representative each, or to agree among themselves to appoint common representatives. Each representative shall have one vote for every 1% guaranteed by his Government.

Article 7. The method of application of the guarantee, the conditions of the loan, the issue price, the rate of interest, the amortisation, the expenses of issue, of negotiation and of delivery, shall be submitted for the approval of the Committee of Control constituted by the guarantor States. The amount of the annuity necessary for the service of interest and amortisation of the loan shall likewise be approved by the Committee of Control. Every loan proposed by the Austrian Government, and not falling within the conditions of the program contemplated in Protocol No. III, shall first be submitted for the approval of the Committee of Control.

Article 8. The Committee of Control shall determine the conditions under which the advances by the Governments should be effected in the event of the guarantee coming into operation, and the method of repaying such advances.

Article 9. Within the limits fixed by the contracts under which they are issued, the Austrian Government shall have the right to effect conversion of the loans with the consent of the Committee of Control; it shall be obliged to exercise this power on the request of the Committee of Control.

Article 10. The Committee of Control shall have the right to require the production of periodical statements and accounts and any other information urgently needed in regard to the administration of the revenues assigned as security; it may bring to the attention of the Commissioner-General any administrative changes and improvements calculated to increase their productivity. Any changes in the rates producing such revenues which might be such as to reduce their minimum total yield, expressed in gold, as this may be determined before the issue of the loans in order to provide the necessary annuities, shall first be submitted for the approval of the Committee of Control. The same rule shall apply to proposed contracts for the concession or farming out of those revenues.

Article 11. In case the yield of the assigned revenues should be insufficient and should involve a possibility of bringing into operation the guarantee of the Governments, the Committee of Control may require that other revenues sufficient to meet the service of the annuity shall be assigned as security.

Any draft instrument or contract which is likely materially to change the nature, condition or administration of the public domain of Austria shall be communicated to the Committee three weeks before the instrument becomes final.

Article 12. The Committee of Control shall meet from time to time at such . dates as it may itself determine, preferably at the seat of the League of Nations. It shall communicate only with the Commissioner-General, who shall be present or shall be represented at the meetings of the Committee of Control. The decisions of the Committee shall be taken by an absolute majority of the votes present; provided always that a majority of two-thirds of the votes present shall be required for any decisions under Articles 7 and 8.

An extraordinary meeting of the Committee of Control shall be convened on a request supported by not less than ten votes.

Article 13. The Committee of Control, or any one of its members, may demand any information or explanations as to the elaboration and the execution of the programme of financial reform. The Committee may address any observations or make any representations to the Commissioner-General which it recognised to be necessary to safeguard the interests of the guarantor Governments.

Article 14. In the event of abuse, the Committee of Control or any guarantor State may appeal to the Council of the League of Nations, which shall give its decision without delay.

Article 15. In the event of any difference as to the interpretation of this Protocol, the parties will accept the opinion of the Council of the League of Nations.

In faith whereof the undersigned, duly authorised for this purpose, have signed the present Protocol.

Done at Geneva in a single copy, which shall be deposited with the Secretariat of the League of Nations and shall be registered by it without delay, on the fourth day of October, one thousand nine hundred and twenty-two.

(Signed) BALFOUR. (Signed) SEIPEL.
G. HANOTAUX.
IMPERIALI
KRČMÁŘ.
POSPÍŠIL.

ANNEXES TO PROTOCOL NO. II.

1. The guarantee granted by the States signatories of Protocol No. II shall be employed for an Austrian loan of 650 million gold crowns, bonds for which shall all be of the same character and shall offer the same security, the Financial Committee having calculated that the Austrian deficit needs to be increased from 520 to 650 million gold crowns so as to take into account the advances made by certain Governments in the course of this year, which carry the right to repayment either from the proceeds of the loan organised by the League of Nations, or in securities enjoying the same guarantees and the same advantages.

2. In order, however, that the advances which may result from the guarantee of that part of the Austrian loan which should be devoted to the repayment of advances already made may not devolve on States not interested in this repayment, and in order that the sacrifices which may ultimately have to be asked of those States should not be greater than those which would be entailed in the guarantee by them of a loan of 520 milhon gold crowns, the Governments entitled to repayments from the Austrian Government (the British, French, Italian and Czechoslovak Governments) have laid down the provisions which form the subject of Annex B.

ANNEX A.

The French, Italian and Czechoslovak Governments undertake to assign for the guarantee of the issues of Treasury bonds or similar Treasury operations, guaranteed by the gross receipts of the Customs and tobacco monopolies and envisaged in the report of the Financial Committee for the period previous to the Vote by the various Parliaments of authority for the guarantees, the balance of the advances promised in 1922 to the Austrian Government, the total amount of which was fixed at

France 55 million francs.

Italy 70 million lire.

Czechoslovakia 500 million Czechoslovak crowns.

By the word "balance" should be understood not only the sums not yet paid in respect of the above totals, but those which, having been paid, might be capable, by reason of their present employment, of being liberated for a different use with the consent of the Austrian Government. As soon as this has been obtained, the balances, as here defined, should be placed without delay at the disposal of the Austrian Government to be utilized—under the authority of the Commissioner-General or of the Provisional Delegation of the Council—in the Treasury operations referred to above.

As soon as the legislation voted by the various Parliaments authorising guarantees shall have obtained a total of at least 80 %, the balances of the advances thus utilised as guarantees shall be liberated and reimbursed to the Governments interested.

Done at Geneva on October the fourth, one thousand nine hundred and twenty-two.

(Signed) BALFOUR.
G. HANOTAUX.
IMPERIALI.
KRČMÁŘ.
POSPÍŠIL.

ANNEX B.

The apportionment of the guarantee between the four Governments, British, French, Italian and Czechoslovak, provided for in Article 5 of Protocol II and paragraph 2 of the preamble, shall take place in accordance with the following provisions:

(1) The guarantee of the annuities corresponding to the sum of 130 millions required for the reimbursement of the advances referred to in the first paragraph of the preamble, shall be apportioned as to one-third to each of the British, French and Czechoslovak Governments.

(2) With regard to the sum required for the reimbursement of the Czechoslovak credit, mounting to about 80 million gold crowns, the Czechoslovak Government undertakes to limit to 60 million gold crowns the total of the reimbursement which it will have the right to claim from the proceeds of the loan. It will accept in payment of this share of 60 millions, bonds of this loan issued over and above the total of the effective subscriptions. With regard to the balance of this claim, it will be satisfied that it should be covered by securities in Czechoslovak crowns and enjoying the same rights and guarantees as the bonds of the loan, but it is understood that these securities shall not benefit by the guarantee of the other Governments, and may be issued in excess of the sum of 650 millions.

The British and French Governments, which are entitled, by the terms of their contracts, to complete reimbursement of the amount of their advances out of the proceeds of the first loan, accept a scale of progressive repayment, charging the larger part of the repayment on the later instalments of the loan.

Italy shall have the right of reimbursement out of the proceeds of the loan, in accordance with a scale of payment identical with that adopted for the English claim, on that part of its advance which shall not have been repaid after having been utilised in accordance with the terms in Annex A. In the case of the guarantee coming into force, Italy shall, in respect of the guarantee of the 130 million, be responsible only for the liability appertaining to that part of the annuity of the loan which corresponds to the total.

To the extent to which Italy shall thus be led to assume a portion of the guarantee of the 130 millions, the share of the guarantee borne by France, Czecho-slovakia and Great Britain shall be correspondingly diminished.

Done at Geneva, the fourth day of October, one thousand nine hundred and twenty-two.

(Signed) BALFOUR.
G. HANOTAUX.
IMPERIALI.
KRČMÁŘ.
POSPÍŠIL.

EXPLANATORY NOTE.

From a comparison of Article 5 of Protocol No. II (which fixes at a maximum of 84% the guarantee to be given by the four Governments and to be apportioned as may be arranged) with the Preamble and with Annex B, it follows:

That each of the four Governments undertakes to guarantee 20% of the annuity corresponding to the capital of the loan floated to meet the deficit of 520 millions;

That the apportionment of the guarantee for the remainder of the annuity, which corresponds to the difference (130 millions) between the total of 650 and this sum of 520 millions, will be made in accordance with Annex B.

(Signed) BALFOUR.
G. HANOTAUX.
IMPERIALI.
KRČMÁŘ.
POSPÍŠIL.
Geneva, October 4th, 1922.

Protocol no. III.

The under signed, acting in the name of the Austrian Government, and duly authorised for this purpose, declares that he accepts the following obligations:

(1) The Austrian Government will ask its Parliament to ratify the political declaration signed by it which is the subject of Protocol No. I.

(2) The Austrian Government will, within one month, in collaboration either with the Commissioner-General, whose functions form the subject of paragraph 4 below, or with such provisional delegation of the Council of the League of Nations as may be appointed for the purpose, draw up a program of reforms and improvement, to be realised by stages and designed to enable Austria to re-establish

a permanent equilibrium of her budget within two years, the general outline of which is defined in the report of the Financial Committee (Annex). This program must place Austria in a position to satisfy her obligations by the augmentation of her receipts and the reduction of her expenditure; it will exclude any recourse to loans except under the conditions determined by it; it will prohibit, by the terms of the statutes to be drawn up for the Bank of Issue, which is to be created, any further monetary inflation.

It should further enable Austria to assure her financial stability on a permanent basis by a series of measures leading to a general economic reform. The report of the Economic Committee dealing with this aspect of the problem shall be duly communicated to the Commissioner-General.

It is understood that, if the first program should appear in practice to be insufficient to re-establish permanent equilibrium of the budget within two years, the Austrian Government will be bound, in agreement with the Commissioner-General, to introduce therein the modifications appropriate to the result which it is essential to attain. The Austrian Government will ask its Parliament to approve the above-mentioned plan.

(3) The Austrian Government will forthwith lay before the Austrian Parliament a draft law giving, during two years, to any Government which may then be in power, full authority to take all measures, within the limits of this program, which in its opinion may be necessary to assure at the end of the period mentioned the re-establishment of budgetary equilibrium without there being any necessity to seek for further approval by Parliament.

(4) Austria accepts the nomination by the Council of the League of Nations of a Commissioner-General who shall be responsible to the Council and removable by it. His functions are defined in broad outline in the report of the Financial Committee.

His duty will be to ensure that the program of reforms is carried out and to supervise its execution. The Commissioner-General shall reside at Vienna. He may provide himself with the necessary technical personnel. The expenses of the Commissioner-General and of his office shall be approved by the Council and supported by the Austrian Government. The Commissioner-General shall present monthly to the Council a report upon the progress of the reforms and the results achieved. This report shall be communicated without delay to the members of the Committee of Control.

The Austrian Government agrees that it may not dispose of any funds derived from loans, or undertake any operation with a view to discounting the proceeds of loans, except by authorisation of the Commissioner-General; provided that the conditions which the Commissioner-General may attach to such authorisation shall have no other object than that of assuring the progressive realisation of the program of reforms and of avoiding any deterioration of the assets assigned for the service of the loan.

If the Austrian Government considers that the Commissioner-General has abused his authority, it may appeal to the Council of the League of Nations.

The functions of the Commissioner-General shall be brought to an end by a decision of the Council of the League of Nations, when the Council shall have ascertained that the financial stability of Austria is assured, without prejudice to any special control of the assets assigned for the service of the loan.

(5) The Austrian Government will furnish as securities for the guaranteed loan, the gross receipts of the Customs and of the tobacco monopoly, and, if the Commissioner-General should deem it necessary, other specific assets determined in agreement with him. It will not take any measure which in the opinion of the Commissioner-General would be such as to diminish the value of such assets so as to threaten the security of the creditors and of the guarantor States. In particular, the Austrian Government may not, without the approval of the Com missioner-General, introduce into the rates producing the revenues assigned as security any changes which might be such as to reduce their minimum total yield expressed in gold as this may be determined, before the issue of the loans, in order to provide for the necessary annuities.

The yield of the gross revenues assigned as security will be paid into a special account, as and when collected, for the purpose of assuring the service of the annuity of the loans. The Commissioner-General may alone control this account. The Commissioner-General may require such modifications and improvements as may increase the productivity of the revenues assigned as security. If, not-withstanding such representations, it should appear to him that the value of these assets is seriously prejudiced by their management by the Austrian Government, he may require that this management shall be transferred to a special administration, either by the constitution of a Government monopoly or by the grant of concessions or of leases.

6 (a). The Austrian Government undertakes to grant no concessions which, in the opinion of the Commissioner-General, might be such as to compromise the execution of the program of reforms.

(b) The Austrian Government will surrender all right to issue paper money and will not negotiate or conclude loans except in conformity with the program above set out and with the authorisation of the Commissioner-General. If the Austrian Government should consider itself obliged to envisage the issue of loans not covered by the conditions of the program contemplated in this Protocol, it would first submit such plans for the approval of the Commissioner-General and of the Committee of Control.

(c) The Austrian Government will ask its Parliament to make such modifications as are considered necessary, in accordance with the report of the Financial Committee (Annex), both in the statutes of the Bank of Issue and, should the occasion arise, in the Law of July 24th, 1922 (Bulletin des Lois No. 490). The statutes of the Bank of Issue shall assure it complete autonomy in its relations with the Government. The Bank should be responsible for the cash transactions of the State, it should centralise the Government's receipts and payments and should furnish periodical financial statements at the dates and in the form which may be determined in agreement with the Commissioner-General.

(d) The Austrian Government will take and carry out all decisions necessary for the full realisation of the program of reforms, including all necessary administrative reforms and the indispensable alterations in the legislation.

(7) The Austrian Government will take all measures necessary to ensure the maintenance of public order.

(8) All obligations defined above relating to the functions of the Commissioner-General or to financial or administrative reforms, so far as they relate to a period subsequent to January 1st, 1923, are conditional and shall not become finally binding until the British, French, Italian and Czechoslovak Governments have confirmed their promised guarantees by the approval of their respective Parliaments.

Nevertheless, the Austrian Government definitely undertakes:

(a) to take as from the present date all measures in its power to reduce the deficit; these measures are to include, in particular, increases in the railway, postal and telegraphic rates, and in the sale prices of the products of the monopolies;

(b) to submit immediately to the Austrian Parliament the draft law contemplated in paragraph (3), which will give for two years to the Government now in office, or to any succeeding Government, full authority to take all measures which in its opinion may be necessary to assure the re-establishment of budgetary equilibrium at the end of that period;

(c) to prepare immediately a program of reform, to set in motion the necessary legislative action and to apply the first measures of execution contemplated by the program, between the present date and January 1st, 1923.

(9) In the event of any difference as to the interpretation of this Protocol, the parties will accept the opinion of the Council of the League of Nations.

The present Protocol shall be communicated to those States which have signed Protocol No. II signed at Geneva on October 4th, 1922.

In faith whereof the undersigned, duly authorised for this purpose, has signed the present Protocol, Done at Geneva in a single copy, which shall be deposited with the Secretariat of the League of Nations and shall be registered by it without delay, on the fourth day of October, nineteen hundred and twenty-two.

(Signed) SEIPEL.

Reply of the Financial Committee to questions referred by the Austrian Committee of the Council

The Financial Committee has the honour to report that it has studied the questions referred to it by the Austrian Committee of the Council, in consultation with the Austrian representatives, and is now able to submit the following replies, which represent the unanimous opinion of the Committee.

QUESTION 1. *The Financial Committee is requested to consider, in consultation with the Austrian representatives, what measures are required and are practicable to secure budget equilibrium, and after what period it considers that, with these measures, the result desired should be obtained.*

ANSWER.

The answer to this question cannot be given with certainty, for the period depends essentially upon the resolution and the authority of the Austrian Government in carrying out the drastic reforms recommended. But if this vital condition is realised, the Committee considers that it should be possible to attain budget equilibrium in two years, and it is on this basis that the further recommendations are made.

The main measures required for this purpose are:

(a) Reform of State Industrial Enterprises.

State industrial enterprises should be either suppressed if merely useless, or run by the State upon a commercial, i. e., paying, basis, or, in suitable cases, transferred to private management by concessions. The abolition of loss under these heads would involve a total annual saving of about 170 million gold crowns. The most important instance is that of the railways, which at present involve a deficit of 124 million gold crowns. The reason is partly the excessive number of employees, which should be reduced, and partly the low tariffs. While wages follow the cost-of-living index, the tariffs have only been raised to about one-fifth of what they would be on this basis. Under the Treaty of St-Germain, these low tariffs apply also to transit trade, and, therefore, benefit the foreigner. The Committee considers that the railways should cease to involve loss within the period of two years, and, in view of the important transit trade, should ultimately be a source of profit.

(b) Reduction of Officials. Vienna, as the capital of a country of 6 millions, has more State employees than when she was the capital of an empire of over 50 millions. The Committee considers that an effective reduction of gold expenses by at least one-third should be effected within the transition period.

In addition, the subventions to the local administrations to assist them in paying their own officials on the basis of the cost-of-living index should be suppressed.

These reforms would give an annual saving of 130 million gold crowns.

The replies to questions 1, 2, 3 and 4 give only the summarised conclusions of the Committee, and not the detailed reports on which they are based.

QUESTION 2. *The Financial Committee is requested to consider what deficit, in terms of gold, must be contemplated as necessary during the intervening period.*

ANSWER.

The Committee estimates the total deficit during the period of two years as 520 million gold crowns, to which must be added the sum required to reimburse certain advances made this year, raising the total to 650 million gold crowns. To enable the reforms to be effected, this sum must be available from credits.

This estimate is based upon the following "normal budget", which allows for the above reforms:

Expenditure (normal budget).	Millions of gold crowns.
Public debt	52
Pensions	42
Civil service	100
Army	20
Social assistance	23
	237

It should be possible to obtain 237 million gold crowns in taxation by the end of two years. This amounts to only 40 gold crowns per head and should be ultimately capable of increase; but the difficulties which now result from low assessment during a period of depreciation and those of a different kind which follow immediately upon a stabilisation make the full attainment of this figure at an earlier date improbable.

QUESTION 3. *What securities can Austria offer for private credits and what is their approximate gold value?*

ANSWER.

The most suitable securities should, with the necessary administrative reforms, yield the following annual returns:

		Millions of gold crowns.
1.	Forests and domains	1
2.	Salt	1
3.	Customs	40
4.	Tobacco	40

Of these, the first three are assigned as security in connection with the new Bank of Issue under the Austrian Government's plan for the Bank. On a conservative estimate, however, of these claims, this would leave 28 millions of the Customs available as a second-rank security, in addition to the 40 millions from the tobacco monopoly as a first-rank security.

Moreover, the Committee considers (cf. answer to Question 4) that the plan for the new Bank of Issue can safely be modified so as to leave the whole of the Customs as a first-rank security for the credits required for the transition period.

In addition, the *impôt foncier* should, if necessary, be available (with reform) as a further first-rank security.

The service of a loan amounting even to the maximum of 650 million gold crowns should not exceed about 70 million gold crowns.

In the unanimous opinion of the Committee, therefore, the securities are ample for the credits required for the transition period, on the vital conditions that the reforms recommended are carried through (and the necessary measures taken to ensure sufficient authority to give confidence that they will be carried through) and that external and internal order are assured.

QUESTION 4. *The views of the Financial Committee are requested on the proposed Bank of Issue for Austria.*

ANSWER.

The Committee considers that the establishment of a Bank of Issue is a useful and indeed vital part of the measures required for Austria's re-establishment.

The Committee considers, however, that:—

(a) The capital proposed, 100 million gold francs, is altogether excessive: 30 millions should suffice.

(b) The guarantee by the State of the capital of the Bank and of an adequate return upon it, secured by a first charge on the Customs, should be relinquished. This should be possible if the other measures for the re-establishment of Austria's finances are adopted.

(c) The capital should be raised by private subscriptions. If public funds must be used, the public interests should be sold out to private holders at the earliest opportunity.

(d) The present provision that directors and substitutes elected by general meeting require the confirmation of the Federal Government should be eliminated.

The Committee desires, however, to emphasise the fact that the Bank can only be of use in re-establishing Austria's credit organisation if the drastic reforms required to establish budget equilibrium are also taken (and the necessary credits for the transition period are obtained); and that, even so, it cannot be permanently successful unless her economic position is also gradually established.

QUESTION 5. *Under what conditions can means be proposed for covering the deficit during the period of transition?*

ANSWER.

I. The Financial Committee estimated that the deficit to be covered by means of loans during the first two years is in the neighbourhood of 520 million gold crowns, plus a sum to cover certain advances made this year which raises the total to 650 million gold crowns. This is a budget deficit, and, in the first instance, it is Austrian currency, not foreign currency, which is required to meet it. It may be expected, therefore, that, once Austria's internal credit is re-established, a considerable proportion of the deficit will be covered by internal loans. But at present Austria's credit is non-existent, and neither internal nor external borrowing is possible for her until the following financial conditions have been satisfied:

(1) The Austrian Government must forthwith (without waiting for any decision by the League of Nations) take all measures within its power to prevent an increase of the deficit (such as raising of railway, postal, telegraph, and telephone charges, increases in the prices at which the products of the tobacco and salt monopolies are sold, etc.).

(2) A control must be organised and set to work, and evidence must be given of the full co-operation of the Austrian Government in securing its efficient functioning.

(3) The Customs revenues and the tobacco monopoly, subject to the necessary improvements in administration, must be allocated as security for loans.

The re-establishment of Austria's credit is further dependent on the adoption of various other measures already under discussion by the Austrian Committee of the Council, such as: the guaranteeing of Austria's territorial and economic integrity, under the auspices of the League of Nations; the improvement of Austria's economic international relations, as well as of her internal economic structure; the establishment of an efficient gendarmery throughout Austria; the establishment of the proposed Bank of Issue; and the cessation of new issues of paper money.

When all these measures have been taken and have proved their value, it is reasonable to hope that Austria may be in a position to borrow, both internally and externally, on her own credit. But it would be vain to expect that such reforms could be effectively initiated unless, at the time of their initiation, the Austrian Government and people were able to look forward with some certainty to the achievement of their final purpose of re-establishing financial and economic equilibrium. Moreover, the deficit begins to accrue at once, and the necessary credit on which loans can be issued to provide ways and means for covering the deficit will not exist for many months unless some basis for credit is found from outside Austria.

The Financial Committee is therefore driven to the conclusion that a successful reconstruction of Austria is impossible unless some of the Powers are prepared to guarantee the loans required to cover the anticipated deficit. It is recognised that such guarantees cannot be given in most cases without the consent of the Parliaments of the guaranteeing Powers, but, if promises of guarantees subject to parliamentary confirmation can be secured at once, these would provide the necessary basis of credit on which the initiation of the reforms depends. The guarantees must cover the full maximum deficit, since it would be both difficult and perilous to embark on the full program of reform if the means for completing it were not visible from the beginning. This does not necessarily mean that the guarantees for the whole sum will actually come into operation, and it may well prove that the guarantees eventually involve no actual cash liability upon the guarantors. If the reform program succeeds, there is reason to hope that some part of the maximum deficit can be provided internally or without external guarantees, and that the revenues of the Austrian State will amply secure the service of the guaranteed loans without recourse to the guarantors. But it remains true that guarantees covering the whole total are an essential pre-requisite. The larger the number of guaranteeing Powers, the broader will be the basis of confidence.

II. We proceed now to sketch the practical steps to be taken to deal with the deficit, on the assumption that the reforms indicated are initiated and promises of guarantees up to the total of the deficit have been given by various Powers.

The period of transition can best be examined in four stages, viz.:

First stage: from the Promise of Guarantees till the Initiation of the Control.

During the first stage, it is essential that the Austrian Government should take all possible measures for reducing the deficit, but otherwise no change from present conditions will be possible.

Second stage: from the Initiation of the Control till the Ratification of the Guarantees by the respective Parliaments, say December 31st, 1922.

It is assumed that the new Bank of Issue will open its doors within a few weeks, and the control to be set up under the auspices of the League of Nations will begin to function. We estimate that from 120 to 160 million gold crowns will be required to cover the deficit during this second period.

We believe that this sum can be met, so far as it is not covered by the reserve at the disposal of the Austrian Government at the moment of the initiation of the control, on the following lines: There are available out of the unspent portion of the French, Italian, and Czechoslovak credits, sums understood at the date of this report to amount to about 45 million gold crowns.

If the lending Governments agree, these sums could be used as part security for three- or six-months Treasury Bills (expressed in gold crowns, or in some foreign currency) to be issued in Austria by the Austrian Government and purchased by the Austrian banks. The Bills might be further secured by a first charge on the Customs and on the tobacco monopoly. Possibly the gold belonging to the old Austro-Hungarian Bank might also temporarily be used as security for these Treasury Bills, instead of being deposited in the new Bank of Issue. It would be a matter for arrangement between the Government and the banks, which are largely concerned in the Bank of Issue, which of the two uses for the gold is preferred. The Austrian banks might reasonably be asked to accept these conditions as their contribution to the success of the reforms.

Third stage: from Ratification of the Guarantees to the Issue of a Long-term Loan. As soon as the Government guarantees become available, Austrian Treasury Bills in gold crowns or foreign currencies can be issued, subject to right of redemption out of the proceeds of the prospective loan, secured either as proposed during the second period or by the guarantees of the Powers. The method of using the guarantees can best be discussed in connection with the fourth period. It is important that action by the Parliaments of the guaranteeing Powers should not be delayed beyond December 31st, 1922.

Fourth stage: from the Issue of the Loan to the End of the Transition Period, December 31st, 1924.

If any guaranteeing Government so prefers, it can, of course, obtain power to lend money direct to the Austrian Government out of its own resources. We assume, however, that most Governments will prefer to confine their assistance to the grant of a guarantee. There are at least three alternative forms under which such guarantees could be given:

(a) Each of the guaranteeing Powers might assume a joint and several responsibility for Austrian loans to be issued up to a maximum total of 650 million gold crowns. Such a guarantee would ensure the placing of the loans on the most favourable terms, but we are of opinion that it is politically impossible to secure such a joint and several guarantee.

(b) Each Government might guarantee a loan to be issued by Austria on the security of the pledged Austrian assets, plus its own guarantee, up to a given maximum, which would be an agreed proportion of the total required; e.g., supposing that ten Powers agreed to give such guarantees in equal proportions, there would be ten types of Austrian loans, all secured on the same Austrian assets but guaranteed separately by different Powers. Such a plan would greatly restrict the market for Austrian loans and postpone for a long period the date at which Austrian credit could be expected to be strong enough for an Austrian loan to be placed without external guarantee.

(c) The guaranteeing Powers might agree to guarantee an agreed proportion of a single Austrian loan, issuable in one or more instalments as required; e. g., supposing, again, that there were ten Powers giving guarantees in equal proportions, each instalment would be guaranteed as to 10 % by each Power, and while the pledged assets would be security for the whole, the individual guarantors would be responsible to the extent of 10 % only.

We are inclined to favour this alternative, but the exact application of the guarantees is a matter which can best be determined by the issuing house, or group of issuing houses, which will be called upon to carry through the actual operation of issuing a long-term loan. An early decision will, however, be necessary as to the form in which the guarantees are to be applied to the issue of Treasury Bills proposed during the third period.

It is unnecessary to pursue these technical details further at the present stage. Our object in alluding to them is to indicate generally the nature of the guarantees which must be asked for from the various Governments, and the necessity for the legislation which authorises such guarantees being drawn in terms sufficiently wide to cover various eventualities. We are convinced, however, that, if such guarantees are given, there will be no insuperable obstacles in placing all necessary loans in due course either in Austria or in money markets outside Austria, provided always that the Austrian Government and people have, in the meanwhile, proved that they are deserving of the assistance proposed by contributing by all means in their power to the efficient working of the reform plans and of the control established by the League of Nations.

QUESTION 6. *The Financial Committee is requested to state its opinion as to the conditions which are essential in any control that may be instituted in order to give effect to the recommendations made by the Committee with regard to the reestablishment of Austria's budget equilibrium and her credit.*

ANSWER.

The aim of the controlling authority should be to assist the Austrian Government and collaborate with it in carrying out the program of radical reform upon the realisation of which depends the possibility of borrowing.

This program must be adopted in advance by the Austrian Government, sanctioned by the Council of the League of Nations, or its Austrian Committee, and voted by the Austrian Parliament. But the vote of the Austrian Parliament cannot be regarded as a mere approval of general principles, which will leave the Austrian Government under the obligation of applying for specific legislative authority to carry out the series of measures of reform, involving reduction of expenditure and increase of taxation, which will have to be taken to put the plan into effect. The initial approval should be clearly understood as conferring on the Government full powers to take decisions of every kind in agreement with the Controlling Authority, provided that they are in conformity with the approved program and are directed to giving effect to it.

This program, which will have been sanctioned by the League of Nations, will, further, become the charter of the Controlling Authority and the source of its powers. The Controlling Authority's task will be to ensure that it is carried into effect, but it will have no mandate to insist upon measures which go outside the limits of the program or are contradictory to it.

In order to be in a position to fulfil its mission, the Controlling Authority must have the right to determine the nature and form of the accounts, statements or periodical returns which it will require to be submitted to it; to ask for any information which it may regard as useful from any departments of Government; to verify, or cause to be verified, any accounts which it may think fit; and to make investigations on the spot if it so desires. The Bank of Issue, which will be the cashier of the State, should centralise all the accounts of receipts and expenditure and submit periodical returns to the Controlling Authority, certifying receipts, expenditure and credit balances of the various departments of the Austrian State. No borrowing operation of any kind should be carried out without the prior authorisation of the Controlling Authority.

The produce of the revenues pledged for the various loans and the produce of any loans should be placed to the credit of special accounts in the Bank of Issue, and such accounts should not be allowed to be drawn upon without the prior authorisation of the Controlling Authority.

QUESTION 7. *The Financial Committee is requested to draw up a detailed report on the nature of the control to be established in Austria.*

ANSWER.

In compliance with this desire, the Financial Committee has the honour to commend to the attention of the Austrian Committee of the Council the following observations, which express its unanimous opinion. The organisation of a form of control to be applied to Austria raises new problems,—for the solution of which precedents can only be appealed to with the greatest caution.

The functions of control, as the Austrian Sub-Committee has already defined them, on the recommendation of the Financial Committee, are to be imposed in accordance with a detailed scheme invested with a twofold authority: that of the Council of the League of Nations and that of the Austrian Parliament.

As regards the Austrian Government, which is to be endowed with full powers to give effect to this scheme, it is the duty of the Control Authority to insist upon the execution of the scheme.

Hence it follows that: (1) the appointment and the dismissal of the agents of the Control Authority must rest entirely in the hands of the Council of the League of Nations, under the authority of which the execution of the scheme is to be carried out; and (2) that the Council cannot regard the execution of the scheme as a matter with which it has no further concern, and that periodical reports ought to be submitted to it setting out the progress of the work of reform.

It may, however, be asked whether the Council ought to confine its duties within these limits.

It would appear that, if defects or abuses should be ascertained in carrying out this scheme, the Council should continue to be the supreme authority to consider them.

It is, however, desirable that the agents of the Control Authority should have undivided responsibility, and that the Council should not be involved, as the result of constant or frivolous petitions, in interference in the financial administration of Austria. Only by defining in accurate terms the cases where an appeal can be made to the Council for a decision and the party to whom this right of appeal should be granted, will it prove possible to eliminate these disadvantages.

Among the parties interested, the first place must be given to the Austrian Government.

Consideration, however, should also be given to the rights of the guarantor Governments. The latter, indeed, cannot remain indifferent to the progress of a policy which aims at healthier conditions. They will wish to know whether the latter will have the effect of diminishing or increasing the risks attaching to their guarantees, but it must be clearly understood that only abuses which are of a nature to endanger the satisfactory execution of the program should give rise to an appeal.

How can the guarantor Governments be enabled to protect their interests, which demand that the program of supervision should be properly carried out? It would appear prima facie that the duty of supervision cannot be entrusted to representatives of the guarantor Governments. The supervision must be carried out under the control of the Council of the League of Nations alone. In the interests of Austria herself, in order that the Council may fully maintain its superior authority and carry out its role of arbiter, it would be impracticable to confuse the task of supervision, which is to be accomplished in its name, with the representation of the Governments concerned, which possess a recognised right of appeal. It would, however, be reasonable that the representatives of the guarantor Governments should form a committee and should have the right to examine the execution of the program and to receive necessary information for their enlightenment.

What relations would in that case be established between this committee and the supervising authority?

If the Council is to remain the supreme authority, it would no doubt be undesirable that this committee should be in daily communication with the Controller. We therefore propose that the committee should meet periodically—every three or six months, for example—and for preference at the seat of the League of Nations. In any conference with the representatives of the Control Authority, the committee would be entitled to ask for any information or explanation, but it would not have the right to give instructions. If any serious difficulties should arise, or should there be any question of serious abuse, the Council would be called upon to arbitrate in the matter.

The further question arises whether the duty of supervision should be entrusted to a single agent or to a body of persons. In order to reduce to a minimum the expenses of control and to ensure the necessary uniformity of view, a single controller would be highly preferable. It should be open to him to secure the help of technical assistants.

The costs of control would be fixed by a decision of the Council of the League of Nations, and would be charged upon the Austrian budget.

The control would come to an end, as a result of a decision of the Council of the League of Nations, when that body was of opinion that the financial stability of Austria had been attained by the execution of reforms, without prejudice to any special control of the guarantees given to secure the interest on the loan.

General Statement as to Austria's position (1922)

The Financial Committee has necessarily confined its examination of the measures required to re-establish Austrian finances within the sphere of financial considerations. It recognises that, apart from these considerations, there remains the problem of the fundamental economic position of Austria. Austria cannot permanently retain a sound financial position, even if she attains it for the time, and maintain her present population, unless her production is so increased and adapted as (with due allowance, of course, for her important invisible exports) to give her equilibrium also in her trade balance.

This balance is at present seriously adverse, partly, but certainly not wholly as a result of inflation and currency dislocation. All possible measures, whether by the amelioration of the international economic relations, the encouragement of the conditions which would increase Vienna's *entrepôt*, financial, and transit business, and of those which will attract further private capital towards the development of her productive resources, are, therefore, of the greatest importance.

These are, however, outside the Financial Committee's province. If the appropriate financial policy is adopted and maintained, the Austrian economic position will adjust itself to an equilibrium, either by the increase of production and the transfer of large classes of its population to economic work, or economic pressure will compel the population to emigrate or reduce it to destitution. At the worst, this would be better than the wholesale chaos and impoverishment of the great mass of the town population which must result from the continuance of the present financial disorganisation, which affords no basis for such economic adaptation as is possible.

The Committee feels bound, in conclusion, to issue one word of grave warning. Austria has for three years been living largely upon public and private loans, which have voluntarily or involuntarily become gifts, upon private charity and upon losses of foreign speculators in the crown. Such resources cannot, in any event, continue and be so used. Austria has been consuming much more than she has produced. The large sums advanced, which should have been used for the re-establishment of her finances and for her economic reconstruction, have been used for current consumption. Any new advances must be used for the purposes of reform; and within a short time Austria will only be able to consume as much as she produces. The period of reform itself, even if the new credits are forth-coming, will necessarily be a very painful one. The longer it is deferred the more painful it must be. At the best, the conditions of life in Austria must be worse next year, when she is painfully re-establishing her position, than last year, when she was devoting loans intended for that purpose to current consumption without reform.

The alternative is not between continuing the conditions of life of last year or improving them. It is between enduring a period of perhaps greater hardship than she has known since 1919 (but with the prospect of real amelioration—thereafter the happier alternative) or collapsing into a chaos of destitution and starvation to which there is no modern analogy outside Russia.

There is no hope for Austria unless she is prepared to endure and support an authority which must enforce reforms entailing harder conditions than those at present prevailing, knowing that in this way only can she avoid an even worse fate.

The following members constituted the Financial Committee when studying the above questions:

Chairman: M. JANSSEN.

Members: M. ARAL.
                       M. AVENOL.
                       Sir Basil BLACKETT.
                       Mr. Fass (substitute for Sir Basil Blackett).
                       Dr. POSPISIL.
                       Sir Henry STRAKOSCH.
Temporary members: M. Maggiorino FERRARIS.
                       M. A. SARASIN.

Appendix D

Draft Budget for 1924 in Austrian Crowns

Total expenditures	8,065,010,501,000
Total revenues	6,817,067,787,000
Preliminary deficit	−1,247,042,714,000
Revenue from monopolies	1,300,484,701,000
Subsidies to federal enterprises	−38,263,180,000
Subsidies to federal railways	−482,441,360,000
Subsidies to Südbahn	−231,000,000,000
Subsidies to other railways	−138,478,462,000
Final deficit	−836,741,015,000

Source: Nicole Piétri. "La réconstruction économique et financière de l'Autriche par la Société des Nations (1921–1926)" (doctoral thesis, Université de Paris I, 1981), based on Bundesministerium für Finanzen Wien. Präs./889/1823. Department 1A, Finanzgesetz für 1924, 5 December 1923.

Abbreviations

Archives

AdR	Archiv der Republik Österreich, Vienna
ANB	Austrian National Bank Archive, Vienna
BdF	Archives de la Banque de France, Paris
BEA	Bank of England Archives, London
BISA	Bank for International Settlements Archives, Basel
CA	Historical Archives of Credit-Anstalt, Vienna
DNB	Dutch National Bank Archives, Amsterdam
ILO	Archives of the International Labour Organization, Geneva
JPM	J. P. Morgan & Co. Archive, New York
LNA	League of Nations Archive, Geneva
NA	National Archives, London
RAL	The Rothschild Archive, London
SNB	Swiss National Bank Archive, Zurich
TA	Tagblatt Archiv, Vienna

Newspapers

AZ	*Arbeiterzeitung*
NFP	*Neue Freie Presse*
ÖVW	*Der Österreichische Volkswirt*
RP	*Reichspost*

Banks and Other Institutions

ANB	Austrian National Bank, Vienna
BdF	Banque de France, Paris

BIS   Bank for International Settlements, Basel
BKA   Boden-Kredit Anstalt, Vienna
BoE   Bank of England, London
CA   Credit-Anstalt für Handel und Gewerbe, Vienna
FED   Federal Reserve Bank, New York
JPM   J. P. Morgan & Co., New York
NMR   N. M. Rothschild, London
SdN   Société des Nations
SMR   S. M. Rothschild, Vienna
SNB   Swiss National Bank
VSE   Vienna Stock Exchange
WBV   Wiener Bankverein

Notes

Introduction

Epigraph: Eric Hobsbawm, *The Age of Extremes: A History of the World, 1914–1991* (New York, 1994), p. 104.

1. Walter Goldinger and Dieter A. Binder, *Geschichte der Republik Österreich 1918–1931* (Munich, 1992), pp. 100–120; Lajos Kerekes, *Von St. Germain bis Genf: Österreich und seine Nachbarn 1918–1922* (Vienna, 1979).

2. Jan van Walré de Bordes, *The Austrian Crown: Its Depreciation and Stabilization* (London, 1924).

3. Hans Kernbauer, Eduard März, and Fritz Weber, "Die wirtschaftliche Entwicklung," in *Österreich, 1918–1938: Geschichte der Ersten Republik*, vol. 1, ed. Erika Weinzierl and Kurt Skalnik (Graz, 1983), pp. 343–358. See also in Emmerich Tálos, Herbert Dachs, Ernst Hanisch, and Anton Staudinger, eds., *Handbuch des politischen Systems Österreichs* (Vienna, 1995), the contributions of Fritz Weber ("Die wirtschaftliche Entwicklung," pp. 23–42, and "Staatliche Wirtschaftspolitik in der Zwischenkriegszeit," pp. 531–551) and Hans Kernbauer ("Österreichische Währungs-, Bank- und Budgetpolitik in der Zwischenkriegszeit," pp. 552–569).

4. Karl Bachinger and Herbert Matis, "Die österreichische Nachkriegsinflation 1918–1922," *Beiträge zur Historischen Sozialkunde* 16, no. 3 (1986): 83–91; Alice Teichova, "Die Inflation der 1920er Jahre in Mitteleuropa im Vergleich," *Beiträge zur Historischen Sozialkunde* 16, no. 3 (1986): 67–68.

5. Hans Kernbauer and Fritz Weber, "Die Wiener Grossbanken in der Nachkriegsinflation (1914–1922)," in *Die Erfahrung der Inflation im internationalen Zusammenhang und Vergleich*, ed. Gerald D. Feldman, Carl Ludwig Holtfrerich, Gerhard A. Ritter, and Peter-Christian Witt (Berlin, 1984), pp. 142–188; Jonathan Bloomfield, "Surviving in a Harsh World: Trade and Inflation in the Czechoslovak and Austrian Republics 1918–1926," in Feldman et al., *Die Erfahrung der Inflation*, pp. 228–268; Elmus Wicker, "Terminating Hyperinflation in the Dismembered Habsburg Monarchy," *American Economic Review* 76, no. 3 (1986): 350–364; Dieter Stiefel, "Konjunkturelle Entwicklung und struktureller Wandel der österreichischen

Wirtschaft in der Zwischenkriegszeit," Institut für Höhere Studien, Forschungsbericht no. 135 (Vienna, 1978).

6. For a general discussion, see Pierre Siklos, "Hyperinflations: Their Origins,
Development and Termination," *Journal of Economic Surveys* 4, no. 3 (1990):
225–248.

7. Phillip Cagan, "The Monetary Dynamics of Hyperinflation," in *Studies in
the Quantity Theory of Money*, ed. Milton Friedman (Chicago, 1956), pp. 25–117.

8. Thomas J. Sargent, "The End of Four Big Inflations," in *Inflation: Causes and
Effects*, ed. Robert Ernest Hall (Chicago, 1982), pp. 41–93; Rüdiger Dornbusch,
"Lessons from the German Inflation Experience of the 1920s," in *Macroeconomics
and Finance: Essays in Honor of Franco Modigliani*, ed. Rüdiger Dornbusch, Stanley
Fischer, and John Bossons (Cambridge, MA, 1987), pp. 409–439; Rüdiger Dornbusch
and Stanley Fischer, "Stopping Hyperinflations Past and Present," National Bureau of
Economic Research Working Paper 1810 (Cambridge, MA, 1986); Andrés Solimano,
"Inflation and the Costs of Stabilization: Historical and Recent Experiences and
Policy Lessons," *World Bank Research Observer* 5, no. 2 (July 1990): 167–685.

9. Barry Eichengreen, "Rational Expectations and Inflation (T. J. Sargent): A
Review," *Journal of Economic Literature* 24 (1986): 1812–1815. Gustavo H. B.
Franco, "Fiscal Reforms and Stabilisation: Four Hyperinflation Cases Examined,"
Economic Journal 100, no. 399 (1990): 176–187, argues that the fiscal deficit in Austria
would have been manageable.

10. Gottlieb Ladner, *Seipel als Überwinder der Staatskrise vom Sommer 1922*
(Vienna, 1964) or Fritz Weber, *Vor dem grossen Krach. Österreichs Bankwesen der
Zwischenkriegszeit am Beispiel der Credit-Anstalt für Handel und Gewerbe* (Vi-
enna, 2016), pp. 44–48.

11. Louis W. Pauly, *The League of Nations and the Foreshadowing of the International Monetary Fund* (Princeton, NJ, 1996).

12. Patricia Clavin and Jens-Wilhelm Wessels, "Transnationalism and the
League of Nations: Understanding the Work of Its Economic and Financial Organisation," *Contemporary European History* 14, no. 4 (2005): 465–492; Patricia
Clavin and Jens-Wilhelm Wessels, "Another Golden Idol? The League of Nations
Gold Inquiry and the Great Depression, 1929–32," *International History Review* 26,
no. 4 (2004): 765–795; Patricia Clavin, *Securing the World Economy: The Reinvention
of the League of Nations, 1920–1946* (Oxford, 2013); Martin David Dubin, "Transgovernmental Processes in the League of Nations," *International Organization*
37, no. 3 (1983): 469–493. See also Robert O. Keohane and Joseph S. Nye, "Transgovernmental Relations and International Organizations," *World Politics* 27, no. 1
(1974): 39–62.

13. Andrew Webster, "The Transnational Dream: Politicians, Diplomats, and
Soldiers in the League of Nations' Pursuit of International Disarmament, 1920–
1938," *Contemporary European History* 14, no. 4 (2001): 493–518; Jo-Anne Pem-

berton, "New Worlds for Old: The League of Nations in the Age of Electricity," *Review of International Studies* 28, no. 2 (2002): 311–336.

14. F. L. Carsten, *The First Austrian Republic, 1918–1938: A Study Based on British and Austrian Documents* (Aldershot, UK, 1986), p. 97.

15. Kernbauer, März, and Weber, "Die wirtschaftliche Entwicklung." See also Hans Kernbauer, "Österreichische Währungs-, Bank- und Budgetpolitik in der Zwischenkriegszeit," in *Handbuch des politischen Systems Österreichs: Erste Republik, 1918–1933,* ed. Emmerich Tálos, Herbert Dachs, Ernst Hanisch, and Anton Staudinger (Vienna, 1995), pp. 552–569.

16. Goldinger and Binder, *Geschichte der Republik Österreich,* pp. 106–133. Elmus Wicker has tried to assess the cost of stabilization by looking at its effect on employment and argues that it was dire in Austria (and even more so in Hungary and Poland). But in Austria, at least, the unemployment effect observed by Wicker cannot be termed endogenous. Rather, it was the consequence of the massive reduction of state workers prescribed by the Geneva Protocol, not a direct consequence of the currency's stabilization. See Elmus Wicker, "Terminating Hyperinflation in the Dismembered Habsburg Monarchy," *American Economic Review* 76, no. 3 (1986): 350–364.

17. The authors identify General Commissioner Rudolph Zimmerman as the most powerful figure in Austria at the time. Karl Bachinger and Herbert Matis, *Der österreichische Schilling: Geschichte einer Währung* (Graz, 1974), p. 65.

18. Karl Ausch, *Als die Banken fielen: Zur Soziologie der politischen Korruption* (Vienna, 1968), pp. 115–191. Mention should be made of an early work by Dieter Stiefel, where the author noted that Austrian economic policy continued to focus on stable exchange rates even after the end of League control. Dieter Stiefel, "Konjunkturelle Entwicklung und struktureller Wandel der österreichischen Wirtschaft in der Zwischenkriegszeit," Institut für Höhere Studien, Forschungsbericht no. 135 (Vienna, 1978), p. 27n45.

19. Margaret G. Myers, "The League Loans," *Political Science Quarterly* 60, no. 4 (1945): 492–526.

20. Pauly, "The League of Nations."

21. Peter M. Garber and Michael G. Spencer, *The Dissolution of the Austro-Hungarian Empire: Lessons for Currency Reform* (Princeton, NJ, 1994).

22. Julio A. Santaella, "Stabilization Programs and External Enforcement: Experience from the 1920s," *International Monetary Fund Staff Papers* 40, no. 3 (1993): 584–621. Beth A. Simmons has argued that any form of "commitment technology," such as the League's, might be illusory and that governments abide to agreements because breaking credibility is costly. Beth A. Simmons, "International Law and State Behavior: Commitment and Compliance in International Monetary Affairs," *American Political Science Review* 94, no. 4 (2000): 819–835.

23. Zara Steiner's justly hailed work on interwar Europe devotes just a few pages to Austrian reconstruction. Zara Steiner, *The Lights That Failed: European International History, 1919–1933* (New York, 2005), pp. 279–281.

24. Nicole Piétri, "La réconstruction économique et financière de l'Autriche par la Société des Nations (1921–1926)" (doctoral thesis, Université de Paris I, 1981), pp. 1437–1438.

25. J. L. J. Bosmans, *De Nederlander Mr. A. R. Zimmerman als Commissaris-Generaal van de Volkenbund in Oostenrijk 1922–1926* (Nijmegen, 1973), p. 286.

26. Michel Fior, "Institution globale, transition et pouvoir: La Société des Nations et la reconstruction de l'Europe (1918–1931)" (doctoral thesis, Université de Neuchâtel, 2006), pp. 289–301, published as *Institution globale et marchés financiers: La Société des Nations face à la reconstructions de l'Europe 1918–1931* (Bern, 2008).

27. Jens-Wilhelm Wessels, *Economic Policy and Microeconomic Performance in Inter-War Europe: The Case of Austria, 1918–1938* (Stuttgart, 2007), pp. 32–73.

28. Robert Boyce, "The Significance of 1931 for British Imperial and International History," *Histoire@Politique: Politique, culture, société* 11 (2010): 2.

29. Most recently Konrad H. Jarausch, *Out of Ashes: A New History of Europe in the Twentieth Century* (Princeton, NJ, 2015), pp. 209–210.

30. "The run on Austria triggered others in Hungary, Czechoslovakia, Rumania, Poland, and Germany," Charles P. Kindleberger, *A Financial History of Western Europe* (London, 1985), p. 372.

31. Barry Eichengreen, "The Origins and Nature of the Great Slump Revisited," *Economic History Review* 45, no. 2 (1992): 213–239.

32. "Another run on the German banks resulted from the Austrian banking crisis of May 1931, when the Creditanstalt of Vienna collapsed, due in part to the actual or rumored recall of short-term lendings by French depositors to force the abandonment of the projected customs union between the Reich and Austria." Karl Hardach, *The Political Economy of Germany in the Twentieth Century* (Berkeley, CA, 1980), p. 41. "The closure on May 11, 1931, of Austria's largest deposit bank, the *Credit-Anstalt* in Vienna, triggered a four-month international financial frenzy that ended only when the British pound was devalued and untied from gold in September," Robert O. Paxton and Julie Hessler, *Europe in the Twentieth Century* (Wadsworth, CA, 2012), p. 265. "This, then, was the state of international relations in May 1931, when the Credit-Anstalt collapse triggered a crisis that even today can still be regarded as 'the mother of all financial crises.'" Gianni Toniolo with the assistance of Piet Clement, *Central Bank Cooperation at the Bank for International Settlements, 1930–1973* (Cambridge, 2005), p. 88. A notable exception is Harold James, "The 1931 Central European Banking Crisis Revisited," in *Business in the Age of Extremes*, ed. Hartmut Berghoff, Jürgen Kocka, and Dieter Ziegler (Cambridge, 2013), pp. 119–132.

Prologue

Epigraph: Ludwig von Mises, *Memoirs* (Auburn, AL, 2009), p. 21.

1. "Ein farbenfrohes Märchen," *Neuigkeits-Weltblatt,* "Die grosse Kaiser-Jubiläumshuldigung der Völker," 13 June 1908; "Ein Schauspiel, aber ach, ein Schauspiel nur!," *NFP,* Morgenblatt, 13 June 1908; "Ein schöner Traum? Vieleicht; aber ein Wahrtraum," *Neues Wiener Journal,* "Leuchtende Spuren," 13 June 1908. Unless otherwise indicated, all translations from the German are mine.

2. "Zug der Vergangenheit," *AZ,* Morgenblatt, 13 June 1908.

3. Steven Beller, "Kraus's Firework," in *Staging the Past: The Politics of Commemoration in Habsburg Central Europe, 1848 to the Present,* ed. Maria Bucur and Nancy M. Wingfield (West Lafayette, IN, 2001), p. 47.

4. Daniel L. Unowsky, *The Pomp and Politics of Patriotism: Imperial Celebrations in Habsburg Austria, 1848–1916* (West Lafayette, IN, 2005).

5. In solidarity, the Cracow city theater and the Slovenian provincial theater also canceled planned performances in the capital, and Czech nationalists called for a boycott of everything German. Nancy M. Wingfield, *Flag Wars and Stone Saints: How the Bohemian Lands Became Czech* (Cambridge, MA, 2007).

6. Beller, "Kraus's Firework," pp. 62–65.

7. "Wien, 27. Juli.," *NFP,* Morgenblatt, 28 July 1914.

8. Lisa Silverman, *Becoming Austrians: Jews and Culture between the World Wars* (Oxford, 2012).

9. Hugo Bettauer, *Der Kampf um Wien: Ein Roman vom Tage* (Hamburg, n.d.), p. 330.

1. Making Sense of Hyperinflation

Epigraph: RAL, XI / III / 214, "SM von Rothschild re Austria; Albert v. Goldschmidt-Rothschild; Louis v. Rothschild; Eugene v. Rothschild": Letter from Eugen von Rothschild (Vienna) to Anthony de Rothschild (London), 17 September 1921.

1. "Die Wertlosigkeit des Geldes könnte im weiteren Verlaufe zu dem vollständigen Versagen der inneren Kaufkraft der Krone führen. Aber die Abgeordneten haben nichts anderes zu tun, als sich mit Theaterklatsch abzugeben und Lokalereignisse zu Staatsaffären aufzubauschen." "Die Abgeordneten und der 'Reigen,'" *NFP,* 12 February 1921, p. 1; "Der Reigen um die Latrine," *RP,* 12 February 1921, p. 1. Schnitzler's *Der Reigen* was banned in Imperial Germany in 1904 because of its perceived immoral content. It opens with the seduction of an Austrian soldier by a Vienna prostitute and exposes the shallowness of relationships based on seduction, adultery, and lust. In 1921, *Der Reigen* was also being staged

at the Kleine Schauspielhaus in Berlin, and on 22 February 1921 a group of demonstrators similarly disrupted the performance there with shouts and stink bombs.

2. Otto P. Schinnerer, "The History of Schnitzler's Reigen," *PMLA* 46, no. 3 (1931): 839–859.

3. "Gewaltsame Verhinderung der heutigen 'Reigen'-Aufführung," *NFP*, 17 February 1921, p. 1; "Die angespritzten 'Reigen' Besucher," *Die Neue Zeitung*, 17 February 1921, p. 3; "Sturm gegen die Reigen-Aufführungen," *RP*, 17 February 1921, p. 5.

4. "Sturm gegen die Reigen-Aufführungen."

5. Even the liberal *Neue Freie Presse* at one point opined that after incurring heavy political and economic losses, Austria was now also losing its moral standards, with 5 percent of Vienna's population indulging in luxury products, erotic dances, half-naked women, and vulgar language. "Was ist zu tun?—Die Notwendigkeit privater und öffentlicher Sparsamkeit," 2 February 1921, p. 1.

6. Lisa Silverman, *Becoming Austrians: Jews and culture between the World Wars* (New York, 2015); C. M. Peniston-Bird, "The Debate on Austrian National Identity in the First Republic (1918–1938)" (doctoral thesis, University of St. Andrews, 1997).

7. Adam Tooze and Ted Fertik, "The World Economy and the Great War," *Geschichte und Gesellschaft* 40, no. 2 (2014): 214–238.

8. Charles Kindleberger, *A Financial History of Western Europe* (Oxford, 1993), pp. 319–323.

9. Nathan Marcus, "Hyperinflation as a Catalyst of Transformations: Path Dependence through Accelerated Dynamics in Post–First World War Austria," *European Review of History* 23, no. 4 (2016): 595–609, discusses the long-term political effects of hyperinflation's acceleration of time.

10. On the question of Austrian viability, see Bruce F. Pauley, "The Social and Economic Background of Austria's Lebensunfähigkeit," in *The Austrian Socialist Experiment: Social Democracy and Austromarxism, 1918–1934*, ed. Anson Rabinbach (Boulder, CO, 1985), pp. 21–37, which innovatively argues that Austria might have been *psychologically* unviable.

11. Klemens von Klemperer points out that any history of the Austrian Republic has to bear in mind that Austrians chose to ignore reality and to reject their new state. They focused on finding salvation abroad and "lived in a never-never land, not in the here and now. Hence the incidence of the 'politics of unreality' and the ascendency of myth over reality, of metapolitics over politics," while politics was "removed from the realm of the practical and subordinated to a ready-made ideological schema." Klemens von Klemperer, "The Habsburg Heritage: Some Pointers for a Study of the First Austrian Republic," in *The Austrian Socialist Experiment: Social Democracy and Austromarxism, 1918–1934*, ed. Anson Rabinbach (Boulder, CO, 1985), pp. 11–20.

12. Anschluss, much discussed on all levels of society, was at the same time understood as impractical and undesirable by many members of the catholic Christian-Social party. While the Socialists officially desired unification with Germany, they also admitted that it was not practically feasible in the immediate future.

13. David Hackett Fischer, *The Great Wave: Price Revolutions and the Rhythm of History* (New York, 1996), p. 169.

14. Karl Bachinger and Herbert Matis, "Die österreichische Nachkriegsinflation 1918–1922," *Beträge zur Historischen Sozialkunde* 16, no. 3 (1986): 83–91.

15. Heinrich Benedikt, ed., *Geschichte der Republik Österreich* (Vienna, 1954), pp. 117–118; Charles A. Gulick, *Austria: From Habsburg to Hitler*, vol. 1 (Berkeley, CA, 1948), p. 158.

16. Walther Federn, "W. F.: Zum Jahreswechsel," and Gustav Stolper, "Aus der Woche," both in *ÖVW* 13, no. 14 (1 January 1921); Gustav Stolper, "Dr. G. St.: Aufbaupläne," *ÖVW* 13, no. 15 (8 January 1921); Walther Federn, "Der Kurssturz der Krone," *ÖVW* 13, no. 17 (22 January 1921); and Gustav Stolper, "Auslandskredit und Anschlussbewegung," *ÖVW* 13, no. 18 (29 January 1921).

17. Walther Federn, "Völkerbundkredit und Devisenkurse," *ÖVW* 13, no. 29 (16 April 1921); Gustav Stolper: "Anschlussverbot und Völkerbundhilfe," *ÖVW* 13, no. 30 (23 April 1921); Gustav Stolper, "Die Hilfsaktion des Völkerbundes," and Walther Federn, "Die Vorgänge auf dem Devisenmarkt," both in *ÖVW* 13, no. 33 (14 May 1921). These views were echoed by the Pan-German *Wiener Mittag* in "Was sie zu bieten wagen!" on 2 May 1921, which accused the delegation of presenting old ideas but no news on necessary credits, leaving Austrians in a state created against their will, which would be ruined until only Anschluss could save it.

18. Walther Federn, "Fortdauer der Devisenpanik," *ÖVW* 13, no. 45 (6 August 1921); "W. F.: Wohlleben und drohende Katastrophe," *ÖVW* 13, no. 46 (13 August 1921); "Völkerbundkredit und Devisenkurse," *ÖVW* 13, no. 47 (20 August 1921); and "Die Völkerbundaktion," *ÖVW* 13, no. 48 (27 August 1921).

19. Gulick, *Austria,* pp. 158–159.

20. Gustav Stopler, "Dr. Gustav Stolper: Vorbemerkungen zu einem Finanzplan. II," *ÖVW* 14, no. 2 (8 October 1921); Gustav Stolper, "Das Finanzprogramm Dr. Gürtlers," and Walther Federn, "Das Devisenchaos," both in *ÖVW* 14, no. 4 (22 October 1921).

21. Walther Federn: "Der Volkswirt.—Das sozialdemokratische Finanzprogramm," *Neues Wiener Tagblatt,* 8 October 1921.

22. Dr. Gustav Stolper, "Die Gefahren des neuen Finanzprogrammes," *Der Morgen,* 30 October 1921.

23. Walther Federn, "Das alte Elend," *ÖVW* 14, no. 15 (7 January 1922); "A. B.: Allgemeiner Lohnabbau oder Massenelend," *ÖVW* 14, no. 16 (14 January 1922);

Gustav Stolper, "Bankrotte Finanzpolitik," *ÖVW* 14, no. 18 (28 January 1922); Gu-lick, *Austria*, p. 162.

24. Gustav Stolper, "Kredithifle," *ÖVW* 14, no. 20 (11 February 1922), and "Der Rücktritt Dr. Rosenbergs," *ÖVW* 14, no. 21 (18 February 1922).

25. "Noch niemals [hat] eine Sanierungsaktion so vollständig Schiffbruch erlitten, noch nie [haben] verantwortliche Staatsmänner so unverantwortlich leichtfertig mit einem anvertrauten Land verfahren," Gustav Stolper, "Dr. G. St.: Finanzpolitische Ratlosigkeit," *ÖVW* 14, no. 34 (20 May 1922); Walther Federn, "Dr. Gürtlers Rücktritt," *ÖVW* 14, no. 33 (13 May 1922); Walther Federn, "W. F.: Wirtschaftspolitischer Absolutismus," *ÖVW* 14, no. 32 (6 May 1922).

26. Benedikt, *Geschichte der Republik Österreichs*, pp. 123–125; Gustav Stolper, "Kredithilfe und Notenbank," *ÖVW* 14, no. 35 (27 May 1922); Gustav Stolper, "Dr. G. St.: An der Wende?," *ÖVW* 14, no. 36 (3 June 1922).

27. Walther Federn, "W. F.: Finanzplan und Wirklichkeit," *ÖVW* 14, no. 42 (15 July 1922).

28. Gustav Stolper, "Dr. G. St.: Deutschösterreichs Aussenhandel," *ÖVW* 13, no. 34 (20 May 1921); see also Gustav Stolper, "Dr. G. St.: Deutschösterreichs Aus-senhandel. II," *ÖVW* 13, no. 35 (28 May 1921); "Dr. G. St.: Deutschösterreichs Aussenhandel. III," *ÖVW* 13, no. 36 (4 June 1921); "Dr. G. St.: Deutschösterreichs Aussenhandel. IV," *ÖVW* 13, no. 37 (11 June 1921).

29. Jan van Walré de Bordes, *The Austrian Crown: Its Depreciation and Stabi-lization* (London, 1924), pp. 144–153. A notable exception to Austria's conserva-tive parties were the Pan-Germans, who naturally argued that the problem *was* the trade balance and Austria therefore had to join Germany.

30. Walter Goldinger and Dieter A. Binder, *Geschichte der Republik Oester-reich, 1918–1938* (Munich, 1992), p. 102.

31. "Eine Schuldenlast von über hundert Milliarden.—Mitteilungen des Prä-sidenten der Ersparungskommission Beck in der Eröffnungsrede. Defizit im Staatshaushalte: Dreissig Billionen," *NFP*, 8 February 1921, p. 1; "Ein Defizit von etwa vierzig Milliarden," *NFP*, Abendblatt, 9 February 1921, p. 1; "Einundsiebzig Mil-liarden Ausgaben, zweiundvierzig Milliarden Defizit," *NFP*, 11 February 1921, p. 1; "Die Pariser Finanzkonferenzen über Oesterreich," *NFP*, 20 February 1921, p. 3.

32. Richard Kerschagl, "Das Wirtschaftsproblem der Inflation und Deflation," *ÖVW* 13, no. 15 (8 January 1921).

33. Wilhelm Rosenberg, "Für eine innere Anleihe," *NFP*, 12 January 1921, pp. 1–2. The agriculturalist Siegfried Strakosch also identified the budget deficit as the main reason behind the increase in note circulation: Siegfried Strakosch, "Der Economist.—Selbsttäuschung ein Hindernis des wirtschaftlichen Wieder-aufbaues," *NFP*, 22 February 1921, pp. 9–10. Two foreign opinions that concurred with Rosenberg and Strakosch were G. J. van der Heyden, "Gedanken zur Sanie-rung des österreichischen Finanz- und Geldwesens," *NFP*, 16 January 1921,

pp. 2–3, and William Goode, in a conversation with the French *Journal de Débats*, summarized in "Sir William Goode über das österreichische Wirtschaftsproblem," *NFP*, 17 January 1921, p. 3.

34. "Das Jahr der Entscheidungen," *NFP*, 4 January 1921, p. 1; see also "Die grosse Finanzkrise—Die Pflichten der Entente gegen Österreich," *NFP*, 10 January 1921, p. 1.

35. Van Walré de Bordes, *The Austrian Crown*, pp. 144–153.

36. In the 1970s, the Austrian economist Christian Suppanz analyzed data on money supply, prices, and the exchange rate to confirm the finding of van Walré de Bordes that depreciation had outpaced and preceded the rise in prices and circulation. Although Suppanz concluded that depreciation of the crown had been the main force behind Austrian inflation, he ignored the role of capital flows and instead put equal blame on the current account deficit, the growth in money supply, and an increase in domestic import demand. Christian Suppanz, *Die österreichische Inflation 1918–1922*, Forschungsbericht No. 111, Institut für Höhere Studien (Vienna, 1976). Today we know that prices react simply slower than the exchange rate to changes in expectations, something economists call the "stickiness" of prices. See also Karl Bachinger and Herbert Matis, *Der österreichische Schilling: Geschichte einer Währung* (Graz, 1974); Karl Bachinger and Herbert Matis, "Die österreichische Nachkriegsinflation, 1918–1922," *Beiträge zur Historischen Sozialkunde* 16, no. 3 (1986): 83–91. One historian who should not go unnoted is Alice Teichova, who succinctly wrote that Austrian postwar inflation was due at first to increased demand facing reduced supply, then to increased circulation because of governmental deficit spending, and finally to the lack of confidence in Austria's viability and the conviction among Austrians that only a foreign loan could restore stability. Alice Teichova, "Die Inflation der 1920er Jahre in Mitteleuropa im Vergleich," *Beiträge zur historischen Sozialkunde* 16, no. 3 (1986): 67–68.

37. In what represented a turnaround on his earlier views, Walther Federn admitted in a special edition of the *Österreichische Volkswirt* on the tenth anniversary of the Empire's dissolution in 1928, that expectations had been key to the eventual termination of Austrian inflation in 1922. According to Federn, stabilization occurred once Austrians expected that the loan, which would be floated with help of the League, was large enough to successfully defend the currency on the exchanges and simultaneously cover the budget deficit for several years. Walther Federn, "Österreichs Währung, Notenbank und Geldmarkt," *ÖVW, Almanach 1908–1918–1928 10 Jahre Nachfolgestaaten* (Vienna, 1928), pp. 39–41.

38. Van Walré de Bordes, *The Austrian Crown*, pp. 163–164.

39. "Hilfe oder Anschluss an Deutschland.—Unwahrscheinlichkeit der grossen Kredite," *NFP*, 9 January 1921, p. 1.

40. Hertz argued that since circulation was 40 times higher than in 1913 and world market prices had increased by a factor of 3, prices in Austria should have been only 13 times higher than before the war. Friedrich Hertz, "Der Economist.—Entspricht der Kurswert der Krone unserer wirtschaftlichen Lage?," *NFP*, 18 January 1921, p. 10.

41. "Im September [1920] findet vorübergehend eine erhebliche Besserung des Kronenkurses statt, weil auf eine internationale Intervention und auf eine grosse Auslandsanleihe gerechnet wird. Der starke Rückgang der Krone in der ersten Dezemberhälfte ist die Folge von Gerüchten über eine bevorstehende Notenabstempelung, für die eine Strömung innerhalb der Regierung bestehe. Auf das förmliche Dementi der Gerüchte tritt eine Erholung des Kronenkurses ein." *Die Bank, Monatshefte für Finanz- und Bankwesen,* "Deutsch-Österreich" (January 1921).

42. "In der Bewertung des Geldes gegenüber den Waren und gegenüber dem ausländischen Gelde ist stets auch ein spekulatives Moment enthalten, das heisst, es wird in ihr immer auch schon die voraussichtliche künftige Gestaltung der Verhätlnisse mit in Betracht gezogen. Wenn anzunehmen ist, dass die Geldentwertung fortschreiten wird, weil die Regierung in der Inanspruchnahme der Notenpresse nicht Mass zu halten gewillt ist, dann wird die Geldeinheit niedriger bewertet werden als es geschehen wäre, wenn man mit keiner weiteren Inflation zu rechnen hätte. Da man erwartet, dass die Geldentwertung fortgehen wird, sucht man sich so schnell als möglich durch den Ankauf von Waren, von Wertpapieren oder von ausländischem Geld des inländischen Geldes, das von Tag zu Tag in der Kaufkraft sinkt, zu entledigen." Ludwig Mises, "Inflation und Geldknappheit.—Gegen eine weitere Verwendung der Notenpresse," *NFP*, 11 March 1922, p. 2.

43. See, for example, Ben Bernanke, "Inflation Expectations and Inflation Forecasting," Speech at the Monetary Economics Workshop of the National Bureau of Economic Research Summer Institute, Cambridge, Massachusetts, 10 July 2007.

44. The real cash balance of an economy is the total real value of cash circulating outside the bank of issue. It can be estimated by dividing money supply with the price level or the exchange rate. During periods of high inflation, both circulation and prices increase, but prices increase faster, reducing the real value of money supply. By September 1922 Austria's real cash balance was about one-third of its level in 1914. Phillip Cagan, "The Monetary Dynamics of Hyperinflation," in *Studies in the Quantity Theory of Money,* ed. Milton Friedman (Chicago, 1956), pp. 25–117. The decline in real cash balances did not go unnoticed by Wilhelm Rosenberg. In an article he pointed out that before the war Austrian circulation was 500 million Swiss francs, whereas in May 1922 it stood at only 200 million Swiss francs. Wilhelm Rosenberg, "Amerikanischer Vorschuss und Notenbank," *NFP*, 24 May 1922, pp. 1–2.

45. Cagan's model used adaptive expectations; that is, the expected rate of inflation was estimated based on weighted averages of past price changes, which is not of much help when the factors that determine expectations are the focus of inquiry. In fact, Cagan himself noted that an undue increase in money supply or a sudden depreciation of the exchange rate alters the expected rate of inflation.

46. Historians of Weimar inflation will be familiar with this argument from Steven B. Webb, *Hyperinflation and Stabilization in Weimar Germany* (New York, 1989). Webb showed that rates of expected inflation estimated by way of forward exchange discounts were well explained by news regarding Germany's total accumulated and future budget deficit. Increases in government debt explained the declines in real cash balances, and thus the rate of inflation. When the real value of Germany's debt increased, individuals expected inflation to rise, sold Treasury Bills and cash for real assets, and thus bid up prices, decreasing the real value of public debt. The note issue, Webb concluded, did not determine rates of German inflation. It was the expected rate of inflation, which itself was based on total accumulated, present, and anticipated real government debt. See also Webb, "Fiscal News and Inflationary Expectations in Germany after World War I," *Journal of Economic History* 46, no. 3 (September 1986): 769–794, and his "Government Debt and Inflationary Expectations as Determinants of the Money Supply in Germany, 1919–1922," *Journal of Money, Credit and Banking* 17 (November 1985, part 1): 479–492.

47. The results of a regression of the change in circulation on the change in Treasury Bills for the period from the first week of June 1921 until the last week of July 1922 provide a reasonable R-square value. Thus increase in government debt produced similar changes in money supply and moved economic agents to bid up prices until they reached their desired level of real cash balances.

48. According to some estimates, Austria was able to repay its depreciated war and prewar debt at 0.3 percent of its original cost. Fritz Weber, *Vor dem grossen Krach. Österreichs Bankwesen der Zwischenkriegszeit am Beispiel der Credit-Anstalt für Handel und Gewerbe* (Vienna, 2016), p. 42.

49. Georg Simmel, *Philosophie des Geldes* (Leipzig, 1900), pp. 506–554.

50. Van Walré de Bordes, *The Austrian Crown*, pp. 163–164.

51. Maria Jahoda, Paul Lazarsfeld, and Hans Zeisel, *Die Arbeitslosen von Marienthal: Ein soziographischer Versuch über die Wirkungen langdauernder Arbeitslosigkeit* (Frankfurt a. M., 1975), pp. 83–92; Henri F. Ellenberger, "A Clinical Introduction to Psychiatric Phenomenology and Existential Analysis," in *Existence,* ed. Rollo May, Ernest Angel, and Henri F. Ellenberger (Northvale, NJ, 1994), p. 106.

52. Paul Neurath, "Sixty Years since Marienthal," *Canadian Journal of Sociology/Cahiers canadiens de sociologie* 20, no. 1 (1995): 91–105.

53. Eugène Minkowski, *Le temps vécu, études phénoménologiques et psychopathologiques* (Paris, 1933).

54. In 1904, births out of wedlock had made up 30.5 percent of total births. After reaching its nadir in 1922, this figure gradually rose back to 24 percent by 1932. Abortion was illegal in Austria, and abortion arrests increased from 288 in 1921 to 376 in 1922 and 460 in 1923. See Robert Hofstätter, *Die arbeitende Frau: Ihre wirtschaftliche Lage, Gesundheit, Ehe und Mutterschaft* (Vienna, 1929); *Statistisches Jahrbuch der Stadt Wien, für das Jahr 1908* (Vienna, 1910), p. 58; *Statistisches Handbuch für die Republik Österreich*, vol. 14 (Vienna, 1933), p. 17; Kammer für Arbeiter und Angestellte für Wien, *Wirtschaftsstatistisches Jahrbuch 1926* (Vienna, 1927).

55. People were sensitive to the changes in tobacco prices. The *Neue Freie Presse* published a report on 9 November that rumors about an increase in tobacco prices were not accurate, and reported on 20 October that tobacco prices would be increased by 25 to 30 percent within two days. "Keine Erhöhung der Preise für Rauchmaterialien," *NFP*, Morgenblatt, 9 November 1922, p. 9; "Neuerliche Erhöhung der Rauchwarenpreise," *NFP*, Morgenblatt, 20 October 1922, p. 11. Another *Neue Freie Presse* article observed that in middle-class districts consumption of higher quality products had fallen, while in working-class neighborhoods expensive tobaccos were being consumed, and that the number of female smokers had increased, too. "Die Erhöhung der Rauchwarenpreise," *NFP*, Nachmittagsblatt, 23 October 1922, p. 5.

56. Bernd Widdig, *Culture and Inflation in Weimar Germany* (Berkeley, CA, 2001); see also Martin H. Geyer, *Verkehrte Welt*, Kritische Studien zur Geschichtswissenschaft 128 (Göttingen, 1998).

57. Widdig, *Culture and Inflation in Weimar Germany*, pp. 213–215. While his claim that in Germany gambling, prostitution, and conspicuous consumption increased during hyperinflation remains tenuous, in Vienna prostitution did indeed grow. See Harold James's review of Widdig in the *Journal of Economic History* 62, no. 1 (March 2002): 239; for prostitution in Vienna, see Oskar Dressler and Hugo Weinberger, "Die Geschlechtsmoral," in *Geldentwertung und Stabilisierung in ihren Einflüssen auf die soziale Entwicklung in Österreich*, ed. Julius Buntzel, Schriften des Vereins für Sozialpolitik 169 (Munich, 1925), pp. 323–326; see also Bachinger and Matis, *Der Österreichische Schilling*, p. 47; and Peter Eigner, "Spekulanten, 'graue Eminenzen' und der Untergang des Altwiener Patriziats; Thesen zum österreichischen Wirtschaftsbürgertum in der Zwischenkriegszeit," in *Auf Heller und Cent: Beiträge zur Finanz- und Währungsgeschichte*, ed. Karl Bachinger, Dieter Stiefel, and Charlotte Natmessnig (Vienna, 2001), pp. 345–370.

58. Sigmund Freud, *Der Witz und seine Beziehung zum Unbewussten* (Leipzig, 1905). Thus a sexual joke is funny when it provides the listener and joker with the image of a sexual act that they long for, but are prevented from engaging in, or when it relieves them from a suppressed sexual fear.

59. Geheimnisse: "Was hast du dir gedacht wie dein Bankier sein Vermögen verloren hat?—Ich habe gedacht: Merkwürdig wie rasch Liebe vergeht!," *Die Bombe*, 15 October 1921, p. 4.

60. Zeichen der Zeit: "Weist Du Lizzi, die Geschäfte müssen miserabel gehen: alle Ehemänner, die ich kenne, sind wieder in ihre Frauen verliebt," *Die Bombe,* 15 December 1922, p. 8.

61. Willkommen: "Er nennt sich Mister Dollar.—Dann lassen Sie ihn rein—der Name ist versprechend," *Die Bombe,* 1 June 1921, p. 5.

62. Kennzeichen: "Was für ein Herr ist das wieder?—Ich weiss nur, dass er eine ganz neue Valuta hat," *Die Bombe,* 15 January 1921, p. 5.

63. Besorgt: "Alice, lassen Sie sich nicht mit dem Amerikaner ein, alles an ihm ist falsch.—Schrecklich, am ende [*sic*] auch die Dollar-Schecks?," *Die Bombe,* 15 April 1921, p. 8.

64. Konjunktur: "Ach Lizzi, all Frauenartikel steigen jetzt im Preise.—Folglich die Frauen selbst auch," *Die Bombe,* 15 April 1921, p. 4.

65. Ein Zufriedener: "Wir Frauen werden bald nichts zum Anziehen haben.—Das ist noch das beste an der gegenwärtigen Lage," *Die Bombe,* 1 October 1922, p. 4.

66. Freud writes that while jokes often satisfy sexual desires, they can also address wants and fears relating to race or class, and both the prostitute and the Jew are commonly used allegorical figures of modernity. Freud, *Der Witz und seine Beziehung zum Unbewussten,* chap. 3.

67. This identity was explicitly evoked by Christian-Social politicians who blamed inflation not on note issue but on speculation, which they identified with Jews. The national government refrained from singling out Jews when attacking speculators, but on the local party level such allegations were frequent. In January 1921, the *Neue Freie Presse* reported on a debate in the Vienna parliament in which the Christian-Social deputy, Leopold Kunschak, demanded the expulsion or internment of Jewish refugees living on usury and "Hasardspiel." He was corrected by the Socialist governor, Neumann, who told him that among the "parasites" devouring Austria were not only Jews but many non-Jews and Aryans as well. "Wiener Landtag: Eine Ostjudendebatte," *NFP,* 15 January 1921, p. 6. When inflation and depreciation reached unprecedented heights in October 1921, Kunschak told an assembly of Christian-Social workers in Vienna that the current panic was caused by rumors that had been planted by the Jewish press and Socialist Party, and, invoking medieval prejudices, warned them that their actions hurt state and people and were "poisoning the wells from which they took their water" ("Wer die Kreditaktion trifft, der trifft daher nicht die christlichsoziale Partei, der trifft den Staat, das Volk, der vergiftet den Brunnen, aus dem er selbst sein Wasser bezieht"). "Kreditaktion, Bankgesetze und Westungarn," *RP,* 3 October 1921, p. 2. Other articles identified Jews with black-marketers or the interests of high finance. "Das Programm des Finanzministers," *AZ,* 14 October 1921, p. 3; "Kriegshetzte und Kurssturz," *RP,* 31 October 1921, p. 2.

68. "Wenn die österreichische Krone noch tiefer sinkt, und wir können aus Paris kein Parfüm mehr kaufen—was fangen wir denn dann an?!," *RP,* 7 August 1922, p. 1.

69. "Da les' i grade, dass es jetzt in Österreich 60.000 Arbeitslose geben soll. Ob sie uns zwei mitgezählt haben, Sami?," *RP,* 18 April 1922, p. 1.

2. The Road to Geneva

Epigraph: BEA, OV/28/52, Austrian Rehabilitation: Letter from Young to Treasury, 18 March 1922.

1. See Charles à Court Repington, *After the War: London–Paris–Rome–Athens–Prague–Vienna–Budapest–Bucharest–Berlin–Sofia–Coblenz–New York–Washington* (London, 1922), p. 133; and Stephen Graham, *Europe—Whither Bound? Being Letters of Travel from Capitals of Europe in the Year 1921* (Toronto, 1922), p. 103.

2. The Bank's Governor at the time, Alexander Spitzmüller, remembered this in his memoirs as follows: "Im Finanzministerium war man der Anschauung, dass der Notendruck fortgesetzt werden müsse, da das Gleichgewicht im Budget ohne Auslandshilfe, das ist Gewährung einer Auslandsanleihe, nicht hergestellt werden könne. Bis zum Zeitpunkte der Gewährung dieser Anleihe setzte das Finanzministerium seine grosszügige Ausgabenpolitik fort und bestand kaum in irgend einem Sektor auf ausgiebigen Ersparungen. . . . Bis dahin wurde geradezu mit voller Absicht eine Politik der Devaluierung der Krone betrieben. . . . Die Situation hatte sich in den ersten Monaten des Jahres 1922 in valutarischer Beziehung geradezu katastrophal gestaltet. Die Krone war infolge des permanenten Notendruckes zur Deckung des Defizits in der bedenklichsten Weise gefallen." Alexander Spitzmüller, . . . *Und hat doch Ursach es zu lieben* (Vienna, 1955), pp. 333.

3. Mauro Megliani, *Sovereign Debt: Genesis–Restructuring–Litigation* (Cham, Switzerland, 2015), pp. 68–71; Ali Coşkun Tunçer, *Sovereign Debt and International Financial Control: The Middle East and the Balkans, 1870–1914* (Houndmills, UK, 2015).

4. Barbara Susan Warnock, "The First Bailout—The Financial Reconstruction of Austria 1922–1926" (doctoral thesis, Birbeck College, University of London, 2015), pp. 49–50.

5. *Memorandum from the British Representative Regarding Financial Measures Urgently Necessary,* 15 September 1920, enclosed with NA, T 160/57/2073/1: Letter from John Bradbury to Treasury, 3 November 1920. Further parts of the proposal included funding of services of Austrian foreign debt and debt of the City of Vienna, assurances of additional supply of 200,000 tons of coal and coke monthly, development of Austrian water power by foreign capital primarily for industrial purposes, a suggested transitory customs tariff, a nonpartisan budget commission to effect state, provincial, and municipal economies, and a reduction of Austrian armed forces, as well as the management of state monopolies and enterprises by private capital.

6. NA, T 160 / 57 / 2073 / 1: Communication from Blackett to Chamberlain, 12 November 1920. According to a memo prepared by Waley for Blackett, measures taken in favor of Austria in 1919 had been a joint relief credit with France and Italy of $48 million for cereals from the United States, paid for by the Americans. In 1920–1921, the United Kingdom had voted £10 million for relief in Austria and Poland, of which £5.5 million were already sanctioned for Austria. The Americans had contributed $25 million, but the French had only provided an office, "consisting of a flat on the 6th floor of an Annex to the French Foreign Office," and there had been no contribution from Italy.

7. NA, T 160 / 57 / 2073 / 1: *Cabinet Decision,* 17 December 1920, and *Note of a Conversation between the Chancellor of the Exchequer, Sir Hugh Levick and Sir William Goode,* 24 November 1920.

8. NA, T 160 / 57 / 2073 / 2: *Second Cabinet Decision,* 30 December 1920.

9. AdR, 01 / 9, Ges. London, Telegramme 1920–1923, Karton 18: Telegram from Simon to Finanzministerium, 4 December 1920.

10. AdR, Staatsamt für Finanzen, 67 / 3666 / 21, "Eingabe an den Völkerbund wegen Hilfe für Oesterreich": Telegram from Simon to Schwarzwald, 10 January 1921, and letter, 31 December 1920. The Austrian Government followed Simon's advice and informed the Entente missions of the dangers if credits were delayed, but did not threaten to resign. See AdR, 01 / 9, Ges. London, Telegramme 1920–1923 / Karton 18, "Herein 1921": Telegram from Aussenamt to Franckenstein, 13 January 1921.

11. NA, T 160 / 57 / 2073 / 2, "Austrian Reconstruction": Letter from Goode to Niemeyer, 11 January 1921.

12. At the conference, the Germans eventually agreed to pay £11.3 billion over forty-two years.

13. NA, T 160 / 57 / 2073 / 2: *Draft: British Secretary's Notes of an Allied Conference Held in the Salle de l'Horloge, Quai d'Orsay, Paris, on Tuesday, January 25th, 1921 at 11 A.M.*

14. LNA, S 143, "Crédits Internationaux / International Credits in Austria (File II)": *Procès-verbal de la séance du 25 janvier 1921.* Dr. Giannini represented Italy. The French members were Seydoux, de Mones, and Bexon, while the British were represented by Sir Goode, Sir Llewellyn Smith, Chief Economic Advisor to the British Government, and British Treasury Representative H. E. Fass.

15. NA, T 160 / 57 / 2073 / 2: Telegram from Hardinge to King and Cabinet, 25 January 1921.

16. LNA, S 143, "Crédits Internationaux / International Credits in Austria (File II)": *Procès-verbal de la séance du 25 janvier 1921.*

17. NA, T 160 / 57 / 2073 / 2, "Austrian Reconstruction": *Report of the Committee on Austria.—Secret,* 29 January 1921.

18. The Italian financial attaché was most probably Amadeo Giannini, who went on to have a career in Italian politics and diplomacy. AdR, 1, Ges. London

Polit. Berichte 1920–1923 / Zl. 5 / P: Letter from Franckenstein to Foreign Ministry, 4 February 1921.

19. AdR, 1, Ges. London Polit. Berichte 1920–1923 / 11 / P: Letter from Franckenstein to Foreign Ministry, 15 February 1921.

20. NA, T 160 / 57 / 2073 / 2, "Austrian Reconstruction": Memo by Blackett for Chamberlain, 14 February 1921; AdR, 01 / 9, Ges. London, Telegramme 1920–1923 / Karton 18, "Hinaus 1921": From Franckenstein, 16 February 1921; AdR, 1 Ges. London Polit. Berichte 1920–1923 / 9 / P: Letter from Franckenstein to Foreign Ministry, 8 February 1921.

21. AdR, 01 / 9, Ges. London, Telegramme 1920–1923 / Karton 18, "Herein 1921": Telegram from Foreign Ministry to Schüller, 25 February 1921, from Mayr to Schüller, 1 March 1921, and from Aussenamt to Schüller, 8 March 1921; AdR, 01 / 9, Ges. London, Telegramme 1920–1923, Karton 18, "Hinaus 1921": Telegram from Schüller to Vienna, 1 March 1921, and from Franckenstein to Vienna, 1 March 1921; AdR, 1 Ges. London Polit. Berichte 1920–1923 / 19 / P.: Letter from Franckenstein to Aussenamt, 4 March 1921; NA, T 160 / 57 / 2073 / 2, "Austrian Reconstruction": Memo by Waterlow, 1 March 1921, and telegram to Ambassadors, 2 March 1921. On the energetic Richard Schüller, see Jürgen Nautz, *Unterhändler des Vertrauens: Aus den nachgelassenen Schriften von Sektionschef Dr. Richard Schüller* (Vienna, 1990).

22. NA, T 160 / 57 / 2073 / 2, "Austrian Reconstruction": *Text of Speech Delivered by the Austrian Chancellor, Dr. Mayr, before the Supreme Council, London, March 12th, 1921.*

23. NA, T 160 / 57 / 2073 / 3, "Austrian Reconstruction": *British Secretary's Notes of an Allied Conference Held in St. James's Palace, S.W., on Saturday, 12th. March, 1921 at 12.45 P.M.*

24. NA, T 160 / 57 / 2073 / 3, "Austrian Reconstruction": Note by Chamberlain for Blackett, 10 March 1921, and note by Blackett, 11 March 1921.

25. NA, T 160 / 57 / 2073 / 3, "Austrian Reconstruction": *British Secretary's Draft Notes of a Meeting on Financial Experts, Conference Held in the Board Room, Treasury, on Saturday, 12th March, 1921 at 3.0. P.M.* The Allied representatives were Loucheur, Saint-Aulaire, Avenol, and Seydoux for France; della Toretta and Meda for Italy; Nagai for Japan; and Chamberlain, Blackett, Lindley, and Goode for Britain. The Austrian delegation consisted of Chancellor Mayr, Finance Minister Grimm, Food Minister Grünberger, Foreign Ministry trade expert Schüller, Treasury delegate Simon, and envoy Franckenstein. The annual Austrian trade deficit was estimated at $50–60 million.

26. NA, T 160 / 57 / 2073 / 3, "Austrian Reconstruction": *British Secretary's Draft Notes of a Meeting on Financial Experts, Conference Held in the Board Room, Treasury, on Saturday, 12th March, 1921 at 3.0. P.M.*; AdR, 01 / 9, Ges. London, Telegramme 1920–1923 / Karton 18, "Hinaus 1921": Telegram from Franckenstein, 12

March 1921; also, AdR 67 / 41662 / 21, *Bericht des Bundesministers für Finanzen über die Londoner Reise.*

27. NA, T 160 / 57 / 2073 / 3, "Austrian Reconstruction": *British Secretary's Notes of a Meeting of Financial Experts, Conference Held in the Board Room, Treasury, on Monday, 14th. March, 1921 at 3.0. P.M.* The experts were Saint-Aulaire, Avenol, and Fevre for France; della Toretta and Giannini for Italy; Mori for Japan; and Blackett, Lindley, and Goode for Britain.

28. AdR, 01 / 9, Ges. London, Telegramme 1920–1923 / Karton 18, "Hinaus 1921": Telegram from Franckenstein to Vienna, 14 March 1921; NA, T 160 / 57 / 2073 / 3, "Austrian Reconstruction": *British Secretary's Notes of a Meeting of Financial Experts, Conference Held in the Board Room, Treasury, on Monday, 14th. March, 1921 at 3.0. P.M.*

29. NA, T 160 / 57 / 2073 / 3, "Austrian Reconstruction": *British Secretary's Notes of a Meeting of Financial Experts, Conference Held in the Board Room, Treasury, on Monday, 14th March, 1921 at 5. P.M.* On the aborted Ter Meulen plan, see Royall Tyler, *The League of Nations Reconstruction Schemes in the Inter-War Period* (Geneva, 1945), pp. 13–15.

30. NA, T 160 / 57 / 2073 / 3, "Austrian Reconstruction": *British Secretary's Verbatim Notes of a Meeting of Financial Experts, Held in the Board Room, Treasury, on Thursday, 17th. March, 1921 at 11.15 A.M.*

31. AdR, 67 / 41662 / 21, *Bericht des Bundesministers für Finanzen über die Londoner Reise,* and telegram from Austrian Embassy to Foreign Ministry, Vienna, 18 March 1921, as well as telegram from Mayr to Vice-Chancellor Breisky, 18 March 1921

32. LNA, E.F.S. 1 - G.P.V. 1, Comité Économique, Documents, Tôme 1, 1920–23 (LNA, 1055, E.F.S. 1–23): *Compte rendu des Travaux de la Commission économique et financière provisoire (première session) Genève, Novembre–Décembre 1920.*

33. LNA, S 143, Crédits Internationaux / International Credits in Austria (File II): *The League and Austria,* 7 February 1921.

34. That the Supreme Council's decision did not come as a surprise to Nixon is attested by a letter to him from his colleague at the Financial Section's London Office, which read, "Today came the news you expected." LNA, S 143, Crédits Internationaux: Letter from Jacobson to Nixon, 16 March 1921.

35. LNA, S 143, Crédits Internationaux: *Austria* by Nixon, 17 March 1921; LNA, S 143, Crédits Internationaux / International Credits in Austria (File II): Memo sent by Loveday to Nixon, 25 March 1921.

36. Arthur Salter, *Slave of the Lamp: A Public Servant's Notebook* (London, 1967), p. 97. See also Sidney Aster, *Power, Policy and Personality: The Life and Times of Lord Salter, 1881–1975* (n.p., 2016).

37. LNA, S 143, Crédits Internationaux / International Credits in Austria (File II): Letter from Salter to Nixon, 14 April 1921.

38. LNA, S 143, Crédits Internationaux / International Credits in Austria (File II): Memo sent by Loveday to Nixon, 26 March 1921. See also LNA, A.36 (LNA 1299 A36–A56, April–May 1921): *Memorandum on the Finances of Austria—Facts and Comments*, 1 April 1921. Loveday argued that the reforms necessitated the initial loan to be administered by an international body and that Austria would have to "accept the position of a company in liquidation" and that of the controlling organ "similar to the position of Lord Cromer in the early days of his administration in Egypt." LNA, A.1 (LNA 1298 A1–A35, October 1920–March 1921): Letter from Avenol to Members of the Financial Section of the Provisional Economic and Financial Committee, 17 March 1921; LNA, S 143, Crédits Internationaux: Letter from Avenol to Ter Meulen, 17 March 1921.

39. LNA, A.42 (LNA 1299 A36–A56, April–May 1921): *Note of an Interview between M. Leon Bourgeois and the Finance Section of the Provisional Economic Financial Committee*, 31 March 1921, and letter from Nixon, 11 April 1921. The Financial Committee members present in Paris were Strakosch, Antonucci, Avenol, Janssen, Ter Meulen, Mori, Niemeyer, Pospíšil, and Fraser.

40. AdR, 67 / 41662 / 21, "31. März 1921": Memo, 31 March 1921; and LNA, A.37 (LNA 1299 A36–A56, April–May 1921): *Conditions Attached to the Grant of Credits to Austria*, 1 April 1921.

41. AdR, 67 / 34419 / 21, "Hilfe an Oesterreich durch Völkerbund": Copy of communication from Eichhoff to Foreign Ministry, 3 April 1921.

42. AdR, 67 / 67Z 29482 / 21, Telegram from Grimm to Eichhoff, 30 March 1921.

43. LNA, A.57 (LNA 1299 A36–A56, April–May 1921): *Commission of Enquiry into the Question of the Application in Austria of International Credits under the Ter Meulen Scheme, April 14–May 10, 1921*, 23 April 1921.

44. LNA, S 106, Sir Arthur Salter's Private Papers, Austria No. 3, "Reports of Meetings and Evidence given to Commission in Vienna [April 1921]": *Compte-rendu de l'entretien avec M. Schwarzwald le 17 avril 1921* and *Conseiller de Ministère Dr. Patzauer, 16.4.1921.*

45. LNA, S 106, Sir Arthur Salter's Private Papers, Austria No. 3, "Reports of Meetings and Evidence given to Commission in Vienna [April 1921]": *Compte-rendu de l'entretien avec M. Schüller le 17 avril 1921*, and *Compte-rendu de l'entretien avec Excellence Sieghart le 20 avril 1921.*

46. LNA, S 106, Sir Arthur Salter's Private Papers, Austria No. 3, "Reports of Meetings and Evidence given to Commission in Vienna [April 1921]": *Compte-rendu de l'entretien avec Directeur Rosenberg le 19 avril 1921*, and *Compte-rendu de l'entretien avec Directeur Feilschenfeld le 19 avril 1921*, as well as *Compte-rendu de l'entretien avec H. Simon le 19 avril 1921*; *Compte-rendu de l'entretien avec Directeur Neurath le 19 avril 1921*, and *Compte-rendu de l'entretien avec Directeur Maxime v. Krassny le 19 avril 1921.*

47. LNA, A.57 (LNA 1299 A36–A56, April–May 1921): *Second Memorandum of the Delegates, April 25th, 1921*, pp. 75–78.

48. LNA, S 106, Sir Arthur Salter's Private Papers, Austria No. 3, "Reports of Meetings and Evidence given to Commission in Vienna [April 1921]": 21 April 1921; LNA, A.34: *First Memorandum of the Delegates, April 23rd, 1921,* pp. 72–74.

49. AdR, 67 / 38680 / 21, "Völkerbund. Entwurf eines Finanzplanes": *Entwurf,* 26 April 1921; AdR, 67 / 41662 / 21, *Budgetäre Massnahmen auf Grund des Finanzplanes,* 9 May 1921.

50. AdR, 67 / 41662 / 21, "Ministerratsprotokoll Nr. 81": *Antwortnote an die Delegierten der Finanzkommission des Völkerbundes,* 9 May 1921; LNA, S 106, Sir Arthur Salter's Private Papers, Austria No. 3, "Reports of Meetings and Evidence given to Commission in Vienna [April 1921]": *Entrevue au Ministère des Affaires Étrangères, 23 Avril 1921.*

51. AdR, 67 41663 / 21, *An die Herren Delegierten des Finanzkomitees des Völkerbundes M. J. Avenol, Sir Drummond-Fraser und Staatsrat E. Glückstadt derzeit in Wien,* 9 May 1921.

52. LNA, S 106, Sir Arthur Salter's Private Papers, Austria No. 3, Letter from Avenol to Blackett, 2 May 1921. Avenol felt that the delegation had changed the whole situation by making the demand for foreign credits no longer the only feature, but rather one among a number of features of a constructive reconstruction program that included budget reform, the establishment of a new central bank, and the organization of control.

53. NA, T 160 / 57 / 2073 / 5, "Austrian Reconstruction": Letter from Lindley to Curzon, 11 May 1921.

54. LNA, A.57 (LNA 1299 A36–A56, April–May 1921): *Commission of Enquiry into the Question of the Application in Austria of International Crédits under the Ter Meulen Scheme, April 14–May 10, 1921;* LNA, 1148 Autriche II Mai 1921: *Extrait des procès-verbaux de la 4ième session du Comité Financier. 1ère séance tenue le 23 mai à 11 et 15h.,* pp. 511–513.

55. Bradley Bordiss and Vishnu Padayachee, "'A Superior Practical Man': Henry Strakosch, the Gold Standard and Monetary Policy Debates in South Africa, 1920–23," *Economic History of Developing Regions* 26, no. 1 (2011): 114–122.

56. LNA, A.58 (LNA 1299 A36–A56, April–May 1921): *Report of Commission of Enquiry in Vienna;* LNA, 1148 Autriche II Mai 1921: *Commission provisoire économique et financière. Séction financière. 4ème session. Londres. 2ème réunion, 25 Mai 1921. à 10 heures 30 et 15 heures,* pp. 515–533. It appears that Glückstadt's bank had bought Austrian crowns in expectation of such a decision being taken, in hope of making a profit from the consequent appreciation of the Austrian currency.

57. LNA, 1148 Autriche II Mai 1921: *Commission provisoire économique et financière. Séction financière. 4ème session. Londres. 3ème réunion, 25 Mai 1921. à 10 heures 30, et 15 heures,* pp. 535–545, and *Commission provisoire économique et financière. Séction financière. 4ème session. 6ème réunion, 28 mai 1921, 10h 30,*

pp. 556–565. Meanwhile, Giannini had arrived as representative of the absent Italian Financial Committee member Balzarotti. Giannini reminded the members of the Italian view that any attitude toward the Austrian question should bring in the Americans and not make cooperation with them more difficult. The proposals of the Supreme Council of 17 March had never been accepted by the Italian government, he claimed, and his presence was not to be seen as any kind of approval of the Committee's work. Strakosch agreed that all were of the view that American participation was indispensable and explained that the Committee had tried in vain to get an American representative to join. However, the request for a report had come from the Supreme Council and the Austrian government and was approved by the League Council. It was necessary to publish the report, so that the Supreme Council could make a definite decision regarding the suspension of liens. Moreover, Strakosch stressed, the Committee was purely advisory, and its members did not represent their governments but were there as technical experts voicing their personal opinions.

58. LNA, 1148 Autriche II Mai 1921: *Commission provisoire économique et financière. Section financière. 4ème session du Comité Financier. 7ème séance, 30 Mai 1921. à 10.30 et 15 h.,* pp. 567–568.

59. LNA, 1148 Autriche II Mai 1921: *Commission provisoire économique et financière. Section financière. 4ème session. 8ème séance–31 Mai, 1921 à 10h. 30.,* p. 570. Toward the end of the session, on 29 May, Strakosch, Avenol, Blackett, Glückstadt, and Monnet visited Governor Norman. The League wanted the Governor to take the initiative and sponsor a public issue of Austrian Treasury Bills of £2 million, underwriting £750,000 while the Treasury would underwrite the remainder. Norman wrote to other central banks to get their assistance, but felt that the League scheme, because of French influence, would turn out to serve French interests instead of focusing on economic issues. When the question came to who would oversee reforms in Vienna, Norman, who wanted a neutral autocrat, clashed with the French, who wanted a commission with French and Italian members. The plan collapsed. R. S. Sayers, *The Bank of England,* vol. 1 (Cambridge, 1976), pp. 164–165. Ter Meulen also opposed the constitution of the Ter Meulen Bond committee because he thought its political character posed a dangerous precedent.

60. AdR, 67 / 41662 / 21, Letter from Simon to Vienna, 30 March 1921; AdR, 01 / 9, Ges. London, Telegramme 1920–1923, Karton 18, "Hinaus 1921": Telegram from Kunz to Hofrat Ludwig, 31 May 1921; NA, T 160 / 57 / 2073 / 3, "Austrian Reconstruction": Letter from Niemeyer to Foreign Office, 2 April 1921; LNA, A.48 (LNA 1299 A36–A56, April–May 1921): Telegram from Imperiali to Drummond, 28 April 1921.

61. AdR, 67 / 52023 / 21, "Kreditaktion des Völkerbundes; Ersuchen an die Mächte um Rückstellung des Generalpfandrechtes": *Abschrift eines Telegrammes*

der österr. Gesandschaft in Paris vom 9. Juni 1921, and *Entwurf eines an die österr. Vertretungsbehörden zu richtendes Telegramm,* 25 June 1921, as well as telegram from Eichhoff to Vienna, 25 June 1921. See also AdR, 01 / 9 Ges. London, Telegramme 1920–1923, Karton 18: Telegram from Schober to Franckenstein, 25 June 1921; AdR, 1 Ges. London Polit. Berichte 1920–1923 / 54 / P: Letter from Franckenstein to Aussenamt, 16 June 1921; NA, T 160 / 572073 / 5, "Austrian Reconstruction": Letters from Blackett to the British Delegation on the Reparations Commission, to Nixon, and to Crowe, all three 17 June 1921.

62. NA, T 160 / 57 / 2073 / 5, "Austrian Reconstruction": Telegram from Hardinge to Foreign Office, 1 July 1921; LNA, R 2941 / Registry Files 1928–1932, "Situation juridique du comité financier": *Secret Resolution of Ambassadors Conference,* 2 July 1921; LNA, R 2941 / Economic and Financial: Finance / 10 E. / 11579 / 1303: Telegram from Foreign Office to Geddes, 2 July 1921.

63. AdR, 65127 / 21, *Verbalnote des Vertreters des Völkerbundes Dr. Riis-Hansen, überreicht dem Finanzminister 12. Juli 1921,* and Riis Hansen, Memorandum, 26 July 1921

64. AdR, 67 / 65478 / 21: Riis Hansen, Memorandum, 26 July 1921. A draft agreement was worked out between Riis Hansen and the Austrian Finance Ministry's Herman Patzauer, on how the Financial Committee would place £5 million of Austrian Treasury bonds abroad and regularly provide the funds to the Austrian government to be used for food imports. Once the larger loan was issued, its proceeds would be used to repay the advances, and should no loan be forthcoming, the bonds could be renewed. Custom revenues would be pledged as security and be paid into a special account under the control of the representative of the Committee of Control, but the Commission did not desire to take over the administration of the revenues and preferred to leave them in the hands of the Austrians.

65. The Austrian food minister argued that many measures had been taken at the time the delegation visited Vienna and that others were currently being implemented. Only flour intended for private use was still subsidized, and meat, fat, and milk prices had all been successively increased. Bread prices would be increased generally but not reach market prices before the year was over, while an end to meat subsidies could not occur before the next year and only once an increase in supply made subsidies unnecessary. AdR, 67 / 65478 / 21, "Ministerratsprotokoll Nr. 106": *Information für den Vertreter des Finanzkomitees des Völkerbundes Dr. Riis-Hansen über die Durchführung des Finanzprogrammes,* and *An den Vertreter des Finanzkomitees des Völkerbundes Herrn Dr. K. Riis-Hansen zur Zeit Wien, Neues Bristol,* 25 July 1921, as well as *Notiz für Herrn Riis-Hansen betr. die vorläufige Kontrolle in Oesterreich,* 26 July 1921; AdR, 67 / 65127 / 21, *Verbalnote des Vertreters des Völkerbundes Dr. Riis-Hansen, überreicht dem Finanzminister 12. Juli 1921.* See also LNA, A.83 (LNA 1301 A81–A128, July–December 1921): *Note for Mr. Riis-Hansen regarding the provisional control in Austria,* 26 July 1921.

66. NA, T 160/58/2073/6, "Austrian Reconstruction": Letter from Lindley to Curzon, 28 July 1921, and letter from Schober to Lindley, 29 July 1921.

67. NA, T 160/58/2073/6, "Austrian Reconstruction": Telegram from Lindley to Foreign Office, 8 August 1921; AdR, 01/9, Ges. London, Telegramme 1920–1923, Karton 18, "Hinaus 1921": Telegram from Franckenstein, 4 August 1921.

68. AdR, 71012/21, *Ministerratsprotokoll Nr. 110 vom 13. August 1921;* AdR, 01/9, Ges. London, Telegramme 1920–1923, Karton 18, "Hinaus 1921": Telegram from Grimm to Vienna, 29 August 1921, and telegram from Franckenstein to Vienna, 31 August 1921; AdR, 01/4, 41 Völkerrecht/unnumbered/1921, "Finanzen Völkerbund": Letter from Pflügl to Foreign Ministry, 1 September 1921; NA, T 160/58/2073/6, "Austrian Reconstruction": Letter from Nixon to Niemeyer, 10 September 1921, and telegram from Keeling to Foreign Office, 2 September 1921.

69. NA, T 160/58/2073/6, "Austrian Reconstruction": Letter from Keeling to Curzon, 30 September 1921.

70. NA, T 160/58/2073/6, "Austrian Reconstruction": Letter from Franckenstein to Niemeyer, 5 October 1921.

71. AdR, 01/9, Ges. London, Telegramme 1920–1923, Karton 18, "Hinaus 1921": Telegrams from Franckenstein to Vienna, 20 September 1921, 21 September 1921, and 24 September 1921, and "Herein 1921": Telegram from Aussenamt to Franckenstein, 20 September 1921. Franckenstein had earlier received assurance from the Treasury that the British would match any advance from the French, who appeared willing to advance £250,000, but on the condition that the Austrian government make acceptable propositions regarding the regulation of Austrian prewar debts. The Austrian government argued that the sum was insufficient, since monthly wheat imports alone cost four times the amount. Chancellor Schober asked Franckenstein to intervene for an advance of £1 million and to assure the amount was kept secret, as announcement of such a meager figure would provoke problems in Austria. Franckenstein was later informed that the Treasury approved the advance of £250,000 and that it supported Austrian attempts to convince the French of the impracticality of linking advances to prewar debts. NA, T 160/58/2073/6, "Austrian Reconstruction": Letter from Waterlow to Niemeyer, 7 October 1921; AdR, 67/90001/21, "Kreditvorschüsse": Note by Lindley for Schober, 17 October 1921, and letter from Schober to Lindley, 18 October 1921.

72. NA, T 160/58/2073/6, "Austrian Reconstruction": Letters from Waterlow to Curzon, 21 October 1921 and 23 October 1921.

73. NA, T 160/58/2073/7, "Austrian Reconstruction," Telegram from Keeling to Foreign Office, 2 December 1921.

74. AdR, 01/9, Ges. London, Telegramme 1920–1923, Karton 18, "III Herein 1922": Telegrams from Schober to Franckenstein, 24 January 1922; AdR, 1 Ges. London Polit. Berichte 1920–1923: Letter from Franckenstein to Lloyd George, 25 January 1922.

75. AdR, 1 Ges. London Polit. Berichte 1920–1923, 39 / P: Letter from Franckenstein to Foreign Ministry, 25 January 1922; AdR, 01 / 9, Ges. London, Telegramme 1920–1923, Karton 18, "III Hinaus 1922": Telegrams from Franckenstein to Foreign Ministry, 25 January 1922 and 26 January 1922; NA, FO 371 / 7335 / C 1282: Letter from Franckenstein to Curzon, 25 January 1922.

76. Together with the £250,000 advance of October, the total sum advanced came to £2,393,617. NA, FO 371 / 7335 / C 1962: Telegram from Foreign Office to Akers-Douglas, 9 February 1922, and / C 1975: Letters from Treasury to Foreign Office, 9 February 1922 and from Waterlow to Franckenstein 10 February 1922; NA, FO 371 / 7336 / C 2347: Letter from Beneš to Curzon, 13 February 1922; AdR, 01 / 9, Ges. London, Telegramme 1920–1923, Karton 18, "III Hinaus 1922": Telegram from Franckenstein to Foreign Ministry, 7 February 1922.

77. AdR, 01 / 9, Ges. London, Telegramme 1920–1923, Karton 18, "III Hinaus 1922": Telegram from Franckenstein to Foreign Ministry, 8 February 1922.

78. The French eventually refused their advance against the Gobelins because they considered them not sufficiently valuable. NA, FO 371 / 7337 / C 7445: Letter from Austrian Foreign Minister to French legation enclosed with letter from Akers-Douglas to Curzon, 19 May 1922.

79. NA, FO 371 / 7335 / C 1950: Letter from Treasury to Curzon, 9 February 1922; LNA, Documents du Comité Financier, vol. V., A.143 (LNA 1302 A129–A169, January–May 1922): Letter from Beneš to the President of the League Council, 17 February 1922, and Agenda of Meeting, 6th Session, 23 February 1922.

80. LNA, 1151 Autriche II Février 1922, pp. 71–75: *Extrait des procès-verbaux de la 6ème session du comité financier, 2ème séance, tenue à Londres, le 24 février à 10 et 16 h.*; LNA, Documents du Comité Financier, vol. V., A.146 (LNA 1302 A129–A169, January–May 1922): Letter from Ador to Franckenstein, 23 February 1922; AdR, 01 / 9, Ges. London, Karton 101, Finanzsachen 1920–1923, "Rekonstruktion 1922": Telegram from Franckenstein to Chancellery, 24 February 1922; AdR, 01 / 9, Ges. London, Telegramme 1920–1923, Karton 18, "III Hinaus 1922": Telegram from Franckenstein to Foreign Ministry, 25 February 1922, and "III Herein 1922": Telegram from Foreign Ministry to Franckenstein, 25 February 1922.

81. LNA, 1151 Autriche II Février 1922, pp. 95–102 P.V. 6 (Procès-verbaux de la 6ième session du CF): *Comité financier 6ème session, Londres, février–mars 1922. 6ème séance, 1. mars 1922 à 11 h. et 3 h.30.*; LNA, Documents du Comité Financier, vol. V., A.151 (LNA 1302 A129–A169, January–May 1922): Letter from Ador to Grimm, 28 February 1922; AdR, 01 / 9, Ges. London, Telegramme 1920–1923, Karton 18, "III Hinaus 1922": Telegram from Franckenstein to Aussenamt, 1 March 1922.

82. "Die Rede des Bundeskanzlers," *RP,* 4 March 1922, pp. 1–2. The Socialist *Arbeiterzeitung* agreed that the foreign exchange should be used to stabilize the

currency and balance the budget. "Finanzpläne," *AZ*, 4 March 1922, p. 1; Ludwig Mises, "Inflation und Geldknappheit.—Gegen eine weitere Verwendung der Notenpresse," *NFP*, 11 March 1922, p. 2.

83. NA, FO 371/7336/C 3175: Telegram from Akers-Douglas to Foreign Office, 3 March 1922, and/C 3735: Letter from Akers-Douglas to Curzon, 10 March 1922, as well as/C 4058: Telegram from Young to Blackett, 10 March 1922.

84. Chancellor Schober had increasingly faced political difficulties after signing the Lana agreement with Czechoslovakia in December 1921, and although the Pan-Germans had remained in his coalition, they refused to cooperate with him, so that his parliamentary majority had melted down to three votes. Not least because of this continued political crisis, no measures to check the issue of paper money or balance the budget were taken.

85. Young himself commented "the political heavens will be rent with outcries against foreign intervention, which is unfortunately the thing that every non-political Austrian is praying for." NA, FO 371/7336/C 4121: Letter from Young to Treasury, 15 March 1922, and letter from Akers-Douglas to Curzon, 20 March 1922.

86. NA, FO 371/7336/C 3970: Telegram from Akers-Douglas to Foreign Office, 16 March 1922.

87. LNA, S 108, Sir Arthur Salter's Private Papers, Austria No. 5: Letter from Nixon to Loveday, 12 July 1921.

88. LNA, S 108, Sir Arthur Salter's Private Papers, Austria No. 5: Letter from Nixon to Blackett, 11 July 1921.

89. NA, T 160/58/2073/6, "Austrian Reconstruction": Letter from Norman to Balfour, 15 July 1921.

90. LNA, S 108, Sir Arthur Salter's Private Papers, Austria No. 5: Letter from Nixon to Avenol, 11 July 1921.

91. AdR, Finanzen, Dpt. 17/Frieden, Karton 84, "Englisch-amerik. Kreditverhandlungen in London": Letter from Norman to Goode, 2 March 1922 (also in NA, T 160/58/2073/8, "Austrian Reconstruction").

92. JPM, ARC 1221 (35), Morgan Bank European papers, "Austrian bonds, 1919–1926": Telegram from Morgan Grenfell to J. P. Morgan, 21 March 1922; AdR, 01/9, Ges. London, Telegramme 1920–1923, Karton 18, "III Herein 1922": Foreign Ministry to Franckenstein, 31 March 1922.

93. AdR, 01/9, Ges. London, Telegramme 1920–1923, Karton 18, "III Hinaus 1922": Telegram from Franckenstein to Foreign Ministry, 4 April 1922; JPM, ARC 1221 (35), Morgan Bank European papers "Austrian bonds, 1919–1926": Telegram from Morgan Grenfell to J. P. Morgan, 4 April 1922.

94. As quoted by Nicole Piétri, "La reconstruction économique et financière de l'Autriche par la Société des Nations (1921–1926)" (doctoral thesis, Université de Paris I, 1981, p. 237); DNB, Norman to Vissering, 12 October 1921, in Internationale Besprekingen 2, Doss. 16.

95. Promising negotiations for a Czech loan issued by Baring Brothers and Rothschild's and endorsed by the Chancellor of the Exchequer, Sir Robert Horne, also commenced in January 1922. The £10 million loan was delayed because the banks were dissatisfied with the securities offered, demanding a specific authorization from parliament, which the Czechs felt humiliating. Finally, a solution was found by appointing the League of Nations as arbitrator in case of future disputes with bondholders. Anne Orde, "Baring Brothers, the Bank of England, the British Government and the Czechoslovak State Loan of 1922," *English Historical Review* 106, no. 418 (1991): 27–40; and Louis W. Pauly, "The League of Nations and the Foreshadowing of the International Monetary Fund," International Finance Section, Department of Economics, Princeton University, 1999; NA, FO 371 / 7335 / C 74: Letter from Geddes to Curzon, 22 December 1922; C 640: Letter from Hardinge to Curzon, 11 January 1922; and C 466: Letter from Saint-Aulaire to Curzon, 8 January 1922; AdR, 1 Ges. London Polit. Berichte 1920–1923 / 157 / P: Letter from Franckenstein, 23 December 1921; AdR, 01 / 9, Ges. London, Telegramme 1920– 1923, Karton 18, "Hinaus 1921": Telegrams from Franckenstein, 23 December 1921 and 30 November 1921, from Kunz to Foreign Ministry, 5 January 1922, and from Franckenstein to Foreign Ministry, 13 January 1922; JPM, ARC 1214 (16), Vincent P. Carosso Papers, "Morgan & Co.—Foreign Loans, Austria. File 2": Letter from Grenfell to Franckenstein, 9 December 1921; JPM, ARC 1221 (35), Morgan Bank European papers, "Austrian Bonds, 1919–1926": Telegrams from Morgan Grenfell to J. P. Morgan, 5 and 9 January 1922, and from Morgan Harjes to J. P. Morgan, 10 and 12 January 1922. See also Stephen A. Schuker, "American Policy towards Debts and Reconstruction at Genoa, 1922," in *Genoa, Rapallo, and European Reconstruction in 1922*, ed. Carole Fink, Axel Frohn, and Jürgen Heideking (Cambridge, 1991), pp. 95–130; and Kathleen Burk, *Morgan Grenfell, 1838–1988* (Oxford, 1989), p. 140.

96. AdR, 01 / 9, Ges. London, Telegramme 1920–1923, Karton 18, "III Hinaus 1922": Telegram from Franckenstein to Foreign Ministry, 6 April 1922; AdR, Finanzen, Dpt. 17 / Frieden, Karton 84, "Englisch-amerik. Kreditverhandlungen in London": Morgan Grenfell to Franckenstein, 7 April 1922; JPM, ARC 1221 (35), Morgan Bank European papers, "Austrian Bonds, 1919–1926": Telegram from Morgan Grenfell to J. P. Morgan, 7 April 1922. See also *Papers Relating to the Foreign Relations of the United States, 1922*, vol. 1 (Washington, DC, 1938), pp. 617–618.

97. NA, FO 371 / 7337 / C 4699: Telegram from Akers-Douglas to Foreign Office, 29 March 1922, and / C 6079: Letter from McFadyean to Waley, 19 April 1922; LNA, S 106, Sir Arthur Salter's Private Papers, Austria no. 3, "Austria and Genoa": Memo by van Walré de Bordes, *The Austria Scheme and Genoa*, 31 March 1922.

98. Carole Fink, *The Genoa Conference: European Diplomacy, 1921–1922* (Syracuse, NY, 1993).

99. NA, FO 371 / 7337 / C 6079: *Austria: Suspension of Liens in Respect of Reparations and Relief Credits*, Report enclosed with letter from Wigram to Barber, 26 April 1922. The failure of the Genoa conference to advance the reconstruction of Austria might have been due to the fact that Eastern European countries felt alienated after being excluded from discussions on currency and exchange.

100. NA, FO 371 / 7337 / C 6079 and T 160 / 58 / 2073 / 8: Blackett, *Austrian Reconstruction*, 23 April 1922. In fact, Blackett thought it best to wipe out all claims for reparations from Austria-Hungary and all liberation bonds.

101. The League of Nations did not partake in the conference but had representatives in town. LNA, S 145, Brussels 1920, "Reports on the Situation in Genoa": *Extract of the Minutes of the Meeting of the League Representatives at Genoa, held on 27th April 1922,* and letter from Nixon to Drummond, 24 April 1922, as well as *Resolutions and Report of the Financial Commission of the Conference.* In his memoirs, Schüller wrote: "Wir fuhren in Extrazügen nach Genua, hatten nichts zu tun, besichtigten die schöne Stadt und ihre Paläste. Abends spielte Schober und ich tanzte mit der schönen Frau des Hoteliers." Nautz, *Unterhändler des Vertrauens,* p. 126.

102. NA, FO 371 / 7337 / C 6760: Letter from Akers-Douglas to Curzon, 8 May 1922.

103. Morgan, Grenfell had wanted to use Rosenberg to investigate on their behalf in Vienna, but Norman had insisted Rosenberg be appointed Austrian negotiator so as to "eliminate" Goode following his misrepresentations in New York. JPM, ARC 1214 (16), Vincent P. Carosso Papers, "Morgan & Co.—Foreign Loans, Austria. File 2": Letter from Morgan Grenfell to J. P. Morgan, 11 April 1922. At the Foreign Office they noted that "This I suppose is the end of Sir W. Goode" and that "Sire W. Goode hanged himself when he went to the U.S." NA, FO 371 / 7337 / C 5934; AdR, Finanzen, Dpt. 17 / Frieden, Karton 84, "Englisch-amerik. Kreditverhandlungen in London": Telegram from Franckenstein to Foreign Ministry, 24 April 1922, and letter from Morgan Grenfell to Franckenstein, 12 April 1922; AdR, 01 / 9, Ges. London, Telegramme 1920–1923, Karton 18, "III Herein 1922": Foreign Ministry to Franckenstein, 6 May 1922.

104. AdR, 01 / 9, Ges. London, Telegramme 1920–1923, Karton 18, "III Hinaus 1922": Telegram from Rosenberg to Foreign Ministry, 11 May 1922; AdR, Finanzen, Dpt. 17 / Frieden, Karton 84, "Englisch-amerik. Kreditverhandlungen in London": Letter from Patzauer, 11 May 1922 and 16 May 1922.

105. JPM, ARC 1221 (35), Morgan Bank European papers, "Austrian bonds, 1919–1926": Letter from Lamont to Harjes, 17 May 1922.

106. JPM, ARC 1214 (16), Vincent P. Carosso Papers, "Morgan & Co.—Foreign Loans, Austria. File 3": Murrow to Fosdick, 15 May 1922. Lamont himself had voiced similar views, writing earlier to London partners that "over here we have an earnest desire to be of assistance in it simply because proposed operation or

something similar seems to us necessary part of the general settlement which we all want to see, and which we therefore want to do." JPM, ARC 1221 (35), Morgan Bank European papers, "Austrian bonds, 1919–1926": Telegram from Thomas Lamont to Morgan Grenfell, 4 April 1922.

107. JPM, ARC 1221 (35), Morgan Bank European papers, "Austrian bonds, 1919–1926": Letter from Lamont to Harjes, 17 May 1922 and from Whigham to Harjes, 1 June 1922; AdR, 01 / 9, Ges. London, Telegramme 1920–1923, Karton 18, "III Hinaus 1922": Telegrams from Franckenstein to Foreign Ministry, 31 May 1922 and 3 June 1922; AdR, Finanzen, Dpt. 17 / Frieden, Karton 84, "Englisch-amerik. Kreditverhandlungen in London": Letter from Franckenstein to Foreign Ministry, 3 June 1922; RAL, XI / III / 189, "Special Correspondence re Austria (Loan)": Letter from Grenfell to N. M. Rothschild, 31 May 1922; NA, T 160 / 58 / 2073 / 8, "Austrian Reconstruction": Communication from Akers-Douglas to Balfour, 9 June 1922.

108. AdR, Finanzen, Dpt. 17 / Frieden, Karton 84, "Englisch-amerik. Kreditverhandlungen in London": Minutes of Ministerrat, 8 June 1922.

109. "Die Kreditfrage," *RP*, 9 June 1922, p. 2; "Verhandlungen mit der Morgan-Gruppe," *Deutsches Volksblatt*, 9 June 1922, p. 1; "Die Verhandlungen über die Amerikanischen Kredite," *NFP*, 9 June 1922, p. 5.

110. AdR, Finanzen, Dpt. 17 / Frieden, Karton 84, "Englisch-amerik. Kreditverhandlungen in London": *Minutes of Meetings Held on 13. and 14. 6.1922*, and *Minutes of Meeting Held on 16.6.1922*, as well as *Minutes of Meeting Held on 17.6.1922*, and further *Minutes of Meeting Held on 21.6.1922*, as well as *Minutes of Meeting Held on 22.6.1922*, and *Minutes of Meeting Held on 24.6.1922*. G. M. Young, according to the minutes, was mostly silent during the meetings. During his previous stay in Vienna, he had been treated by Sigmund Freud for a stutter. See letters from Ernest Jones to Sigmund Freud, 3 February 1921, and from Freud to Jones, 28 January 1921 and 7 February 1921, published in Ernest Jones and R. Andrew Paskauskas, *The Complete Correspondence of Sigmund Freud and Ernest Jones, 1908–1939* (Cambridge MA, 1993), pp. 405–412.

111. RAL, XI / III / / 189, "Special Correspondence re Austria (Loan)": Letter and memorandum from Young to Whigham, 23 June 1922; NA, T 160 / 58 / 2073 / 8, "Austrian Reconstruction": Telegram from Akers-Douglas to Foreign Office, 25 June 1922; for memorandum see also NA, FO 371 / 7338 / C 9482.

112. RAL, XI / III / 189, "Special Correspondence re Austria (Loan)": Letter from Young to Whigham, 15 June 1922.

113. RAL, XI / III / 189, "Special Correspondence re Austria (Loan)": Letter from Young to Whigham, 23 June 1922.

114. JPM, ARC 1214 (16), Vincent P. Carosso Papers, Morgan & Co.—Foreign Loans, Austria. File 2: Letter from Morgan Grenfell to J. P. Morgan, 7 July 1922, and from Morgan Grenfell to Franckenstein, 8 July 1922; AdR, NPA, 286 Liasse Oesterreich 1921–1922 8 / IV / 216, "Liasse Oesterreich 1921–1922": Telegram from

· Franckenstein to Foreign Ministry, 8 July 1922; AdR, 01/9, Ges. London, Telegramme 1920–1923, Karton 18, "III Hinaus 1922": Telegram from Franckenstein to Foreign Ministry, 8 July 1922; RAL, XI/III/189, "Special Correspondence re Austria (Loan)": Letters from Whigham to N. M. Rothschild, 3 and 8 July 1922.

115. NA, T 160/58/2073/8, "Austrian Reconstruction": Note by Blackett, 5 July 1922, and letter from Blackett to MacFadyean, 5 July 1922.

116. AdR, 1 Ges. London Polit. Berichte 1920–1923/325/P.: Letter from Franckenstein to Foreign Ministry, 25 July 1922; AdR, NPA, 286 Liasse Oesterreich 1921–1922 8/IV: Telegram from Franckenstein to Wildner; AdR, 01/9, Ges. London, Telegramme 1920–1923, Karton 18, "III Hinaus 1922": Telegram from Franckenstein to Foreign Ministry, 24 July 1922; NA, FO 371/7338/C 10080: Memo from Vansittart for Crowe, 12 July 1922, as well as/C 10304: Telegrams from Keeling to Foreign Office, 18 July 1922, and from Foreign Office to Akers-Douglas, 22 July 1922.

117. NA, T 160/58/2073/8, "Austrian Reconstruction": Letter from MacFadyean to Waley, 29 May 1922; NA, FO 371/7337/C 6548: Letters from Treasury to Foreign Office, 3 May 1922, and from Waley to Lampson, 3 May 1922. The French ambassador in London suggested in April that the Reparations Commission be asked to consent to the raising of liens on Austrian assets for twenty years and the Little Entente states be outvoted by Italy, France and Great Britain, but the Treasury favored a unanimous decision and so the Foreign Office had replied that it wanted to await the outcome of negotiations taking place at Genoa.

118. The Reparations Commission consisted of a British, Italian, French, and Belgian member. The Belgian member was largely under French control. The Chair was French and in that capacity had a casting vote. NA, T 160/58/2073/8, "Austrian Reconstruction": Letters from Wiley to McFadyean, 31 May 1922, and from McFadyean to Blackett, 26 and 30 June 1922, as well as communications from Blackett to Under Secretary of State, 31 May 1922, and from Akers-Douglas to Balfour, 9 June 1922; NA, FO 371/7337/C 7977: Letter from Lampson to Hardinge, 7 June 1922.

119. NA, FO 371/7338/C 9866: Communication from Blackett to Foreign Office, 11 July 1922.

120. AdR, 01/1, NPA, 287/632, "Liasse Oesterreich 8/IV Sek Schmid Fol. 523–733": Letter from Schüller to Vienna, 4 August 1922.

121. AdR, 01/1, NPA, 287/629, "Liasse Oesterreich 8/IV Sek Schmid Fol. 523–733": Minutes of a meeting held on 3 August 1922, and letter from Franckenstein to Lloyd George, 7 August 1922, from Franckenstein to Foreign Minister, 8 August 1922, as well as telegram from Franckenstein to Foreign Minister, 9 August 1922; AdR, NPA, 286 Liasse Oesterreich 1921–1922 8/IV, "Liasse Oesterreich 1921–1922": Telegram from Franckenstein, 7 August 1922, and telegram from Franckenstein and Schüller to Wildner, 11 August 1922; AdR, 01/9, Ges. London,

Telegramme 1920–1923, Karton 18, "III Hinaus 1922": Telegram from Francken-stein to Foreign Ministry, 3 August 1922; NA, FO 371/7338/C 11106: Note by Lampson, 3 August 1922, and/C 11182: Letter from Grigg to Franckenstein, 11 August 1922.

122. During the conference, the French demanded the appropriation of German property and capital on the left bank of the Rhine. Germany had been granted a six-month moratorium on reparations payments following the collapse of its cur-rency. The British rejected the French demands and the French refused granting a moratorium to Germany. NA, FO 371/7339/C 11706: Extract of I.C.P. 253, *British Secretary's Notes of an Allied Conference held at 10 Downing Street, S.W., on Monday, 14th August, 1922, at 5 P.M.*

123. Avenol, who was present at the meeting, wrote to Salter: "Pourquoi nous demande-t-on de nous occuper de l'Autriche? Parce que l'on n'avait aucune autre idée et qu'il fallait clore." LNA, S 106, Sir Arthur Salter's Private Papers, Austria No. 3, "Austria—Memoranda etc.": Letter from Avenol to Salter, 18 August 1922; AdR, NPA, 286 Liasse Oesterreich 1921–1922 8/IV/309, "Liasse Oesterreich 1921–1922": Letter from Eichhoff to Foreign Ministry, 5 September 1922.

124. AdR, 67/81566/22, "Schreiben Lloyd Georges betreffend Ablehnung der Kredite an Oesterreich": Letter from Llyod George to Franckenstein, 15 August 1922.

125. The statement that given the right conditions governmental guarantees might be considered was not meant as a sign of encouragement but due to a For-eign Office suggestion to have the referral to the League look less "absurd." NA, T 160/64/2073/021, "Austrian Reconstruction": Note from Niemeyer to Blackett, 2 September 1922; AdR, NPA, 286 Liasse Oesterreich 1921–1922 8/IV, "Liasse Oesterreich 1921–1922": Letter from Franckenstein to Foreign Ministry, 15 August 1922.

126. AdR, NPA, 286 Liasse Oesterreich 1921–1922 8/IV, "Liasse Oesterreich 1921–1922": Telegram from Franckenstein and Schüller to Wildner, 15 August 1922.

127. NA, T 160/58/2073/8, "Austrian Reconstruction": Letter from Akers-Douglas to Curzon, 17 August 1922.

128. NA, T 160/58/2073/8, "Austrian Reconstruction": Letter from Akers-Douglas to Curzon, 17 August 1922.

129. AdR, NPA, 286 Liasse Oesterreich 1921–1922 8/IV, "Liasse Oesterreich 1921–1922": Fernspruch from Foreign Ministry to the Austrian ambassadors in Paris, London, Berlin, and Rome, 19 August 1922; AdR, 01/9, Ges. London, Tele-gramme 1920–1923, Karton 18, "III Herein 1922": Telegram from Foreign Ministry to Franckenstein, 19 August 1922.

130. AdR, 01/1, Karton 408: Wildner, *Aufzeichnung über die Reise des Bundes-kanzlers Dr. Seipel nach Prag, Berlin und Verona. 20. bis 27. August 1922.*

131. To help Austria, Beneš agreed to advance up to 175 billion Austrian crowns within a week. NA, FO 371/7339/C 12182: Letter from Clark to Curzon, 22 August 1922, and/C 11946: Telegram from Clerk to Foreign Office, 22 August 1922.

132. AdR, 01/1, Karton 408: Wildner, *Aufzeichnung über die Reise des Bundeskanzlers Dr. Seipel nach Prag, Berlin und Verona. 20. bis 27. August 1922*; NA, FO 371/7339/C 11981: Telegram from Lord D'Abernon to Foreign Office, 22 August 1922.

133. According to Schüller's memoirs, he was called to attend the meeting in Verona from his vacation at Tegernsee in Bavaria. He claims to have drafted the scheme for a customs and monetary union on the night-train from Munich to Verona. He then proceeded to Rome to begin negotiations. See Nautz, *Unterhändler des Vertrauens*, pp. 127–128; AdR, 01/1, Karton 408, Wildner, *Aufzeichnung über die Reise des Bundeskanzlers Dr. Seipel nach Prag, Berlin und Verona. 20. bis 27. August 1922*; NA, FO 371/7339/C 12115: Telegram from Kennard, 26 August 1922.

134. Schüller says there was no wily intention behind Seipel's trips and that the Austrian government was simply doing what it felt was necessary, as it did not think the League would produce any results. However, they then found the League scheme to be no worse than their own. Nautz, *Unterhändler des Vertrauens*, pp. 129–130. In his speech before the League Council on September 6, Seipel said retrospectively: "The visit had, however, I frankly admit, yet another object. The Austrian people, rather than perish in isolation, will do everything in their power to make a last effort to break the chains which are oppressing and strangling them. It is for the League of Nations to see that this effort does not endanger the peace of the world or our relations with our neighbours." *League of Nations—Official Journal*, November 1922, p. 1449; AdR, NPA, 286 Liasse Oesterreich 1921–1922 8/IV/272–3,"Liasse Oesterreich 1921–1922": Letter from Grünberger to Austrian ambassadors in Paris, London, Rome, Berlin, Prague, Belgrade, and Budapest, 28 August 1922.

135. NA, FO 371/7340/C 12894: Letter from Schanzer to Lloyd George, 29 August 1922.

136. LNA, S 106, Sir Arthur Salter's Private Papers, Austria No. 3, "Austria and Genoa": Memo by van Walré de Bordes, *The Austria Scheme and Genoa*, 31 March 1922.

137. LNA, S 59, M. de Bordes Files, Box 6, Austria 1922–1926, "Various Papers September 1922 & 1921": *Le Triple aspect du problème autrichien*; LNA, S 108, Sir Arthur Salter's Private Papers, Austria No. 5, "Austria—League of Nations' scheme for the financial Reconstruction of Austria": Memorandum by van Walré de Bordes, 2 August 1922.

138. According to the memoires of Jean Monnet, Balfour and Bourgeois, the British and French Council members, decided in August that the problem needed to be approached by politicians and tackled successfully. Monnet, *Mémoire* (Paris,

1976), pp. 107–111. Arthur Salter also claimed that the fact that the Council included first rank statesmen allowed the League to save Austria, since by the virtue of their national positions, they were able to assure acceptance of an agreed upon policy in their respective capitals. Salter, *Memoirs of a Public Servant* (London, 1961), p. 177; LNA, C.580.1922 in LNA, 1154 Autriche, Septembre 1922: Note from Secretary General to Council, 28 August 1922; LNA, Documents du Comité Financier, vol. VI., A.191 (LNA 1303 A170–A215, Juin–Dec 1922): Speech by the President of the Council, 31 August 1922; *League of Nations—Official Journal,* November 1922, pp. 1443–1444; NA, FO 371/7340/C 12402: Telegram from Balfour to Secretariat of Cabinet, 31 August 1922.

139. Salter, *Memoirs of a Public Servant,* p. 176.

140. Otto Niemeyer tried to convince the Chancellor of the Exchequer not to send a Treasury representative despite Balfour's appeal. According to Niemeyer, Austria would be united either with Italy or, under French auspices, with Czechoslovakia. Thus the whole question was more political than financial and the Financial Committee would simply state that nothing could be done without governmental guarantees. As we shall see, Austrian reconstruction would preoccupy his time for many years, and he might have wished he had been right. NA, T 160/64/2073/021, "Austrian Reconstruction": Note from Niemeyer to Blackett, 2 September 1922, and note from Niemeyer for the Chancellor of the Exchequer, 31 August 1922; NA, FO 371/7340/C 12894: Note by Lampson, 11 September 1922; NA, FO 371/7339/C 12214: Telegram from Balfour to Foreign Office, 30 August 1922, as well as telegrams from Foreign Office to Akers-Douglas, and to Lord Balfour, both 1 September 1922.

141. Before his departure, British envoy Akers-Douglas noted, the Chancellor had seemed "very pleased that the Austrian question loomed so large in the proceeding of the League of Nations and attributed this to his recent journey, particularly to his visits to Czecho-Slovakia and Verona which had caused wholesome fright among Austria's neighbours." NA, FO 371/7340/C 12982: Letter from Phillpotts to Akers-Douglas, 7 September 1922.

142. NA, FO 371/7340/C 13124: Letter from Akers-Douglas to Curzon, 19 September 1922.

143. LNA, C 36, Reconstruction financière de l'Autriche 1922–1925: "Mins: Aust. Comm. of Council (Sept) '22": *Procès-verbal provisoire de la première séance du Sous-Comité du Conseil tenue le vendredi 8 septembre 1922, à 17 h.30.* France was represented by Hanotaux, Italy by the Marquis Imperiali, Austria by Foreign Minister Grünberger, and Czechoslovakia by Prime Minister Beneš.

144. LNA, document du Comité Financier, vol. VI., A.194: *Note on the Past Activities of the Financial Committee Regarding the Reconstruction of Austria, and on Certain Recent Developments in That Question,* 2 September 1922, and A.198: *Report on the Economic & Financial Conditions in Austria,* 2 September 1922.

145. Pierre Quesnay wrote a memo for Salter on the Austrian problem that outlined the necessary measures for a solution, namely a plan of reform and control and a plan to then obtain the necessary credits. Political guarantees would be necessary for the future of Austria as well as financial guarantees for the loan in form of a control commission entitled to withhold loan funds if reforms were not implemented. LNA, S 106, Sir Arthur Salter's Private Papers, Austria No. 3: *Position du problème autrichien by Pierre Quesnay*, 13 September 1922; LNA, 1154 Autriche Septembre 1922, E.F.S. / Finance / 9th Session / P.V.8: *8th Meeting Held on Friday, September 15th, 1922, at 10.30.A.M.*

146. The following members were present on the Financial Committee: Arai (Japan), Avenol (France), Bianchini (Italy), Blackett (United Kingdom), Janssen (Belgium), Pospíšil (Czechoslovakia), and Strakosch (South Africa). Austria was represented by Brauneis and Gruber and the League by Salter, Dufour, and van Walré de Bordes. The Italian Council member, Ferraris, who had recently been to Vienna, was invited to participate in the proceedings. Presented with estimates of revenue and expenditure by the Austrians, Avenol and Blackett decided to study the budgetary questions, while their Czech colleague, Pospíšil, would look into the question of securities, with Strakosch and the Belgian banker Albert Janssen dealing with the creation of the new central bank. LNA, 1154 Autriche, Septembre 1922: *Preliminary Meeting Held Saturday, September, 9th. at 10.30. A.M.*; LNA, Documents du Comité Financier, vol. VI., A.204 (LNA 1303 A170–A215, Juin–Dec 1922): *Comité Financier. 9ème session, septembre 1922. 1ère séance, samedi 9 septembre à 12h.*, and *Prévisions pour le budget autrichien établies d'après les chiffres actuels en couronne papier et en couronnes or au 9 septembre 1922*. See also LNA, S 106, Sir Arthur Salter's Private Papers, Austria No. 3: *Observations on the Budget in Gold Crowns Transmitted by the Austrian financial Experts to the financial Committee, on September 9th, 1922*; NA, FO 371 / 7340 / C 13332: Letter from Phillpotts to Akers-Douglas, 10 September 1922.

147. LNA, 1154 Autriche, September 1922, E.F.S. / Financial / 9th Session / P.V.5: *5th Meeting, Held Wednesday, 13th September at 10.30 A.M.*, and LNA, E.F.S. / Financial / 9th Session / P.V.6: *6th Meeting, Held Wednesday, 13th September at 4.30 P.M.*, as well as LNA, E.F.S. / Financial / 9th Session / P.V.9: *9th Meeting Held on Friday, September 15th, 1922, at 3.30 P.M.*

148. LNA, 1154 Autriche, September 1922: *3ème séance, tenue le lundi 11 septembre à 16 heures 15*, and *Procès-verbal de la 2ème séance du Sous-comité du Conseil tenue le lundi 11 septembre 1922 à 17 h. 30*, as well as *Fourth Meeting, Held on Tuesday, 12th September, at 10.30 A.M.*

149. On 13 September, the Ausschuss für Äusseres of the Austrian parliament discussed Chancellor Seipel's report on his journey to Geneva. Socialist Party leader Bauer wanted clarifications on the nature of the control, as foreign press reports indicated that it would be extensive. There was a heated debate. Seitz ac-

cused Seipel of wanting control in order to make his ruling easier, something Seipel denied. In the parliamentary debate that followed, Seipel's report was approved and even Bauer was not categorically against international financial control. AdR, 01 / 2, NPA, Karton 1, "Sitzungen des Ausschusses für Aeusseres": 13 September 1922; AdR, NPA, 286 Liasse Oesterreich 1921–1922 8 / IV / 321, "Liasse Oesterreich 1921–1922": Telegram from Seipel, 14 September 1922.

150. LNA, 1154 Autriche Septembre 1922, E.F.S. / Finance / 9th Session / P.V.7: *7th Meeting Held on Thursday, 14th September, at 3.30 P.M.*

151. NA, FO 371 / 7340 / C 13213: Enclosure I: *Austria—Memorandum by Sir Cecil Hurst,* 13 September 1922.

152. LNA, 1154 Autriche, Septembre 1922, E.F.S. / Finance / 9th Session / P.V.10: *10th Meeting Held on Saturday, September 16th, 1922, at 3.30 P.M.*

153. LNA, C 36, "Reconstruction financière de l'Autriche 1922–1925.": *Procès-verbal de la 5ème séance du Sous-Comité du Conseil chargé d'examiner la question de la reconstruction financière de l'Autriche, tenue le mardi, 19 septembre 1922, à 10.h.30.*

154. NA, FO 371 / 7341 / C 13399: Letter from Phillpotts to Akers-Douglas, 20 September 1922.

155. NA, FO 371 / 7340 / C 13213: Enclosure II, *Austria,* 15 September 1922.

156. NA, T 160 / 64 / 2073 / 021, "Austrian Reconstruction": Letter from Blackett to Niemeyer, 23 September 1922.

157. NA, FO 371 / 7341 / C 13547: Letter from Blackett to the Chancellor of the Exchequer, 25 September 1922, and / C 13429: Telegram from Balfour to Cabinet, 25 September 1922, as well as / C 13460: Telegram from Chancellor of the Exchequer to Balfour, 25 September 1922; NA, T 160 / 64 / 2073 / 021: Letter from Niemeyer to Wigram, 25 September 1922.

158. LNA, 1154 Autriche Septembre 1922, C. / S.C.A. / P.V.7: *Procès-verbal provisoire de la 7e séance du Sous-Comité du Conseil, chargé d'examiner la question de la reconstruction financière de l'Autriche (Mercredi 27 Septembre 1922, à 16 heures).*

159. NA, FO 371 / 7341 / C 13845: Letter from Phillpots to Akers-Douglas, 29 September 1922.

160. NA, FO 371 / 7341 / C 13845: Letter from Phillpots to Akers-Douglas, 30 September 1922.

161. J. A. Salter, "The Financial Reconstruction of Austria," *American Journal of International Law* 17, no. 1 (1923): 116–128.

162. This claim was already made by Frank Beyersdorf, "'Credit or Chaos?' The Austrian Stabilisation Programme of 1923 and the League of Nations," in *Internationalism Reconfigured: Transnational Ideas and Movements between the World Wars,* ed. Daniel Laqua (London, 2011), pp. 134–157.

163. William H. Wynne, *State Insolvency and Foreign Bondholders: Selected Case Histories of Governmental Foreign Bond Defaults and Debt Readjustments*

(New Haven, CT, 1951); Tunçer, *Sovereign Debt and International Financial Control.*

164. League of Nations, *The Restoration of Austria: Agreements Arranged by the League of Nations and Signed at Geneva on October 4th, 1922 with the Relevant Documents and Public Statements* (Geneva, 1922), p. 35.

165. Susan Pedersen, *Guardians: The League of Nations and the Crisis of Empire* (New York, 2015).

3. How to Kill a Hyperinflation

Epigraph: LNA, S 100 / Mr. Nixon, Box No. 4: Austria, L.o.N.'s financial Delegation in Vienna: *Letter from Pelt (Vienna) to Salter*, 23 October 1922. Adrianus Pelt (1892–1981) had worked as a journalist before joining the League of Nations in 1920. From 1922 to 1924 he was the League Secretariat's representative among Alfred Rudolph Zimmerman's staff in Vienna. He served as the Director of the United Nations European Office from 1952 to 1957. J. Bosmans, "Pelt, Adrianus (1892–1981)," in *Biografisch Woordenboek van Nederland*, vol. 2, ed. Johannes Charité and Ivo Schöffe ('s-Gravenhage, 1985).

1. The events began to unfold the previous week, when Jewish and German students at Vienna's College for International Trade got into a fight over the distribution of foreign relief funds. The representative of the German student union Deutschvölkische Studentenschaft felt insulted by a colleague from the Jewish student union Judäa, who called him a *Lausbub* (rascal). Despite an imminent apology, the German students insisted on the immediate resignation of the Jewish representative and of Judäa's chairman. Fearing an escalation of unrest, the College's Rector closed the campus for the remainder of the week. See Bruce F. Pauley, who quotes an internal document at the Central Zionist Archive, CZA, Z$_4$/2094 I: "Memorandum on the Background to Incident at the Social Welfare Office (Wirtschaftsstelle) of College of International Trade, 22 December 1922," and "Sperrung der Hochschule für Welthandel," *Neues 8 Uhr Blatt*, 27 November 1922. See also Bruce F. Pauley, *From Prejudice to Persecution: A History of Austrian Anti-Semitism* (Chapel Hill, NC, 1998), pp. 92–99; Bruce F. Pauley, "Political Antisemitism in Interwar Vienna," in *Jews, Antisemitism, and Culture*, ed. Ivar Oxaal, Michael Pollak, and Gerhard Botz (London, 1987), pp. 153–173.

2. Pauley, *From Prejudice to Persecution*, p. 94. Article 66 of the peace treaty of Saint-Germain outlawed discrimination among Austrians based on religion, and students from the successor states had to be treated equally with Austrians, too. Among the 12,000 students studying in Vienna in 1922, no fewer than 5,000 came from the successor states of the former empire. See "Der Zusammenbruch Oesterreichs und die Wiener Universität," *NFP*, Morgenblatt, 15 October 1922. See also "Demonstrationen der deutschvölkischen Studentenschaft in Wien. Sis-

tierung der Vorlesungen an der Technik und an der Hochschule für Welthandel,"
NFP, Morgenblatt, 28 November 1922; "Die deutsche Studentenschaft gegen ihre
Beschimpfung," *RP,* 28 November 1922.

3. "Die Vorgänge an den Wiener Hochschulen, "*NFP,* Morgenblatt, 29 November 1922; "Die Wiener Hochschulen geschlossen. Deutschnationale Demonstrationen," *Neues 8 Uhr Blatt,* 28 November 1922; "Wiederaufnahme des
Hochschulbetriebes," *NFP,* Morgenblatt, 30 November 1922.

4. The delegation's secretary, Adrianus Pelt, described the atmosphere
among the delegates as "excellent," and considered Avenol, Sarasin. and Strakosch as "without doubt the most constructive minds of the gathering. . . .
Pospisl [*sic*] and Niemeyer have also thrown themselves wholeheartedly into the
job and the only dissonant is Ferraris," who "makes the impression of being very
much annoyed that he is obliged to play this part, personally he is full of good-
will, but he seems to be bound by very stringent instructions of his government,
and when I count the many times I see him together with the Italian Ambassador he must be controlled constantly." LNA, S 100, Mr. Nixon, Box No. 4:
Austria, "L.o.N.'s financial Delegation in Vienna": Letter from Pelt to Salter, 23
October 1922.

5. Heinrich Benedikt, *Geschichte der Republik Österreich* (Vienna, 1954),
p. 130. See also the identical text in Walter Goldinger and Dieter A. Binder, *Geschichte der Republik Österreich* (Vienna, 1992), p. 117; Charles A. Gulick, *Austria,
from Habsburg to Hitler,* vol. 1, *Labor's Workshop of Democracy* (Berkeley, CA,
1948). Anne Orde's excellent *British Policy and European Reconstruction after the
First World War* (Cambridge, 1990) does not mention the League delegation either.
Zara S. Steiner, *The Lights That Failed: European International History, 1919–1933*
(New York, 2005), p. 279, ascribes a central role to the Financial Committee of the
League of Nations in organizing the international loan for Austria but does not
provide any details on what its role entailed. F. L. Carsten, *The First Austrian
Republic 1918–1938: A Study Based on British and Austrian Documents* (Cam-
bridge 1986), pp. 50–52, mentions the delegation in passing, while Klaus Koch,
Walter Rauscher, Arnold Suppan, eds., *Aussenpolitische Dokumente der Republik
Österreich 1918–1938, Band 5: Unter der Finanzkontrolle des Völkerbundes: 7. No-
vember 1922 bis 15. Juni 1926* (Vienna, 2002) makes no reference to it. J. L. J. Bosmans, *De Nederlander Mr. A. R. Zimmerman als Commissaris-Generaal van de
Volkenbund in Oostenrijk 1922–1926* (Nijmegen, 1973), pp. 34–37, provides only a
short overview of the delegation's achievements, and Finance Minister Victor
Kienböck's *Das österreichische Sanierungswerk* (Stuttgart, 1925), pp. 22–31, only
credits the Delegation with a marginal role. Eduard März, *Austrian Banking and
Financial Policy: Credit-Anstalt at a Turning Point, 1913–1923* (New York, 1984),
pp. 499–505, also does not make much of the League delegation.

6. A good example is Klaus Berchtold, *1918–1933: Fünfzehn Jahre Verfassungskampf* (Vienna, 1998).

7. Karl Ausch, *Als die Banken fielen: Zur Soziologie der politischen Korruption* (Vienna, 1968), chapter 3, "Es begann in Genf," pp. 75–113.

8. Otto Bauer, *Die österreichische Revolution* (Vienna, 1923).

9. Victor Kienböck, *Das österreichische Sanierungswerk* (Stuttgart, 1925), esp. pp. 22–31.

10. LNA, S 106, Sir Arthur Salter's Private Papers, Austria No. 3, "Austria—Miscellaneous Papers": Note by Denis, 19 October 1922.

11. "Oesterreichisch-ungarische Bank. Notenumlauf 2453, Zunahme 176 Billionen Kronen," *NFP*, Morgenblatt, 15 October 1922. The increase in circulation was significantly lower than in September, and although 80 billion of the 176 billion crowns in new notes were printed for government expenditure, the other half were to satisfy private discounts (23 billion), cash withdrawals (23 billion), Kassenscheine (25 billion), and other passiva (23 billion).

12. *Reply of the Financial Committee to questions referred by the Austrian Committee of the Council*, 4 October 1922 (see Appendix C in this volume).

13. The loan was to be against the security of unused French and Italian advances, which, in fact, had only been given on paper. Only French delegate Avenol rightly argued at the time that the real value of circulation had declined so drastically that increases in notes did not only provide no danger, but were actually necessary. LNA, C 34, *La reconstruction financière de l'Autriche 1922–1922: Procès-verbal de la 2ème réunion tenue le 18 octobre 1922 à midi*; and *Procès-verbal de la 3ème réunion tenue le 18 octobre 1922 à 4h40, Hôtel Impérial, Vienne*.

14. "Die Erledigung des Kreditermächtigungsgesetztes im Nationalrat," *NFP*, Abendblatt, 20 October 1922.

15. "Die Erledigung des Kreditermächtigungsgesetztes im Nationalrat," *NFP*, Abendblatt, 18 November 1922. "Ein Goldkredit von 30 Millionen bei den Wiener Banken.—Beratung im Finanzministerium," *NFP*, 19 October 1922, erroneously argued that the Delegation was in favor of delaying the central bank's foundation and thus Vienna's banks could be released from their pledge.

16. In fact, the delegates stressed that getting the Vienna banks to lend to the government against Treasury Bills would prepare the ground for the guaranteed loan and be "a non-negligible effort [which would] make a great impression abroad," especially if the Treasury Bills were secured by the same revenues from tobacco and customs, with which it was planned to secure the guaranteed loan as well. LNA, C 34, Reconstruction financière de l'Autriche 1922–1922: *Procès-verbal de la 4ème réunion tenue le 18 octobre 1922 à 18"*; *Procès-verbal de la 5ème réunion tenue le 19 octobre 1922 à 5h, Hôtel Impérial, Vienne*; *Procès-verbal de la 8ème réunion tenue le samedi matin 21 octobre 1922 à 11h, Hôtel Impérial, Vienne*; *Procès-verbal de la 12ème réunion tenue le lundi matin, 9h:30, le 23 octobre, Hôtel Impérial, Vienne*.

17. LNA, C 34, Réconstruction financière de l'Autriche 1922–1922: *6ème séance de la délégation tenue le 20 octobre 1922 à 10h.45, Hôtel Imperial; Procès-*

verbal de la 12ème réunion tenue le lundi matin, 9h:30, le 23 octobre, Hôtel Impérial, Vienne.

18. LNA, C 34, Reconstruction financière de l'Autriche 1922–1922: *Procèsverbal de la 11ème réunion tenue 22 octobre 1922 à 9h.45 au Ministère des Finances,* and *Aide-Memoire* by Niemeyer, 23 October 1922. The Bills were to be secured on revenues from tobacco and customs and repayable from the first issue of the international loan. The banks initially proposed to provide only the originally pledged amount of 345.6 billion crowns and still demanded to be released from their pledge to finance part of the new central bank's capital. The press reported the agreement still needed to be discussed with the League Delegation. See also "Wien. 20. Oktober. Die Verhandlungen mit den Banken über die Gewährung eines Interimkredites," *NFP,* Morgenblatt, 21 October 1922, and "Wien. 23. Oktober. Eine Erweiterung der Interimskredite," *NFP,* 24 October 1922.

19. LNA, C 34, Reconstruction financière de l'Autriche 1922–1922: *Procèsverbal de la 4ème réunion tenue le 18 octobre 1922 à 18",* and 8 / 4 V: *Procès-verbal de la 5ème réunion tenue le 19 octobre 1922 à 5h, Hôtel Impérial, Vienne.*

20. LNA, C 34, Réconstruction financière de l'Autriche 1922–1922: *6ème séance de la délégation tenue le 20 octobre 1922 à 10h.45, Hôtel Impérial.* The reduction was recommended so as to make it easier to raise the funds entirely in Austria and eliminate the need for foreign capital, which would have made foreign banks shareholders of the new central bank and given them seats on its board.

21. LNA, S 106, Sir Arthur Salter's Private Papers, Austria No. 3, "Miscellaneous Correspondence and Memoranda": *Note by Mr. Niemeyer,* 26 October 1922.

22. LNA, S 100, Mr. Nixon, Box No. 4: Austria, "L.o.N.'s financial Delegation in Vienna": Letter from Pelt to Salter, 23 October 1922; LNA, C 34, Réconstruction financière de l'Autriche 1922–1922: *Procès-verbal de la 8ème réunion tenue le samedi matin 21 octobre 1922 à 11h, Hôtel Impérial, Vienne.* The government took umbrage with the role foreign banks were given on the central bank's board, the power of veto of board members, and felt most humiliated by the clause requiring the bank to hold its reserves abroad. A compromise was reached, which allowed for half of the bank's reserves to be kept in Austria, or all of the reserves if the entire capital was raised within Austria itself. This popular fear of foreign domination was echoed in the comments of Gustav Stolper upon the Protocols' publication. He argued that it was important that the central bank did not become an instrument of foreigners, and that capital and administration were Austrian, linking the potential intrusion of foreign capital with Austrian moral decay: "Ist die Herrschaft über Deutschösterreich erst einmal an unverantwortliche ausländische Finanzkräfte ausgeliefert, dann muss sich über dieses Land eine Atmosphäre bereiten, in der man nicht mehr leben kann. Dann kommt der Verfall der letzten moralischen Kräfte, dann wird der Dienst am Gemeinwesen, die Sorge um

das Gemeinwohl zur Farce. Dann mag die Konjunktur der Geschäftemacher blühen, aber ein ganzes Volk bezahlt es mit seiner sittlichen Existenz." "Dr. G. St.: Die Genfer Protokolle," *ÖVW* 15, no. 2 (14 October 1922).

23. LNA, C 44, Réconstruction financière de l'Autriche 1922–1926, "Minutes of Sub-Committees": *Procès-verbal de la séance du Comité pour la Banque d'Émission tenue le 30 octobre 1922 à 31/2 h. Hôtel Impérial*; LNA, C 34, Réconstruction financière de l'Autriche 1922–1922: *20ème séance (vendredi) 27 octobre 1922, 4h. Hôtel Impérial.*

24. LNA, C 34, Réconstruction financière de l'Autriche 1922–1922: *Procès-verbal de la 8ème réunion tenue le samedi matin 21 octobre 1922 à 11h, Hôtel Impérial, Vienne.* Ségur wanted the minimum coverage changed from one-third to one-fifth, while Ferraris desired a limit of emissions if there was not to be a gold standard, but the other members did not agree.

25. LNA, C 34, Réconstruction financière de l'Autriche 1922–1922: *30ème séance, tenue le vendredi 3 novembre à 9 h.30.*, and *31ème séance tenue le vendredi 3 novembre à 11 h.*

26. LNA, C 34, Réconstruction financière de l'Autriche 1922–1922: *32ème séance, tenue le 3 novembre 1922, à 151/21 h., Hôtel Impérial; 36ème séance tenue le 6 novembre à 11 h., Hôtel Impérial; 37ème séance tenue le lundi 6 novembre 1922 à 51/2 heures, Hôtel Impérial.* An important last-minute revision was Strakosch's proposal to add Austria's provinces and communes to the government, which could not borrow from the bank without offering foreign exchange or commercial paper as security.

27. Janssen and Strakosch thought this would reduce Vienna banks' influence on the directorate. LNA, C 44, Réconstruction financière de l'Autriche 1922–1926, "Minutes of Sub-Committees": *Procès-verbal de la séance du Comité pour la Banque d'Émission tenue le 30 octobre 1922 à 31/2 h., Hôtel Impérial;* LNA, C 34, Réconstruction financière de l'Autriche 1922–1922: *Procès-verbal de la 12ème réunion tenue le lundi matin, 9h:30, le 23 octobre, Hôtel Impérial, Vienne;* and Strakosch's memos: *Bank of Issue* and *Treasury Bills*, both 23 October 1922; LNA, C 43, Réconstruction financière de l'Autriche 1923–1925, "Divers": Letter from Niemeyer to Blackett, 24 October 1922.

28. LNA, C 34, Réconstruction financière de l'Autriche 1922–1922: *Procès-verbal de la 23ème séance du 30 octobre à 17 heures.*

29. "Das Sanierungsprogramm der Regierung" and "Das grosse Finanzprogramm,—Defizit dieses Jahres 4,5 Billionen. Neue Einnahmen für die nächsten zwei Jahre von 3,8 Billionen," *NFP*, 20 October 1922. The program was leaked to the press by Chancellor Seipel himself, probably to weaken the position of the delegation, revealing his intentions and souring relations from the start.

30. LNA, C 34, Réconstruction financière de l'Autriche 1922–1922: *Procès-verbal de la 2ème réunion tenue le 18 octobre 1922 à midi.*

31. LNA, C 34, Réconstruction financière de l'Autriche 1922–1922: *6ème séance de la délégation tenue le 20 octobre 1922 à 10h.45, Hôtel Impérial.* Swiss delegate Sarasin thought the plan provided a good basis, though the Austrians had purposely omitted figures. His Italian colleague, Maggiorino Ferraris, concurred that with a stable crown, which would need artificial support, the plan would be a success. The plan was however strongly criticized by Walter Federn, "Das Finanzprogramm," *ÖVW* 15, no. 4 (28 October 1922), in which he deplored that once again the old measures to try to fool the public and the League were being employed by working with unreliable and false figures.

32. LNA, C 34, Réconstruction financière de l'Autriche 1922–1922: *7ème réunion tenue le 20 octobre 1922 à 16h.30, Hôtel Impérial.*

33. LNA, C 34, Réconstruction financière de l'Autriche 1922–1922: *Procèsverbal de la 4ème réunion tenue le 18 octobre 1922 à 18".*

34. LNA, C 34, Réconstruction financière de l'Autriche 1922–1922: Niemeyer, *Annexe 2* to *Procès-verbal de la 13ème réunion tenue le 23 octobre 1922 à 16h30, Hôtel Impérial.* The headings for expenditure were public debt, pensions, army, social welfare, and administration, as well as the contributions to provinces and communes and coverage of the losses of railways and other state enterprises. The headings for revenues were customs, consumption tax, direct taxes, and receipts from state monopolies and enterprises. Finally, figures were included of the approximate numbers of employees paid by the state and employed by the railways, army, police and general administration as well as the estimated cost of compensation and pension for retrenched officials.

35. "Eine Woche der Beratungen.—Der Einfluss der Vorgänge in England," *NFP,* Nachmittagsblatt, 23 October 1922, erroneously reported that negotiations were proceeding well and that the delegates proved elastic regarding the large figures proposed. The new plan received strong criticism in "Dr. G. St.: Das Reform- und Sanierungsprogramm," *ÖVW* 15, no. 5 (4 November 1922). Stolper called the new plan a disaster, unprofessional, and argued that it would not produce the desired effect but rather destroy the economy.

36. Paul Grünwald-Ehren, a Ministerialrat with the Ministry of Finance, had published calculations in the *Neue Freie Presse,* according to which prewar taxation in Austria had been as high as 35.32 gold crowns per capita in direct taxes, but those had been quite different times. Niemeyer thought that the maximum level of total taxation was 40 to 45 gold crowns per person. "Die Steuerbelastung in Oesterreich einst und jetzt," *NFP,* Morgenblatt, 22 October 1922, and "Die Steuerbelastung in Oesterreich einst und jetzt," *NFP,* Morgenblatt, 24 October 1922.

37. LNA, C 34, Réconstruction financière de l'Autriche 1922–1922: *19ème séance du vendredi le 27 octobre 1922 à 91/2, Hôtel Impérial.* Ferraris agreed that there was not enough will for radical reforms or savings and that Austrian reforms

appeared costly in pensions and indemnities, so he favored a maximal increase in taxation, but Avenol noted that since Swiss tax revenue had been a mere 43 francs per capita in 1921 and 54 francs in 1922, one could not hope for more than 50 francs per capita in Austria (about 45 gold crowns).

38. LNA, C 34, Réconstruction financière de l'Autriche 1922–1922: *19ème séance du vendredi le 27 octobre 1922 à 91/2, Hôtel Impérial;* "Abänderungen im Vorentwurfe des Sanierungsprogramms.—Mitteilungen des Bundeskanzlers im Sonderausschuss," *NFP,* 25 October 1922; "Die Beratungen über das Sanierungsprogramm," *NFP,* Nachmittagsblatt, 30 October 1922; "Abschluss der Vorverhandlungen über das Sanierungsprogramm. Einbringung der Regierungsvorlagen in der Samstagsitzung des Nationalrates," *NFP,* 31 October 1922.

39. LNA, C 34, Réconstruction financière de l'Autriche 1922–1922: *19ème séance du vendredi le 27 octobre 1922 à 91/2, Hôtel Impérial* ;and *Procès-verbal de la 22ème séance tenue le 30 octobre à 10 heures.*

40. At the same time, Austrians were told by Chancellor Seipel that a program would be presented on time, and the press even reported that negotiations with the delegation were completed. "Die Besprechungen mit den Völkerbunddelegierten," *NFP,* Nachmittagsblatt, 30 October 1922; "Abschluss der Vorverhandlungen über das Sanierungsprogramm. Einbringung der Regierungsvorlagen in der Samstagsitzung des Nationalrates," *NFP,* 31 October 1922.

41. Savings Commission President Max Wladimir Beck, who had been Austrian Prime Minister from 1906 to 1908 and now served as President of the Austrian Court of Audits, was the man charged by the government to develop and propose ways to achieve reductions in expenditure. Beck termed the Austrian plan a "heroic and considerable effort," but argued outright that, given strong Socialist opposition, two years were simply not enough to balance the budget. Transport Minister Franz Odehnal (Christian-Social party) admitted that the Austrian railways faced exaggerated expenses for materiel and personnel due to the empire's collapse, and that it did not charge enough for tickets from customers. But while he could gradually reduce personnel to 60,000 and even lay off 8,000 workers by year's end, there was nothing he could do to raise tariffs, which required a parliamentary decision. Commerce Minister Alfred Grünberger (Christian-Social party) suggested that he reduce the number of personnel at customs and borders and at the road administration, and privatize the statistics service. The delegates told Minister of Justice Leopold Waber (Pan-German) that the army had to be reduced to its smallest possible size and told Interior Minister Felix Frank (Pan-German) to provide the Delegation with plans on fiscal and administrative reforms in provinces and communes. LNA, C 34, Réconstruction financière de l'Autriche 1922–1922: *Procès-verbal de la 25ème séance tenue le 31 octobre à 15 heures.*

42. LNA, C 34, Réconstruction financière de l'Autriche 1922–1922: *Procès-verbal de la 26ème réunion, tenue le 1er novembre à midi, Hôtel Impérial.* Ferraris

agreed with Niemeyer that the plan was drafted hastily, but was in doubt whether they could demand a budget reduction to 350 million gold crowns without proposing ways to achieve this. It was thus better to accept a tax level of 80 gold crowns per head and a budget of almost 500 million. Even Strakosch was skeptical and feared that 350 million gold crowns might be too low.

43. AdR, 68 Finanzen, Völkerbundskreditaktion vom Jahre 1922: Letter from delegates to Seipel, *Aide Mèmoire: Stellungnahme zum zweiten Sanierungsprogramm der Regierung,* 2 November 1922; LNA, C 34, Réconstruction financière de l'Autriche 1922–1922: *27ème réunion, tenue le 1er novembre à 8 heures, Hôtel Impérial;* and *31eme séance tenue le vendredi 3 novembre à 11 h.* Moreover, the delegates were prepared to exclude the exact figures from the reform program and reform law itself, and make them part of a separate agreement with the League Delegation. Meanwhile, the *Neue Freie Presse* erroneously reported that negotiations with the League's delegates were making good progress due to a complete understanding on reducing the budget and a quick reduction of officials, and that the Socialists had promised to oppose but not delay passage of the program. "Die parlamentarische Beratung des Sanierungspgrogramms," *NFP,* 1 November 1922; "Die Beratungen der Völkerbunddelegierten," *NFP,* 2 November 1922.

44. LNA, C 34, Réconstruction financière de l'Autriche 1922–1922: *27ème réunion, tenue le 1er novembre à 8 heures, Hôtel Impérial.*

45. LNA, C 34, Réconstruction financière de l'Autriche 1922–1922: *Procès-verbal de la 2ème réunion tenue le 18 octobre 1922 à midi;* LNA, C 34, Réconstruction financière de l'Autriche 1922–1922: *20ème séance (vendredi) 27 octobre 1922, 4h., Hôtel Impérial.* British ambassador Akers-Douglas speculated that they might even demand Seipel's resignation in return for their vote. NA, FO 371/7342/C 14079: Telegram from Akers-Douglas to Foreign Office, 10 October 1922.

46. LNA, C 34, Réconstruction financière de l'Autriche 1922–1922: *Procès-verbal de la 24ème séance du 31 octobre à 9 h. 1/2 du matin.*

47. The delegation also wished it to state that no new laws could be introduced by parliament that were bound to detrimentally change expected revenues or expenses without the government's agreement. AdR, 68 Finanzen, Völkerbundskreditaktion vom Jahre 1922: Letter from delegates to Seipel, 2 November 1922.

48. LNA, S 100, Mr. Nixon, Box No. 4: "Austria, L.o.N.'s financial Delegation in Vienna": Communication from Pelt to van Walré de Bordes, 2 November 1922.

49. LNA, S 100, Mr. Nixon, Box No. 4: Austria, "L.o.N.'s financial Delegation in Vienna": Letter from van Walré de Bordes to Pelt, 1 November 1922.

50. NA, FO 371/7343/C 15230: Letter from Keeling to Curzon, 5 November 1922. This meeting is also discussed in Carsten, *The First Austrian Republic,* p. 52.

51. LNA, S 100, Mr. Nixon, Box No. 4: Austria, "L.o.N.'s financial Delegation in Vienna": Communication from Pelt to van Walré de Bordes, 2 November 1922.

Pelt noted that they had arrived at an impasse despite what he considered good-will on behalf of the Austrian government. LNA, C 34, Réconstruction financière de l'Autriche 1922–1922: *31ème séance tenue le vendredi 3 novembre à 11 h.*

52. *Bundesverfassungsgesetz vom 26. November 1922 über die Ausübung der ausserordentlichen Vollmachten, die der Bundesregierung gemäss dem Genfer Protokoll Nr. III vom 4. Oktober 1922 eingeräumt werden,* Bundesgesetzblatt für die Republik Österreich, 3 December 1922.

53. See Appendix C in this volume.

54. The *Neue Freie Presse* commented widely on the new bank statutes and welcomed the revisions to reduce the influence of private banks and the threat of the bank's foreign domination: "Der Economist.—Das Statut der Notenbank. Einstellung der Notenpresse in der nächsten Woche.—Mitteilungen von hervorragend informierter Seite," *NFP,* Morgenblatt, 5 November 1922; "Der Economist.—Das neue Bankstatut," *NFP,* Morgenblatt, 7 November 1922; "Das neue Bankstatut," *NFP,* Abendblatt, 7 November 1922.

55. LNA, C 34, Réconstruction financière de l'Autriche 1922–1922: *34ème séance, tenue le 3 novembre, 1922, à 21h;1/2, Hôtel Impérial.* The Socialists had formulated their official position on the Geneva Protocols one week before the League delegate's arrival at a party convention. Party president Karl Seitz had stressed that Austria stood at a turning point and did not need a foreign loan to be saved. Socialist Otto Bauer had spoken in favor of rejecting the League loan and compared the Socialist convention to a war council charged to discuss the means by which to defend the Republic against the imminent dangers of Seipel's authoritarianism. The assembled party delegates voted to oppose the ratification of the Geneva Protocols and to organize mass activities across Austria to "fight" the impending foreign domination, beginning with demonstrations, but keeping the alternative of violent means open for the future. "Sozialdemokratischer Parteitag," *NFP,* Abendblatt, 14 October 1922; "Vereinte Arbeit oder unfruchtbarer Streit. Die Rede Dr. Bauers auf dem sozialdemokratischen Parteitag," *NFP,* Morgenblatt, 15 October 1922.

56. "Negative Kritik.—Die Reden des Bundeskanzlers und des Abgeordneten Dannenberg," *NFP,* Morgenblatt, 7 November 1922.

57. LNA, C 44, Réconstruction financière de l'Autriche 1922–1926, Delegation Reports, Status of Work etc.: Letter from Pelt to Salter, 21 November 1922; LNA, C 34, Réconstruction financière de l'Autriche 1922–1922, 8/4 50: *50eme séance tenue le 18 Novembre 1922.*

58. The program foresaw the right to implement the customs tariffs of 1906, which could include the introduction of tariffs on food imports, a measure certain to harm consumers but in the interest of farmers. Similarly, the alcohol tax was ostensibly increased to fight alcoholism, but the one on wine produced in Aus-

tria had been lowered by one-third from the initial proposal to favor local wine producers.

59. The words of Dannenberg's speech illustrate the charged atmosphere that surrounded the debate: "In Wahrheit ist dieses Programm nur ein Feigenblatt für den Absolutismus *(Zustimmung bei den Sozialdemokraten),* der nur vergleichbar ist mit einer Aera, die es irgendeinmal in der Habsburgerzeit gegeben hat. Glauben Sie nicht, dass wir, wenn die Bureaukraten das in ein paar Wochen ersonnen haben, gesonnen sind, dazu einfach ja und amen zu sagen und uns mit irgendwelchen Drohungen mit denen der Bundeskanzler heute begonnen hat, irgendwie einschüchtern lassen werden, die Interessen zu vertreten, die die Regierung hätte vertreten sollen. Was da vorliegt, ist kein Finanzplan, das ist eine Spottgeburt bei der das Feuer fehlt *(Heiterkeit bei den Sozialdemokraten),* ist ein Machwerk, das entstanden ist aus bureaukratischem Dünkel und bureaukratischer Unwissenheit, aus agrarischem Hochmut, aus bürgerlicher Steuerscheu, aus Tücke gegen die Städte und gegen die Industrie und aus einem infernalischen Hass gegen die Arbeiter. *(Lebhafter Beifall bei den Sozialdemokraten.)* Wenn niemand sich in Oesterreich für die Entwicklung und die Zukunft der industrie, für das Schicksal der Städte einsetzten wird—die Arbeiter und Angestellten sind bereit, einzutreten in den Kampf für einen wirklichen Sanierungsplan für diese Republik." *(Stürmischer, anhaltender Beifall und Händeklatschen bei den Sozialdemokraten.)* "Gegen den Absolutismus des Ermächtigungsgesetzes," *NFP,* 7 November 1922, p. 7.

60. "Das Wiederaufbaugesetz im Nationalrat.—Fortsetzung der ersten Sitzung," *NFP,* Morgenblatt, 8 November 1922. Renner further attacked Seipel for turning to Austria's former enemies first, instead of discussing his plans in parliament, so that it ended up being drafted in favor of foreign and Austrian capitalists instead of the Austrian people!

61. "Nationalrat. Abschluss der ersten Lesung des Wiederaufbaugesetzes," *NFP,* Abendblatt, 8 November 1922; "Beginn der Verhandlungen über das Sanierungsprogramm im Finanzausschuss. Abschluss der ersten Lesung im Nationalrat," *NFP,* Morgenblatt, 9 November 1922; "Der Verlauf der Sitzung," *NFP,* Morgenblatt, 9 November 1922. The bank statutes were quickly accepted and returned to the Nationalrat for their second reading. They were ratified on 15 November. On the second day of the debate, Leopold Kunschak (Christian-Social) accused the Socialists of not doing their part and attacking the government instead of increasing the productivity of Austrian labor; he defended the empowerment law as necessary but not absolutist, and limited to the time it would take to raise money to pay back the international loan. Karl Seitz accused Seipel of selling Austria and Germany into bondage and slavery and promised to fight the planned introduction of the customs tariff of 1906, repeating the Socialist claim that 520 million gold crowns could have been found in Austria as well. The Socialists

declared that they would fight the reform program to prevent Austria from becoming a country of farmers and petty commerce.

62. Since no Kabinettsrat had been foreseen in the Geneva Protocols, Joost
Adriaan van Hamel, Director of the League Secretariat's Legal Section and later
the League's High Commissioner of Danzig, arrived in Vienna to confidentially
study the proposed solution. Van Hamel disliked the draft being negotiated by Socialists and Christian-Socials and noted that it failed to state that "full powers"
were being given to the government. The Socialists wanted the law to include only
measures with an immediate effect on expenditure, while the delegates suggested
limiting the measures to those that had a fiscal goal. LNA, C 34, Réconstruction
financière de l'Autriche 1922–1922: *42ème séance tenue le 13 novembre 1922 à 18
heures, Hôtel Impérial; 44ème séance tenue le 14 Novembre 1922 à 23.30; 45ème séance tenue le 15 Novembre 1922 à 17h, 45; 48ème séance tenue le 18 novembre à
10 h.15, Hôtel Impérial; 49ème séance tenue le 18 Novembre 1922 à 15 heures, Hôtel
Impérial.*

63. LNA, C 2, Réconstruction financière de l'Autriche 1922–1927, "re Récon-
struction Law,—Text etc.": Letter from delegates to Seipel, 20 November 1922;
LNA, C 18, Réconstruction financière de l'Autriche 1922–1928, "Stopping Bank-
Note Printing-Press": Letter from Avenol to Niemeyer, 20 November 1922; "Die
Gefahr einer Verzögerung der Hilfsaktion. Ein Schreiben der Völkerbunddele-
gierten an den Bundeskanzler," *NFP,* Morgenblatt, 21 November 1922.

64. "Die Verabschiedung der Wiederaufbaugesetze in den Ausschüssen," "Das
Wiederaufbaugesetz im Finanzausschusse," and "Sonderausschuss zur Beratung
der Genfer Konvention," all from *NFP,* Morgenblatt, 22 November 1922. Upon request of the opposition, the debate on the Ermächtigungsgesetz had been postponed to Wednesday to allow the Socialist Party council to discuss it beforehand.
Both parties publicly promised to pass the laws by the delegates' deadline, so that
the *Neue Freie Presse* prematurely declared the crisis over. "Fertigstellung des Finanzprogramms in dieser Woche: Ein wichtiges Schreiben der Finanzdelegierten
des Völkerbundes an die Regierung," *NFP,* Morgenblatt, 21 November 1922;
LNA, C 34, Réconstruction financière de l'Autriche 1922–1922: *51ème séance du
lundi, 20 Octobre [sic] 1922, 16 h.*

65. LNA, C 44, Réconstruction financière de l'Autriche 1922–1926, "Delegation Reports, Status of Work etc.": Letter from Pelt to Salter, 21 November 1922.

66. LNA, C 34, Réconstruction financière de l'Autriche 1922–1922: *52ème
séance tenue chez le Dr. Seitz. Président du parti social-démocratie, le 21 novembre
à 4 h. 1/2.* The other Socialists present were Renner and Bauer. The only delegates
present were Avenol and Ferraris.

67. The *Neue Freie Presse* quite rightly assumed that the slow proceedings were
simply meant to give the parties enough time to find a compromise on the Ermächtigungsgesetz, and knew to report that Chancellor Seipel and Socialist Party

President Seitz had recently met to discuss possible solutions. "Die Ueberwachung der Durchführung der Vollmachten," *NFP*, 16 November 1922; "Die Verhandlungen über das Sanierungsprogramm," *NFP*, Morgenblatt, 14 November 1922; "Das Wiederaufbaugesetz," *NFP*, Morgenblatt, 14 November 1922.

68. LNA, C 44, Reconstruction financière de l'Autriche 1922–1926, "Delegation Reports, Status of Work, etc.": Letter from Pelt to Salter, 21 November 1922. The *Neue Freie Presse* reported on a meeting between Avenol, Ferraris, Seitz, and Bauer, but could only speculate about its essence, which it believed was to convince the opposition of the necessity to compromise and the dire consequences for Austria if it did not. "Die Konferenz zwischen den Finanzdelegierten und Führern der Sozialdemokraten. Anlässlich der bevorstehenden Erledigung des Finanzprogramms," *NFP*, Morgenblatt, 22 November 1922, as well as "Die Verabschiedung der Wiederaufbaugesetze in den Ausschüssen," "Verhandlungen der Völkerbunddelegierten mit den Führern der Sozialdemokraten," and "Abschluss der auschussberatungen über das Sanierungsprogramm.—Alle Vorlagen für die Verhandlungen im Nationalrat fertiggestellt," all in *NFP*, 23 November 1922; "Der Sieg der Regierung.—Die Beschlüsse des sozialdemokratischen Parteirates," *NFP*, Abendblatt, 23 November 1922.

69. Around 1:00 A.M., after the vote on the first part of the reform program (administrative reform and savings) passed, Socialist Victor Adler requested the closure of the meeting, but was opposed by Christian-Social party whip Jodok Fink. The majority parties had revoked their right to speak and only Socialists took to the podium, speaking in front of an almost empty assembly. By 2:00 A.M., black coffee and cognac were sold out and almost all parliamentarians were standing in the surrounding hallways, talking or playing cards, with only Chancellor Seipel present in the plenary hall all night. The majority parties intended to pass all second readings and the Ermächtigungsgesetz, but shortly after 5:00 A.M. the opposition and majority parties had to agree to a recess, forced by the stenographers, who could no longer continue their work. The reconstruction law was voted upon and the vote on the Ermächtigungsgesetz postponed for Sunday afternoon. The final third readings and votes were scheduled for a formal meeting on Monday. "Die Genfer Vorlagen im Nationalrate. Eine authentische Interpretation des Genfer Übereinkommens durch den Bundeskanzler," *NFP*, Morgenblatt, 25 November 1922; "Die Verabschiedung der Genfer Vereinbarungen im Nationalrate. Grosse Lärmszenen in der Sonntagsitzung," *NFP*, Nachmittagblat, 27 November 1922.

70. *Bundeskanzler Dr. Seipel:* Welche Hoffnungen haben wir für die Zukunft? Mein Vorredner hat gemeint, wir wollen, dass dieses Volk dezimiert werden soll. Ich sage Ihnen: meine Hoffnung ist eine andere. Dieses Volk soll auf seinem Boden wieder leben können, aber es soll ja nicht das eintreten müssen, was neulich derselbe Redner von der Opposition

hier einem grossen Teile von Volksgenossen zugerufen hat: "Sie hätten
doch auswandern sollen!" *(Stürmischer Beifall rechts. Lebhafte
Zwischenrufe links. Pfuirufe rechts. Grosser Lärm)*
Präsident (das Glockenzeichen gebend): Ich bitte um Ruhe, der Bundes-
kanzler hat das Wort. *(Anhaltende Zwischenrufe. Rufe: Verdrehung!)*
Bundeskanzler Dr. Seipel: Das hohes Haus, hat er gerade einem wichtigen
Teile unseres bodenständigen deutschen christlichen Volkes zugerufen.
*(Erneuter stürmischer Beifall und Händeklatschen rechts. Stürmische
Zwischenrufe links.)*
"Die Verabschiedung der Genfer Vereinbarungen im Nationalrate. Grosse Lärm-
szenen in der Sonntagsitzung," *NFP,* Nachmittagblat, 27 November 1922.

71. "Die Verabschiedung der Genfer Vereinbarungen im Nationalrate. Grosse
Lärmszenen in der Sonntagsitzung," *NFP,* Nachmittagblat, 27 November 1922;
"Die Genfer Vorlagen im Bundesrate," *NFP,* Morgenblatt, 28 November 1922; NA,
FO 371/7343/C 16217: Telegram from Keeling to Foreign Office, 24 No-
vember 1922; LNA, C 34, Réconstruction financière de l'Autriche 1922–1922:
55ème séance tenue le 25 novembre 1922 à 18 heures.

72. There were 23 Christian-Social, 2 Pan-German, and 24 Socialist members
in the Bundesrat. Because the Bundesrat's Christian-Social chairman had no vote,
the opposition and the government parties tied. If matters were left unresolved
that way, the laws would automatically be resent to the Nationalrat at the end of
eight weeks where, after a further three readings, they would become law. Alter-
natively, the laws could be rejected in the Bundesrat, which would resend them to
the Nationalrat sooner, where, after a further three readings, they would also become law. But still this meant a delay of probably at least 1–2 days. LNA, C 34, Réconstruction financière de l'Autriche 1922–1922: *56ème séance du 29 Novembre
1922;* LNA, S 106, Sir Arthur Salter's Private Papers, Austria No. 3, "Telegrams
dispatched and received": Telegram from Avenol to Denis, 26 November 1922; NA,
FO 371/7344/C 16532: Letter from Keeling to Foreign Office, 30 November 1922;
NA, FO 371/7344/C 16967: Letter from Keeling to Curzon, 8 December 1922;
"Ratifizierung der Genfer Vorlagen durch den Bundesrat. Bedenken gegen die
Aufteilung der Abgabenanteile," *NFP,* Abendblatt, 28 November 1922.

73. "Schwierigkeiten bei der Erledigung der Genfer Vorlagen im Bundesrate"
and "Die Verhandlung über die Genfer Protokolle im Bundesrate," both in *NFP,*
Morgenblatt, 29 November 1922.

74. Had the Pan-Germans and Christian-Socials voted for the laws, it would
have led to a tie, which would have meant a delay of eight weeks until the law
would have become effective. This way it was returned immediately to the Nationalrat and if it decided to keep its decision, the law became effective immediately,
which this still meant a delay of a few days. "Einspruch des Bundesrates gegen die
Genfer Vorlagen. Absentierung der Regierungsparteien vor der Abstimmung,"
NFP, Morgenblatt, 30 November 1922.

NOTES TO PAGE 130

75. Salter himself credits the delegation: "We stopped the printing press (though after taking the precaution, I confess on my initiative, of first working it overtime before the date of closing, so that we might have some reserve for an emergency); and of course publicly announced this decisive step." Arthur Salter, *Memoirs of a Public Servant* (London, 1961), p. 179.

76. LNA, C 34, Réconstruction financière de l'Autriche 1922–1922: *48ème séance tenue le 18 novembre à 10 h.15 Hôtel Impérial.*

77. LNA, C 34, Réconstruction financière de l'Autriche 1922–1922: *50ème séance tenue le 18 Novembre 1922;* LNA, C 18, Réconstruction financière de l'Autriche 1922–1928, "Stopping Bank-Note Printing-Press": Letter from Avenol to Niemeyer, 20 November 1922; "Die Einstellung der Notenprese.—Ein Notenwechsel zwischen Finanzminister und den Delegierten des Völkerbundes," *NFP*, Nachmittagblatt, 20 November 1922; "Wien, 20. November.—Die Stillegung der Notenpresse," *NFP*, 21 November 1922; "Oesterreichisch-ungarische Bank. Notenumlauf 3133 Billionen, Abnahme 28 Billionen Kronen," *NFP*, Morgenblatt, 28 November 1922. Not only did the state cease to use the bank's discount window, it bought back 1 billion crowns of discounted Treasury Bills, so that the balance sheet of the Austrian section of the Austro-Hungarian Bank, published on 28 November 1922, showed a first reduction of circulation.

78. "Die Subskription auf die Golschatzscheine und die Aktien der Nationalbank," *NFP*, Morgenblatt, 30 November 1922.

79. LNA, C 34, Réconstruction financière de l'Autriche 1922–1922: *54ème séance du 25 novembre 1922 à 10 h.30.*

80. This sum excludes some subscriptions at banks, which came in five days later. LNA, C 34, Réconstruction financière de l'Autriche 1922–1922: *57ème séance tenue le 30 Novembre 1922 à 16 h. Hôtel Impérial.* The return of confidence is also reflected in a letter from London Rothschild's correspondent in Vienna, Paul Kern, who wrote on 11 December 1922 that he considered the 8 percent national gold loan "to be one of the best present investments." RAL, XI / III / 189, "Special Correspondence re Austria (Loan)": Letter from Paul Kern to RAL, 11 December 1922.

81. LNA, S 106, Sir Arthur Salter's Private Papers, Austria No. 3, "Miscellaneous Correspondence and Memoranda": Letter from Salter to Niemeyer, 21 December 1922; LNA, C 4, Réconstruction financière de l'Autriche 1922–1926: "Credits—Account B—Trance II—Subscriptions etc.": Telegram from Salter to Avenol, 19 December 1922; and "Credits—Account B—Tranche I: Zahlungseingänge für die 8%ige öst. Dollar Anleihe." The loan was floated at 8 percent interest and with the favorable exchange rate of 70,000 crowns per U.S. dollar, to be repaid in dollars on 1 June 1923 and including the option to acquire central bank shares. On 22 December, the first shareholder meeting of the Austrian National Bank was held, by which time capital of 20,731,321.97 gold crowns (more than $4 million) had successfully been raised. AdR, 01 / 9, Ges. London, Karton 101, Finanzsachen 1920–1923, "Finanzen 1923": Runderlass from Bundespressedienst,

Vienna sent to Franckenstein, 5 December 1922; NA, FO 371 / 8538 / C 1160: Otto Niemeyer, *Note on a Program for Geneva,* 18 January 1923; and NA, FO 371 / 8538 / C 1305: Letter from Akers-Douglas to Marquess Curzon, 19 January 1923.

82. BEA, OV 28 / 54, Austrian Rehabilitation: Letter from Strakosch to Norman, 30 December 1922. Norman was in the United States at the time.

83. BEA, OV / 28 / 53, Austrian (Rehabilitation): Letter from Spencer-Smith to Norman, 6 December 1922.

84. See, e.g., Goldinger and Binder, *Geschichte der Republik Österreich.*

85. Brendan Brown, *Monetary Chaos in Europe* (London, 1988), p. 122. Gulick (*Austria,* p. 167) does not explain how stabilization was achieved, but he claims that it was a consequence of Seipel's campaign. Benedikt (*Geschichte der Republik Österreich,* pp. 127-129) does not discuss stabilization either, and neither does Carsten (*The First Austrian Republic*).

86. Thomas Sargent, *Rational Expectations and Inflation* (New York, 1986), pp. 47-55.

87. Ibid., p. 97.

88. Leo Pasvolsky, *Economic Nationalism of the Danubian States* (New York, 1928), p. 116. Garber and Spencer do write that stabilization was only initiated by the Protocols' signing in October and that not until the Austrian government stopped borrowing, in mid-November, did the currency stabilize. See Peter Garber and Michael Spencer, "The Dissolution of the Austro-Hungarian Empire: Lessons for Currency Reform." International Monetary Fund Working Paper 92 / 66, 1992, pp. 29-30.

89. This view is also shared by Dieter Stiefel, "Konjunkturelle Entwicklung und struktureller Wandel der österreichischen Wirtschaft in der Zwischenkriegszeit," Forschungsbericht Nr. 135 (November 1978), p. 28: "Schon die Nachricht über die Absicht des Völkerbundes, eine Sanierungsaktion für Österreich einzuleiten, genügte um der [sic] weiteren Kurssturz der Krone Einhalt zu gebieten."

90. Some examples: "In August 1922, however, the Austrian crown was abruptly stabilized and the 'Austrian inflation was essentially stopped cold'" (Herbert Matis, *The Economic Development of Austria since 1870* [Aldershot, UK, 1994], p. 488); "The fiscal and monetary reforms that stopped inflation in Austria in August 1922 are an example.... When the announcement of the agreement was made, inflation came to a screeching halt before its details became public and before implementation began" (George Macesich, *Successor States and Cooperation Theory: A Model for Eastern Europe* [Westport, CT, 1994], p. 5); Larry Allen, "The depreciation of the crown in foreign exchange markets stopped abruptly in August 1922, and the upward spiral in retail prices ended the following month" (*The Encyclopedia of Money* [Santa Barbara, CA, 2009], pp. 207-208).

91. Rudiger Dornbusch, Federico Sturzenegger, and Holger Wolf, "Extreme Inflation: Dynamics and Stabilization," *Brookings Papers on Economic Activity* 2 (1990): 1-65; Rüdiger Dornbusch and Stanley Fischer, "Stopping Hyperinflations

Past and Present," National Bureau of Economic Research Working Paper 1810 (Cambridge, MA, 1986); Rüdiger Dornbusch, "Lessons from Experiences with High Inflation," *World Bank Economic Review* 6, no. 1 (January 1992): 13–31; Andrés Solimano, "Inflation and the Costs of Stabilization—Historical and Recent Experiences and Policy Lessons," *World Bank Research Observer* 5, no. 2 (July 1990): 167–185.

92. März, *Austrian Banking and Financial Policy*, p. 503. Van Walré de Bordes writes that stabilization was "effected artificially" (*The Austrian Crown: Its Depreciation and Stabilization* [London, 1924], p. 204). The Devisenzentrale's official name was "Österreichische Zentralstelle für den Zahlungsverkehr mit dem Ausland." A number of articles against the Devisenzentrale appeared in *Neue Freie Presse* on 3 November 1922 under the heading "Die schweren Schäden der Devisenzwangswirtschaft. Aeusserungen hervorragender Fachmänner." See also "Die Missbräuche der Devisenzwangswirtschaft. Die Auswirkung der verschärften Devisenordung auf Arzneiwaren." *NFP*, Morgenblatt, 18 November 1922.

93. Friedrich Gärtner, "Die Stabilisierung der Österreichischen Krone," *Schriften des Vereins für Socialpolitik* 165 (1923): 49–77.

94. This is further supported by the editor of the *Österreichische Volkswirt*, Gustav Stolper: "Dr. G. St.: Der Kampf um Genf," *ÖVW* 15, no. 6 (11 November 1922). Stolper wrote that foreign exchange rates showed no new confidence in Austria, since the crown had not appreciated and it seemed unlikely the Devisenzentrale was simply throwing out foreign currency, given that it was still unable to supply sufficient foreign exchange to satisfy all domestic demand. But this is exactly what it was doing!

95. Van Walré de Bordes, *The Austrian Crown*, p. 205.

96. The *Neue 8 Uhr Blatt* of 27 November 1922 also reported that the DZ planned to increase its supply of foreign exchange for imports in face of the increased supply of foreign currencies ("Erhöhung der Devisenzuteilungen").

97. "Die Konferenz zwischen den Finanzdelegierten und Führern der Sozialdemokraten. Anlässlich der bevorstehenden Erledigung des Finanzprogramms," "Die Verabschiedung der Wiederaufbaugesetze in den Ausschüssen," and "Verhandlungen der Völkerbunddelegierten mit den Führern der Sozialdemokraten," all in *NFP*, Morgenblatt, 22 November 1922.

4. The Inception of Control

Epigraph: LNA, C 41, Reconstruction financière de l'Autriche 1923–1927, "re Trade congresses etc": speech by General Commissioner Alfred Rudolph Zimmerman in front of the International Chamber of Commerce visiting Vienna on 29 March 1923.

1. Zimmerman had to be pressured by Blackett, Niemeyer, and Norman to take the job, and at first only agreed to do so until 1 April 1923. See Nicole Piétri,

"La réconstruction économique et financière de l'Autriche par la Société des Nations (1921–1926)" (doctoral thesis, Université de Paris I, 1981), pp. 635–636.

2. LNA, S 106, Sir Arthur Salter's Private Papers, Austria No. 3: *Letter from Salter to Niemeyer*, 21 December 1922; "Die Ankunft des Generalkommissärs Dr. Zimmerman," *NFP*, 16 December 1922, p. 4.

3. The American candidate was Roland W. Boyden, U.S. observer at the Reparations Commission. Boyden misread a reserved telegram from the U.S. State Department as an instruction not to take the job. Zimmerman was the second choice, but the one preferred by Norman and Blackett. Both knew him from the Brussels Conference in 1920 and he had already been briefly considered as controller in February 1922. In his memoirs, Arthur Salter, who had hoped the General Commissioner would bring about cooperation between Christian-Socials and Socialists, termed Boyden's mistaken understanding of the telegram a "tragic misinterpretation." Salter, *Memoirs of a Public Servant* (London, 1961), p. 179; LNA, S 106, Sir Arthur Salter's Private Papers, Austria No. 3, "Telegrams despatched and received": Telegram from Salter to Monnet, 11 November 1922. On Zimmerman, see Bosmans, "Alfred Rudolph Zimmerman," in *Biografisch Woordenboek van Nederland*, vol. 1, ed. Jan Charité (Den Haag, 1979), pp. 678–679, as well as Bosmans, *De Nederlander Mr. A. R. Zimmerman als Commissaris-Generaal van de Volkenbond in Oostenrijk 1922–1926* (Nijmegen, 1973).

4. League of Nations, *The Restoration of Austria: Agreements arranged by the League of Nations and signed at Geneva on October 4th 1922 with the relevant documents and public statements* (Geneva, 1922). See Appendix C in this volume.

5. *Bundesverfassungsgesetz vom 26. November 1922 über die Ausübung der ausserordentlichen Vollmachten, die der Bundesregierung gemäss dem Genfer Protokolle Nr. III vom 4. Oktober 1922 eingeräumt werden.*, Bundesgesetzblatt für die Republik Österreich, 3 December 1922; *Bundesgesetz vom 27. November 1922 über die zur Aufrichtung der Staats- und Volkswirtschaft der Republik Österreich zu treffenden Massnahmen (Wiederaufbaugesetz).*, Bundesgesetzblatt für die Republik Österreich, 3 December 1922.

6. Harold James argues in this context that during the interwar years, short-term capital flows moved mainly in reaction to news on government deficits. Harold James, "Financial Flows across Frontiers during the Interwar Depression," *Economic History Review*, n.s., 45, no. 3, European Special Issue (1992): 594–613.

7. Michael Spencer-Smith of the Anglo-Austrian bank told Chancellor Seipel during a visit to Vienna in December 1922 that since getting an international loan would be very difficult it was best to make the League commit itself to Austria to such an extent that the former's very existence depended on the scheme going through. BEA, OV/28/53, "Austrian (Rehabilitation)": Letter from Spencer-Smith to Norman, 4 December 1922.

8. Over the first six months of 1923, the deficit declined and Zimmerman advanced a total of only 4 billion crowns (about $55,000) from tobacco and customs revenues under his control to cover it. Piétri, "La réconstruction économique," p. 653.

9. Frank Beyersdorf, " 'Credit or Chaos?' The Austrian Stabilisation Programme of 1923 and the League of Nations," in *Internationalism Reconfigured: Transnational Ideas and Movements between the World Wars*, ed. Daniel Laqua (London, 2011), p. 140.

10. Zimmerman wrote to Seipel that the placement of Treasury Bills abroad would be made much easier if a foreigner was placed at the head of the bank. LNA, S 59, M. De Bordes Files, Box 6, Austria 1922–1926 "Austria": Letter from Zimmerman to Seipel, 19 December 1922; BEA, OV/28/53, "Austrian (Rehabilitation)": Letter from Spencer-Smith to Norman, 4 December 1922, and from Norman to Spencer-Smith, 7 December 1922.

11. NA, FO 371/7343/C 15784: Telegram from Salter to Niemeyer, 18 November 1922; BEA, OV/28/53, "Austrian (Rehabilitation)": Letter from Niemeyer to Norman, 27 November 1922.

12. BEA, OV/28/53, "Austrian (Rehabilitation)": Letter from Norman to L. van der Rest, 11 December 1922.

13. BEA, OV/28/53, "Austrian (Rehabilitation)": Letter from Norman to Franckenstein, 22 December 1922.

14. "Die Präsidentschaft der neuen Notenbank," *NFP*, 27 November 1922, p. 5: "In parlamentarischen Kreisen wird behauptet, dass die Präsidentschaft der neuen Notenbank in die Hände eines Ausländers gelangen solle. Es ist gewiss in keinem Lande der Welt der Fall, dass der Präsident der Emissionsbank ein Ausländer ist; sicherlich würde eine solche Besetzung zu schweren Bedenken Anlass geben. Da ohnedies vier Stellen im Generalrate Ausländern vorbehalten sind und der Generalkommissär die Oberaufsicht über die gesamte Finanzgebarung führt, so ist nicht einzusehen, wozu das Ausland eine noch stärkere Vertretung im Generalrate haben und warum uns die Demütigung auferlegt werden soll, dass die Leitung der Bankpolitik in fremde Hände gelegt wird." See also "Der Präsident der Nationalbank," *NFP*, Abendblatt, 30 November 1922, p. 3: "Die Konstituierung der neuen österreichischen Nationalbank soll nach den Mitteilungen, die in der Pressekonferenz seitens des Bundeskanzlers Dr. Seipel gemacht worden sind, noch vor Weihnachten erfolgen. Bis dorthin wird auch über die Besetzung der Stelle des Präsidenten entschieden sein. Die von manchen Seiten gemachte Anregung, dass für eine Übergangzeit ein Ausländer an die Spitze der Nationalbank gestellt werden soll, hat in weiten Kreisen Befremden erregt. Die Bank wird mit österreichischem Kapital ins Leben gerufen. Sie ist berufen, das Geldwesen Österreichs zu regulieren, den Kredit für österreichische Unternehmungen zuzumessen, und so ist der Wunsch wohl berechtigt, dass an *ihre Spitze ein Österreicher gestellt*

werde, der in unseren inneren Verhältnissen bewandert und erfahren ist, die Bedürfnisse und die vorhandenen Quellen der Befriedigung aus eigener Erfahrung kennt. Hoffentlich wird es gelingen, die Demütigung eines ausländischen Präsidenten der österreichischen Nationalbank abzuwehren und diese Stelle mit einem Österreicher zu besetzen." (Emphasis in the original.)

15. BEA, OV / 28 / 53, "Austrian (Rehabilitation)": Letter from Norman to Spencer-Smith, 6 December 1922: "You know that as a matter of fact I am supporting the appointment of Mr. Janssen as head of the Bank although he is personally scarcely known to me. But he has, I believe, the unanimous approval of all those who have been concerned with the League Scheme for Austria. And I mistrusted every word that these two Hebrews said to me."

16. NA, FO 371 / 7344 / C 17537: Telegram from Foreign Office to Keeling, 22 December 1922; AdR, NPA, 286, Liasse Oesterreich 1921–1922 8 / IV, "Liasse Oesterreich 1921–1922": Telegram from Franckenstein to Aussenamt, 22 December 1922.

17. Envoy Franckenstein immediately left for Vienna to learn why British wishes had been ignored. Upon return he explained to Norman that the appointment of Reisch was not the fault of the Austrian government, but that Italian pressure to appoint an Italian, and public opinion, which was strongly opposed to a foreigner, had forced the government's hand. Furthermore, the Austrian government had never promised to appoint a foreigner, but had merely been told by Avenol and Strakosch that it was advisable. BEA, OV 28 / 54, "Austrian Rehabilitation": Letter from Franckenstein to Norman, 5 January 1922; NA, FO 371 / 7344 / C 17515: Telegram from Keeling to Foreign Office, 21 December 1922.

18. LNA, S 59, M. De Bordes Files, Box 6, Austria 1922–1926 "Austria": *Note pour M. Avenol sure une conversation avec Sir Arthur Salter,* 21 December 1922.

19. LNA, S 107, Sir Arthur Salter's Private Papers, Austria No. 4, "Austria— Correspondence with and regarding the Provisional Delegation of the League in Vienna, up to December 15th, 1922": Letter from Niemeyer to Salter, 27 December 1922.

20. LNA, S 108, Sir Arthur Salter's Private Papers, Austria No. 5, "Austria— Bank of Issue": Letter from Niemeyer to Zimmerman, 13 January 1923. The following were present: Lord Cullen, Deputy Governor of the Bank of England; Henry Strakosch; Albert Janssen; Arthur Salter; and Jan van Walré de Bordes.

21. The Conseiller had the right to partake in all meetings of the General Assembly, the Council, and the Directors, as well as to call a meeting of the latter two. In cases where the President's vote was decisive in the Council, he had to first obtain the Conseiller's approval. This also held true for his decisions on the admission of securities as collateral for loans to banks, or if he decided to reduce ANB reserves held abroad before the bank took up gold payment. Conseiller approval was further necessary on all decisions pertaining to the execution of the

Geneva Protocols and the ANB's relations with the government, provinces, communes, and municipalities. In effect he did little but sit at his desk and look out the window. See Chapter 5 in this volume.

22. The memoirs of Arthur Salter support this view. Accordingly, Norman cabled Salter on Christmas Day that the Bank of England had dropped its participation in the scheme. Salter was certain that the plan would collapse without Norman, but he considered Norman and the Bank too far committed and interested in the scheme to really abandon Austria and thus decided to keep the cable secret from Zimmerman, who he feared would otherwise get up and return to Holland immediately. Salter, *Memoirs of a Public Servant*, p. 180.

23. P. L. Cottrell, "Norman, Strakosch and the Development of Central Banking: From Conception to Practice, 1919–1924," in *Rebuilding the Financial System in Central and Eastern Europe, 1918–1944*, ed. Philip L. Cottrell (Aldershot, UK, 1997), pp. 29–73.

24. Beyersdorf, "'Credit or Chaos?'"

25. LNA, S 109, Sir Arthur Salter's Private Papers, Austria No. 6, "Austria— Correspondence etc. with Commissioner-General and Staff at Vienna": Letter from Zimmerman to Seipel, 5 January 1923; LNA, C 21, Réconstruction financière de l'Autriche 1922–1928, "Simplification of Administration": Letters from Zimmerman to Frank and from Frank to Zimmerman, both 5 January 1923, as well as Zimmerman's report: "Financial Reconstruction of Austria. First Report by the Commissioner-General of the League of Nations at Vienna, submitted to the Council on February 1st, 1923," published in *League of Nations Official Journal* 4 (March 1923): 307–343.

26. LNA, C 21, Réconstruction financière de l'Autriche 1922–1928, "Simplification of Administration": Letter from Frank to Zimmerman, 5 January 1923, and from Zimmerman to Frank, 9 January 1923.

27. The reconstruction law passed in 1922 included a list of reforms to reduce government expenditure. The most important among them were the amalgamation of ministries, reforms at the war ministry, reduction of the number of civil servants, reorganization of state enterprises, and restructuring of the fiscal relationship between the state and its provinces. Zimmerman asked to be given a Kalendarium, a calendar listing all the planned reforms with dates as to when they would be completed. Interior Minister Frank presented the General Commissioner with a Kalendarium on 15 February 1922, and it foresaw a complete implementation of all reforms by the scheduled end of League control on 31 December 1924. But four days later Zimmerman wrote to Seipel that he was "obliged to admit that at the end of this first period, apart from the fiscal measures, not one of the important reforms decided upon has yet been carried out, the few administrative reforms which have been accomplished are of a minor character. This fact is particularly to be regretted, because it shows that, if better results are not obtained

within a very short time, the progress of the work of reconstruction may be delayed." LNA, C 21, Réconstruction financière de l'Autriche 1922–1928, "Simplification of Administration": Letter from Zimmerman to Seipel, 19 January 1923.

28. LNA, C 21, Réconstruction financière de l'Autriche 1922–1928, "Simplification of Administration": Letter from Seipel to Zimmerman, 18 January 1923.

29. LNA, S 113, Sir Arthur Salter's Private Papers, Austria No. 10, "Austria—Miscellaneous. Various memoranda on situation in Austria etc. etc.": Letter from Salter to Drummond, 16 January 1923; NA, FO 371/8538/C 1160: Niemeyer, *Note on a Programme for Geneva*, 18 January 1923; AdR, 01/9, Ges. London, Telegramme 1920–1923, Box 18: Telegram from Franckenstein to Vienna, 17 January 1923.

30. The Control Committee was chaired by the Italian Pantaleoni and included Roos (Czechoslovakia), Niemeyer (United Kingdom), Avenol (France), Janssen (Belgium), and Botella (Spain), while Wallenberg (Sweden) and Patyn (Netherlands), whose countries had not yet ratified their guarantee laws, participated as observers. The Austrian delegation, which appeared before the Committee in the afternoon, consisted of Herman Patzauer, Richard Reisch, and Richard Schüller. Upon Pantaleoni's request, a passage was introduced into the resolution, which noted that the Austrian parliament had failed to grant the government extraordinary powers. LNA, C 39, Réconstruction financière de l'Autriche 1922–1928, "Mins. Control Committee (Paris) January 1923": *Procès-verbal des séances du comité de contrôle de l'Autriche du 27 janvier 1923*; AdR, 01/9, Ges. London, Telegramme 1920–1923, Box 18: Telegram from Franckenstein to Vienna, 17 January 1923; AdR, 01/9, Ges. London, Telegramme 1920–1923, Box 18, "IV Herein 1923": Telegram from Aussenamt to Franckenstein, 24 January 1923; LNA, C 39, Réconstruction financière de l'Autriche 1922–1928, "Mins. Control Committee (Paris) January 1923": Letter from Seipel to Zimmerman, 26 January 1923.

31. Zimmerman reported that at a meeting held with government officials on 29 December 1922, the Vice-Chancellor had failed to show up, that he had since insisted on the energetic application of reforms, which included merging the War and Interior Ministries, and that he considered creating a reliable armed force through merging the Interior Ministry's gendarmerie with the War Ministry's army a precondition for the energetic measures to be undertaken. Not only in the Extraordinary Cabinet Council, but also in relation to the army, Socialist influence was the reason for government's inaction. Seipel confirmed that it was Socialist opposition that prevented him from closing the Ministry of Social Affairs and amalgamating the War and Interior Ministries, while it was the Pan-Germans who opposed the abolition of the Ministry of Agriculture. The Council's Sub-Committee meetings were attended by Balfour (United Kingdom), Viviani (France), Salandra (Italy), and Pospíšil (Czechoslovakia, in lieu of Beneš). The Austrian delegation consisted of Chancellor Seipel and Foreign Minister Alfred

Grünberger. LNA, S 111 Sir Arthur Salter's Private Papers, Austria No. 8, "Austria—Sub Committee of Council": *Speech by M. Zimmerman, commissioner-General of the League of Nations at Vienna, to Sub Cttee of council*, 31 January 1923; AdR, NPA, 289 Liasse Oesterreich 8/IV Genf fol. 352–552, "Paris Februar 1923": *Rapport du Comité de Contrôle pour l'Autriche au Sous-comité d'autriche du conseil de la société des Nations*, 30 January 1923; NA, FO 371/8538/C 1964: *Report No. 1.* from Phillpotts (Paris) to Akers-Douglas, 31 January 1923.

    32. Such was also the assessment of the British envoy to Vienna. NA, FO 371/8538/C 1305: Letter from Akers-Douglas to Marquess Curzon, 19 January 1923.

    33. Austrian Finance Ministry official Herman Schwarzwald had earlier informed the Bank of England that his government was running out of funds and that, to safeguard the scheme, London banks should be ready to agree on a loan proposal by the time of the League meeting in Paris at the end of January. Schwarzwald's colleague, Sztankowitz, wrote a similar memo for Zimmerman and the Bank of England in which he described the catastrophic consequences that further delays would entail. Only if there were no further setbacks would confidence persist and foreign capital be repatriated; otherwise there would be a run for foreign currency and a sudden depreciation of the crown not unlike the one experienced in April 1922. Zimmerman, worried by the memo, telegraphed Salter that he felt uneasy about a decline in Austrian confidence, should the meeting not produce tangible results. Niemeyer instructed Balfour to counter any Austrian claim in Paris that the country had done its part but the loan was still outstanding by insisting on the punctual performance of reforms and by pointing out that raising the loan was Austria's job, neither that of the League nor that of any of the guarantor states. BEA, OV 28/54, Austrian Rehabilitation: Schwarzwald, *Memorandum über die gegenwärtige Lage in Oesterreich.*, and telegram from Bank of England to Norman (USA), 10 January 1923; NA, FO 371/8538/C 1160: Niemeyer, *Note on a Programme for Geneva*, 18 January 1923 (see also the copy held at BEA, OV 28/54, which identifies it as drafted for Lord Balfour); AdR, Box 68 fasz. 50/IV, "Voelkerbundkreditaktion vom Jahre 1922": Schwarzwald, *Finanzielle Programmpunkte für Genf*, 22 January 1923; AdR, 01/9, Ges. London, Box 101, Finanzsachen 1920–1923, "Finanzen 1923": Letter from Franckenstein, 16 January 1923; AdR, 01/9, Ges. London, Telegramme 1920–1923, Box 18, IV "Herein 1923": Telegram from Aussenamt to Franckenstein, 14 January 1923; LNA, C 36, Réconstruction financière de l'Autriche 1922–1925, "Meetings & Annexes—Meetings Aust-Sub-Committee. Paris Jan '23": Letter from Pantaleoni to Zimmerman, 27 January 1923, and *Rapport du Comité de Contrôle pour l'Autriche au sous-comité d'autriche du conseil de la société des Nations*, 30 January 1923; LNA, S 113, Sir Arthur Salter's Private Papers, Austria No. 10, "Austria—Miscellaneous. Various memoranda on situation in Austria etc. etc.": Letter from Salter to Drummond, 16

January 1923; LNA, C 7, Réconstruction financière de l'Autriche 1921–1928, "Balance Sheets (small) Issue Bank": Memorandum by Sztankowitz, 5 January 1923; LNA, C 4, Réconstruction financière de l'Autriche 1922–1926, "Credits Operations (General)": Telegram from Zimmerman to Salter, 12 January 1923.

34. In its resolution the Sub-Committee demanded that the Austrian government refrain from using the Extraordinary Cabinet as an excuse for further delays, and its French Chairman, Viviani, called upon Austria to overcome party strife because any further criticism from the Commissioner General would negatively impact the confidence of foreign lenders. LNA, C 36, Réconstruction financière de l'Autriche 1922–1925, "Meetings & Annexes—Meetings Aust-Sub-Committee, Paris Jan '23": Draft Resolution, 30 January 1923.

35. LNA, 1156 Juin 1923 II: Autriche, "1st Report; incl CONFIDENTIAL annexes": First Report of the Commissioner-General of the League of Nations at Vienna—Period December 15th, 1922 to January 15th, 1923.

36. Ibid., p. 10.

37. Zimmerman would not resist those changes, but demanded that in the future any concessions be made only after consulting with his office. LNA, C 3, Réconstruction financière de l'Autriche 1922–1927, "re Abbau Law": Memo from Zimmerman to Frank; LNA, C 21, "Simplification . . .": Unterredung mit Herrn Vize-Kanzler Dr. Frank am 9. Februar 1923.

38. In a letter to Seipel, Zimmerman pointed to an article in the Neue Wiener Zeitung that reported on protests at the Vienna garrison on 11 February 1923, during which a resolution had been passed declaring the unbreakable loyalty of the army to the Austrian working class—illustrating, according to Zimmerman, the worthlessness of the army to the state. LNA, C 3, Réconstruction financière de l'Autriche 1922–1927, "re Austrian Army": Unterredung mit dem Bundeskanzler Dr. Seipel am 10. Februar 1923, and Letter from Zimmerman to Seipel, 12 February 1923.

39. LNA, C 5, Réconstruction financière de l'Autriche 1922–1924, "Negotiations for Long-Term Loan": Letters from van Walré de Bordes to Niemeyer, 7 March 1923, and from Zimmerman to Niemeyer, 14 March 1923.

40. Addressing the Committee of Control in January 1924, Zimmerman would state that "il est juste de dire que, pendant la période d'émission de l'emprunt, les réformes on été ralenties, car il était nécessaire d'éviter tout conflit pouvant créer à l'étranger une impression défavorable." LNA, C 39, Réconstruction financière de l'Autriche 1922–1928, "Proces-Verbal—Control Committee—Geneva September & December 1923": Procès-verbal de la deuxième séance, tenue à Paris le mercredi 19 décembre 1923, à 10 h. 1/2.

41. The reduction would be made up by discharging 3,130 men who had served for more than twelve years and 4,246 men who had served over six years and who were above the age of thirty-eight, and by canceling the annual recruitment in

September set at 3,100 men. LNA, C 3, Réconstruction financière de l'Autriche 1922–1927: *Unterredung, 17 February 1923.*

42. LNA, C 3, Réconstruction financière de l'Autriche 1922–1927, "re Austrian Army": *Conversation between Zimmerman and Vaugoin, 24 February 1923.*

43. LNA, C 3, Réconstruction financière de l'Autriche 1922–1927, "re Austrian Army": *Unterredung mit dem Bundeskanzler Dr. Seipel von Herren General-Kommissaer Dr. Zimmermann [sic], am 17. Maerz 1923.*

44. LNA, C 3, Réconstruction financière de l'Autriche 1922–1927, "re Austrian Army": Letters from Zimmerman to Seipel, 26 March 1923, and from Seipel to Zimmerman, 27 March 1923.

45. LNA, C 222. 1923. II: *Financial Reconstruction of Austria, Third Report by the Commissioner-General of the League of Nations for Austria,* May 1923.

46. Present were Pantaleoni (Italy), Roos (Czechoslovakia), Strakosch (United Kingdom), Bexon and Felcourt (France), Janssen (Belgium), Botella (Spain), Patjin (Netherlands), Boheman (Sweden), and Dinichert (Switzerland). LNA, C 39, Réconstruction financière de l'Autriche 1922–1928, "Minutes—Control Committee—April 1923—Geneva": *Procès-verbal de la première séance tenue à Genève le samedi 14 avril 1923 à midi,* Annex I.

47. The following delegates were present: Wood (United Kingdom), Hanotaux (France), Salandra (Italy), Pospíšil (Czechoslovakia), Seipel and Grünberger (Austria), General Commissioner Zimmerman, and League Secretary General Eric Drummond. Zimmerman specifically deplored the linkage between state workers' wages and the official price index, which made precise budgeting impossible. LNA, C 36, Réconstruction financière de l'Autriche 1922–1925, "Minutes—Austrian Sub-Committee": *Procès-verbal de la séance du dimanche 22 avril 1923, tenue à Genève à 11 heure,* and "Resolutions, etc. Geneva Council Meetings (April 1923 & July 1923)": *Discours de M. Zimmerman au Conseil de la Société des Nations.*

48. LNA, 1156 Juin 1923 II: Autriche: *PV of 12th Meeting of 24th Session of Council,* 22 April 1923.

49. The conflict between Zimmerman and War Minister Carl Vaugoin over downsizing the Austrian army also continued. Zimmerman complained in May that measures to reduce military expenses remained dismal, and he suggested the closure of garrisons and the amalgamation of army academies. The General Commissioner was told again that nothing in the Geneva Protocols made reducing the number of soldiers compulsory, and that any reduction achieved over the summer would be made ineffective by recruitments in the fall. Figures presented by Zimmerman that the army's administrative apparatus could be reduced were simply dismissed by Vaugoin as erroneous, and Vaugoin declared himself unwilling to cancel recruitment in 1923. As a concession to Zimmerman, the new soldiers would, however, not be enlisted until January 1924, and the administration shed 1,000 men. LNA, C 3, Réconstruction financière de l'Autriche 1922–1927, "re Austrian

Army": Letters from Zimmerman to Vaugoin, 4 May 1923 and 1 July 1923, from Vaugoin to Zimmerman, 23 May 1923 and 26 July 1923, and from Kienböck to Zimmerman, 12 May 1923, as well as *Unterredung des Herrn Generalkommissaers Dr. Zimmerman mit dem Bundesminister für Heerwesen Vaugoin am 25. Juli 1923.*

50. Over the first six months of 1923, prices in Austria rose by 25 percent. NA, FO 371 / 8542 / C 10583: Letter from Akers-Douglas to Curzon, 15 June 1923.

51. LNA, C 24, Réconstruction financière de l'Autriche 1923–1925, "Salaries State Employees A": *Unterredung am 9. Mai mit dem Finanzminister Dr. Kienböck (von Herrn General-Kommissär Dr. Zimmerman),* 9 May 1923, and H. Patzauer, *Erhöhung der Bezüge der Bundesangestellten,* 11 May 1923.

52. LNA, C 24, Réconstruction financière de l'Autriche 1923–1925, "Salaries State Employees A": Letter from Zimmerman to Kienböck, presented as a memorandum at their meeting on 15 May 1923.

53. LNA, C 24, Réconstruction financière de l'Autriche 1923–1925, "Salaries State Employees A": *Unterredung des Herrn General-Kommissärs Dr. Zimmerman mit dem Finanzminister Dr. Kienböck, am 3. Juli 1923,* and letters from Kienböck to Zimmerman, 13 July 1923, and from Zimmerman to Kienböck, 18 June 1923.

54. LNA, C 24, Réconstruction financière de l'Autriche 1923–1925, "Salaries State Employees A": *Unterredung mit dem Finanzminister Dr. Kienböck über Beamtenfrage und Reform der Bundesbahnen,* 13 July 1923.

55. LNA, C 21, Réconstruction financière de l'Autriche 1922–1928, "Simplification of Administration": Letters from Frank to Zimmerman, 27 July 1923, from Zimmerman to Frank, 8 August 1923, and from Seipel to Zimmerman, 24 August 1923.

56. Zimmerman also pointed to other positive indicators, such as the increase of motorcars on Vienna's streets and the high number of travelers visiting Austria and he further acknowledged the rapid fall of unemployment between March and May. Only the slow pace of dismissals of state workers was serious enough to cause regret and possibly jeopardize "the execution of a very important part of the reconstruction programme" in the future. Summing up, the report stated: "These few indications of an economic revival in conjunction with the very favorable state of affairs as regards the actual diminution of the State deficit strengthen my confidence in our work. At the moment when the subscription of the great reorganization loan is about to open, I can only express the hope that its success will respond to our expectations. The results obtained hitherto are encouraging, those that are yet to come can only be so after the credit operations have been actually entered into. If subscribers give proof of confidence, it will give new force to the energies and courage of those who are conducting and supporting the work of reconstruction in Vienna." LNA, C 367, 1923. II: *Financial Reconstruction of Austria: Fourth Report of the Commissioner-General of the League of Nations for Austria (Period March 15th to April 15th, 1923),* published in *League of Nations Official Journal* 4 (July 1923): 772–834.

57. LNA, C 20, Réconstruction financière de l'Autriche 1922–1927, "Austrian Budget 1924": Letter from Zimmerman to Seipel, 6 July 1923.

58. LNA, C 24, Réconstruction financière de l'Autriche 1923–1925, "Salaries State Employees A": Letter from Zimmerman to Kienböck, 15 November 1923, and Patzauer, *Gehaltsreform*, 10 November 1923; LNA, C 20, Réconstruction financière de l'Autriche 1922–1927, "Austrian Budget 1924": *Unterredung mit dem Herrn Finanzminister Dr. Kienböck, am 10. November 1923*; Piétri, "La réconstruction économique," p. 788.

59. The Delegation's plan foresaw an annual deficit of approximately 300 billion crowns at the end of 1923 (about $4 million) and of 146.7 billion crowns at the end of 1924 (about $2 million). See Appendix D in this volume for the draft budget agreed upon.

60. Piétri, "La réconstruction économique," pp. 777, 783–784.

61. LNA, C 24, Réconstruction financière de l'Autriche 1923–1925, "Salaries State Employees A": *Unterredung des Herrn Generalkommissärs mit dem Herrn Bundesminister für Finanzen am 22. November 1923*, and Patzauer, *Gehaltsreform und Steuerteilung*, 27 November 1923.

62. Complications to the agreement with state workers arose when Georg Günther, head of the federal railways, made a slightly more generous offer to his own workers. The railways had become autonomous under the condition that Zimmerman's authority not be affected, but Günther had not consulted him. Zimmerman was opposed to Günther's proposal because the railways were still running at a loss, had too many workers, and, above all, because the government would find it impossible to withhold making the same offer to its state workers. Günther, however, had already made his proposal public, and Kienböck felt compelled to increase his own offer at an additional annual cost of 74 billion crowns (about $1 million). Zimmerman acquiesced as long as the cost was fully covered and the railways shed at least 18,000 workers by the end of the year, but on 6 December 1923, workers at the post and telegraph authorities went on strike, demanding the additional Christmas advance of 480,000 crowns ($6.5 per person) granted by the railways. The Socialist Party further demanded a special increase in the salaries of the lower ranks of state workers and declared itself opposed to the Ertragsanteile law, which was to finance the wage increases. Seipel decided to raise Kienböck's offer somewhat, but threatened to step down if the budget and the law on wages (Besoldungsnovelle) and transfers (Ertragsanteile) were not passed. To gain Socialist support, Kienböck considered offering revenues from an increase in the beverage tax to the municipalities, but Zimmerman opposed, viewing an increase in taxes to pay for new expenses inacceptable. While the wage-reform law was adopted, the one on Ertragsanteile remained an object of much debate and only passed on 6 June 1924. LNA, C 24, Réconstruction financière de l'Autriche 1923–1925, "Salaries State Employees A": Letter from Zimmerman to Kienböck, 11 December 1923, and *Unterredung des Herrn Generalkommissärs mit*

dem Generaldirektor der Oest. Bundesbahnen, Ing. Siegmund, 3 December 1923, as well as *Gehaltsreform und Steuerteilung,* 1 December 1923, and *Unterredung des Herrn Generalkommissärs mit Herrn Bundeskanzler Dr. Seipel und Herrn Bundesminister für Finanzen, Dr. Kienböck,* 6 December 1923; LNA, C 20, Réconstruction financière de l'Autriche 1922–1927, "Austrian Budget 1924": *Unterredung des Generalkommissärs mit dem Herrn Finanzminister Dr. Kienböck am 13. November 1923,* and letter from Zimmerman to Salter, 20 November 1923, as well as *Unterredung des Herrn Generalkommissärs mit Finanzminister Dr. Kienböck,* 5 December 1923; LNA, C 4, Réconstruction financière de l'Autriche 1922–1926, "Taxation in Austria at 1st Sept 1923 & Proposed Steuerverteilungsgesetz": Patzauer, *Reform der Steuerertragsanteile,* 7 December 1923.

63. Norman asked that Reisch intervene with the Austrian government and ensure it observed its original commitment to balance the budget by the end of 1924. Reisch found Norman's doubts baseless and wrote that it made a "painful impression" if Austrian efforts were so little appreciated in London. There also seems to have been some heavy pressure on the *Times* of London to change its tone on Austria. At first the *Times* reported positively that although Austria would have a deficit of £2.5 million instead of the contemplated surplus of £480,000, the draft deficit still represented a 68 percent reduction from the 1923 deficit of £8 million, and that Kienböck planned to decrease it by end of 1924 to £441,000 through administrative retrenchment, an increase in customs duties and large monopoly takings. "Thus Dr. Seipel's government will have performed the task it assumed from the League of Nations only six months behind the time." "Deficit Largely Reduced," *Times,* 22 November 1923. However, only four days later, the *Times* was decidedly less optimistic and reported that while the deficit for 1924 had been reduced by 68 percent, the Geneva Protocols had contemplated a balanced budget by end of year. It stressed that the expenditure side of the budget had not received the attention it deserved, "and we would urge Austria to realize that it is very important that she should fulfill to the letter the terms of the Geneva convention. It would be a pity if, for the lack of a small additional effort, the programme should not be fulfilled by the end of 1924 as originally intended." "Austrian Budget 1923," *Times,* 26 November 1923. A letter to the editor by Franckenstein pointed out that the Finanzgesetz obliged the Austrian government to hold the deficit for 1924 within the 146.7 billion crowns prescribed by the League delegates in October 1922 and was eventually followed by a more positive City Note in the *Times* on 29 November 1923. BEA, OV 28/58, "Austrian Rehabilitation": Telegrams from Norman to Reisch, 23 and 26 November 1923, as well as letter from Reisch to Norman, 3 December 1923; NA, FO 371/8543/C 20382: Telegram from Niemeyer to Zimmerman, 23 November 1923; LNA, C 20, Réconstruction financière de l'Autriche 1922–1927, "Austrian Budget 1924": Letter from Niemeyer to Zimmerman, 30 November 1923.

64. "I have no reason whatever to doubt that this end will be reached and in this way the reconstruction scheme fully realized." LNA, C 20, Réconstruction financière de l'Autriche 1922–1927, "Austrian Budget 1924": Letter from Zimmerman to Norman, 27 November 1923; BEA, OV 28 / 58, "Austrian Rehabilitation": Telegram from Reisch to Norman, 28 November 1923, and letter from Norman to Reisch, 10 December 1923; NA, T 160 / 58 / 2073 / 10–11: Telegram from Zimmerman to Niemeyer, 24 November 1923, as well as letter from Zimmerman to Niemeyer, 12 December 1923; NA, FO 371 / 8543 / C 20427: Telegram from Niemeyer to Zimmerman, 26 November 1923.

65. LNA, C 39, Réconstruction financière de l'Autriche 1922–1928, "Proces-verbal—Control Committee—Geneva September & December 1923": *Procès-verbal de la première séance tenue à Paris le lundi 17 décembre 1923, à 11 heures,* and *Procès-verbal de la deuxième séance, tenue à Paris le mercredi 19 décembre 1923, à 10 h.1 / 2.* The meetings were attended by President Pantaleoni (Italy), Vice-President Roos (Czechoslovakia), Andersen (Denmark), Botella (Spain), Janssen (Belgium), Count Lagerbielke (Sweden), Niemeyer (United Kingdom), Patijn (Netherlands), Seydoux (France), Dinichert (Switzerland), and Zimmerman. No Austrians were invited.

66. LNA, C 19, Réconstruction financière de l'Autriche 1922–1925, "Agreement Aust. gov. re Budget": Letters from Zimmerman to Kienböck, 31 January 1924.

67. LNA, C 4, Réconstruction financière de l'Autriche 1922–1926, "Taxation in Austria at 1st Sept 1923 & Proposed Steuerverteilungsgesetz": *Unterredung des Herrn Generalkommissaers mit Bundeskanzler Dr. Seipel und Finanzminister Dr. KienBoEck,* 9 January 1923, and *Unterredung des Herrn Generalkommissaers Dr. Zimmerman mit dem Bundesminister fuer Finanzen am 17. Jaenner 1924,* as well as letter from Zimmerman to Seipel, 12 January 1924.

68. For the police, however, Zimmerman agreed to additional annual wage payments of 6 billion crowns (£183,476), under the condition that the amount be saved elsewhere. Then he reminded Kienböck to never again make public any proposals he had not seen or commented on. LNA, C 24, Réconstruction financière de l'Autriche 1923–1925, "Salaries State Employees B": *Unterredung des Herrn Generalkommissärs Dr. Zimmerman mit dem Bundesminister für Finanzen Dr. Kienböck am 9. Februar 1924,* and Zimmerman to Kienböck, *note verbale,* 13 February 1924, as well as letter from Zimmerman to Kienböck, 5 February 1924.

69. Zimmerman also requested British envoy Akers-Douglas to warn Seipel that if he failed to sufficiently reduce expenditure and the number of state workers (esp. at the railways), Austria would face a rude awakening once trade fell or prices rose. LNA, S 113, Sir Arthur Salter's Private Papers, Austria No. 10, "Austria—Miscellaneous. Various memoranda on situation in Austria etc. etc.": Letter from Akers-Douglas to Curzon, 9 January 1924; LNA, S 108, Sir Arthur Salter's Private Papers, Austria No. 5, "Austria—Bank of Issue": Letter from Zimmerman to Salter,

1 February 1924; LNA, C 3, Réconstruction financière de l'Autriche 1922–1927, "re Austrian Army": Zimmerman to Seipel, *note verbale*, 18 February 1924.

70. Piétri, "La réconstruction économique," pp. 645–647.

71. LNA, C 4, Réconstruction financière de l'Autriche 1922–1926, "Credits Operations (General)": Letter from Spencer-Smith to Rosenberg, 10 January 1923.

72. Present were Lord Revelstoke and Gaspard Farrer of Barings, Baron Schröder, Anthony de Rothschild, Vivian Smith, and Charles Whigham of Morgan Grenfell, as well as Niemeyer, Strakosch, Bark, and the Bank of England Deputy Governor.

73. Some of their reluctance was certainly feigned, possibly to get later concessions out of the Bank of England. After all, each of the four banks was already invested in Austria and thus interested in seeing it return to prosperity. The London and Vienna Rothschild houses were in fact preparing for the loan already before the meeting. JPM, Vincent P. Carosso Papers, ARC 1214 (17): "Morgan & Co.— Boden Credit Anstalt": *Memo from January 1923*, and letter from E. C. Grenfell to Baron Bruno Schröder, 26 February 1923; RAL, XI / III / 189, "Special Correspondence re Austria (Loan)": Telegram from Whigham (Morgan Grenfell) to Young, 1 January 1923, and telegram from Vienna to London, 4 January 1923.

74. RAL, XI / III / 189, "Special Correspondence re Austria (Loan)": Telegram from Morgan Grenfell to J. P. Morgan, 16 January 1923.

75. BEA, OV 28 / 54, "Austrian Rehabilitation": *Meeting at the Bank—15th January, 1923*, and letter from Strakosch to Niemeyer, 15 January 1923; LNA, S 113, Sir Arthur Salter's Private Papers, Austria No. 10, "Austria—Miscellaneous. Various memoranda on situation in Austria etc. etc.": Letter from Salter to Drummond, 16 January 1923; AdR, 01 / 9, Ges. London, Telegramme 1920–1923, Box 18, "IV Hinaus 1923": Telegram from Franckenstein to Aussenamt, 19 January 1923.

76. Extracts from the reply by J. P. Morgan are worth quoting verbatim: "We feel too that if some such Austrian plan were to be successfully carried out it might possibly show the way to a similar operation in Germany. . . . We must however point out that we can give no encouragement to the idea that the United States Markets will absorb any material amount of the proposed long time loan in April or May. . . . Under fortunate conditions and after results in Austria had shown the value of the liens this situation might conceivably change but we see little chance for early American participation on any considerable scale." If the London houses nevertheless decided to issue a loan, J. P. Morgan would take some of *their* commitment. RAL, XI / III / 189, "Special Correspondence re Austria (Loan)": Telegrams from Morgan Grenfell to J. P. Morgan, 16 January 1923, and from J. P. Morgan to Morgan Grenfell, 18 January 1923; BEA, OV 28 / 54, "Austrian Rehabilitation": Telegrams from Deputy Governor to Norman, 17 January 1923, and from Morgan Grenfell to J. P. Morgan, 18 January 1923, as well as from J. P. Morgan to Vivian H. Smith and to Charles F. Whigham, 17 January 1923.

77. The smaller interim loan was meant to prepare the markets for the international long-term loan and to get investors accustomed again to buying Austrian securities. The conditions put down for the loan were similar to those envisioned for the larger long-term loan: Exemption from all taxes in Austria on capital and interest and covered 100 percent both by pledged revenues and by the guaranteeing states. Tranches were to be denominated in the currency of the country where issued and convertible into bonds of the long-term loan. Because some guarantees were still outstanding and others were doubtful, Niemeyer arranged that Britain, France, Italy, and Czechoslovakia each took over 25 percent of any deficit in the guarantees existing by the time of issue. BEA, OV 28/54," Austrian Rehabilitation": Letter from Niemeyer to Norman, 27 January 1923.

78. The committee was chaired by the Italian Pantaleoni and included Roos (Czechsolovakia), Niemeyer (United Kingdom), Avenol (France), Janssen (Belgium), and Botella (Spain), while Wallenberg (Sweden) and Patyn (Netherands), whose countries had not yet ratified their guarantee laws, participated as observers. The Austrian delegation consisted of Herman Patzauer, Richard Reisch, and Richard Schüller. AdR, 01/9, Ges. London, Box 102, Finanzsachen 1923–1931, 1938–1939, "Interimsanleihe 1923": Seipel to Franckenstein, 27 January 1923, and letter from Pantaleoni, 27 January 1923; LNA, C 39, Réconstruction financière de l'Autriche 1922–1928, "Mins. Control Committee (Paris) January 1923": *Procès-verbal des séances du comité de contrôle de l'Autriche du 27 janvier 1923.*

79. LNA, S 111, Sir Arthur Salter's Private Papers, Austria No. 8, "Austria—Sub Committee of Council": *Speech by M. Zimmerman, commissioner-general of the League of Nations at Vienna, to Sub Cttee of council,* 31 January 1923; LNA, C 36, Réconstruction financière de l'Autriche 1922–1925, C./S.C.A./P.V.11, "Meetings & Annexes—Meetings Aust-Sub-Committee. Paris Jan '23": *Draft Resolution,* 30 January 1923; AdR, NPA, 289 Liasse Oesterreich 8/IV Genf fol. 352–552, "Paris Februar 1923": *Rapport du Comité de Contrôle pour l'Autriche au Sous-comité d'Autriche du conseil de la société des nations,* 30 January 1923.

80. AdR, Box 68 fasz. 50/IV, "Völkerbundkreditaktion vom Jahre 1922": *Conseil de la Société des Nations—Déclération de Mgr Seipel, Chancelier d'Autriche,* 1 February 1923; LNA, 1156 Juin 1923 II: Autriche, pp. 807–838: *Extracts from the 23rd Council Session: Minutes,* 1 February 1923.

81. AdR, 01/9, Ges. London, Telegramme 1920–1923, Box 18, "IV Hinaus 1923": Franckenstein's telegrams, 2 February 1923.

82. JPM, ARC 1214 (16), Vincent P. Carosso Papers, "Morgan & Co.—Foreign Loans, Austria. File 2": Letter from Charles F. Whigham to N. D. Jay, 2 February 1923, and letter from Morgan Grenfell to N. D. Jay, 3 February 1923.

83. AdR, NPA, 289 Liasse Oesterreich 8/IV Genf fol. 352–552, "Paris Februar 1923": Telegram from Kienböck to Seipel, 6 February 1923; AdR, 01/9, Ges.

London, Telegramme 1920–1923, Box 18, "IV Hinaus 1923": Telegram from Franckenstein, 6 February 1923.

84. Norman had sent telegrams to all relevant central banks, asking them to receive an Austrian delegation. Apart from agreeing with the banks in the various financial centers on the amount and interest rate of the respective tranches to be floated, it was necessary that the governments prepare collateral bonds and get the Reparations Committee to settle the formal release of reparation liens and any claims from relief credits, too. This work was all done by Niemeyer from his desk at the Treasury with help of the Foreign Office. BEA, OV 28/54, "Austrian Rehabilitation": Telegrams from Norman to Msrs L. Van der Rest and Moll (Rijksbank, Sweden), to Vissering (Dutch National Bank), to Swiss National Bank, and to Governor Robineau (Banque de France), all 7 February 1923; and letters from Norman to Reisch and Kienböck, 7 February 1923; NA, FO 371/8539/C 2757: Telegram from Niemeyer to Zimmerman, 13 February 1923; AdR, 1 Ges. London Polit. Berichte 1920–1923: *Minutes of Meeting Held on 7.2.1923 at Austrian Legation in London*, and letter from Norman to Reisch, 7 February 1923; see also AdR, NPA, 289 Liasse Oesterreich 8/IV Genf fol. 352–552, "Paris Februar 1923": Norman, *Government of Austria Short-Term Loan*, to Franckenstein and Reisch, 8 February 1923, and letter from Franckenstein to Grünberger, 8 February 1923; AdR, 01/9, Ges. London, Telegramme 1920–1923, Box 18, "IV Hinaus 1923": Telegram from Kienböck, 6 February 1923.

85. The French considered an interest rate of 8 percent adequate, but upon learning that Norman envisioned 8 percent for the British tranche, demanded 9 percent. The setting of the interest rate was the most delicate, important, and probably arbitrary decision that had to be made. It influenced or even set the future rate of interest at which the Austrian state, Austrian firms and banks, and other countries as well would be allowed to borrow in London. The first tranche of the Czechoslovak loan issued at 8 percent by Barings in 1922 served as the relevant precedent. On the Czechoslovak loan, see Anne Orde, "Baring Brothers, the Bank of England, the British Government and the Czechoslovak State Loan of 1922," *English Historical Review* 106 (1991): 27–40, and Gerald J. Protheroe, *A Biography of Sir George Russell Clark: Nation-Building and the Limits of Personal Diplomacy* (London, 2004), pp. 74–129; BEA, OV 28/54, "Austrian Rehabilitation": Telegram from Norman to Bark, 12 February 1923, and telegrams from Bark to Norman, 10, 13, and 17 February 1923; AdR, 01/9, Ges. London, Box 102, Finanzsachen 1923–1931, 1938–1939, "Interimsanleihe 1923": Telegram from Reisch (Paris) to Franckenstein, 13 February 1923.

86. An emission in Norway proved impossible because of the state's bad economic situation. BEA, OV 28/54, "Austrian Rehabilitation": Letter from Norman to Kienböck, 8 February 1923, and from Vissering to Norman, 7 and 14 February 1923, as well as telegrams from Strakosch to Norman, 12 and 13 February

1923, letter from SNB to Norman, 8 February 1923, and telegrams from Schnyder von Wartensee and Bark to Norman, 15 and 17 February 1923; AdR, NPA, 289 Liasse Oesterreich 8 / IV Genf fol. 352–552, "Paris Februar 1923": Telegrams from Kienböck (The Hague) to Seipel, 13 February 1923, from Duffek (The Hague) to London, 14 February 1923, from Di Pauli (Berne), 15 and 17 February 1923, and from Patzauer (Stockholm), 15 February 1923, as well as letters from Patzauer, 15, 17, and 19 February 1923. See also AdR, 01 / 9, Ges. London, Telegramme 1920–1923, Box 18, "IV Herein 1923": Telegrams from Kienböck to Franckenstein, 13 February 1923, and from Patzauer (Copenhagen) to Franckenstein and Kienböck, 21 and 22 February 1923; AdR, 01 / 9, Ges. London, Telegramme 1920–1923, Box 18 "IVa 1923 Claris Tel Hinaus und Herein": Reisch (Geneva) to London, 16 February 1923.

87. Niemeyer, who had coordinated efforts toward the liberation of Austrian assets for the duration of the long-term loan, complained a few days before the issue that he could no longer "undertake to continue more or less permanently as financial agent for the austrian [sic] Government". He did not fail to point out that "the real credit for the success rests with the governor at the Bank of England. He has devoted an enormous amount of time to the Austrian affair and has used his influence both in England and outside it to carry the matter to a success.... I am certain that but for that assistance not a penny would have been raised for Austria." The Austrians "had no notion whatever of how to negotiate loans of this character and did not know in the least what they wanted. In consequence the whole work has had to be done for them." NA, FO 371 / 8539 / 3603: Letter from Niemeyer to Zimmerman, 24 February 1923; AdR, 68, 18130 / 23, "Generalpfandrecht": Letter from Reparations Commission Secretary General Andrew McFadyean, 21 February 1923.

88. The London issue received 367 public subscriptions totaling £3,107,500. J. P. Morgan eventually stayed out of the loan, but the London banks still participated. The New York firm of Kuhn, Loeb & Co. also turned down requests from the French Banque de Paris et des Pays Bas and from Max Warburg to join the short-term loan; BEA, OV 28 / 54, "Austrian Rehabilitation": Telegrams from Federal Reserve Bank of New York to Norman, 9 February 1923, from Norman to Bark and from Bark to Norman, both 15 February 1923, and from J. P. Morgan to Norman, 16 February 1923, as well as letters from E. C. Grenfell to Norman, 14 February 1923, from Ter Meulen to Norman, 28 February 1923, and from Norman to Moll, Vissering, Van der Rest, Robinau, and Schnyder von Wartensee, all 1 March 1923; AdR, 01 / 9, Ges. London, Telegramme 1920–1923, Box 18, "IV Hinaus 1923": Telegram from Franckenstein to Foreign Ministry, 28 February 1923; AdR, 01 / 9, Ges. London, Box 102, Finanzsachen 1923–1931, 1938–1939, "Interimsanleihe 1923": Letters from Sir Ernest Harvey (BoE) to Franckenstein, 2 March 1923, from Austrian Ministry of Finance to Harvey (BoE), 27 April 1923, and from

Wallenberg (Stockholm Enskilda Bank) to Franckenstein 22 March 1923; JPM, ARC 1214 (16), Vincent P. Carosso Papers, "Morgan & Co.—Foreign Loans, Austria"; JPM, MG&Co. Papers, Loans & Options, Hist. Box 33.

89. Piétri, "La réconstruction économique," p. 730.

90. LNA, C 39, Réconstruction financière de l'Autriche 1922–1928, "Minutes— Control Committee—April 1923—Geneva": *Procès-verbal de la première séance tenue à Genève le samedi 14 avril 1923 à midi:* Annex I., and *Procès-verbal de la troisième séance tenue à Genève, le dimanche 15 avril 1923, à 11 h.,* as well as *Procès-verbal de la quatrième séance, tenue à Genève, le Dimanche 15 avril 1923, à 16.30 heures,* and letter from Pantaleoni to Zimmerman, 15 April 1923; NA, FO 371 / 8540 / C 6908: Telegram from Strakosch to Niemeyer, 17 April 1923.

91. AdR, 01 / 9, Ges. London, Telegramme 1920–1923, Box 18 "IV Hinaus 1923": Telegram from Franckenstein to Foreign Ministry, 27 March 1923; LNA, C 5, Réconstruction financière de l'Autriche 1922–1924, "Negotiations for Long-Term Loan": Letter from Trotter (BoE) to Zimmerman, 29 March 1923.

92. BEA, OV 28 / 55, "Austrian Rehabilitation": Letters from Norman to Bark, 6 April 1923, from Vissering to Norman, 25 May 1923, from Schnyder von Wartensee to Norman, 23 May 1923, from Bark (Paris) to Trotter (BoE), 8, 12, and 14 April 1923, and from Bark to Simon (Anglo-Austrian Bank, Vienna), 20 June 1923, as well as telegrams from Bark (Brussels) to BEA, 9 April 1923, and from Bark to Norman, 19 April and 19 May 1923; AdR, Box 68 fasz. 50 / IV, "Voelkerbundanleihe 1923": Letters from Franckenstein to Grünberberger, 9 and 11 April 1923, and letter from Franckenstein (Geneva) to Grünberger and Kienböck, 16 April 1923; AdR, NPA, 289, Liasse Oesterreich 8 / IV Genf fol. 553–715, "Neue Kreditverhandlungen Voelkerbund April 1923": Telegram from Franckenstein (The Hague) to Vienna, 10 April 1923.

93. BEA, OV 28 / 55, "Austrian Rehabilitation": Telegram from J. P. Morgan to Morgan, Grenfell & Co., 19 April 1923; AdR, Box 68 fasz. 50 / IV, "Voelkerbundanleihe 1923": Letter from Franckenstein (Geneva) to Grünberger and Kienböck, 21 April 1923.

94. The sudden change of mind in New York makes it appear all too likely that the exchange of telegrams was in fact staged and was meant to impress on the Austrians the sway Norman held over the U.S. capital market.

95. The syndicate included Kuhn Loeb, First National Bank, National City Bank, Guaranty Trust and Bankers Trust. BEA, OV 28 / 55, "Austrian Rehabilitation": Telegram from J. P. Morgan to Morgan, Grenfell & Co., 28 April 1923.

96. To convince Lamont, Arthur Salter asked Zimmerman's aide-de-camp, Pierre Quesnay, to draw up the latest information on pledged revenues, the budget position, taxation and on how the Austrian economy was being affected by the situation in Germany. LNA, S109, Sir Arthur Salter's Private Papers, Austria, No. 6, "Austria—Correspondence etc. with Commissioner-General and Staff at Vienna":

Telegram from Salter to Zimmerman, 30 April 1923, and letter from Salter to Quesnay, 30 April 1923; BEA, OV 28/55, "Austrian Rehabilitation": Telegram from Morgan, Grenfell & Co. to J. P. Morgan, 21 April 1923, and telegrams from J. P. Morgan to Morgan, Grenfell & Co., 23 and 24 April 1923, as well as telegram from Norman to Bark, 25 April 1923; AdR, 01/9, Ges. London, Telegramme 1920–1923, Box 18, "IV Hinaus 1923": Telegram from Franckenstein to Foreign Ministry, 22 April 1923; AdR, "Box 68 fasz. 50/IV": Letter from Franckenstein to Kienböck, 26 April 1923.

97. Lamont telegraphed New York that he favored the business and that "knowing your great desire and especially that of J. P. Morgan to assist in this matter we have taken it very seriously here and believe it must be now handled by New York as a matter of immediate and prime interest." BEA, OV 28/56, "Austrian Rehabilitation": Telegrams from Lamont to J. P. Morgan, 6, 7, and 9 May 1923, telegrams from J. P. Morgan to Lamont (Paris), 9 May 1923, and to Morgan, Grenfell & Co., 18 May 1923, as well as letter from Bark to Norman, 10 May 1923; LNA, C 5, Réconstruction financière de l'Autriche 1922–1924, "Negotiations for Long-Term Loan": Nixon (Paris) to Zimmerman, 8 May 1923; LNA, S 109, Sir Arthur Salter's Private Papers, Austria No. 6, "Austria—Correspondence etc. with Commissioner-General and Staff at Vienna": Letter from Salter to Quesnay, 9 May 1923; AdR, 01/9, Ges. London, Telegramme 1920–1923, Box 18, "IV Hinaus 1923": Telegram from Franckenstein to Foreign Ministry, 18 May 1923; see also the *Times,* City Notes: *American Bankers and Austria: Participation in Loan,* 14 May 1923.

98. In Bark's eyes, the French still viewed Austria as an enemy, which made negotiations difficult, and he wrote that only following pressure from London was the demand surmounted. AdR, Box 68 fasz. 50/IV, "Voelkerbundanleihe 1923": Letters from Franckenstein to Grünberger and Kienböck, 20 and 21 April 1923; NA, FO 371/8540/C 6908: Telegram from Strakosch to Niemeyer, 17 April 1923; BEA, OV 28/56, "Austrian Rehabilitation": Letter from Bark to Norman, 9 May 1923, and from Bark to Simon (Anglo-Austrian Bank, Vienna), 20 June 1923.

99. AdR, Box 68 fasz. 50/IV, "Voelkerbundanleihe 1923": Telegrams from Franckenstein (The Hague) to Kienböck, 1 and 3 May 1923, as well as from Franckenstein to Foreign Ministry, 6 June 1923; AdR, 01/9, Ges. London, Telegramme 1920–1923, Box 18, "IV Herein 1923": Telegram from Foreign Ministry to London, 22 May 1923; BEA, OV 28/56, "Austrian Rehabilitation": Letters from Vissering to Norman, 28 April and 3 May 1923, from Bark to Norman, 3 and 30 May 1923, from Ter Meulen to Norman, 7 May 1923, from Ter Meulen to Franckenstein, 9 May 1923, from Moll (Sveriges Riksbank) to Norman, 5 and 12 May 1923, from Bark to Norman, 9 May 1923, from Bark to Simon, 20 June 1923, and from Norman to Ter Meulen, 9 May 1923, as well as telegrams from Reisch to Norman, 23 May 1923, from Norman to Vissering, 7 May 1923, from Vissering

to Norman, 7 May 1923, and from Norman to Bark, 9 May 1923; JPM, ARC 1221 (Box 35) Morgan Bank European papers: "Austrian Bonds, 1919–1926": Letter from Kienböck to Janssen, 18 June 1923.

100. Piétri, "La réconstruction économique," p. 744.

101. BEA, OV 28/56, "Austrian Rehabilitation": *Speech Made by Dr. Zimmerman, Commissioner General of the League of Nations in Vienna, to American Press Representatives London, June 4th, 1923.*

102. AdR, 01/9, Ges. London, Telegramme 1920–1923, Box 18, "IV Hinaus 1923": Telegram from Franckenstein to Foreign Ministry, 6 June 1923. The British issue of £3,232,000 was three times oversubscribed.

103. NA, FO 371/8542/C 10613: Telegram from Barclay to Curzon, 12 June 1923.

104. On the eve of the American subscription, Norman released the following press release to the United States: "Within Austria great elements of strength are already appearing. With some help from outside in financial matters, which a democratic world bent on co-operation are not only willing but anxious to supply, the new Austrian Republic has convinced the investors of the world that, whatever its past, it is now deserving of credit. Consequently, credit has been forthcoming." BEA, OV 28/56, "Austrian Rehabilitation": *Press Release for US Press for Monday Morning 11.6.1923*; NA, FO 371/8542/C 10996: Letter from Chilton (Washington, DC) to Curzon, 15 June 1923.

105. AdR, Box 68 fasz. 50/IV, "Voelkerbundanleihe 1923": Telegram from Duffek to Grünberger, 16 June 1923; BEA, OV 28/56, "Austrian Rehabilitation": Telegram from Ter Meulen to Norman, 16 June 1923, and letters from Norman to Ter Meulen, and from Vissering to Norman, both 18 June 1923.

106. BEA, OV 28/56, "Austrian Rehabilitation": Telegram from Bark to Norman, 18 June 1923. The British Board of Trade could not believe this figure, which it thought ought to read 30 million Swiss francs, but inquiries by the Foreign Office confirmed it. NA, FO 371/8542/C 13602: Letter from Scott to Curzon, 14 July 1923, and /C 18571: Letter from Chancery to Central Department, 21 August 1923.

107. This is not to say that economic conditions were generally good in Austria in 1923. In fact, Karl Ausch defined them as "schizophrenic," since the stable exchange rates resulted in prosperity for banks and speculators but deprived exporting industries of the "inflation premium." Stable exchange rates resulted in a fall of production for certain industries, while hyperinflation in Germany and the continued depreciation of the French, Czech, Hungarian, and Polish currencies did much to further reduce Austrian exports. Furthermore, difficulties for Austrian producers were exacerbated by the French invasion of the Ruhr and the resulting higher price for coal. The occupation of the Ruhr did, however, have some positive effects on unemployment, because Austrian steel producers received

orders that otherwise would have gone to Westphalia. Quesnay argued that that the drop in unemployment from 170,000 in February to 149,000 in April 1923 was partially due to difficulties in Germany and Czechoslovakia. Industrial stagnation is reflected in the fact that the Austrian industry consumed markedly less coal and the federal railways transported significantly less goods in 1923. See Kernbauer, *Währungspolitik in der Zwischenkriegszeit: Geschichte der Österreichischen Nationalbank von 1923 bis 1938* (Vienna, 1991), pp. 89–92; März, *Österreichische Bankenpolitik in der Zeit der gossen Wende, 1913–1923: Am Beispiel der Credit-Anstalt für Handel und Gewerbe* (Munich, 1981), pp. 538–542; Ausch, *Als die Banken fielen: Zur Soziologie der politischen Korruption* (Vienna, 1968), pp. 126, 133–140; LNA, S 113, Sir Arthur Salter's Private Papers, Austria No. 10, "Austria—Miscellaneous. Various memoranda on situation in Austria etc. etc.": Quesnay, *Note relative aux répercussions de la situation allemande sur la vie économique autrichienne*, 2 May 1923.

108. Speculators' demand for credit supported the high interest rate level and Austrian companies, unable to borrow, took advantage of the rally to raise capital by going public or issuing new shares. The VSE witnessed 236 capital increases in 1922, another 151 in 1923, but only 34 in 1924. Similarly, the number of new public companies was 265 in 1922 and 250 in 1923, but only 148 in 1924. Kernbauer, *Währungspolitik in der Zwischenkriegszeit*, pp. 93–94.

109. Unfortunately, Swiss commercial banks, whose historical archives hold much valuable information about the global size of Austrian flight capital, as a rule only grant access to their own internal historians.

110. Schnyder von Wartensee gave the deficit as £6–8 million. According to calculations by Zimmerman's office, however, the Austrian balance of payments would have shown an enormous deficit if the Austrian government had been forced to pay its interest on foreign debt by obtaining the necessary foreign exchange on the market instead of taking it from the loan proceeds. NA, T 160/584/2073/021/9, "Austrian Reconstruction": Letter from Schnyder von Wartensee to Norman, 24 July 1923; LNA, C 43, Réconstruction financière de l'Autriche 1923–1925, "Miscellaneous Documents on Statistics": Letter to Loveday, 9 July 1924.

111. Wolfgang Zipser, *Auf der Suche nach Stabilität: Das Zentralbankgeldangebot der Österreichischen Nationalbank 1923 bis 1937* (Frankfurt am Main, 1997).

112. According to Schnyder von Wartensee, the invisible exports included revenues from the movement of foreigners, purchases of foreigners in Austria not controlled by customs, compensation of work done by Vienna banks or merchants for foreigners, transit trade, return of emigrated capital to Austria and investments from foreign capital in Austrian shares, real estate, mortgages, etc. The reserve stock from the Devisenzentrale transferred to the ANB at the end of 1923

was 100 million gold crowns (almost $20 million), of which two-thirds were included in the official balance sheet. LNA, C 11, Réconstruction financière de l'Autriche 1922–1926, "Use of Reserve Funds": Letter from Schnyder von Wartensee to Zimmerman and Norman, 28 December 1923, and his report, *Impression about the Austrian National Bank and questions Concerning the Austrian Exchange during the First Exercise of the Bank*; LNA, C 4, Réconstruction financière de l'Autriche 1922–1926, "Credits Operations (General)": Telegram from Zimmerman to Salter, 12 January 1923; ANB, IV / 9, "Monatsberichte des Beraters bei der OeNB an den Generalkommissär des Völkerbundes": Conseiller Report No. 1, 10 July 1923, pp. 6–7.

113. LNA, C 20, Réconstruction financière de l'Autriche 1922–1927, "Austrian Budget 1924": *Unterredung mit Kienböck*, 5 December 1923; LNA, C 24, Réconstruction financière de l'Autriche 1923–1925, "Salaries State Employees A": Letter from Zimmerman to Kienböck, 6 December 1923; NA, FO 371 / 8543 / C 21284: Letter from Akers-Douglas to Curzon, 6 December 1923; BEA, OV 28 / 43, "Oesterreichische Nationalbank": Telegram from Reisch to Norman, 10 December 1923, and from Norman to Reisch, 11 December 1923, as well as untitled memorandum, 13 December 1923; BEA, OV 28 / 58, "Austrian Rehabilitation": Telegram from Bank of England to Reisch, 7 December 1923.

114. ANB, IV / 9, "Monatsberichte des Beraters bei der OeNB an den Generalkommissär des Völkerbundes": Conseiller Report No. 2, 10 August 1923.

115. To Norman, however, he wrote that "I am very glad to tell you that I have a good impression of the progress of Austria. Confidence is returning and the people out of work are diminishing. There is one black point: the boom of the Stock exchange, may it last? It is justified? The enclosed tableau 'Börse' shows you the evaluation of the principal shares. Everybody buys shares and few put their money into Savings Banks." NA T 160 / 584 / 2073 / 021 / 9, "Austrian Reconstruction": Letter from Schnyder von Wartensee to Norman, 24 July 1923. By October, Schnyder von Wartensee was decidedly more critical: "Bei der Unmasse von neuen Banken, Bankhäusern und Vermittlern, die als Parasiten am Volkswirtschaftskörper nagen, ist es begreiflich, dass diese Stimmung aufrecht gehalten wird, denn je mehr Leute sich dafür interessieren, je mehr Zwischengewinner [sic] werden eingeheimst, und die Ersparnisse oder mit Mühe geretteten Gelder aus der Valutenkatastrophe fliessen als Quelle in die Taschen dieser Leute, ohne den geringsten Nutzen für die Volkswirtschaft im Gegenteil zum grossen Schaden der moralischen Entwicklung des Landes." ANB, IV / 9, "Monatsberichte des Beraters bei der OeNB an den Generalkommissär des Völkerbundes": Conseiller Report No. 4, 10 October 1923, p. 21.

116. Kernbauer, *Währungspolitik in der Zwischenkriegszeit*, p. 97. The deficit mainly stemmed from the costs of the Ruhr occupation, expenses on reconstruction, and indemnities to war invalids, and many believed that the French currency would depreciate just as the Austrian, German, Polish, and Hungarian had already done. In December, 100 French francs were still worth 30 Swiss francs, but on

11 March 1923, their value had fallen to 21 Swiss francs. Viennese speculators participated in this run on the franc, by engaging in deals by which they would sell francs for dollars in the present, but supply the francs in the future, hoping that the downward trend would continue. Others took out loans in French francs and it was also common to buy goods from France that had only be paid three months in the future.

117. Jean-Noël Jeanneney, "La spéculation sur les changes comme arme diplomatique—A propos de la première 'bataille du franc' (novembre 1923–mars 1924)," *Relations internationales* 13 (1978): 5–27; Jean Claude Débeir, "La crise du franc de 1924—Un exemple de spéculation 'internationale,'" *Relations internationales* 13 (1978): 29–49.

118. In Vienna, the first to close were the Allgemeine Industriebank, Austro-Polnische Bank, Austro-Orientbank, and Kolmar und Co., while Kettner and Brüder Nowak were in trouble. The related problems at Postsparkasse and Union Bank would only be revealed at a later date.

119. LNA, S 109, Sir Arthur Salter's Private Papers, Austria No. 6, "Austria—Correspondence etc. with Commissioner-General and Staff at Vienna": Letter from Zimmerman to Drummond, 12 December 1923.

120. Zimmerman had written to Salter in January 1923 that it was desirable to obtain definite guarantees towards foreign credits because Austrians would otherwise grow nervous and the government's position would be weakened. He went on to state that "in the meantime I try as best I can to play the role of Janus, the man with the two faces: only with this difference—if I recollect rightly the two faces of Janus were exactly the same, whereas I have to show a face with a certain expression to the Austrian Government, and a face with an utterly different expression to the public and to all who can influence the good will of the financiers." LNA, S 109, Sir Arthur Salter's Private Papers, Austria No. 6 "Austria—Correspondence etc. with Commissioner-General and Staff at Vienna": Letter from Zimmerman to Salter, 12 January 1923.

5. Reconstructions at the Crossroad

Epigraph: NA, FO 371 / 9653 / C 17573: Letter from Niemeyer to Franckenstein, 7 November 1924.

1. "Vom Herzen, mit Schmerzen, ein wenig oder gar nicht," *Sporttagblatt,* 1 January 1924, pp. 1–2; "Die Vienna in Paris," *Illustriertes Sportblatt,* 5 January 1924, p. 9.

2. "Vienna in Paris," *Sporttagblatt,* 3 January 1924, pp. 1–2.

3. LNA, S 108, Sir Arthur Salter's Private Papers, Austria No. 5, "Austria": Charles Rist, *Report on His Mission to Austria,* 10 January 1923. Published versions of the report can be found as "Le relèvement politique de l'Autriche et de la reprise de son commerce extérieur," in *La Revue politique et parlementaire,* 10 June 1923,

and "La situation économique de l'Autriche en 1922," in his *Essais sur quelques problèmes économiques et monétaires* (Paris, 1933), pp. 344–382. See also Nicole Piétri, "La réconstruction économique et financière de l'Autriche par la Société des Nations (1921–1926)" (doctoral thesis, Université de Paris I, 1981), p. 978.

4. Louis von Rothschild was asked to relay the same information to his London cousins: "Werde von massgebender Stelle ersucht euch mitzuteilen dass hiesige Börsensituation in dortigen Zeitungen anscheinend unrichtig dargestellt wurde. Börse nach einigen flauen Tagen wieder wesentlich fester kein Grund zu Beunruhigung stop Kann meinerseits vorstehendes voll Bestätigen." RAL, XI/84/37 1924: Telegram from S. M. Rothschild to N. M. Rothschild, 7 April 1924. See also RAL, XI/III/297, "SM von Rothschild": Letter from Louis von Rothschild to N. M. Rothschild, 3 April 1924, in which Louis reported a heavy fall on the VSE, but that a "crisis was averted as sufficient means are at the disposal of the market": LNA, C 11, Réconstruction financière de l'Autriche 1922–1926, "Temporary Use of Loan Money. Börse Unterstützung etc.": Letter from Kienböck to Zimmerman, 26 March 1924.

5. LNA, C 7, Réconstruction financière de l'Autriche 1921–1928, "Adviser to Bank": *Unterredung des Herrn Generalkommissaers Dr. Zimmerman mit Herrn Praesidenten dr. Reisch, Praesident der Nationalbank, am 9. Mai 1924;* LNA, C 11, Réconstruction financière de l'Autriche 1922–1926, "Temporary Use of Loan Money. Börse Unterstützung etc.": Telegram from Quesnay to Denis, 8 May 1924, and letters from Zimmerman to Brauneis, 14 April 1924, from Grimm to Zimmerman, 13 April 1924, from Kienböck to Zimmerman, 29 April 1924, and from Zimmerman to Kienböck, 1 May 1924; LNA, S 110, Sir Arthur Salter's Private Papers, Austria No. 7, "Austria—Enquiry by C. G. & Financial Cttee into present financial position & possible modification in reform programme. Preliminary investigations": Letter from Felkin to Salter, 15 April 1924; NA, FO 371/9651/C 7833: Phillpotts, memorandum on VSE, 9 May 1924.

6. In June, the Wiener Escompte und Lombard Bank shut its doors, as did the Adriatische Bank, while the Biedermann Bank, experiencing heavy withdrawals from depositors, was initially saved with assistance from the ANB, but closed in 1927. The Depositenbank was at first bailed out by larger banks but eventually was forced to close its doors, too. BEA, OV 9/384, "Sir Otto Niemeyer's Files: Austria National Bank": Telegram from Reisch to Norman, 1 July 1924, and letter from Young to Niemeyer, 7 August 1924.

7. LNA, C 11, Réconstruction financière de l'Autriche 1922–1926, "Temporary Use of Loan Money. Börse Unterstützung etc.": Letter from ANB Directors to Zimmerman, 24 May 1924.

8. BEA, OV 9/384, "Sir Otto Niemeyer's files: Austria National Bank": Letter from Zimmerman to Strakosch, 4 August 1924 (also in LNA, C 32, Réconstruction financière de l'Autriche 1923–1927, "Geldinstitut Centrale").

9. In June the Control Committee of Guarantor States would discuss Zimmerman's unorthodox employment of the loan to support the Vienna market and

agree to leave future decisions of that kind to Zimmerman. LNA, C 39, Réconstruction financière de l'Autriche 1922–1928, "Committee of Control—Procès-verbal & résolution (June 1924; September 1924)": *Procès-verbal définitif, 6ème session, première séance, tenue à Genève le mercredi 11 juin 1924 à 11 heures,* and *deuxième séance, tenue à Genève le jeudi 12 juin 1924 à 10 heures;* LNA, C 11, Réconstruction financière de l'Autriche 1922–1926, "Temporary Use of Loan Money. Börse Unterstützung etc.": Letter from ANB to Zimmerman, 24 May 1924, and letter from Kienböck to ANB, 30 May 1924.

10. ANB, VI/9 "Monatsberichte des Beraters bei der OeNB an den Generalalkommissär des Völkerbundes": Conseiller reports for 1924.

11. LNA, S 122, Sir Arthur Salter's Private Papers, No. 18, "Delegation of Financial Committee [to] Vienna, August–September 1924.—Notes on Meetings": *Brauneis,* 30 August 1924; LNA, R 512 "Modification of the Program of Reform": *4ème séance tenue à Vienne le 28 août 1924, à 11 heures.*

12. Kernbauer, *Währungspolitik in der Zwischenkriegszeit: Geschichte der Österreichischen Nationalbank von 1923 bis 1938* (Vienna, 1991), pp. 96, 98, 131, puts the capital outflow due to failed speculation between $6 and $9 million. Ausch, *Als die Banken fielen: Zur Soziologie der politischen Korruption* (Vienna, 1968), p. 139, estimates that because of French franc speculation $7 million was lost abroad.

13. "Es ist ja auch Ihnen, hochverehrter Herr Minister bekannt, dass die wirtschaftliche Lage unseres Landes es unbedingt erforderlich erscheinen lässt, unseren heimischen Unternehmungen fremdes, wenn möglich westländisches Kapital zuzuführen. Nur mit Hilfe der billiger verzinslichen ausländischen Gelder wird es möglich sein, durch Investitionen die Productionsfähigkeit unserer Industrie auf eine konkurrenzfähige Höhe zu bringen." AdR, 01/9, Ges. London, Karton 102, Finanzsachen 1923–1931; 1938–1939, "Finanzen Allg. 1924": Letter from Vienna Chamber of Commerce to Franckenstein, 26 June 1924.

14. "On the other hand I am afraid that the situation of our industries will not really improve owing to the terrible scarcity of capital, and particularly to the fact that credits from abroad are only obtainable for short periods, whilst our industries want their working capital for at least one year, and in many cases even for a longer period. This I consider at present as the greatest difficulty, and unless it is solved I am afraid that no progress in the industrial situation will be achieved." BEA, OV 28/59, "Austrian Rehabilitation": Letter from Simon to Norman, 31 May 1924.

15. RAL, XI/III/297, "SM von Rothschild": Letter from London to Louis v. Rothschild, 10 April 1924; AdR, 01/9, Ges. London, Karton 102, Finanzsachen 1923–1931; 1938–1939, "Finanzen Allg. 1924": Letter from Franckenstein to Chancellery, 31 July 1924.

16. AdR, 01/9, Ges. London, Karton 101, Finanzsachen 1920–1923, "Finanzsachen: Reconstruktion 1921": Letter from Franckenstein to Chancellery, 7 April 1924; AdR, 01/9, Ges. London, Karton 102, Finanzsachen 1923–1931; 1938–

1939, "Finanzen Allg. 1924": Letter from Harvey to Franckenstein, 10 July 1924, and letter from Tugendhat to Benedikt, 4 July 1924.

17. Norman had not been available to discuss the question with Franckenstein. AdR, 01 / 9, Ges. London, Karton 102, Finanzsachen 1923-1931; 1938-1939, "Finanzen Allg. 1924": Letters from Franckenstein to Chancellery with copies to Harvey and Vienna Chamber of Commerce, from Strakosch to Franckenstein, and from Franckenstein to Chancellery, all on 18 July 1924.

18. AdR, 01 / 9, Ges. London, Karton 102, Finanzsachen 1923-1931; 1938-1939, "Finanzen Allg. 1924": Letter from Schröder to Franckenstein, 14 July 1924.

19. Van Gijn, a former Finance Minister and Member of Parliament, was also a professor and a Royal Commissioner of the Dutch National Bank. He had taken up office on 13 May 1924. LNA, C 9, Réconstruction financière de l'Autriche 1923-1928, "Monthly Reports on Austrian National Bank by Schnyder": Memo by Anton van Gijn, May 1924; LNA, C 11, Réconstruction financière de l'Autriche 1922-1926, "Use of Reserve Funds": Letter from Reisch to Zimmerman, 10 May 1924; LNA, C 11, Réconstruction financière de l'Autriche 1922-1926, "Temporary Use of Loan Money. Börse Unterstützung etc.": Telegram from Reisch to Norman, 2 May 1924; NA, FO 371 / 9651 / C 7222: Telegram from Zimmerman to Norman, 25 April 1924, and / C 7402: Telegram from Norman to Zimmerman, 6 May 1924; BEA, OV 28 / 59, "Austrian Rehabilitation": Letter from Franckenstein to Norman, 8 July 1924, and Memorandum: *The Austrian Gold Crown*, 10 July 1924; AdR, 01 / 9, Ges. London, Karton 102, Finanzsachen 1923-1931; 1938-1939, "Finanzen Allg. 1924": Letter from Deputy Governor Lubbock to Franckenstein, 21 July 1924, and letter from Kienböck to Franckenstein, 25 June 1924; JPM, ARC 1221 (Box 35) Morgan Bank European papers, File 5: Austrian Bonds 1924, "Austrian bonds, 1919-1926": Letter from Arragon to Garr, 30 August 1924.

20. NA, FO 371 / 9651 / C3894: Lampson, *Conversation*, 6 April 1924; NA, HW 12 / 56 / 016023: Telegram from Arlotta to Toretta, 29 February 1924; AdR, 01 / 9, Ges. London, Karton 19: Telegramme 1924-1938, "1924 Herein Ziffer": Telegram from Foreign Ministry to Franckenstein, 6 March 1924.

21. NA, T 160 / 59 / 2073 / 11, "Austrian Reconstruction": Note by Niemeyer, 1 January 1924, and letters from Salter to Niemeyer, 18 and 29 February 1924, as well as note from Niemeyer to Parmoor, *Austrian Reconstruction*, 4 March 1924, and note from Rowe-Dutton to Phillips, 23 January 1924; NA, FO 371 / 9651 / C 3789: Letter from Rowe Dutton to Lampson sent by Niemeyer to Parmoor, 5 March 1924; BEA, OV 28 / 58, "Austrian Rehabilitation": Letters from Salter to Niemeyer, 15 February 1924, and from Niemeyer to Salter, 18 February 1924.

22. Present: Salandra (Italy, Chair), Beneš (Czechoslovakia), Grünberger (Austria), Hanotaux (France), Lord Parmoor (United Kingdom), and Zimmerman. LNA, C / S.C.A. / 4ème session / P.V.1., in LNA, 1164 Juin 1924 II: Autriche, *Procès-verbal provisoire de la séance tenue à Genève le mercredi 12 mars 1924, à 15 h. 30*; LNA, C

19, Réconstruction financière de l'Autriche 1922–1925, "Agreement Aust. gov. re Budget": Letter from Grünberger to Zimmerman, 10 March 1924.

23. "The functions of the Commissioner-General shall be brought to an end . . . when the Council shall have ascertained that the financial stability of Austria is assured," Geneva Protocols, III/4 (see Appendix C of this volume); LNA, C/S.C.A./4ème session/P.V.1., in LNA, 1164 Juin 1924 II: Autriche, *Proces-verbal provisoire de la séance tenue à Genève le mercredi 12 mars 1924, à 15 h. 30.*

24. AdR, NPA, 288, fol. 241: "Layton u. Rist Genfer Verhandlungen fol. 160–257": Letter from Pflügl to Schüller, 15 April 1924; NA, FO 371/9651/C4527: Telegram from British Consul (Geneva), 12 March 1924.

25. The Council pointed "out that: (a) The original programme adopted by the Austrian Government constitutes a solemn undertaking the execution of which remains obligatory unless modified with the consent of all the Contracting Parties; (b) Under the terms of the Protocols, the control can only be withdrawn when permanent equilibrium is re-established in the Austrian budget and the financial stability of Austria is assured; (c) Under the terms of the Protocols and of the prospectus for the flotation of the various blocks of the loan, i.e., of the undertakings entered into towards the guarantor States and the bondholders, the total yield of the loan can only be employed under the control of, with the authorisation of, and for purposes approved by the Commissioner-General," LNA, 1164 Juin 1924 II: Autriche: *P.V.5 of 28th Session of Council,* 12 March 1924, and *Resolution by League of Nations Council on Austria,* 12 March 1924.

26. LNA, C 31, Réconstruction financière de l'Autriche 1923–1928, "New Programme—Austrian Government": Letters from Salter to Zimmerman, 15 and 29 April 1924; AdR, NPA, 288, fol. 241–: "Layton u. Rist Genfer Verhandlungen fol. 160–257": Letter from Salter to Schüller, 15 April 1924.

27. Socialist leader Bauer correctly reported to Seipel that, according to his informants, the League had not yet decided whether to continue control over Austria and that the decision would possibly be postponed. Seipel forwarded a copy to Foreign Minister Grünberger, commenting that Bauer's letter "schon als Tatsache, abgesehen vom Inhalt, besonders beachtenswert erscheint." AdR, NPA, 288, "Layton u. Rist Genfer Verhandlungen fol. 160–257": Communication from Bauer to Seipel, and from Seipel to Grünberger, both 28 April 1924.

28. Zimmerman, "Financial Reconstruction of Austria (Second Year)—Thirteenth Report by the Commissioner-General of the League of Nations for Austria (Period December 15th, 1923, to January 15, 1924—First Month of the Third Stage)," *League of Nations—Official Journal* 5 (April 1924): 630–656.

29. Zimmerman, "Financial Reconstruction of Austria (Second Year).—Fourteenth Report by the Commissioner-General of the League of Nations for Austria (Period January 15th to February 15th, 1924.—Second Month of the Third Stage)," *League of Nations—Official Journal* 5 (April 1924): 657–682.

30. LNA, S 110, Sir Arthur Salter's Private Papers, Austria No. 7, "Austria—
Enquiry by C. G. & Financial Cttee into present financial position & possible
modification in reform programme: Preliminary investigations": *Discussion between the Commissioner-General Dr. Zimmerman, the Chancellor Dr. Seipel and
the Finance Minister, Dr. Kienboeck. On the 17th May, 1924;* LNA, C 31, Réconstruction financière de l'Autriche 1923–1928, "New Programme—Austrian Government": *Unterredung des Herrn Generalkommissärs Dr. Zimmerman mit dem
Budneskanzler Dr. Seipel und dem Finanzminister Dr. Kienböck, am 17. Mai 1924;*
NA, FO 371 / 9652 / C 9257: Letter from Akers-Douglas to MacDonald, 6 June 1924.
    31. LNA, C 24, Réconstruction financière de l'Autriche 1923–1925, "Salaries
State Employees B": Patzauer, *Pensionskürzungsgesetz,* 8 April 1924; LNA, 21, Réconstruction financière de l'Autriche 1922–1928, "Simplification of Administration": Letter from Zimmerman to Seipel, 11 April 1924, and letter from Seipel to
Zimmerman, 14 April 1924.
    32. Both Seipel and Kienböck thought it politically impossible to reform the
financial relationship between the state and its provinces and communes, which
required changing the constitution. The Anglo-Austrian Bank's Simon expressed
the same view to Norman, namely that the government had tried hard to meet
Zimmerman's views, but that its chief difficulty was the lack of influence over the
local authorities, in particular Vienna, which meant that it could not keep total
taxation within reasonable limits. BEA, OV 28 / 59, "Austrian Rehabilitation":
Letter from Simon to Norman, 31 May 1924; LNA, S 110 Sir Arthur Salter's Private Papers, Austria No. 7, "Austria—Enquiry by C.G. & Financial Cttee into
present financial position & possible modification in reform programme. Preliminary investigations": *Discussion between the Commissioner-General Dr. Zimmerman, the Chancellor Dr. Seipel and the Finance Minister, Dr. Kienbock. On the
17th May, 1924;* LNA, C 31, Réconstruction financière de l'Autriche 1923–1928,
"New Programme—Austrian Government": *Unterredung des Herrn Generalkommissärs Dr. Zimmerman mit dem Budneskanzler Dr. Seipel und dem Finanzminister Dr. Kienböck, am 17. Mai 1924.*
    33. While real prices were higher in postwar Vienna, state officials' wages in
the new Republic were significantly lower than they had been in Imperial Vienna,
particularly for the higher ranks, which often made less than half their prewar
salaries after adjusting for inflation. "Das neue Besoldungssystem und die Fami-
lienerhalter," *Reichspost,* 1 June 1924, pp. 3–4.
    34. LNA, C 24, Réconstruction financière de l'Autriche 1923–1925, "Salaries
State Employees B": *Unterredung des Herrn Generalkommissärs Dr. Zimmerman
mit dem Bundesminister für Finanzen Dr. Kienböck am 4. April 1924;* LNA, C 21,
Réconstruction financière de l'Autriche 1922–1928, "Simplification of Adminstra-
tion": *Unterredung des Herrn Generalkommissärs Dr. Zimmerman, mit Herrn
Bundekanzler Dr. Seipel, am 5. Mai 1924;* LNA, C 7, Réconstruction financière de
l'Autriche 1921–1928, "Adviser to Bank": *Unterredung mit dem Finanzminister*

Dr. Kienboeck von Herrn Generalkommissaers Dr. Zimmerman, am 8. Mai 1924; NA, FO 371/9651/C 6955: Letter from Akers-Douglas to MacDonald, 25 April 1924.

35. Seipel had changed his tone and now stated that he wished to have regular conversations with Zimmerman to minimize conflicts. He claimed that he had not had enough time previously and that furthermore the General Commissioner had shown a tendency to take plans as promises. LNA, C 31, Réconstruction financière de l'Autriche 1923-1928, "New Programme—Austrian Government": *Résumé d'une conférence qui a eu lieu entre: M. Zimmerman, M. Seipel et M. Kienböck. le 20 mai 1924;* LNA, C 24, Réconstruction financière de l'Autriche 1923-1925, "Salaries State Employees B": *Unterredung des Herrn Generalkommissärs mit dem Herrn Bundeskanzler und dem Herrn bundesmininster für Finanzen,* 26 May 1924.

36. Zimmerman attacked Kienböck for not consulting him, but the Finance Minister argued that he had informed Patzauer. Patzauer himself commented, "Dies ist ein Irrtum!" LNA, C 24, Réconstruction financière de l'Autriche 1923-1925, "Salaries State Employees B": Zimmerman, *Note verbale,* 24 May 1924, and *Unterredung des Herrn Generalkommissärs Dr. Zimmerman und dem Finanzminister Dr. Kienböck am 22. Mai 1924;* LNA, C 31, Réconstruction financière de l'Autriche 1923-1928, "New Programme—Austrian Government": *Unterredung des Herrn Generalakommissärs am 22. Mai im Finanzministerium mit dem Bundeskanzler und dem Finanzminister.*

37. The Foreign Ministser had no qualms raising public hopes that the meeting might result in an end of the League intervention in Austria. Grünberger wrote in the *Reichspost* that "die Beschlüsse, die Oesterreich in den nächsten Wochen auf der Junitagung des Völkerbundes zu erreichen hofft, sollen es ermöglichen, das Genfer Werk zu vollenden, die Kontrolle zu beschließen, für einen geordneten Staatshaushalt die volle Freiheit des Handelns wieder zu gewinnen." "Zwei Jahre," *Reichspost,* 1 June 1924, pp. 1-2, 2.

38. LNA, C 31, Réconstruction financière de l'Autriche 1923-1928, "New Programme—Austrian Government": Letters from Salter to Zimmerman, 15 and 29 April 1924; LNA, S 110, Sir Arthur Salter's Private Papers, Austria No. 7, "Austria—Meeting on June 11th 1924 of Financial Cttee and Cttee of Control with reference to Enquiry in Austria": A. Pelt, *Memorandum on the Policy to be Followed by the Council of the League of Nations at its Next Meeting, June 1924, in Regard to the Austrian Reconstruction Problem,* 29 May 1924.

39. LNA, 1164 Juin 1924 II: Autriche, 11 June 1924: *Exposé de M. Janssen sur la situation monétaire à Vienne.*

40. "Der Generalkomissär billigt ausdrücklich die Vereinbarung zwischen den Parteien über das Normalbudget. Er stellt sich der in diesem Beschlusse festgelegten Summe von fünfhundertzwanzig Millionen Goldkronen nicht entgegen, er betrachtet die Kundgebung der Parteien keineswegs als eine Kriegserklärung, sondern als eine gute Basis der Diskussion in der Genfer Beratung." NFP, "Gute

Hoffnungen für Genf. Wichtige Mitteilungen des Generalkommissärs Dr. Zimmerman," 8 June 1924, pp. 1-2.

41. LNA, S 110, Sir Arthur Salter's Private Papers, Austria No. 7, "Austria—Meeting on June 11th 1924 of Financial Cttee and Cttee of Control with reference to Enquiry in Austria": "Very confidential" letter from Zimmerman to Salter, 30 May 1924.

42. The meeting was attended by Ter Meulen, Bianchini, Janssen, Niemeyer, Parmentier, Pospíšil, and Strakosch. Salter, Zimmerman, Loveday, and Jacobson were also present. LNA, F 156 (LNA 1397 [146-169]): *Rapport préparé par le Commissaire Général en Autriche,* 9 June 1924; LNA, F 157 (LNA 1397 [146-169]): *Avant-projet de Rapport commun au conseil du Commissaire Général de la Société des Nations en Autriche et du Comité Financier de la Société des Nations sur les demandes du gouvernement autrichien,* 10 June 1924; LNA, S 110, Sir Arthur Salter's Private Papers, Austria No. 7, "Austria—Meeting on June 11th 1924 of Financial Cttee and Cttee of Control with reference to Enquiry in Austria": Letter from Zimmerman to Salter, 30 May 1924; LNA, C 31, Réconstruction financière de l'Autriche 1923-1928, "New Programme—Austrian Government": Letter from Zimmerman to Niemeyer, 9 April 1924; LNA, Documents du Comité Financier, vol. XII, F.153 (LNA 1309 F120-F153, Janvier-Mai 1924), *Preliminary Draft Budget prepared by the Austrian Government.*

43. LNA, F / 15ème session / P.V. 3 (1) in LNA, 1164 Juin 1924 II: Autriche: *Procès-verbal de la 3ème séance, tenue à Genève, le jeudi 12 juin 1924 à 10 heures (première partie),* and *Procès-verbale de la 5ième session à 19 heures (seconde partie).*

44. LNA, F / 15ème session / P.V. 7 (1) in LNA, 1164 Juin 1924 II: Autriche: *Procès-verbal de la septième séance, tenue à Genève le vendredi 13 juin 1924, à 17 heures.*

45. LNA, F 165 (SdN 1397 [146-169]): *Memorandum confidentiel remie le 13 iuin au Comite financier par les representants du Govuernement autrichien.*

46. LNA, F / 15ème session / P.V.10 (1) in LNA, 1164 Juin 1924 II: Autriche: *PV—Réconstruction Financière de l'Autriche—Questions du Rélèvement des Traitments.*

47. LNA, F / 15ème session / P.V. 4(1) in LNA, 1164 Juin 1924 II: Autriche: *Procès-verbal de la 4ème séance, tenue à Genève, le jeudi 12 juin 1924 à 15 heures.*

48. LNA, F 164 (SdN 1397 [146-169]): Zimmerman, *L'augmentation des traitements et des pensions,* 16 June 1924.

49. LNA, F / 15ème session / P.V. 6 (1) in LNA, 1164 Juin 1924 II: Autriche: *Procès-verbal de la 6ème séance, vendredi matin 13 juin;* LNA, F 162: *Austria. Confidential Report by the Financial Committee,* 14 June 1924.

50. LNA, F 161 (SdN 1397 [146-169]) and LNA, S.C.A. 32: *Austria. Report by Financial Committee and the Commissioner General to the Council,* 14 June 1924;

LNA, C 47 / "Report by Financial Committee and Commissioner General to Council. June 1924": *Avant-projet de Rapport commun au conseil du Commissaire Général de la Société des Nations en Autrich et du Comité Financier de la Société des Nations sure les demandes du Gouvernement Autrichien,* 10 June 1924.

51. The Control Committee had previously expressed its agreement with the Financial Committee's proposal and had, given the legal hurdles to the usage of the loan remainder, suggested that the Council begin addressing the matter so that progress on it could be made before September. However, it would be necessary to consider all the information of the prospectus regarding the usage of the loan money as well as all other rights and interests involved, which meant the conditions from reparations and relief, so that it was by no means certain that the balance could be used by the government for productive investments. LNA, C 39, Réconstruction financière de l'Autriche 1922–1928, "Committee of Control — Procès-verbal & résolution (June 1924; September 1924)": *Troisième séance tenue à Genève le vendredi 13 juin 1924 à 18 heures.,* and *Resolution adoptée le 13 juin 1924 par le Comité de Control des états garants de l'emprunt Autrichien,* 13 June 1924.

52. LNA, F 161 (SdN 1397 [146–169]): *Report by Financial Committee and the Commissioner General forwarded by the Austrian Committee to the Council,* 14 June 1924; LNA, C 47 / "Reports by Financial Committee & Commissioner General to Council. June 1924": *Austria. Confidential Report by the Financial Committee,* 14 June 1924; LNA, C / S.C.A. / 5e session / P.V.1. 14 June 1924: *Sous-Comité d'Auriche. séance du samedi 14 juin 1924, à 16 heures.*

53. LNA, F / 15ème session / P.V. 4 (1) in LNA, 1164 Juin 1924 II: Autriche: *Procès-verbal de la 4ème séance, tenue à Genève, le jeudi 12 juin 1924 à 15 heures,* and *PV— Réconstruction financière de l'Autriche—Questions du rélèvement des traitements;* LNA, C 24, Réconstruction financière de l'Autriche 1923–1925, "Salaries State Employees C": *Unterredung des Herrn Generalkommissärs Dr. Zimmerman mit dem Vizekanzler Dr. Frank und dem Finanzminister Dr. Kienböck am 23. Juni 1924;* LNA, S 109, Sir Arthur Salter's Private Papers, Austria No. 6, "Austria—Correspondence etc. with Commissioner-General and Staff at Vienna": Letter from Zimmerman to Salter, 26 June 1924; LNA, C 31, Réconstruction financière de l'Autriche 1923–1928, "New Programme—Austrian Government": *Unterredung des Herrn Generalkommissärs mit dem Vizekanzler Dr. Frank am 28. Juni 1924.*

54. Schüller welcomed the visit of the Financial Committee, which he thought was wrongly informed about the Austrian situation, not least due to Zimmerman's official reports! AdR, 01 / 9, Ges. London, Karton 102, Finanzsachen 1923–1931; 1938–1939, "Finanzen Allg. 1924": Letter from Schüller to Franckenstein, 25 June 1924.

55. NA, FO 371 / 9652 / C 10050: Letter from Akers-Douglas to MacDonald, 21 June 1924.

56. LNA, C 4, Réconstruction financière de l'Autriche 1922–1926, "Taxation in Austria at 1st Sept 1923 & Proposed Steuerverteilungsgesetz": Letter from Zimmerman to Kienböck, 17 June 1924; LNA, C 31, Réconstruction financière de l'Autriche 1923–1928, "New Programme—Austrian Government": *Unterredung des Herrn Generalkommissärs mit Herrn Dr. Viktor Kienböck, am 4. Juli 1924;* LNA, C 24, Réconstruction financière de l'Autriche 1923–1925, "Salaries State Employees C": Patzauer, *Aufhebung der Pensionsautomatik,* 22 July 1924.

57. LNA, C 31, Réconstruction financière de l'Autriche 1923–1928, "New Programme—Austrian Government": Letter from Zimmerman to Frank, 25 June 1924.

58. BEA, OV 9/384, "Sir Otto Niemeyer's files: Austria National Bank": Letter from Zimmerman to Strakosch, 4 August 1924; LNA, S 109, Sir Arthur Salter's Private Papers, Austria No. 6, "Austria—Correspondence etc. with Commissioner-General and Staff at Vienna": Letter from Zimmerman to Salter, 26 June 1924.

59. Characteristically, Niemeyer, who had been given a room on the first floor on which the meeting room and secretariat were located and which Janssen and Pospíšil had also chosen, moved to the cheaper second floor on which the lower functionaries of the League and Zimmerman's office were quartered. LNA, C 47, Reconstruction fiancière de l'Autriche 1924–1925, "Documents submitted to Del. of Finance Committee": *Numéros des chambres à l'hôtel Impérial.*

60. The delegates split into five subcommittees: Niemeyer, Paramentier, and Ter Meulen were to study the budget and the Treasury position; Dubois, Mazzucchelli, and Parmentier would review the railways, state enterprises, and postal, telephone, and telegraph authorities; Janssen and Pospíšil would preoccupy themselves with the relationship of the government and local authorities; and on the ANB and economic questions, Dubois, Janssen, and Niemeyer, and possibly also Ter Meulen and Pospíšil, would write a report.

61. A total of eight meetings were held interviewing ANB President Reisch, General Manager Brauneis, and Conseiller van Gijn; the Verband der Oesterreichischen Banken und Bankiers; the Kammer für Arbeiter und Angestellte; the Hauptverband der Industrie Oesterreichs; the Hauptverband der Oesterreichischen Kaufmannschaft; the Oesterreichische Landwirtschaftsgesellschaft und Kammer für Landwirtschaft; the Verband der Baumeister Oesterreichs together with other trade associations; and representatives of the textile industry of Vorarlberg. LNA, S 122, Sir Arthur Salter's Private Papers, No. 18, "Delegation of Financial Committee [to] Vienna, August–September 1924.—Notes on Meetings," 30 August 1924. See also LNA, C 41, Réconstruction financière de l'Autriche 1923–1927, "Economic & Industrial Crisis": Kammer für Handel, Gewerbe und Industrie in Wien, *Exposé,* 12 August 1924; LNA, C 47, Réconstruction financière de l'Autriche 1924–1925, "Documents submitted to Del. of Finance Committee": Verband österreichischer Banken und Bankiers, *Exposé sur la crise économique et bancaire en Autriche,* 25 August 1924, and *Exposé on Taxation of Banks,* 7

June 1924, as well as *Denkschrift der Wiener Kammer für Arbeiter und angestellte über die Frage des Zinsfusses,* 1 September 1924.

62. The delegation proposed that the ANB conduct its discount policy so as to maintain stability not only with gold but also with commodity prices, and that it create a small executive body to take rapid decisions to allow it to do so. Because companies' balance sheets were still drawn up in devaluated paper crowns and provided unreliable information to foreign lenders, the delegates suggested that gold balance sheets be introduced soon and the crown legally put on gold. An internal memo by Hawtrey at the Bank of England, however, saw no reason for concern over ANB policy. BEA, OV 9/384, "Sir Otto Niemeyer's files: Austria National Bank": Hawtrey, *Austrian Currency and the National Bank,* 12 August 1924; LNA, C 32, Réconstruction financière de l'Autriche 1923–1927, "Geldinstitut Centrale": Letters from Zimmerman to Strakosch, 4 August 1924, and from Strakosch to Zimmerman 14 August 1924.

63. It expected the government to abolish the tax on banking and foreign-exchange transactions, reduce corporate taxation, and introduce legal reforms to facilitate the issue of industrial bonds. The list of economies included amalgamating federal and provincial administrations in the provinces, regulating the fiscal relationship between federal government and local authorities, reducing taxation in Vienna, cutting the number of officials on war-invalid commissions, reforming the agrarian administration and administration of state buildings, providing better control over the observance of work hours in government offices, and transforming numerous state enterprises into autonomous bodies. LNA, C 41, Réconstruction financière de l'Autriche 1923–1927, "Economic & Industrial Crisis": *Report of Sub Committee IV to Delegation of Finance Committee,* 12 August 1924; LNA, C 47, Réconstruction financière de l'Autriche 1924–1925, "re Delegation of Financial Committee": Letter from Avenol to Zimmerman, 14 August 1924, Niemeyer, *Notes sur les conclusions provisoires du sous-comité I.,* 1 September 1924, and *Liste provisoire des conclusions,* 2 September 1924; LNA, 1167 Septembre 1924 II: Autriche: *Procès-verbal de la 16ème séance tenue à Genève le 9 septembre 1924 à 15 h 30;* LNA, Documents du Comité Financier, vol. XIV F 179 (LNA 1398 [170–200]): FC Delegation to Vienna and Zimmerman, *Réconstruction de l'Autriche,* 8 September 1924.

64. NA, FO 371/9652/C 14586: Letter from Akers-Douglas to MacDonald, 9 September 1924; LNA, S 122, Sir Arthur Salter's Private Papers, No. 18, "Delegation of Financial Committee [to] Vienna, August–September 1924—Notes on Meetings": *Rough Notes,* 30 August 1924.

65. AdR, 01/1, NPA 287, "Liasse Oesterreich 8/IV 1923–25 Fol. 1–458": Telegram from Seipel to Frank, 2 September 1924.

66. The meeting was chaired by Ter Meulen (Netherlands) and attended by Bianchini (Italy), Dubois (Switzerland), Janssen (Belgium), Niemeyer (United Kingdom), Strakosch (South Africa), Sekiba (Japan), and Wallenberg (Sweden).

LNA, 1167 Septembre 1924 II: Autriche: *Procès-verbal de la deuxième séance, tenue à Genève, le mercredi 10 septembre 1924, à 10 h. 30.*

67. LNA, 1167 Septembre 1924 II: Autriche: *Procès-verbal de la quatrième séance tenue à Genève le 11 septembre 1924 à 10 heures.*

68. LNA, 1167 Septembre 1924 II: Autriche: *Procès-verbal de la cinquième séance tenue à Genève le jeudi 11 septembre 1924 à 16 heures.*

69. LNA, 1167 Septembre 1924 II: Autriche: *Procès-verbal de l 6ème séance tenue à Genève, le vendredi 12 septembre 1924 à 10 h.45.*

70. Government papers in Vienna reacted positively to the results obtained and pointed to the impending relaxation of control, while opposition papers declared that the government had been utterly defeated. AdR, NPA, 289 Liasse Oesterreich 8/IV Genf fol. 1—381, "Genf Maerz und Juni 1924": *Discours Pronince par M. Zimmerman au Conseil,* and *Discours de Mgr. Seipel,* 16 September 1924; NA, FO 371/9652/C 14749: Telegram from British Delegation to Foreign Office, 18 September 1924, and/C 14902: Letter from Coote to MacDonald, 18 September 1924, as well as/C 15256: Letter from Keeling to MacDonald, 26 September 1924; LNA, S 110, Sir Arthur Salter's Private Papers, Austria No. 7, "Enquiry into Financial position and possible modifications in Reform Program": Letters from Ter Meulen to Chancellor Seipel and from Seipel to Financial Committee, 15 September 1924; LNA, F188 (LNA 1398 [170–200]), *Rapport commun du Comité Financier et du Commissaire Général à Vienne,* 12 September 1924.

71. On Monday, 15 September 1924, the Committee of Control had a meeting to discuss and approve the report before it was presented to the Council. The following members were present at the meeting: President Pantaleoni (Italy), Roos (Czechoslovakia), Andersen (Denmark), de Felcourt (France), de la Huerta (Spain), Lagerbielke (Sweden), Melot (Belgium), Niemeyer (United Kingdom), Patijn (Netherlands), and Dinichert (Switzerland). President Pantaleoni attacked the report, which he considered incomplete, and Lagerbielke found it too optimistic but was of the opinion that the Control Committee could not but accept the agreement. It was defended by Niemeyer, Zimmerman and Patijn, who stated that one could not ask more from Austria than from another country, and that the most important thing was that the security of the loan remain assured. It was obvious to Andersen that the Austrian budget level had to be increased. The committee demanded that all reforms listed in the report be executed without delay. LNA, C.G.A./7ème session/ P.V.1 (1): *Procès-verbal—séance du lundi 15 Septembre 1924 à 15 heures 30.*

72. LNA, SCA 34: "Joint Report by the Financial Committee and the Commissioner-General in Vienna," 15 September 1924 (C.496.1924/II.), p. 2.

73. Ibid., p. 3.

74. An exception here is Peter Berger in his book on Zimmerman's Dutch assistant, Meinoud Rost van Tonningen, *Im Schatten der Diktatur* (Wien, 2000), p. 80: "In Wahrheit war Alfred Rudolf Zimmerman nicht der unumschränkte Fi-

nanzdiktator, als den ihn vor allem die zeitgenössische Linkspresse porträtierte." See also Peter Berger, "The League of Nations and Interwar Austria: Critical Assessment of a Partnership in Economic Reconstruction," in *The Dolfuss-Schuschnigg Era in Austria: A Reassessment*, ed. Günther Bischof, Anton Pelinka, and Alexander Lassner (New Brunswick, NJ, 2003), pp. 73–92. Ausch, *Als die Banken fielen*, writes: "Dr. Zimmerman fühlte sich, wie man sieht, als der Finanzdiktator Österreichs, als der Mann von dem die ganze Gewalt ausging und dem sich Parlament, Regierung und Gewerkschaften einfach unterzuordnen hatten. Er nahm für sich Machtbefugnisse in Anspruch, die so gut wie keine Grenzen hatten und die zweifellos in Widerspruch zu dem standen, was offiziell von der österreichischen Regierung gelegentlich der Unterzeichnung der Genfer Protokolle erklärt worden war" (p. 110). Karl Bachinger and Herbert Matis, *Der österreichische Schilling: Geschichte einer Währung* (Graz, 1974), p. 65, define him as the most powerful man in Austria. Wolfgang Fritz, *Für Kaiser und Republik: Österreichs Finanzminister seit 1848* (Vienna, 2003), p. 173, regards him as "ein wahrer Finanzdiktator im Interesse des internationalen Finanzkapitals."

75. J. L. J. Bosmans, *De Nederlander Mr. A. R. Zimmerman als Commissaris-Generaal van de Volkenbund in Oostenrijk, 1922–1926* (Nijmegen, 1973).

76. George E. Berkley, "Vienna and Its Jews: The Solitary Scapegoat in Postwar Vienna," in *Hostages of Modernization*, ed. Herbert A. Strauss (Berlin, 1993), pp. 797–810.

77. "Ankunft des Generalkomissärs in Wien," *NFP*, 15 December 1922, p. 1. The original text read: "Der Generakomissär wird nicht den Tyrannen spielen, er wird nur der Regierung das Rückgrat stärken, er wird ihr die moralische Autorität geben das zu tun, was sie selber tun will und was sie tun muss, um ihren Pflichten zu genügen und den Rückfall in die Versumpfung und Bankerottierwirtschaft zu verhindern." True to its political orientation, the Socialist *Arbeiterzeitung* ignored Zimmerman's arrival and the following day chose to mock the *Neue Freie Presse*'s adulations, commenting that with the General Commissioner's appearance, Austria had ceased to be a "free and independent state." "Die Ankunft," *AZ*, 16 December 1922, p. 3.

78. *Der Götz von Berlechingen—Eine lustige Streitschrift gegen Alle*, "Die drei scheinheiligen Könige aus dem Borgenlande," 4 January 1924, p. 1: "Das ist nicht der richtige Zimmerman für uns!"

79. "Ein armer sanierter Staat bitt' gar schön," *Der Morgen*, 7 January 1924, p. 14: "Wir wollen durch die Stadt marschieren, Mit dem Fechten unser Glück probieren. Und will einer uns grad' nichts spendieren, Na so betteln wir an Andern an. Wissenschaft und Kunst—wird bei uns verhunzt. Und dem Zimmermann— liegt da gar nix dran. Darum nur munter fortsanieren, Auf die Kunst im Fechten kommt es an."

80. "Also sprach der Herr Dr Zimmermann," *AZ*, 24 February 1924, p. 7: "Jehova, der eifervolle Gott aus Rotterdam."

81. "Karikatur der Woche. Generalkommissär Dr. Zimmerman," *Der Morgen*, 25 February 1924, p. 5: "Was sagt der Prediger? Contenti estote, Begnügt euch mit eurem Kommissbrote: Seid zufrieden mit eurer Löhnung, Und verflucht jede böse Angewöhnung! Lasst euch vom Sparsinn leiten bloss: So kommt ihr sicher in Abrahams Schoss! (Er nimmt bei den letzten Worten in seinem achtzylindrigen Auto Platz und fährt fort—seine bescheidene Monatslöhnung zu beheben.)

82. "Wer vom Zimmermann isst . . . ," *Arbeiterwille*, 21 March 1924, p. 3: "Jetzt wissen Sie es, mein lieber Herr Bundeskanzler, dass Sie mich nur dann loskriegen, wenn mir anderswo ebenso hohe Bezüge wie in Österreich garantiert werden."—"Ja, Ja, Sie haben recht. Aber ich habe es nicht glauben können, dass dem lieben Gott der Bürgermeister von Amsterdam mehr gilt als der Prälat des Herrn."

83. "Die Wissenden," *AZ*, 21 March 1924, p. 7: "Wenn wir uns auch über den Weg ein bisschen streiten, über das Ziel sind wir uns einig: Auf unserem Posten bleiben so lange als möglich!"—"Im alten Rom sagte man: Wenn zwei Auguren einander begegnen, lächeln sie . . ."

84. "Whoever eats my flesh and drinks my blood has eternal life." John 6:54.

85. "Nach der Schlacht von Genf," *AZ*, 25 June 1924, p. 7: "Der Sieger": "Die hab'n a nokan g'fressen."—"Uns kann ohnehin nichts mehr schaden."

86. "Schnorrituri Te Salutant," *Der Morgen*, 7 July 1924, p. 16.

87. LNA C 47, Réconstruction financière de l'Autriche 1924–1925, "re Delegation of Financial Committee": Letter from Zimmerman to Drummond, 8 August 1924; LNA, C 47, Réconstruction financière de l'Autriche 1924–1925, "Documents submitted to Del. of Finance Committee": Letter from Reisch to Zimmerman and League of Nations' Delegation, 22 August 1924, published in the Vienna press the next day; BEA, OV 9 / 384: Memorandum, 27 August 1924; NA, FO 371 / 9652 / C 13953: Letter from Akers-Douglas to MacDonald, undated.

88. This seems to have been the view of President Reisch and Director Brauneis. Traditionally, facing financial crisis, the policy of a "peripheral" central bank such as the Austro-Hungarian was to intervene on the exchange markets, possibly with help of emergency credits from other central banks, until confidence returned. Matthias Morys, "Monetary Policy under the Classical Gold Standard (1870s–1914)" (Working Paper, Department of Economics and Related Studies, University of York, 2010); Kernbauer, *Währungspolitik in der Zwischenkriegszeit*, pp. 134, 148.

89. LNA, C 9, Réconstruction financière de l'Autriche 1923–1928, "Raising of Discount of the 'National Bank'": *Unterredung des Herrn Generalkommissaers in der Nationalbank mit Vize-Praesident Thaa, Generaldirektor Brauneis und dem Berater, Prof van Gyn*, 4 August 1924.

90. LNA, C 11, Réconstruction financière de l'Autriche 1922–1926, "Temporary Use of Loan Money. Börse Unterstützung etc.": *Unterredung mit dem Bundesminister für Finanzen Dr. Kienböck*, 22 September 1924.

91. The *Times* of London, which often reflected Norman's views, wrote on 30 October 1924 that the "Austrian Bank has not been very happy in its Bank rate policy. It failed to take action in time to check the speculation which brought about serious troubles earlier in the year, and led to the withdrawal of a considerable amount of foreign credit. Now it proposes to reduce the rate just at the moment when it is beginning to do its work. Doubtless a reduction will suit the speculators admirably and those people who thrive on an active Bourse: but the gains of private interests are not necessarily consistent with national advantage. In view of the financial crisis in the spring, the National Bank would be wiser not to be in too great a hurry to reduce its rate." *Times,* "City Notes, Prospective Capital Operations: Austrian Monetary Policy"; BEA, OV 9/391, "Sir Otto Niemeyer's files: Austria 1925": Letters from Niemeyer to Kienböck and Franckenstein, 31 October 1924; BEA, OV 9/384, "Sir Otto Niemeyer's files: Austria National Bank": Letter from Norman to van Gijn, 25 October 1924.

92. The ANB's General Council was split, with five members in favor of reducing the rate to 12 percent and five in favor of leaving it unchanged. Reisch, who had initially favored reducing the rate to 12 percent, finally cast his decisive vote for 13 percent. AdR, 2 Ges. London Polit. Akten 1923–4, "298/Pol": Telegram from Grünberger to Franckenstein, 5 November 1924; LNA, C 9, Réconstruction financière de l'Autriche 1923–1928, "Raising of Discount of the 'National Bank'": Letter from Zimmerman to Niemeyer, 6 November 1924; Kernbauer, *Währungspolitik in der Zwischenkriegszeit,* p. 152; Piétri, "La réconstruction économique," p. 921.

93. AdR, 01/9, Ges. London, Karton 102, Finanzsachen 1923–1931; 1938–1939, "Finanzen Allg. 1924": Letter from Reisch to Franckenstein, 24 November 1924; AdR, 2 Ges. London Polit. Akten 1923–4, 321: Letters from Franckenstein to Norman, 28 November 1924, and from Norman to Franckenstein, 1 December 1924, as well as telegram from Franckenstein to Reisch, 1 December 1924.

94. Van Gijn had not thought Austrian prices too high and believed the high rate of 15 percent could be safely abandoned because it attracted no new foreign capital. BEA, OV 9/391, "Sir Otto Niemeyer's files: Austria 1925": Letter from Strakosch to van Gijn, 13 November 1924, and letter from van Gijn to Norman, 5 November 1924, as well as telegram from van Gijn to Norman, 5 November 1924; BEA, OV 28/60, "Austrian Rehabilitation": Letter from Strakosch to van Gijn, 6 December 1924, and letter from van Gijn to Strakosch, 22 November 1924, as well as Memorandum: *Austria. Strakosch versus Van Gijn,* 26 November 1924, and Memorandum: *Strakosch v. Van Gijn,* 8 December 1924.

95. BEA, OV28/29, "Oesterreichische Nationalbank": Memorandum: *Dr. Reisch's visit—possible subjects for discussion,* 9 December 1924; AdR, 2 Ges. London Polit. Akten 1923–4, Pol. 339: Letter from Franckenstein to Mataja, 11 December 1924.

96. JPM, ARC 1214 (16) Vincent P. Carosso Papers, "Morgan & Co.—Foreign Loans, Austria. File 3": Letter from Whigham to Lamont, 16 December 1924.

97. BEA, OV28/29, "Oesterreichische Nationalbank": *Second Interview with Dr. Reisch*, 10 December 1924; AdR, 2 Ges. London Polit. Akten 1923–4, 339/Pol.: Osborne, *Interview with Dr. resich* [sic] *9th December*, 9 December 1924; as well as Letters from Reisch, 10 December 1924, and from Franckenstein to Mataja, 11 December 1924.

98. LNA, S 113, Sir Arthur Salter's Private Papers, Austria No. 10, "Austria—Miscellaneous Memoranda on Austrian Situation from January 1925": Van Walré de Bordes, *The Austrian Price Level*, 14 January 1925; LNA, S 111, Sir Arthur Salter's Private Papers, Austria No. 8, "Situation in Austria—Events subsequent to Assembly 1924": Van Walré de Bordes, *The Dispute between the Bank of England and the Austrian National Bank*, 17 January 1925; AdR, 2 Ges. London Polit. Akten 1923–4: Letter from Reisch, 10 December 1924, and letter from Franckenstein to Mataja, 11 December 1924.

99. AdR, 2 Ges. London Polit. Akten 1923–4: Letter from Franckenstein to Mataja, 11 December 1924.

100. BEA, OV 9/391, "Sir Otto Niemeyer's files: Austria 1925": Letter from Norman to van Gijn, 17 December 1924, and letter from Strakosch to van Gijn, 16 December 1924.

101. NA, FO 371/9653/C 19219: Letter from Akers-Douglas to Chamberlain, 18 December 1924.

102. AdR, 2 Ges. London Polit. Akten 1923–4: Letter from Franckenstein to Mataja, 22 December 1924.

103. "Es ist gewiss möglich, dass wir in theoretischen Kenntnissen im Grossen und Ganzen den Engländern überlegen sind; . . . Die alles überragende Frage ist jedoch: Benötigen wir die britische Sympathie, das angelsächsische Kapital, das Vertrauen der Welt und die Hilfsbereitschaft des mächtigsten Finanzmannes, unseres bewährten grossen Freundes Mr. Norman? Wenn ja, so müssen wir Eitelkeit, Empfindlichkeit und Misstrauen ablegen und den gegebenen Machtverhältnissen zum Wohle des Vaterlandes mit Mut und Entschlossenheit Rechnung tragen." AdR, 01/9, 2 Ges. London Polit. Akten 1923–4, Pol. 339: Franckenstein to Mataja, 11 December 1924.

104. LNA, S 60, M. de Bordes Files—Box 7, "Financial Adviser": Letter from Quesnay to van Walré de Bordes, 22 January 1925.

105. BEA, OV 9/391, "Sir Otto Niemeyer's files: Austria 1925": Letter from Niemeyer to Lampson, 16 December 1924.

106. Comité Olympique Français, *Les jeux de la VIIIe Olympiade Paris 1924* (Paris, 1924), p. 79; "Die Pariser Olympiade," *Neues Montagblatt*, 3 March 1924, p. 10; "Beteiligung Oesterreichs an der Pariser Olympiade," *NFP*, 8 May 1924, pp. 11–12.

107. "Wo die Sportbegeisterung endet," *Sporttagblatt*, 9 April 1924, pp. 1–2; "Die Fussball-Olympiade," *Sporttagblatt*, 6 June 1924, pp. 5–6.

108. "Die achte bürgerliche Olympiade in Paris," *AZ*, 2 August 1924, p. 9.

109. "Die sportliche Völkerschlacht in Paris," *NFP*, 25 July 1924, p. 3.

6. The Politics of Control

Epigraph: LNA, C 43, Réconstruction financière de l'Autriche 1923–1925, "Projected American & Foreign Loans": Letter from Zimmerman to Speyer, 28 July 1925.

1. Ulrike Felber, "Der Schilling—eine Antwort auf die 'österreichische Frage,'" in *Vom Schilling zum Euro*, ed. Klaus Liebscher and Wilfried Seipel (Vienna, 2002), pp. 98–110.

2. LNA, C 24, Réconstruction financière de l'Autriche 1923–1925, "Salaries of Railway Employees": *Unterredung des Herrn Generalkommissärs mit dem Generaldirektor der Bundesbahnen, Dr. Siegmund, & Finanzdirektor hofrat Maschat. (Dr. Rost),* 4 November 1924, and *Unterredung des Generalkommissärs Dr. Zimmerman mit dem Finanzminister Dr. Kienböck, am 5. November 1924;* LNA, C 20, Réconstruction financière de l'Autriche 1922–1927, "Preliminary Budget 1925": *Unterredung des Herrn Generalkomissärs mit dem Finanzminister Dr. Kienböck, am 20. Oktober 1924;* LNA, C 21, Réconstruction financière de l'Autriche 1922–1928, "Amalgamation of Provincial Administrations": *Unterredung de Generalkommissärs Dr. Zimmerman mit dem Bundesminister für Finanzen, Dr. Kienböck, am 3. October 1924;* NA, FO 371/9652/C 16478: Letter from Keeling to MacDonald, 22 October 1924.

3. LNA, C 24, Réconstruction financière de l'Autriche 1923–1925, "Salaries of Railway Employees": *Unterredung des Generalkommissärs Dr. Zimmerman mit dem Finanzminister Dr. Kienböck, am 10. November 1924,* and *Unterredung des Generalkommissärs Dr. Zimmerman mit Dr. Günther. Präsident der österreichischen Bundesbahnen, am 10. November 1924,* as well as H. Patzauer, *Eisenbahnstreik, finanzielle Wirkungen,* 14 November 1924.

4. LNA, C 11, Réconstruction financière de l'Autriche 1922–1926," Release of Funds (1 July–)": *Unterredung des Herrn Generalkommissärs Dr. Zimmerman mit Herrn Finanzminister Dr. Kienböck am 14. November 1924.*

5. LNA, C 21, Réconstruction financière de l'Autriche 1922–1928, "Amalgamation of Provincial Administrations": *Unterredung des Generalkommissärs Dr. Zimmerman mit dem Bundesminister für Finanzen, Dr. Kienböck, am 17. November 1924;* AdR, 2 Ges. London Polit. Akten 1923–4, 315: Telegram from Grünberger to Franckenstein, 17 November 1924.

6. NA, T 160/60/2073/19, "Austrian Reconstruction": Telegram from Akers-Douglas to Foreign Office, 18 November 1924.

7. On Rudolf Ramek (1881–1941), see Walter Goldinger, "Rudolf Ramek," in *Österreichisches Biographisches Lexikon*, vol. 8 (Vienna, 1983). On Heinrich Mataja (1877–1937), see E. Jellinek and J. T. Lilla, "Heinrich Mataja," in *Österreichisches Biographisches Lexikon*, vol. 6 (Vienna, 1975). On Jakob Ahrer (1888–1962), see Jakob Ahrer, *Erlebte Zeitgeschichte* (Vienna, 1930) and Wolfgang Fritz, "Jakob Ahrer: Ein glückloser Finanzminister," in Wolfgang Fritz, *Für Kaiser und Republik, Österreichs Finanzminister seit 1848* (Vienna, 2003).

8. BEA, OV 28/60, "Austrian Rehabilitation": Letter from Zimmerman to Gordon Leith, 24 February 1925.

9. Jürgen Nautz, "Die Entwicklung der Handelsbeziehungen Österreichs zu den Nachfolgestaaten nach dem Ersten Weltkrieg," *Wirtschaft und Gesellschaft* 18, no. 4 (1992): 539–559. Austria had the lowest tariffs among successor states, and, after Belgium, Britain, Sweden, and Switzerland, the fifth-lowest in Europe. Fritz Weber, *Vor dem grossen Krach: Österreichs Bankwesen der Zwischenkriegszeit am Beispiel der Credit-Anstalt für Handel und Gewerbe* (Vienna, 2016), p. 12.

10. This is not to say that trade with the Successor States declined across the board. Exports to Italy, Czechoslovakia, and Hungary rose during the 1920s, as did those to Western Europe. But increasing or at least stabilizing exports to the rest of the Danubian region was considered the ideal way to cut Austria's trade deficit. See Jens Wilhelm Wessels, *Economic Policy and Microeconomic Performance in Inter-War Europe: The Case of Austria 1918–1938* (Stuttgart, 2007), pp. 22–25; Jürgen Nautz, *Die österreichische Handelspolitik der Nachkriegszeit 1918–1923: Die Handelsbeziehungen zu den Nachfolgestaaten* (Vienna, 1994); Nautz, "Die Entwicklung der Handelsbeziehungen."

11. According to Nicole Piétri, "La réconstruction économique et financière de l'Autriche par la Société des Nations (1921–1926)" (doctoral thesis, Université de Paris I, 1981), p. 1361, the annual trade deficit of roughly 700 million gold crowns (about $142 million) was exacerbated by foreign debt payments of 111 million gold crowns per year (76 million for public debt, 35 million for other loans, totaling about $22 million annually), turning the current account negative.

12. Meinoud Rost van Tonningen would remain in Vienna after Zimmerman's departure, return to Austria as the League's representative in the 1930s and later head the Dutch National Bank under German occupation. See Peter Berger, *Im Schatten der Diktatur* (Vienna, 2000).

13. LNA, C 11, Réconstruction financière de l'Autriche 1922–1926, "Use of Reserve Funds & Funds of Account B": Letter from Reisch to Zimmerman, 23 July 1924. Estimates by Rudolf Nötel suggest that Austria never suffered from a negative balance of payments in the 1920s, but that most of the capital inflow was indeed short-term. Rudolf Nötel, "Money, Banking and Industry in Interwar Austria and Hungary," *Journal for European Economic History* 13, no. 2 (1984): 137–202, 157. The economists Charles Rist and Friedrich Hertz also estimated that

much of the trade deficit could be covered by invisible exports. See Fritz Weber, *Vor dem grossen Krach*, p. 34.

14. A review of the League of Nations economic interventions judged its failure to solve trade problems a cardinal mistake. Royall Tyler, *The League of Nations Reconstruction Schemes in the Interwar Period* (Geneva, 1945), pp. 139–159.

15. Piétri, "La réconstruction économique et financière," p. 992, 1355–1360. Piétri quotes Friedrich Hertz, *Zahlungsbilanz und Lebensfähigkeit Österreichs* (Munich, 1925). Hertz suggested that once a general agreement on lowering tariffs were obtained and if more foreign capital could be brought to Austria to increase production, increased exports might make the deficit disappear. The *Volkswirt*'s editors, Walter Federn and Gustav Stolper, naturally disagreed, still arguing that Austria was not viable because it would never attract sufficient foreign exchange to finance its trade deficit (Stolper put his money where his mouth was and moved to Berlin in 1925 to found the *Deutsche Volkswirt*). See their articles on the Layton-Rist report in issues of *Der Österreichische Volkswirt*, September 1925. Information on the balance of payments assembled by Austria's Finance Ministry for the League's official publication remained unsatisfactory. *Memorandum sur le commerce international et sur les balances des paiements (1923–1927)* (Geneva, 1928).

16. NA, T 160/60/2073/19, "Austrian Reconstruction": Letter from Lampson to Niemeyer, 20 February 1925.

17. NA, T 160/60/2073/19, "Austrian Reconstruction": Letter from Niemeyer to Lampson, 24 February 1925.

18. BEA, OV 9/394, "Sir Otto Niemeyer's files: Austria—Economic Barriers 1925": Letter from Niemeyer to Lampson, 24 February 1925.

19. BEA, OV 28/61, "Austrian Rehabilitation": Letter from Bark to Norman, 2 July 1925.

20. An exception is Peter Berger, "The League of Nations and Interwar Austria: Critical Assessment of a Partnership in Economic Reconstruction," in *The Dollfuss/Schuschnigg Era in Austria: A Reassessment*, ed. Günther Bischof, Anton Pelinka, and Alexander Lassner (New Brunswick, NJ, 2003), pp. 73–92, 80: "Nevertheless, if we look at the whole period between March 1924 and August 1925, it seems unwarranted to speak of the presence of deflation in a technical sense. Austrian banknote circulation, instead of contracting, remained stable. And the cost of living measured by the consumer price index even increased, from 126 to 143 (January 1923=100)." But see Karl Bachinger and Herbert Matis, *Der österreichische Schilling: Geschichte einer Währung* (Graz, 1974), p. 105, who identify Austria's deflationary policy as its main problem and a consequence of League intervention and Austrian attitudes. Karl Ausch, *Als die Banken fielen: Zur Soziologie der politischen Korruption* (Vienna, 1968), p. 106, calls the Austrian budgetary policy under Zimmerman "deflationary." It is of course true that a fixed exchange rate regime such as the gold exchange standard is "deflationary" and that cutting

public expenses has a deflationary effect, but that is not the same as saying the ANB pursued a policy of deflation. It certainly did not.

21. Mataja and Ahrer also visited Norman in London during March 1925. Mataja's trip was kept secret; Ahrer invited himself. BEA, OV 28/29, "Oesterreichische Nationalbank": *Conversation between the Governor and Sir Henry Strakosch 25th February 1925;* AdR, 4 Ges. London Polit. Akten 1925: Letter from Reisch to Franckenstein, 12 February 1925; Franckenstein to Mataja, 17 March 1925, telegram from Franckenstein to Ahrer, 13 March 1925; NA, FO 371/10660/C 13831: Letter from Selby to Lampson, 13 March 1925; LNA, S 111, Sir Arthur Salter's Private Papers, Austria No. 8, "Situation in Austria—Financial Committee Meeting of February 1925 and Events subsequent thereto": Letter from Niemeyer to Zimmerman, 27 March 1925.

22. BEA, OV 28/30, "Oesterreichische Nationalbank": Memorandum: *Dr. Resich's* [sic] *letter,* 3 January 1925; *Preliminary Memo before meetings,* 16 March 1925; BEA, OV 9/394, "Sir Otto Niemeyer's files: Austria—Economic Barriers 1925": Letter from Niemeyer to Zimmerman, 9 March 1925.

23. Reisch, Brauneis, Norman, Niemeyer, Strakosch, van Walré de Bordes, Mill, and Franckenstein were present. AdR, 4 Ges. London Polit. Akten 1925: Letter from Franckenstein to Mataja, 16 March 1925.

24. BEA, OV 28/30 and AdR, 4 Ges. London Polit. Akten 1925: Memorandum by Franckenstein, Reisch, and Brauneis, 17 March 1925.

25. LNA, S 60, M. de Bordes Files—Box 7, "Financial Adviser": Memorandum, 16 March 1925; LNA, S 111, Sir Arthur Salter's Private Papers, Austria No. 8, "Situation in Austria—Financial Committee Meeting of February 1925 and Events subsequent thereto": Letter from van Walré de Bordes to Salter, 20 March 1925; LNA, C 28, Réconstruction financière de l'Autriche 1922–1928, "Devisenzentrale—regulations re.—": Letter from van Gijn to Zimmerman, 19 February 1925, and *Unterredung am 21. Februar 1925 von Herrn Generalkommissär Dr. Zimmerman mit den Herren: Dr. Reisch, Präsident der Nationalbank, Dr. Brauneis, Generaldirektor der Nationalbank, Exzell. van Gijn, Berater der Nationalbank.*

26. BEA, OV 28/30, "Oesterreichische Nationalbank": *Interview between Baron Franckenstein, Dr. Reisch, Dr. Brauneis and the Governor—17th March, 1925, Morning.*

27. AdR, 4 Ges. London Polit. Akten 1925: Letter from Franckenstein to Mataja, 17 March 1925.

28. AdR, 01/9, 4 Ges. London Polit. Akten 1925: Letters from Franckenstein to Mataja, 25 April 1925 and 31 March 1925.

29. LNA, C 28, Réconstruction financière de l'Autriche 1922–1928, "Devisenzentrale—regulations re.—": Bousquet, *Les nouvelles mesures financières,* 3 April 1925; AdR, 4 Ges. London Polit. Akten 1925: Letter from Brauneis to Franckenstein, 25 March 1925.

30. ANB, I / 4b: *Protokoll der 28. am 23. März abgehaltenen Sitzung des Gener-*
alrates der Oesterreichischen Nationalbank.

31. AdR, 4 Ges. London Polit. Akten 1925: Letter from Franckenstein to
Mataja, 25 April 1925; AdR, 01 / 9, Ges. London, Karton 19: Telegramme 1924
1938, "1925 Herein": Telegram from Franckenstein to Vienna, 22 April 1925.

32. Curiously, the *Times* was less reserved about a reduction. It reported on 22
April 1925 that "A reduction in the Austrian Bank rate from 13 to 11 per cent is
foreshadowed in a telegram from Vienna. A downward movement would cause no
surprise in London. On the contrary, in some quarters a reduction had been looked
for some weeks ago; but the ANB are undoubtedly wise, in view of certain tenden-
cies that have only lately been reversed, to proceed cautiously lest they encourage
a renewal of speculative activity such as was responsible for the troubles of a year
ago." *Times*, "City Notes," 22 April 1925, p. 20; BEA, OV 28 / 30, "Oesterreichische
Nationalbank": *Memorandum*, 29 April 1925; ANB, I / 4b: *Protokoll der 29. am 24.*
April abgehaltenen Sitzung des Generalrates der Oesterreichischen Nationalbank.

33. BEA, OV 28 / 30, "Oesterreichische Nationalbank": *Interview with Dr. Re-*
sich [sic], Dr. Thaa (Vice-President) and Dr. Brauneis 12th June, 1925, and Memorandum, 30 June 1925; ANB, 1138 / 1925, Memorandum, 13 June 1925.

34. Wolfgang Zipser, *Auf der Suche nach Stabilität: Das Zentralbankgeldan-*
gebot der Österreichischen Nationalbank 1923 bis 1937 (Frankfurt am Main,
1997).

35. LNA, S 113, Sir Arthur Salter's Private Papers, Austria No. 10, "Austria—
Miscellaneous Memoranda on Austrian Situation from January 1925": Letter from
Krabbe to van Walré de Bordes, 7 May 1925, and from van Walré de Bordes to
Salter, 11 May 1925.

36. BEA, OV 28 / 61, "Austrian Rehabilitation": Letter from Norman to Salter,
11 May 1925, and *Interview with Dr. Günther, Morning 17th March 1925,* as well as
letter from Norman to Zimmerman, 8 May 1925, and from Norman to Salter, 11
May 1925.

37. LNA, S 60, M. de Bordes Files, Box 7, Austria 1925-1928, "Austrian Loan
Negotiations": Letter from van Walré de Bordes to Barrington, 24 April 1925, and
from Nigel L. Campbell to van Walré de Bordes, 30 April 1925.

38. Norman wrote to the London Stock Exchange on the matter. BEA, OV
28 / 60: Letters from Niemeyer to Norman, 4 October 1924, Norman to Morgan, 4
October 1924, Lamont to Norman, 7 October 1924, and Satterwhaite to Norman,
13 October 1924, as well as Memorandum: *Austrian Provincial & Municipal Loans,*
13 October 1924; JPM, ARC 1221 (Box 35), Morgan Bank European papers, File 5:
Austrian Bonds 1924, "Austrian Bonds, 1919-1926": Letter from Zimmerman to
Niemeyer, 26 September 1924.

39. LNA, C 43, Réconstruction financière de l'Autriche 1923-1925," Projected
American & Foreign Loans": Letters from F. Forbes Morgan to Zimmerman, 31
October 1924, from Zimmerman to Gordon Leith Co, 30 January 1925, from

Schlegel to Zimmerman, 6 October 1924, and from Zimmerman to Schlegel, 8 October 1925, as well as *Unterredung des Herrn Generalkommissärs Dr. Zimmerman mit dem Amerikanischen Gesandten Mr. Washburn am 29. Jänner 1925,* and *Unterredung des Herrn Generalkommissäsr Dr. Zimmerman mit dem Amerikansichen Gesandten Mr. Washburn am 2. Februar 1925;* LNA, C 43, Réconstruction financière de l'Autriche 1923–1925, "Water Power Exploitation": Letter from Chargé d'Affaires at U.S. Legation to Zimmerman, 15 July 1924, and *Unterredung des Herrn Generalkommissärs mit mr. Upson, Handelssekretär der amerikanischen Gesandtschaft und R. E. Desvernin, Rechtsanwalt der Bankgrupp livermore Morgan, 24, Broad Street, New York City,* 6 August 1924; LNA, C 18, Réconstruction financière de l'Autriche 1922–1928, "Advances from Konto B, to Länder for Electrification Purposes": Letter from Schlegel to Zimmerman, 31 October 1924, and from Zimmerman to Schlegel, 18 November 1924.

40. In April 1925, Speyer returned to conclude a loan for Vienna and start negotiating a joint loan of £2–3 million to Austria's provinces along Zimmerman's lines, but Oberösterreich opted for an uncontrolled loan with the American bank Morgan, Livermore, and so negotiations between Speyer and the remaining provinces were broken off again. LNA, C 43, Réconstruction financière de l'Autriche 1923–1925, "Projected American & Foreign Loans": *Unterredung von Herrn Generalkommissär Dr. Zimmerman mit dem Bundeskanzler Dr. Ramek am 29. Jänner 1925; Loan Negotiations,* 29 January 1925, and *Unterredung von Generalkommissär Dr. Zimmerman mit dem amerikanischen Gesandten Mr. Washburn am 8. Mai 1925,* as well as *Unterredung des Generalkommissärs Dr. Zimmerman mit den Herren Forbes Morgan und Desvernine am 9. Mai 1925,* and further *Unterredung des Generalkommissärs Dr. Zimmerman mit den Herren Anton Spak und Rimmelmoser, Landtagsabgeordnete in Steiermark, am 9. Mai 1925,* as well as *Unterredung von Herrn Generalkommissär Dr. Zimmerman, mit den Herren Georg A. Kurz und F. C. Schwedtman, am 27. Mai 1925,* and *Unterredung von Generalkommissär Dr. Zimmerman, mit den Herren: Lloyd Gilmour, Clare M. Torrey, von der Firma Blyth, Witters & Co, Raoul E. Desvernine, Verteter der Firma Morgan Livermore, am 28. Juli 1925,* and further letter from Gordon Leith & Co. to Zimmerman, 15 January 1925; BEA, OV 28/61, "Austrian Rehabilitation": Letter from Clarke M. Torrey to Norman, 8 May 1925, and Memo, 24 June 1925; BEA, OV 28/60, "Austrian Rehabilitation": Letter from Gordon Leith to Norman, 3 February 1925, and telegram from Speyer to Gordon Leith, 3 February 1925; LNA, S 60, M. de Bordes Files, Box 7, Austria 1925–1928, "Austrian Loan Negotiations": Letter from van Walré de Bordes to Salter, 3 July 1925.

41. LNA, S 115, Sir Arthur Salter's Private Papers, No. 10, Correspondence Letter-book 1923–30, "Correspondence 1925": Letter from Salter to Norman, 5 May 1925; LNA, C 43, Réconstruction financière de l'Autriche 1923–1925, "Projected American & Foreign Loans": *Unterredung des Generalkommissärs Dr. Zim-*

merman mit Mr. James Speyer aus New York, am 22. Februar 1925, and *Unterre-dung von Herrn Generalkommissär Dr. Zimmerman mit Landeshauptmann Dr. Rintelen (Steiermakr) und Landeshauptmannstellvertreter Dr. Schlegle (Oberös-terreich) am 25. Februar 1925,* as well as *Unterredung des Herrn Generalkommissärs Dr. Zimmerman am 23. März 1925 A. mit dem Landeshauptmann von Steiermark Dr. Rintelern. B. mit den Herren Gordon Leith und Marx,* and further *Unterredung des Generalkommissärs Dr. Zimmerman mit dem amerikanischen Gesandten Mr. Washburn,* 9 April 1925, as well as *Unterredung des Herrn Generalkommissäsr [sic] mit Mr. Bertram a. Marx am 21. Februar 1925*; BEA, OV 28/60, "Austrian Rehabilitation": Letter from Zimmerman to Gordon Leith, 24 February 1925; BEA, OV 9/392, "Sir Otto Niemeyer's files: Austrian Money Market 1925": Letter from Zimmerman to Norman, 16 April 1925.

42. NA, FO 371/10660/C 12913: Akers-Douglas to Chamberlain, *Memo by Mr. Akers-Douglas on the Present Position of Austria,* 28 February 1925.

43. BEA, OV 9/394, "Sir Otto Niemeyer's files: Austria—Economic Barriers 1925": Letter from Zimmerman to Niemeyer, 26 February 1925; AdR, C 30, Ré-construction financière de l'Autriche 1923–1926, "Monetary Questions+Issue of Metal Money": Bousquet, *Note sur le Marché de l'Argent (No. II),* 8 April 1925.

44. The Foreign Office preferred working through the League because other-wise "our friends would at once begin their little games of political intrigue which they can never avoid." Niemeyer replied "The trouble about working through the League is the excessively cumbersome nature of the machinery and the endless op-portunities for any single malcontent to put sand in it. Its pace is that of the slowest partner." Salter did not believe the Council could discuss the matter at its upcoming session in March, though he would talk to Beneš and he had already tried to pressure Bethlen. BEA, OV 9/394, "Sir Otto Niemeyer's files: Austria—Economic Barriers 1925": Letter from Lampson to Niemeyer, 28 February 1925, and letters from Niemeyer to Lampson and Salter, both 2 March 1925, as well as letters from Lampson to Crewe (Paris), Dodd (Prague), Leeper (Vienna), and Bar-clay (Budapest), all 2 March 1925; LNA, S 115, Sir Arthur Salter's Private Papers, No. 10, Correspondence Letter-book 1923–30, "Correspondence 1925": Letter from Salter to Niemeyer, 6 March 1925.

45. "Im Ganzen ist es jetzt so: In der Kreditfrage *will* man uns nicht helfen und wirkt uns sogar entgegen, in der handelspolitischen Frage *kann* man uns nicht helfen." AdR, 4 Ges. London Polit. Akten 1925: Letter from Schüller to Francken-stein, 24 February 1925; NA, T 160/60/2073/19, "Austrian Reconstruction": Letter from Lampson to Niemeyer, 20 February 1925.

46. AdR, 4 Ges. London Polit. Akten 1925: Letter from Franckenstein to Ahrer, 6 April 1925; AdR, 3 Ges. London Polit. Akten 1924–5: Letter from Franckenstein to Norman, 6 April 1925, and Schüller, *Memorandum,* undated; LNA, S 115, Sir Arthur Salter's Private Papers, No. 10, Correspondence Letter-book 1923–30,

"Correspondence 1925": Letters from Salter to Layton, 17 April 1925, Salter to Ter Meulen, 20 April 1925, and Salter to Layton and Niemeyer, both 27 April 1925; BEA, OV 9/394, "Sir Otto Niemeyer's files: Austria—Economic Barriers 1925": Letters from Salter to Niemeyer, 8 and 24 April 1925, from Zimmerman to Niemeyer, 26 February 1925, and from Drummond to Chamberlain, 24 April 1925.

47. LNA, F 238, and S.C.A. 77ème session P.V. 1: *Comité d'Autriche—Séance du Lundi, 8 Juin 1925*; LNA, S 115, Sir Arthur Salter's Private Papers, No. 10, Correspondence Letter-book 1923–30, "Correspondence 1925": Letter from Salter to Ter Meulen, 4 May 1925, as well as letter and telegram from Salter to Niemeyer, both 7 May 1925; NA, FO 371/10661/C 16513: Memo from Howard Smith for Chamberlain, *Economic Situation in Austria*, 7 May 1925; AdR, 5 Ges. London Polit. Akten 1925–6: Letter from Schüller to Franckenstein, 20 April 1925.

48. LNA, 1180 décembre 1925 II: Autriche, E.244.(1): *Supplementary Information collected by the Secretariat covering the Period since the Publication of the Layton-Rist Report*, 28 November 1925; LNA, E/17th Session P.V. 2(1) in LNA, 1180 décembre 1925 II: Autriche: *Second Meeting, Held at Geneva, on Monday, 30th November, 1925 at .3.30 P.M.*; LNA, E/17th Session P.V. 3 (1) in LNA, 1180 décembre 1925 II: Autriche: *Third Meeting held in Geneva on Tuesday, December 1st 1925 at 10.30 A.M.*, and *Fourth Meeting, Held at Geneva at 5 P.M. on December 1st 1925*; LNA, c.7097.1925.ii (f.263): *Arrangements Consequent upon the Approaching Limitation and Termination of the Commissioner-General's Control*, 10 December 1925; AdR, O 1/9 Ges. London, Karton 19: Telegramme 1924 1938, "Herein 1925": Telegram from Franckenstein to Vienna, 5 November 1925; AdR, 3 Ges. London Polit. Akten 1924–5: Letters from Schüller to Franckenstein, 29 October 1925, and from Franckenstein to Mataja, 26 November 1925.

49. LNA, C 4, Réconstruction financière de l'Autriche 1922–1926, "Sickness & Unemployment Insurance Laws": *Unterredung von Herrn Generalkommissaer Dr. Zimmerman mit dem Minister fuer Soziale Fuersorge Dr. Resch am 25. November 1924*, and *Unterredung von Herrn Generalkommissaer Dr. Zimmerman mit dem Finanzminister Dr. Ahrer am 25. November 1924*; LNA, C 20, Réconstruction financière de l'Autriche 1922–1927, "Budget 1925": *Note Verbal von Dr. Zimmerman verlesen in Ministerialrat am 6.12.1924*; LNA, C 24, Réconstruction financière de l'Autriche 1923–1925, "Salaries State Employees C": *Unterredung des Generalkommissärs Dr. Zimmerman mit dem Finanzminister, Dr. Ahrer, am 1. December 1924*.

50. Piétri, "La réconstruction économique et financière," pp. 1052–1110.

51. LNA, C 4, Réconstruction financière de l'Autriche 1922–1926, "Taxation in Austria at 1st Sept 1923 & Proposed Steuerverteilungsgesetz": *Unterredung des Herrn Generalkomissaers mit Bundeskanzler Dr. Ramek*, 7 April 1925; Piétri, "La réconstruction économique et financière," p. 1160.

52. Piétri, "La réconstruction économique et financière," pp. 1888–1890.

53. The Financial Committee also commented unfavorably on the ANB's *Kostgeschäft*, asked that credit be curtailed, and recommended close cooperation with the Bank of England.

54. NA, FO 371 / 10660 / C 15332: Letter from Akers-Douglas to Chamberlain, 15 April 1925; Piétri, "La réconstruction économique et financière," p. 1383.

55. LNA, C 11, Réconstruction financière de l'Autriche 1922–1926, "Release of Funds (July 1–)": *Unterredung von Generalkommissär Dr. Zimmerman mit dem Finanzminister Dr. Ahrer, am 29. Mai 1925;* LNA, C 23, Réconstruction financière de l'Autriche 1924–1928, "Budget Figures—April 1925": Letters from Ahrer to Zimmerman, 7 April 1925, and from Zimmerman to Ahrer, 8 April 1925, and *Unterredung des Generalkommissärs mit dem Finanzminister Dr. Ahrer, am 28. April 1925;* LNA, C 20, Réconstruction financière de l'Autriche 1922–1927, "Budget 1925": Letter from Zimmerman to Ahrer, 23 April 1925, and *Unterredung von Generalkommissär Dr. Zimmerman mit dem finanzminister Dr. Ahrer, am 8. Mai 1925.*

56. NA, FO 371 / 10660 / C 15332: Letter from Akers-Douglas to Chamberlain, 15 April 1925; LNA, C 4, Réconstruction financière de l'Autriche 1922–1926, "Taxation in Austria at 1st Sept 1923 & Proposed Steuerverteilungsgesetz": *Unterredung des Herrn Generalkomissaers mit Bundeskanzler Dr. Ramek, 7 April 1925;* LNA, C 47, Réconstruction financière de l'Autriche 1922–1926, "Commissioner General's Report to the Financial Committee—June 1925": *Rapport du Commissaire General en Autriche au Comité Financier du Conseil de la Société des Nations,* undated; LNA, F / 18ème session / P.V. (3). in LNA, 1174 Juin 1925 II: Autriche: *Procès-verbal provisoire de la 3ème séance—1ère partie 5 juin, matin: 10 h.30.* The following delegates participated: Ter Meulen (Netherlands), de Chalendar (France), Dubois (Switzerland), Mazzuchelli (Italy), Niemeyer (United Kingdom), Wallenberg (Sweden), Warland (Belgium), and Yamaji (Japan).

57. The difference of 90 million gold crowns was partly due to the considerable increase in unemployment, which required additional expenses of 13.5 million gold crowns, and the appreciation of pound sterling, which increased prewar debt payments by 2.8 million gold crowns.

58. LNA, F. 236: *Electrification des Chemins de Fer Autrichiens: Rapport présenté au Comité financier par M. Léopold Dubois,* 22 May 1925.

59. Bankers Wallenberg (Sweden) and Ter Meulen (Netherlands) both disliked using loan funds for anything but covering future deficits, but the Financial Committee followed Niemeyer. Present were Roos (Czechoslovakia), Andersen (Denmark), De vos van Steenvyk (Netherlands), Leith-Ross (United Kingdom), de la Huerta (Spain), Lagerbielke (Sweden), Perrier (Belgium), and Seydoux (France). The Swiss delegate Dinichert was unable to attend. LNA, C 39, Réconstruction financière de l'Autriche 1922–1928, "Minutes & Resolutions—Committee of Control (Paris, May 1925. Geneva, December 1925)": *Resolutionen des Kontrollkomitees,*

2 May 1925, *Procès-verbal de la première séance tenue à Paris, le 1er mai 1923* [*sic*], *à 15 heures*, and *Procès-verbal de la deuxième et dernière séance tenue à Paris, le 2 mai 1925, à 15 heures*, as well as letter from Chancellor Ramek to General Commissioner Zimmerman, 24 April 1925; LNA, F/18ème session/P.V.7 (1) (3ème Partie), in LNA, 1174 Juin 1925 II: Autriche: *Procès-verbal de la 7ème séance, 3ème partie tenue le dimanche 7 juin à 10 h 30 du matin;* LNA, C 48/Report for Committee of Control Meeting—Paris—May 1st 1925; LNA, S 60/M. de Bordes Files—Box 7, "Financial Adviser": Van Walré de Bordes, Memorandum, 17 March 1925; LNA, S 59, M. de Bordes Files, Box 6, Austria 1922–1926, "Austria": Letter from van Walré de Bordes to Salter, 20 March 1925; AdR, 3 Ges. London Polit. Akten 1924–5: Letters from Franckenstein to Mataja, 18 March 1925, from Kunz to Franckenstein, 29 April 1925, from Mataja to Franckenstein 22 and 24 April 1925, from Schüller to Franckenstein, 24 April 1925, and from Günther to Franckenstein, 22 April 1925, as well as telegram from Kunz to Franckenstein, 29 April 1925; BEA, OV 9/390, "Sir Otto Niemeyer's files: Austria—Committee of Control, May 1925": Leith Ross, *Austrian Committee of Control. Meetings of 2nd and 3rd May, 1925*.

60. NA, FO 371/10661/C 18553: Aveling, *Expert Enquiry into Austrian Economic Conditions*, 23 June 1925; NA, FO 371/10660/C 15992: Letter from Foreign Office (Harold Nicolson) to British Ambassadors in Vienna, Budapest, Belgrade, and Bucharest, 21 May 1925; NA, T 160/60/2073/21, "Austrian Reconstruction": Letter from Fountain to Under Secretary of State, 4 May 1925.

61. Piétri, "La réconstruction économique et financière," p. 962, quotes from Rist's memoirs that the French economist was under the impression that the inquiry would lead to the termination of Zimmerman's control and give Austria back its freedom in matters of finance. Luigi Enaudi et al., "Charles Rist, 1874–1955. L'homme, la pensée, l'action," *Revue d'Economie Politique* 65 (1955): 884–1025, 1021.

62. LNA, C 43, Réconstruction financière de l'Autriche 1923–1925: Letter from Zimmerman to Speyer, 28 July 1925; LNA, S 109, Sir Arthur Salter's Private Papers, Austria No. 6, "Question of Termination of Control in Austria": Letter from Salter to Zimmerman, 19 August 1925.

63. LNA, S 109, Sir Arthur Salter's Private Papers, Austria No. 6, "Question of Termination of Control in Austria": Letter from Salter to Leith-Ross, 19 August 1925.

64. BEA, OV 28/61, "Austrian Rehabilitation": Letter from Salter to Niemeyer, 24 August 1925, and Salter, *Austrian Reconstruction: Termination or Transformation of Control*, 24 August 1925.

65. NA, T 160/65/2073/029/1, "Economic situation of Austria. Report presented to League of Nations by Mssrs Layton and Rist": Letter from Niemeyer to Salter, 26 August 1925; LNA, S 109, Sir Arthur Salter's Private Papers, Austria No. 6, "Question of Termination of Control in Austria": Letter from Zimmerman

to Salter, 14 August 1925; BEA, OV 9/395, "Sir Otto Niemeyer's files: Austria September 1925": Letter from Zimmerman to Niemeyer, 14 August 1925; BEA, OV 28/61, "Austrian Rehabilitation": Letter from Niemeyer to Salter, 21 August 1925.

66. LNA, C./S.C.A. 8ème session, P.V. 1(1) in LNA, 1177 Septembre 1925 II: Autriche: *Procès-verbal de la première séance tenue le vendredi 4 septembre 1925, à 17 heures;* NA, FO 371/10661/C 11365: C. Howard Smith, *Report on Austrian Economic Situation,* 3 September 1925.

67. J. L. J. Bosmans, *De Nederlander Mr. A. R. Zimmerman als Commissaris-Generaal van de Volkenbund in Oostenrijk, 1922–1926* (Nijmegen, 1973), pp. 247–249.

68. According to Piétri it was the Italian delegate, Vittorio Scialoja, and not the French delegate, Painlevé. However, J. L. J. Bosmans agrees with my reading of the sources. See his excellent treatment of the subject in "Innen- und Aussenpolitische Probleme bei der Aufhebung der Völkerbundkontrolle in Österreich 1924–1926," *Zeitgeschichte* 9, no. 6 (1982): 189–201.

69. NA, T 160/65/2073/029/1, "Economic Situation of Austria: Report Presented to League of Nations by Mssrs Layton and Rist": Telegram from Mr. London to Foreign Office, 5 September 1925; AdR, 4 Ges. London Polit. Akten 1925: Letter from Franckenstein to Mataja, 30 September 1925.

70. The following synthesis is based on the verbal protocols of the meetings of the Financial Committee in September 1925, held in LNA, 1177 Septembre 1925 II: Autriche: F. 19ème session.

71. LNA, F. 19ème session/P.V. 7 (1) in LNA, 1177 Septembre 1925 II: Autriche: *Procès-verbal de la septième séance, tenue le 5 septembre 1925, à 15 heures.30.*

72. LNA, C 20, Réconstruction financière de l'Autriche 1922–1927, "Budget 1925": *Unterredung von Generalkommissär Dr. Zimmerman mit dem Bundeskanzler Dr. Ramek, am 12. Juni 1925,* and *Unterredung von Herrn Generalkommissär Dr. Zimmerman mit dem Finanzminister Dr. Ahrer, am 15. Juni 1925;* LNA, C 22, Réconstruction financière de l'Autriche 1923–1926, "Konzentration der Konten bei der Nationalbank": *Unterredung von Herrn Generalkommissär Dr. Zimmerman mit dem Finanzminister Dr. Ahrer, am 15. Juni 1925;* LNA, C 31, Réconstruction financière de l'Autriche 1923–1928, "Postsparkasse Administration": Letter from Zimmerman to Ramek, 17 July 1925; LNA, 1177 Septembre 1925 II: Autriche: *Procès-verbal de la 6ème séance, tenue le 5 septembre 1925 à 10 h.30,* and *Rapport Confidentiel du Commissaire Général au Comité Financier de la Société des Nations,* undated; Piétri, "La réconstruction économique et financière," pp. 1199, 1215, 1240.

73. LNA, F. 19ème session/P.V. 11 (1) in LNA, 1177 Septembre 1925 II: Autriche: *Procès-verbal de la 11e séance tenue à Genève, le mardi 8 septembre 1925 à 11 h. 30.*

74. LNA, F. 19ème session/P.V. 12 (1) in LNA, 1177 Septembre 1925 II: Autriche: *Procès verbal de la douzième séance, 1ère partie, tenue le mardi 8 septembre 1925, à 15 heures.*

75. LNA, F. 19ème session/P.V. 11 (1) in LNA, 1177 Septembre 1925 II: Autriche: *Procès-verbal de la douzième séance—troisième partie, tenue le 8 septembre 1925, à 18 H.30.*

76. LNA, F. 19ème session/P.V. 14 1ère partie in LNA, 1177 Septembre 1925 II: Autriche: *Procès-verbal de la quatorzième séance—1ère partie, tenue le 9 septembre 1925, à 3h.*

77. LNA, C.526.1925.II: Speech by the Austrian delegate.

78. NA, FO 371/10661/C 11365: C. Howard Smith, *Report on Austrian Economic Situation,* 3 September 1925; LNA, S 115, Sir Arthur Salter's Private Papers, No. 10, Correspondence Letter-book 1923-30, "Correspondence 1925": Letter from Salter to Niemeyer, 24 September 1925; LNA, S 109, Sir Arthur Salter's Private Papers, Austria No. 6, "Question of Termination of Control in Austria": Letter from Niemeyer to Salter 17 September 1925; AdR, 4 Ges. London Polit. Akten 1925: Letter from Franckenstein to Mataja, 30 September 1925.

79. LNA, S 115, Sir Arthur Salter's Private Papers, No. 10, Correspondence Letter-book 1923-30, "Correspondence 1925": Letter from Salter to Seydoux, 15 September 1925.

80. BEA, OV 28/61, "Austrian Rehabilitation": Telegram from Morgan, Harjes (Paris) to J. P. Morgan, 12 September 1925; JPM, ARC 1221 (Box 35) Morgan Bank European papers "Austrian Bonds, 1919-1926": Letter from Weems to Jay, 24 September 1925; JPM, ARC 1224 (16) Vincent P. Carosso Papers "Morgan & Co.— Foreign Loans, Austria. File 2": Letter from Whigham to J. P. Morgan, 25 September 1925.

81. Lojkó Miklós, *Meddling in Middle Europe: Britain and the "Lands Between," 1929-1925* (Budapest, 2006), pp. 114-115; Martin Hill, *The League of Nations and the Work of Refugee Settlement and Financial Reconstruction in Greece, 1922-1930* (Jena, 1931), p. 281; George J. Andreopoulos, "The International Financial Commission and Anglo-Greek Relations (1928-1933)," *Historical Journal* 3, no. 2 (1988): 341-364; Emily S. Rosenberg, *Financial Missionaries to the World: The Politics and Culture of Dollar Diplomacy* (Durham, NC, 2003), pp. 180-181, 220; see also Kirsten Wandschneider, "Central Bank Reaction Functions during the Inter-war Gold Standard: A View from the Periphery," in *The Origins and Development of Financial Markets and Institutions: From the Seventeenth Century to the Present,* ed. Jeremy Attack and Larry Neal (Cambridge, 2009), pp. 388-415, 412. On Bulgaria, see Adam Tooze and Martin Ivanov, "Disciplining the 'Black Sheep of the Balkans': Financial Supervision and Sovereignty in Bulgaria, 1902-38," *Economic History Review* 64, no. 1 (2011): 30-51. On Poland, see Daniel Stone, "The Big Business Lobby in Poland in the 1920s," *Canadian Slavonic Papers* 32, no. 1 (1990): 41-58, 53.

82. Germany, following that same reasoning, was spared a foreign adviser because it was dealt with outside the League and accredited the status of a former Power. But reforms of the Reichsbank in 1924, passed in return for a reduction in

reparation payments, included the appointment of a foreign commissioner for the note issue there, too. Kenneth Mouré, "French Money Doctors, Central Banks, and Politics in the 1920s," in *Money Doctors: The Experience of International Financial Advising 1850–2000*, ed. Marc Flandeau (London, 2003), pp. 138–165, 144; Carl-L. Holtfrerich and Toru Iwami, "Post-war Central Banking Reform: A German-Japanese Comparison," in *The Emergence of Modern Central Banking from1918 to the Present*, ed. Carl-L. Holtfrerich and Jaime Reis (Aldershot, UK, 2016), pp. 69–101.

83. György Péteri, "Central Bank Diplomacy: Montagu Norman and Central Europe's Monetary Reconstruction after World War I," *Contemporary European History* 1, no. 3 (2005): 233–258.

84. Thus in December 1923 Zimmerman raised suspicions that the Austrian Federal Railways might be discounting bills at the ANB; these suspicions were quickly set to rest by Schnyder von Wartensee. LNA, C 9, Réconstruction financière de l'Autriche 1923–1928, "Monthly Reports on Austrian National Bank etc by Schnyder": Letter from Schnyder von Wartensee to Zimmerman, 11 December 1923.

85. Schnyder von Wartensee wrote that "I am very glad to tell you that I have a good impression of the progress of Austria. Confidence is returning and the people out of work are diminishing. There is one black point: the boom of the Stock exchange, may it last? It is justified?" NA, T 160/584/2073/021/9, "Austrian Reconstruction": Letter from Schnyder von Wartensee to Norman, 24 July 1923; ANB, VI/9, "Monatsberichte des Beraters bei der OeNB an den Generalkommissär des Völkerbundes": Conseiller Report No. 2, 10 August 1923; LNA, C 43, Réconstruction financière de l'Autriche 1923–1925, "Miscellaneous documents on Statistics": Letter to Loveday, 9 July 1924.

86. LNA, C 9, Réconstruction financière de l'Autriche 1923–1928, "Monthly Reports on Austrian National Bank etc by Schnyder": Letter from Schnyder von Wartensee to Zimmerman, 30 January 1924.

87. LNA, C 11, Réconstruction financière de l'Autriche 1922–1926, "Use of Reserve Funds": Schnyder von Wartensee, *Impression about the Austrian National Bank and questions concerning the Austrian exchange during the first exercise of the Bank*, encl. with his letters to Zimmerman and Niemeyer, both 28 December 1923.

88. LNA, C 9, Réconstruction financière de l'Autriche 1923–1928, "Monthly Reports on Austrian National Bank etc by Schnyder": Letter from Schnyder von Wartensee to Norman, 21 January 1924.

89. When Schnyder von Wartensee spoke out against the ANB's continued discounting of financial bills, the ANB's management proposed to the General Directorate to reduce them. LNA, C 9, Réconstruction financière de l'Autriche 1923–1928, "Monthly Reports on Austrian National Bank etc by Schnyder": Letter from Schnyder von Wartensee to Zimmerman, 15 December 1923.

90. LNA, C 28, Réconstruction financière de l'Autriche 1922–1928, "Devisenzentrale—regulations re.—": Letter from Schnyder von Wartensee to Zimmerman, 17 December 1923.

91. BEA, OV 28/27, "National Bank of Austria": Letter from Schnyder von Wartensee to Norman, 27 November 1923.

92. BEA, OV 9/384, "Sir Otto Niemeyer's files: Austria National Bank": Letter from van Gijn to Norman, 5 August 1924.

93. BEA, OV 9/391, "Sir Otto Niemeyer's files: Austria 1925": Telegram from van Gijn to Norman, 5 November 1924, and his letter to Norman of the same date.

94. LNA, C 11, Réconstruction financière de l'Autriche 1922–1926, "Use of Reserve Funds & Funds of Account B": Letter from van Gijn to Zimmerman, 23 April 1925

95. LNA, C 11, Réconstruction financière de l'Autriche 1922–1926, "Use of Reserve Funds & Funds of Account B": Letter from van Gijn to Zimmerman, 22 December 1925.

96. Van Gijn saw no reason to keep funds liquid for defense of the Austrian currency because he thought foreign reserves at the ANB were ample enough in that respect. LNA, C 11, Réconstruction financière de l'Autriche 1922–1926, "Temporary Use of Loan Money. Börse Unterstützung etc": Letter from van Gijn to Zimmerman, 21 May 1924; LNA, C 11, Réconstruction financière de l'Autriche 1922–1926, "Use of Reserve Funds": Letter from van Gijn to Zimmerman (undated); LNA, C 11, Réconstruction financière de l'Autriche 1922–1926, "Use of Reserve Funds & Funds of Account B": Letter from van Gijn to Zimmerman, 9 October 1925.

97. BEA, OV 28/61, "Austrian Rehabilitation": Letter from van Gijn to Niemeyer, 22 September 1925.

98. BEA, OV 28/1, "Austria": Letters from Kay to Norman, 13 and 21 January 1927; BEA, OV 28/32, "Oesterreichische Nationalbank": Letter from Kay to Norman, 10 March 1926; BEA, OV 28/42, "Austria Gold": Extract from a letter by Charles Kay, 23 March 1926.

99. BEA, OV 28/31 "Oesterreichische Nationalbank": Letter from Kay to Norman, 31 March 1926.

100. BEA, OV 28/32 "Oesterreichische Nationalbank": Letter from Kay to Norman, 20 September 1926.

101. BEA, OV 28/1, "Austria": Letters from Kay to Norman, 17 and 28 September 1926.

102. BEA, OV 28/1, "Austria": Letter from Kay to Norman, 11 June 1927.

103. BEA, OV 28/1, "Austria": Letter from Kay to Norman, 19 July 1927.

104. BEA, G1/536, "Austrian Rehabilitation": Communication between Kay and Norman, 14 September 1928.

105. LNA, R 2940, Registry Files 1928–1932 "Dates sur le budget et la situation économique de l'Autriche" publiées par le ministère des finances d'Autriche": Resignation of Mr. R. Kay, 23 June 1929.

106. AdR, O 1/9 Ges. London, Karton 19: Telegramme 1924 1938, "1925 Herein": Telegram from Foreign Ministry to Franckenstein, 28 October 1925; Piétri, "La réconstruction économique et financière," p. 1274.

107. Ramek retorted somewhat disingenuously that he knew very well that the loan was impossible and he had only looked for a way to quiet state workers. LNA, C 24, Réconstruction financière de l'Autriche 1923–1925, "Salaries State Employees C": *Unterredung des Generalkommissärs Dr. Zimmerman mit dem Bundeskanzler Dr. Ramek, am 31. Oktober um 21h30,* and letter from Zimmerman to Ramek, 29 October 1925; AdR, 4 Ges. London Polit. Akten 1925: Telegram from Foreign Ministry to Franckenstein, 4 November 1925, letter from Chancellery to Franckenstein, 2 November 1925, and letter from Franckenstein to Niemeyer, 6 November 1925; NA, FO 371/10661/C 14627: Letter from Akers-Douglas, 11 November 1925.

108. NA, T 160/65/2073/029/1 and AdR, 4 Ges. London Polit. Akten 1925: Letter from Niemeyer to Franckenstein, 9 November 1925.

109. LNA, S 109, Sir Arthur Salter's Private Papers, Austria No. 6, "Question of Termination of Control in Austria": Letter from Niemeyer to Salter, 10 November 1925.

110. NA, FO 371/10661/C 14815: Letter from Niemeyer to Lampson, 18 November 1925.

111. LNA, F. 20ème session/P.V. 3(1) in LNA, 1180 décembre 1925 II: Autriche: *Procès-verbal de la 3ème séance, tenue le vendredi 4 décembre 1925, à 15 h.*

112. LNA, F. 20ème session/P.V. 4(1) in LNA, 1180 décembre 1925 II: Autriche: *Procès-verbal de la quatrième séance tenue le samedi 5 décembre 1925, à 11 heures;* LNA, 1180 décembre 1925 II: Autriche: *Proposal on Loan Reliquat,* 5 December 1925.

113. LNA, S 108, Sir Arthur Salter's Private Papers, Austria No. 5, "Austria—Trustees for Long Term Loan": Telegram from Jay to Janssen, 5 December 1925; LNA, S 109, Sir Arthur Salter's Private Papers, Austria No. 6, "Question of Termination of Control in Austria": *Record of a Conversation between Sir Arthur Salter, Sir Henry Strakosch and Sir Otto Niemeyer,* 12 October 1925; LNA, F. 20ème session/P.V. 8(1) in LNA, 1180 décembre 1925 II: Autriche: *Procès-verbal de la 8ème séance, tenue le lundi 7 décembre 1925, à 12 heures;* AdR, 5 Ges. London Polit. Akten 1925–6: Letter from Schüller to Franckenstein, 3 November 1925.

114. From the remainder the Austrians intended to use 118 million gold crowns on electrification, keep 52 million gold crowns as cash reserves (17 million with the Treasury, 21 million at the PSK, and 14 million as special reserves for advances from the Austrian government to state enterprises), and earmark 48 million gold crowns for investments in 1927. LNA, 1180 décembre 1925 II: Autriche: F. 20ème session/P.V. 5 (1) *Procès-verbal de la 5ème séance, tenue le samedi 5 décembre 1925, à 15 heures 30,* and P.V. 6 (1) *Procès-verbal de la sixième séance, tenue le dimanche 6 décembre 1925 à 10 heures,* as well as P.V. 8 (1) *Procès-verbal de la 8ème séance,*

tenue le lundi 7 décembre 1925, à 12 heures, and further P.V. 10 (1) *Extrait du procès-verbal de la 10ème séance, tenue le 8 dèc 1925 à 15 heures.* The members present were Chamberlain (United Kingdom), Clauzel (France), Scialoja (Italy), Beneš (Czechoslovakia), and Mataja (Austria). Dubois, Zimmerman, and Salter were also present. LNA, C / S.C.A. / 9ème session / P.V. 1 (1) in LNA, 1180 décembre 1925 II: Autriche: *Première séance tenue à Genève le 9 décembre 1925 à 15 heures sous la présidence de Sir Austen Chamberlain.*

115. The socialist proposal suggested that the Austrian government promise to avoid inflation, to offer new securities if the pledged revenues became insufficient, and to accept a new Conseiller if the exchange rate dropped below the gold point for more than a week.

116. The members present were President Dubois (Switzerland), Takashi Aoki (Japan), Bianchini (Italy), de Chalendar (France), Ter Meulen (Netherlands), Niemeyer (United Kingdom), Pospíšil (Czechoslovakia), Strakosch (South Africa), and Wallenberg (Sweden). LNA, F / 22eme Session / P.V. 5 (1) in LNA, 1183 Juin 1926 II: Autriche: *Extrait du procès-verbal de la 5ème séance, tenue le 5 juin 1926 à 11 heures.*

117. LNA, S 115, Sir Arthur Salter's Private Papers, No. 10, Correspondence Letter-book 1923–30, "Correspondence 1926": Letter from Salter to Williams, 22 March 1926.

118. LNA, S 115, Sir Arthur Salter's Private Papers, No. 10, Correspondence Letter-book 1923–30, "Correspondence 1926": Letter from Felkin to Salter, 22 March 1926.

119. LNA, C / S.C.A. / 11ème Session P.V.1 in LNA, 1183 Juin 1926 II: Autriche: *Comité d'Autriche du Conseil, 11ème session . . . séance tenue le jeudi, 8 juin, 1926, à 11 heures 45;* LNA, 1183 Juin 1926 II: Autriche: C.348.1926.II: *Report of the Financial Committee to the Council,* 7 June 1926, and C.352.M127.1926. II: *Council resolutions adopted on 8. and 9.6.1926.*

120. LNA, C 11 Réconstruction financière de l'Autriche 1922–1926, "Use of Reserve Funds & Funds of Account B": Letter from Reisch to Zimmerman, 9 November 1925.

121. LNA, C 11 Réconstruction financière de l'Autriche 1922–1926, "Use of Reserve Funds & Funds of Account B": Letter from Brauneis to van Gijn, 4 April 1925.

122. LNA, C 11 Réconstruction financière de l'Autriche 1922–1926, "Use of Reserve Funds & Funds of Account B": Letter from van Gijn to Zimmerman, 22 December 1925.

123. LNA, R 522, "Economic situation of Austria—Archives of the Rist-Layton Mission. 1925.—General": *Notes on conversation between Mr. Layton and Dr. Heinzheimer, of the wiener Bankverein, Vice President of the Federation of Bankers, and Dr. Neurath, of the Credit Anstalt, on Thursday, August 6th, 1925.*

124. For a recent and overall positive assessment of the League-sponsored interwar loans, see Juan H. Flores Zendejas and Yann Decorzant, "Going Multilat-

eral? Financial Markets' Access and the League of Nations Loans, 1923–8," *Economic History Review* 60, no. 2 (2016): 653–678.

125. "Der Abschied des Generalkommissärs Dr. Zimmerman," *RP,* 30 June 1926, p. 3.

126. "Der Abschied des Generalkommissärs," *NFP,* 30 June 1926, pp. 1–2.

127. "Die Abreise eines Besiegten," *AZ,* 6 July 1926, pp. 1–2.

128. "Eine Auszeichnung für Generalkommissär Dr. Zimmerman," *Wiener Zeitung,* 2 June 1926, p. 1; "Abreise des Generalkommissärs Dr. Zimmerman." *RP,* 5 July 1926, p. 1.

7. The Precedence of Politics

Epigraph: NA, FO 371 / 13566: Telegram from Phipps to Henderson, 25 November 1929.

1. NA, FO 371 / 12079: Letter from Leeper to Chamberlain, 16 July 1927, as quoted by F. L. Carsten, *The First Austrian Republic, 1918–1938: A Study Based on British and Austrian Documents* (Aldershot, UK, 1986), p. 121.

2. "Die Mörder von Schattendorf freigesprochen!," *AZ,* 15 July 1925, pp. 1–2: "Die bürgerliche Welt warnt immerzu vor dem Bürgerkrieg; aber ist diese glatte, diese aufreizende Freisprechung von Menschen, die Arbeiter getötet haben, weil sie Arbeiter getötet haben, nicht schon selbst der Bürgerkrieg? Wir warnen sie alle, denn aus einer Aussaat von Unrecht, wie es gestern geschehen ist, kann nur schweres Unheil entstehen."

3. The most important works are Norbert Leser and Paul Sailer-Wlasits, eds., *1927, als die Republik brannte: Von Schattendorf bis Wien* (Vienna, 2002); Rudolf Neck and Adam Wandruszka, eds., *Die Ereignisse des 15. Juli 1927: Protokoll des Symposiums in Wien am 15. Juni 1977* (Vienna, 1979); *80 Jahre Justizpalastbrand: Recht und gesellschaftliche Konflikte* (Vienna, 2008); Gerhard Botz, *Gewalt in der Politik: Attentate, Zusammenstösse, Putschversuche, Unruhen in Österreich 1918 bis 1938* (Munich, 1983).

4. A copy of the police report is kept at the Archives of the Vienna Landespolizeidirektion: "Juliereignisse 1927," Box 2: *Ausschreitungen in Wien am 15. Und 16. Juli 1927,* 2 August 1927.

5. See the protocols of the Socialist Party Leadership meeting held on Monday morning, 18 July 1927, Socialist party archives, Vienna, Partei-Archiv vor 1934, Mappe 4: *Protokoll über die Sitzung des Parteivorstandes;* AdR, 01 / 9, 7 Ges. London Polit. Berichte 1926–1927: Telegrams from Bratislava to Franckenstein, 16 and 17 July 1927, and from Prague to Franckenstein, 17 July 1927; Gerhard Botz, "Der '15. Juli 1927,' seine Ursachen und Folgen," in *Österreich 1927 bis 1938* (Protokoll des Symposiums in Wien 23. bis 28. Oktober 1972) (Munich, 1973), pp. 43–67;

Charles Gulick, *Austria from Habsburg to Hitler*, vol. 1 (Berkeley, CA, 1948), pp. 717–751; Carsten, *The First Austrian Republic*, pp. 121–128.

6. Oliver Kühschelm, "Implicit Boycott: The Call for Patriotic Consumption in Interwar Austria," *Management & Organizational History* 5, no. 2 (2010): 165–195.

7. Despite the bankruptcy of one of Vienna's oldest merchant houses in early June, with an exposure of $1 million in London alone, the violent events did not provoke a dangerous flight of capital from Austria. AdR, 01/9, 7 Ges. London Polit. Berichte 1926–1927: Letter from Franckenstein to Seipel, 18 July 1927, and letter from Franckenstein, 29 July 1927; AdR, 01/9, Ges. London, Karton 19, Telegram 1924–1938, "VIII 1927 Hinaus": Telegram from Franckenstein to Seipel, 18 July 1927; AdR 01/4, 42 Voelkerrecht, "Berichte aus London 1927 IV–XII": Letter from Franckenstein to Seipel, 26 July 1927; BEA, OV 28/1, "Austria": Letters from Kay to Norman, 11 and 22 June 1927, and from Norman to Kay, 13 June 1927.

8. On the German Institute, see Adam Tooze, "Weimar's Statistical Economics: Ernst Wagemann, the Reich's Statistical Office, and the Institute for Business-Cycle Research, 1925–1933," *Economic History Review* 52, no. 2 (1999): 523–543; and Bernd Kulla, *Die Anfänge der empirischen Konjunkturforschung in Deutschland 1925–1933* (Berlin, 1996). On the U.S. Institute see Thomas A. Stapleford, "Business and the Making of American Econometrics, 1910–1940," *History of Political Economy* 49, no. 2 (2017): 233–265; and Walter Friedman, *Fortune Tellers: The Story of America's First Economic Forecasters* (Princeton, NJ, 2014).

9. Carl Theodore Schmidt, "The Austrian Institute for Business Cycle Research," *Journal of Political Economy* 39, no. 1 (1931): 101–103.

10. Hayek warned that recent declines in economic activity were not just a necessary adjustment to new realities, but also were due to the recurring phenomenon of recession, and that the current return to growth in Austria did not mean that all structural hurdles had been dismantled. Whether the Austrian economy existed and would persist to do so was not questioned. See *Monatsberichte des österreichischen Institutes für Konjunkturforschung* 1, no. 9 (1927): 71–72; Karl Aiginger, "85 Jahre WIFO: Gedanken zu Geschichte und Zukunft des Institutes," *WIFO Monatsbericht* 6 (2012): 497–510.

11. Angelina Keil, "85 Jahre WIFO: Die Publikationstätigkeit," *WIFO Monatsbericht* 6 (2012): 551–555.

12. "Die Abweichung von diesem typischen Bild des Konjunkturverlaufes in den grossen Industriestaaten festzustellen, die vielleicht die Konjunkturbewegung in Österreich zeigt, wird eine der Aufgaben der Untersuchungen des Institutes sein." *Monatsberichte des österreichischen Institutes für Konjunkturforschung* 1, no. 1 (1927): 3.

13. *Monatsberichte des österreichischen Institutes für Konjunkturforschung* 1, nos. 1–9 (1927).

14. *Monatsberichte des österreichischen Institutes für Konjunkturforschung* 2, no. 2 (1928).

15. *Monatsberichte des österreichischen Institutes für Konjunkturforschung* 1, nos. 11–12 and 2, no. 1 (1927–1928).

16. *Monatsberichte des österreichischen Institutes für Konjunkturforschung* 2, nos. 3–4 (1928).

17. *Monatsberichte des österreichischen Institutes für Konjunkturforschung* 2, nos. 6–7 (1928).

18. *Monatsberichte des österreichischen Institutes für Konjunkturforschung* 2, nos. 8–12 (1928).

19. *Monatsberichte des österreichischen Institutes für Konjunkturforschung* 3, no. 1 (1929).

20. *Monatsberichte des österreichischen Institutes für Konjunkturforschung* 3, nos. 2–3 (1929).

21. *Monatsberichte des österreichischen Institutes für Konjunkturforschung* 3, no. 4 (1929).

22. *Monatsberichte des österreichischen Institutes für Konjunkturforschung* 3, nos. 5–6 (1929).

23. *Monatsberichte des österreichischen Institutes für Konjunkturforschung* 3, nos. 8–9 (1929).

24. Jens-Wilhelm Wessels, *Economic Policy and Microeconomic Performance in Inter-War Europe: The Case of Austria, 1918–1938* (Stuttgart, 2007), pp. 156–218.

25. Dieter Stiefel, "Konjunkturelle Entwicklung und struktureller Wandel der österreichischen Wirtschaft in der Zwischenkriegszeit," Institut für Höhere Studien, Forschungsbericht 135, Vienna, November 1978, p. 40; Hans Bayer, *Strukturwandlungen der österreichischen Volkswirtschaft nach dem Kriege* (Leipzig, 1929).

26. Dieter Stiefel, *Arbeitslosigkeit: Soziale, politische und wirtschaftlich Auswirkungen—am Beispiel Österreichs 1918–1938*, Schriften zur Wirtschafts- u. Sozialgeschichte 31 (Berlin, 1979); Dieter Stiefel, "Der Arbeitsmarkt in Österreich in der Zwischenkriegszeit," *Studia Germanica et Austriaca* 1, no. 2 (2002): 1–12; Eduard März, "Die grosse Depression in Österreich: 1930–1933," *Wirtschaft und Gesellschaft* 16, no. 3 (1990): 409–438.

27. Fritz Weber, *Vor dem grossen Krach: Österreichs Bankwesen der Zwischenkriegszeit am Beispiel der Credit-Anstalt für Handel und Gewerbe* (Vienna, 2016), p. 57.

28. Karl Ausch, *Als die Banken fielen: Zur Soziologie der politischen Korruption* (Vienna, 1968), pp. 201–245, provides further details about the Österreichische Industrie & Handelsbank, the Niederösterreichische Bauernbank and Steierbank.

29. NA, FO 371 / 11213: Letter from Chilston to Chamberlain, 7 July 1926; LNA, C 10, Réconstruction financiere de l'Autriche 1922–1928, "Gestion du Reliquat de

l'Emprunt": Letters from Rost van Tonningen to Dubois, 2 and 16 July 1926, and from Dubois to Rost van Tonningen, 16 July 1926; LNA, C 32, Réconstruction fiancière de l'Autriche 1923–1927, "Zentral Bank Deutscher Sparkassen (Juillet 1926–)": Letter from Rost van Tonningen to Niemeyer, 16 July 1926.

30. LNA, C 32, Réconstruction financière de l'Autriche 1923–1927, "Zentral Bank Deutscher Sparkassen (Juillet 1926–)": Letters from Niemeyer to Rost van Tonningen and Kay, 17 July 1926.

31. NA, FO 371 / 11213: Letter from Leeper to Chamberlain, 1 September 1926.

32. According to Hans Kernbauer, *Währungspolitik in der Zwischenkriegszeit: Geschichte der Österreichischen Nationalbank von 1923 bis 1938*. (Vienna, 1991), p. 270, the accumulated losses of the Postsparkasse eventually turned out to be sch.319.4 million ($45 million). Further problems also surfaced at the semipublic Dorotheum, where only a third of assets were liquid and a reasonable withdrawal of deposits could not be faced. Finance Minister Jakob Ahrer, who was personally involved in the scandals surrounding the Postsparkasse, ran away to Cuba. See also Niko Wahl, "Kaffeehäuser zu Bankfilialen: Ein kurzer Abriss der Wiener Spekulation," in *Das Werden der Republik . . . Der Rest is Österreich*, ed. Helmut Konrad and Wolfgang Maderthaner, vol. 2 (Vienna, 2008), pp. 49–66; LNA, C 10, Réconstruction financière de l'Autriche 1922–1928, "Gestion du Reliquat de l'Emprunt": Letter from Rost van Tonningen to Dubois, 24 July 1926; NA, FO 371 / 11213: Letter from Chilston to Chamberlain, 11 November 1926.

33. BEA, OV 9 / 399 and LNA, C 1, Réconstruction financière de l'Autriche 1926–1928, "Reports to Sir Arthur Salter": Letters from Rost van Tonningen to Salter, 16 October 1926 and 24 November 1926.

34. Gulick, *Austria from Habsburg to Hitler*, vol. 1. pp. 689–713.

35. BEA, OV 28 / 1, 2 "Austria": Letter from Kay to Norman, 5 November 1926.

36. BEA, OV 28 / 1: Letter from Kay to Norman, 27 November 1926; Gulick, *Austria from Habsburg to Hitler*, vol. 1, pp. 245–246, 709.

37. LNA, C 1, Réconstruction financière de l'Autriche 1926–1928: *Notes sur la période du 30 novembre 1926 jusqu'au 28 février 1927.*

38. The Socialists' party program predicted that gaining power over Austria by democratic means would provoke attempts to establish a "monarchal or fascist dictatorship," making civil war inevitable. *Programm der Sozialdemokratischen Arbeiterpartei Österreichs, beschlossen vom Parteitag zu Linz am 3, November 1926.*

39. AdR, 01 / 4, 42 Voelkerrecht, "Berichte aus London 1927 IV–XII": Letter from Franckenstein to Seipel, 3 May 1927; BEA, OV 28 / 1: Letter from Kay to Norman, 27 November 1926.

40. Telegrams from Vienna, sent via Bratislava and Prague, to Ambassador Franckenstein, though meant to pacify concerns, drew a frantic picture of events in the Austrian capital. AdR, 01 / 9, 7 Ges. London Polit. Berichte 1926–1927: Telegrams from Bratislava to Franckenstein, 16 July 1927, and from Prague to Franckenstein, 17 July 1927.

41. AdR, 01/9, 7 Ges. London Polit. Berichte 1926–1927: Letter from Franckenstein to Seipel, 18 July 1927; AdR, 01/9 Ges. London, Karton 19: Telegram 1924–1938, "VIII 1927 Hinaus": Telegram from Franckenstein to Seipel, 18 July 1927; AdR, 01/4, 42 Voelkerrecht, "Berichte aus London 1927 IV–XII": Letter from Franckenstein to Seipel, 26 July 1927.

42. According to information obtained by the British embassy in 1927, reserves amounted to $122 million. NA, FO 371/12080: Memo by Phillpotts, 31 July 1927; BEA, OV 28/2, "Austria": *Extracts from the Report on the Financial and Commercial Situation of Austria by O. S. Phillpotts O.B.E. Issued by the Department of Overseas Trade.*

43. BEA, OV 28/1, "Austria": Letter from Kay to Norman, 19 July 1927; BEA, OV 28/33, "Oesterreichische Nationalbank": *Further Points Which Arose in Conversation with Dr. Braunesi [sic] on the 12th October, 1927.*

44. Ulrich Kluge, *Bauern, Agrarkrise und Volksernährung in der Europäischen Zwischenkriegszeit: Studien zur Agrargesellschaft und -wirtschaft der Republik Österreich 1918 bis 1938* (Stuttgart, 1988), pp. 319–320; Heinrich Benedikt, ed., *Geschichte der Republik Österreich* (Munich, 1977), pp. 362–363; John T. Lauridsen, *Nazism and the Radical Right in Austria 1918–1934* (Copenhagen, 2007).

45. The marches provoked an increase in public demand for dollars and some flight of capital from Austria. *Die Bilanzen, Beilage zum oesterreichischen Volkswirt,* October 1928, pp. 19–20; C. A. Macartney, "Austria since 1928," *Slavonic and East European Review* 7 (1928/1929): 288–303.

46. Robert Kriechbaumer, *Die grossen Erzählungen der Politik: Politische Kultur und Parteien in Österreich von der Jahrhundertwende bis 1945* (Vienna, 2001), pp. 276–278; Gulick, *Austria from Habsburg to Hitler,* vol. 2, pp. 806–808.

47. Benedikt, *Geschichte der Republik Österreich,* p. 162; Walter Wiltschegg, *Die Heimwehr: Eine unwiderstehliche Volksbewegung?* (Vienna, 1985).

48. Seipel's diary entries do indicate that he was done with politics and looked to concentrate on his spiritual well-being. Klemens von Klemperer, *Ignaz Seipel, Staatsmann einer Krisenzeit* (Vienna, 1976), pp. 276–295; Lauridsen, *Nazism and the Radical Right;* Ludwig Reichhold, *Ignaz Seipel* (Vienna, 1988); Friedrich Rennhofer, *Ignaz Seipel* (Vienna, 1978).

49. The Heimwehr were receiving financial support from Italy and Hungary to instigate a putsch. See Lajos Kerekes, *Abenddämmerung einer Demokratie: Mussolini, Gömbös und die Heimwehr* (Vienna, 1966); Benedikt, *Geschichte der Republik Österreich,* p. 163.

50. Benedikt, *Geschichte der Republik Österreich,* p. 163; Von Klemperer, *Ignaz Seipel,* p. 295.

51. Charlotte Natmessnig, "Wege zur Währungssanierung und Beginn der Bankenkonzentration auf dem Wiener Platz," in *Bank Austria Credit-Anstalt: 150 Jahre österreichische Bankengeschichte im Zentrum Europas,* ed. Oliver Rathkolb,

Theodor Venus, and Ulrike Zimmerl (Vienna, 2005), pp. 162–179. See also Kernbauer, *Währungspolitik in der Zwischenkriegszeit,* pp. 276–279.

52. Gulick, *Austria from Habsburg to Hitler,* vol. 2, p. 859.

53. Ibid., pp. 870–871.

54. Natmessnig, "Wege zur Währungssanierung und Beginn der Bankenkonzentration." See also Kernbauer, *Währungspolitik in der Zwischenkriegszeit,*
pp. 276–279.

55. Wolfgang Zipser, *Auf der Suche nach Stabilität: Das Zentralbankgeldangebot der österreichischen Nationalbank 1923 bis 1937* (Frankfurt am Main, 1997),
p. 122; Rudolf Nötel, "Money, Banking and Industry in Interwar Austria and Hungary," *Journal of European Economic History* 13, no. 2 (1984): 160.

56. Fritz Weber, "Grosse Hoffnungen und k(l)eine Erfolge": Zur Vorgeschichte
der österreichischen Finanzkrise von 1931," in *Bank Austria Credit-Anstalt: 150
Jahre österreichische Bankengeschichte im Zentrum Europas,* ed. Oliver Rathkolb,
Theodor Venus, and Ulrike Zimmerl (Vienna, 2005), pp. 180–195. See also Weber,
Vor dem grossen Krach; "Allgemeine Österreichische Boden-Credit Anstalt," *Die Bi-
lanzen Beilage zum Österreichischen Volkswirt* 21, no. 24 (16 March 1929): 258–260.

57. Weber, "Grosse Hoffnungen un k(l)eine Erfolge." See also Weber, *Vor dem
grossen Krach,* p. 331.

58. BEA, OV 28/34, "Oesterreichische Nationalbank": Letter from Brauneis
to Siepman, 12 October 1929; ANB, 1256/1929, "Diverse unnummerierte Beilagen
zum Akt Nr. 1256/1929": Letters from ANB to CA, 9 October 1929, from ANB to
Ministerialrat Rizzi, 16 October 1929, and from ANB to CA, 8 October 1929; ANB,
1256/1929, "Giroausweise betr. das Eskont-, Lombard- und Devisengeschäft,"
16/1930: *Stand des Sonderkredites (verschiedene Anlagen) am 31. Jänner 1930;* NA,
FO 371/13567: Letters from Phipps to Henderson, 17 and 24 October 1929, and
from Le Rougetel to Henderson, 8 October 1929; Kernbauer, *Währungspolitik in
der Zwischenkriegszeit,* p. 276.

59. BEA, OV 28/34, "Oesterreichische Nationalbank": Letter from Brauneis to
Siepman, 12 October 1929; Kernbauer, *Währungspolitik in der Zwischenkriegszeit,*
pp. 276–282. Kernbauer repeated his account in "Österreichische Währungs-,
Bank- und Budgetpolitik in der Zwischenkriegszeit," in *Handbuch des politischen
Systems Österreichs: Erste Republik 1918–1933,* ed. Emerich Tálos, Herbert Dachs,
Ernst Hanisch, and Anton Staudinger (Vienna, 1995), p. 563.

60. Peter Eigner and Peter Melichar, "Das Ende der Boden-Credit-Anstalt 1929
und die Rolle Rudolf Siegharts," *Österreichische Zeitschrift für Geschichtswissen-
schaften* 19, no. 3 (2008): 56–114.

61. Of course, many recent works still fail to provide an exact reason for the
timing of BKA's collapse. For example, Natmessnig, "Wege zur Währungssanierung und Beginn der Bankenkonzentration," pp. 162–179, 178. In the same
volume see Herbert Matis, "Österreichs Wirtschaft in der Zwischenkriegszeit:
Desintegration, Neustrukturierung und Stagnation," pp. 124–147, 137; and Weber,

"Grosse Hoffnungen und k(l)eine Erfolge," pp. 180–195, 180–181. See also Fritz Weber, "Die wirtschaftliche Entwicklung," in Dachs et al., *Handbuch des politischen Systems Österreichs*, pp. 23–42, and similarly Hans Kernbauer, Eduard März, and Fritz Weber, "Die wirtschaftliche Entwicklung," in *Österreich 1918–1938: Geschichte der Ersten Republik*, ed. Kurt Skalnik and Erika Weinzierl (Graz, 1983), pp. 343–379, 366.

62. Zipser, *Auf der Suche nach Stabilität*, p. 122.

63. Nötel, "Money, Banking and Industry," p. 160; see also Gulick, *From Habsburg to Hitler*, vol. 2, pp. 856–861; and Karl Ausch, *Als die Banken fielen* (Vienna, 1968), pp. 307–334.

64. Weber, "Grosse Hoffnungen und k(l)eine Erfolge."

65. Weber, *Vor dem grossen Krach*, pp. 365–366.

66. The ANB was ready to place the following amounts abroad: $3 million with Guaranty Trust Company, $3 million with Chase National Bank, $5 million with National City Bank, $1.5 million with New York Trust Company, $2.5 million with Nederlandsche Handel-Maatschappij, $1 million with Lippman, Rosenthal & Co., $1 million with Nederlandsche Indische Handelsbank, $5 million with N. M. Rothschild & Sons, $0.5 million with S. Japheth & Co., and $0.5 million with Schweizerische Bankgesellschaft. The placements would be reduced from $15 million to $11 million after the first year and from $11 million to $7 million after the second year. After the third year, the CA could ask for $3.5 million to be renewed. ANB, 1256/1929, "Diverse unnummerierte Beilagen zum Akt Nr. 1256/1929": Letter from ANB to CA, 9 October 1929; NA, FO 371/13567: Letter from Phipps to Henderson, 17 October 1929.

67. NA, FO 371/13567: Letter from Le Rougetel to Henderson, 8 October 1929.

68. Weber, *Vor dem grossen Krach*, pp. 347–348, 358.

69. Ibid., p. 331.

70. Central banks can shift gains and losses from one month to the next and enjoy broad freedom as to how they categorize their assets. This means, for example, they are free to choose whether to include foreign currency among their official reserves or to report them under *other assets*.

71. P. L. Cottrell with C. J. Stone, "Credits, and Deposits to Finance Credits," in *European Industry and Banking, 1920–1939: A Review of Bank Industry Relations*, ed. P. L. Cottrell, Håkan Lindgren, and Alice Teichova (Leicester, 1992), pp. 43–78.

72. *Monatsberichte des österreichischen Institutes für Konjunkturforschung* 4, no. 2 (1929).

73. *Monatsberichte des österreichischen Institutes für Konjunkturforschung* 3, nos. 10–12 (1929).

74. According to Phillpotts, sch.700 million were held by big banks, 150 million by small banks, and 200 million by industry and other concerns. Currency in circulation was sch.840 million. NA, FO 371/12077: Letter from Phillpotts to

Foreign Office, 5 October 1927; BEA, OV 28/1, "Austria," and BEA, OV 28/31, "Oesterreichische Nationalbank": Letter from Kay to Norman, 10 March 1927.

75. BEA, OV 28/33, "Oesterreichische Nationalbank": *Note of a Conversation with Dr. Brauneis, the Managing Director of the Austrian National Bank.*

76. BEA, OV28/1, "Austria": Letters from Norman to Kay, 21 March 1927, from Kay to Siepman, 28 October 1927, and from Siepman to Kay, 4 November 1927.

77. NA, FO 371/13566: E. Phipps, *Austria—Annual Report 1928.*

78. NA, FO 371/12080: Memo by Phillpotts, 31 July 1927; BEA, OV 28/2, "Austria": *Extracts from the Report on the Financial and Commercial Situation of Austria by O. S. Phillpotts O.B.E. Issued by the Department of Overseas Trade.* Further estimates are discussed by Weber, *Vor dem grossen Krach,* pp. 265–267.

79. LNA, S 109, Sir Arthur Salter's Private Papers, Austria No. 6, "Austria—Correspondence etc. with Commissioner-General and Staff at Vienna": Letter from Rost van Tonningen to Niemeyer, 1 October 1927.

80. NA, T 160/65/2073/029/1, "Austria. Financial Reconstruction: League of Nations Scheme. Termination of Control": Letter from Strakosch to Schwarzwald, 13 October 1925, and from Niemeyer to Schwarzwald, 14 October 1925; AdR, 4 Ges. London Polit. Akten 1925: Letters from Bark to Franckenstein and Ahrer, 7 October 1925; CA, Bankverein—Protokollbuch, September bis Dezember 1925, 30 October 1925.

81. LNA, *Procès-verbal définitif de la quinzième session tenue à Madrid, le mardi 26 mars 1929, à 19 heures.* The following members were present: Alberti (Italy), Roos (Czechoslovakia), Andersen (Denmark), de Borchgrave (Belgium), Bernix-Carrasco (Spain), Thierry (France), Niemeyer (United Kingdom), Zimmerman (Netherlands), and Gisle (Spain). Nathan Marcus, "The Austrian Minority of South Tyrol and the Investitionsanleihe of 1930," in *National Economies: Volkswirtschaft, Racism and Economy in Europe between the Wars, 1918–1939,* ed. Christoph Kreutzmüller, Michael Wildt, and Mosche Zimmerman (Newcastle upon Tyne, 2015), pp. 229–238.

82. Norman pointed out that such an arrangement would require exclusive relations between the two central banks, something Reisch opposed. BEA, OV 28/31, "Oesterreichische Nationalbank": Letter from Norman to Kay, 27 January 1926, and from Kay to Norman, 5 February 1926.

83. Norman congratulated Reisch on the occasion of the termination of League control and assured him of his "desire to cooperate at all times." BEA, OV 28/31, "Oesterreichische Nationalbank": Letter from Kay to Norman, 24 March 1926; BEA, OV 28/62, "Austrian Rehabilitation": Telegram from Norman to Reisch, 10 June 1926; AdR, 1 Ges. London Polit. Akten 19: Letter from Reisch to Norman, 10 February 1926; AdR, 6 Ges. London Polit. Akten 1926: Letters from Norman to Reisch, 9 March 1926, from Reisch to Norman, 22 March 1926, and from Franckenstein to Ramek, 10 June 1926.

84. BEA, OV 28/2, "Austria": Letter from Siepman to Kay, 22 October 1927.

85. BEA, OV 28/34, "Oesterreichische Nationalbank": Letter from Siepman to Kay, 22 March 1929.

86. "Krawalle an der Technik und der Universität," *NFP*, 29 October 1929.

87. "Studentenprügeleien an der Technik und an der Universität," *NFP*, 29 October 1929.

88. "Gegen die Prügeleien an der Universität—Energisches Einschreiten erforderlich" and "Studentenkrawalle auf der Universitätsrampe," *NFP*, Abendblatt, 5 November 1929.

89. "Prügeleien und kein Ende" and "Neuerliche Tumulte an der Universität," *NFP*, Abendblatt,7 November 1929; "Die Wiener Hochschulen geschlossen" and "Die gestrigen Tumulte an der Universität," *NFP*, Abendblatt, 8 November 1929.

8. The Credit-Anstalt Crisis and the Collapse of the Gold Exchange Standard

Epigraph: BEA, OV 28/5, "Austria": Letter from Niemeyer to Meinl, 25 November 1931.

1. Ernest Llewellyn Woodward and Rohan Butler, eds., *Documents of British Foreign Policy*, vol. 2 part 4 (London, 1947), pp. 71–77; Paul Schmidt, *Statist auf diplomatischer Bühne 1923–1945: Erlebnisse des Chefdolmetschers im Auswärtigen Amt mit den Staatsmännern Europas* (Bonn, 1953), p. 211. The incident is not mentioned in either of the two detailed accounts of the meeting cited hereafter: Edward Bennett, *Germany and the Diplomacy of the Financial Crisis, 1931* (Cambridge, MA, 1962); William L. Patch Jr. and William L. Patch, *Heinrich Brüning and the Dissolution of the Weimar Republic* (Cambridge, 2006). Norman might have purposefully exaggerated given that the Credit-Anstalt never closed its doors and in fact even extended working hours to satisfy withdrawing customers. See Aurel Schubert, "The Causes of the Austrian Currency Crisis of 1931," in *Economic Development in the Habsburg Monarchy and in the Successor States*, ed. John Komlos (New York, 1990), pp. 89–131, 330n11.

2. Thus for example: "The fundamental problems triggering the crisis / crises were too large and the initial reactions by both the domestic and foreign authorities too hesitant to stop the flow of events once the avalanche had been set in motion." Aurel Schubert, "Torn between Monetary and Financial Stability: An Analysis of Selected Episodes of Austrian Central Banking History," in *Finance and Modernization: A Transnational and Transcontinental Perspective for the Nineteenth and Twentieth Centuries*, ed. Gerald Feldman and Peter Hertner (Farnham, UK, 2008), p. 71; or "The accidental collapse of the Austrian Kreditanstalt in May 1931 finally set a chain reaction in motion: the run on the German

banks (June–July), the withdrawals from London and the devaluation of sterling (September), the largescale withdrawals from New York (September–October), and another series of bank failures in the United States (October–January 1932)." Roland Vaubel, "International Debt, Bank Failures, and the Money Supply: The Thirties and the Eighties," *Cato Journal* 4, no. 1 (1984): 259.

3. Warren J. Samuels, "Melchior Palyi: Introduction and Biography," in *Documents from F. Taylor Ostrander,* ed. Warren J. Samuels (Bingley, UK, 2005), pp. 305–306.

4. Charles Kindleberger, *The World in Depression, 1929–1939* (Berkeley, CA, 1986), p. 148. It is difficult to assess those claims without actual data. To evaluate the effects of the Credit-Anstalt crisis, Hanan Morsy has looked at the returns of global stock markets and concluded that it did trigger a worldwide downturn in equities, but that generally the Vienna Stock Exchange had an impact only on the New York Stock Exchange (where Credit-Anstalt shares were the first foreign shares to be quoted) and then only mildly. Hanan Morsy, "International Financial Crisis Contagion" (mimeo, Department of Economics, George Washington University, 2002). Albrecht Ritschl and Samad Sarferaz found spillover effects from Germany to the U.S. Albrecht Ritschl and Samad Sarferaz, "Currency versus Banking in the Financial Crisis of 1931," *International Economic Review* 55, no. 2 (2014): 349–373.

5. Walter Goldinger and Dieter Binder, *Geschichte der Republik Österreich, 1918–1938* (Oldenbourg, 1992), p. 180.

6. Karl Ausch, *Als die Banken fielen: Zur Soziologie der politischen Korruption,* (Vienna, 1968), p. 338; Rudolf Nötel, "Money, Banking and Industry in Interwar Austria and Hungary," *Journal of European Economic History* 13, no. 2 (1984): 168.

7. Barry Eichengreen, *Golden Fetters: The Gold Standard and the Great Depression, 1919–1939* (New York, 1992), pp. 270–273. Alec Cairncross and Barry Eichengreen also write that the CA's collapse set off a chain reaction of withdrawals all over Europe. Alec Cairncross and Barry Eichengreen, *Sterling in Decline* (Oxford, 1983), 62; see also Fritz Weber, "The Creditanstalt from the 1870s to the 1930s," in *Finance and Modernization: A Transnational and Transcontinental Perspective for the Nineteenth and Twentieth Centuries,* ed. Gerald D. Feldman and Peter Hertner (Farnham, UK, 2008), pp. 72–96. Classic accounts of the German crisis also located its origins in Austria. See R. E. Lüke, *Von der Stabilisierung zur Krise* (Zurich, 1958) or K. E. Born, *Die deutsche Bankenkrise 1931: Finanzen und Politik* (Munich, 1967).

8. Liaquat Ahamed, *Lords of Finance: The Bankers Who Broke the World* (New York, 2009), p. 404. Such claims have trickled down into less accurate understandings of the crisis. John Mackintosh wrote in the *Financial Times* in March 2015 that "in 1931, the failure of Austria's Creditanstalt led to bank runs across Europe—and arguably turned a post-crash recession into the Great Depres-

sion." Three years earlier, its monetary affairs analyst, Martin Wolf, similarly opined that "it is often forgotten that the failure of Austria's Creditanstalt in 1931 led to a wave of bank failures across the continent." In July 2015, *USA Today* published a piece that stated with incredible inaccuracy that "it was the failure of a German bank in 1931 that led to the collapse of the large Austrian bank, Creditanstalt, setting off a global chain reaction of bank failures that led to a new phase of the Great Depression." Finally, writing for the BBC in 2011, Paul Mason made the largest leap, claiming that the "Credit Anstalt bank in Vienna sparked the 1931 banking crisis, which quickly spread to Bank of the United States." James Mackintosh, "Imposing Losses on Bank Bondholders Is No Bad Thing," *Financial Times*, 2 March 2015; Martin Wolf, "Panic Has Become All Too Rational," *Financial Times*, 5 June 2012; Darrell Delamaide, "Portugal Flashes EU Bank Worries," *USA Today*, 10 July 2014; Paul Mason, "Thinking Outside the 1930s Box," BBC News, 7 October 2011, http://www.bbc.co.uk/news/business-15217615.

9. Charles H. Feinstein, Peter Temin, and Gianni Toniolo, "International Economic Organization: Banking, Finance, and Trade in Europe between the Wars," in *Banking, Currency and Finance in Europe between the Wars,* ed. Charles H. Feinstein (Oxford, 1995), p. 10.

10. Peter Temin, "Transmission of the Great Depression," *Journal of Economic Perspectives* 7, no. 2 (1993): 95.

11. "It was the common nature of the causes of the crisis that provided the link, the only substantial link, between the German and Austria crises after 11 May 1931." Harold James, "The Causes of the German Banking Crisis of 1931." *Economic History Review* 37, no. 1 (1984): 81; see also Harold James, *The German Slump: Politics and Economics, 1924–1936* (Oxford, 1986).

12. Fritz Weber, *Vor dem grossen Krach: Österreichs Bankwesen der Zwischenkriegszeit am Beispiel der Credit-Anstalt für Handel und Gewerbe,* (Vienna, 2016), pp. 533–534, 475–476.

13. BEA, OV 9/151, "Sir Otto Niemeyer's Files: Austrian Releases 1929": Letter from Juch to Niemeyer, 25 January 1930.

14. AdR, 29 Ges. London Polit. u Adm. Korr. 1930: Letters from Schüller to Franckenstein, 31 January 1930 and 7 March 1930; AdR, 01/1, Ges. London, Box 11, Polit. Akten 1930–32: Letter from Juch to Franckenstein, 25 March 1930.

15. AdR, 0 1/9 Ges. London, Karton 19: Telegramme 1924–1938, "XI 1930 Hinaus": Telegrams from Juch to Schober, 21 June and 22 June 1930; AdR, 29 Ges. London, Polit. u Adm. Korr. 1930: Telegram from Juch to Franckenstein, 24 March 1930, and letter from Morgan, Grenfell to Juch, 3 April 1930; AdR, 01/1, Ges. London, Box 11, Polit. Akten 1930–32: Letters from Reisch to Juch, 28 March 1930, Franckenstein to Juch, 31 March 1930 and 1 April 1930, Franckenstein to Schober, 2 April 1930 and 20 March 1930, Reisch to Juch, 2 April 1930, Juch to Franckenstein, 25 March 1930, and Engerth to Juch, 15 March 1930; BEA, OV 9/151, "Sir Otto Niemeyer's Files: Austrian Releases 1929": Letters from

Niemeyer to Juch, 6 February 1930, Niemeyer to de Chalendar, 20 March 1930, and de Chalendar to Niemeyer, 21 March 1930; RAL, XI / III / 395, Austria, proposed loan, 1927 Austrian Govt International 7 percent loan, 1930 (1927–1930): Louis von Rothschild to N. M. Rothschild, 25 March 1930; JPM, ARC 1214 (31) Vincent P. Carosso Papers, "Morgan & Co.—Foreign Loans, Austria, 1930's File 2": Letter from Whigham to Jay, 17 June 1930; Gianni Toniolo, *Central Bank Cooperation at the Bank for International Settlements 1930–1973* (Cambridge, 2005), pp. 70–71.

16. BEA, OV 28 2, "Austria": *Note of a Conversation with Dr. Juch on Saturday, the 5th July, 1930*, and Siepman, *Conversation with Dr. Juch, 9th July 1930*; AdR, O 1 / 1, Ges. London, Box 11, Polit. Akten 1930–32: Phone conversations with Grünberger, 4 and 7 July 1930; AdR, 01 / 9 Ges. London, Karton 19, Telegramme 1924–1938, "XI 1930 Hinaus": Telegram from Juch to Schober, 27 June 1930 and 1 July 1930; NA, FO 371 / 14309: Letter from Phipps to Henderson, 17 July 1930.

17. The loan was divided as follows: United States $24 million, United Kingdom $14.6 million, Austria $6.8 million, Italy $5.3 million, Switzerland $4.9 million, Sweden $2.7 million, and the Netherlands $2.4 million. BEA, OV 28 / 3, "Austria": *Austrian Government International Loan 1930*, 14 January 1931; BEA, OV 28 / 2, "Austria": *Telephone Message from Dr. Juch*, 10 July 1930; NA, FO 371 / 14309: Letter from Rougetel to Henderson, 19 July 1930; CA, Bankverein—Protokollbuch, July–September 1930, 18 June and 21 July 1930; AdR, O 1 / 9 Ges. London, Karton 19, Telegramme 1924–1938, "XI 1930 Hinaus": Telegram from Juch to Schober, 10 July 1930; RAL, XI / III / 395 Austria, proposed loan, 1927 Austrian Govt International 7 percent loan, 1930 (1927–1930): Telegrams between N. M. Rothschild and S. M. Rothschild, 10 July and 11 July 1930.

18. AdR, 31 Ges. London Adm. Korr. 1931, "Zollunion": Letter from Schüller to Franckenstein, 17 March 1931.

19. AdR, 31 Ges. London Adm. Korr. 1931, "Zollunion": Letter from Schüller to Franckenstein, 12 March 1931 and from Peter to Franckenstein, 4 April 1931; Anne Orde, "The Origins of the German-Austrian Customs Union Affair of 1931," *Central European History* 13, no. 1 (1980): 34–59.

20. AdR, 31 Ges. London Adm. Korr. 1931, "Zollunion": *Demarche* by Franckenstein to Vansittart, 21 March 1931; AdR, O 1 / 9 Ges. London, Karton 19, Telegramme 1924–1938, "XII 1931 Hinaus": Telegram from Franckenstein to Foreign Ministry, 21 and 24 March 1931.

21. AdR, 31 Ges. London Adm. Korr. 1931, "Zollunion": Letters from Franckenstein to Schober, 26 March, 27 April, and 6 May 1931, as well as letter from Seligman to Franckenstein, 10 April 1931; AdR, O 1 / 9 Ges. London, Karton 19, Telegramme 1924–1938, "XII 1931 Hinaus": Telegrams from Franckenstein to Foreign Ministry, 4 and 26 March 1931; JPM, ARC 1221, Box 36, Morgan Bank European papers, "Austrian Bonds, 1929–30": *Proposed Austro-German Customs Union: Remarks on certain legal and political aspects of the Question*, 28 April 1931,

and F. C. W., *Austrian View of Proposed Customs Union.* Sent to Leffingwell, 7 May 1931.

22. NA, FO 371 / 15150: Letter from Phipps to Henderson, 15 June 1931.

23. RAL, XI / III / 700 (b), "S.M. v. Rothschild. Vienna": *Interview with Dr. Reisch, President of the Austrian National Bank,* 23 June 1931.

24. These "cross-deposits" are mentioned both by Hans Rutkowski, *Der Zusammenbruch der Österreichischen Credit-Anstalt für Handel und Gewerbe und ihre Rekonstruktion: Ein Beitrag zur österreichischen Bankenkrise* (Bottrop, 1934) and by Hans Kernbauer, *Währungspolitik in der Zwischenkriegszeit: Geschichte der Österreichischen Nationalbank von 1923 bis 1938* (Vienna, 1991). Iago Gil Aguado's claim that his discovery of said cross-deposits requires a revision of the narrative is exaggerated. Iago Gil Aguado, "The Credit-Anstalt Crisis of 1931 and the Failure of the Austro-German Customs Union Project," *Historical Journal* 44, no. 1 (2001): 199–221.

25. AdR, 31 Ges. London Adm. Korr. 1931, "Finanzpolitisch Oesterreich II Credit-Anstalt": Phone conversation between Fuchs and Franckenstein, 12 May 1931; NA, FO 371 / 15150: Letter from Phipps to Henderson, 12 May 1931; RAL, XI / III / 521 (b) Austrian Credit-Anstalt: Phone call from Fuchs, 12 May 1931, and telegram from Credit-Anstalt, 12 May 1931.

26. Detailed accounts are given by Philip L. Cottrell, "The Bank of England and Credit-Anstalt's Collapse, Spring 1931," in *Auf Heller und Cent: Beiträge zur Finanz- und Währungsgeschichte,* ed. Karl Bachinger, Dieter Stiefel, and C. Natmessnig (Vienna, 2001), pp. 407–433, and Aurel Schubert, *The Credit-Anstalt Crisis of 1931* (Cambridge, 1991).

27. Weber, *Vor dem grossen Krach,* pp. 497, 523.

28. RAL, XI / III / 521 (b) Austrian Credit-Anstalt: Letter from Max Warburg to Anthony de Rothschild, 16 May 1931, and phone call from Erik Warburg, 13 May 1931; NA, FO 371 / 15150: Telegram from Phipps to Henderson, 12 May 1931; CA, Bankverein–Protokollbuch, April–June 1931: 12 May 1931, p. 79; BEA, OV 28 / 3, "Austria": *Note,* 13 May 1931.

29. Beth A. Simmons, "Why Innovate? Founding the Bank for International Settlements," *World Politics* 45, no. 3 (1993): 361–405; Frank Costigliola, "The Other Side of Isolationism: The Establishment of the First World Bank, 1929–1930," *Journal of American History* 59, no. 3 (1972): 602–620.

30. Barry Eichengreen and Harold James, "Monetary and Financial Reform in Two Eras of Globalization" (unpublished paper), p. 11.

31. Eleanor Lansing Dulles, "The Bank for International Settlements in Recent Years," *American Economic Review* 28, no. 2 (1938): 295; Stephen Clarke, *Central Bank Cooperation: 1924–31* (New York, 1967), p. 147.

32. "Obituary: Lord Renell of Rodd, KBE, CB, JP," *The Geographical Journal* 144, no. 2 (1978): 392–393; Kathleen Burk, "Rodd, Francis James Rennell, Second

Baron Rennell (1895–1978)," in *Oxford Dictionary of National Biography* (Oxford, 2004).

33. BISA, 7.18 (9) (ROD1): Telegrams from Rodd to Fraser, 12 May 1931.

34. Archive de la Banque de France (BdF), MA.A.16.E.1, 1489200303 / 162: *Table Dictated by Telephone from Vienna by Mr. Rodd*, 1 June 1931.

35. BEA, OV 28/3, "Austria": Note, 13 May 1931, and Norman, *Note*, 15 May 1931; BEA, OV 28/35: Siepman, *Credit Anstalt*, 14 May 1931, and "Oester-reichische Nationalbank": Siepman, *Memorandum*, 14 May 1931; BdF, MA.A.16.E.1, 1489200303 / 162: *Réunion des Gouverneurs*, 17 May 1931.

36. BEA, OV 28/3, "Austria": Norman, *Note on the Meeting of Governors Held in Basle on Sunday, the 17th May 1931.*

37. BdF, MA.A.16.E.1, 1489200303 / 162: *Réunion des Gouverneurs*, 17 May 1931.

38. BISA, 1.38 Minutes of Directorate February 1930–March 1932, Board of Directorate Minutes, 18 May 1931; Toniolo, *Central Bank Cooperation*, pp. 92, 91.

39. BISA, 7.18(2) MCG 1 "McGarrah / Fraser 2": Telegram from BIS to FED, 18 May 1931.

40. JPM, ARC 1221 (Box 36), Morgan Bank European papers, "Austrian Bonds, 1929–30": Telegram from CA to Morgan & Cie. Paris, sent on to J. P. Morgan, New York, 19 May 1931.

41. BISA, 7.18 (9) (ROD1): Telegram from Simon to Rodd, 16 May 1931.

42. BEA, OV 28/3, "Austria": Siepman, *Note of a Telephone Conversation with Dr. Brauneis at 11.15 A.M. on the 26th May, 1931.*

43. BISA, 7.18 (2) MCG 1 "Austria—Credit Anstalt Crisis": Telegram from ANB to BIS, 22 May 1931.

44. BISA, 7.18(2) MCG 1 "McGarrah / Fraser 1": Telegram from Simon to Fraser, 19 May 1931; BISA, 7.18 (9) (ROD1) "Confidential Papers on Austria and Hungary—Mr Rodd": Cable no. 4 from Simon to Fraser, 20 May 1931.

45. BISA, 7.18 (9) (ROD1) "Confidential Papers on Austria and Hungary—Mr Rodd": Decoded Telegram from Simon to Fraser, 19 May 1931; AdR, O 1/9 Ges. London, Karton 19, Telegramme 1924–1938, "XII 1931 Herein": Telegrams from Foreign Ministry to Franckenstein, 18 May 1931, and from Wimmer to Foreign Ministry, 19 May 1931; AdR, 31 Ges. London Adm. Korr. 1931, "Finanzpolitisch Oesterreich II Credit-Anstalt," and JPM, ARC 1221 (Box 36), Morgan Bank Euro-pean papers, "Austrian Bonds, 1929–30": Telegrams from Credit-Anstalt to Morgan, Harjes & Cie., 19 May 1931, from J. P. Morgan to Credit-Anstalt, 20 May 1931, and from Morgan, Grenfell to J. P. Morgan, 18 May 1931.

46. NA, FO 371/15150: Note by Leith-Ross for Cadogan, 22 May 1931; BEA, OV 28/3, "Austria": Telegram from Lionel Rothschild to van Hengel, 3 June 1931; JPM, ARC 1214 (31) Vincent P. Carosso Papers, "Morgan & Co.—Foreign Loans, Austria, 1930's. File 2": Telegram from Morgan, Grenfell to J. P. Morgan, 1 June 1931; JPM, ARC 1221 (Box 36), Morgan Bank European papers, "Austrian

Bonds, 1929–30": Telegram from Morgan, Grenfell to J. P. Morgan, 25 May 1931, and from J. P. Morgan to Morgan, Grenfell, 27 May 1931; RAL, XI/III/521 (b) "Austrian Credit-Anstalt": Telegrams from N. M. Rothschild to S. M. Rothschild, 8 June 1931 and 26 May 1931; RAL, XI/III/480 De Rothschild Frères: general: N. M. Rothschild to Rothschild Frères, 26 May 1931, Edouard de Rothschild to N. M. Rothschild, 27 May 1931, and N. M. Rothschild to Edouard de Rothschild, 1 June 1931; BEA, OV 28/3, "Austria": Gunston, *Memo,* 6 June 1931, London Committee, *Credit Anstalt,* 9 June 1931, and Siepman, *Credit Anstalt,* 10 June 1931.

47. RAL, XI/III/183 [000/205], "Credit Anstalt Correspondence/telegrams with NMR": Telegram from N. M. Rothschild to Credit-Anstalt, 20 May 1931, and telegram from N. M. Rothschild to Creditanstalt, 28 May 1931; RAL, XI/III/521 (b) "Austrian Credit-Anstalt": Memorandum, 23 May 1931, and letter from N. M. Rothschild to Fuchs, 22 May 1931; NA, FO 371/15150: Letter from Leith-Ross to Vansittart, 27 May 1931; BEA, OV 28/3, "Austria": Telegram from Norman to Bark, 21 May 1931, and *Further Telephone Message from Mr. Rodd at 12.30 P.M.,* 23 May 1931, as well as note from Rist for Norman, 3 June 1931; JPM, ARC 1214 (31) Vincent P. Carosso Papers, "Morgan & Co.—Boden Credit Anstalt": Letter from Morgan, Grenfell to E. C. Grenfell, 28 May 1931; JPM, ARC 1214 (31) Vincent P. Carosso Papers, "Morgan & Co.—Foreign Loans, Austria, 1930's. File 2": Telegram from J. P. Morgan to Morgan, Grenfell, 29 May 1931; JPM, ARC 1221 (Box 36), Morgan Bank European papers, "Austrian Bonds, 1929–30": Telegram from J. P. Morgan to Credit-Anstalt, 20 May 1931.

48. BISA, 7.18 (9) (ROD1) "Confidential Papers on Austria and Hungary—Mr Rodd 3": Note by Rodd, 28 May 1931.

49. BISA, 7.18 (9) (ROD1) "Confidential Papers on Austria and Hungary—Mr Rodd 3": Telegram from BIS to ANB, 25 May 1931.

50. BISA, 7.18 (2) MCG 1 "McGarrah/Fraser 1": Telegrams from BIS to ANB, 28 May 1931; BISA, 7.18 (9) (ROD1) "Confidential Papers on Austria and Hungary—Mr Rodd 3": Summary of phone conversation with Director Brauneis, 28 May 1931, and telegram from BIS to ANB, 28 May 1931.

51. BISA, 7.18 (9) (ROD1) "Confidential Papers on Austria and Hungary—Mr Rodd 3": Press Communiqué, 29 May 1931; BEA, OV 28/3, "Austria": Siepman, *Kredit Anstalt,* 29 May 1931, and Press Communiqué, 29 May 1931; Toniolo, *Central Bank Cooperation,* p. 93; Dieter Stiefel, *Finanzdiplomatie und Weltwirtschaftskrise: Die Krise der Credit-Anstalt für Handel und Gewerbe 1931* (Frankfurt am Main, 1989), pp. 33, 50–53.

52. J. P. B. Jonker, "HENGEL, Adrianus Johannes van (1886–1936)," in *Biografisch Woordenboek van Nederland,* vol. 6., ed. Klaas van Berkel ('s-Gravenhage, 2008).

53. Hajo Brugmans, *Persoonlijkheden in het Koninkrijk der Nederlanden in woord en beeld: Nederlanders en hun werk* (Amsterdam, 1938), p. 258; Bob Moore, "Bruins' Berlijnse besprekingen: Een selectie uit het archief van prof. mr. dr. G.W.J.

Bruins, in het bijzonder de jaren, 1924–1930," *The English Historical Review* 108, no. 429 (1993): 1069–1070.

54. See, e.g., Toniolo, *Central Bank Cooperation*, pp. 93–94, or Stephen Clarke, *Central Bank Cooperation: 1924–31* (New York, 1967), p. 187.

55. BISA, 7.18 (9) (ROD1) "Confidential Papers on Austria and Hungary—Mr Rodd 3": Foreign Exchange Position of To-day, 1 June 1931.

56. BEA, OV 28/3, "Austria": Siepman, *Memorandum,* 2 June 1931, Gunston, *Oesterreichische Credit Anstalt,* 2 June 1931, Siepman, *Austria,* 3 June 1931, Rodd, *Austria,* 5 June 1931, Gunston, *Memo,* 6 June 1931, Siepman, *Telephone message from Mr. Rodd at Vienna at 1.30 P.M. on the 5th June, 1931,* and *Telephone message from Mr. Rodd in Vienna received at 6.45 P.M. on the 5th June, 1931,* as well as *Telephone message from Mr. Siepman at Basle—5 P.M.–8th June, 1931, Credit Anstalt,* 9 June 1931, *Credit Anstalt,* 10 June 1931, Siepman, *Credit-Anstalt,* 11 June 1931, and Siepman, *Memorandum,* 12 June 1931.

57. BISA, 1.38 Minutes of Directorate February 1930–March 1932, "Board of Directorate Minutes": Minutes 8 June 1931; BISA, 7.18 (9) (ROD1) "Confidential Papers on Austria and Hungary—Mr Rodd 2": Telephone message from BIS to Rodd, 4 June 1931.

58. BdF, MA.A.16.E.1, 1489200303/162: *Banque National d'Autriche.*

59. BISA, 7.18 (9) (ROD1) "Confidential Papers on Austria and Hungary—Mr Rodd 2": Letter from Bruins to Juch, 12 June 1931; BISA, 7.18 (2) MCG 1 "Mc-Garrah/Fraser 1": McGarrah to Finlayson, 13 June 1931.

60. BISA, 6/30 b "Granting of credit of 100,000,000 schillings to Austrian National Bank": Letter from Juch to Bruins, 13 June 1931.

61. BEA, OV 28/3, "Austria": Siepman, *Credit Anstalt,* 11 and 12 June 1931.

62. German Bundesarchiv Berlin-Lichterflede, R 43 I; BISA, 7.18 (9) (ROD1) "Confidential Papers on Austria and Hungary—Mr Rodd 2": Telephone message from Rodd to BIS, 4 June 1931; BISA, 7.18 (2) MCG 1 "McGarrah/Fraser 2": Telegram from Kindersley to Norman, 15 June 1931; JPM, ARC 1221 (Box 36), Morgan Bank European papers, "Austrian Bonds, 1929–30": Telegrams from Morgan, Grenfell to J. P. Morgan, 8 and 10 June 1931, and from Norman to Whigham, 13 June 1931, as well as Jay, *Austria,* sent to Arragon and Morize, 15 June 1931, and telegrams from Morgan, Grenfell to J. P. Morgan, 15 June 1931; BEA, OV 28/3, "Austria": Siepman, *Credit Anstalt,* 11 June 1931.

63. AdR, 01/9 Ges. London, Karton 19, Telegramme 1924–1938, "XII 1931 Hinaus": Telegrams from Franckenstein to Juch, 11, 12, and 13 June 1931; AdR, 31 Ges. London Adm. Korr. 1931, "Finanzpolitisch Oesterreich I": Letter from Whigham to Franckenstein, 12 June 1931, and from Franckenstein to Norman, 15 June 1931; BEA, OV 28/3, "Austria": Siepman, *Note of a telephone conversation with Monsieur Lacour-Gayet at 12.45 P.M. on the 15th June, 1931,* and Siepman, *Memorandum,* 15 June 1931; NA, FO 371/15150: Telegrams from Phipps to Henderson, 16 June 1931.

64. NA, FO 371 / 15151, Francis Rodd, Memorandum, 20 June 1931. Hence, Dieter Stiefel is not quite right if he writes that there is no truth at all to the claim that the French were partially to blame for the financial crisis. Stiefel, *Finanzdiplomatie und Weltwirtschaftskrise*, pp. 75–79. For Aguado, the behavior of Länderbank and Živnostenská indicates a concerted effort by the French to pressure the Austrians into abandoning the customs-union project. Iago Gil Aguado, "The Credit-Anstalt Crisis of 1931 and the Failure of the Austro-German Customs Union Project," *Historical Journal* 44, no. 1 (2001): 199–221.

65. BISA, 7.18 (2) MCG 1 "McGarrah / Fraser 2": Memorandum by Rodd, 20 June 1931. Neither of the banks, which had strong foreign backing and few foreign commitments, needed the foreign exchange.

66. BISA, 7.18 (2) MCG 1 "McGarrah / Fraser 2": Telegram from BIS to Bruins, 16 June 1931; BEA, OV 28 / 4, "Austria": Telegrams from Norman to Bruins, 18 June 1931, from Bruins to Norman, 19 June 1931, and from Kindersley to Norman, 19 June 1931, as well as Siepman, *Austria,* 19 June 1931, Gunston, *Telephone message from Dr. Bruins at Vienna,* 17 June 1931, and Siepman, *Telephone conversation with Dr. Bruins,* 20 June 1931 and *Note of a telephone conversation with Dr. Bruins at 12.15 p.m. on 20th June, 1931*; NA, FO 371 / 15151: Letter from Phipps to Henderson, 18 June 1931, and NA, FO 371 / 15150: Letter from Phipps to Henderson, 19 June 1931.

67. BISA, 7.18 (2) MCG 1 "McGarrah / Fraser 2": Telegram from Kindersley to Norman, 15 June 1931.

68. AdR, 01 / 1, Ges. London, Box 11, Polit. Akten 1930–32: Peter, *Amtsvermerk,* 16 June 1931; BEA, OV 28 / 44: Letter from Snwoden to Norman 15 June 1931; BEA, OV 28 / 4, "Austria": Gunston, *Telephone message from Mr. Rodd for the Governor sent from the National Bank at Vienna,* 17 June 1931; Stiefel, *Finanzdiplomatie und Weltwirtschaftskrise,* pp. 59, 150–167. Stiefel stressed that Norman was acting in the interest of the international creditors, but he might as well have tried simply to prevent a moratorium. Charles Kindleberger, *The World in Depression, 1929–1939* (Berkeley, CA, 1973), p. 147, makes the point that Norman only lent sch.50 million ($7 million), so little that it marks the end of the Bank as lender of last resort. But this followed the original request of Austria for another BIS loan of double that amount and the BIS decision to allow an advance if secured against ANB's gold in London, which totaled only £3 million. See BEA, OV 28 / 3, "Austria": Siepman, *Note of the meeting of Governors held in Basle on Sunday, the 7th, and Monday, the 8th June 1931,* 11 June 1931.

69. NA, FO 371 / 15151: Letter from Phipps to Henderson, 17 June 1931; BEA, OV 28 / 4, "Austria": Lionel Rothschild to National City Bank, New York, and Commercial National Bank, 18 June 1931, and letter from Butler to Gunston, 20 June 1931.

70. BEA, OV 28 / 4, "Austria": Siepman, *Note of a telephone conversation and telephone Message from Sir Robert Kindersley at 5.30 P.M. on the 22nd June, 1931*;

Siepman, *Telephone Message from Mr. Rodd received at 4.30 P.M. on the 23rd June, 1931 and with Dr. Bruins at 12.15 P.M. on 20th June, 1931*; Siepman, *Austria*, 24 June 1931; Siepman, *Telephone message from Dr. Bruins at 6 P.M. on 22/6/31*, *Note of a telephone conversation with Dr. Bruins at 5 P.M. on 23rd June, 1931*, and *Note of a telephone conversation with Dr. Bruins at 5.15 P.M. on the 26th June, 1931*; NA, FO 371/15151: Letters from Phipps to Henderson, 24 June 1931, and from Phipps to Henderson, 27 June 1931.

71. BEA, OV 28/4, "Austria": Letter from Bruins to McGarrah, 18 July 1931.

72. BEA, OV 28/4, "Austria": Siepman, *Telephone message from Mr. Rodd received at 4.30 P.M. on the 23rd June, 1931* and *Note of a telephone conversation with Mr. Rodd at 12 P.M. on 4th July, 1931*; AdR, 01/9 Ges. London, Karton 19, Telegramme 1924–1938, "XII 1931 Hinaus": Telegram from Franckenstein to Juch, 20 June 1931; RAL, XI/III/700 (b), "S. M. v. Rothschild. Vienna": *Visit to Redlich, Minister of Finance—June 23rd, 1931*.

73. Peter Temin, "Transmissions of the Great Depression," in *Journal of Economic Perspectives* 7, no. 2 (1993): 87–102. Temin identified three main ways by which panic could propagate across borders. First, financial panic could spread from one country to another through a "contagion of fear." Second, foreign banks might have bought illiquid assets during a financial panic, but then faced a run when their own depositors realized they were illiquid. Finally, short-term capital flows might have been a major factor spreading financial crises.

74. Ben Bernanke and Harold James, "The Gold Standard, Deflation, and Financial Crisis in the Great Depression: An International Comparison," in *Financial Markets and Financial Crises*, ed. R. Glenn Hubbard (Chicago, 1991), pp. 33–68.

75. Olivier Accominotti, "London Merchant Banks, the Central European Panic, and the Sterling Crisis of 1931," *Journal of Economic History* 72, no. 1 (2012): 1–43. See also William A. Allen and Richhild Moessner, "The International Propagation of the Financial Crisis of 2008 and a Comparison with 1931," *Financial History Review* 19, no. 2 (2012): 123–147.

76. Joh de Vries, *Geschiedenis van der Nederlandsche Bank v 1914–1948*, vol. 5, part 2 (Amsterdam, 1994), p. 55.

77. Eduard März, *Österreichische Bankenpolitik in der Zeit der grossen Wende 1913–1923—Am Beispiel der Creditanstalt für Handel und Gewerbe* (Munich, 1981), p. 449. Amstelbank was to function as an acceptance bank for trade bills, but it engaged more in industrial credit than trade financing. The *New York Times* in 1923 reported that "private Vienna banks [were] resuming their pre-war financing of central Europe" and called Amstelbank "the intermediary bank between Western and Central Europe." *New York Times*, 10 December 1923. Willard Hurst, "Holland, Switzerland and Belgium and the English Gold Crisis of 1931," *Journal of Political Economy* 40, no. 5 (1932): 638–660.

78. NMR, 87/44 Box 1 of 2.

79. NMR, 87 / 44 Box 1 of 2: 17 June 1931.

80. Ibid.

81. Michael Collins, "English Bank Development within a European Context, 1870–1939," *Economic History Review* 51, no. 1 (1998): 1–24.

82. BEA, OV 28 / 5 and OV 28 / 2, "Austria": Niemeyer, *Aide Memoire, Vienna 12th December 1928.* Hajdú had been a director of the Anglo-International Bank in Vienna and Budapest before the BoE had him appointed one of the CA's directors in 1929. Harold James, *The End of Globalization: Lessons from the Great Depression* (Cambridge, MA, 2002), p. 53; Harold James, *The Creation and Destruction of Value* (Cambridge, MA, 2012), pp. 76–77; Weber, *Vor dem grossen Krach,* p. 257.

83. DNB, 9.2 / 43 / 1; DNB, 9.2 / 56 / 1; DNB, 9.2 / 57 / 1.

84. DNB, 9.2 / 43 / 1; DNB, 9.2 / 56 / 1; DNB, 9.2 / 57 / 1; DNB, 9.2 / 57 / 1: *Note in zake de N. V. Amstelbank te Amsterdam,* 27 June 1927.

85. The two largest corporate withdrawals were Mundus Allgemeine Industrie & Handels A.G., withdrawing $321,007 between 23 May and 4 June, and the Dutch N.I. Handelsbank, withdrawing $227,273 on 9 June 1931. DNB 9.2 / 58 / 1.

86. According to the *Wall Street Journal,* Amstelbank's announcement did not come as a surprise, since it was common knowledge that the "bank was the Dutch subsidiary of the Austrian Creditanstalt and bankers here stated that it was a foregone conclusion that the bank would run into trouble as soon as the extent of the difficulties were known. It is believed here that the reorganization committee of the Creditanstalt found it advisable to let the Dutch institution go as guarantors were unwilling to extend their guarantees to creditors." *Wall Street Journal,* 20 June 1931. The *Times* of London reported that Amstelbank's directors had decided to ask for a moratorium following "heavy withdrawals of deposits" and voiced hope that an agreement would be reached "from creditors to abstain from withdrawing credits." *Times* (London), 22 June 1931.

87. The notion of such a self-justifying run on banks was formalized by Douglas Diamond and Philip Dybvig, "Bank Runs, Deposit Insurance and Liquidity," *Journal of Political Economy* 91, no. 3 (1983): 401–419.

88. NMR, 87 / 44 Box 1 of 2: 4 July 1931 and 30 July 1931.

89. BISA, 7.18 (2) MCG 1 "McGarrah / Fraser 1": Telegram from Harrison to McGarrah, 26 May 1931.

90. BISA, 7.18 (2) MCG 1 "McGarrah / Fraser 1": Telegrams from Harrison to McGarrah, 27 May 1931, and from McGarrah to Harrison, 27 May 1931.

91. BISA, 7.18 (2) MCG 1 "McGarrah / Fraser 1": Letter from van Hengel to McGarrah, 11 June 1931.

92. BISA, 7.18 (9) (ROD1) "Confidential Papers on Austria and Hungary—Mr Rodd 2": Phone message from Rodd to BIS, 3 June 1931; BISA, 7.18 (2) MCG 1 "McGarrah / Fraser 2": Telegram from Gannon to Wiggin, 16 June 1931; BISA, 3 / 12

"Opening by BIS of Special Account for Maintenance of Gold Standard of Various Currencies June 1931–August 1931": Letter from Norman to McGarrah, 16 June 1931.

93. BISA, 7.18 (2) MCG 1 "McGarrah / Fraser 1": Telegrams from Banque de Grèce to BIS, 25 May 1931, and from McGarrah to Banque de Grèce, 26 May 1931.

94. Bundesarchiv Berlin, BA R 43 I.

95. Kindleberger, *The World in Depression*, pp. 149–150.

96. Ibid., pp. 149–151.

97. BISA, 7.18 (9) (ROD1) "Confidential Papers on Austria and Hungary—Mr Rodd 1": Letter from Kindersley to Rodd, 20 June 1931, and letter from McGarrah to Harrison, 20 June 1931; BISA, "3 / 12 Opening by BIS of Special Account for maintenance of Gold Standard of various currencies June 1931–August 1931": Letter from Banque Nationale du Royaume de Yougoslavie to BIS, 29 June 1931, and from Latvijas Banka to BIS, 2 July 1931.

98. Weber provides information according to which CA's discounting with ANB, after growing almost six-fold in May, fell slightly during June. Weber, *Vor dem grossen Krach*, p. 477.

99. BISA, 7.18 (9) (ROD1) "Confidential Papers on Austria and Hungary—Mr Rodd 1": Phone messages from Bruins to BIS, 3 and 6 July 1931.

100. BISA, 7.18 (9) (ROD1) "Confidential Papers on Austria and Hungary—Mr Rodd 1": Telegram from Bruins to BIS, 8 July 1931.

101. BISA, 1.38 Minutes of Directorate February 1930–March 1932, "Board of Directorate Minutes": Minutes 13 July 1931.

102. NA, FO 371 / 15151: Telegram from Hadow to Henderson, 14 July 1931; BISA, 7.18 (9) (ROD1) "Confidential Papers on Austria and Hungary—Mr Rodd 1": Bruins, Report no. 2, 30 July 1931.

103. NA, FO 371 / 15151: Letter from Hadow to Henderson, 16 July 1931; BEA, OV 28 / 4, "Austria": Siepman, Phone call from Bruins, 16 July 1931.

104. NA, FO 371 / 15151: Letter from Hadow to Henderson, 16 July 1931; BEA, OV 28 / 4, "Austria": Siepman, Phone call from Bruins, 16 July 1931.

105. BISA, 7.18 (9) (ROD1) "Confidential Papers on Austria and Hungary—Mr Rodd 1": Telegram from BIS to Harrison, 14 July 1931; BEA, OV 28 / 4, "Austria": Letter from Bruins to McGarrah, 18 July 1931, and Siepman, *Note of a telephone conversation with Mr. Rodd at 6.20 P.M. on 17th July 1931*; PRO, FO 371 / 15151: Telegram from Hadow to Foreign Office, 18 July 1931.

106. BISA, 6 / 30 b "Granting of Credit of 100,000,000 Schillings to Austrian National Bank": Letter from Simon to Juch, 14 July 1931.

107. BISA, 7.18 (9) (ROD1) "Confidential Papers on Austria and Hungary—Mr Rodd 1": Telegram from McGarrah to Bruins, 15 July 1931; BISA, 7.18 (2) MCG 1 "BIS MCG": Letter from McGarrah to Bruins, 16 July 1931.

108. BISA, 7.18(2) MCG 1 "McGarrah / Fraser 2": Telegram from Bruins to BIS, 16 July 1931.

109. BEA, OV 28 / 4, "Austria": Siepman, *Note of a telephone conversation with Mr. Rodd at 11.40 A.M. on 16th July, 1931.*

110. NA, FO 371 / 15152: Letter from Hadow to O'Malley, 4 August 1931.

111. BISA, 3 2(r) 1 "Liaison with Oesterreichische Nationalbank 1930–1b 1f": Telegram from ANB to BIS, 22 July 1931.

112. BEA, OV 28 / 5, "Austria": Siepman, *Note of a telephone conversation with Dr. Bruins at 6.30 P.M. on Friday, 7th August 1931;* NA FO 371 / 15152: Letter from Hadow to Henderson, 12 August 1931; ANB, 1138 / 1925: Letters from ANB to BEA, 17 August 1931, and from BEA to ANB, 20 August 1931.

113. A recent and excellent account of the British crisis is James Ashley Morrison, "Shocking Intellectual Austerity: The Role of Ideas in the Demise of the Gold Standard in Britain," *International Organization* 70, no. 1 (2016): 175–207.

114. Cairncross and Eichengreen, *Sterling in Decline,* p. 63.

115. Ibid.

116. Morrison, "Shocking Intellectual Austerity," p. 16.

117. Cairncross and Eichengreen, *Sterling in Decline,* pp. 70–71.

118. Morrision, "Shocking Intellectual Austerity," pp. 20–21.

119. NA, FO 371 / 15152: Telegram from Hadow to Foreign Office, 5 August and 30 July 1931, letter from Hadow to O'Malley, 4 and 11 August 1931, letter from Hadow to Sargent, 24 August 1931, and telegram from Hadow to Foreign Office, 22 August 1931; BEA, OV 28 / 5, "Austria": Letter from van Walré de Bordes to Siepman, 7 August 1931, and Siepman, *Note of a conversation with Baron Franckenstein at 6.15 P.M. on Monday, the 10th August 1931.*

120. LNA, C 1639, Investigations re: banking Austria 23, "Austria": *Valutarischer Nostrostand der Oesterr. Nationalbank am 7. / 10.1931;* NA, FO 371 / 15153: Letter from Phipps to Reading, 8 October 1931.

121. Aurel Schubert, *The Credit-Anstalt Crisis of 1931* (Cambridge, 1991), pp. 49–65; Aurel Schubert, "The Causes of the Austrian Currency Crisis of 1931," in *Economic Development in the Habsburg Monarchy and in the Successor States,* ed. John Komlos (Boulder, CO, 1983), pp. 89–113; Aurel Schubert, "Torn between Monetary and Financial Stability: An Analysis of Selected Episodes of Austrian Central Banking History," in *Finance and Modernization: A Transnational and Transcontinental Perspective for the Nineteenth and Twentieth Centuries,* ed. Gerald D. Feldman and Peter Hertner (Farnham, UK, 2008), pp. 51–74.

122. Schubert, *The Credit-Anstalt Crisis,* p. 61. Schubert is mistaken in thinking that opposed to the 1923 League loan, the international Investment loan was not a gold loan. The Austrian tranche was issued in gold schillings and ranked second right after the League loan. It was also serviced from the same tobacco and customs revenues as the League loan. The yield spread thus reflected only the absence of international guarantees.

123. Schubert, *The Credit-Anstalt Crisis*, p. 62.

124. Schubert, *The Credit-Anstalt Crisis*, p. 61.

125. Barry Eichengreen, "The Origins and Nature of the Great Slump Revisited," *Economic History Review* 45, no. 2 (1992): 213–239. Eichengreen's analysis that the Banque de France and the New York Federal Reserve failed to inflate their economies in the face of gold inflows and thereby put strains on the international financial system is of course correct.

126. Charles Kindleberger, *The World in Depression, 1929–1939* (Berkeley, CA, 1986), p. 151.

127. BEA, OV 28 / 5, "Austria": Niemeyer, *Interview between Profesor Bruins and M. van Hengel and League Representatives at Vienna, Friday, 23d October, 1931,* and *Note of conversation with the Austrian Chancellor and the Austrian Finance Minister on Saturday, October 24th 1931 (Dr. Juch came in towards the end).*

128. BEA, OV 28 / 5, "Austria": *Note of conversation with the Austrian Chancellor and the Austrian Finance Minister on Saturday, October 24th 1931 (Dr. Juch came in towards the end).*

129. NA, FO 371 / 15155 / C 9748: Letter from Phipps to Sargent, 29 December 1931; BEA, OV 28 / 5, "Austria": Niemeyer, *Interview between Professor Bruins and M. van Hengel and League Representatives at Vienna, Friday, 23d October, 1931.*

130. NA, FO 371 / 15154: Telegram from Phipps to Foreign Office, 15 October 1931.

131. Peter Berger, "The League of Nations and Interwar Austria: Critical Assessment of a Partnership in Economic Reconstruction," in *The Dolfuss-Schuschnigg Era in Austria: A Reassessment,* ed. Günther Bischof, Anton Pelinka, and Alexander Lassner (New Brunswick, NJ, 2003), pp. 73–92.

132. LNA, C 72, Réconstruction financière de l'Autriche 1931–36, "League's Financial Committee Documents concerning Austria, up to 30th Sept. 1931": Janssen, *Note,* 15 September 1931.

133. NA, FO 371 / 15153: Letter from Niemeyer to Cadogan, 19 September 1931; LNA, A.55 (b).1931.II in SdN, 1248 Septembre 1931 III: Autriche, "Report to the Council": *1. Austria,* 19 September 1931.

134. RAL, XI / III / 480 De Rothschild Frères: general: Letter from N. M. Rothschild to Rothschild Frères, 4 November 1931; NA, FO 371 / 15154: Leith-Ross, *Note of a meeting in Sir F. Leith Ross's room—14th November, 1931.* The meeting was attended by Leith-Ross, Niemeyer, Waley, Cowan, Bewley, and Loveday.

135. NA, FO 371 / 15155 / C 8925: Cowan, *Minutes,* 16 November 1931.

136. BEA, OV 28 / 5, "Austria": Telegram from Morgan, Grenfell to J. P. Morgan, 27 November 1931, and Norman, *Note,* 27 November 1931. Present were E. C. Grenfell, C. F. Whigham, and Otto Niemeyer.

137. BEA, OV 28 / 5, "Austria": Telegrams from Whigham to J. P. Morgan, 28 November 1931, from Peacock to E. C. Grenfell, 30 November 1931, from J. P.

Morgan to Morgan, Grenfell, 30 November 1931, and from Morgan, Grenfell to J. P. Morgan, 4 December 1931.

138. NA, FO 371 / 15155 / C 9468: Letter from Phipps to Simon, 12 December 1931.

139. BEA, OV 28 / 5, "Austria": Letter from Rost van Tonningen to Niemeyer, 9 December 1931.

140. RAL, XI / III / 456 "Austria 1931–2": Telegrams from ANB to Holland-Martin, 5 January 1931.

141. LNA, C 84 / Réconstruction financière de l'Autriche 1931–1936, "Austrian Guaranteed Loan 1932–1943": *Memorandum on the Loan Issued in Austria under the Auspices of the League of Nations* and *Telephonische Information des Finanzministeriums,* 11 July 1933. Significantly smaller tranches were planned for Switzerland, Belgium, and the Netherlands. RAL, XI / III / 456 "Austria 1931–2": *Synopsis of Events since Outbreak of CA Crisis,* 15 March 1932, and *Austria,* undated; BEA, OV28 / 51, "Austria—Standstill Negotiations": Letter from Guinness to Niemeyer, 2 January 1935, and Norman, *Short-Term Foreign Indebtedness of Austrian Banks,* 18 August 1932.

Conclusion

Epigraph: Eric Hobsbawm, *Interesting Times: A Twentieth-Century Life* (New York, 2003), p. 47.

1. Ernst Kieninger, Nikola Langreiter, Armin Loacker, and Klara Löffler, eds., *1. April 2000* (Vienna, 2000).

2. David Art, *The Politics of the Nazi Past in Germany and Austria* (New York, 2006).

3. Those opposed to Anschluss in 1938 for the most part hid their views. Robert Breuer, *Nacht über Wien* (Vienna, 1988); Ilana Offenberger, *The Jews of Nazi Vienna, 1938–1945* (Cham, Switzerland, 2017).

4. Jennifer Rankin, "Eurozone Crisis: Which Countries Are for or against Grexit," *Guardian,* 12 July 2015, https://www.theguardian.com/business/2015/jul/12/eurozone-crisis-which-countries-are-for-or-against-grexit.

5. Heena Smith, "Alexis Tsipras: 'The Worst Is Clearly behind Us,'" *Guardian,* 24 July 2017, https://www.theguardian.com/world/2017/jul/24/alexis-tsipras-the-worst-is-clearly-behind-us.

6. Jamie Martin, "The Colonial Origins of the Greek Bailout," *Imperial & Global Forum,* 27 July 2015, https://imperialglobalexeter.com/2015/07/27/the-colonial-origins-of-the-greek-bailout/.

7. Rupert Neate, "Growing Anti-German Feeling on Streets of Greece," *Guardian,* 27 February 2017, https://www.theguardian.com/business/2012/feb/27/growing-anti-german-feeling-streets-greece.

8. "#ThisIsACoup: Germany Faces Backlash over Tough Greece Bailout Demands," *Guardian*, 13 July 2015, https://www.theguardian.com/business/2015/jul/13/thisisacoup-germany-faces-backlash-over-tough-greece-bailout-demands. Mohamed A. El-Erian tweeted on 13 July 2015: "The sad reality of #Greece & #Europe: Its [*sic*] not long now until historians draw a parallel with historical episodes of "gunboat diplomacy.""" https://twitter.com/elerianm/status/620547739244322816?lang=ms.

9. Graeme Wearden and Helen Davidson, "Greek Debt Crisis: Deal Reached after Marathon All-Night Summit—as It Happened," *Guardian*, 13 July 2015, https://www.theguardian.com/business/live/2015/jul/12/greek-debt-crisis-eu-leaders-meeting-cancelled-no-deal-live.

10. "Protocols of the Elders of Zion Read Aloud in Greek Parliament," *Haaretz*, 26 October 2012, http://www.haaretz.com/jewish/news/protocols-of-the-elders-of-zion-read-aloud-in-greek-parliament-1.472552; "Greek Neo-Nazi Lawmaker Indicates He Is a Holocaust Denier," *Haaretz*, 7 June 2013, http://www.haaretz.com/misc/haaretzcomsmartphoneapp/dailybrief/1.528483.

11. Helena Smith, "Greece's Golden Dawn Party Describes Hilter as 'Great Personality,'" *Guardian*, 16 April 2014, https://www.theguardian.com/world/2014/apr/16/greece-golden-dawn-hitler; "Greek Government Censures Neo-Nazi Party Head over Holocaust Comment," *Times of Israel*, 16 May 2012, http://www.timesofisrael.com/greek-government-censures-neo-nazi-party-head-over-holocaust-comment/.

12. Alana Goodman, "Poll: 85% of Greeks Believe the Jews Have Too Much Power over Global Finance," *Washington Free Beacon*, 30 June 2015, http://freebeacon.com/issues/poll-85-of-greeks-believe-the-jews-have-too-much-power-over-global-finance/.

13. Karin Riss and Maria Sterkl, "Blauer Klub in Burschenschafterhand," *Der Standard*, 25 October 2017, http://derstandard.at/2000066617298/Blauer-Klub-in-Burschenschafterhand.

14. "Why Is Greece the Most Anti-Semitic Country in Europe?," *Haaretz*, 20 May 2014, http://www.haaretz.com/jewish/features/1.591841.

15. Carmen M. Reinhart and Kenneth S. Rogoff, *This Time is Different: Eight Centuries of Financial Folly* (Princeton, NJ, 2009), pp. 92, 98.

16. Michaela Seiser, "Mit dem Vermögen der Genossen Casino gespielt," *Frankfurter Allgemeine Zeitung*, 9 February 2009, http://www.faz.net/aktuell/finanzskandale/finanzskandale-3-die-bawag-im-casino-mit-dem-vermoegen-der-genossen-casion-gespielt-1149375/helmut-elsner-vor-gericht-1671842.

17. "Korruptionsvorwürfe: Anklage gegen Grasser, Meischberger und Co," *Der Standard*, 21 July 2016, http://www.derstandard.at/2000041517255/Anklage-gegen-Grasser-Meischberger-und-14-weitere-Personen.

18. Jakob Zirm "Hypo: Versagen auf allen Linien," *Die Presse,* 2 December 2014, http://www.diepresse.com/home/wirtschaft/economist/4610315/Hypo_Versagen -auf-allen-Linien.

19. Dimitrii Georgievich Tomashevskii, *Lenin's Ideas and Modern International Relations* (Moscow, 1974), p. 62.

20. Thomas H. Huxley, "On Descartes' 'Discourse Touching the method of using one's reason rightly and of seeking scientific truth'" (Address, Cambridge Young Men's Christian Society, 24 March 1870), in *Essays* (London, 1894), pp. 166–198, 168.

Bibliography

Accominotti, Olivier. "London Merchant Banks, the Central European Panic, and the Sterling Crisis of 1931." *Journal of Economic History* 72, no. 1 (2012): 1–43.

Addis, Charles Stewart. "The Outlook for International Cooperation in Finance." *Proceedings of the Academy of Political Science* 14, no. 2 (1931): 96–105.

Aguado, Iago Gil. "The Credit-Anstalt Crisis of 1931 and the Failure of the Austro-German Customs Union Project." *Historical Journal* 44, no. 1 (2001): 199–221.

Ahamed, Liaquat. *Lords of Finance: The Bankers Who Broke the World*. New York, 2009.

Ahrer, Jakob. *Erlebte Zeitgeschichte*. Vienna, 1930.

Aiginger, Karl. "85 Jahre WIFO: Gedanken zu Geschichte und Zukunft des Institutes." *WIFO Monatsbericht* 6 (2012): 497–510.

Aldcroft, Derek H., and Michael J. Oliver. *Exchange Rate Regimes in the Twentieth Century*. Cheltenham, UK, 1998.

Allen, Larry. *The Encyclopedia of Money*. Santa Barbara, CA, 2009.

Allen, William A., and Richhild Moessner. "The International Propagation of the Financial Crisis of 2008 and a Comparison with 1931." *Financial History Review* 19, no. 2 (2012): 123–147.

Andreopoulos, George J. "The International Financial Commission and Anglo-Greek Relations (1928–1933)." *Historical Journal* 3, no. 2 (1988): 341–364.

Art, David. *The Politics of the Nazi Past in Germany and Austria*. New York, 2006.

Aster, Sidney. *Power, Policy and Personality: The Life and Times of Lord Salter, 1881–1975*. N.p., 2016.

Ausch, Karl. *Als die Banken fielen: Zur Soziologie der politischen Korruption*. Vienna, 1968.

———. *Genfer Sanierung und der 12. Februar 1934 in Österreich: 1927 bis 1938*. Munich, 1973.

Bachinger, Karl, and Herbert Matis. *Der österreichische Schilling—Geschichte einer Währung*. Graz, 1974.

———. "Die österreichische Nachkriegsinflation, 1918–1922." *Beiträge zur historischen Sozialkunde* 16, no. 3 (1986): 83–91.

Bachinger, Karl, Dieter Stiefel, and Charlotte Natmessnig. *Auf Heller und Cent: Beiträge zur Finanz- und Währungsgeschichte.* Vienna, 2001.

Barker, Elisabeth. *Austria 1918–1972.* London, 1973.

Bauer, Otto. *Die österreichische Revolution.* Vienna, 1923.

———. *Die Wirtschaftskrise in Österreich.* Vienna, 1925.

Bayer, Hans. *Strukturwandlungen der österreichischen Volkswirtschaft nach dem Kriege.* Leipzig, 1929.

Bayoumi, Tamim, Barry Eichengreen, and Mark P. Taylor, eds. *Modern Perspectives on the Gold Standard.* Cambridge, 1996.

Beller, Steven. "Kraus's Firework." In *Staging the Past: The Politics of Commemoration in Habsburg Central Europe, 1848 to the Present,* edited by Maria Bucur and Nancy M. Wingfield. West Lafayette, IN, 2001.

Benedikt, Heinrich. *Geschichte der Republik Österreich.* Vienna, 1954.

Bennett, Edward. *Germany and the Diplomacy of the Financial Crisis, 1931.* Cambridge, MA, 1962.

Berchtold, Klaus. *1918–1933: Fünfzehn Jahre Verfassungskampf.* Vienna, 1998.

Berend, Ivan T., and Györgi Ranki. *Economic Development in East-Central Europe in the 19th and 20th Centuries.* New York, 1974.

Berger, Peter. "The Austrian Economy, 1918–1938." In *The Economic Development in the Habsburg Monarchy and in the Successor States,* edited by John Komlos, pp. 270–284. New York, 1990.

———. *Im Schatten der Diktatur.* Vienna, 2000.

———. "The League of Nations and Interwar Austria: Critical Assessment of a Partnership in Economic Reconstruction." In *The Dolfuss-Schuschnigg Era in Austria: A Reassessment,* edited by Günther Bischof, Anton Pelinka, and Alexander Lassner, pp. 73–92. New Brunswick, NJ, 2003.

———. "Ökonomische Macht und Politik." In *Handbuch des politischen Systems Österreichs, Erste Republik 1918–1933,* edited by Emerich Tálos, Herbert Dachs, Ernst Hanisch, and Anton Staudinger, pp. 395–411. Vienna, 1995.

Berkley, George E. "Vienna and Its Jews: The Solitary Scapegoat in Post-war Vienna." In *Hostages of Modernization,* edited by Herbert A. Strauss, pp. 797–810. Berlin, 1993.

Bernanke, Ben. "Inflation Expectations and Inflation Forecasting." Speech at the Monetary Economics Workshop of the National Bureau of Economic Research Summer Institute, Cambridge, Massachusetts, 10 July 2007.

Bernanke, Ben, and Harold James. "The Gold Standard, Deflation, and Financial Crises in the Great Depression: An International Comparison." In *Financial Markets and Financial Crises,* edited by Glenn R. Hubbard, pp. 33–68. Chicago, 1991.

Bettauer, Hugo. *Der Kampf um Wien: Ein Roman vom Tage.* Hamburg, n.d.

Beyersdorf, Frank. " 'Credit or Chaos?' The Austrian Stabilisation Programme of 1923 and the League of Nations." In *Internationalism Reconfigured: Transna-*

tional Ideas and Movements between the World Wars, edited by Daniel Laqua, pp. 134–157. London, 2011.

Birn, Donald S. *The League of Nations Union, 1918–1945.* Oxford, 1981.

Bloomfield, Arthur. *Monetary Policy under the International Gold Standard, 1880–1915.* New York, 1959.

Bloomfield, Jonathan. "Surviving in a Harsh World: Trade and Inflation in the Czechoslovak and Austrian Republics 1918–1926." In, *Die Erfahrung der Inflation im internationalen Zusammenhang und Vergleich*, edited by Gerald D. Feldman, Carl Ludwig Holtfrerich, Gerhard A. Ritter, and Peter-Christian Witt, pp. 228–268. Berlin, 1984.

Bordiss, Bradley, and Vishnu Padayachee. "'A Superior Practical Man': Henry Strakosch, the Gold Standard and Monetary Policy Debates in South Africa, 1920–23." *Economic History of Developing Regions* 26, no. 1 (2011): 114–122.

Bordo, Michael D., and Ronald MacDonald. "The Inter-War Gold Exchange Standard: Credibility and Monetary Independence." National Bureau of Economic Research Working Paper 8429. Cambridge, MA, 2001.

Born, K. E. *Die deutsche Bankenkrise 1931: Finanzen und Politik.* Munich, 1967.

Bosmans, J. L. J. "Alfred Rudolph Zimmerman." In *Biografisch Woordenboek van Nederland*, vol. 1, edited by Johannes Charité. Den Haag, 1979.

——. *De Nederlander Mr. A. R. Zimmerman als Commissaris-Generaal van de Volkenbund in Oostenrijk, 1922–1926.* Nijmegen, 1973.

——. "Innen- und Aussenpolitische Probleme bei der Aufhebung der Völkerbundkontrolle in Österreich 1924–1926." *Zeitgeschichte* 9, no. 6 (1982): 189–201.

——. "Pelt, Adrianus (1892–1981)." In *Biografisch Woordenboek van Nederland*, vol. 2, edited by Johannes Charité and Ivo Schöffer. 's-Gravenhage, 1985.

Botz, Gerhard. "Der '15. Juli 1927,' seine Ursachen und Folgen." In *Österreich 1927 bis 1938* (Protokoll des Symposiums in Wien 23. bis 28. Oktober 1972), pp. 43–67. Munich, 1973.

——. *Gewalt in der Politik: Attentate, Zusammenstösse, Putschversuche, Unruhen in Österreich 1918 bis 1938.* Munich, 1983.

Boyce, Robert. "The Significance of 1931 for British Imperial and International History." *Histoire@Politique: Politique, culture, société* 11 (2010): 2.

Breuer, Robert. *Nacht über Wien.* Vienna, 1988.

Brown, Brendan. *Monetary Chaos in Europe.* London, 1988.

Brugmans, Hajo. *Persoonlijkheden in het Koninkrijk der Nederlanden in woord en beeld: Nederlanders en hun werk.* Amsterdam, 1938.

Burk, Kathleen. "Money and Power: The Shift from Great Britain to the United States." In *Finance and Financiers in European History, 1880–1960*, edited by Youssef Cassis, pp. 360–369. Cambridge, 1992.

——. *Morgan Grenfell, 1838–1988.* Oxford, 1989.

———. "Rodd, Francis James Rennell, second Baron Rennell (1895–1978)." In *Oxford Dictionary of National Biography*. Oxford, 2004.

Butschek, Felix. *Die österreichische Wirtschaft im 20. Jahrhundert*. Stuttgart, 1985.

Cagan, Phillip. "The Monetary Dynamics of Hyperinflation." In *Studies in the Quantity Theory of Money*, edited by Milton Friedman, pp. 25–117. Chicago, 1956.

Cairncross, Alec, and Barry Eichengreen. *Sterling in Decline*. Oxford, 1983.

Capie, Forrest, Charles Goodhart, and Norbert Schnadt. "The Development of Central Banking." In *The Future of Central Banking: The Tercentenary Symposium of the Bank of England*, edited by Forrest Capie, Charles Goodhart, Stanley Fischer, and Norbert Schnad, pp. 1–97. Cambridge, 1994.

Capie, Forrest, Terence Mills, and Geoffrey Wood. "What Happened in 1931?" In *Financial Crises and the World Banking System*, edited by Forrest Capie and Geoffrey E. Wood, pp. 120–159. New York, 1986.

Carsten, F. L. *The First Austrian Republic, 1918–1938: A Study Based on British and Austrian Documents*. Aldershot, UK, 1986.

Cassis, Youssef, ed. *Finance and Financiers in European History, 1880–1960*. Cambridge, 1992.

Chancellor, Edward. *Devil Take the Hindmost: A History of Financial Speculation*. London, 1999.

Clarke, Stephen V. O. *Central Bank Cooperation: 1924–31*. New York, 1967.

Clavin, Patricia. "The Austrian Hunger Crisis and the Genesis of International Organization after the First World War." *International Affairs* 90, no. 2 (2014): 265–278.

———. *Securing the World Economy: The Reinvention of the League of Nations, 1920–1946*. Oxford, 2013.

Clavin, Patricia, and Jens-Wilhelm Wessels. "Another Golden Idol? The League of Nations Gold Inquiry and the Great Depression, 1929–32." *International History Review* 26, no. 4 (2004): 765–795.

———. "Transnationalism and the League of Nations: Understanding the Work of Its Economic and Financial Organisation." *Contemporary European History* 14, no. 4 (2005): 465–492.

Collins, Michael. "English Bank Development within a European Context, 1870–1939." *Economic History Review* 51, no. 1 (1998): 1–24.

Comité Olympique Français. *Les jeux de la VIIIe Olympiade Paris 1924*. Paris, 1924.

Costigliola, Frank C. "Anglo-American Financial Rivalry in the 1920s." *Journal of Economic History* 37, no. 4 (1977): 911–934.

———. "The Other Side of Isolationism: The Establishment of the First World Bank, 1929–1930." *Journal of American History* 59, no. 3 (1972): 602–620.

Cottrell, P. L., with C. J. Stone. "Credits, and Deposits to Finance Credits." In *European Industry and Banking, 1920–1939: A Review of Bank Industry*

Relations, edited by P. L. Cottrell, Håkan Lindgren, and Alice Teichova, pp. 43–78. Leicester, 1992.

Cottrell, Philip L. "The Bank of England and Credit-Anstalt's Collapse, Spring 1931." In *Auf Heller und Cent: Beiträge zur Finanz- und Währungsgeschichte*, edited by Karl Bachinger, Dieter Stiefel, and Charlotte Natmessnig, pp. 407–433. Vienna, 2001.

———. "Norman, Strakosch and the Development of Central Banking: From Conception to Practice, 1919–1924." In *Rebuilding the Financial System in Central and Eastern Europe, 1918–1944*, edted by Philip L. Cottrell, pp. 29–73. Aldershot, UK, 1997.

Débeir, Jean Claude. "La crise du franc de 1924—Un exemple de spéculation 'internationale.'" *Relations internationales* 13 (1978): 29–49.

Dexter, Byron. *The Years of Opportunity: The League of Nations, 1920–1926.* New York, 1967.

Diamond, Douglas, and Philip Dybvig. "Bank Runs, Deposit Insurance and Liquidity." *Journal of Political Economy* 91, no. 3 (1983): 401–419.

Dornbusch, Rüdiger. "Lessons from the German Inflation Experience of the 1920s." In *Macroeconomics and Finance: Essays in Honor of Franco Modigliani*, edited by Rüdiger Dornbusch, Stanley Fischer, and John Bossons, pp. 409–439. Cambridge, MA, 1987.

———. "Monetary Problems of Post-Communism: Lessons from the End of the Austro-Hungarian Empire." *Weltwirtschaftliches Archiv* 28 (1992): 391–424.

Dornbusch, Rüdiger, and Stanley Fischer. "Stopping Hyperinflations Past and Present." National Bureau of Economic Research Working Paper 1810, Cambridge, MA, 1986.

Dornbusch, Rudiger, Federico Sturzenegger, and Holger Wolf, "Extreme Inflation: Dynamics and Stabilization." *Brookings Papers on Economic Activity* 2 (1990): 1–65.

Dressler, Oskar and Hugo Weinberger. "Die Geschlechtsmoral." In *Geldentwertung und Stabilisierung in ihren Einflüssen auf die soziale Entwicklung in Österreich*, edited by Julius Buntzel, pp. 323–326. Munich, 1925.

Dubin, Martin David. "Transgovernmental Processes in the League of Nations." *International Organization* 37, no. 3 (1983): 469–493.

Dulles, Eleanor Lansing. "The Bank for International Settlements in Recent Years." *American Economic Review* 28, no. 2 (1938): 290–304.

Ebner, Monika. *Der Bankenzusammenbruch des Jahres 1931 in Österreich.* Phil. diss., University of Vienna, 1969.

Eichengreen, Barry. "The Bank of France and the Sterilization of Gold, 1926–1932." *Explorations in Economic History* 23 (1986): 56–84.

———. "Conducting the International Orchestra: Bank of England Leadership under the Classical Gold Standard." *Journal of International Money and Finance* 45, no. 2 (1987): 5–29.

———. *Elusive Stability: Essays in the History of International Finance, 1919–1939.* Cambridge, 1990.

———. *Golden Fetters: The Gold Standard and the Great Depression, 1919–1939.* New York, 1992.

———. "The Origins and Nature of the Great Slump Revisited." *Economic History Review* 45, no. 2 (1992): 213–239.

———. "Rational Expectations and Inflation (T. J. Sargent): A Review." *Journal of Economic Literature* 24 (1986): 1812–1815.

Eichengreen, Barry, and Harold James. "Monetary and Financial Reform in Two Eras of Globalization." Unpublished paper.

Eichengreen, Barry, and Jeffrey Sachs. "Exchange Rates and Economic Recovery in the 1930s." *Journal of Economic History* 45 (1985): 925–946.

Eichengreen, Barry, and Peter Temin. "The Gold Standard and the Great Depression." *Contemporary European History* 9, no. 2 (2000): 183–207.

Eichengreen, Barry, with Mark W. Watson and Richard S. Grossman. "Bank Rate Policy under the Interwar Gold Standard: A Dynamic Probit Model." *Economic Journal* 95 (1985): 725–745.

80 Jahre Justizpalastbrand: Recht und gesellschaftliche Konflikte. Vienna, 2008.

Eigner, Peter. "Bank-Industry Networks: The Austrian Experience, 1895–1940." In *Rebuilding the Financial System in Central and Eastern Europe, 1918–1994,* edited by Philip L. Cottrell, pp. 91–114. Aldershot, UK, 1997.

———. "Spekulanten, 'graue Eminenzen' und der Untergang des Altwiener Patriziats; Thesen zum österreichischen Wirtschaftsbürgertum in der Zwischenkriegszeit." In *Auf Heller und Cent: Beiträge zur Finanz- und Währungsgeschichte,* edited by Karl Bachinger, Dieter Stiefel, and Charlotte Natmessnig, pp. 345–370. Vienna, 2001.

Eigner, Peter, and Peter Melichar, "Das Ende der Boden-Credit-Anstalt 1929 und die Rolle Rudolf Siegharts." *Österreichische Zeitschrift für Geschichstwissenschaften* 19, no. 3 (2008): 56–114.

Eijffinger, Sylvester C. W., and Benedik Goderis. "Currency Crises, Monetary Policy, and Corporate Balance Sheet Vulnerabilities." Tilburg University Center Discussion Paper no. 2005-113, 2005.

Einzig, Paul. *The Fight for Financial Supremacy.* London, 1931.

———. *Foreign Dollar Loans in Europe.* London, 1965.

Ellenberger, Henri F. "A Clinical Introduction to Psychiatric Phenomenology and Existential Analysis." In *Existence,* edited by Rollo May, Ernest Angel, and Henri F. Ellenberger, pp. 92–126. Northvale, NJ, 1994.

Enaudi, Luigi, et al. "Charles Rist, 1874–1955. L'homme, la pensée, l'action." *Revue d'Economie Politique* 65 (1955): 884–1025.

Eybl, Peter. *Die Wirtschafts- und Bankenkrise des Jahres 1931 unter besonderer Berücksichtigung der Sanierung der Credit Anstalt.* Linz, 1993.

Falter, Jurgen, Thomas Lindenberger, and Siegfried Schumann. *Wahlen und Abstimmungen in der Weimarer Republik.* Munich, 1986.

Federn, Walter. *Der Zusammenbruch der österreichischen Kreditanstalt.* Tübingen, 1932.

Feinstein, Charles H., Peter Temin, and Gianni Toniolo. "International Economic Organization: Banking, Finance and Trade in Europe between the Wars." In *Banking, Currency and Finance in Europe between the Wars,* edited by Charles H. Feinstein, pp. 9–76. Oxford, 1995.

Feinstein, Charles H., and Katherine Watson. "Private International Capital Flows in Europe in the Inter-War Period." In *Banking, Currency, and Finance in Europe between the Wars,* edited by Charles H. Feinstein, pp. 94–130. Oxford, 1995.

Feis, Herbert. *Europe, the World's Banker, 1870–1914: An Account of European Foreign Investment and the Connection of World Finance with Diplomacy before World War I.* Clifton, NJ, 1974.

Felber, Ulrike. "Der Schilling—eine Antwort auf die "österreichische Frage."" In *Vom Schilling zum Euro,* edited by Klaus Liebscher and Wilfried Seipel, pp. 98–110. Vienna, 2002.

Ferguson, Niall. "Constraints and Room for Manoeuvre in the German Inflation of the Early 1920s." *Economic History Review* 49, no. 4 (1996): 635–666.

Ferguson, Thomas, and Peter Temin. "Comment on 'The German Twin Crisis of 1931.'" *Journal of Economic History* 64, no. 3 (2004): 872–876.

———. "Made in Germany: The German Currency Crisis of July 1931." *Research in Economic History* 21 (2003): 1–53.

Fink, Carole. *The Genoa Conference: European Diplomacy, 1921–1922.* Syracuse, NY, 1993.

Fior, Michel. "Institution globale, transition et pouvoir: La Société des Nations et la reconstruction de l'Europe (1918–1931)." Doctoral thesis, Université de Neuchâtel, 2006. Published as *Institution globale et marchés financiers: La Société des Nations face à la reconstructions de l'Europe 1918–1931.* Bern, 2008.

Fischer, David Hackett. *The Great Wave: Price Revolutions and the Rhythm of History.* New York, 1996.

Flandreau, Marc, and John Komlos. "Target Zones in Theory and History: Credibility, Efficiency, and Policy Autonomy." [Unpublished.]

Flores Zendejas, Juan H., and Yann Decorzant. "Going Multilateral? Financial Markets' Access and the League of Nations Loans, 1923–8." *Economic History Review* 60, no. 2 (2016): 653–678.

Franco, Gustavo H. B. "Fiscal Reforms and Stabilisation: Four Hyperinflation Cases Examined." *Economic Journal* 100, no. 399 (1990): 176–187.

Freud, Sigmund. *Der Witz und seine Beziehung zum Unbewussten.* Leipzig, 1905.

Friedman, Walter. *Fortune Tellers: The Story of America's First Economic Forecasters.* Princeton, NJ, 2014.

Fritz, Wolfgang. *Für Kaiser und Republik: Österreichs Finanzminister seit 1848.* Vienna, 2003.

Garber, Peter, and Michael Spencer. *The Dissolution of the Austro-Hungarian Empire: Lessons for Currency Reform.* Princeton, NJ, 1994.

Garrett, John R. "Monetary Policy and Expectations: Market-Control Techniques and the Bank of England, 1925–1931." *Journal of Economic History* 55, no. 3 (1995): 612–636.

Gärtner, Friedrich. "Die Stabilisierung der Österreichischen Krone." *Schriften des Vereins für Socialpolitik* 165 (1923): 49–77.

Geng, Karl Heinz. "Der Zusammenbruch der Credit-Anstalt und die Sanierungsmassnahmen der Bundesregierung." Unpublished thesis, University of Vienna, 1969.

Geyer, Martin H. *Verkehrte Welt.* Göttingen, 1998.

Goldinger, Walter. "Rudolf Ramek." In *Österreichisches Biographisches Lexikon,* vol. 8. Vienna, 1983.

Goldinger, Walter, and Dieter A. Binder. *Geschichte der Republik Österreich, 1918–1938.* Munich, 1992.

Graham, Stephen. *Europe—Whither Bound? Being Letters of Travel from Capitals of Europe in the Year 1921.* Toronto, 1922.

Green, E. H. H. "The Influence of the City over British Economic Policy c. 1880–1960." In *Finance and Financiers in European History, 1880–1960,* edited by Youssef Cassis, pp. 193–218. Cambridge, 1992.

Gulick, Charles. *Austria from Habsburg to Hitler,* 2 vols. Berkeley, CA, 1948.

Hanisch, Ernst. *Der lange Schatten des Staates: Österreichische Gesellschaftsgeschichte im 20. Jahrhundert.* Vienna, 1994.

Hardach, Karl. *The Political Economy of Germany in the Twentieth Century.* Berkeley, CA, 1980.

Herz, Bernhard, and Hui Tong. "The Interactions between Debt and Currency Crises: Common Causes or Contagion?" Department of Economics, University of Bayreuth, Discussion Paper 17, 2004.

Herz, Frederick. *The Economic Problem of the Danubian States: A Study in Economic Nationalism.* London, 1947.

Hill, Martin. *The Economic and Financial Organization of the League of Nations: A Survey of Twenty-Five Years' Experience.* Washington, DC, 1945.

———. *The League of Nations and the Work of Refugee Settlement and Financial Reconstruction in Greece, 1922–1930.* Jena, 1931.

Hobsbawm, Eric. *The Age of Extremes: A History of the World, 1914–1991.* New York, 1994.

———. *Interesting Times: A Twentieth-Century Life.* New York, 2003.

Hofstätter, Robert. *Die arbeitende Frau: Ihre wirtschaftliche Lage, Gesundheit, Ehe und Mutterschaft.* Vienna, 1929.

Holtfrerich, Carl-L., and Toru Iwami. "Post-war Central Banking Reform: A German-Japanese Comparison." In *The Emergence of Modern Central Banking from 1918 to the Present*, edited by Carl-L. Holtfrerich and Jaime Reis, pp. 69–101. Aldershot, UK, 2016.

Huber, Ulrike. "Österreich und der Völkerbund in den 20er Jahren." PhD. thesis, University of Vienna, 1991.

Hurst, Willard. "Holland, Switzerland and Belgium and the English Gold Crisis of 1931." *Journal of Political Economy* 40 (1932): 638–660.

Huxley, Thomas H. "On Descartes' 'Discourse Touching the Method of Using One's Reason Rightly and of Seeking Scientific Truth.'" Address, Cambridge Young Men's Christian Society, 24 March 1870. In *Essays*, pp. 166–198. London, 1894.

Jacobsson, Erin E. *A Life for Sound Money*. Oxford, 1979.

Jacobsson, Per. *The Economic Consequences of the League*. London, 1927.

Jahoda, Maria, Paul Lazarsfeld, and Hans Zeisel. *Die Arbeitslosen von Marienthal: Ein soziographischer Versuch über die Wirkungen langdauernder Arbeitslosigkeit*. Frankfurt a. M., 1975.

James, Harold. Book review of Bernd Widdig, *Culture and Inflation in Weimar Germany. Journal of Economic History* 62, no. 1 (March 2002): 239.

——. "The Causes of the German Banking Crisis of 1931." *Economic History Review* 37, no. (1984): 68–87.

——. *The Creation and Destruction of Value*. Cambridge, MA, 2012.

——. *The End of Globalization: Lessons from the Great Depression*. Cambridge, MA, 2002.

——. "Financial Flows across Frontiers during the Interwar Depression." *Economic History Review* 45, no. 3 (1992): 594–613.

——. *The German Slump: Politics and Economics, 1924–1936*. Oxford, 1986.

——. "The 1931 Central European Banking Crisis Revisited." In *Business in the Age of Extremes*, edited by Hartmut Berghoff, Jürgen Kocka, and Dieter Ziegler, pp. 119–132. Cambridge, 2013.

Jarausch, Konrad H. *Out of Ashes: A New History of Europe in the Twentieth Century*. Princeton, NJ, 2015.

Jeanneney, Jean-Noël. "La spéculation sur les changes comme arme diplomatique—A propos de la premiere 'bataille du franc' (novembre 1923–mars 1924)." *Relations internationales* 13 (1978): 5–27.

Jellinek, E., and J. T. Lilla. "Heinrich Mataja." In *Österreichisches Biographisches Lexikon*, vol. 6. Vienna, 1975.

Jobst, Clemens. "Revisiting the Gold Points: Myths and Realities of Central Bank Intervention under the Gold Standard, the Austro-Hungarian Example 1892–1914." Working Paper, Chaire Finances Internationales, Institut d'Études Politiques de Paris, 2007.

Jones, Ernest, and R. Andrew Paskauskas. *The Complete Correspondence of Sigmund Freud and Ernest Jones, 1908–1939.* Cambridge MA, 1993.

Jonker, J. P. B. "HENGEL, Adrianus Johannes van (1886–1936). In *Biografisch Woordenboek van Nederland*, vol. 6, edited by Klaas van Berkel. 's-Gravenhage, 2008.

Jonker, Joost, and Jan Luiten van Zanden. "Method in the Madness? Banking Crises between the Wars, an International Comparison." In *Banking, Currency, and Finance in Europe between the Wars*, edited by Charles H. Feinstein, pp. 77–94. Oxford, 1994.

Kaldor, Nicholas. "The Economic Situation in Austria." *Harvard Business Review*, October 1932: 23–34.

Karner, Stefan. "From Empire to Republic: Economic Problems in a Period of Collapse, Reorientation, and Reconstruction." In *The Economic Development in the Habsburg Monarchy and in the Successor States*, edited by John Komlos, pp. 251–269. New York, 1990.

Keil, Angelina. "85 Jahre WIFO: Die Publikationstätigkeit." *WIFO Monatsbericht* 6 (2012): 551–555.

Keohane, Robert O., and Joseph S. Nye. "Transgovernmental Relations and International Organizations." *World Politics* 27, no. 1 (1974): 39–62.

Kerekes, Lajos. *Abenddämmerung einer Demokratie: Mussolini, Gömbös und die Heimwehr.* Vienna, 1966.

———. *Von St. Germain bis Genf: Österreich und seine Nachbarn, 1918–1922.* Vienna, 1979.

Kernbauer, Hans. "Österreichische Währungs-, Bank- und Budgetpolitik in der Zwischenkriegszeit." In *Handbuch des politischen Systems Österreichs*, edited by Emerich Tálos, Herbert Dachs, Ernst Hanisch, and Anton Staudinger, pp. 552–569. Vienna, 1995.

———. *Währungspolitik in der Zwischenkriegszeit: Geschichte der Österreichischen Nationalbank von 1923 bis 1938.* Vienna, 1991.

Kernbauer, Hans, Eduard März, and Fritz Weber. "Die wirtschaftliche Entwicklung." In *Österreich, 1918–1938: Geschichte der Ersten Republik*, edited by Erika Weinzierl and Kurt Skalnik, vol. 1, pp. 343–379. Graz, 1983.

Kernbauer, Hans, and Fritz Weber. "Die Wiener Grossbanken in der Nachkriegsinflation." In *Die Erfahrung der Inflation im internationalen Zusammenhang und Vergleich*, edited by Gerald Feldman, Carl-Ludwig Holtfrerich, Gerhard A. Ritter, and Peter-Christian Witt, pp. 141–148. Berlin, 1984.

Khoudour-Castéras, David. "Labor Immobility and Exchange Rate Regimes: An Alternative Explanation for the Fall of the Interwar Gold Exchange Standard." *Journal of European Economic History* 38, no. 1 (2009): 13–47.

Kienböck, Victor. *Das österreichische Sanierungswerk.* Stuttgart, 1925.

Kieninger, Ernst, Nikola Langreiter, Armin Loacker, and Klara Löffler, eds. *1. April 2000.* Vienna, 2000.

Kindleberger, Charles. *A Financial History of Western Europe*. London, 1984.

——. *Manias, Panics and Crashes: A History of Financial Crises*. 3rd ed. New York, 1996.

——. *The World in Depression, 1929–1939*. Berkeley, CA, 1986.

Kitchen, Martin. *The Coming of Austrian Fascism*. London, 1980.

Klausinger, Hansjörg. "The Austrian School of Economics and the Gold Standard Mentality in Austrian Economic Policy in the 1930s." Working Paper 02-2. Center for Austrian Studies, December 2002.

Klemperer, Klemens von. "The Habsburg Heritage: Some Pointers for a Study of the First Austrian Republic." In *The Austrian Socialist Experiment: Social Democracy and Austromarxism, 1918–1934*, edited by Anson Rabinbach, pp. 11–20. Boulder, CO, 1985.

——. *Ignaz Seipel, Staatsmann einer Krisenzeit*. Vienna, 1976.

Klingstein, Grete. *Die Anleihe von Lausanne: Ein Beitrag zur Geschichte der Ersten Republik in den Jahren 1931–1934*. Vienna, 1965.

Kluge, Ulrich. *Bauern, Agrarkrise und Volksernährung in der Europäischen Zwischenkriegszeit: Studien zur Agrargesellschaft und -wirtschaft der Republik Österreich 1918 bis 1938*. Stuttgart, 1988.

Koch, Klaus, Walter Rauscher, and Arnold Suppan, eds. *Aussenpolitische Dokumente der Republik Österreich 1918–1938, Band 5: Unter der Finanzkontrolle des Völkerbundes: 7. November 1922 bis 15. Juni 1926*. Vienna, 2002.

Kriechbaumer, Robert. *Die grossen Erzählungen der Politik: Politische Kultur und Parteien in Österreich von der Jahrhundertwende bis 1945*. Vienna, 2001.

Kühschelm, Oliver. "Implicit Boycott: The Call for Patriotic Consumption in Interwar Austria." *Management & Organizational History* 5, no. 2 (2010): 165–195.

Kulla, Bernd. *Die Anfänge der empirischen Konjunkturforschung in Deutschland 1925–1933*. Berlin, 1996.

Kunz, Diane. *The Battle for Britain's Gold Standard in 1931*. London, 1987.

Lackner, Andreas: *Der Zusammenbruch der Credit-Anstalt 1931: Eine Literaturübersicht*. Vienna, 1993.

Ladner, Gottlieb. *Seipel als Überwinder der Staatskrise vom Sommer 1922*. Vienna, 1964.

Lane, Philip R., and Gian Maria Milesi-Ferretti. "The Transfer Problem Revisited: Net Foreign Assets and Real Exchange Rates." International Monetary Fund Working Paper WP/00/123, 2000.

Lauridsen, John T. *Nazism and the Radical Right in Austria 1918–1934*. Copenhagen, 2007.

Laursen, Karsten, and Jørgen Pedersen. *The German Inflation 1918–1923*. Amsterdam, 1964.

League of Nations. *Memorandum sur le commerce international et sur les balances des paiements (1923–1927)*. Geneva, 1928.

———. *The Restoration of Austria: Agreements Arranged by the League of Nations and Signed at Geneva on October 4th 1922 with the Relevant Documents and Public Statements*. Geneva, 1922.

Leser, Norbert, and Paul Sailer-Wlasits, eds. *1927, als die Republik brannte: Von Schattendorf bis Wien*. Vienna, 2002.

Lewis, Jill. *Fascism and the Working Class in Austria, 1918–1934: The Failure of Labour in the First Republic*. New York: Berg, 1991.

Lüke, R. E. *Von der Stabilisierung zur Krise*. Zurich, 1958.

Macartney, C. A. "Austria since 1928." *Slavonic and East European Review* 7 (1928 / 1929): 288–303.

Macesich, George. *Successor States and Cooperation Theory: A Model for Eastern Europe*. Westport, CT, 1994.

Madsen, Jakob B. "Agricultural Crises and the International Transmission of the Great Depression." *Journal of Economic History* 61, no. 2 (2001): 327–365.

Marcus, Nathan. "The Austrian Minority of South Tyrol and the Investitionsanleihe of 1930." In *National Economies: Volkswirtschaft, Racism and Economy in Europe between the Wars, 1918–1939*, edited by Christoph Kreutzmüller, Michael Wildt, and Mosche Zimmerman, pp. 229–238. Newcastle upon Tyne, 2015.

———. "Hyperinflation as a Catalyst of Transformations: Path Dependence through Accelerated Dynamics in Post–First World War Austria." *European Review of History* 23, no. 4 (2016): 595–609.

März, Eduard. *Austrian Banking and Financial Policy: Credit-Anstalt at a Turning Point, 1913–1923*. New York, 1984.

———. "Die grosse Depression in Österreich: 1930–1933," *Wirtschaft und Gesellschaft* 16, no. 3 (1990): 409–438.

———. "Economic Policy in the Crises of 1920 and 1929: Comment." In *Financial Crises: Theory, History and Policy*, edited by Charles P. Kindleberger and Jean-Pierre Laffargue, pp. 187–194. Cambridge, 1982.

———. *Österreichische Bankenpolitik in der Zeit der gossen Wende, 1913–1923: Am Beispiel der Credit-Anstalt für Handel und Gewerbe*. Munich, 1981.

März, Eduard, and Fritz Weber. "The Antecedents of the Austrian Financial Crash of 1931." *Zeitschrift für Wirtschafts- und Sozialwissenschaften* 103, no. 5 (1983): 497–519.

———. "Commentary to Article by Dieter Stiefel." In *International Business and Central Europe, 1918–1939*, edited by Alice Teichova and P. L. Cottrell, p. 430. New York, 1983.

Matis, Herbert. *The Economic Development of Austria since 1870*. Aldershot, UK, 1994.

———. "Österreichs Wirtschaft in der Zwischenkriegszeit: Desintegration, Neustrukturierung und Stagnation." In *Bank Austria Credit-Anstalt: 150 Jahre österreichische Bankengeschichte im Zentrum Europas*, edited by Oliver Rathkolb, Theodor Venus, and Ulrike Zimmerl, pp. 125–147. Vienna, 2005.

Mattl, Siegfried. "Die Finanzdiktatur: Wirtschaftspolitik in Österreich 1933–1938." In *Austrofaschismus: Beiträge über Politik, Ökonomie und Kultur, 1934–1938,* edited by Emerich Tálos and Wolfgang Neugebauer, pp. 133–159. Vienna, 1984.

McNeil, William C. *American Money and the Weimar Republic.* New York, 1986.

Megliani, Mauro. *Sovereign Debt: Genesis—Restructuring—Litigation.* Cham, Switzerland, 2015.

Miklós, Lojkó. *Meddling in Middle Europe: Britain and the "Lands Between," 1929–1925.* Budapest, 2016.

Minkowski, Eugène. *Le temps vécu, études phénoménologiques et psychopathologiques.* Paris, 1933.

Mises, Ludwig von. *Memoirs.* Auburn, AL, 2009.

Mitchell, Timothy. "Fixing the Economy." *Cultural Studies* 12, no. 1 (1998): 82–101.

Moggridge, D. E. *British Monetary Policy, 1924–31.* London, 1969.

———. "The 1931 Financial Crisis: A New View." *The Banker* 120 (August 1970): 832–839.

Monnet, Jean. *Mémoire.* Paris, 1976.

Mooij, Joke. "Corporate Culture of Central Banks: Lessons from the Past." De Nederlandsche Bank, Working Paper, no. 6, July 2004.

Moore, Bob. "Bruins' Berlijnse besprekingen: Een selectie uit het archief van prof. mr. dr. G.W.J. Bruins, in het bijzonder de jaren, 1924–1930." *The English Historical Review* 108, no. 429 (1993): 1069–1070.

Morrison, James Ashley. "Shocking Intellectual Austerity: The Role of Ideas in the Demise of the Gold Standard in Britain." *International Organization* 70, no. 1 (2016): 175–207.

Morsy, Hanan. "International Financial Crisis Contagion." Mimeo, Department of Economics, George Washington University, 2002.

Morys, Matthias. "Monetary Policy under the Classical Gold Standard (1870–1914)." Working Paper, Department of Economics and Related Studies, University of York. 2010.

Mouré, Kenneth. "French Money Doctors, Central Banks, and Politics in the 1920s." In *Money Doctors: The Experience of International Financial Advising 1850–2000,* edited by Marc Flandeau, pp. 138–165. London, 2003.

———. "The Limits to Central Bank Co-operation, 1916–37." *Contemporary European History* 1, no. 3 (1992): 259–279.

Myers, Margaret G. "The League Loans." *Political Science Quarterly* 60, no. 4 (1945): 492–526.

Natmessnig, Charlotte. "Wege zur Währungssanierung und Beginn der Bankenkonzentration auf dem Wiener Platz." in *Bank Austria Credit-Anstalt, 150 Jahre österreichische Bankengeschichte im Zentrum Europas,* edited by Oliver Rathkolb, Theodor Venus, and Ulrike Zimmerl, pp. 162–179. Vienna, 2005.

Nautz, Jürgen. "Die Entwicklung der Handelsbeziehungen Österreichs zu den Nachfolgestaaten nach dem Ersten Weltkrieg." *Wirtschaft und Gesellschaft* 18, no. 4 (1992): 539–559.

———. *Die österreichische Handelspolitik der Nachkriegszeit 1918–1923: Die Handelsbeziehungen zu den Nachfolgestaaten.* Vienna, 1994.

Neck, Rudolf, and Adam Wandruszka, eds. *Die Ereignisse des 15. Juli 1927: Protokoll des Symposiums in Wien am 15. Juni 1977.* Vienna, 1979.

———. *Unterhändler des Vertrauens: Aus den nachgelassenen Schriften von Sektionschef Dr. Richard Schüller.* Vienna, 1990.

Neurath, Paul. "Sixty Years Since Marienthal." *Canadian Journal of Sociology / Cahiers canadiens de sociologie* 20, no. 1 (1995): 91–105.

Northedge, F. S. *The League of Nations: Its Life and Times, 1920–1946.* New York, 1986.

Nötel, Rudolf. "International Capital Movements and Finance in Eastern Europe 1919–1949." *Vierteljahrschrift für Sozial- und Wirtschaftsgeschichte* 61 (1974): 65–112.

———. "Money, Banking and Industry in Interwar Austria and Hungary." *Journal of European Economic History* 13, no. 2 (1984): 137–202.

Obstfeld, M., and A. M. Taylor. "Sovereign Risk, Credibility and the Gold Standard: 1870–1913 versus 1925–31." *Economic Journal* 113 (April 2003): 1–35.

Obstfeld, Maurice, Jay C. Shambaugh, and Alan M. Taylor. "Monetary Sovereignty, Exchange Rates, and Capital Controls: The Trilemma in the Interwar Period." National Bureau of Economic Research, Working Paper 10393. Cambridge, MA, March 2004.

Offenberger, Ilana. *The Jews of Nazi Vienna, 1938–1945.* Cham, Switzerland, 2017.

Orde, Anne. "Baring Brothers, the Bank of England, the British Government and the Czechoslovak State Loan of 1922." *English Historical Review* 106, no. 418 (1991): 27–40.

———. *British Policy and European Reconstruction after the First World War.* Cambridge, 1990.

———. "The Origins of the German-Austrian Customs Union Affair of 1931." *Central European History* 13, no. 1 (1980): 34–59.

Patch, William L., Jr., and William L. Patch. *Heinrich Brüning and the Dissolution of the Weimar Republic.* Cambridge, 2006.

Pauley, Bruce F. *From Prejudice to Persecution: A History of Austrian Anti-Semitism.* Chapel Hill, NC, 1992.

———. "Political Antisemitism in Interwar Vienna." In *Jews, Antisemitism, and Culture*, edited by Ivar Oxaal, Michael Pollak, and Gerhard Botz, pp. 153–173. London, 1987.

———. "The Social and Economic Background of Austria's Lebensunfähigkeit." In *The Austrian Socialist Experiment: Social Democracy and Austromarxism, 1918–1934*, edited by Anson Rabinbach, pp. 21–37. Boulder, CO, 1985.

Pauly, Louis W. *The League of Nations and the Foreshadowing of the International Monetary Fund*. Princeton, NJ, 1996.

Pasvolsky, Leo. *Economic Nationalism of the Danubian States*. New York, 1928.

Paxton, Robert O., and Julie Hessler. *Europe in the Twentieth Century*. Wadsworth, CA, 2012.

Pedersen, Susan. "Back to the League of Nations." *American Historical Review* 112, no. 4 (2008): 1091–1117.

Pemberton, Jo-Anne. "New Worlds for Old: The League of Nations in the Age of Electricity." *Review of International Studies* 28 (2002): 311–336.

Peniston-Bird, C. M. "The Debate on Austrian National Identity in the First Republic (1918–1938)." Doctoral thesis, University of St. Andrews, 1997.

Péteri, György. "Central Bank Diplomacy: Montagu Norman and Central Europe's Monetary Reconstruction after World War I." *Contemporary European History* 1, no. 3 (1992): 233–258.

Piétri, Nicole. "La réconstruction économique et financière de l'Autriche par la Société des Nations (1921–1926)." Doctoral thesis, Université de Paris I, 1981.

———. "L'œuvre d'un organisme technique de la Société des Nations: Le Comité Financier et la reconstruction de l'Autriche (1921–1926)." In *The League of Nations in Retrospect: Proceedings of the Symposium*, pp. 319–342. Berlin, 1983.

Pohl, Manfred. *Einführung in die deutsche Bankengeschichte*. Frankfurt am Main, 1989.

Pollard, Sidney, ed. *The Gold Standard and Employment Policies between the Wars*. London, 1970.

Protheroe, Gerald J. *A Biography of Sir George Russell Clark: Nation-Building and the Limits of Personal Diplomacy*. London, 2004.

Rabinbach, Anson. *The Crisis of Austrian Socialism: From Red Vienna to Civil War, 1927–1934*. Chicago, 1983.

Reichhold, Ludwig. *Ignaz Seipel*. Vienna, 1988.

Reinhart, Carmen M., and Kenneth S. Rogoff. *This Time is Different: Eight Centuries of Financial Folly*. Princeton, NJ, 2009.

Rennhofer, Friedrich. *Ignaz Seipel*. Vienna, 1978.

Repington, Charles à Court. *After the War: London–Paris–Rome–Athens–Prague–Vienna–Budapest–Bucharest–Berlin–Sofia–Coblenz–New York–Washington*. London, 1922.

Rist, Charles. *Essais sur quelques problèmes économiques et monétaires*. Paris, 1933.

Ritschl, Albrecht, and Samad Sarferaz. "Currency versus Banking in the Financial Crisis of 1931." *International Economic Review* 55, no. 2 (2014): 349–373.

Rosenberg, Emily S. *Financial Missionaries to the World: The Politics and Culture of Dollar Diplomacy*. Durham, NC, 2003.

Rothschild, K. W. *Austria's Economic Development between the Two Wars*. London, 1947.

Rutkowski, Hans. *Der Zusammenbruch der Österreichischen Credit-Anstalt für Handel und Gewerbe und ihre Rekonstruktion: Ein Beitrag zur österreichischen Bankenkrise.* Bottrop, Germany, 1934.

Salter, Arthur. *Memoirs of a Public Servant.* London, 1961.

———. *Slave of the Lamp: A Public Servant's Notebook.* London 1967.

Salter, J. A. "The Financial Reconstruction of Austria." *American Journal of International Law* 17, no. 1 (1923): 116–128.

Samuels, Warren J. "Melchior Palyi: Introduction and Biography." In *Documents from F. Taylor Ostrander*, edited by Warren J. Samuels, pp. 305–306. Bingley, UK, 2005.

Sandgruber, Roman. *Ökonomie und Politik: Österreichische Wirtschaftsgeschichte vom Mittelalter bis zur Gegenwart.* Vienna, 1995.

Santaella, Julio A. "Stabilization Programs and External Enforcement: Experience from the 1920s." *International Monetary Fund Staff Papers* 40, no. 3 (1993): 584–621.

Sargent, Thomas. "The Ends of Four Big Inflations." In *Inflation: Causes and Effects*, edited by Robert E. Hall, pp. 41–97. Chicago, 1982.

———. *Rational Expectations and Inflation.* New York, 1986.

Sayers, Richard Sidney. *The Bank of England, 1891–1944.* 3 vols. Cambridge, 1976.

Schinnerer. Otto P. "The History of Schnitzler's Reigen." *PMLA* 46, no. 3 (1931): 839–859.

Schmidt, Carl Theodore. "The Austrian Institute for Business Cycle Research." *Journal of Political Economy* 39, no. 1 (1931): 101–103.

Schmidt, Paul. *Statist auf diplomatischer Bühne 1923–1945: Erlebnisse des Chefdolmetschers im Auswärtigen Amt mit den Staatsmännern Europas.* Bonn, 1953.

Schnabel, Isabel. "The German Twin Crisis of 1931." *Journal of Economic History* 64, no. 3 (2004): 822–871.

———. "The Great Banks' Depression: Deposit Withdrawals in the German Twin Crisis of 1931." SFB 504 Working Paper no. 03–11, Mannheim University, 2003.

———. "Reply to Ferguson and Temin." *Journal of Economic History* 64, no. 2 (2004): 877–878.

Schöpfer, Gerald. "Möglichkeiten einer aktiven Konjunkturpolitik im Österreich der 20er-Jahre." *Geschichte und Gegenwart, Vierteljahresschrift für Zeitgeschichte, Gesellschaftsanalyse und politische Bildung* 2, no. 1 (1983): 24–46.

Schubert, Aurel. "The Causes of the Austrian Currency Crisis of 1931." In *Economic Development in the Habsburg Monarchy and in the Successor States*, edited by John Komlos, pp. 89–131. New York, 1990.

———. *The Credit-Anstalt Crisis of 1931.* New York, 1991.

———. "Torn between Monetary and Financial Stability: An Analysis of Selected Episodes of Austrian Central Banking History." In *Finance and Modernization: A Transnational and Transcontinental Perspective for the Nineteenth and Twentieth Centuries*, edited by Gerald D. Feldman and Peter Hertner, pp. 51–74. Farnham, UK, 2008.

Schuker, Stephen. "American Policy towards Debts and Reconstruction at Genoa, 1922." In *Genoa, Rapallo, and European Reconstruction in 1922*, edited by Carole Fink, Axel Frohn, and Jürgen Heideking, pp. 95–130. Cambridge, 1991.

Scott, George. *The Rise and Fall of the League of Nations*. London, 1973.

Sharma, Shiva-Kumar. *Der Völkerbund und die Grossmächte: Ein Beitrag zur Geschichte der Völkerbundpolitik Grossbritanniens, Frankreichs und Deutschlands, 1929–1933*. Frankfurt am Main, 1978.

Siklos, Pierre. "Hyperinflations: Their Origins, Development and Termination." *Journal of Economic Surveys* 4, no. 3 (1990): 225–228.

Silverman, Lisa. *Becoming Austrians: Jews and Culture between the World Wars*. New York, 2012.

Simmel, Georg. *Philosophie des Geldes*. Leipzig, 1900.

Simmons, Beth A. "International Law and State Behavior: Commitment and Compliance in International Monetary Affairs." *American Political Science Review* 94, no. 4 (2000): 819–835.

———. "Rulers of the Game: Central Bank Independence during the Interwar Years." *International Organization* 50, no. 3 (Summer 1996): 407–443.

———. *Who Adjusts? Domestic Sources of Foreign Economic Policy during the Interwar Years*. Princeton, NJ, 1994.

———. "Why Innovate? Founding the Bank for International Settlements." *World Politics* 45, no. 3 (1993): 361–405.

Skalnik, Kurt, and Erika Weinzierl. *Österreich 1918–1938: Geschichte der Ersten Republik*. Graz, 1983.

Solimano, Andrés. "Inflation and the Costs of Stabilization: Historical and Recent Experiences and Policy Lessons." *World Bank Research Observer* 5, no. 2 (July 1990): 167–185.

Spitzmüller, Alexander. *. . . und hat auch Ursach es zu lieben*. Vienna, 1955.

Stapleford, Thomas A. "Business and the Making of American Econometrics, 1910–1940." *History of Political Economy* 49, no. 2 (2017): 233–265.

Steiner, Zara. *The Lights That Failed: European International History, 1919–1933*. New York, 2005.

Stiefel, Dieter. *Arbeitslosigkeit: Soziale, politische und wirtschaftlich Auswirkungen— am Beispiel Österreichs 1918–1938*. Schriften zur Wirtschafts-u. Sozialgeschichte 31. Berlin, 1979.

———. "The Bankers' View: Austria's Economic and Political Development and the Role of the Banks." In *Finance and Modernization: A Transnational and Transcontinental Perspective*, edited by Gerald Feldman and Peter Hertner, pp. 3–28. Farnham, UK, 2008.

———. "Der Arbeitsmarkt in Österreich in der Zwischenkriegszeit." *Studia Germanica et Austriaca* 1, no. 2 (2002).

———. *Die Grosse Krise in einem kleinen Land: Österreichische Finanz- und Wirtschaftspolitik 1929–38*. Vienna, 1988.

———. "Die Sanierung und Konsolidierung der österreichischen Banken 1931 bis 1934." In *Bank Austria Credit-Anstalt, 150 Jahre österreichische Bankengeschichte im Zentrum Europas,* edited by Oliver Rathkolb, Theodor Venus, and Ulrike Zimmerl, pp. 196–211. Vienna, 2005.

———. *Finanzdiplomatie und Weltwirtschaftskrise: Die Krise der Credit-Anstalt für Handel und Gewerbe 1931.* Frankfurt am Main, 1989.

———. "The Great Depression in a Small Country: Austria, the World Economic Crisis of the 1930s, and Its Significance for the Present Day." In *The Impact of the Great Depression of the 1930s and Its Relevance for the Contemporary World,* edited by Ivan T. Berend and Knut Borchardt, pp. 472–488. Budapest, 1986.

———. "Konjunkturelle Entwicklung und struktureller Wandel der österreichischen Wirtschaft in der Zwischenkriegszeit." Institut für Höhere Studien, Forschungsbericht 135. Vienna, November 1978.

———. "Managementprobleme und die österreichische Bankenkrise des Jahres 1931." In *Management und Organisation: Veröffentlichungen des Vereins der wissenschaftlichen Forschung auf dem Gebiete der Unternehmensbiographie und Firmengeschichte,* vol. 10. Vienna, 1983.

Stone, Daniel. "The Big Business Lobby in Poland in the 1920s." *Canadian Slavonic Papers* 32, no. 1 (1990): 41–58.

Suppanz, Christian. *Die österreichische Inflation 1918–1922.* Vienna, 1976.

Tálos, Emerich, Herbert Dachs, Ernst Hanisch, and Anton Staudinger, eds. *Handbuch des politischen Systems Österreichs, Erste Rpublik 1918–1933.* Vienna, 1995.

Teichova, Alice. "Banking and Industry in Central-East Europe in the First Decades of the 20th Century." In *Bank Austria Credit-Anstalt, 150 Jahre österreichische Bankengeschichte im Zentrum Europas,* edited by Oliver Rathkolb, Theodor Venus, and Ulrike Zimmerl, pp. 148–161. Vienna, 2005.

———. "Die Inflation der 1920er Jahre in Mitteleuropa im Vergleich." *Beiträge zur Historischen Sozialkunde* 16, no. 3 (1986): 67–68.

———. "Versailles and the Expansion of the Bank of England into Central Europe." In *Recht und Entwicklung der Grossunternehmen im 19. und frühen 20. Jahrhundert,* edited by Norbert Horn and Jürgen Kocka, pp. 366–387. Göttingen, 1979.

Temin, Peter. *Lessons from the Great Depression.* Cambridge, MA, 1989.

———. "Transmission of the Great Depression." *Journal of Economic Perspectives* 7, no. 2 (1993): 87–102.

Tomashevskii, Dimitrii Georgievich. *Lenin's Ideas and Modern International Relations.* Moscow, 1974.

Toniolo, Gianni, with the assistance of Piet Clement. *Central Bank Cooperation at the Bank for International Settlements, 1930–1973.* Cambridge, 2005.

Tooze, Adam. "Weimar's Statistical Economics: Ernst Wagemann, the Reich's Statistical Office, and the Institute for Business-Cycle Research, 1925–1933." *Economic History Review* 52, no. 2 (August 1999): 523–543.

Tooze, Adam, and Ted Fertik. "The World Economy and the Great War." *Geschichte und Gesellschaft* 40, no. 2 (2014): 214–238.

Tooze, Adam, and Martin Ivanov. "Disciplining the 'Black Sheep of the Balkans': Financial Supervision and Sovereignty in Bulgaria, 1902–38." *Economic History Review* 64, no. 1 (2011): 30–51.

Tunçer, Ali Coşkun. *Sovereign Debt and International Financial Control: The Middle East and the Balkans, 1870–1914.* Houndmills, UK, 2015.

Tyler, Royall. *The League of Nations Reconstruction Schemes in the Inter-War Period.* Geneva, 1945.

Unowsky, Daniel L. *The Pomp and Politics of Patriotism: Imperial Celebrations in Habsburg Austria, 1848–1916.* West Lafayette, IN, 2005.

Van Walré de Bordes, Jan. *The Austrian Crown: Its Depreciation and Stabilization.* London, 1924; reprint, New York, 1983.

Vaubel, Roland. "International Debt, Bank Failures, and the Money Supply: The Thirties and the Eighties." *Cato Journal,* 4 no. 1 (1984): 249–267.

Vries, Joh de. *Geschiedenis van der Nederlandsche Bank 1914–1948,* vol. 5 part 2. Amsterdam, 1994.

Wahl, Niko. "Kaffeehäuser zu Bankfilialen: Ein kurzer Abriss der Wiener Spekulation." In *Das Werden der Republik . . . Der Rest is Österreich,* edited by Helmut Konrad and Wolfgang Maderthaner, vol. 2, pp. 49–66. Vienna, 2008.

Wandschneider, Kirsten. "Central Bank Independence and Policy Performance Central-East Europe 1919–1939." Doctoral thesis, University of Illinois at Urbana–Champaign, 2003.

———. "Central Bank Reaction Functions during the Inter-war Gold Standard: A View from the Periphery." In *The Origins and Development of Financial Markets and Institutions: From the Seventeenth Century to the Present,* edited by Jeremy Attack and Larry Neal, pp. 388–415. Cambridge, 2009.

Warnock, Barbara Susan. "The First Bailout—The Financial Reconstruction of Austria 1922–1926." Doctoral thesis, Birbeck College, University of London, 2015.

Webb, Steven B. "Fiscal News and Inflationary Expectations in Germany after World War I." *Journal of Economic History* 46, no. 3 (September 1986): 769–794.

———. "Government Debt and Inflationary Expectations as Determinants of the Money Supply in Germany, 1919–1922." *Journal of Money, Credit and Banking* 17 (November 1985, part 1): 479–492.

———. *Hyperinflation and Stabilization in Weimar Germany.* New York, 1989.

Weber, Fritz. "The Creditanstalt from the 1870s to the 1930s." In *Finance and Modernization: A Transnational and Transcontinental Perspective for the Nineteenth and Twentieth Centuries,* edited by Gerald D. Feldman and Peter Hertner, pp. 72–96. Farnham, UK, 2008.

———. *Die Krise des österreichishen Bankwesens in den zwanziger Jahren.* Habilitation, University of Vienna, 1991 [unpublished].

——. "Die writschaftliche Entwicklung." In *Handbuch des politischen Systems Österreichs*, edited by Emerich Tálos, Herbert Dachs, Ernst Hansich, and Anton Staudinger, pp. 23–42. Vienna, 1995.

——. "Staatliche Wirtschaftspolitik in der Zwischenkriegszeit." In *Handbuch des politischen Systems Österreichs*, edited by Emerich Tálos, Herbert Dachs, Ernst Hansich, and Anton Staudinger, pp. 531–551. Vienna, 1995.

——. *Vor dem grossen Krach: Österreichs Bankwesen der Zwischenkriegszeit am Beispiel der Credit-Anstalt für Handel und Gewerbe*. Vienna, 2016.

Webster, Andrew. "The Transnational Dream: Politicians, Diplomats and Soldiers in the League of Nations' Pursuit of International Disarmament, 1920–1938." *Contemporary European History* 14, no. 4 (2001): 493–518.

Weinzierl, Erika, and Kurt Skalnik. *Österreich, 1918–1938: Geschichte der Ersten Republik*. Graz, 1983.

Wessels, Jens-Wilhelm. *Economic Policy and Microeconomic Performance in Inter-War Europe: The Case of Austria, 1918–1938*. Stuttgart, 2007.

Wicker, Elmus. "Terminating Hyperinflation in the Dismembered Habsburg Monarchy." *American Economic Review* 76, no. 3 (1986): 350–364.

Widdig, Bernd. *Culture and Inflation in Weimar Germany*. Berkeley, CA, 2001.

Williams, David. "London and the 1931 Financial Crisis." *Economic History Review* 15, no. 3 (1963): 513–528.

Williamson, Philip. "A 'Bankers' Ramp'? Financiers and the British Political Crisis of August 1931." *English Historical Review* 99, no. 393 (1984): 770–806.

Wiltschegg, Walter. *Die Heimwehr: Eine unwiderstehliche Volksbewegung?* Vienna, 1985.

Wingfield, Nancy M. *Flag Wars and Stone Saints: How the Bohemian Lands Became Czech*. Cambridge, MA, 2007.

Wittgenstein, Ludwig. *Tractatus Logicus Philosophicus*. Vienna, 1922.

Wolf, Nikolaus. "Europe's Great Depression: Coordination Failure after the First World War." Centre for Economic Policy Research, Discussion Paper Series 7957, August 2010.

Woodward, Ernest Llewellyn, and Rohan Butler, eds. *Documents of British Foreign Policy*, vol. 2, part 4. London, 1947.

Wynne, William H. *State Insolvency and Foreign Bondholders: Selected Case Histories of Governmental Foreign Bond Defaults and Debt Readjustments*. New Haven, CT, 1951.

Zimmermann, Horst. *Die Schweiz und Österreich während der Zwischenkriegszeit: Eine Studie und Dokumentation internationaler Beziehungen im Schatten der Grossmächte*. Wiesbaden, 1973.

Zipser, Wolfgang. *Auf der Suche nach Stabilität: Das Zentralbankgeldangebot der Österreichischen Nationalbank 1923 bis 1937*. Frankfurt am Main, 1997.

Acknowledgments

I have spent a large part of the last ten years studying, researching, and writing this book. Teachers, colleagues, friends, and family accompanied and supported this endeavor, and I am grateful to have the space and time to thank them here.

At New York University, where I began this project, Professor Mary Nolan very warmly welcomed me to the history department after I fled differential equations and I remain inspired by her combination of personal engagement and academic rigor. I also wish to thank Jess Benhabib, who let me escape economics, and the history department faculty, particularly Yanni Kotsonis, Brigitte Bedos-Rezak, Herrick Chapman, and Marion Kaplan, for accepting my conversion. Shortly thereafter, a walk and talk with Niall Ferguson, then at NYU Business School, provided the very idea for this book, followed by many encouraging comments and helpful conversations over the years. As a teaching assistant to Larry Wolff I not only learned about the cultural history of Freud's Vienna, but also how to teach it. Harold James at Princeton devoted much time and careful thought to my work on interwar financial history. At NYU I also benefited greatly from my interactions with Guy Ortolano and John Shovlin, and I remain indebted to the support of Nicole Davidson, Ali Salamey, and Kit Frick.

My studies at NYU were generously funded by a MacCracken Fellowship. An Austrian Ernst Mach Grant financed my first six months of research in Vienna, where I profited especially from conversations with Oliver Rathkolb, Dieter Stiefel, and Niko Wahl. I completed the draft of the manuscript during a Max Weber Fellowship at the European University Institute in Fiesole, where I benefited from the scholarly supervision of Ramon Marimon and Youssef Cassis, and I remain indebted to Karin Tilmans, Ognjen Aleksic, and Sarah Simonsen. At the Hebrew University of Jerusalem, where I spent time as a Golda Meir Fellow, I gained from conversations with Yossi Zeira and Eli Lederhendler. I was also a fellow at the Basel Institute for European Global Studies, where I enjoyed fruitful discussions with Madeleine Herren, Isabelle Löhr, Georg Kreis, and Laurent Goetschel. Finally, I must thank the Institute for New Economic Thinking, which provided generous financial support as I completed this book.

Many fellow colleagues and scholars read drafts, heard conference presentations, or discussed this project with me privately over the years. I would particularly like to thank Alexandre Afonso, Rebecca Alderdice, Giulia Andrighetto, Benny Arbel, Lorans Baruh, Stefano Battilossi, Noah Benninga, Seth Bernstein, Alexey Bessudnov, Hubert Bonin, Patricia Clavin, Chris Colvin, Cécile D'Albis, Willem Martijn Dekker, Elise Dermineur, Mehmet Dosemeci, Vincent Duchaussoy, Sarah Easterby-Smith, Haggay Etkes, Franziska Exeler, Elaine Fahey, Tami Fakhoury, Olivier Feiertag, Gerald Feldman, Michel Fior, Marc Flandreau, Juan Huitzilihuitl Flores, Lior Herman, Daniel Hershenzon, Ana Hosne, Davide Franco Jabes, Erin Jenne, Clemens Jobst, Masanori Kashiwagi, Izabela Kazejak, Reuben Kline, Jan Klingelhöfer, Pavel Kolář, Christian Kühner, Florian Kührer-Wielach, Daniel Lee, Gerardo Leibner, Sarah Lemmen, Stefan Link, Flora Macher, Raphael Magarik, Noam Maggor, Hassan Malik, Ronen Mandelkern, Kobi Metzer, Eric Monnet, James Morrison, Jürgen Nautz, Stefan Nikolič, Stéphanie Novak, Michael Ottolenghi, Zoltán Peterecz, Helmut Portele, Amalia Ribi, Anne-Isabelle Richard, Albrecht Ritschl, Daniel Ritter, Georg Schimd, Uditi Sen, Glenda Sluga, Yannay Spitzer, Tobias Straumann, Kristin Surak, Nathan Sussman, Yane Svetiev, Martin van Creveld, Dean Vuletic, Paul Wachtel, Blaz Zakelj, Moshe Zimmermann, and Mordechai Zucker. Colleagues in Professor Nolan's reading group at NYU gave valuable feedback on my earliest drafts. Special thanks to Elisabetta Bini, Maggie Clinton, Sasha Disko, Daniella Doron, Thomas Fleischman, Laura Honsberger, Lauren Kaminsky, Shira Klein, Andrew Lee, Tristan Kirvin, Quinn Slobodian, and Shirley Ye.

This work would not have seen the light of day without the helpful assistance of the historians' guardian angels, the archivists. At the archives of the League of Nations in Geneva, Berhardine Pejovic and Jacques Oberson guided me masterfully through the collection. I wish to thank Renée Berthon at the International Labour Organization archives in Geneva; Ulrike Zimmerl at the historical section of Bank Austria, Vienna; Rudolf Jeřábek and Hubert Steiner at the Austrian National Archives in Vienna; Walter Antonowicz and Bernhard Mussak at the Vienna archives of the Austrian National Bank; Jakub Kunert at the historical archives of the Czech National Bank in Prague; Roger Nougaret and Fabrice Reuzé at the French National Bank Archives in Paris; G. J. M. Boerlage at the archives of the Dutch National Bank in Amsterdam; Piet Clement, Maria Friesen, and Claire Whitfield at the archives of the Bank for International Settlements in Basel; Patrick Halbeisen at the archives of the Swiss National Bank in Zurich; Ben White at the Archives of the Bank of England in London; Melanie Aspey, Victor Grey, and Chiara Scesa at the Rothschild Archives in London; Stephen Freeth and Wendy Hawke at the Manuscript Section of London's Guildhall Library; the archivists at the Churchill Archives in Cambridge; the archivists at the New York Federal Reserve; and Inge Dupont and Maria Molestina at the Morgan Library & Museum Reading Room in New York.

Many friends have supported me over the years with boundless hospitality and friendship. In Switzerland, these include Ramin Akbarzadeh; Alex Barbier; Nino Brunner and Melanie Rui; Jerome Leupin; Thierry Thorman and Simon Schweingruber; Stefanie Baumgartner; Annie Cottier; Nicole Curti; Claire and Geraint Davies; Janine Dumont; Frank (a.k.a. Jack); Nathalie Geiser; Stephen Greis; Olivier Josefowitz; Alain Kahn; José and Evelyn Kaufmann; Melanie Kohli; Diana Krebs; Selma Kuyas; Minh Ly; Hillel Neuer; Alain, Philippe, and Yves Nordman; Marcela Oancea; Claude Recher; Nili Shemesh; Orly Saso; Esra and Hannah Weill; Charles and Helena Wiener; Nitzan Weiss; and the crew at Cargo Bar, Basel.

In New York, around Washington Square and beyond: Matt Embrey, Simon Jackson, Anastasios Karantounias, Paul Kershaw, Olga Kirschbaum, David Koffman, Sadi Ozelge, Gabrielle Sims, Susan Valentine, Matt Watkins, David Weinfeld, and Emma Winter. And my gratitude also to many extramural friends: Leah Albek, the Appels, Liran Avisar, Yair Barzilai, Marc Benda, Philip Berkowitsch, Noah and Nadia Bickart, David Bliah, David Cannata, Armando Cohen, Sy Cohen, Sarah Dunitz, Zachary Edinger, the Farbers, David Flatto, Billie Florsheim, Itsik and Michal Francis, Edwin Goodgold, the Gottesmans, Wendy and Sholom Greenbaum, David Grosgold, Daniel Hofbauer, David Horowitz, Elyakim Kislev, Sascha Knobloch, Etai Kramer, the Kramers, Yuri Kruman, Michael Lewkowicz, Tizpora Lubarr, Natalia Matas, Jesse Mermelstein, Rivka Namdar, Elise and Lauren Ohayon, Michael Ottolenghi, Keith and Sarah Palmer, Tamar Rosenthal, Atara Schultz, Sara Sharf, Pete Silverman, Henry Stimler, Rebecca Strapp, Nomi Strauss, Yitz Treitel, Yossi Tzur, Chaim Zelinger, and the crew of Musical Box.

In Israel: Yonatan Adiri, Michael Alyoshin, Yoav Ashkenazy, Kevin Baxpehler, Assaf Ben-Shoham, the Berry clan, János Chiálá, Hila Cohen, Emanuel Cohn, Tessa Dopheide, Leo Doron, Moshe Edri, Roy Eitani, Yonatan Ellert, Odelia Englander, Olivier Fitoussi, Linda Fried, Noam Ginossar, Yehonatan Givati, Patrick Shmuel Goldfein, Sharon Gordon, Malca and Devora Greenberg, Hadasa Greenberg-Yaakov, Michèle Hasson, Benjamin Huguet, Stefan Ihrig, Andi Kaufman, Dan Keynan, Limor Komornik, Danishay Kornbluth, Louise Le Marie, Haran Levaot, Adi Leviatan, Arnon Levy, Micki Melzer, Benaiah Moses, Udi Nachmany, Michael Ottolenghi, Jaron Pazi, Illia Rainer, Fawaz Ramzi, Shai Ron, Daphné Rousseau, Sinai Rusinek, Daniel Schvarcz, Chen Shtauber, Sharon Teich Sommer, Shelly Steinberg, Michal Strassberg, Yan Tales, Ilan Tojerow, Yakov Tolstoy, Shulim Vogelman, Noa Yeheskel, Lior, Rayzel, Eli Shargo, and the crew from Sira Bar.

In Vienna: Michael Aletrakis, Monika Berger, Roni Dauber, Ariel Edelman, Denise Feiger, Elad Gadot, Benno Gammerl, Franz Gotsmy, Alex Haber, Amir Havelka, Ke-chin Hsia, Robin Kratz, Mara Kronick, Leon und Zila Lewkowicz, Hanna and Bernhard Morgenstern, George and Dorit Muzicant, Benjamin Neufeld, Ilana Offenberger, Rabbiner Josef Pardess, Johanna Rainio, Becky Sandorffy, Hannes Schafelner, Andres Schenker, Daniel Schustermann, Rafael Schwarz, Ronny Slomovits, Michael Teichner, Efraim Fritzi Zethofer, and the team at Loos Bar.

In Berlin: Hannah Boie, Margot Effertz, Roni Fuss, Paula Hettich, the Kvariani sisters, Oded Libhaber, the Marcus clan, Clemens Meier-Wolthausen, Marek Polewski, Raphael Prejs, Daniel Reiter, Sweeny Westphal, Stefan Zanev, and the Tuesday crew at Cookies.

In Amsterdam: Sanne Boswijk, Vera Ebels, Max van Weezel, and Anet Bleich.

In London: Aaron Begner, Chantal and Eliot Bishop, Richard Clayton, Benjy Cuby, the Erdoshes, Jean-Baptiste Giraud, the Hofbauers, Aliza and Martin Kander, Sarah Laitner, Eli Luzac, Michael Ottolenghi, Philippe Volpe, Ruth Waiman, and Sandy Wilheim.

In Florence: Matteo Albanese, Henrik Forshamn, Francesco "Flask" Gnot, Igor Guardiancich, Agostino Inguscio, Tomas Simcha Jellinek, Iassen Punky Lazarov, Rabbi Joseph Levi and Shulamit Furstenberg-Levi, Mariangela Martire, Luan Nikolli, Marco Rizzi, Bat Hen Shneor, Adam Smulevich, Niccolò Tognarini, Rabbi Levi Wolvovsky, and the crowd at Sant'Ambrogio.

In St. Petersburg: Kostas Afantitis, Layla Baichorova, Illia Bazarsky, Alexander Boltyan, Tatiana Borisova, Jason Cieply, Maxim Denim, Anna Fedyunina, Gamliel Fishkin, Elazar Goldberg, Vera Guseva, Misha Gutenkov, Igal Halfin, Levon Israelyan, Viktor Kaploun, Tatiana Karasik, Maria Kattsova, Angelus Klein, Anton Kotenko, Sergei Levin, Alex Marshalsky, German Moyzhes, Beila Nepomniaschaia, Osher Nudelman, Rabbi M. M. Pewzner, Yakov Pichkhadzeh, Anatoly Pinsky, Zvi and Dina Pinsky, Victor Pliner, Ivan Pushkin, Shneor Reinitz, Liza Reutova, Alexander Semyonov, Pavel Sergeev, Karina Sevoyan, Anna Skrikulak, Semyon and Nataliya Smushkin, Nikolai Ssorin-Chaikov, George Tshakadiashvili, Dietmar Wulff, and the crew from Bekitzer.

A big shout-out to Jerzy Łazor, Jamie Martin, and David Petruccelli, who read, commented on, and discussed the final draft with me. And many thanks to Michael Burri, Reuven Brenner, and Jonathan Zatlin for their ongoing involvement with this project. Above all, I wish to thank my parents, my brothers, and my extended family—the Marcuses and Pezls—around the world for their support and sustained enthusiasm about Austrian history. To my father, who has critically read almost everything I have ever written, I owe particular thanks. Last but not least, a heartfelt thank you to Michael Aronson, Thomas LeBien, and Kathi Drummy at Harvard University Press, and to John Donohue and Allison Anderson at Westchester Publishing Services, for shepherding this book and its author so smoothly and pleasantly to the shores of his first monograph.

Jerusalem, on the eve of the new year 5778
ירושלים עיה"ק ת"ו ערב ר"ה תשע"ח

Index